SATELLITE COMMUNICATIONS

SATELLITE COMMUNICATIONS

Robert M. Gagliardi

CBS PUBLISHERS & DISTRIBUTORS PVT. LTD.

New Delhi • Bangalore • Pune • Cochin • Chennai (India)

ISBN : 81-239-0919-5

First Indian Edition : 1987
Reprint : 2000, 2002, 2004

This edition has been reprinted in India by arrangement with
Van Nostrand Reinhold Company Inc., USA

Published by Satish Kumar Jain and produced by V.K. Jain for
CBS Publishers & Distributors Pvt. Ltd.,
CBS Plaza, 4819/XI Prahlad Street, 24 Ansari Road, Daryaganj,
New Delhi - 110002, India. • Website: www.cbspd.com
e-mail: delhi@cbspd.com, cbspubs@airtelmail.in
Ph.: 23289259, 23266861, 23266867 • Fax: 011-23243014

Branches:

- ***Bengaluru:*** Seema House, 2975, 17th Cross, K.R. Road,
  Bansankari 2nd Stage, Bengaluru - 560070
  • Ph.: +91-80-26771678/79 • Fax: +91-80-26771680
  • E-mail: cbsbng@gmail.com, bangalore@cbspd.com
- ***Pune:*** Bhuruk Prestige, Sr. No. 52/12/2+1+3/2,
  Narhe, Haveli (Near Katraj-Dehu Road By-pass), Pune - 411041
  • Ph.: +91-20-64704058/59, 32342277 • E-mail: pune@cbspd.com
- ***Kochi:*** 36/14, Kalluvilakam, Lissie Hospital Road,
  Kochi - 682018, Kerala • Ph.: +91-484-4059061-65
  • Fax: +91-484-4059065 • E-mail: cochin@cbspd.com
- ***Chennai:*** 20, West Park Road, Shenoy Nagar, Chennai - 600030
  Ph.: +91-44-26260666, 26208620 • Fax: +91-44-42032115
  • E-mail: chennai@cbspd.com

Printed at :
Nikunj Print Process, Delhi

In dedication to the memory of my beloved mother and father,
Louise Musco Gagliardi and Michael Gagliardi,
Hamden, Connecticut

Contents

Preface

Communication via orbiting satellites is now an important part of today's technology. Such systems have unique communication link models, complete with their own inherent characteristics, constraints, limitations, and design procedures. As a result an area of communication engineering has emerged that is now referred to simply as "Satellite Communications."

OBJECTIVES

The objectives of this book run as follows:

- To present a unified approach to a general study of the satellite communication field
- To provide classroom, at-home, or on-the-job reading aid for students, engineers, or scientists entering the satellite communication field
- To help readers become aware of the terminology, models, analysis methodology, and principal design directions of a modern satellite link
- To stress system analysis and block diagram design as opposed to operational and hardware details or circuit description, to focus on satellite communications and not communication satellites (satellite circuit design changes at such a rapid rate that descriptions of specific hardware are soon found to be out of date)

AUDIENCE

The material is presented at a senior or first-year graduate level and will assume the reader has experienced something of a modern electrical engineering curriculum. A necessary background would probably include knowledge of basic Fourier transform analysis, some electromagnetics and electronics, and elementary probability and noise theory. Previous course work in communications and modulation theory would also be advantageous but not strictly necessary.

With more and more emphasis being placed on worldwide satellite communications, it is hoped that this book will assist in the formulation of new and innovative courses in a graduate engineering curriculum. The book should also have direct application to continuing education and in-house training courses, both of which have become extremely prevalent over the past several years. The uninitiated scientist should also benefit from this book as he or she follows material that is unified in its format, that begins with the simplest satellite systems and builds up to the more complex models. The practicing engineer will find the text useful for review, for aiding in analytical studies and performance evaluation, and for addressing issues posed by newer satellite concepts.

ORGANIZATION

Chapter 1 introduces and summarizes the various types of satellite links and their key parameters and constraints. Chapter 2 acts as a basic review of modulation, encoding, and decoding for both analog and digital systems, especially those properties of prime importance to the satellite links. (Appendices A and B serve as a back-up for this review.) Chapter 3 reviews and applies basic link-power analysis for idealized and simplified satellite models, pointing out the key design equations, system trade-offs, and inherent problem areas characteristic of all satellite links. Chapter 4 examines the inherent structure of satellite payloads, allowing for more realistic link modeling and modifying the earlier results in Chapter 3. In addition, Chapter 4 (in conjunction with Appendix D) introduces the details of satellite waveforms, signal processing, and device nonlinearities.

With these extended models, the specific analyses of the various multiple-accessing formats can then be carried out. Chapter 5 considers the FDMA format, Chapter 6 the TDMA format, and Chapter 7 the CDMA and SSMA formats. Since satellite ranging is an important auxiliary communication operation within these formats, a separate discussion of satellite-ranging subsystems is presented in Appendix C.

Chapters 8 and 9 are two innovative chapters dealing with special topics in satellite links. Chapter 8 concentrates on the basic phase-coherency problem associated with any satellite links, and discusses the accepted procedures and difficulties in establishing phase coherency between remote terminals. The chapter is divided into three basic parts: it describes the subsystems used for carrier generation and their inherent phase stability; it describes the mechanism used for establishing phase coherency at the remote terminal; and it applies this analysis to several basic link configurations. Chapter 9 deals with the new and growing field of laser light-wave technology for satellite crosslinks. This chapter summarizes the characteristics and differences of an optical link vis-à-vis an RF link, and shows how to apply these results to typical satellite-crosslink analysis.

Homework problems are included at the end of each of these nine chapters to provide an opportunity for additional study and to review key equations and theory.

PROCEDURES

In putting together a manuscript of this type, the most difficult task lies not in determining what should be covered but rather in deciding what need not be covered. A separate book could easily be written on the topic of each individual chapter. My most time-consuming effort was devoted to filtering through the abundance of available material on each topic so as to present, in the number of pages available to me, that portion that allowed the highest level of general understanding for the reader.

In any systems book of this type there is always the question of the amount of detailed mathematics to be included. It is well known that the key to satellite communication design and future development is to be found in the physical theory and mathematical formulae underlying device performance and communication analysis. To avoid these formulae (and so emphasize word descriptions) is both inadequate and useless, since many of the modern design directions are influenced entirely by the bottom-line mathematics. However, to simply list these formulae is equally inadequate, and in fact dangerous, since many of the assumptions in their derivation may be violated in certain applications. I have tried, therefore, to find an adequate balance of mathematical statement and formula derivation that will allow the systems engineer to move somewhat efficiently through the topics without bogging down on a lot of epsilon-delta gymnastics.

Several sections were purposely intended to be mathematically complex in order to show explicitly the degree of sophistication sometimes necessary for accurate performance evaluation and design; these sections can easily be skipped.

I have also tried to relegate much of the mathematical detail to appendices or references; in this way a reader or instructor can choose either to pass over or to study in detail the appropriate mathematical derivations.

ACKNOWLEDGMENTS

An effort of this type is of course the result of many years of head-banging with colleagues, engineers, and scientists throughout the academic and industrial world. I wish to thank the many excellent and assiduous technical staff members of the various companies with whom I have consulted over the years for helping me to understand a little more about satellite communications, and for influencing my teaching in this area. In addition, I wish to acknowledge the help of my fellow faculty at USC, UCLA, and Cal Tech., and the many graduate students who suffered through seminars, graduate courses, and summer short courses during the preparation of this book. I also wish to thank personally Ms. Georgia Lum, Ms. Mildred Montenegro, and Ms. Shérri Gagliardi for diligently typing the manuscript, and Ms. Carol Dondrea for undangling my participles and reconnecting my infinitives during final editing. Finally, I wish to thank several anonymous reviewers whose suggestions concerning topics and additions were greatly appreciated.

Robert M. Gagliardi
Professor of Electrical Engineering
University of Southern California

1

Satellite Systems

The use of orbiting satellites as an integral part of worldwide communication systems has progressed rapidly over the last several decades. As the technology and hardware of such systems continues to make significant advancements, it is expected that satellites will continue to play an ever-increasing role in the future of long-range communications. Each new generation of satellite is more technologically sophisticated than its predecessors, and each undoubtedly will have significant impact on the development and capabilities of military, domestic, and international communication systems.

To the communication engineer, satellite communications has presented a special type of communication link, complete with its own design formats, analysis procedures, and performance characterizations. In one sense, a satellite system is simply an amalgamation of basic communication systems, with slightly more complicated subsystem interfacing. On the other hand, the severe constraints imposed on system design by the presence of a spaceborne vehicle makes the satellite communication channel somewhat special in its overall fabrication. In this book we address some of the salient features of satellite communications and the corresponding design approaches that have evolved.

1.1 HISTORICAL DEVELOPMENT OF SATELLITES

Long-range communications via modulated microwave electromagnetic fields were first introduced in the 1920s. With the rapid development of microwave technology, these systems rapidly became an important part of our terrestrial (ground-to-ground) and near-earth (aircraft) communication system. These systems, however, were, for the most part, restricted to line-of-sight links. This meant that two stations on Earth, located over the horizon from each other, could not communicate directly, unless by ground transmission relay methods. The use of tropospheric and ionospheric scatter

Table 1.1. Communication Satellites

Satellite	*Launch Date*	*Launch Weight, Lbs.*	*Number of Transmitters*	*Total RF Bandwidth, MHz*
Echo	1956	100	0	—
Score	1958	90	1	4
Courier	1960	500	2	13.2
Telstar	1962	170	2	50
Syncom	1963	86	2	10
Intelsat I	1965	76	2	50
II	1966	190	2	130
III	1968	270	4	450
IV	1971	1400	12	500
ATS, A, B, C, D	1966–1969	700	2	50
Telesat	1972–1975	1200	12	500
Westar	1974	1200	12	500
Globecom	1975	1400	24	1000
DSCS, I, II, III	1980–1981	2300	6	500
TDRSS	1980	1600	30	1200
Intelsat V	1981–1983	2000	35	2300
VI	1986	3600	77	3366

to generate reflected skywaves for the horizon links tend to be far too unreliable for establishing a continuous system.

In the 1950s a concept was proposed for using orbiting space vehicles for relaying carrier waveforms to maintain long-range, over-the-horizon communications. The first version of this idea appeared in 1956 as the Echo satellite—a metallic reflecting balloon placed in orbit to act as a passive reflector of ground transmissions to complete long-range links. Communications across the United States and across the Atlantic Ocean were successfully demonstrated this way. In the late 1950s new proposals were presented for using active satellites (satellites with power amplification) to aid in relaying long-range transmissions. Early satellites such as Score, Telstar, and Relay verified these concepts. The successful implementation of the early Syncom vehicles proved further that these relays could be placed in fixed (geostationary) orbit locations. These initial vehicle launchings were then followed by a succession of new generation vehicles, each bigger and more improved than its predecessors (see Table 1.1 and Figure 1.1). Today satellite

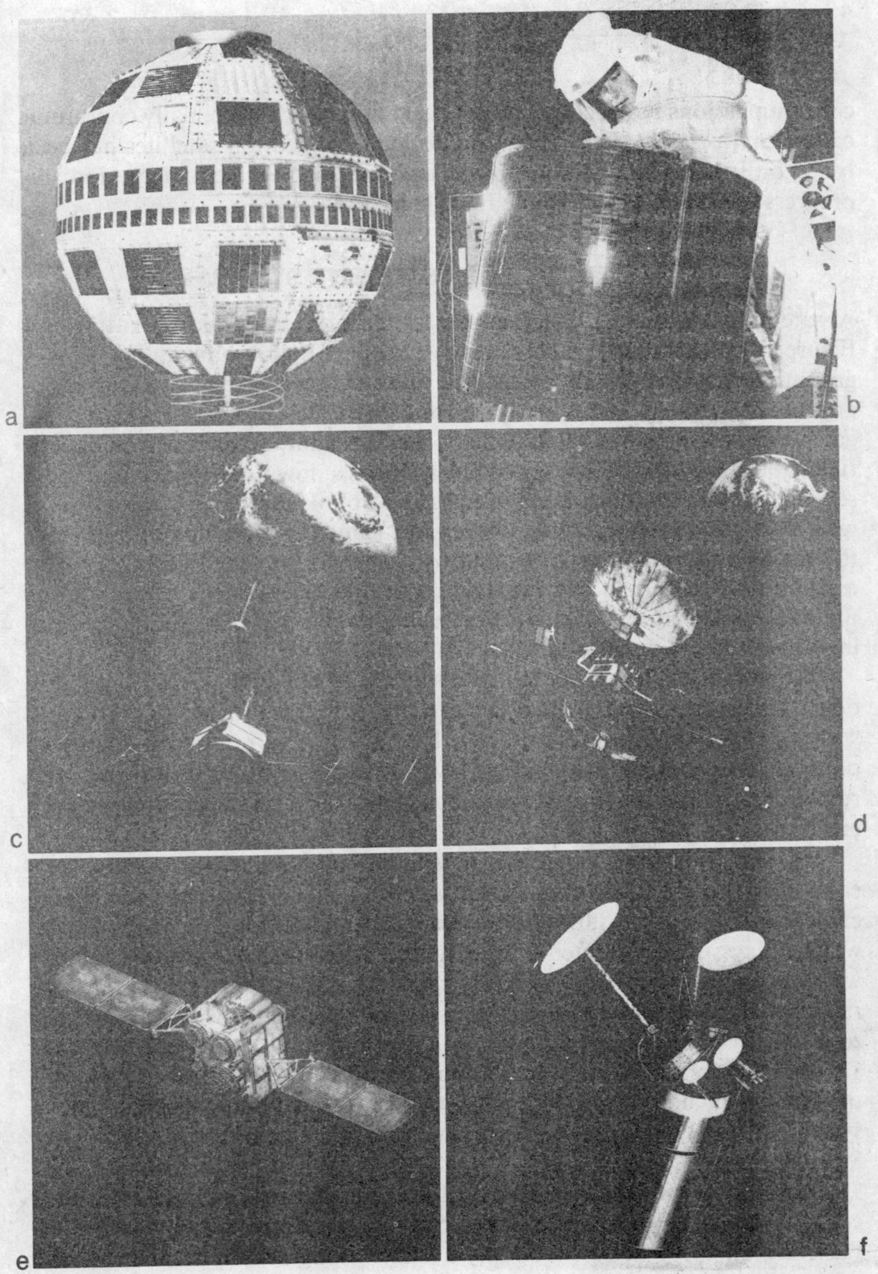

Figure 1.1. Communication satellites. (a) Telstar. (b) Early Bird. (c) Fleetsatcom. (d) TDRSS. (e) DSCS-III, (f) Intelsat VI. Courtesy of Bell Telephone Labs., AT&T, Hughes Aircraft Co., TRW, and General Electric

communications has become a basic part of our worldwide, daily communication environment. Each generation of communication satellites has been based on increasingly more refined and sophisticated technology, and this progress is expected to continue into the future.

1.2 COMMUNICATION SATELLITE SYSTEMS

A satellite communication system can take on several different forms. Figure 1.2 summarizes the basic types. System I shows an uplink from a ground-based earth station to satellite, and a downlink from satellite back to ground. Modulated carriers in the form of electromagnetic fields are propagated up to the satellite. The satellite collects the impinging electromagnetic field, and retransmits the modulated carrier as a downlink to specified earth stations. A satellite that merely relays the uplink carrier as a downlink is referred to as a **relay satellite**, or **repeater satellite**. More commonly, since the satellite *transmits* the downlink by *responding* to the uplink, it is also called a **transponder**. A satellite that electronically operates on the received uplink to reformat it in some way prior to retransmission is called a **processing satellite**.

System II shows a satellite crosslink between two satellites prior to downlink transmission. Such systems allow communication between earth stations not visible to the same satellite. By spacing multiple satellites in proper orbits around the Earth, worldwide communications between remote earth stations in different hemispheres can be performed via such crosslinks.

System III shows a satellite relay system involving earth stations, near-earth users, (aircraft, ships, etc.) and satellites. An earth station communicates to another earth station or to a user by transmitting to a relay satellite, which relays the modulated carrier to the user. Since an orbiting satellite will have larger near-earth visibility than the transmitting earth station, a relay satellite allows communications to a wider range of users. The user responds by retransmitting back through the satellite to the earth station. The link from earth station to relay to user is called the **forward link,** while the link from user to satellite back to Earth is called the **return link**. A system of this type is the basis for the TDRSS (Tracking and Data Relay Satellite System; see Table 1.1).

Earth stations form a vital part of the overall satellite system, and their cost and implementation restrictions must be integrated into system design. Basically, an earth station is simply a transmitting and/or receiving power station operating in conjunction with an antenna subsystem. Earth stations are usually categorized into large and small stations by the size of their radiated power and antennas. Larger stations may use antenna dishes as

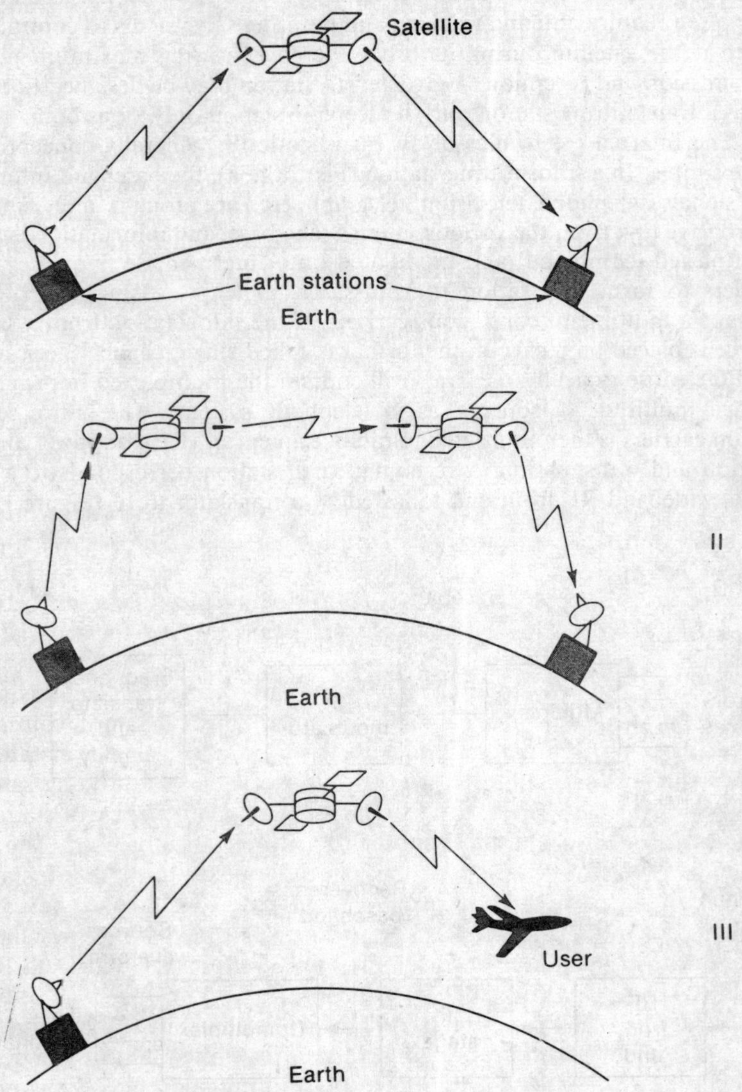

Figure 1.2. Satellite systems. I. Ground–ground, II. Ground–crosslink–ground, III. Ground–user relay.

large as 30 meters in diameter. Smaller stations may use antennas of only 3–10 meters, and may in fact be constructed so as to be mobile. Larger stations may often require antenna tracking and pointing subsystems to continually point at the satellite during its orbit, thereby ensuring maximum power transmission and reception. A given earth station may be designed to operate as a transmitting station only, a receiving station only, or as both.

The internal electronics of an earth station is generally conceptually quite simple. In a transmitting station (Figure 1.3a), the baseband information signals (telephone, television, telegraph, etc.) are brought in on cable or microwave link from the various sources. The baseband information is then multiplexed (combined) and modulated onto intermediate frequency (IF) carriers to form the station transmissions, either as a single carrier or perhaps a multiple of contiguous carriers. If the information from a single source is placed on a carrier, the format is called **single-channel-per-carrier (SCPC)**. More typically, a carrier will contain the multiplexed information from a multitude of sources, as in telephone systems. The entire set of station carriers is then translated to radio frequencies (RF) for power amplification and transmission. A receiving earth station corresponds to a low noise, wideband RF front end followed by a translator to IF (Figure 1.3b).

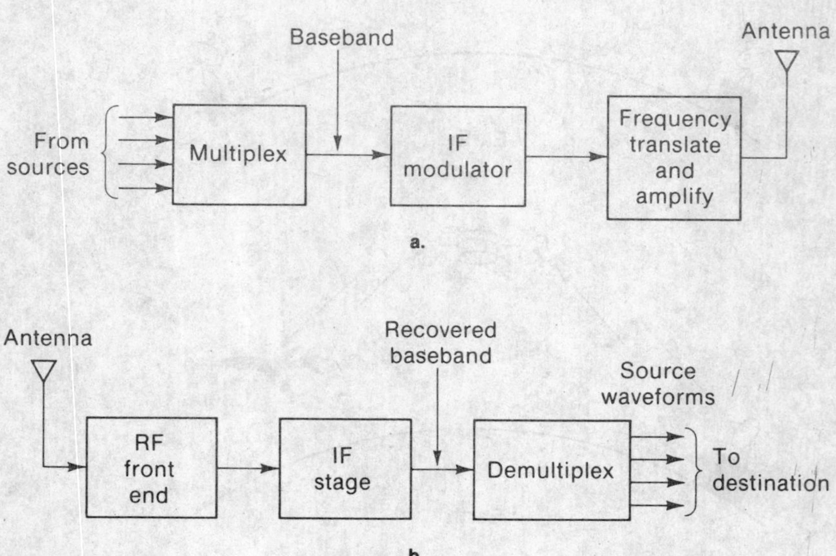

Figure 1.3. Earth-station block diagram. (a) Transmitting. (b) Receiving.

At the IF, the specific uplink carriers wishing to be received are first separated, then demodulated to baseband. The baseband is then demultiplexed (if necessary) and transferred on to the destination.

1.3 COMMUNICATION SATELLITES

A **communication satellite** is basically an electronic communication package placed in orbit around the Earth. The prime objective of the satellite is to aid communication transmission from one point on or near Earth to another. In modern systems this information most often corresponds to voice (telephone), video (television), and digital data (teletype).

A satellite transponder must relay an uplink or forward link electromagnetic field to a downlink, or a return link. If this relay is accomplished by an orbiting passive reflector, as, for example, in the case of the Echo satellite, the power levels of the downlink will be extremely low due to the total uplink-downlink propagation loss (plus the additional loss of a nonperfect reflector). An active satellite repeater aids the relay operation by being able to add power amplification at the satellite prior to the downlink transmission. Hence, an ideal active repeater would be simply an electronic amplifier in orbit, as sketched in Figure 1.4a. Ideally, it would receive the uplink carrier, amplify to the desired power level, and retransmit in the

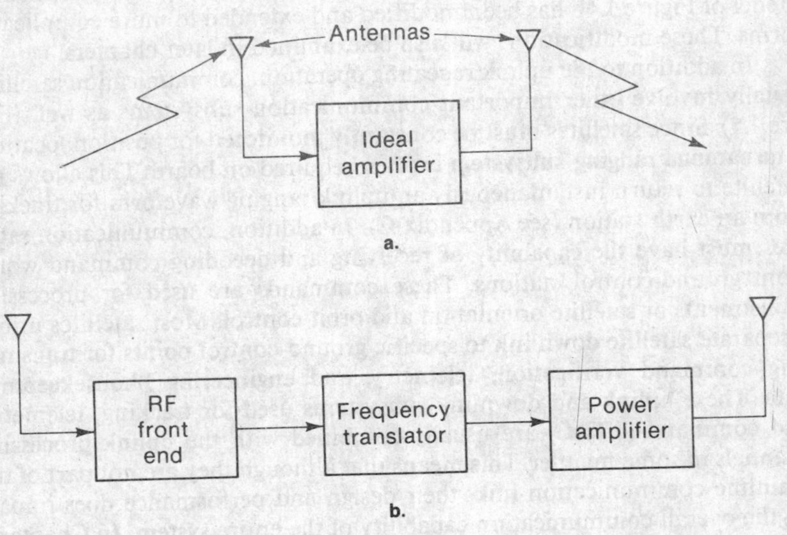

Figure 1.4. Satellite block diagram. (a) Ideal. (b) Repeater.

downlink. Practically, however, trying to receive and retransmit an amplified version of the same uplink waveform at the same satellite will cause unwanted feedback, or **ringaround**, from the downlink antenna back into the receiver. For this reason satellite repeaters must involve some form of frequency translation prior to the power amplification. The translation shifts the uplink frequencies to a different set of downlink frequencies so that some separation exists between the frequency bands. This separation allows frequency filtering at the satellite uplink antenna to prevent ringaround from the transmitting (downlink) frequency band. In more sophisticated processing satellites the uplink carrier waveforms are actually reformatted or restructured, rather than merely frequency translated, to form downlink. Frequency band separation also allows the same antenna to be used for both receiving and transmitting, simplifying the satellite hardware.

The frequency translation requirements in satellites means that the ideal amplifier in Figure 1.4a should instead be reconstructed as in the diagram in Figure 1.4b. The satellite contains a receiving front end that first collects and filters the uplink. The collected uplink is then processed so as to translate or reformat to the downlink frequencies. The downlink carrier is then power-amplified to provide the retransmitted carrier. The details of the hardware circuitry of a transponder of this type will be discussed in Chapter 4. As more sophisticated satellites have evolved, the basic transponder model of Figure 1.4b has been modified and extended to more complicated forms. These modifications will also be examined in later chapters.

In addition to the uplink repeating operation, communication satellites usually involve other important communication subsystems as well (Figure 1.5). Since satellites must be constantly monitored for position location, a **turnaround ranging subsystem** is often required on board. This allows the satellite to return instantaneously an uplink ranging waveform for tracking from an earth station (see Appendix C). In addition, communication satellites must have the capability of receiving and decoding command words from ground-control stations. These commands are used for processing adjustments or satellite orientation and orbit control. Most satellites utilize a separate satellite downlink to specific ground-control points for transmitting command verification, telemetry, and engineering "housekeeping" data. These uplink and downlink subsystems used for tracking, telemetry, and command (**TT&C**) are usually combined with the uplink processing channels in some manner. This means that although they are not part of the mainline communication link, their design and performance does impact on the overall communication capability of the entire system. In Chapter 8 we will discuss some of these alternatives.

The details of the fabrication of a satellite space vehicle is beyond the

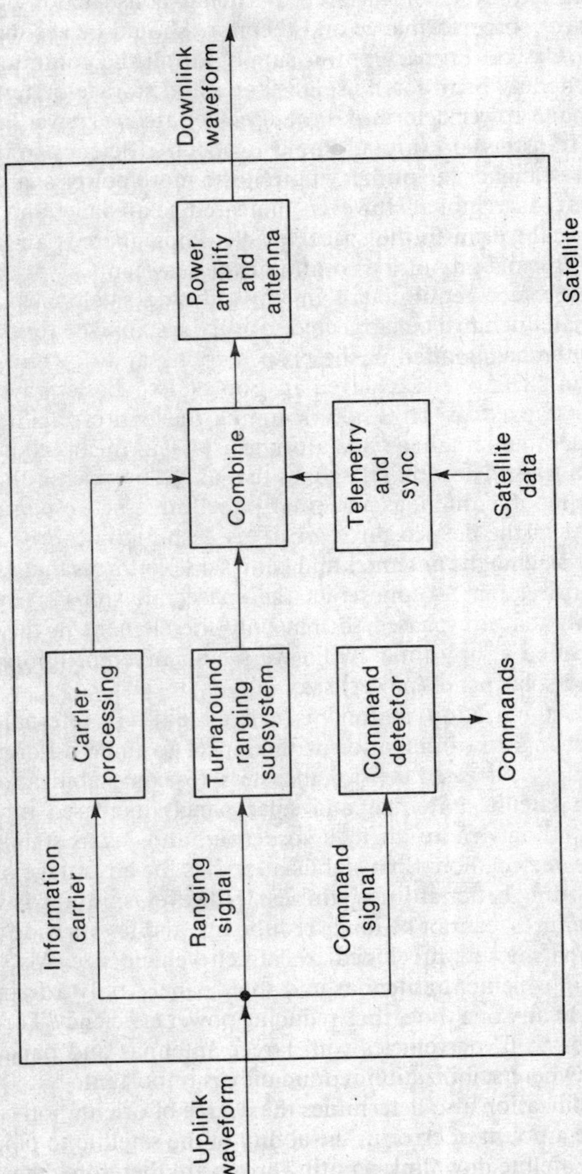

Figure 1.5. Satellite subsystems.

scope of this text. However, some aspects of satellite construction indirectly affect communication performance and therefore should be accounted for in initial system design. Primary power supply for all the communication electronics is generally provided by solar panels and storage batteries. The amount of primary power determines the useable satellite power levels for processing and transmission through the conversion efficiency of the electronic devices. The higher the primary power, the more power available for the downlink retransmissions. However, increased solar panel and battery size adds additional weight to the space vehicle. Thus, there is an inherent limit to the power capability of the communication system.

Another important requirement in any orbiting satellite is attitude stabilization. A satellite must be fabricated so as to be stabilized (oriented) in space with its antennas pointed in the proper uplink and downlink direction. Satellite stabilization is achieved in one of two basic ways. Early satellites were stabilized by physically spinning the entire satellite (spin-stabilized) in order to maintain a fixed attitude axis. This means all points in space will be at a fixed direction relative to that axis. However, if the entire satellite is spinning, the antennas and solar panel must be *despun* so they continually point in the desired direction. This despinning can be accomplished either by placing the antennas and panels on platforms that are spun in the opposite direction to counteract the spacecraft spin, or by using multiple elements that are phased so that only the element in the proper direction is activated at any time. Again we see an inherent limitation to both antenna and solar panel (power) size.

The second stabilization method is carried out via internal gyros, through which changes in orientation with respect to three different axes can be sensed and corrected by jet thrusters (3-axis stabilization). As requirements on satellite antennas and solar panels increased in size, it became correspondingly more difficult to despin, and 3-axis stabilization became the preferred method. Spin stabilization has the advantage of being simpler and providing better attitude stiffness. However, spinning is vulnerable to bearing failures, cannot be made redundant, and favors wide diameter vehicles, which may be precluded by launch vehicle size. Also, when despinning multiple-element antennas and solar panels, only a fraction of each can be used at any one time, thus reducing power efficiency. Three-axis stabilization tends to favor vehicles with larger antennas and panels, and favors operation where stabilization redundancy is important.

Attitude stabilization also determines the degree of orientation control, and therefore the amount of error in the ability of the satellite to point in a given direction. Satellite downlink pointing errors are therefore determined by the stabilization method used. Both methods previously described can be made to produce about the same pointing accuracy, generally about a fraction of a degree. We shall see later that pointing errors directly affect antenna design and system performance, especially in the more sophisticated satellite models being developed.

Satellite power amplifiers provide the primary amplification for the retransmitted carrier, and are obviously one of the key elements in a communication satellite. Power amplifiers, besides having to generate sufficient power levels and amplification gain, have additional requirements for reliability, long life, stability, high efficiency, and suitability for the space (orbiting) environment. These requirements have been sufficiently met by the use of **traveling wave tube amplifiers (TWTA)**, either of the cavity-coupled or helix type [1, 2]. TWTA have been extensively developed, their theory of operation is well understood, and they have been successfully implemented in all types of space missions. For this reason TWTA have emerged as the universal form of both earth station and satellite power amplifier. Even as increased demands on power amplifiers will push them to higher power levels and higher frequencies, the TWTA will undoubtedly continue to be the dominant amplification device. Their continual development has already produced sufficient power levels well into the 30 GHz frequency range.

It is expected that there will be continued effort to develop smaller, lighter-weight solid-state amplifiers, such as Galium Arsenide **field-effect transistors** (GA FET) for future satellite operations [3–5]. These devices, however, have not been established in high-power operating modes with reasonable size bandwidths. They most likely will have future applications with appropriate power-combining, or lower power, multiple-source operations. FET operation is generally confined to upper frequencies of about 30 GHz. For projected amplification above 30 GHz, **impact avalanche transit time (IMPATT)** diode amplifiers are rapidly developing as a capable medium-power amplifier. Such diodes have been developed at frequencies up to about 40 GHz, and it appears they will become extendable to 60 GHz operation in the near future.

1.4 ORBITING SATELLITES

Typical paths of an orbiting satellite are sketched in Figure 1.6. The satellite encircles the Earth with an orbit that can be equatorial, polar, or inclined. The orbit itself may be elliptical or circular. For a circular orbit a satellite must achieve a velocity of:

$$v_s = \sqrt{\frac{g_0}{r_E + h}} \qquad (1.4.1)$$

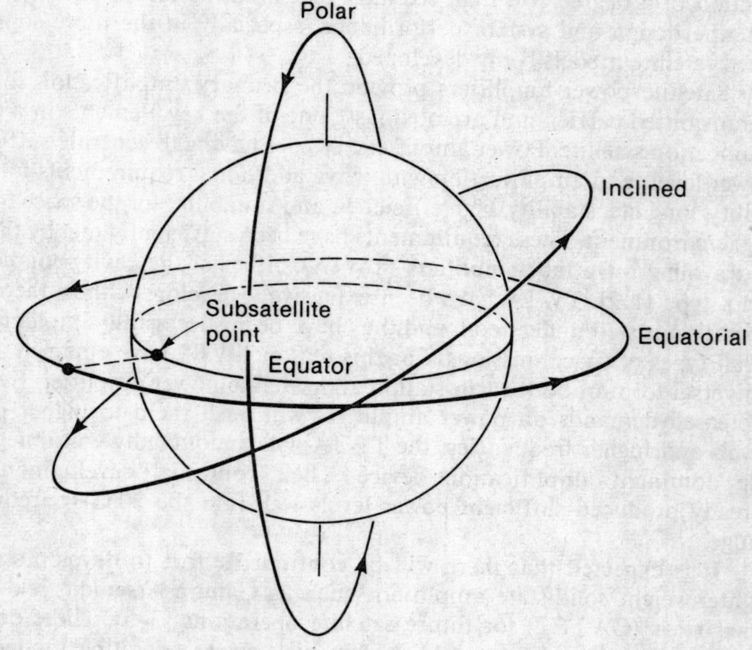

Figure 1.6. Satellite orbits.

where r_E is the Earth's radius, ($r_E = 3444$ nm $= 6378$ km), h is the orbit altitude, and g_0 is the gravitational coefficient,

$$g_0 = (1.4 \times 10^{16})\text{ft}^3/\text{sec}^2 \tag{1.4.2}$$

The time t_s for an orbiting satellite to complete one revolution (orbit period) satisfies $w_s t_s = 2\pi$, where w_s is the angular velocity in radian/sec. Since $v_s = (r_e + h)w_s$, we have

$$\begin{aligned} t_s &= \frac{2\pi}{v_s}(r_E + h) \\ &= \frac{2\pi}{\sqrt{g_0}}(r_E + h)^{3/2} \end{aligned} \tag{1.4.3}$$

Figure 1.7 plots (1.4.1) and (1.4.3) as a function of the orbit altitude h. As the orbit altitude increases, the required satellite velocity decreases while the orbit period increases. If the satellite orbits in a equatorial plane at exactly

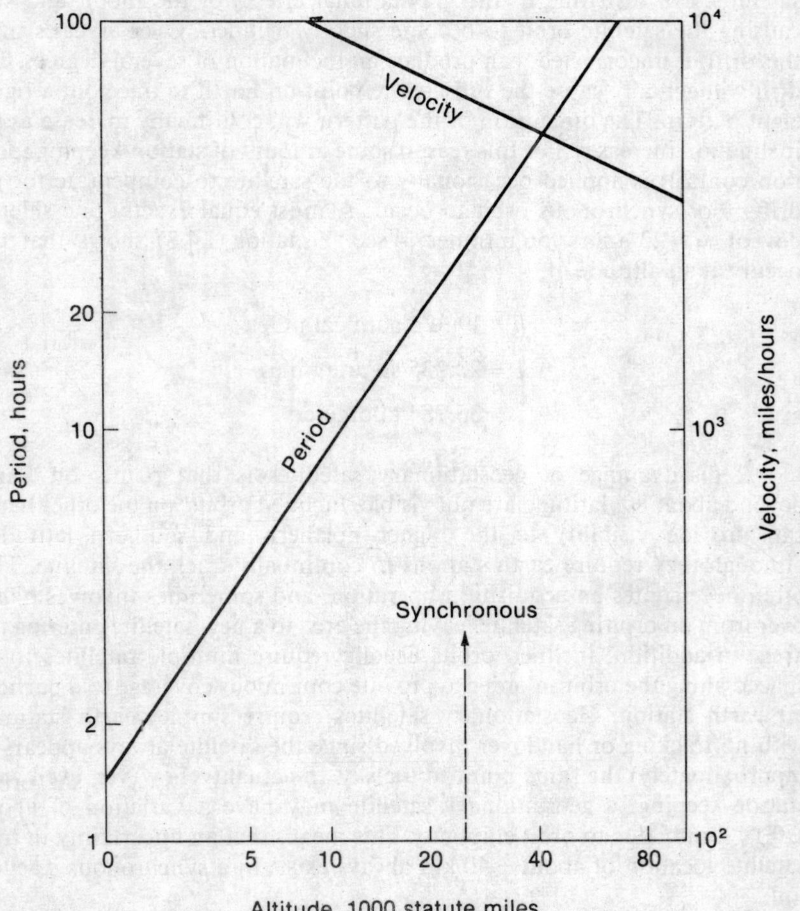

Figure 1.7. Satellite velocity and period as a function of satellite altitude (circular orbit).

the same angular velocity as the Earth rotates, it will appear to be fixed at a specific point in the sky when viewed from the Earth. Such a satellite is said to be in **synchronous**, or **geostationary**, orbit.

If a satellite is in geostationary orbit, and a subsatellite point is projected down normal to the Earth (see Figure 1.6), the subsatellite point will theoretically remain at a fixed point on the equator. However, geostationary satellites can drift due to the gravitational effects of the moon and sun, causing the satellite orbit to become slightly inclined. Over a year's time, this drift, if uncorrected, can produce an inclination of several degrees. The drift will actually cause the subsatellite point on Earth to trace out a figure eight pattern. The dimension of the pattern will continually increase as the inclination increases. For this reason some amount of station-keeping (position control) is applied occasionally to the satellite to compensate for the drifts. For synchronous orbit to occur, t_s must equal exactly one sidereal day of $t_s = 23$ hours, 56 minutes, 4 sec. Equation (1.4.3) shows that this occurs at an altitude of:

$$\begin{aligned} h &= 19{,}322 \text{ nautical miles} \\ &= 22{,}235 \text{ statute miles} \\ &= 35{,}784 \text{ kilometers} \end{aligned} \tag{1.4.4}$$

A disadvantage of geostationary satellites is that points on Earth beyond about 80° latitude are not visible. Inclined orbits, on the other hand, can provide visibility to the higher northern and southern latitudes, although they require earth stations to continually track the satellite. This often necessitates an acquisition operation, and sometimes involves handover from an orbiting satellite leaving the area to a new satellite entering the area. In addition, inclined orbits usually require multiple satellites to be spaced along the orbit in order to provide continuous coverage to a particular earth station. Geostationary satellites require simpler earth stations, with no tracking or handover involved since the satellite always appears at (approximately) the same point in the sky. In actuality, however, even with station-keeping, a geostationary satellite may have a variation of about ± 0.1°, simply due to orbit ellipticity. This means that an uncertainty in true satellite location of about ± 40 km always exists in a synchronous satellite link.

From a communication point of view, there are three key parameters associated with an orbiting satellite: (1) coverage area, or the portion of the Earth's surface that can receive the satellite's transmissions with an elevation angle larger than a prescribed minimum angle, (2) the slant range (actual line-of-sight distance from a fixed point on the Earth to the satellite), and (3) the length of time a satellite is visible with a prescribed elevation angle. Elevation angle is important since communications can be significantly impaired if the satellite must be viewed at a low elevation angle; that is, an angle too close to the horizon. From the diagram in Figure 1.8 we can establish that the coverage area A_{cov} from which the satellite is visible with an elevation angle of at least ϕ_l is given by

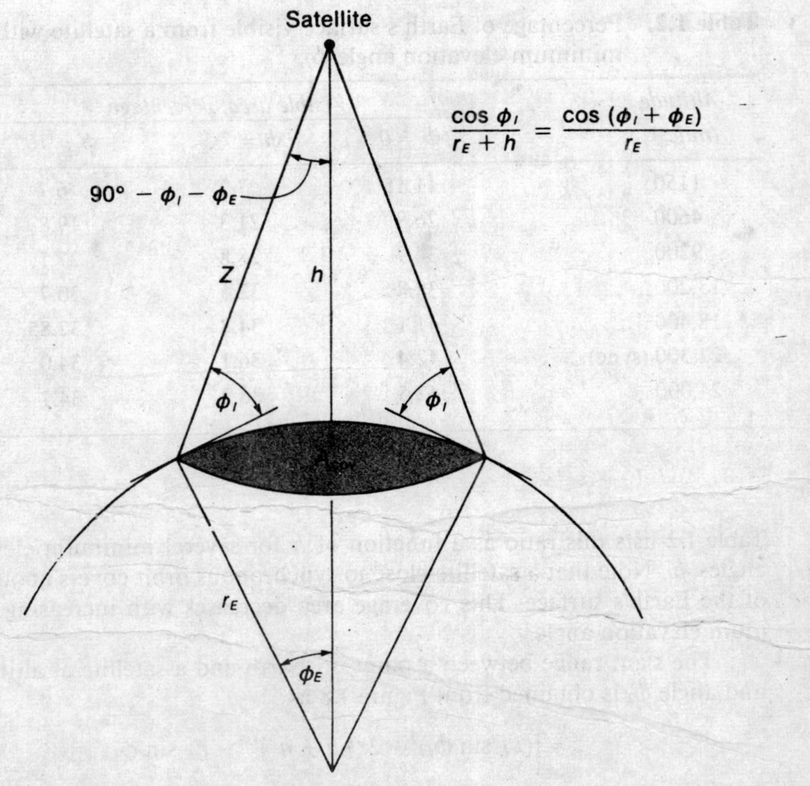

Figure 1.8. Satellite–Earth angles (ϕ_l = elevation angle from ground station).

$$A_{\text{cov}} = (2\pi r_E^2)(1 - \cos \phi_E) \tag{1.4.5}$$

where

$$\phi_E = \cos^{-1}\left(\frac{r_E \cos \phi_l}{r_E + h}\right) - \phi_l \tag{1.4.6}$$

Since the total Earth's surface area is $4\pi r_E^2$, we can rewrite A_{cov} as a fraction of the total earth surface:

$$\frac{A_{\text{cov}}}{4\pi r_E^2} = 0.5(1 - \cos \phi_E) \tag{1.4.7}$$

Table 1.2. Percentage of Earth's surface visible from a satellite with minimum elevation angle ϕ_l.

Altitude (miles)	*Visible area, percentage* $\phi_l = 0$	$\phi_l = 7.5°$	$\phi_l = 10°$
1150	11.15	7.7	6.7
4600	26.9	21.3	19.8
9200	34.9	28.8	27.1
13,200	38.8	32.5	30.7
18,400	41.1	34.8	32.85
22,300 (sync)	42.4	36.1	34.0
24,000	42.5	36.2	34.1

Table 1.2 lists this ratio as a function of h for several minimum elevation angles ϕ_l. Note that a satellite close to synchronous orbit covers about 40% of the Earth's surface. This coverage area decreases with increasing minimum elevation angle.

The slant range between a point on Earth and a satellite at altitude h and angle ϕ_l is obtained from Figure 1.8 as

$$z = [(r_E \sin \phi_l)^2 + 2r_E h + h^2]^{1/2} - r_E \sin \phi_l \tag{1.4.8}$$

This determines the direct propagation length between an earth station and a satellite at altitude h and elevation angle ϕ_l. This slant range will determine the total propagation power loss from earth station to satellite. In addition, the range z determines the propagation time (time delay) over the path. It will take an electromagnetic field

$$\tau_d = (3.83)z \ \mu\text{sec} \tag{1.4.9}$$

to propagate over a path of length z kilometers. Thus it takes approximately 10 msec to transmit to geostationary orbits. Also, since the location of the satellite is uncertain to about $\pm$ 40 km, a delay uncertainty of about $\pm$ 133 μsec is always present in an earth–satellite geostationary propagation path.

If a satellite is in orbit at altitude h, it will pass over a point on Earth with an elevation angle exceeding ϕ_l for a time period

$$t_p = \left(\frac{2\phi_E}{360°}\right)\left(\frac{t_s}{1 \pm (t_E/t_s)}\right) \tag{1.4.10}$$

where t_s is the orbit period, t_E is the rotation period of the Earth (one sidereal day), and ϕ_E is related to ϕ_l by (1.4.6). The ± sign depends on whether the satellite is in a prograde (same direction) orbit or a retrograde (opposite) orbit. For a progradéd geostationary orbit $t_s = t_E$, and $t_p = \infty$. Equation (1.4.10) is important in evaluating the amount of time an earth station has to communicate with an orbiting satellite as it passes overhead.

1.5 SATELLITE FREQUENCY BANDS

The electromagnetic frequency spectrum is shown in Figure 1.9, along with designated frequency bands. The frequencies used for satellite communications should be selected from bands that are most favorable in terms of power efficiencies, minimal propagation distortions, and reduced noise and interference effects. These conditions tend to force operation into particular frequency regions that provide the best trade-offs of these factors. Unfortunately, terrestrial systems (ground-to-ground) tend to favor these same bands. Hence there must be concern for interference effects between satellite and terrestrial systems. In addition, space itself is an international domain, just as are airline airways and the oceans, and satellite use from space must be shared and regulated on a worldwide basis. For this reason, frequencies to be used by satellites are established by a world body known as the International Telecommunications Union (ITU), with broadcast regulations controlled by a subgroup known as the World Administrative Radio Conference (WARC). An international consultative technical committee (CCIR) provides specific recommendations on satellite frequencies under consideration by WARC. The basic objective of these agencies is to allocate particular frequency bands for different types of satellite services, and also to provide international regulations in the areas of maximum radiation levels from space, coordination with terrestrial systems, and the use of specific satellite locations in a given orbit. Within these allottments and regulations, an individual country operating its own domestic satellite system, or perhaps a consortium of countries operating a common international satellite system (e.g., Intelsat), can make its own specific frequency selections based on intended uses and desired satellite services.

The frequency bands allocated by WARC (1979) for satellite communications is summarized in Figure 1.10. The tabulation in Table 1.3 shows the major use of these frequency bands in the US, and the available bandwidth within each band. Use of frequencies has been separated into military and nonmilitary, and services have been designated as **fixed-point** (between ground stations located at fixed points on Earth), **broadcast** (wide-area coverage), and **mobile** (aircraft, ships, land vehicles). **Intersatellite** refers to satellite crosslinks.

Most of the early satellite technology was developed for UHF, C-band,

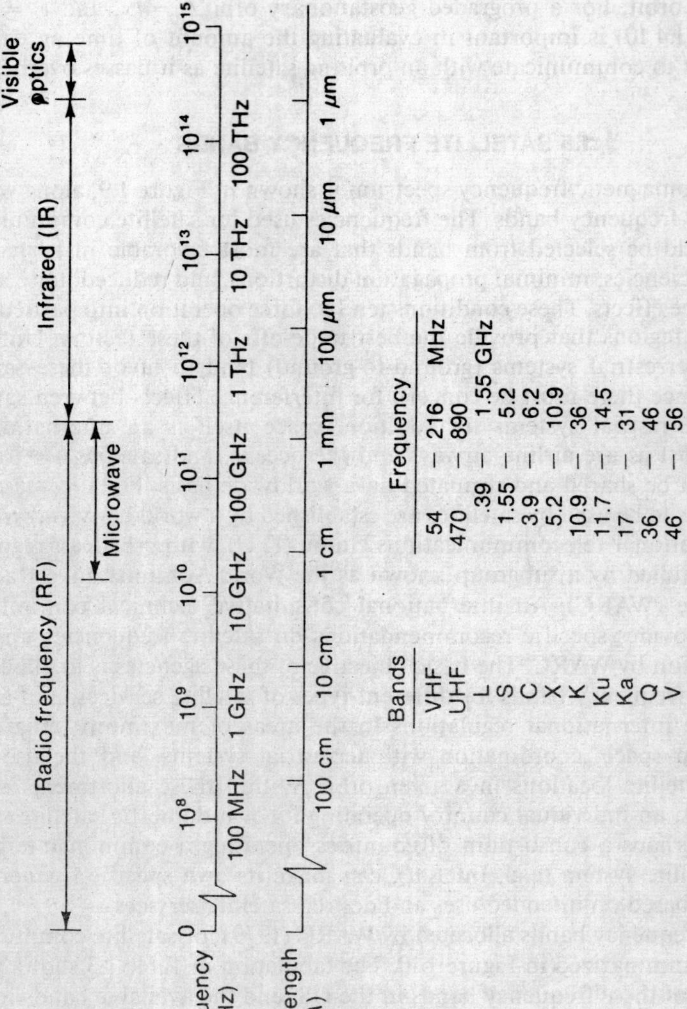

Figure 1.9. Electromagnetic frequency spectrum and designated bands [$\lambda = 3 \times 10^8$/frequency (Hz)].

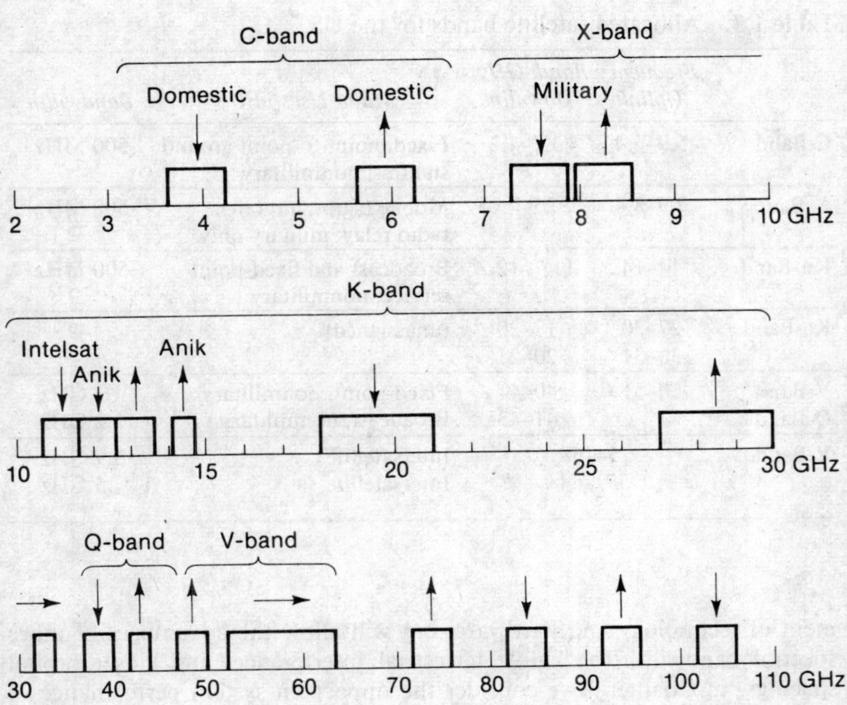

Figure 1.10. Allocated satellite frequency bands, WARC 1979 (↑ = uplink, ↓ = downlink, → = crosslink).

and X-band, which required the minimal conversion from existing microwave hardware. Major problems have been projected in these areas, however, because of the worldwide proliferation of satellite systems in these bands. The foremost problem is the fact that the available bandwidth in these bands will soon be inadequate to meet present and future traffic demands. Further, interference among various independent satellite systems, and between satellite and existing terrestrial systems, will become more severe as additional satellites are put into use. Coordination among independent systems will be difficult to maintain. There can also be serious orbital congestion in the most favorable orbits for systems operating at C- and X-bands (as we shall see in Chapter 3, choice of satellite frequencies dictates acceptable satellite spacing in a given orbit). For these reasons there is continued interest in extending operation to the higher K-band and V-band frequencies (see Figure 1.10). In most cases this means further develop-

Table 1.3. Allocated satellite bands for the US.

	Frequency Band, GHz Uplink	Downlink	*Major Uses in US*	*Bandwidth*
C-Band	5.9–6.4	3.7–4.2	Fixed, point-to-point ground stations; nonmilitary	500 MHz
X-Band	7.9–8.4	7.25–7.75	Mobile (ships, aircraft), radio relay; military only	500 MHz
Ku-Band	14–14.5	11.7–12.2	Broadcast and fixed-point service; nonmilitary	500 MHz
Ka-Band	27–30 30–31	17–20 20–21	(unassigned)	—
V-Band	50–51	40–41	Fixed-point, nonmilitary	1 GHz
Q-Band		41–43	Broadcast, nonmilitary	2 GHz
V-Band	54–58		Intersatellite	3.9 GHz
	59–64		Intersatellite	5 GHz

ment of technology and hardware, but will allow the advantages of more spectral bandwidth, negligible terrestrial interference, and closer orbital spacings. In Chapter 3 we consider the impact on system performance of being able to operate at these higher frequency bands.

An immediate, obvious advantage of using a carrier at a higher frequency is the ability to modulate more information (wider bandwidths) on it. If we assume the bandwidth that can be modulated onto a carrier is a fixed percentage of that carrier frequency, then a carrier at 30 GHz can carry roughly five times the information of a C-band carrier. Thus, while C-band satellite systems can provide bandwidths of 500 MHz (about 10% of the carrier frequency), a K-band carrier frequency would project to about 2.5 GHz of modulation bandwidth. An increase of this proportion would have significant impact on the cost efficiency and capabilities of a satellite link.

1.6 SATELLITE MULTIPLE-ACCESS FORMATS

A communication satellite will invariably be designed to handle many simultaneous uplinks and downlinks, as depicted in Figure 1.11. Here, separate earth stations each transmit their individual carrier waveforms to the satellite, and all are relayed simultaneously to a similar group of separate

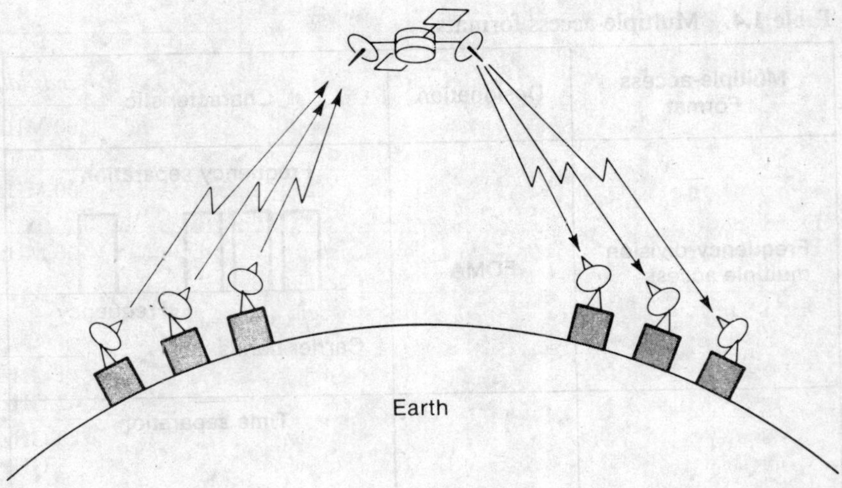

Figure 1.11. Multiple-accessing satellite links.

receiving stations. A given transmitting station may wish to communicate its waveform to one or several different receiving stations. Similarly, a receiving station may wish to receive the transmissions of several different transmitting stations. Since all the uplink carriers must access through a common satellite to complete their downlink transmissions, the overall system operation has been referred to as **multiple-access communications**. In general all receivers observe the same satellite transmissions, and therefore a multiple-access satellite system must allow for separability in the downlink waveforms. That is, multiple accessing must allow a downlink receiver to separate out a desired uplink transmission while tuning out undesired ones. This separability is achieved by requiring the uplink carrier to conform to a specific multiple-access format. The multiple-access format is simply a form of carrier-wave multiplexing that allows many uplink carriers, even when emitted from remotely located ground stations, to pass their waveforms through the satellite electromagnetically so as to be separable during the downlink transmission.

The three most common forms of multiple-accessing formats are summarized in Table 1.4. In **frequency-division multiple access (FDMA)**, earth stations using the satellite are assigned specific uplink and downlink carrier frequency bands within the allotted satellite bandwidth. Station separability is therefore achieved by separation in frequency. After retransmission through the satellite, a receiving station can receive the transmitted

Table 1.4. Multiple-access formats.

Multiple-access Format	Designation	Characteristic
Frequency-division multiple access	FDMA	Frequency separation (Carrier bands; Frequency)
Time-division multiple access	TDMA	Time separation (Carrier time slots; Time)
Code-division multiple access (spread-spectrum multiple access)	CDMA (SSMA)	Waveform separation (Coded carrier spectra; Frequency)

waveform of an uplink station by simply tuning to the proper frequency band. FDMA is the simplest and most basic format to implement since it requires earth station configurations most compatible with existing hardware. FDMA formats are also the most popular, and were used almost exclusively in all early satellite systems. The primary disadvantage of FDMA is its susceptibility to station crosstalk and intercarrier interference from nearby carriers while all are passing through the satellite.

In **time-division multiple access (TDMA)**, each uplink station is assigned a specific time slot in which to use the satellite. Each station must carefully ensure that its waveform passes through the satellite during its prescribed interval only. Receiving stations receive an uplink station by receiving the downlink only at the proper time period. Clearly, TDMA involves more complicated station operations, including some form of precise time synchronization among all users. Frequency crosstalk between users is no longer a problem, since theoretically only one station uses the satellite at a time. Since each station uses the satellite for intermittent time periods, TDMA systems require short burst communications. This type of communications allows each station to transmit a burst of information on its carrier waveform, during its allotted time interval. An operation like this makes TDMA primarily applicable to special purpose systems involving relatively few earth stations.

In **code-division multiple access (CDMA)**, carriers are separated by assigning a specific coded address waveform to each. Information is transmitted by superimposing it onto the addressing waveform, and modulating the combined waveform onto the station carrier. A station can use the entire satellite bandwidth and transmit at any desired time. All stations transmitting simultaneously therefore overlap their carrier waveforms on top of each other. Receiving the entire satellite transmission, and demodulating with the proper address waveform, allows reception of only the appropriate uplink carrier. Accurate frequency and time-interval separation are no longer needed, but station receiver equipment tends to be more complicated in order to carry out the address selection required.

Since addressing waveforms tend to produce carrier spectra over a relatively wide bandwidth, CDMA signals are often called **spread-spectrum signals**, and CDMA is alternatively referred to as **spread-spectrum multiple access (SSMA)**.

The specific implementation and attainable performance associated with these multiple-access formats will be examined in detail in Chapters 5–7. It is first necessary, however, to review carefully the basic properties of modulated carriers, and to develop reliable communication models of the various types of satellite links. These topics will be covered in the next three chapters.

PROBLEMS

1.1 A satellite has a fixed allowable weight of W lb for its communication equipment. Each watt of transmitter power has a communication weight of x lb. Each watt of primary power used will add y lb. The satellite has a power efficiency of ϵ. (ϵ = ratio of useable transmitter power to required primary power.) Plot a curve of available transmitter power vs. satellite efficiency for fixed values of W, x, and y.

1.2 Assume a satellite location is known to within a distance of δr at altitude h. Convert this to angular uncertainty as observed from Earth, and sketch a plot of angle uncertainty vs. position uncertainty for various orbit altitudes.

1.3 Use (1.4.3) to show that synchronous orbit is achieved at the values given in (1.4.4).

1.4 Derive (1.4.5) and (1.4.8) using Figure 1.8.

1.5 Derive an equation for field propagation time in terms of propagation path length, and confirm (1.4.9) using the fact that an electromagnetic wave travels at the speed of light ($c = 3 \times 10^8\ m/s$).

1.6 A low-orbiting satellite has an 8-hour prograde orbit. How long during each orbit will an earth station have to communicate with it above an elevation angle of 15°? Repeat if the orbit is retrograde.

1.7 Carrier wavelength λ is related to carrier frequency f by $\lambda = c/f$, where c is the speed of light. Compute: (a) the carrier frequency corresponding to 1 mm wavelength, (b) the wavelength corresponding to 1 GHz frequency, and (c) the frequency separation corresponding to a given wavelength separation $\delta\lambda = \lambda_1 - \lambda_2$.

REFERENCES

1. M. Howes, and D. Morgan, *Microwave Devices* (New York: Wiley, 1976).

2. R. Strauss, J. Bretting, and R. Metivier, "TWT for Communication Satellites," *Proceedings of the IEEE*, vol. 65 (March 1977), pp. 387–400.

3. W.J. Hoefer, "Microwave Amplifiers," in *Digital Communications-Microwave Applications*, by K. Feher, (Englewood Cliffs, N.J.: Prentice-Hall, 1981), chapter 4.

4. C. Liechti, "Microwave Field Effect Transistors," *IEEE Trans. on Microwave Theory*, vol. MT 24 (June 1976), pp. 279–300.

5. J. Di Lorenzo, "GaAs FET Development," *Microwave Journal*, vol. 21 (February 1978), pp. 39–42.

2

Modulation, Encoding, and Decoding

In this chapter we review the basic properties of the modulated carriers involved in satellite systems. We will temporarily ignore the presence of the satellite here, and simply consider a transmitter generating the modulated carrier, and a receiver processing this carrier. The discussion focuses the analysis then on the basic components of any communication system, and the key elements of modulation theory and receiver performance are directly applicable. We consider specifically those modulation characteristics that are of particular interest to satellite systems.

In communication links, information is transmitted by modulating it onto electromagnetic carriers, which are then propagated to the receiver. At the receiver, the information is demodulated (extracted) from the carrier to complete the link. The objective of any communication system is to transmit the modulated carrier to the receiver as reliably as possible, so that the demodulated information can be satisfactorily recovered. In **analog** modulation systems, the information waveforms (voice, video, teletype, etc.) are modulated directly from the source onto the carrier. In **digital** communication systems, source information is first converted into sequences of digital symbols, which are then encoded into waveforms for carrier modulation. At the receiver, the demodulated waveforms are decoded back into the digital sequence, from which the source information is then retrieved.

Early satellite systems primarily used analog modulation techniques, since their technology and hardware were fully developed for terrestrial microwave systems. Although modern satellite systems are still predominantly analog, the rapid development of high-speed digital circuitry is fostering a trend toward completely digital satellite communications. We here review the basic properties of modulation, encoding, and decoding associated with both these system formats.

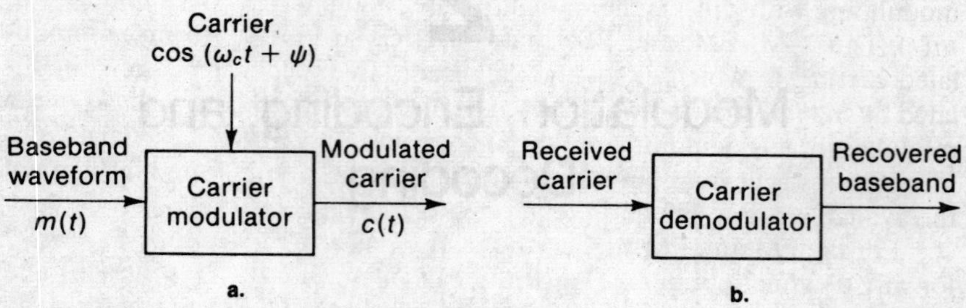

Figure 2.1. Analog communication basic components. (a) Transmitter modulator. (b) Receiver demodulator.

2.1 ANALOG MODULATION

In analog communications, source waveforms are directly modulated onto carriers at the transmitter (Figure 2.1a) using some form of amplitude modulation (AM), frequency modulation (FM), or phase modulation (PM). The carrier can be at RF, or it can be at IF and then frequency-translated to RF, as we showed in Figure 1.3a. At the receiver (Figure 2.1b) the carrier is demodulated to recover directly the source waveforms. Performance of analog modulation systems is usually measured in terms of signal-to-noise ratio (SNR) of the demodulated information waveform relative to any interfering noise. The larger the demodulated SNR, the higher the quality of the communication link.

Modulated Carrier Waveforms

If $m(t)$ represents the information waveform to be transmitted, the modulated carriers (more specifically, the E-field component of the electromagnetic field) for each type of analog modulation take the following forms:

$$\text{AM:} c(t) = A(1 + \Delta_a m(t)) \cos(\omega_c t + \psi) \tag{2.1.1a}$$

$$\text{FM:} c(t) = A \cos\left(\omega_c t + 2\pi\Delta_f \int m(t)dt + \psi\right) \tag{2.1.1b}$$

$$\text{PM:} c(t) = A \cos(\omega_c t + \Delta m(t) + \psi) \tag{2.1.1c}$$

Here A is the carrier amplitude, ω_c the carrier frequency in rad/sec, and ψ the carrier phase angle. The coefficients Δ_a, Δ_f, and Δ are modulation coefficients determining the degree of modulation, and are commonly called the **AM index**, the **frequency-deviation coefficient** (Hz/volt), and the

phase-deviation coefficient (rad/volt), respectively. Note that frequency modulating with $m(t)$ is the same as phase modulating with the integral of $m(t)$. Thus AM, FM, and PM analog carriers are simply forms of modulated carriers in which either the amplitude, frequency, or phase is modulated by the information waveform. Detailed description and analysis of the modulation and demodulation circuitry commonly used in modern communications is beyond our scope here, but can be readily found in many of the available communication textbooks (e.g., references 1–7).

For the FM and PM carrier, the carrier power P_c is given by $P_c = A^2/2$ for any modulation $m(t)$. Hence the carrier amplitude A in (2.1.1b) and (2.1.1c) directly sets the carrier power. For the AM carrier the power is given by $P_c = A^2(1 + \Delta_a^2 P_m)/2$, where P_m is the power in the modulating waveform $m(t)$. Thus the modulation power adjusts the carrier power in AM carriers.

Key Parameters of Modulated Carriers

In satellite communications, the important parameters of a modulated carrier are its bandwidth, the amount of receiver carrier power needed to demodulate, and the resulting demodulated signal-to-noise ratio (SNR_d). These parameters are summarized in Table 2.1 for each type of carrier in (2.1.1). The demodulated SNR_d determines the ultimate performance of the link, indicating how accurately the transmitted baseband information waveform has been recovered. Generally SNR_d values* between 100 (20 dB) and 10^4 (40 dB) are usually required, depending on the specific application. The required carrier power is that which must be provided at the receiver in order to overcome the noise in the demodulator noise bandwidth, while producing a carrier-to-noise ratio (CNR) exceeding a specified threshold. The threshold CNR_T is needed to ensure distortionless demodulation of the information waveform. Carrier bandwidth is the bandwidth that must be provided in the entire satellite RF system in order to avoid carrier distortion.

Angle-modulated carriers (FM and PM) require more carrier bandwidth than AM, but achieve a higher demodulated SNR_d for the same carrier CNR. For angle modulation, two types of demodulators are considered in Table 2.1. The standard demodulator uses conventional frequency or phase detection circuits, and the carrier power must overcome the noise in the entire modulated carrier bandwidth. Feedback tracking demodulators have reduced noise bandwidths, resulting in less required carrier power for a given threshold CNR. However, design of tracking-loop demodulators often

*The decibel (dB) value of a number N is defined as $(N)_{dB} = 10\log_{10}N$.

Table 2.1. Analog demodulation summary.

Type	*Modulated Carrier Bandwidth, Hz*	*Threshold noise Bandwidth, Hz*	*Required Carrier Power*	*Demodulated SNR_d*
AM	$2\ B_m$	$2\ B_m$	$CNR_T \geq 12$ dB	$SNR_d = CNR_T$
FM		$2(\beta + 1)B_m$	$CNR_T \geq 16$ dB	$SNR_d = 6\beta^2(\beta + 1)CNR_T$
Disc. frequency detection	$2(\beta + 1)B_m$ $\beta = \dfrac{\text{Peak frequency deviation}}{B_m}$			
FBFM	$2(\beta + 1)B_m$	$2\left(\dfrac{\beta}{G} + 1\right)B_m$ G = FBFM gain	$CNR_T \geq 16$ dB	$SNR_d = 6\beta^2(\beta + 1)CNR_T$
PM				
Phase detection circuitry	$2(\Delta + 1)B_m$ Δ = Phase deviation	$2(\Delta + 1)B_m$	$CNR_T \geq 12$–16 dB	$SNR_d = 6\ \Delta^2(\Delta + 1)CNR_T$
Phase tracking loop demod	$2(\Delta + 1)B_m$	$2B_m$	$CNR_T \geq 10$ dB	$SNR_d = 6\ \Delta^2(\Delta + 1)CNR_T$

CNR_T = Carrier power to noise power in threshold bandwidth.
B_m = Modulation bandwidth.

becomes extremely sensitive when producing large noise bandwidth reductions.

The carrier and noise bandwidths in Table 2.1 are directly related to the bandwidth B_m of the modulating baseband signal $m(t)$ in (2.1.1). The larger the baseband bandwidth, the more information it will contain, but the required carrier bandwidth is larger. The bandwidth B_m depends on the type of sources, and on the manner in which they may be combined to form $m(t)$. If a single source (video camera, microphone, etc.) is used as the modulating waveform (SCPC carrier), then $m(t)$ has the bandwidth of the source itself. The bandwidth B_m will then correspond to the highest significant frequency in the source spectrum. Table 2.2 lists the frequency bandwidth of some common sources. A voice channel has a bandwidth of about 4 KHz, while a video signal has frequency components out to about 4 MHz. Commercial television channels have been allotted channel bandwidths of 6 MHz to allow for audio and synchronization.

A group of sources can be multiplexed and transmitted simultaneously by modulating each on a separate subcarrier, and summing the subcarriers to form the baseband, as shown in Figure 2.2. This procedure corresponds to a form of **frequency-division multiplexing (FDM)** at a source level, and the baseband in Figure 2.2 is referred to as having an *FDM format*. The entire set of FDM subcarriers is then modulated onto the RF carrier using any of the forms in (2.1.1). The baseband bandwidth will therefore depend on the type and number of sources being multiplexed, the modulation used on the subcarriers, and the spacings between each subcarrier. Table 2.2 also lists the required bandwidth B_m for the FDM of voice channels using single

Table 2.2. Baseband bandwidths.

Type of Baseband	*Bandwidth (B_m)*
Voice	3.5 KHz
Audio channel	4 KHz
Video	4 MHz
Television channel	6 MHz
Multiplexed voice:	
12 channels	48 KHz
40	160 KHz
100	400 KHz
500	2 MHz
1000	4 MHz
2000	8 MHz

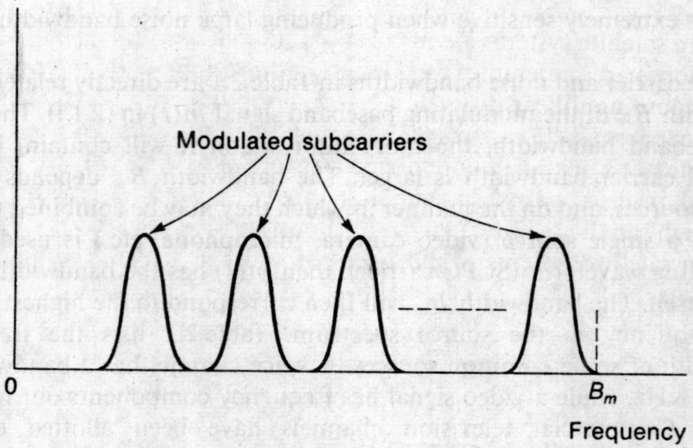

Figure 2.2. FDM baseband spectrum.

sideband amplitude modulation (SSB/AM)* on the subcarriers. Note that close to 1000 voice channels can be multiplexed into the same bandwidth as a single video signal.

As an example, consider a video-modulating waveform of 4 MHz. To achieve high-quality television reception, we need to produce $\text{SNR}_d \geqslant$ 40 dB. If the video is frequency-modulated onto the carrier, and if frequency demodulation requires a CNR_T of 15 dB, Table 2.1 indicates that

$$\text{SNR}_d \approx 6\beta^2(\beta + 1)\text{CNR}_T \tag{2.1.2}$$

For SNR_d = 40 dB, the FM index β must be about 3.5, corresponding to a carrier frequency deviation of 14 MHz. This produces a carrier bandwidth of 2(3.5 + 1)4 = 36 MHz. A standard frequency discriminator would require 15 dB more carrier power at the demodulator input than the noise power generated in this 36 MHz bandwidth. A frequency tracking detector using feedback has a noise bandwidth of only about 2 × 4 = 8 MHz, and would require 36/8 = 4.5 = 6.53 dB less carrier power to operate with the same SNR_d. We point out that the 36 MHz carrier bandwidth of this example is in fact commensurate with typical transponder bandwidths in operating C-band satellites.

*SSB/AM is a modified form of amplitude modulation that produces carriers with one-half the AM bandwidth in Table 2.1. Thus, SSB/AM has a subcarrier bandwidth of about 4 KHz. Circuitry for modulating and demodulating SSB/AM is more complex than for standard AM, and can only be designed for narrow band waveforms, such as voice.

In satellite systems we invariably find that carriers employing constant envelopes are preferable over those that have time-varying envelopes. This is because nonlinear distortion effects are produced on nonconstant envelope carriers as the carriers pass through satellites, a topic to be discussed in Chapter 4. Thus angle-modulated carriers (FM or PM) are usually preferred, instead of amplitude modulation, in transmitting from earth stations through satellites. FM carriers are almost exclusively used in analog modulation satellite systems, while both FM and PM are used in digital satellite systems.

2.2 ANALOG FM CARRIERS

FM carriers, modulated with analog source waveforms, are commonly used in satellite links. FM carriers have the advantage of constant amplitudes and higher demodulated SNR_d, both properties of considerable importance in satellite transmission. In addition, the circuitry and hardware used in FM modulation and demodulation have been well established and technically developed for many decades. FM carriers, however, require more carrier bandwidth than conventional AM carriers. Careful control of the FM carrier spectra is therefore necessary to make maximal use of available satellite bandwidth and to prevent crosstalk between adjacent FM carriers (e.g., as in an FDMA format).

The spectral spread of an FM carrier is difficult to compute precisely due to the nonlinear relation between the carrier $c(t)$ and the modulation $m(t)$. In Table 2.1 the bandwidth of the FM carrier is estimated by using only the peak frequency deviation of the carrier, which in turn determines the FM modulation index. The frequency deviation in (2.1.1b) is given by $\Delta_f m(t)$, and is therefore dependent on the choice of the deviation coefficient and the peak value of the modulation $m(t)$. Unfortunately, peak values of video and audio source waveforms are difficult to estimate in advance. For FM carriers modulated with a single video waveform, it has been found that the FM carrier spectrum is strongly dependent only on the rms (root mean squared) deviation, the latter depending only on the power P_m of the modulating signal $m(t)$. The corresponding rms value of the modulation index β is then

$$\beta_{\text{rms}} = \frac{\Delta_f \sqrt{P_m}}{B_m} \tag{2.2.1}$$

By controlling the power level of the modulation, the FM index can be accurately set. Figure 2.3 shows the resulting shape of the video FM carrier

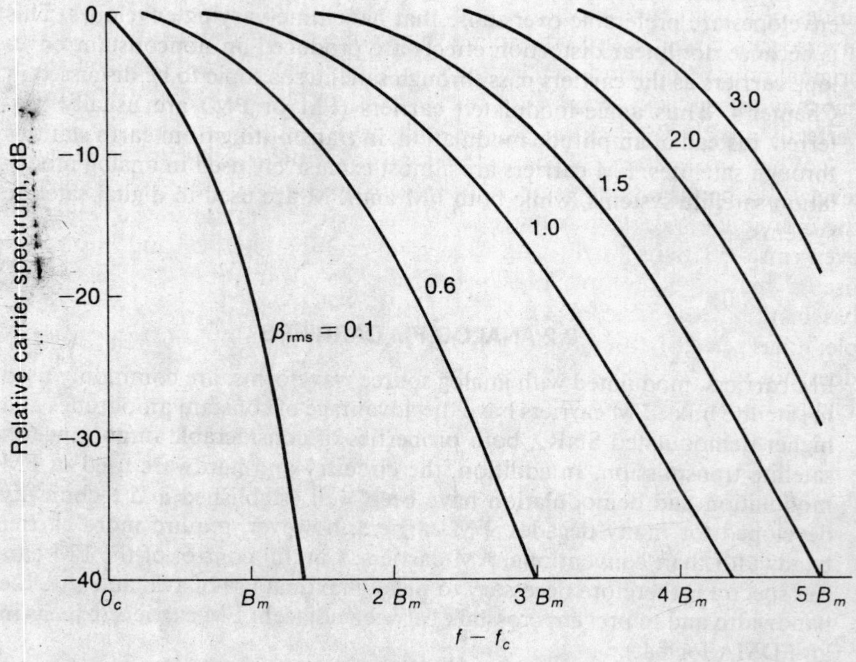

Figure 2.3. FM video carrier spectrum (β_{rms} = rms modulation index).

as a function of the rms β in (2.2.1). The FM carrier bandwidth is often estimated as

$$B_c \approx 2(\beta_{rms} + 1)B_m$$
$$= 2(\Delta_f\sqrt{P_m} + B_m)Hz \tag{2.2.2}$$

For example, if β_{rms} in (2.2.1) is set at 3, Equation (2.2.2) indicates that a carrier bandwidth of 2(4)4 = 32 MHz is required. Figure 2.3, on the other hand, indicates that the FM carrier spectrum will be spread over a bandwidth of only about 2(3.25)4 = 26 MHz. Hence, a slightly smaller bandwidth can generally be used for analog TV transmission than that predicted by (2.2.2).

A source waveform with abnormally large peak deviations may produce spectral components exceeding this rms bandwidth, even though the power is being accurately controlled. As a result, additional circuitry is often used to limit the peak deviations. **Compander** circuits [8] are nonlinear gain networks that are used at the transmitter to compress the extreme peak values of a source waveform prior to FM modulation. At the receiver, an inverse gain circuit is used to expand the compressed waveform back to its original range. Companding allows additional FM carrier spectrum control, but may introduce receiver distortion if the inverse gain functions are not perfectly matched.

When multiplexing voice channels to form the baseband, the power level P_m depends on the number of channels active at any one time and on the individual voice characteristics of each particular audio source. Hence even rms deviations are difficult to set with multiplexed baseband. Instead, use is made of multiplexing *loading factors*, which estimate average baseband power levels as a function of the number of channels. For example, it has generally been found that the power content of multiplexed voice does not increase as fast as expected when more channels are added [9]. Figure 2.4 shows a recommended carrier deviation to be used with FDM

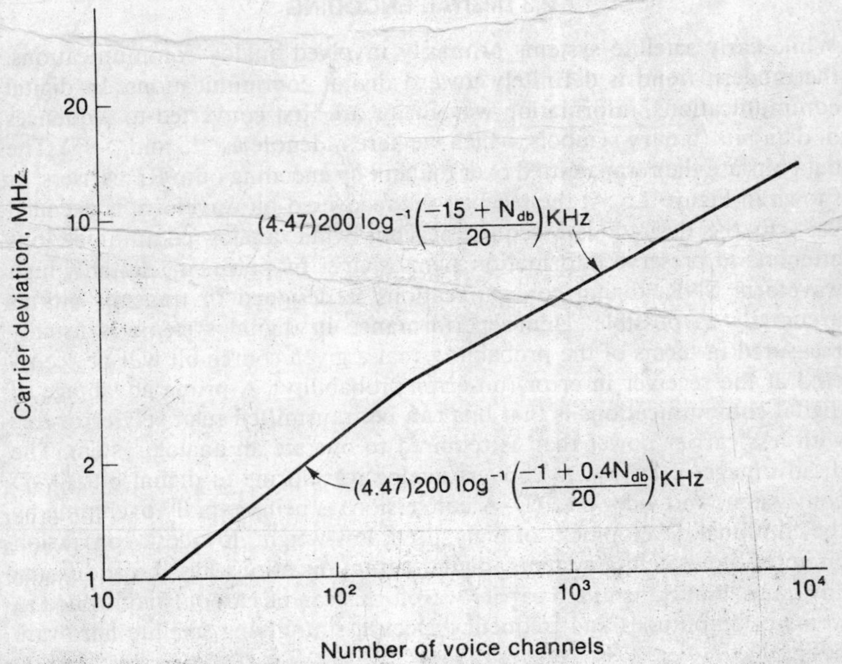

Figure 2.4. Required FM frequency deviation vs. number of multiplexed voice channels.

voice modulation of an FM carrier as a function of the number of voice channels being multiplexed.

A problem with multiplexing large numbers of FDM channels is that the FM demodulated noise spectrum at the receiver tends to increase with frequency [7, Chapter 4]. This means the subcarrier voice channels with the higher frequencies have poorer SNR_d. To combat this, spectral *pre-emphasis* is used at the transmitter. This is a form of nonuniform amplification applied to the multiplexed baseband prior to FM carrier modulation so as to transmit the higher subcarriers with more power. It tends to equalize the individual SNR_d across the entire set of FDM channels after demodulation at the receiver. However, pre-emphasis, being a form of baseband amplification, increases the frequency deviation of the FM carrier, and tends to increase further the resulting FM carrier bandwidth. Thus pre-emphasized FM carriers require slightly more carrier bandwidth than conventional FM carriers.

2.3 DIGITAL ENCODING

While early satellite systems primarily involved analog communications, the modern trend is definitely toward digital communications. In digital communications, information waveforms are first converted to sequences of data bits (binary symbols, which we herein denote as "1" and "−1"). The data bits are then transmitted over the link by encoding onto RF carriers, as shown in Figure 2.5. At the receiver the recovered-bit waveform is decoded back to the desired data sequence. Thus while analog communications attempts to preserve information signal shapes by producing suitably high waveform SNR, digital communications is designed to transmit bits as accurately as possible. Hence performance in digital systems is usually measured in terms of the probability that a given source bit will be recovered at the receiver in error (bit-error probability). A prime advantage of digital communications is that bits can be transmitted relatively error-free with less carrier power than is required to operate an analog system. The disadvantage of having to convert analog waveforms to digital bits (A–D conversion) and vice-versa (D–A conversion) is being rapidly overcome by the continual development of high-speed, low-weight, low-cost, conversion circuitry. For satellite systems, digital communications has the additional advantage that transmitted carrier waveforms can be carefully controlled in terms of amplitudes and frequency spectra, simplifying satellite hardware design.

The rate at which data bits are generated (number of bits per sec) at the transmitter is an important parameter in subsequent digital system design. This rate depends on the desired accuracy built into the A–D conversion of

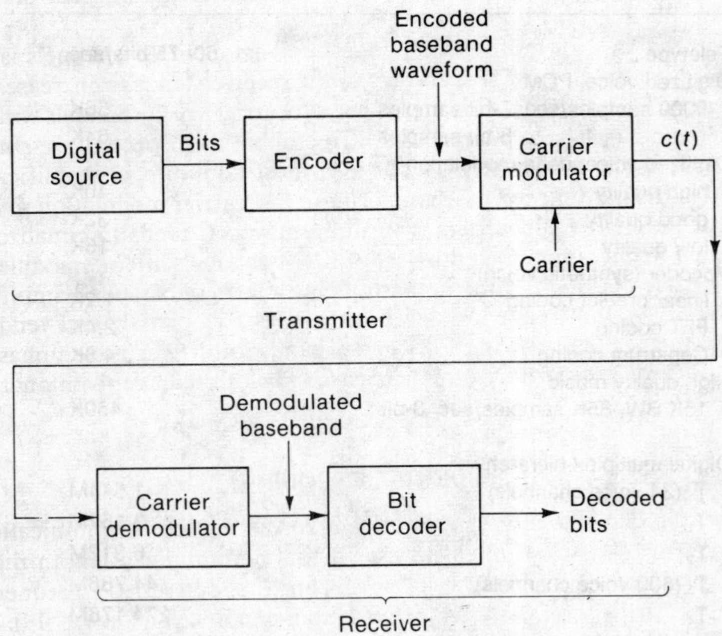

Figure 2.5. Digital communication block diagram.

information waveforms. Box 2.1 lists typical bit rates associated with the A–D conversion of specific types of common information sources. When multiple data sources are serially multiplexed (interlaced in time) to form a combined bit sequence, the resulting bit rate becomes the sum of the individual bit rates of each source.

Encoding Schemes

Several primary types of encoding schemes have emerged for use in satellite digital communications, each with inherent advantages and disadvantages. We review these methods here; a more detailed mathematical discussion can be found in Appendix A. Digital encoding can be visualized in two steps, as we showed in Figure 2.5. First, data bits are converted to baseband waveforms, then the waveforms are modulated onto the IF or microwave carrier for transmission. Either phase or frequency-carrier modulation is typically used in order to maintain the constant carrier envelope condition. Encoding can be either **binary encoding** (bit by bit) or **block encoding**

Teletype	50–75 bits/sec	
Digitized voice, PCM		
8000 samples/sec: 7-bit samples	56K	
8-bit samples	64K	
Digitized voice, delta modulation		
high quality	40K	
good quality	32K	
low quality	16K	
Vocoder (synthetic voice)		
linear predict coding	1.2K	
FFT coding	2.4K	
Cepstrum coding	4.8K	
High quality music		
15K BW, 35K samples/sec, 8-bit	450K	
Digital multiplex hierarchy		
T_1 (24 voice channels)	1.544M	
T_{1c}	3.152M	
T_2	6.312M	
T_3 (600 voice channels)	44.736M	
T_4	274.176M	
Digital TV, high-quality color	92.608M	
reduced resolution (good–excellent)	32 M	
reduced resolution (fair–good)	1.5–4.8M	
transform encoded (good resolution)	6–11M	
Picture phone (video telephone)	6.3M	(T_2)
Imagery	1–6M	

Box 2.1. Digital bit rates.

(groups of bits). Both of these encoding methods may be augmented by forward-error correction techniques (Section 2.6) that improve performance by introducing redundancy. Error correction can involve **fixed-block encoding** or **convolutional encoding**. Both these advanced techniques provide increasing levels of improvement in system performance, but at the same time they involve increasing complexity in system-decoding hardware.

In binary encoding, each data bit of the source sequence is encoded one bit at a time into a preselected baseband waveform prior to carrier modulation. The preferred encoding is via **antipodal** signals, in which a binary 1 is encoded into a specific waveform, and a binary −1 is encoded into the negative of that waveform. Thus, if $p(t)$ is the designated bit waveform, each data bit is sent in sequence by encoding into $\pm p(t)$, depending on the bit. A sequence of data bits $(d_1, d_2, \ldots)$, where $d_i = \pm 1$, will therefore be encoded into a baseband waveform

$$m(t) = \sum_{k=-\infty}^{\infty} d_k p(t - kT_b) \tag{2.3.1}$$

Here T_b is the bit time, that is, the time allocated between each bit. We therefore encode one bit every T_b sec, or at a bit rate of

$$R_b = \frac{1}{T_b} \text{ bits/sec} \tag{2.3.2}$$

To transmit the bit rate of a given source, as in Table 2.3, it is necessary to match the bit time to the desired rate using (2.3.2).

The waveform $p(t)$ is preselected according to ease of generation, spectral shape, and bandwidth, or is perhaps designed to give other advantages, such as improved decoding or synchronization capability. The popular forms in satellite links are NRZ waveforms:

$$\begin{aligned} p(t) &= 1 \qquad 0 \leqslant t \leqslant T_b \\ &= 0 \qquad \text{Elsewhere} \end{aligned} \tag{2.3.3}$$

or Manchester waveforms:

$$\begin{aligned} p(t) &= 1 \qquad 0 \leqslant t \leqslant T_b/2 \\ &= -1 \qquad T_b/2 \leqslant t \leqslant T_b \end{aligned} \tag{2.3.4}$$

NRZ signals are simply rectangular pulses with a time width of one bit time, while Manchester signals contain both a positive and negative pulse within a bit time (Figure 2.6). Both waveforms are exactly T_b sec long, so that (2.3.1) corresponds to sequences of nonoverlapping, unit magnitude, positive and negative pulsed waveforms. The primary difference between the two waveforms is the baseband frequency spectrum that they produce for $m(t)$. Assuming independent, equally likely data bits $\{d_i\}$, the spectrum of $m(t)$ can be shown to be

$$S_m(\omega) = \frac{1}{T_b} |P(\omega)|^2 \tag{2.3.5}$$

where $P(\omega)$ is the Fourier transform of $p(t)$. See Section A.1 of Appendix A. Figure 2.6 sketches the NRZ and Manchester spectra. Note that an NRZ

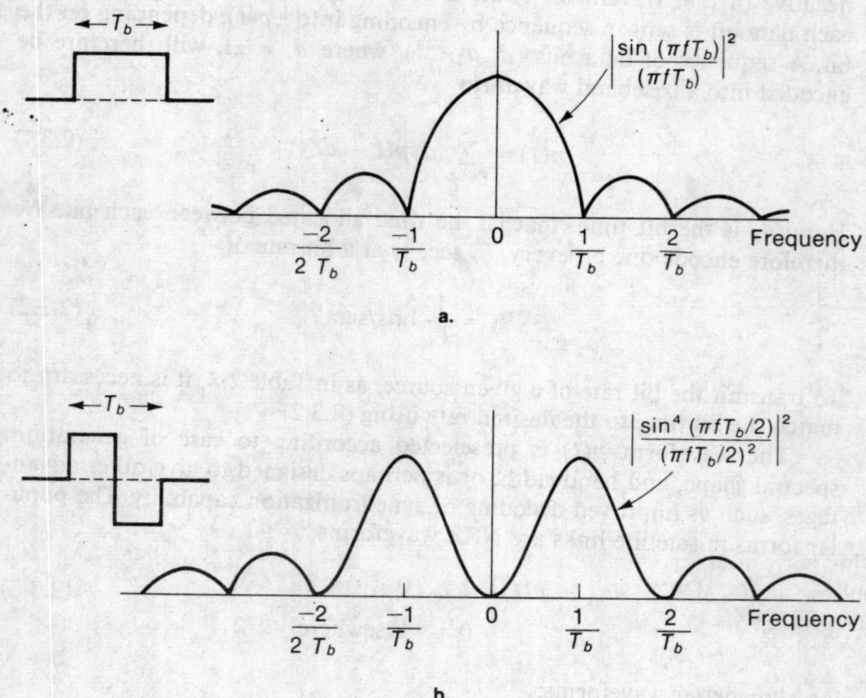

Figure 2.6. Baseband waveforms and spectra. (a) NRZ waveforms. (b) Manchester waveforms.

signal concentrates its spectrum around $f = 0$, with decaying spectral humps extending over all frequencies. The Manchester signal concentrates its spectrum at $f = 1/T_b$, away from zero frequency, which gives it advantages in synchronization and in avoiding low-frequency interference. This synchronization potential is also apparent from the waveshape, which shows that every Manchester bit contains a pulse sign change. Contrast this with long sequences of identical NRZ bits, which would contain no sign change. A sign change occurring once every bit, at exactly mid-bit time, can be used to establish a synchronized receiver clock at precisely the bit time period. Subsystems for establishing bit timing from encoded baseband waveforms are discussed in Appendix B.

Binary Phase Shift Keying. The encoded baseband $m(t)$ is then modulated onto the RF carrier. In **binary phase shift keying (BPSK)** the waveform is used to phase modulate the carrier, forming as in (2.1.1c),

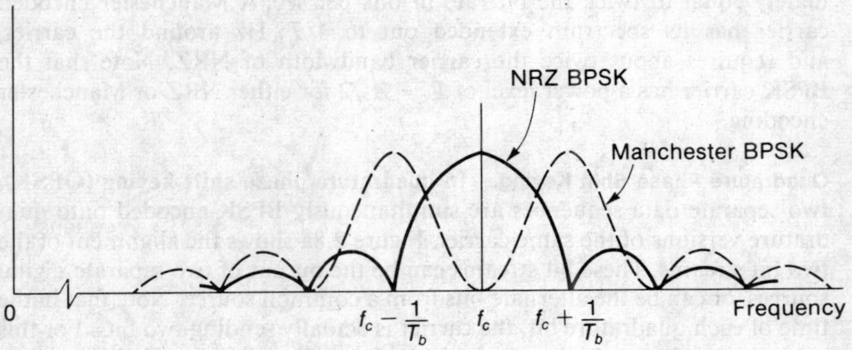

Figure 2.7. BPSK carrier spectra.

$$c(t) = A\cos\left(\omega_c t + \frac{\pi}{2}(1 - m(t)) + \psi\right) \tag{2.3.6}$$

This corresponds to $(0, \pi)$ phase shifts of the RF carrier according to the pulses of $m(t)$. By trigonometrically expanding, using $\cos(a \pm b) = \cos(a)\cos(b) \mp \sin(a)\sin(b)$, we can rewrite (2.3.6) instead as

$$c(t) = Am(t)\cos(\omega_c t + \psi) \tag{2.3.7}$$

Hence, when pulsed waveforms such as NRZ or Manchester signals are phase encoded, the BPSK carrier is identical to an amplitude-modulated carrier in which the baseband waveform $m(t)$ directly multiplies the carrier. This means the BPSK carrier can be formed without directly phase modulating, but instead by waveform multiplication, which simplifies the encoding circuitry. The resulting spectrum of the BPSK carrier is then*

$$S_c(\omega) = \frac{A^2}{4}S_m(\omega \pm \omega_c) \tag{2.3.8}$$

Hence the BPSK carrier spectrum is obtained by merely shifting the spectrum of the baseband amplitude modulation to the carrier frequency. The carrier spectra of NRZ and Manchester encoding is shown in Figure 2.7. Note that for NRZ the spectral hump at f_c occupies a total width of $2/T_b$ Hz, which is generally taken as the required carrier bandwidth needed to transmit the NRZ BPSK carrier. Since $1/T_b$ is also the bit rate in (2.3.2), we see that a BPSK carrier requires a carrier bandwidth in Hz approxi-

*Here the notation $S_m(\omega \pm \omega_c)$ represents the replacement of ω by both $(\omega + \omega_c)$ and $(\omega - \omega_c)$, which corresponds to the shift of the spectrum $S_m(\omega)$ to both ω_c and $-\omega_c$.

mately equal to twice the bit rate in bits per sec. A Manchester encoded carrier has its spectrum extended out to $4/T_b$ Hz around the carrier, and requires about twice the carrier bandwidth of NRZ. Note that the BPSK carrier has a power level of $P_c = A^2/2$ for either NRZ or Manchester encoding.

Quadrature Phase Shift Keying. In **quadrature phase shift keying (QPSK)**, two separate data sequences are simultaneously BPSK-encoded onto quadrature versions of the same carrier. Figure 2.8a shows the alignment of the two bit streams. These bit streams can be the output of two separate digital sources, or can be the alternate bits from a common source. Note that in the time of each quadrature bit, the carrier is actually sending two bits. For this reason we refer to the quadrature bit times T_s as the *symbol* time, and denote the *carrier* bit time as $T_b \triangleq T_s/2$. If $m_c(t)$ and $m_s(t)$ denote the baseband waveforms in (2.3.1) formed from each data sequence, the carrier is then formed as

$$c(t) = Am_c(t) \cos(\omega_c t + \psi) + Am_s(t) \sin(\omega_c t + \psi) \tag{2.3.9}$$

This corresponds to separate amplitude modulation onto the quadrature components (cosine and sine) of the same carrier frequency. The orthogonality of the carrier components allows both modulations to remain orthogonal during transmission and decoding. By combining trigonometrically, the QPSK carrier in (2.3.9) can also be written

$$c(t) = \sqrt{2}\, A\, \alpha(t) \cos(\omega_c t + \theta(t) + \psi) \tag{2.3.10}$$

where

$$\alpha(t) = (m_c^2(t) + m_s^2(t))^{1/2} \tag{2.3.11a}$$

$$\theta(t) = \tan^{-1}\left[\frac{m_s(t)}{m_c(t)}\right] \tag{2.3.11b}$$

Since both $m_c(t)$ and $m_s(t)$ are either ± 1 at every t for either NRZ or Manchester waveforms, $\alpha(t) = 1$ at every t, and the QPSK carrier also has a constant envelope. Equations (2.3.9) and (2.3.10) also show that QPSK carriers can be formed either by combining separate BPSK quadrature carriers (see Figure 2.8b) or by phase shifting a carrier according to the ratio $m_s(t)/m_c(t)$. It can be easily verified that the phase angle θ in (2.3.11b) can take on only one of the four phase angles (45°, 135°, −135°, −45°) during each bit time, depending on the sign of $m_c(t)$and$m_s(t)$. Thus a phase modulation generator of QPSK, as shown in Figure 2.8c, corresponds to hopping the carrier phase between these angles, dependent on the bits of the data sequences of $m_c(t)$ and $m_s(t)$.

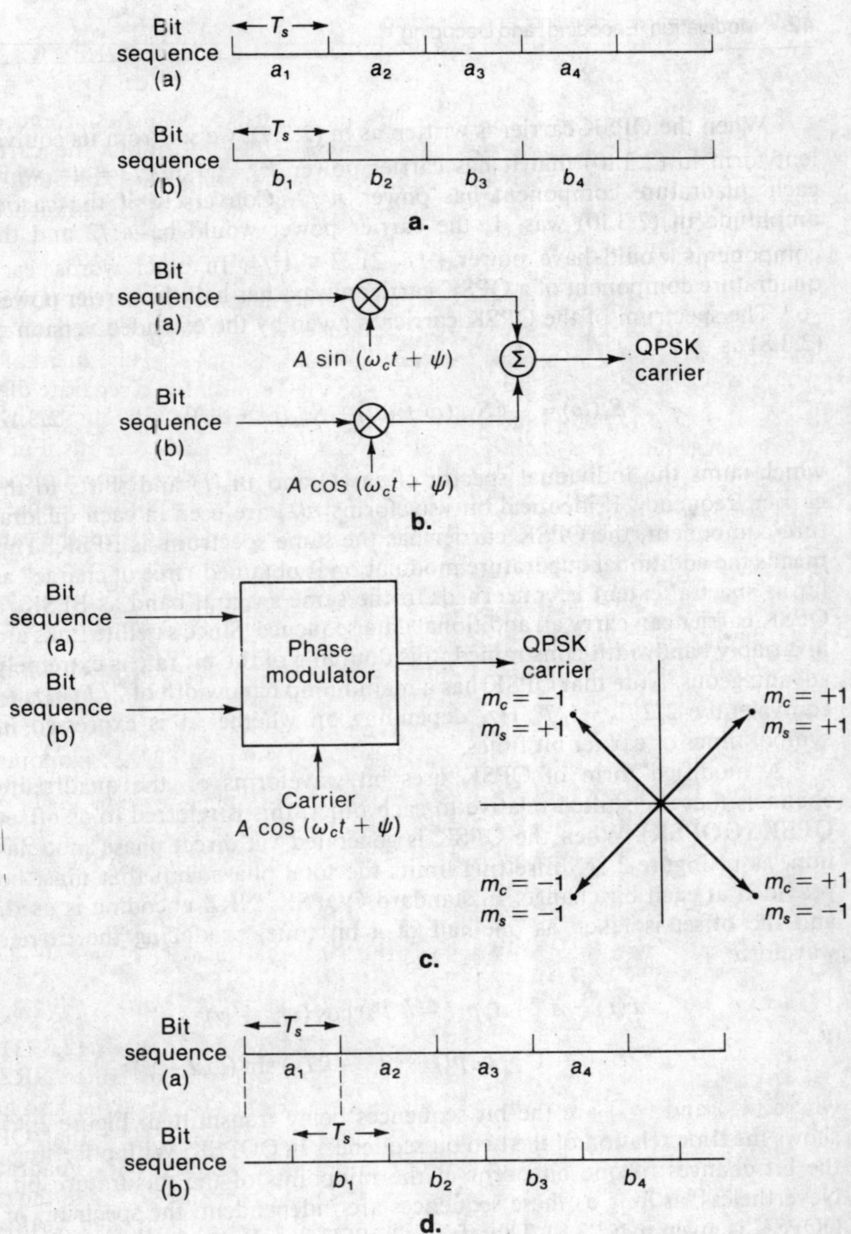

Figure 2.8. QPSK carriers. (a) Bit sequence alignment. (b) Carrier generator using quadrature amplitude modulation. (c) Carrier generator using quadrature phase shifting. (d) Bit sequence alignment for OQPSK.

When the QPSK carrier is written as in (2.3.9), we see from its equivalent form in (2.3.10) that it has carrier power $P_c = (A\sqrt{2})^2/2 = A^2$, while each quadrature component has power $A^2/2$. Conversely, if the carrier amplitude in (2.3.10) was A, the carrier power would be $A^2/2$ and the components would have power $(A/\sqrt{2})^2/2 = A^2/4$. In other words, each quadrature component of a QPSK carrier always has half the carrier power.

The spectrum of the QPSK carrier is given by the extended version of (2.3.8) as

$$S_c(\omega) = \frac{A^2}{4}[S_{m_c}(\omega \pm \omega_c) + S_{m_s}(\omega \pm \omega_c)] \tag{2.3.12}$$

which sums the individual spectra of $m_c(t)$ and $m_s(t)$ and shifts to the carrier frequency. If identical bit waveforms $p(t)$ are used in each quadrature component, the QPSK carrier has the same spectrum as BPSK. This means the additional quadrature modulation is obtained "free of charge" as far as spectral extent is concerned. In the same spectral band as BPSK, a QPSK carrier can carry an additional data sequence. Since satellite links are invariably bandwidth-constrained, this doubling of the bit rate is extremely advantageous. Note that QPSK has a main hump bandwidth of $2/T_s$ Hz, or equivalently, $2/2T_b = 1/T_b$ Hz, depending on whether it is expressed in symbol times or carrier bit times.

A modified form of QPSK uses bit waveforms on the quadrature channels that are shifted relative to each other; this is referred to as **offset QPSK (OQPSK)**. When the QPSK is generated via direct phase modulation, as in Figure 2.8c, offsetting limits the total phase shift that must be provided at each bit change. In standard OQPSK, NRZ encoding is used, and the offset is taken as one-half of a bit time, producing the carrier waveform

$$\begin{aligned} c(t) &= A \sum a_k p(t - kT_s) \cos(\omega_c t + \psi) \\ &\quad + A \sum b_k p(t - \tfrac{1}{2}T_s - kT_s) \sin(\omega_c t + \psi) \end{aligned} \tag{2.3.13}$$

where $\{a_k\}$ and $\{b_k\}$ are the bit sequences being transmitted. Figure 2.8d shows the time relation of the two bit sequences in OQPSK. With offsetting, the bit changes of one bit occur at the midpoints of the quadrature bit. Nevertheless, as long as these sequences are independent, the spectrum of OQPSK is given by (2.3.8). Therefore, OQPSK has the same spectral shape as QPSK and BPSK. An advantage in this is the limited phase shift that must be imparted during modulation. Also, as we shall see later, offsetting also provides spectral and interference advantages during nonideal decoding and nonlinear processing.

Frequency Shift Keying. Constant envelope binary signaling can also be generated from frequency modulation. The NRZ bit waveform is used to shift the carrier frequency between two modulation frequencies according to the bit waveform. The encoding is referred to as **frequency shift keying (FSK)**. The modulated carrier has the form

$$c(t) = A \cos\left(\omega_c t + 2\pi\Delta_f \int m(t)dt + \psi\right) \tag{2.3.14}$$

where $m(t)$ is the bit waveform sequence. This carrier corresponds to the frequency modulation of a carrier at ω_c with the baseband waveform $\Delta_f m(t)$.

Equation (2.3.14) differs from (2.1.1b) for analog modulation because the digital waveform $m(t)$ can be precisely adjusted in amplitude and waveshape. The carrier spectrum is somewhat difficult to compute, but can be estimated by noting that for NRZ bit waveforms, $c(t)$ corresponds to

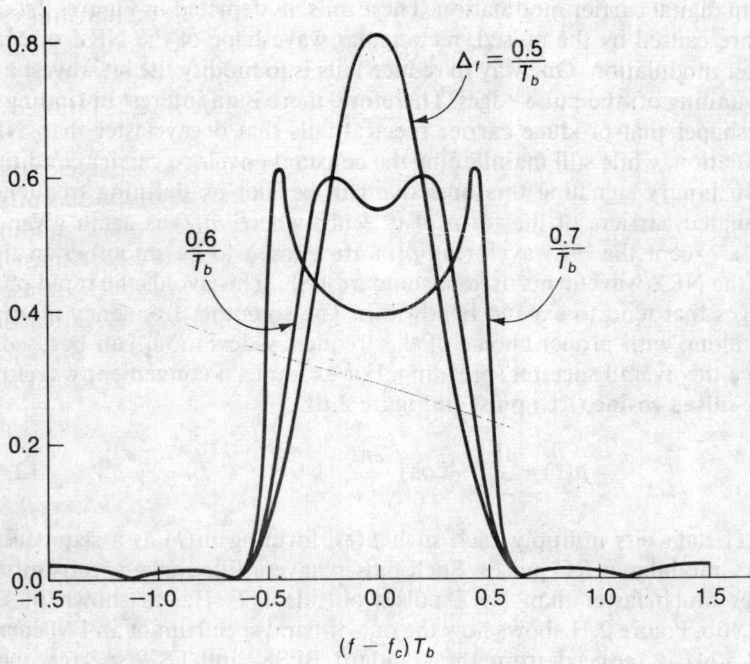

Figure 2.9. Carrier spectra for FSK.

sequences of bursts of a carrier at each of the modulation frequencies $f_c \pm \Delta_f$. Since each burst lasts for a bit time of T_b sec, each such burst produces a spectrum centered at the modulation frequency, with a spectral width corresponding to that of a gating pulse of width T_b sec. Hence, the spectrum of an FSK carrier will appear approximately as a combination of two such spectra, each centered at each of the modulation frequencies, producing the result shown in Figure 2.9. Note that the shape of the spectrum depends on the deviation Δ_f. As the deviation is increased, the two frequencies are further separated, and the ability to distinguish the two frequencies (decode the bit) is improved. However, the resulting carrier spectrum will have a wider main lobe, as shown in Figure 2.9.

2.4 SPECTRAL SHAPING

In modern satellite communications there is usually concern about the spectral tails (spectrum outside the main hump) interfering with other carriers. Hence there is often an interest to reduce the spectral tails generated in digital carrier modulation. These tails, as depicted in Figures 2.7 and 2.9, are caused by the pulsed, rectangular waveshape of the NRZ or Manchester modulation. One way to reduce tails is to modify the bit waveshapes by rounding off the pulse edges. Therefore, there is an interest in finding bit waveshapes that produce carrier spectral tails that decay faster than NRZ modulation, while still maintaining the constant envelope carrier condition.

In binary signaling this objective can be met by defining frequency-modulated carriers of the form of (2.3.14), where $m(t)$ is again given by (2.3.1), except the bit waveforms $p(t)$ are chosen to be smoother in time than the NRZ waveforms used in standard FSK. This avoids the rapid phase changes that tend to expand bandwidth. The smoother frequency modulation, along with proper choice of the frequency deviation, can be used to reduce the overall spectral spreading. For example, a convenient waveform is the **raised cosine (RC)** pulse in Figure 2.10:

$$p(t) = \frac{1}{2}\left[1 - \cos\left(\frac{2\pi t}{T_b}\right)\right], 0 \leqslant t \leqslant T_b \tag{2.4.1}$$

The ± 1 data bits multiply each such $p(t)$, forming $m(t)$ as a sequence of binary modulated RC pulses. Such pulses have a frequency spectrum that decays much faster than NRZ pulses outside $1/T_b$ Hz, as shown in Figure 2.10b. Figure 2.11 shows how the out-of-band spectrum of an FM carrier in (2.3.14) is reduced from the standard BPSK and FSK spectra, when frequency-modulated with binary RC pulses having various deviations Δ_f.

Frequency-shifted carriers have the property that the phase of the

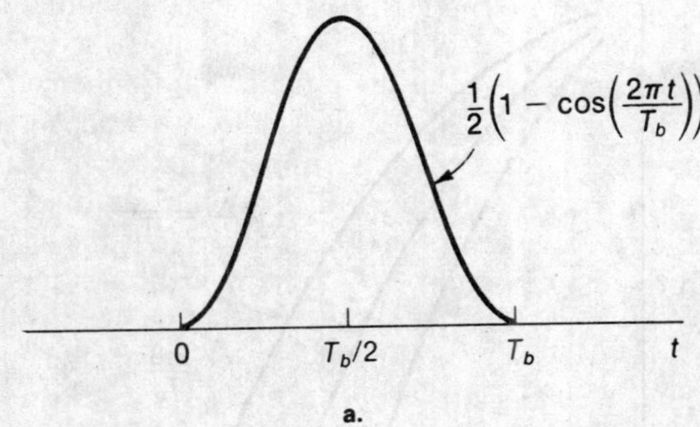

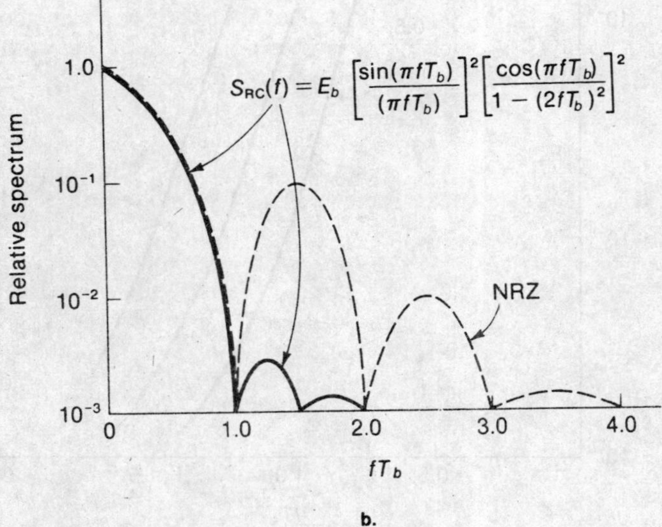

Figure 2.10. Raised cosine pulse. (a) Time waveform. (b) Frequency function.

carrier traces out a continuous phase trajectory in time, according to the modulation sequence, as shown in Figure 2.12. (Recall carrier phase is the integral of the carrier frequency modulation.) This allows binary frequency-modulated carriers to be decoded by phase demodulation, using processing that attempts to track these phase functions. This phase demodulation has decoding advantages over standard frequency detection. For this reason FM

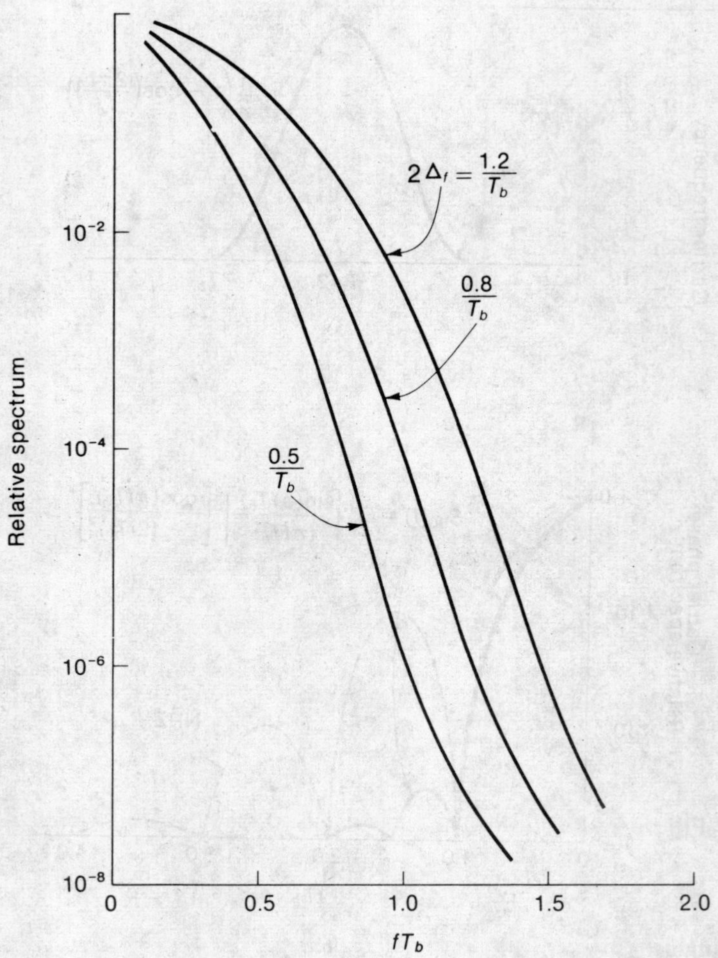

Figure 2.11. Carrier spectrum for FSK with binary raised cosine bit pulses (Δ_f = frequency deviation from carrier).

digital carriers of this type are often referred to as **continuous phase FSK (CPFSK)**. The shape of the phase trajectories depends on the FM pulse waveform, while the separation between two different trajectories depends on the deviation Δ_f. If a smoother frequency modulation is used, as with RC pulses, the phase trajectories tend to become compressed and harder to

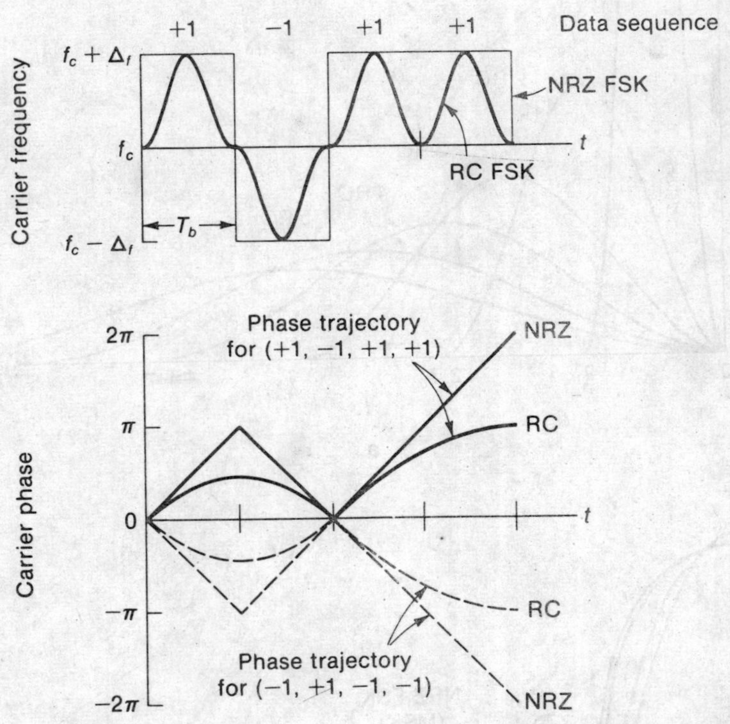

Figure 2.12. Carrier frequency and phase plots for FSK (NRZ = rectangular FM pulses; RC = raised cosine FM pulses).

distinguish (Figure 2.13). Likewise, decreasing the deviation Δ_f to reduce the spectral lobe, as shown in Figure 2.11, also impairs the ability to decode, either by tracking-phase functions or by direct frequency detection.

Carrier bandwidths with FSK using RC pulses can be further reduced using pulses extended over longer time lengths while retaining the same bit rate. Figure 2.13a shows several RC pulses with their time length extended over several bits. Data is transmitted by using one of these waveforms as the bit waveform $p(t)$ frequency-modulating the carrier. The longer RC bit waveform will produce carrier spectra with even less spectral spreading, as depicted in Figure 2.13b. The longer the RC pulse, the less the spectral extent. However, when the RC bit waveform is extended over multiple bit times, intersymbol interference occurs in which the phase of one bit period overlaps into the adjacent bit periods. This complicates the

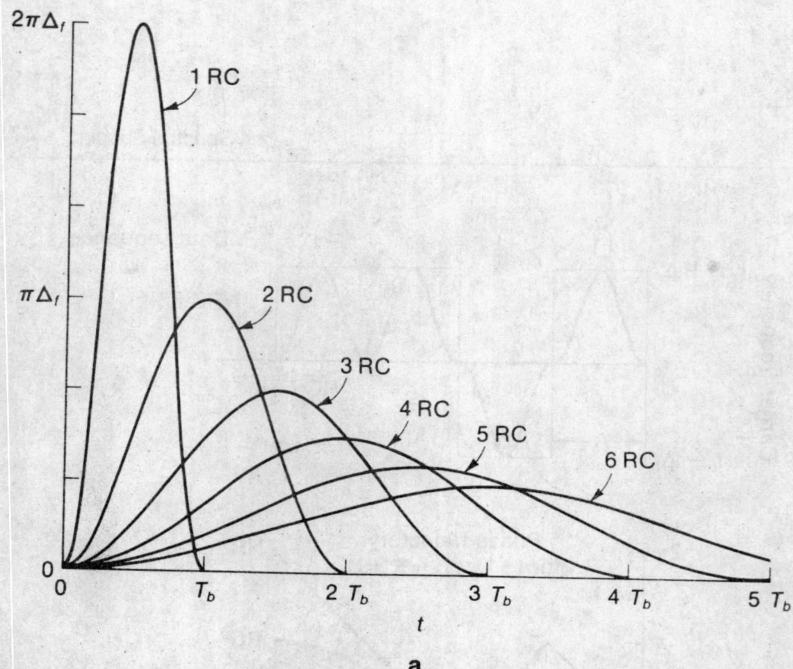

a.

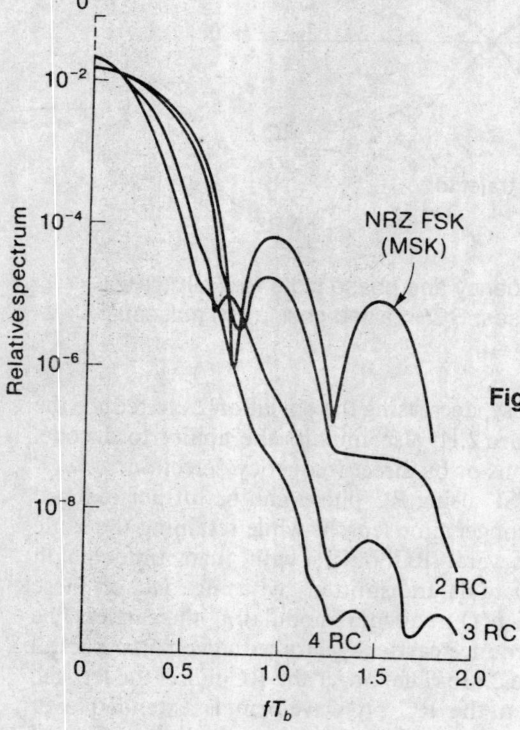

b.

Figure 2.13. Extended raised cosine pulses. (a) Time waveform. (b) Carrier spectrum for FSK with length L, denoted LRC (from Reference 21). $2\Delta_F\ P_b = .5$

corresponding CPFSK phase trajectories and, as we shall see in Section 2.5, results in reduced phase decoding performance.

In QPSK waveforms generated from quadrature multipliers, the use of nonrectangular pulse shapes will generally cause nonconstant envelope carriers to occur. However, offsetting allows use of particular filtered pulse shapes that still retain constant envelopes. One example of filtered OQPSK is the class of **minimum shift-keyed (MSK) carriers** [10]. Here, an OQPSK format is used, with NRZ bits replaced by half-period sine waves (Figure 2.14a). The MSK carrier is generated from pulse-shaped quadrature multipliers (Figure 2.14b) and produces the bit waveform

$$p(t) = \sin\left(\frac{\pi}{T_s}\right)t \qquad 0 \leq t \leq T_s \tag{2.4.2a}$$

and

$$\begin{aligned} p\left(t - \frac{1}{2}T_s\right) &= \sin\left(\frac{\pi}{T_s}\left(t - \frac{1}{2}T_s\right)\right) \\ &= \cos\left(\frac{\pi}{T_s}t\right) \qquad 0 \leq t \leq T_s \end{aligned} \tag{2.4.2b}$$

The MSK carrier is then formed as

$$\begin{aligned} c(t) = {} & A \sum_k a_k \cos\left[\frac{\pi}{T_s}(t - kT_s)\right] \cos(\omega_c t + \psi) \\ & + A \sum_k b_k \sin\left(\frac{\pi}{T_s}(t - kT_s)\right) \sin(\omega_c t + \psi) \end{aligned} \tag{2.4.3}$$

Note that the bit waveforms constituting $m_c(t)$ and $m_s(t)$ still do not overlap. Also at any t, $m_c^2(t) + m_s^2(t) = 1$, so that MSK carriers retain a constant envelope, while producing spectra in (2.3.12) that depend on the modified $p(t)$ of (2.4.2). The resulting MSK spectrum is shown in Figure 2.14c superimposed with OQPSK. Although the main spectral hump has been widened slightly for MSK, a significant reduction has occurred in the out-of-band spectral tails. This makes MSK carriers somewhat more favorable in QPSK systems, where out-of-band spectra control and constant envelope carriers are jointly required.

By trigonometrically expanding, the MSK carrier can also be written as

$$\begin{aligned} c(t) &= A\cos\left(\omega_c t + d_k\left(\frac{\pi}{T_s}\right)(t - kT_s) + x_k\right) \\ & \qquad kT_s \leq t \leq (k+1)T_s \end{aligned} \tag{2.4.4}$$

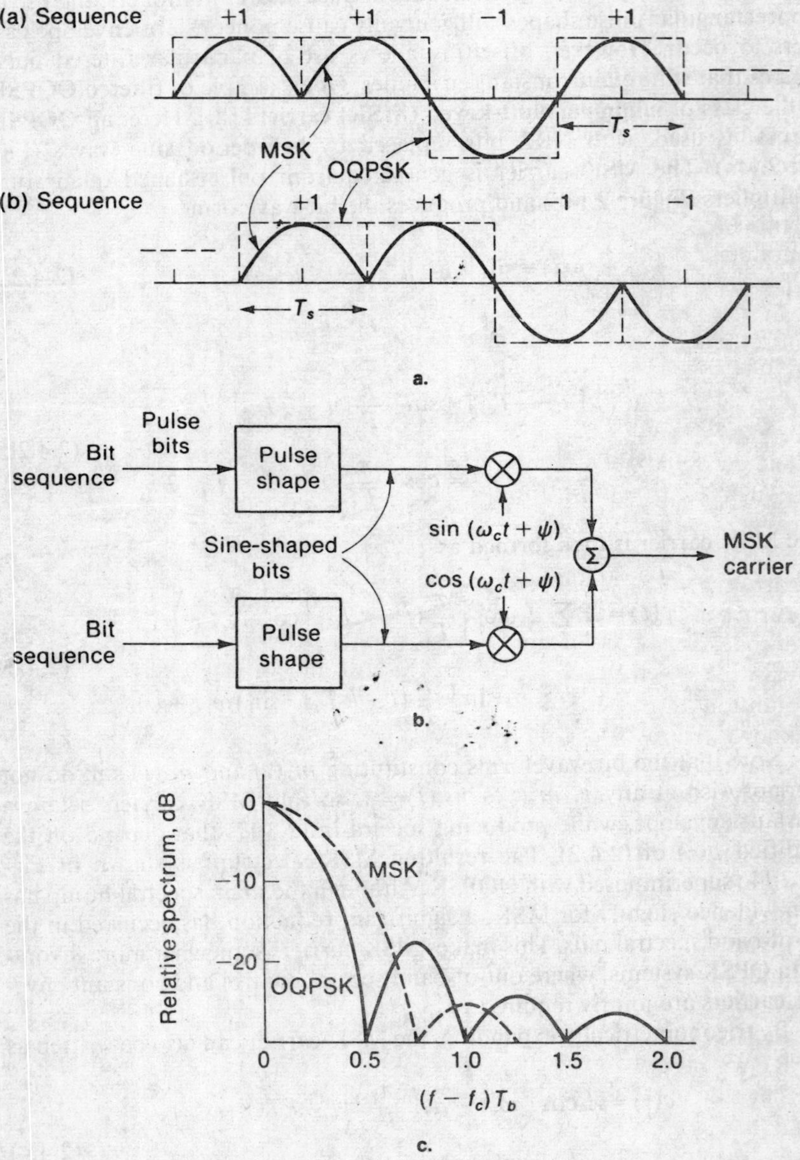

Figure 2.14. Minimum shift-keyed (MSK) signaling. (a) Bit waveforms (b) Encoder. (c) Spectral comparison with QPSK. *Note*: T_s = symbol time, $T_b = T_s/2$ = QPSK bit time.

where

$$d_k = a_k \qquad kT_s/2 \leq t \leq (k+1)T_s/2$$
$$= b_k \qquad (k+1)T_s/2 \leq t \leq (k+2)T_s/2 \tag{2.4.5a}$$

$$x_k = x_{k-1} + \frac{\pi k}{2}(d_{k-1} - d_k) + \psi \tag{2.4.5b}$$

This now has the form of a carrier that is frequency-shifted between $(f_c + 1/2T_s)$ and $(f_c - 1/2T_s)$ at each half bit (offset) time, according to the data bits. The carrier corresponds therefore to an FSK carrier with NRZ frequency modulating bit waveforms and a specific deviation of $\Delta_f T_s = 1/2$. In terms of carrier bit time, $T_b = T_s/2$, this is equivalent to $\Delta_f T_b = 1/4$. Thus MSK is, in fact, a form of a CPFSK carrier, having this particular modulation and deviation. This means, too, that the FSK curves with $\Delta_f = 1/4T_b$ in Figure 2.13b can be similarly labeled as MSK. Note that we can view MSK as either the simultaneous quadrature modulation of two offset bits, or as a CPFSK modulation of the same two bits in sequence.

2.5 DIGITAL DECODING

The decoding operation is the process required to reconstruct the data bit sequence encoded onto the carrier. The lowest probability of decoding a carrier bit in error (bit error probability) occurs if phase coherent decoding is used. Phase coherent decoding requires the decoder to use a referenced carrier at the same frequency and phase as the received modulated carrier during each bit time. That is, in order to optimally decode each bit, the decoder must provide in each bit interval a carrier at the exact frequency ω_c with the exact phase ψ used in the description of each encoded carrier. In addition, the exact timing of the beginning and ending of each bit must be known. This frequency, phase, and timing coherency must be obtained via a separate synchronization subsystem operating in conjunction with the receiver decoder, as shown in Figure 2.15. The synchronization subsystem must extract the required reference and timing from the received modulated carrier itself. These sync subsystems are discussed in Appendix B.

Phase coherent decoding can be used with the phase modulated carriers previously considered. Decoders for BPSK and QPSK carriers are shown in Figure 2.16. In BPSK, the phase coherent carrier reference is first used to multiply (demodulate) the received carrier waveform. The demodulated waveform is then multiplied by the bit waveform $p(t)$ and integrated over each bit time. This effectively corresponds to the correlation of the received RF waveform with the reference waveform $p(t)\cos(\omega_c t + \psi)$ over each bit. The sign of the integrated bit output is then used to decode the bit. In QPSK

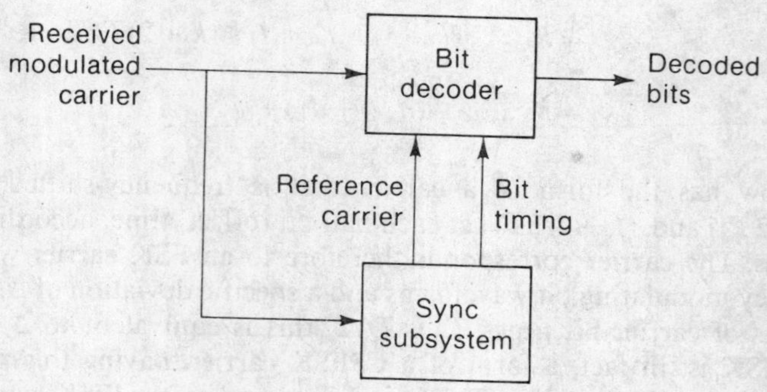

Figure 2.15. Bit decoding subsystem.

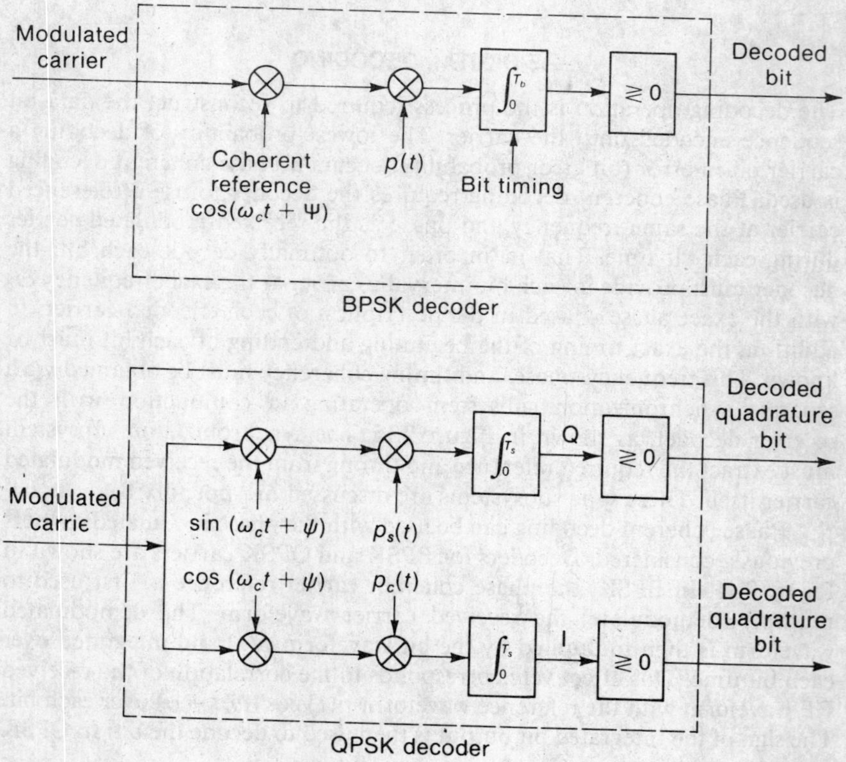

Figure 2.16. BPSK and QPSK decoders.

Table 2.3. Summary of decoding bit-error probabilities.

Binary format	*PE, bit-error probability*
BPSK, QPSK, MSK (phase coherent decoding)	$Q\left(\sqrt{\frac{2E_b}{N_0}}\right)$
FSK (phase coherent frequency detection)	$Q\left(\sqrt{\frac{E_b}{N_0}}\right)$
DPSK	$\frac{1}{2}e^{-E_b/N_0}$
Noncoherent FSK	$\frac{1}{2}e^{-E_b/2N_0}$

E_b = Bit energy

$Q(x) = \frac{1}{2\pi}\int_x^\infty e^{-t^2/2}\,dt$

the received carrier is simultaneously correlated with each phase-referenced quadrature carrier, each with its own bit waveform. Separate symbol integrations in each quadrature arm are then used to decode each quadrature bit simultaneously. Since the bit waveforms are arbitrary, this decoder will have the same form for OQPSK and MSK carriers as well, with the waveforms $p_c(t)$ and $p_s(t)$ matching the transmitted bit waveform shape.

The probability of making a bit error with these decoders is computed in Appendix A. Table 2.3 lists the resulting bit-error probability expressions for decoding in the presence of additive white Gaussian RF noise, along with those expressions of some alternative encoding formats that are to be discussed. The plots of these equations are shown in Figure 2.17. Note that the bit-error probability depends only on the parameter

$$\frac{E_b}{N_0} = \frac{\text{Bit energy of the modulated carrier at decoder input}}{\text{Spectral level of additive noise at decoder input}} \tag{2.5.1}$$

This parameter can be written directly in terms of the decoder carrier power P_c and the carrier bit time T_b as

$$\frac{E_b}{N_0} = \frac{P_c T_b}{N_0} \tag{2.5.2}$$

The fact that the entire class of phase coherent digital systems, when operating in an additive Gaussian white noise environment, has error prob-

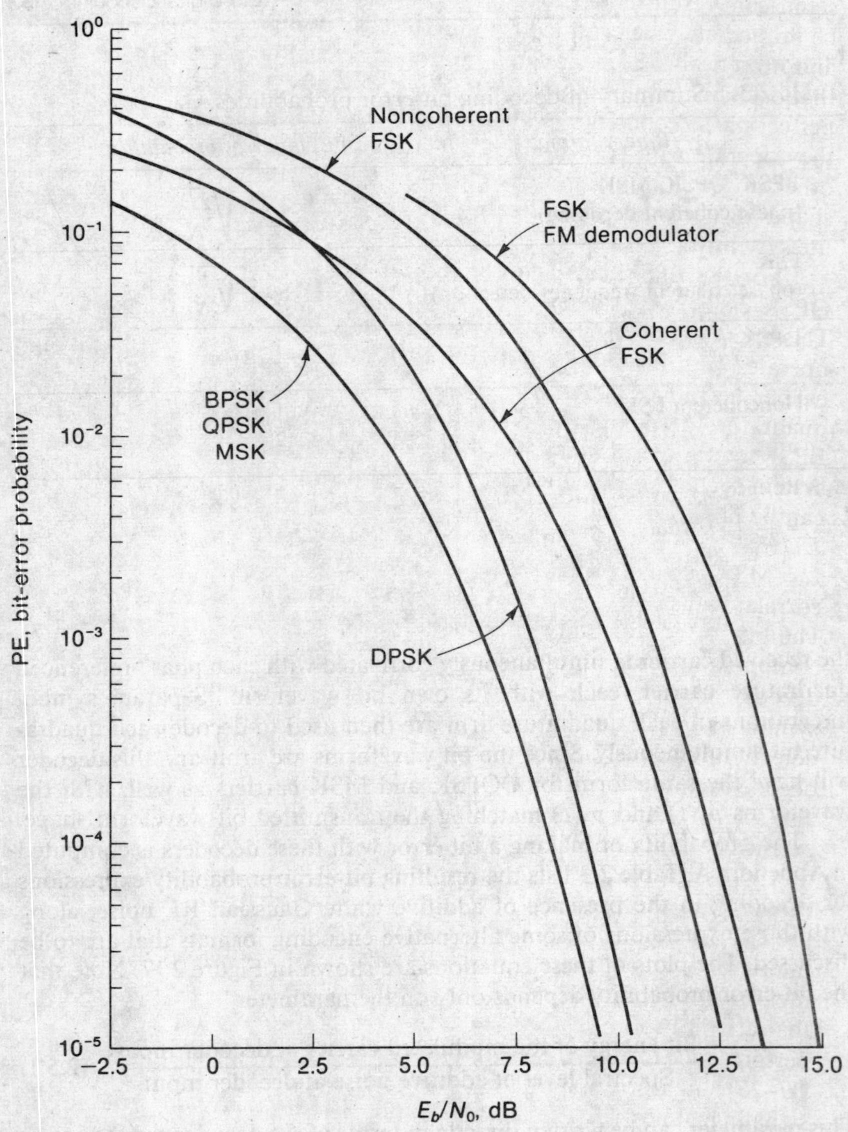

Figure 2.17. Bit-error probabilities vs. E_b/N_0.

abilities dependent on only the single parameter in (2.5.2) is an extremely significant result in decoding theory. It means that digital performance can be immediately determined from knowledge of only decoder carrier power and noise levels. This fact greatly simplifies satellite system analyses. Note that decoding of all binary waveforms previously described, operating with perfect phase coherence, will theoretically produce the same PE as long as they operate with the same E_b/N_0. Thus one waveform is as good as any other in terms of error probability, and those with advantages of spectral shapes or hardware simplification become increasingly important in satellite systems.

For the BPSK carrier in (2.3.7), $P_c = A^2/2$, and $E_b = A^2T_b/2$. For a QPSK carrier P_c is again $A^2/2$, and the carrier symbol energy is $A^2T_s/2$. This energy is divided between the two quadrature components, and each operates with decoding energy $A^2T_s/4 = A^2T_b/2$, where T_b is the QPSK carrier bit time ($T_b = T_s/2$). Thus bit-error probability for either QPSK quadrature decoder can be obtained by reading off the value of PE on a BPSK curve at the value P_cT_b/N_0. Even though a QPSK (or OQPSK) system sends two bits during a symbol time, the PE of each quadrature bit can be obtained from the BPSK curve in Figure 2.17 at the corresponding E_b/N_0.

MSK carriers, being a form of OQPSK, are also decoded by quadrature correlators using pulse matching to the sinusoidal bit waveforms in (2.4.3). The bit-error probability depends on the energy of each quadrature pulse component, which is also given by P_cT_b. Hence, a perfectly matched MSK decoder produces the same PE as a QPSK decoder with the same carrier symbol energy. This MSK decoding can also be viewed as a form of phase detection in which the carrier phase trajectory over a symbol time is used to decode each offset quadrature bit. This interpretation follows since MSK is also a form of CPFSK with NRZ frequency pulses, and the phase trajectory extends continuously over a symbol time. If a smoother frequency modulation is used (e.g., raised cosine pulses for spectral control), the resulting carrier phase trajectories will be harder to decode, as we showed in Figure 2.12. If the RC pulse is extended over several bits, the phase intersymbol interference appears as a form of correlative encoding [11] (i.e., insertion of memory). This can be decoded by introducing elaborate phase algorithms that attempt to unravel the interbit overlap [12–16]. Estimates of bit-error performance for those algorithms have been made via performance bounds [17–23]. Figure 2.18 shows these bounds for various CPFSK raised cosine signaling, along with the previous result for MSK. We note that little degradation relative to MSK is predicted by this encoding, while the encoding simultaneously obtains the spectral reduction. Hence CPFSK carriers with time-extended raised cosine pulse can be made to perform comparable to

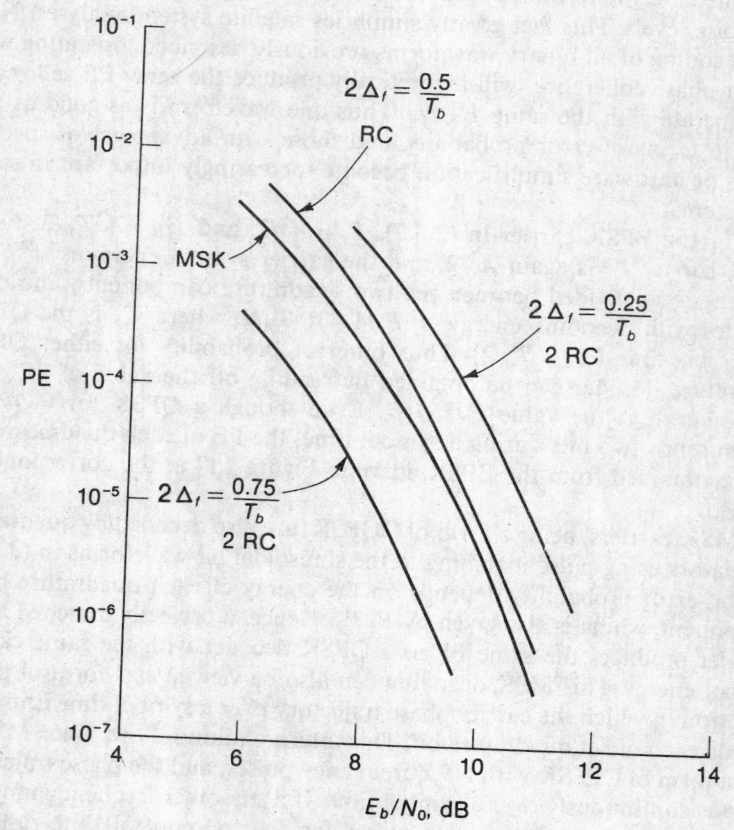

Figure 2.18. CPFSK bit-error probability bounds for binary raised cosine FSK (from Reference 21).

MSK, but at the expense of implementing the decoding algorithms. An assessment of the required decoder hardware is discussed in [16].

Since MSK can also be viewed as an FSK carrier frequency-shifted during each bit time (not symbol time), it can also be decoded by phase coherent frequency detection (see Appendix A) operating over each subsequent carrier bit time. Since only carrier energy in a bit time (instead of symbol time) is used for distinguishing the two frequencies, the decoding will be 3 dB poorer, as evidenced by the curve labeled "Coherent FSK" in Figure 2.17. This degradation can be reduced to about 1 dB for this type of decoding by using an optimal frequency separation of $0.71/T_b$ [7, Chapter 7] instead of the $0.5/T_b$ separation used in MSK.

The previous decoders all assumed perfect phase referencing. If the phase referencing is not perfect (i.e., the decoder carrier used for the correlations in Figure 2.16 does not have the same exact phase as the input modulated carrier), the decoding performance is degraded. Typically the phase error between the received and reference carrier evolves as a random process caused by noise in the phase referencing circuitry in Figure 2.15. As the phase referencing error increases, the decoding bit-error probability is further degraded from that predicted in Figure 2.17, where perfect phase referencing was assumed. Figure 2.19 shows how the BPSK PE varies from the ideal BPSK case as the rms reference phase error increases. Note that phase reference errors can produce bit-error probabilities several orders of magnitude higher than that predicted by the ideal case. Phase errors cause a bottoming of the PE performance that cannot be reduced even if the bit energy E_b is significantly increased. As a rough rule of thumb, if PE performance is to be maintained at 10^{-5} or lower, rms phase reference errors must be limited to about 15° or less.

In some satellite systems it may be advantageous to avoid completely the receiver task of having to generate a phase coherent reference for decoding. Two ways to operate a binary encoder without a phase coherent reference is to do so either by **differential encoding** or by **noncoherent** frequency-shift keyings. In differential PSK encoding (DPSK), a BPSK carrier is used, but the carrier phase of each bit is referenced to the previous bit. A binary +1 or −1 is encoded during a bit time T_b by using either the same phase or a π shift of the previous bit phase, depending on whether the present bit is identical or opposite to the previous bit. This is equivalent to forming the BPSK carrier in (2.3.7) using the NRZ sequence in (2.3.1) with

$$d_k = d_{k-1} a_k \tag{2.5.3}$$

where a_k is the present bit. Decoding is achieved by correlating the present carrier bit with the previous carrier bit over each bit time, and determining if they correlate positively or negatively, as shown in Figure 2.20a. No phase coherent reference is needed (the carrier during the previous bit is effectively used as the reference), but performance is slightly poorer than with a coherent system (see Figure 2.17). Differential decoders can be constructed as the one-bit delay correlator, but can be optimized by using two parallel two-bit correlators [7, Chapter 7] producing the performance curve shown.

A second way to transmit binary data without requiring phase coherent decoding is by the use of the FSK carriers in (2.3.14), except that pure frequency detection is used. Since the bit modulation is inserted onto the frequency of the carrier, the bit can be decoded by making frequency measurements on the received carrier. These frequency measurements can

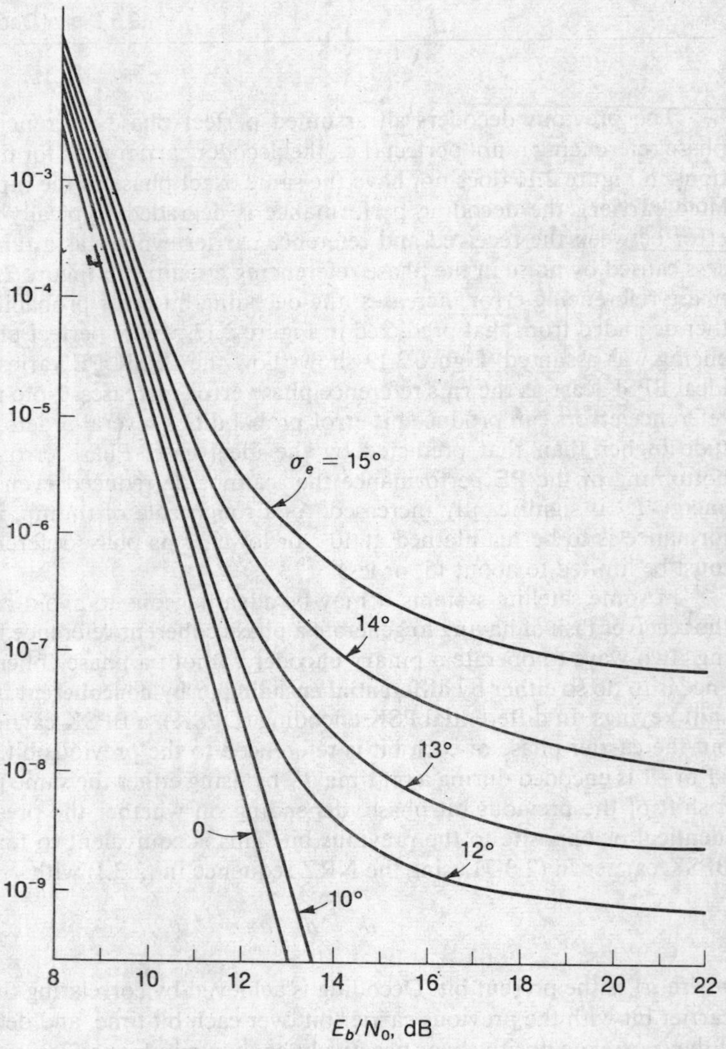

Figure 2.19. BPSK bit-error probability vs. E_b/N_0 and rms phase reference error.

be made without knowledge of the phase. In binary FSK, decoding is accomplished by tuned-matched bandpass filters centered at each of the modulating frequencies, followed by energy detection during each bit time

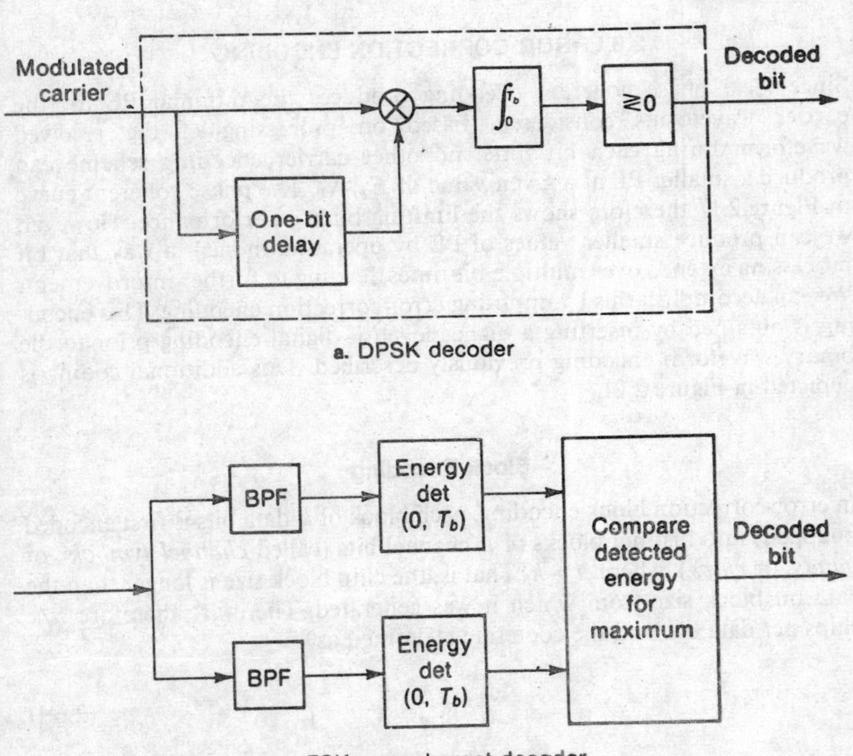

Figure 2.20. DPSK and noncoherent FSK decoders.

to determine which filter contains the most energy (Figure 2.20b). If the frequencies are sufficiently separated, only the correct filter will contain signal carrier energy, while the other filter contains only noise. The resulting bit-error probability is included in Table 2.3 and Figure 2.17. We note that this form of non-coherent frequency decoding again produces poorer (higher) PE at the same carrier bit energy than phase coherent BPSK. FSK is about 4 dB worse at PE = 10^{-3}, and about 3 dB worse at PE = 10^{-5}.

FSK can also be detected by first frequency demodulating the carrier to recover the baseband $m(t)$. The latter is then followed by bit integrations and sign detections over each bit time to determine bits of $m(t)$. Such systems do about 1 dB worse than bandpass filter-energy detection decoders [7, Chapter 7], as shown in Figure 2.17. These FSK degradations in performance again reflect the price of not implementing phase referencing circuitry.

In low-cost receiver design this trade-off of error performance for hardware simplicity may be both desirable and cost efficient.

2.6 ERROR-CORRECTION ENCODING

Since ideal phase coherent decoding produces the minimal PE for the carrier waveforms considered, based on processing of the received waveform during each bit time, no other carrier encoding scheme can produce a smaller PE at a given value of E_b/N_0. The phase coherent curve in Figure 2.17 therefore shows the limiting binary performance. However, we can produce smaller values of PE by operating in such a way that bit processing extends over multiple bit times, leading to further improvement. We can accomplish this by imposing error-correction encoding. This encoding is obtained by inserting a higher level of digital encoding prior to the binary waveform encoding previously described. This additional coding is depicted in Figure 2.21.

Block Encoding

In error-correction block encoding, each block of k data bits is first encoded (mapped) into distinct blocks of n **channel bits** (called *channel symbols*, or *bauds*, or *chips*), where $n > k$. That is, the chip block size is longer than the data bit block size from which it was generated. There are therefore n/k chips per data bit, and the code rate is defined as

$$r = \frac{k}{n} \tag{2.6.1}$$

Each consecutive block of k data bits is converted into a block of n chips, according to the prescribed coding rule. The chips are then sent over the binary channel as if they were data bits. If the n chips are all decoded correctly, the k data bits to which they correspond are immediately identi-

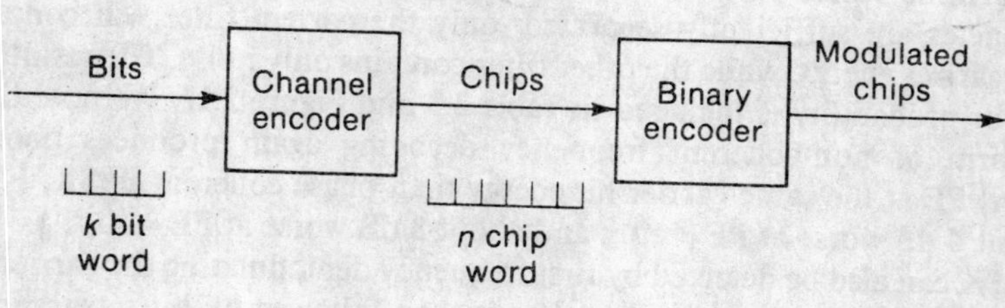

Figure 2.21. Error-correction encoding model.

fied, and the data bits have effectively been correctly transmitted. If some of the n chips are decoded incorrectly, however, the k data bits may still possibly be correctly identified, since "extra" chips are used to represent the k bits. Some of the chips in a block may be decoded incorrectly without decoding the data bit block incorrectly. If this occurs, the resulting bit-error probability of the data will be less than the chip-error probability of the link, for the same chip carrier power. The number of chips that can be in error before a data bit error occurs is related to the coding rule that maps the k bits into the n chips.

The development of the theory of this mapping is beyond our scope here, but for properly selected code (mapping) rules, the number of allowable chip errors will be related to the difference $n - k$. The larger this difference the more chip errors can be made before data bit errors occur. Unfortunately, the larger the values of n and k, the more complex is the implementation of the required coding and decoding hardware.

The probability that a transmitted chip will be decoded in error, using the phase coherent encoding methods of Table 2.4, is given by

$$\epsilon = Q\left(\sqrt{\frac{2E_c}{N_0}}\right) \tag{2.6.2}$$

where E_c is the energy per chip. If the bits are to be sent at a fixed rate, the chips must be sent faster than this rate (shorter chip time and larger carrier bandwidth) since more chips than bits are transmitted. This means the chip time is less than a bit time and

$$E_c = rE_b \tag{2.6.3}$$

where r is again the code rate in (2.6.1). It can be shown [24] that the resulting bit-error probability is accurately bounded by

$$\text{PE} \leqslant 2^{-n(r_0 - r)} \tag{2.6.4}$$

where r_0 is the chip **cut-off rate**, defined by

$$r_0 \triangleq 1 - \log_2[1 + \sqrt{4\,\epsilon(1 - \epsilon)}] \tag{2.6.5}$$

The bit-error probability can therefore be estimated directly from the code parameters. Note that as long as the code rate r is less than the cut-off rate r_0 (the latter dependent on the chip energy through (2.6.5) and (2.6.2)) the bit-error probability can be reduced by increasing the chip block length n (and therefore also increasing data block length k, since $k = rn$). This simply reiterates the fact that for a fixed code rate k/n, the larger the values of k

and n, the larger is the difference $n - k$ and the more chip errors can be tolerated. The number of computations needed to convert the decoded chips into the decoded bits, however, increases as 2^k. Thus, decoding complexity and required processing speed increases exponentially with error-correction block lengths.

Figure 2.22 plots the bound on (2.6.4) as a function of block code length k for several values of r/r_0. Typically, $\epsilon \leqslant 10^{-3}$, for which r_0 in (2.6.5) is about 1, and the ratio r/r_0 is approximately equal to the code rate r in (2.6.1). Note the continual improvement in performance as higher levels of coding are introduced at a fixed rate. However, as stated earlier, the number

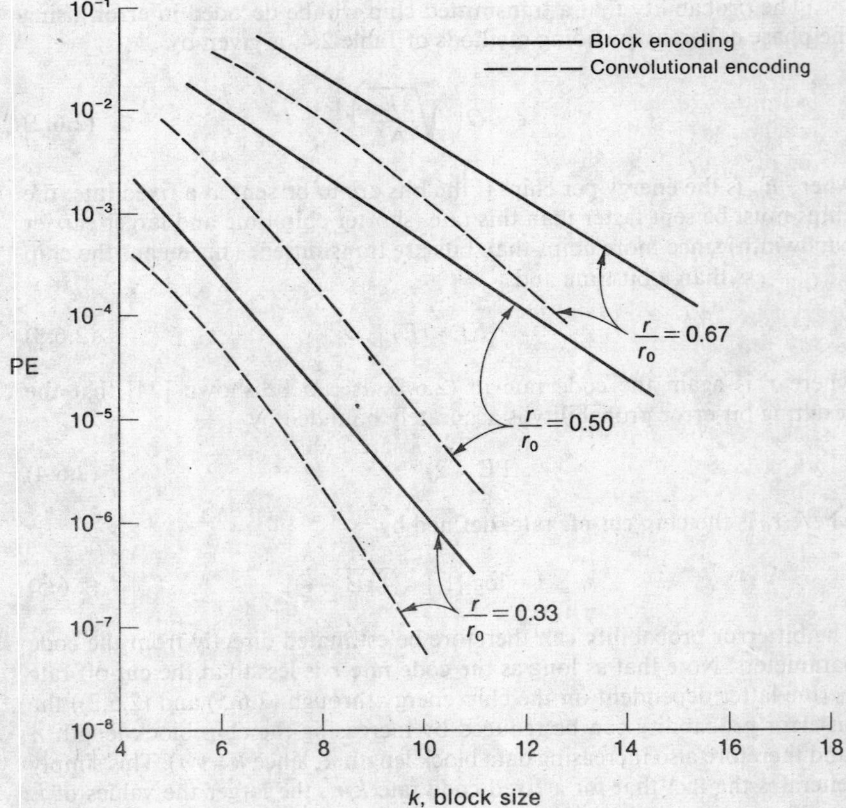

Figure 2.22. PE bound vs. code block length k and r/r_0 (r = code rate = k/n; r_0 = channel cut-off rate).

of computations needed also increases exponentially with k. Thus the price to be paid for PE improvement via error correction is in the decoding complexity that must be implemented. As digital processing capabilities and computation speeds increase through technological advances, higher levels of block lengths can be physically implemented, leading directly to digital performance improvement. It is expected that this push toward faster decoding processing and reduced PE will continue throughout the future of satellite communications.

Convolutional Encoding

An alternative to the block error correcting coding is the use of convolutional coding [24, 25]. Convolutional coding is another technique for encoding data bits into transmission chips, such that subsequent chip decoding leads to improved bit decoding. Rather than coding fixed-data blocks into fixed-chip blocks, each chip is generated instead through a continuous convolution of previous data bits. This convolution leads again to improved performance when operating at the same code rate. Decoding is achieved by detecting one bit at a time in sequence, based on the processing of sliding sequences of received chips. The optimal decoding is obtained by means of a **Viterbi decoding algorithm** [26, 27], which "unconvolves" the bits from the decoded chips.

The convolving property of convolutional encoding produces codes that can be decoded with better bit-error performance than previous block codes with the same rate and block length. Since the convolutional encoders are no more complicated than block encoders, convolutional encoding is the preferred method for forward-error correction. Performance analysis is more difficult, however, due to the interlaced nature of the encoded bits. It has been shown that for a code rate r and **constraint length k** (the number of past bits convolved into each chip), there exists a convolutional code with bit-error probability bounded by

$$\text{PE} \leq \frac{2^{-k(r_0/r)}}{[1-2^{-(r_0/r-1)}]^2} \tag{2.6.6}$$

where r_0 is again given in (2.6.5). Figure 2.22 shows (2.6.6) for the convolutional codes, showing the potential advantage over fixed-length block codes. Convolutional decoding can also be improved by "soft-decisioning" decoding algorithms, which allow the decoder to achieve a finer granularity during the chip processing. This results in an improved chip cut-off rate of approximately

$$r_0 = 1 - \log_2[1 + e^{-rE_b/N_0}] \tag{2.6.7}$$

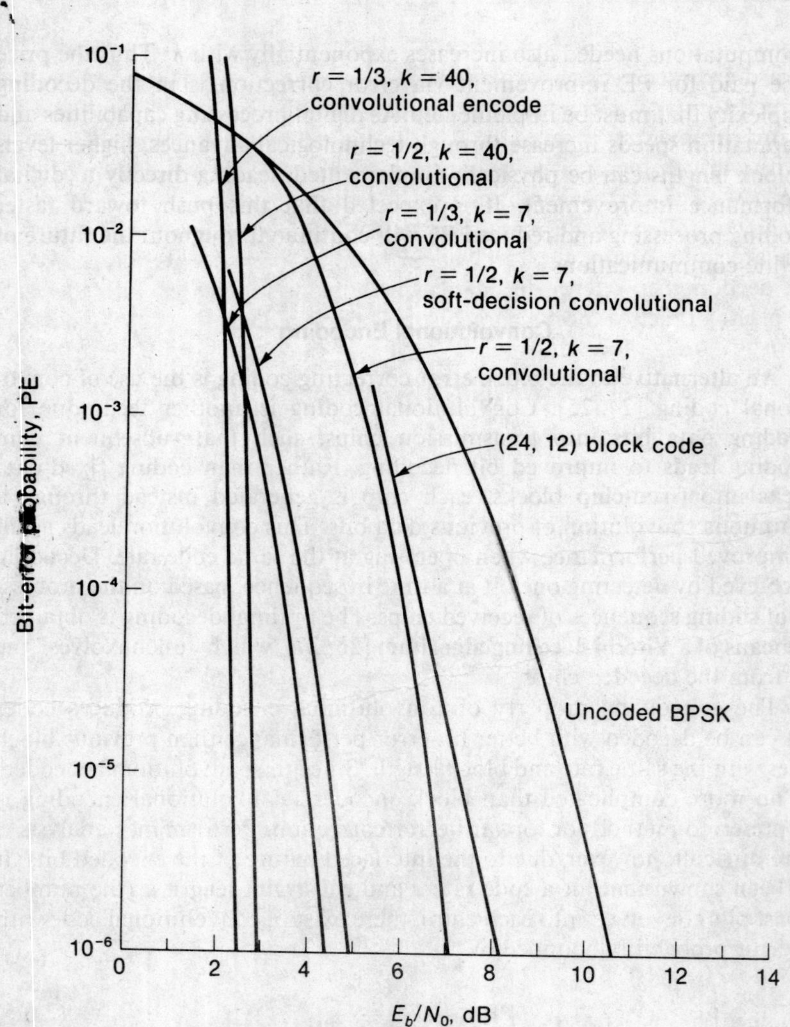

Figure 2.23. Improvement in PE over BPSK with block and convolutional coding.

as compared to (2.6.5). This soft-decision rate yields the same values of r_0 in (2.6.5) with about 2 dB less E_b. Hence, when entering the convolutional coding curves in Figure 2.22, and reading PE at a specific constraint length k and ratio r/r_0, the resulting performance can be achieved with 2 dB less bit energy if soft-decisioning decoding is used. Soft-decision processing however further increases the required decoder complexity.

Forward-error correction, with either block codes or convolutional codes, directly improves the bit-error probability. Figure 2.23 shows the expected improvement over standard BPSK obtained by forward-error correction with various block sizes or constraint lengths k, as a function of channel E_b/N_0. This improvement can be interpreted as a lower PE at the same E_b/N_0, or the same PE at a lower E_b/N_0, as higher levels of error correction are used. Again, the receiver processor complexity required in the block decoding or Viterbi decoder algorithms also increases with the length k, placing practical limits on achievable performance.

2.7 BLOCK WAVEFORM ENCODING

The forward error correction coding just discussed in Section 2.6 is based on binary transmission, where sequences of binary chips are sent over the link and each is separately decoded. Performance improvement is obtained by inserting extra chips, or redundancy, into the transmitted chip waveform. Another way to achieve improvement in bit-error probability is to use higher levels of data transmission by encoding more than binary information on the transmitted carrier at any one time. This is referred to as **block waveform encoding**. It allows blocks of bits (binary *words*) to be transmitted at one time as one particular waveform. This encoding format is shown in Figure 2.24.

Orthogonal Block Encoding

A common block waveform encoding procedure uses phase coherent orthogonal signals to represent the word. The k bit words are encoded into $M = 2^k$ orthogonal sequences of BPSK chips, which are then transmitted as a single waveform to represent the word (Figure 2.25a). At the decoder, the

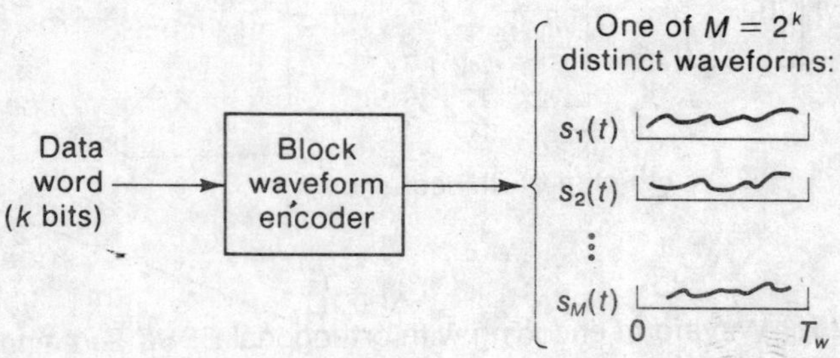

Figure 2.24. Block waveform encoding model.

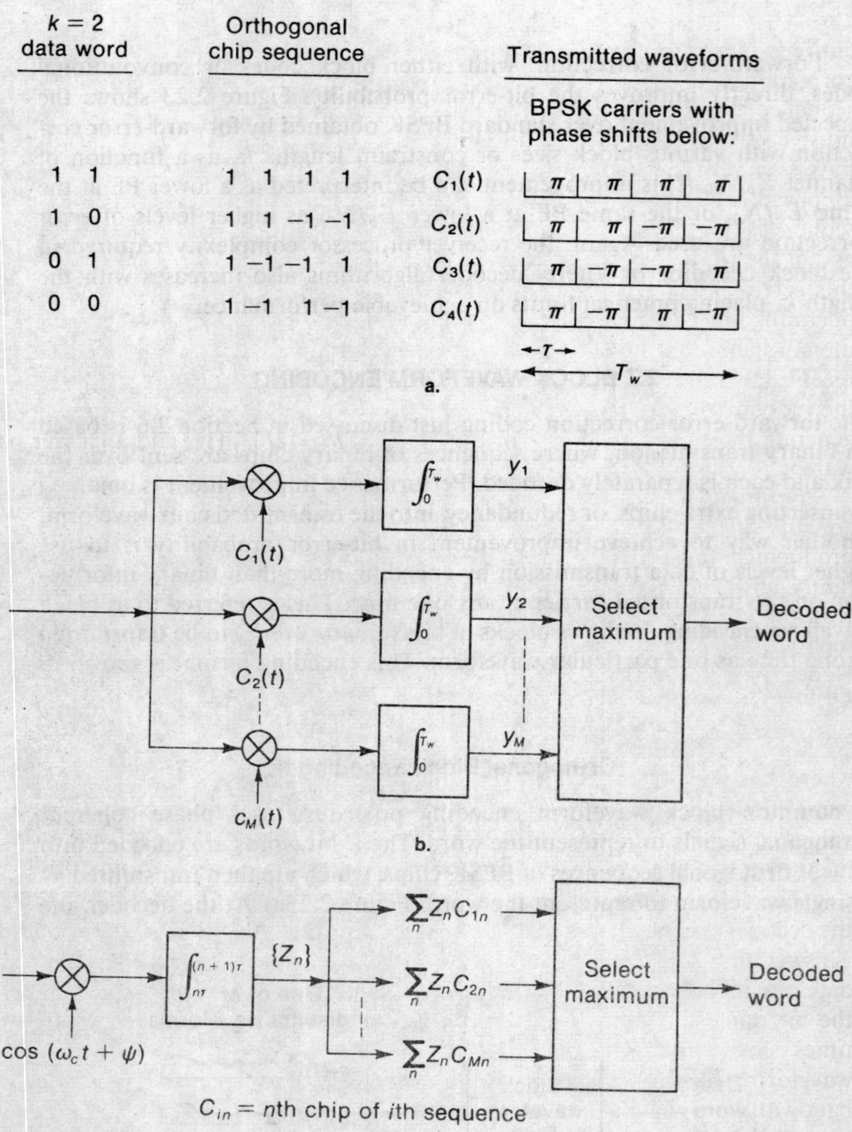

Figure 2.25. Waveform encoding with orthogonal BPSK sequences. (a) Encoding example for $k = 2$. (b) Required block waveform decoder. (c) Alternate decoder model.

entire sequence of chips (rather than one chip at a time, as in forward error correction) is decoded. A single decision concerning the entire received chip sequence is made at the end of the sequence (word) time. The decoder now must have the capability of detecting any of the 2^k sequences that could have been sent for that word. To do this, the decoder must contain a bank of 2^k phase coherent correlations, each looking for one of the possible chip sequences (Figure 2.25b). The correlator producing the largest output at the end of the word correlation time decodes the transmitted words. In practice this set of parallel correlators is constructed as a single chip correlator, operating on each received chip, followed by a bank of sum-and-store memory circuits, as shown in Figure 2.25c. Since the correlation of a received waveform with a sequence of BPSK chips is identical to the sum of the individual correlations of each chip, this sum-and-store procedure will generate the same set of 2^k parallel correlation values with simpler hardware.

Orthogonal waveform encoding has the advantage that the orthogonality of the waveforms reduces the possibility of the correct waveform producing a large correlation value in an incorrect correlator. More importantly, however, it benefits from the fact that a single word decision is made with the combined energy of the *entire* chip sequence, rather than having separate decisions made on each chip using only the energy of a single chip. Hence, in terms of equivalent bit energy, the word decoding energy is

$$E_w = kE_b \tag{2.7.1}$$

where k is the word size. The resulting bit-error probability for orthogonal word encoding is listed in Table 2.4, and shown in Figure 2.26 for several values of k, as a function of the available E_b/N_0 of the link. The improvement over BPSK binary signaling by increasing the block length is apparent.

The disadvantage of the orthogonal sequence waveform system (besides the decoder complexity) is that 2^k chips must be sent to represent the k bits. This requires that the chips must be sent $2^k/k$ times faster if a particular date rate is to be maintained (requiring a bandwidth $2^k/k$ times larger than the bit rate bandwidth). Conversely the transmitted bit rate will be $k/2^k$ times slower than the chip rate permitted by the link. Hence, coded waveform PE improvement is achieved at the expense of channel bandwidth or reduced data bit rate.

Multiple Phase Shift Keying

Another common waveform encoding procedure is **multiple phase shift keying**, MPSK, where the k data bits are transmitted at one time by encoding into one of $M = 2^k$ phase shifts of the same carrier. The system still uses

Table 2.4. Tabulation of word-error probabilities for M-ary block waveform encoding ($M = 2^k$, k = block size).

Block encoding format	*Word-error probability, PWE*
M Orthogonal phase coherent waveforms	$1 - \int_{-\infty}^{\infty} \left[1 - Q\left(\sqrt{2y} + \sqrt{\frac{2E_w}{N_0}} \right) \right]^{M-1} \frac{e^{-y^2/2}}{\sqrt{2\pi}} dy$
MPSK	$\approx Q\left[\left(\frac{2E_w}{N_0} \right)^{1/2} \sin\left(\frac{\pi}{M} \right) \right]$
MFSK	$1 - e^{-\rho^2/2} \sum_{q=0}^{M-1} (-1)^q \binom{M-1}{q} \frac{e^{(\rho^2/2)/1+q}}{1+q}$
MASK	$\frac{M-1}{M} Q\left[\left(\frac{6E_w}{(M^2-1)N_0} \right)^{1/2} \right]$
M-CPFSK	$\leqslant (M-1)\, Q\left[\left(\frac{d_{\min} E_w}{N_0} \right)^{1/2} \right]$
	Bit-error probability, PE
M Orthogonal phase coherent waveforms	$\frac{M/2}{M-1}$ PWE
MPSK	$\approx \frac{\text{PWE}}{\log_2 M}$
MFSK	$\frac{M/2}{M-1}$ PWE
MASK	$\approx \frac{\text{PWE}}{\log_2 M}$
M-CPFSK	$\leqslant \frac{M}{2} Q\left[\left(\frac{d_{\min} E_w}{N_0} \right)^{1/2} \right]$

E_w = word energy = $(\log_2 M) E_b$
$\rho^2 = 2E_w/N_0$

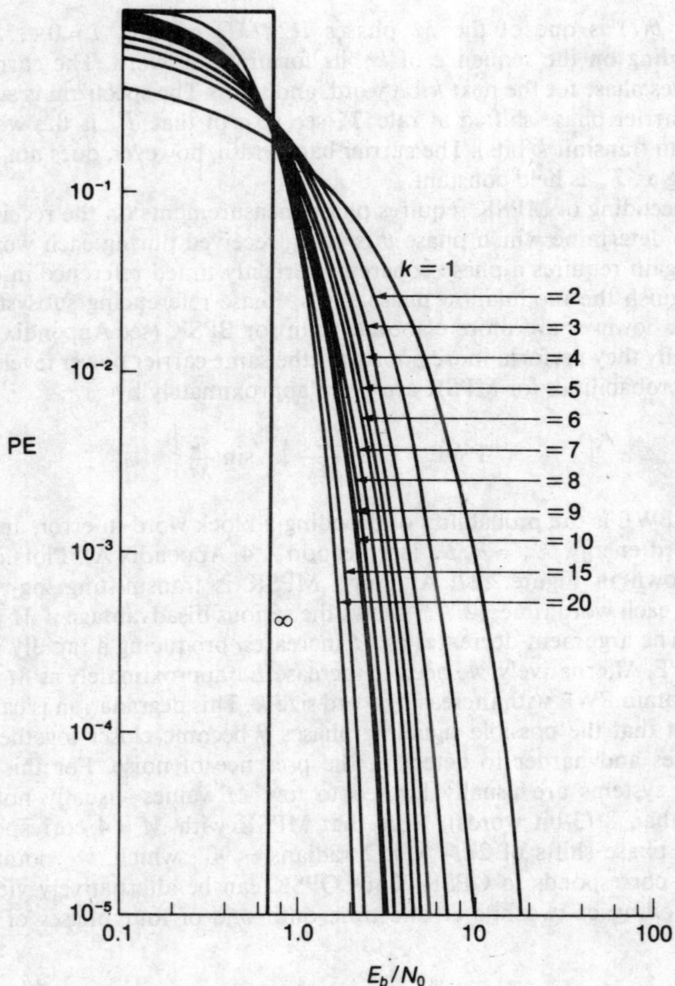

Figure 2.26. Phase coherent orthogonal bit-error probability vs. the equivalent E_b/N_0 for values of block length k ($E_b = E_w/k$).

constant envelope carriers with phase modulation, but the phase modulation can be any one of M phases instead of two phases as in BPSK. During a word transmission time T_w, the carrier again has the form

$$c(t) = A \cos(\omega_c t + \theta(t) + \psi) \tag{2.7.2}$$

where $\theta(t)$ is one of the M phases $i(2\pi/M)$ radians, $i = 0,\ldots, M-1$, depending on the sequence of k bits forming the word. The carrier then switches phase for the next k bit word, and so on. The spectrum is again that of a carrier phase shifted at rate T_w sec, except that T_w is the word time (time to transmit k bits). The carrier bandwidth, however, does not increase as long as T_w is held constant.

Decoding of MPSK requires phase measurements on the received carrier to determine which phase θ is being received during each word time. This again requires a phase coherent, perfectly timed reference in order to distinguish the modulation phase shifts. Phase referencing subsystems for MPSK however are more elaborate than for BPSK (see Appendix B), and generally they perform more poorly for the same carrier power levels. Word-error probabilities for MPSK are given approximately by

$$\text{PWE} = Q\left[\left(\frac{2E_w}{N_0}\right)^{1/2} \sin\frac{\pi}{M}\right] \tag{2.7.3}$$

where PWE is the probability of decoding a block word in error, and E_w is the word energy, $E_w = P_c T_w$ (see Section A.4, Appendix A). Plots of PWE are shown in Figure 2.27. Although MPSK is transmitting $\log_2 M$ bits during each word time, (2.7.3) shows the serious disadvantage if M gets too large. The argument decreases as M increases, producing a rapidly increasing PWE. Alternatively, we need to increase E_w approximately as $M^2 = (2^k)^2$ to maintain PWE with increasing word size k. This degradation is caused by the fact that the possible signaling phases θ become closer together as M increases and harder to detect in the presence of noise. For this reason MPSK systems are usually limited to low M values—usually not much larger than 8 (3-bit words). Note that MPSK with $M = 4$ corresponds to carrier phase shifts of $2\pi/4 = \pi/2$ radians $= 90°$, which, we pointed out earlier, corresponds to QPSK. Thus QPSK can be alternatively viewed as word coding of two bits at one time onto one of four phases of an RF carrier.

Multilevel CPFSK Encoding

Block waveform encoding with constant amplitude carriers can also be achieved by multilevel CPFSK [28–30]. In this case, each data word is encoded into one of M frequency deviations that are used to pulse-frequency-modulate the carrier. If the FM waveform is selected as an extended raised cosine pulse, as in Figure 2.10, the M-ary word encoding can be coupled with the spectral shaping of this format. Phase tracking demodulation can be used to decode the multilevel phase trajectories over the mem-

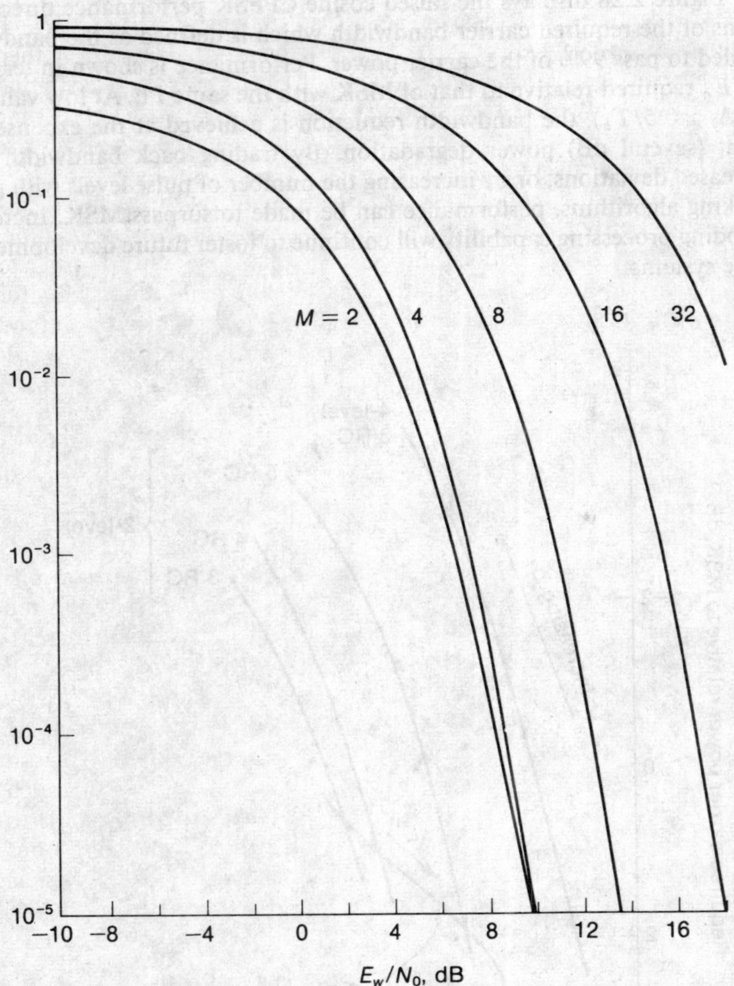

Figure 2.27. MPSK word-error probabilities vs. word energy $E_w = P_c T_w$ (M = number of carrier phases; log M = number of bits in T_w seconds).

ory (number of extended RC bit times) of the encoding. Decoding performance is again estimated by PE bounds, as listed in Table 2.4. These bounds are useful for evaluating the basic bandwidth-error probability trade-off of these types of carriers.

Figure 2.28 displays the raised cosine CPFSK performance directly in terms of the required carrier bandwidth which is defined as the bandwidth needed to pass 99% of the carrier power. Performance is shown in terms of the E_b required relative to that of MSK with the same PE. At low values of Δ_f ($\Delta_f \cong 0.5/T_b$), the bandwidth reduction is achieved at the expense of a slight (several dB) power degradation. By trading back bandwidth with increased deviations, or by increasing the number of pulse levels with phase tracking algorithms, performance can be made to surpass MSK. Increased decoding processing capability will continue to foster future development of these systems.

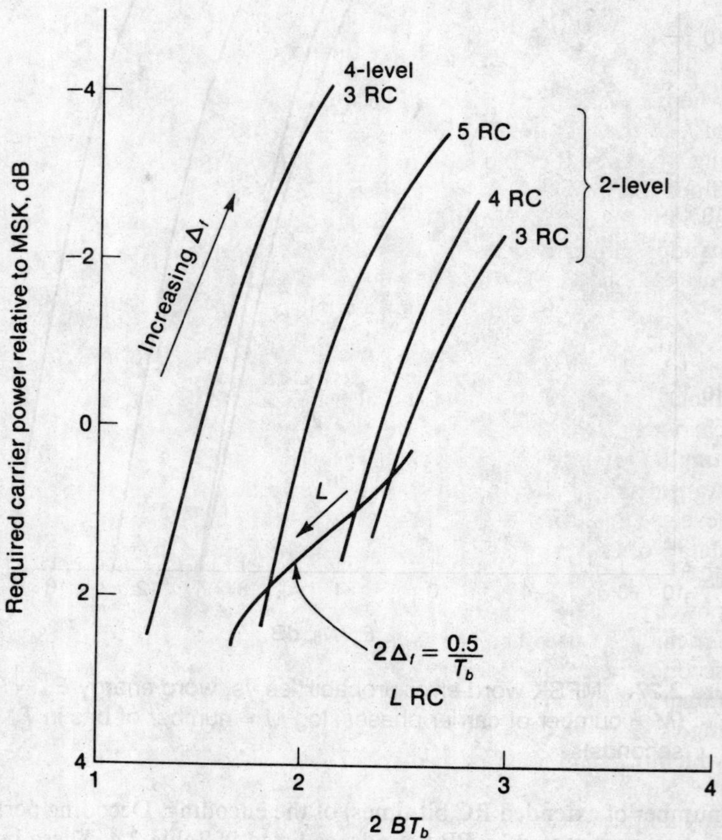

Figure 2.28. Multilevel CPFSK E_b performance relative to MSK vs. 99% carrier bandwidth (from Reference 21).

Multiple Frequency Shift Keying

A word of k bits can be transmitted without the need for phase coherent decoding by the use of **multiple frequency shift keying** (MFSK). The k-bit word is transmitted as a carrier burst at one of $M = 2^k$ different frequencies. The frequencies must be separated by $1/T_w$ Hz to avoid carrier energy from one frequency appearing as energy at another frequency. MFSK can be decoded noncoherently by a bank of tuned bandpass filters at each frequency, followed by an energy comparison. (i.e., the M-ary extension of the binary FSK decoder in Figure 2.20b). The resulting MFSK bit-error probability is computed in Appendix A, and is listed in Table 2.4. It is closely bounded by

$$\text{PE} \leqslant \frac{M}{4} e^{-E_b k/N_0} \tag{2.7.4}$$

where E_b is the carrier energy per bit. Figure 2.29 plots PE for several values of k. Note that unlike MPSK, MFSK performance improves with increasing word size, but the required number of frequencies increases as $M = 2^k$. Since the spacing between frequencies is fixed, the required RF bandwidth also increases with word size. Also, since each frequency requires a separate bandpass filter and energy detector, the complexity of the decoding structure also increases exponentially with block size.

Multiple Amplitude Shift Keying

Block waveform encoding can also be achieved by using a fixed-frequency carrier burst with multiple amplitude levels. This is referred to as **multiple amplitude shift keying (MASK)**. In this format, each k-bit data word is transmitted as a T_w second burst of a carrier with one of $M = 2^k$ amplitude levels. Thus, MASK is a form of amplitude modulation with the encoded data word determining the carrier amplitude every T_w seconds. This means the carrier power varies with the encoding word, and an average carrier power can be determined by averaging over all amplitude levels. Decoding is achieved by using a phase-coherent reference multiplier followed by a T_w second integrator, as in the BPSK decoder in Figure 2.16, but comparing the integrator output to each of the M possible integrator levels. MASK decoding is improved by increasing the separation between amplitude levels, which in turn increases the overall average carrier power.

Since MASK involves amplitude modulation, it is directly affected by any amplitude distortion in the carrier link. For this reason, MASK encoding is generally not used in satellite communications, unless the link can be guaranteed to have little or no amplitude nonlinearities. On the other hand, MASK has the distinct advantage that it can transmit any number of

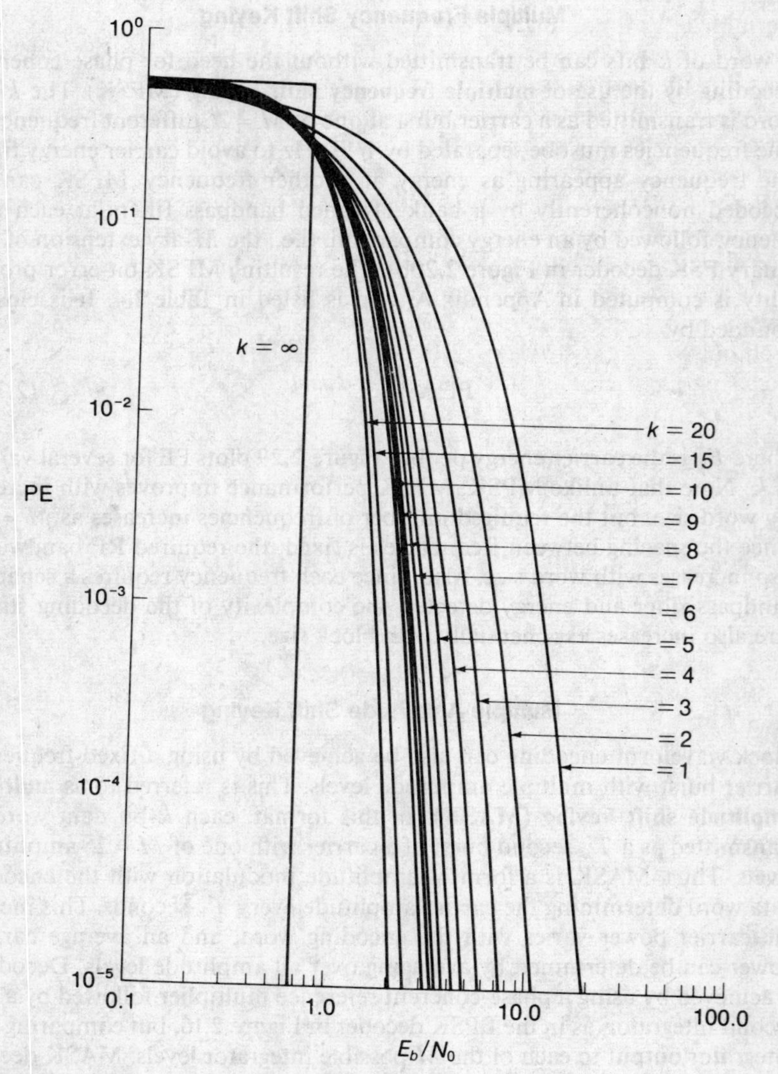

Figure 2.29. Noncoherent MFSK word-error probability vs. equivalent bit energy.

amplitude levels M using a carrier bandwidth that is always about $2/T_w$ Hz, just as in MASK.

Word-error and bit-error probabilities for MASK signaling can be determined by computing the probability that the integrated decoder noise causes the incorrect carrier amplitude to be decided, as shown in Section A.10. The results are listed in Table 2.4, in terms of M and the average word energy E_w (product of average carrier power and T_w). We again see that as M increases (more levels are used with fixed spacing) the average word energy must necessarily increase as M^2 in order to maintain the same PWE performance. This is similar to the MPSK performance, which also uses carrier bursts but has constant amplitudes and slightly more complicated decoder processing.

MASK encoding can be simultaneously applied to quadrature components of a common carrier. Each component is separately encoded in amplitude by a different data word, and the two components are combined into a single carrier. This is referred to as **quadrature amplitude shift keying (QASK)**. QASK is equivalent to the encoding of a $2k$-bit word (or two k-bit words) into one of 2^{2k} joint amplitude values of the two quadrature components. Since each quadrature amplitude pair defines a combined carrier with a specific amplitude and phase, QASK is equivalent to simultaneous amplitude and phase encoding of the carrier. QASK carriers can be decoded by a phase-coherent quadrature correlator, as in Figure 2.16b, followed by separate amplitude decoding in each arm.

2.8 DIGITAL THROUGHPUT

In satellite systems, excessive demand for limited satellite bandwidth forces the communication link to be extremely efficient in the use of this bandwidth. For this reason satellite signaling formats tend toward modulation and coding schemes that combine both power efficiency with bandwidth advantages. In digital systems this bandwidth can be somewhat controlled by proper selection of the waveshapes used for the encoding, as we previously described. If a digital link transmits R bits/sec while requiring a carrier bandwidth of B_c Hz, the bandwidth efficiency is measured by the so-called **channel throughput**, defined as

$$\eta = \frac{R}{B_c} \text{ bit/sec/Hz} \tag{2.8.1}$$

This parameter indicates how well the digital link makes use of the available bandwidth B_c. The larger the throughput, the more bits can be transmitted for a given carrier bandwidth. Since the achievable bit rate is related to the decoding E_b/N_0 via (2.5.1),

$$\frac{E_b}{N_0} = \frac{P_c T_b}{N_0} = \frac{P_c}{N_0 R} \tag{2.8.2}$$

and since the value of E_b/N_0 determines error-probability performance, PE, we see that throughput implicitly depends on the design PE. If we boldly increase bit rate R by simply sending bits at a faster rate through the same carrier bandwidth, we will eventually distort waveshape, and a higher E_b/N_0 will be needed to produce the same PE. This means increased carrier power P_c must be provided to maintain the higher rate at the same PE. We therefore expect that throughput could be increased at the expense of carrier power. In satellite systems operating under bandwidth constraints, this trade-off may in fact be both desirable and cost efficient. The communication design task is then to find signaling formats that provide the best trade-off (greater throughput increase as a function of carrier power).

Consider a standard BPSK system sending bits at a rate $R = 1/T_b$ bps. From Figure 2.7 we require a carrier bandwidth of approximately $B_c = 2/T_b$ Hz, and a carrier power $P_c = (\gamma)N_0B_{RF}$, where γ is the required value of E_b/N_0 to achieve the desired PE, obtained by reading from Figure 2.17. The throughput is then

$$\eta_{\text{BPSK}} = \frac{R}{B_c} = \frac{1/T_b}{2/T_b} = \frac{1}{2}\frac{\text{bps}}{\text{Hz}} \tag{2.8.3}$$

Thus, for example, if one Mbps is to be transmitted, a carrier bandwidth of 2 MHz is required. If we use QPSK, or OQPSK, the bit rate is doubled for the same bandwidth and PE. Hence

$$\eta_{\text{QPSK}} = \frac{2/T_b}{2/T_b} = 1\frac{\text{bps}}{\text{Hz}} \tag{2.8.4}$$

One Mbps can now be transmitted with one MHz of carrier bandwidth.

To further increase the throughput while maintaining the constant envelope property it is necessary either to increase the number of bits encoded onto the carrier burst without increasing bandwidth, or to encode the same number of bits with a reduced bandwidth. The former can be achieved by inserting additional phase states over the QPSK carrier; that is, MPSK. The latter, bandwidth reduction, can be achieved by phase modulation with pulse waveforms extended in time or by the CPFSK waveforms previously described to reduce bandwidth. In MPSK the throughput becomes

$$\eta_{\text{MPSK}} = \frac{\log_2 M}{B_c T_w} = \frac{\log_2 M}{2} \tag{2.8.5}$$

However, the carrier power must be correspondingly increased, as evidenced by (2.7.2), to maintain performance. Figure 2.30 shows how the

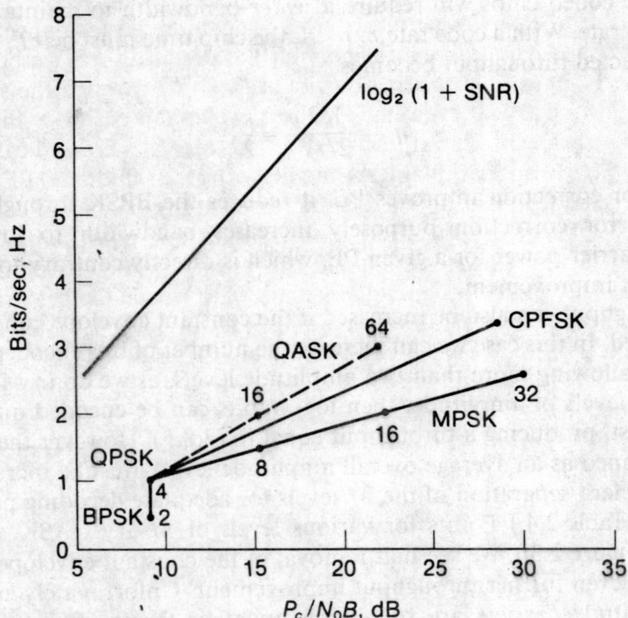

Figure 2.30. Digital throughput (R/B) vs. required CNR (PE = 10^{-5}).

throughput increase in MPSK requires an increasing carrier power to sustain a PE = 10^{-5} as the number of phase states increases. Points for BPSK ($M = 2$) and QPSK ($M = 4$) are included.

MFSK also transmits $\log_2 M$ bits with each T_w sec frequency burst, but requires a bandwidth that increases as $M(2/T_w)$. Hence

$$\eta_{\text{MFSK}} = \frac{\log_2 M}{2M} \tag{2.8.6}$$

and the MFSK throughput actually decreases with increasing M, having a maximum value of $\eta_{\text{MFSK}} = \frac{1}{4}$ at $M = 2$ and 4.

Bandwidth reduction by pulse shaping in frequency-modulation encoding increases throughput, but requires complex decoding and increased carrier power to overcome the resulting intersymbol interference. Points for raised cosine–phase encoding for various symbol extensions are included in Figure 2.30. Note that an improved trade-off of throughput for power is achievable by these methods.

If error-correction encoding is used to reduce the required carrier power, the coded chips will require a *wider* bandwidth to maintain a prescribed bit rate. With a code rate r, $r < 1$, the chip time must be rT_b, and the error-corrected throughput becomes

$$\eta_{ec} = \frac{1/T_b}{2/rT_b} = \frac{r}{2} \tag{2.8.7}$$

While error correction improves PE, it reduces the BPSK throughput. In essence, error correction purposely increases bandwidth to lower the required carrier power for a given PE, which is directly contrary to desired throughput improvement.

Throughput can also be increased if the constant envelope condition is not required. In this case we can increase the number of bits encoded onto a carrier by allowing more than two amplitude levels, as we do in MASK. If we use M levels of amplitude, then $\log_2 M$ bits can be encoded onto each carrier burst, producing a throughput equal to (2.8.5). However the carrier power (defined as an average overall amplitude level) must be increased to allow sufficient separation of the M levels for adequate decoding performance. (See Table 2.4.) Points for various levels of M-ary QASK are also shown in Figure 2.30. We see that removal of the constant envelope condition allows even further throughput improvement. Unfortunately, nonconstant amplitude carriers are susceptible to other forms of distortion in satellite links that may preclude the throughput advantage.

Theoretical analyses in Information Theory has shown that a rigorous upper bound to throughput exists in any digital communication system. In operating over an additive Gaussian white noise channel with carrier power P_c and bandwidth B_c, system throughput is limited by

$$\eta \leqslant \frac{1}{2} \log_2\left(1 + \frac{P_c}{N_0 B_c}\right) \tag{2.8.8}$$

This bound is included in Figure 2.30, and shows the maximum possible throughput achievable by *any* type of encoding and decoding operation. We see that practical encoding methods are generally well below this bound, and approach it rather slowly. However our discussion has shown that any attempts to approach rapidly the maximal available throughput will necessarily be accompanied by increasingly higher levels of decoder processing and the implementation of rather complex decoding equipment.

In summary, we have used this chapter to review the salient features of analog and digital modulation theory that impact most directly on a satellite communication link. The importance of these characteristics and the manner in which they affect overall satellite performance will be continually stressed throughout subsequent chapters. A reader interested in the mathematical derivation and detail of the facts presented here may wish to review

Appendix A or any of the available texts emphasizing these aspects of digital communications, some of which are listed in the references of Appendix A.

PROBLEMS

2.1 Convert the following numbers to decibels:
(a) 200 (b) 0.01 (c) 1/8 (d) 27 (e) 10^4

Convert the following to numbers:
(a) 37 dB (b) 6 dB (c) –6 dB (d) 20 dB (e) –190 dB

2.2 A communication link is to transmit a 6 MHz TV channel over a 36 MHz RF bandwidth. A demodulation input threshold of 12 dB is required. The noise level is –150 dBw/Hz.

(a)How much received carrier power is needed, and what SNR_d will be achieved, if AM is used? (b) Repeat for FM, assuming the maximum possible frequency deviation is used.

2.3 An FM system has a receiver threshold of 15 dB. How much received carrier power and RF bandwidth is needed to transmit a 4-KHz baseband signal with a demodulated SNR_d of 40 dB? ($N_0 = 10^{-10}$w/Hz)

2.4 An FM system transmits a 1-MHz bandwidth waveform with a 10-MHz deviation. (a) If the demodulator requires a threshold of 15 dB, compute the demodulated SNR_d. (b) If the deviation is limited to 1% of the carrier frequency, what is the maximum SNR_d attainable with a 100-MHz RF carrier?

2.5 Let $x(t)$ be a random voltage waveform with probability density $p(x)$ at any t. Determine the compander gain function required to produce an output $y(t)$ that is uniformly distributed over (–1,1) volts. [*Hint*: If $y = g(x)$, then $p(y) = (p(x)/|dg/dx|$ evaluated at $x = g^{-1}(y)$.]

2.6 A voltage waveform is sampled, and each sample is quantized into one of q different levels. If the sampling rate is f_s samples per second, show that the resulting bit rate that will be generated is $R = f_s$ (log q) bits/sec.

2.7 Derive the spectrum of the NRZ and Manchester waveforms in (2.3.3) and (2.3.4) by formally transforming each waveshape.

2.8 Show that a QPSK system achieves twice the bit rate per carrier bandwidth that a binary antipodal PSK system with the same bit-error probability and power level does.

2.9 Derive the spectrum of the raised cosine pulse in (2.4.1). [*Hint*: $p(t)$ in (2.4.1) is also the result of passing an NRZ pulse into a filter with impulse response $h(t) = (\pi/T_b)\sin(2\pi t/T_b), \quad 0 \leq t \leq T_b$.]

2.10 Let a signal $s(t), \quad 0 \leq t \leq T,$ be expandable into the orthonormal set

$$s(t) = \sum_{i=1}^{v} s_i \Phi_i(t) \qquad 0 \leq t \leq T$$

where

$$\int_0^T \Phi_i(t)\Phi_j(t)dt = 1 \qquad i = j$$
$$= 0 \qquad i \neq j$$

We then plot $\mathbf{s} = (s_1, s_2, \ldots, s_v)$ as a point in a vector space of v dimensions. (a) Show that $|\mathbf{s}|^2$ = energy in $s(t)$. (b) Show that for two such expansions, $y(t)$ and $s(t)$, each with energy E, $\int_0^T y(t)s(t)dt = E(\cos\psi)$, where ψ is the angle between the vectors **s** and **y**. (c) Show that any carrier $\cos(\omega t + \theta)$ can be plotted as a unit phasor at angle θ in a two-dimensional space. (d) Use (c) to plot vector points for a BPSK signal pair, a QPSK signal set, and an MPSK signal set.

2.11 An M-ary pulse position modulated (MPPM) system communicates by placing a τ sec carrier pulse in one of M τ sec slots to represent a data word of $\log_2 M$ bits. Use the main hump bandwidth of the carrier to determine the MPPM throughput.

REFERENCES

1. P. Panter, *Modulation, Noise, and Spectral Analyses* (New York: McGraw-Hill, 1965), chapter 6.

2. F. Terman, *Electronic and Radio Engineering* (New York: McGraw-Hill, 1955).

3. H. Taub, and D. Shilling, *Principles of Communication Systems* (New York: McGraw-Hill, 1971), chapter 10.

4. R. Ziemer, and W. Tranter, *Principles of Communications* (Boston: Houghton Mifflin, 1976).

5. B. Lathi, *Modern Digital and Analog Communication Systems* (New York: Holt, Rinehart and Winston, 1983).

6. M. Shwartz, W. Bennett, and S. Stein, *Communication Systems and Techniques* (New York: McGraw-Hill, 1966).

7. R. Gagliardi, *Introduction to Communication Engineering* (New York: Wiley, 1978).

8. R. Freeman, *Telecommunication Transmission Handbook* (New York: Wiley, 1975).

9. Bell Telephone Laboratories, *Transmission Systems for Communications*, 4th ed. (Bell Telephone Laboratories, 1970).

10. S. Gronemeyer, and A. McBride, "MSK and OQPSK Modulation," *IEEE Trans. on Comm.*, vol. Com-24 (August 1976).

11. G. Deshpande, and P. Wittle, "Correlative Encoded Digital FM," *IEEE Trans. on Comm.*, vol. Com-29 (February 1981).

12. C. R. Cahn, "Phase Tracking and Demodulation with Delay," *IEEE Trans. on Information Theory*, vol. IT-20 (January 1974), pp. 50–58.

13. G. Ungerboeck, "New Applications for the Viterbi Algorithm: Carrier Phase Tracking in Synchronous Data-Transmission Systems," *NTC'74 Conference Record*, San Diego, CA, December 1974, pp. 734–738.

14. L. L. Scharf, D. D. Cox, and C. J. Masreliez, "Modulo-2π Phase Sequence Estimation," *IEEE Trans. on Information Theory*, vol. IT-26 (September 1980), pp. 615–620.

15. T. Aulin, "Viterbi Detection of Continuous Phase Modulated Signals," *NTC'80 Conference Record*, Houston, Texas, November 1980, pp. 14.2.1–14.2.7.

16. P. McLane, "Viterbi Receiver for Correlation Encoded MSK Signals," *IEEE Trans. on Comm.*, vol. Com-31 (February 1983).

17. J. B. Anderson, and D. O. Taylor, "A Bandwidth-Efficient Class of Signal-Space Codes," *IEEE Trans. on Information Theory*, vol. IT-24 (November 1978), pp. 703–712.

18. C-E. Sundberg, T. Aulin, and N. Rydbeck, "Recent Results on Spectrally Efficient Constant Envelope Digital Modulation Methods" (pp. 42.1.1–42.1.6), "*M*-ary CPFSK Type of Signalling with Input Data Symbol Pulse Shaping—Minimum Distance and Spectrum" (pp. 42.3.1–42.3.6), and "Bandwidth Efficient Digital FM with Coherent Phase Tree Demodulation" (pp. 42.4.1–42.4.6); *ICC '79 Conference Record*, Boston, MA, June 1979.

19. J. K. Omura, and D. E. Jackson, "Cutoff Rates for Channels Using Bandwidth Efficient Modulations," *NTC '80 Conference Record*, Houston, Texas, November 1980, pp. 14.1.1–14.1.11.

20. J. B. Anderson, C-E. Sundberg, T. Aulin, and N. Rydbeck,

"Smoothed Phase Modulation Codes: Power Vs. Bandwidth," *NTC '80 Conference Record*, Houston, Texas, November 1980, pp. 14.6.1–14.6.6.

21. T. Aulin, N. Rydbeck, and C. Sundberg, "Continuous Phase Modulation—Part I and Part II," *IEEE Trans. on Comm.*, vol. Com-29 (March 1981).

22. D. Muilwijk, "Correlative Phase Shift Keying—A Class of Constant Envelope Modulation Techniques," *IEEE Trans. on Comm.*, vol. Com-29 (March 1981).

23. M. Austin, and M. Chang, "Quadrature Overlapped Raised Cosine Modulation," *IEEE Trans. on Comm.*, vol. Com-29 (March 1981).

24. A. J. Viterbi, and J. K. Omura, *Principles of Digital Communication and Coding* (New York: McGraw-Hill, 1979).

25. W. C. Lindsey, and M. K. Simon, *Telecommunication Systems Engineering* (Englewood Cliffs, N. J.: Prentice-Hall, 1973).

26. A. J. Viterbi, "Error Bounds for Convolutional Codes and an Asymptotically Optimum Decoding Algorithm," *IEEE Transactions on Information Theory*, vol. IT-13 (1967), pp. 250–269.

27. D. Forney, "The Viterbi Algorithm," *Proc. IEEE*, vol. 61 (March 1973).

28. B. Mazur, and D. Taylor, "Demodulation and Carrier Synchronization of Multi-h Phase Codes," *IEEE Trans. on Comm.*, vol. Com-29 (March 1981).

29. G. Wilson, and R. Gaus, "Power Spectra of Multi-h Phase Codes," *IEEE Trans. on Comm.*, vol. Com-29 (March 1981).

30. T. Aulin, N. Rydbeck, C-E. Sundberg, "Performance of Constant Envelope M-ary Digital FM Systems and Their Implementation," *NTC '79 Conference Record*, Washington, DC, November 1979, pp. 55.1.1–55.1.6.

3
The Satellite Channel

Communication between points is achieved by analog or digital modulation of information onto carriers, and by transmission of the carriers as an electromagnetic field from one point to the other. As we discussed in Chapter 2, the amount of received carrier power invariably determines the ability of the receiver to demodulate or decode the information. In satellite systems it is extremely important to know the key parameters that directly determine this received power so that proper trade-off in system design between spacecraft and earth stations can be achieved. In this chapter we examine the basic power flow equations associated with satellite channels.

3.1 ELECTROMAGNETIC FIELD PROPAGATION

Power Flow

A basic communication link is shown in Figure 3.1. The transmitter field is characterized by its **effective isotropic radiated power (EIRP)** defined by

$$\text{EIRP} = P_T g_t(\phi_z, \phi_l) \tag{3.1.1}$$

where P_T is the available antenna input carrier power from the transmitter power amplifier, including circuit coupling losses and antenna radiation losses, and $g_t(\phi_z, \phi_l)$ is the transmitting antenna gain function in the angular direction (ϕ_z, ϕ_l) of the receiver. Here (ϕ_z, ϕ_l) refer to an azimuth and elevation angle, respectively, measured from a coordinate system centered at the transmitting antenna. The **flux density**, or **field intensity** of the electromagnetic field at the receiver due to the transmitter field is then

$$I(z) = \frac{(\text{EIRP})L_a}{4\pi z^2} \tag{3.1.2}$$

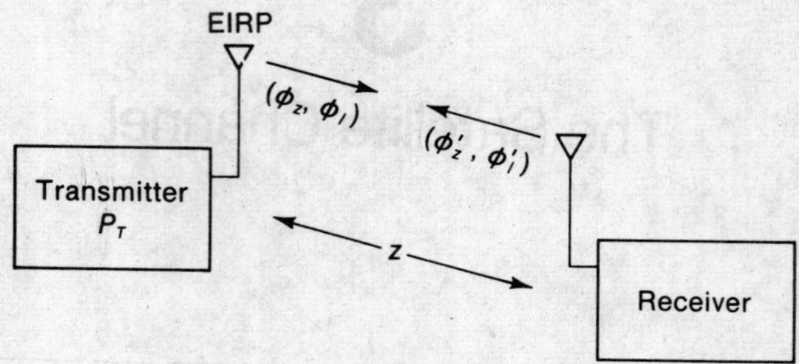

Figure 3.1. Communication link.

where z is the propagation distance to the receiver and L_a accounts for the atmospheric losses during propagation. The received carrier power collected by the receiving antenna having area A_r normal to the direction of the transmitter is then

$$P_r = I(z)A_r = \frac{(\mathrm{EIRP})L_a}{4\pi z^2}A_r \tag{3.1.3}$$

The receiving area A_r can be written in terms of the receiving antenna gain function g_r in the direction of the transmitter:

$$A_r = \left(\frac{\lambda^2}{4\pi}\right)g_r(\phi'_z, \phi'_l) \tag{3.1.4}$$

where λ is the carrier wavelength, and (ϕ'_z, ϕ'_l) are the azimuth and elevation angles of the transmitter relative to the receiver coordinate system. Combining this equation with (3.1.3) allows us to rewrite:

$$P_r = (\mathrm{EIRP})L_a L_p g_r(\phi'_z, \phi'_l) \tag{3.1.5}$$

where we have defined

$$L_p = \left(\frac{\lambda}{4\pi z}\right)^2 \tag{3.1.6}$$

The parameter L_p appears as an effective loss occurring during transmission and is referred to as the **propagation loss** of the link. Note that L_p depends on both the carrier frequency through the wavelength λ and on the distance Z, and its loss is always present, even if there are no atmospheric

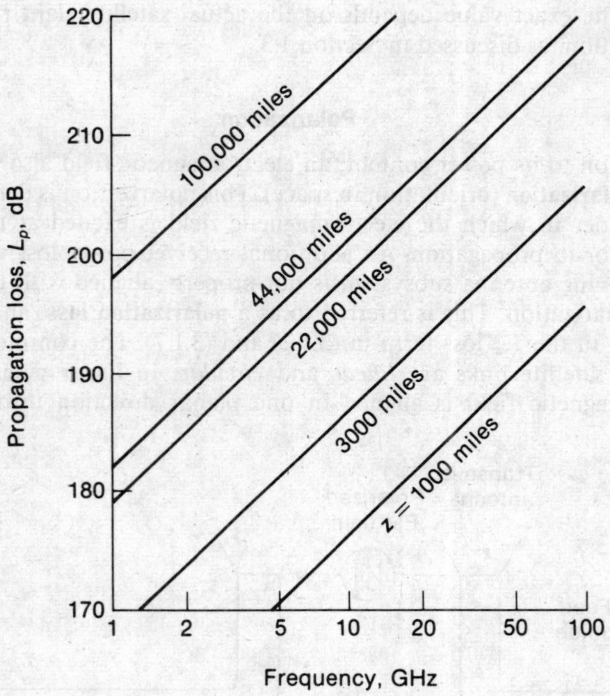

Figure 3.2. Satellite propagation loss.

losses (i.e., if there is free space transmission outside the Earth's atmosphere). We often state P_r in terms of decibels, and write

$$(P_r)_{dB} = (\text{EIRP})_{dB} + (L_p)_{dB} + (L_a)_{dB} + (g_r)_{dB} \tag{3.1.7}$$

where each term is computed in decibels. Note that gain values (greater than 1) are always positive (add) decibels, while attenuation losses (less than 1) are always negative (subtract) decibels. The propagation loss, L_p, when converted to frequency, has the decibel value

$$(L_p)_{dB} = -36.6 - 20 \log_{10}[Z(\text{miles})f(\text{MHz})] \tag{3.1.8}$$

A plot of $(L_p)_{dB}$ for typical satellite distances and satellite frequencies is shown in Figure 3.2. Note that about several hundred dB of propagation loss will generally occur in satellite communication paths for geostationary orbits. The exact value depends on the actual satellite slant range to the earth station, as discussed in Section 1.3.

Polarization

In addition to its power content, an electromagnetic field also has a designated **polarization** (orientation in space). This polarization is determined by the manner in which the electromagnetic field is excited at the antenna feeds prior to propagation. An additional receiver power loss will occur if the receiving antenna subsystem is not properly aligned with the received wave polarization. This is referred to as a **polarization loss**, and should be included in the L_a loss term in (3.1.2) and (3.1.7). The common polarizations in satellite links are *linear* and *circular*. In **linear polarization** the electromagnetic field is aligned in one planar direction throughout the

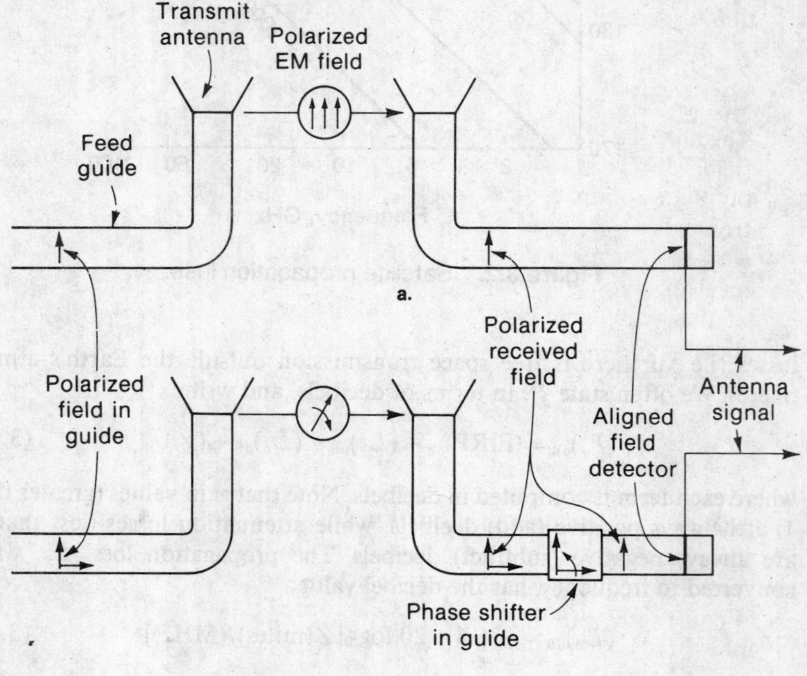

Figure 3.3. Transmitted and detected field polarizations. (a) Linear. (b) Circular.

entire propagation, as shown in Figure 3.3a. These directions are usually designated as horizontal or vertical polarizations (relative to the receiving antenna coordinates). The receiving antenna system must have a matching planar receptor in order to maximize the collected power. For example, terrestrial commercial television is transmitted as a horizontally polarized field, and our rooftop antennas utilize horizontal dipole rods for reception.

In **circular polarization (CP)** the field is excited and transmitted with components in two orthogonal coordinates (one horizontal and one vertical) that are phased so that the combination of the two produces a resultant field polarization that appears to rotate circularly as the wave propagates. (Figure 3.3b) CP reception is achieved by an antenna that feeds both components into an antenna waveguide, and that uses internal phase shifters to reorient one orthogonal polarization back onto the other, thereby collecting the total power available in both components. CP has the advantage that any extraneous rotation of the polarization axis caused by the atmosphere will not affect CP reception, whereas such rotation will produce a polarization loss in a linear polarized system.

3.2 ANTENNAS

The antenna converts electronic carrier signals to polarized electromagnetic fields, and vice-versa. A transmitting antenna is composed of a feed assembly that illuminates an aperture or reflecting surface, from which the electromagnetic field then radiates. A receiving antenna has an aperture or surface focusing an incident radiation field to a collecting feed, producing an electronic signal proportional to the incident radiation. Antennas are one of the key elements in a communication system since their gain values directly determine the amount of received power. Their size and structure are perhaps the easiest to modify from a hardware point of view.

Gain Patterns

Antennas are described by their gain pattern $g(\phi_z, \phi_l)$, which indicates how the gain of the antenna is distributed spatially with respect to the antenna coordinate system. Although a function of the two dimensional angles, gain patterns are often displayed in terms of a single planar angle ϕ, as shown in Figure 3.4. For nonsymmetrical patterns, a separate planar pattern must be shown for both azimuth and elevation.

The most important parameters of an antenna pattern are its **gain** (maximum value of the gain pattern), its **beamwidth** (a measure of the angle over which most of the gain occurs), and its **sidelobes** (amount of gain in off-axis directions). For most communication purposes, desirable antenna

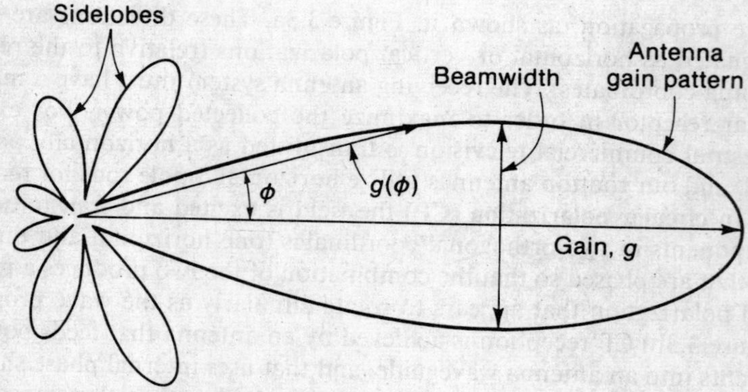

Figure 3.4. Antenna gain pattern.

patterns should be highly directional, with high maximum gain concentrated over a narrow beamwidth with negligibly small sidelobe transmission. As a rough rule of thumb for all antennas, the maximum gain, g, and the half power beamwidth, ϕ_b, in radians are given by

$$g = \rho_a \left(\frac{4\pi}{\lambda^2} \right) A \tag{3.2.1}$$

$$\phi_b \cong \frac{\lambda}{d\sqrt{\rho_a}} \tag{3.2.2}$$

where A is the antenna aperture cross-sectional area, d the cross-sectional diameter, and ρ_a the antenna efficiency factor. The latter is dependent on the type of antenna and on how the antenna aperture is electromagnetically illuminated. Note that the antenna gain is always proportional to the square of the carrier frequency and the antenna size, while the beamwidth varies inversely with frequency and size. Hence the larger the antenna or the higher the frequency, the larger is the gain and the narrower the beamwidth. Thus, a given antenna has an increasingly more directional pattern as higher frequencies are used. At a fixed frequency, the pattern becomes more directional as the antenna is made larger.

Common Antenna Types

In satellite systems the common antenna types are the linear dipole, the helix, the horn, the antenna array, and the parabolic reflector. These are shown in Box 3.1, along with a sketch of their gain patterns and parameter

Antenna type	*Pattern*	*Gain* g	*Half-power beamwidth*
Short dipole $l << \lambda$	$g\cos^2\phi$; Length l	1.5	90°
Long dipole $l >> \lambda$		1.5	47°
$l = \lambda/2$		1.64	78°
Phased array, phase difference $= \frac{2\pi s}{\lambda}\cos\theta_0$	N elements $l = \lambda/2$; S; Φ_o	$\left\{\frac{N\pi s}{1.4\lambda}\right\}^2$	$50°\left\{\frac{\lambda}{Ns}\right\}$ $\theta_0 = 0$
Helix	l; c; Circumference c; Length l	$15\left\{\frac{cl}{\lambda^2}\right\}$	$52°\left\{\frac{\lambda}{c\sqrt{l}}\right\}$
Square horn, dimension d	13 dB; $g\left(\frac{\sin x}{x}\right)^2$; 0; $x = \frac{\pi d}{\lambda}\sin\phi$; Horn direction	$\frac{4\pi d^2}{\lambda^2}$	$\frac{0.88\lambda}{d}$
Circular reflector	17.6 dB; $g\left(\frac{2J_1(x)}{x}\right)^2$; 0; $x = \frac{\pi d}{\lambda}\sin\phi$; Reflector direction	$\left\{\frac{\pi d}{\lambda}\right\}^2$	$\frac{1.02\lambda}{d}$

Box 3.1. Typical antenna patterns.

values. The parabolic reflector is the most common, giving a highly directional, symmetric pattern. The dipole has a pattern that is hemispherical, and produces a propagating field polarized in the direction of the dipole. Helix and horns are smaller antennas with reasonable directivity, but higher sidelobes than parabolic reflectors. A helix antenna produces a circularly polarized field, while a horn is generally used to produce linearly polarized fields. An array is a group of small antennas (dipoles, horns, or helices) properly separated so that if a carrier is phase shifted and individually radiated from each element, the propagating fields will reinforce in some directions and interfere in others. The net result will be a combined beam with directivity. By properly selecting the phase shifts between array elements, the directivity of the beam can be oriented in a given direction. Hence a phased array can theoretically produce beams in arbitrary off-axis directions. As we see from Box 3.1 gain increases with the number of array elements, and thus high gain is achieved with large arrays. The beamwidth changes with the beam direction, being narrowest for broadside beams, and becoming increasingly larger for off-axis beams.

Phased-array antennas on satellites represent a rapidly advancing technology that will continue to undergo substantial development. Phase arrays allow beam steering without physically moving an antenna; they simply readjust phase shifters in the array feed. This electronic steering can be used to advantage to point toward moving transmitters, or to reduce the receiving gain in the direction of noise sources (null steering).

The Parabolic Dish

The most common antenna for satellites and earth stations is the parabolic reflector, or **dish**. Figure 3.5 shows two different feed diagrams for a para-

Table 3.1. Parameter values of parabolic reflector.

Aperture field intensity distribution over dish:

$$\left[1 - \left(\frac{2r}{d}\right)^2\right]^\gamma \qquad r \leq d/2$$

γ	ρ_a, %	ϕ_b, rad	sidelobe, dB	gain g
0	100	$1.02\ \lambda/d$	−17.6	$9.86\ (d/\lambda)^2$
1	75	$1.27\ \lambda/d$	−24.6	$7.39\ (d/\lambda)^2$
2	55	$1.47\ \lambda/d$	−30.6	$5.4\ (d/\lambda)^2$
3	44	$1.65\ \lambda/d$	−40.6	$4.83\ (d/\lambda)^2$

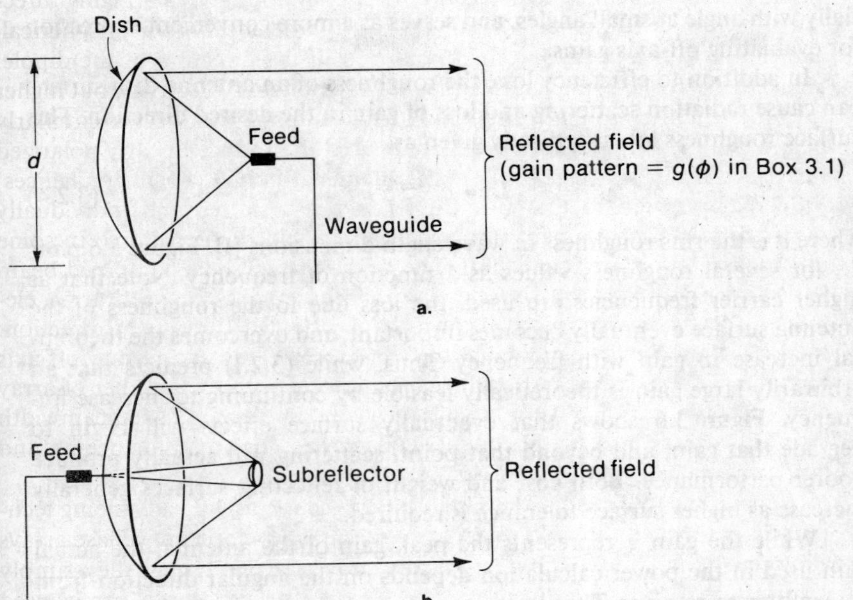

Figure 3.5. Parabolic reflector. (a) Front feed. (b) Rear (Cassagrainian) feed.

bolic dish. The field to be transmitted is excited in the feed waveguide with the desired polarization and is then radiated to the reflector. The feed may be located in front at the focus of the parabolic dish, or it may be fed from behind using a subreflector. If the dish is uniformly illuminated by the feed, the reflected transmitted gain pattern is circular symmetric, as given in Box 3.1. The gain, half-power beamwidth ϕ_b, and the sidelobe gain depend on the manner in which the feed radially distributes the field intensity over the dish. Table 3.1 lists the relation between type of illumination, the resulting aperture efficiency, ρ_a; beamwidth, ϕ_b; and the sidelobe peak values. Note that reduction of sidelobes is accompanied by a spreading of the radiated beam.

For small angles off boresight, such that the pattern skirt is within about 6 dB of the peak value, the parabolic antenna pattern is adequately represented by the simpler relation

$$g(\phi) \approx \rho_a \left(\frac{\pi d}{\lambda}\right)^2 e^{-2.76(\phi/\phi_b)^2} \tag{3.2.3}$$

Equation (3.2.3) states that parabolic gain falls off approximately exponentially with angle at small angles, and serves as a more convenient expression for evaluating off-axis gains.

In addition to efficiency loss, the roughness of an antenna dish surface can cause radiation scattering and loss of gain in the desired direction. This surface roughness loss is typically given as

$$L_r = e^{-(4\pi\sigma/\lambda)^2} \tag{3.2.4}$$

where σ is the rms roughness in wavelength dimensions [1]. Figure 3.6 plots L_r for several roughness values as a function of frequency. Note that as higher carrier frequencies are used, the loss due to the roughness of the antenna surface eventually becomes important, and overcomes the theoretical increase in gain with frequency. Thus, while (3.2.1) predicts that an arbitrarily large gain is theoretically feasible by continuing to increase frequency, Figure 3.6 shows that eventually surface effects will begin to degrade that gain, and beyond that point, scattering will actually produce poorer performance. Both cost and weight of reflecting surfaces generally increase as higher surface tolerance is required.

While the gain g represents the peak gain of the antenna, the actual gain used in the power calculation depends on the angular direction from transmitter to receiver. That is, it depends on how accurately the antennas are pointed at the transmitter and receiver. This accuracy depends, in turn, on the pointing error, which arises from both the inability to aim an antenna in exactly the right direction and the inaccurate knowledge of the

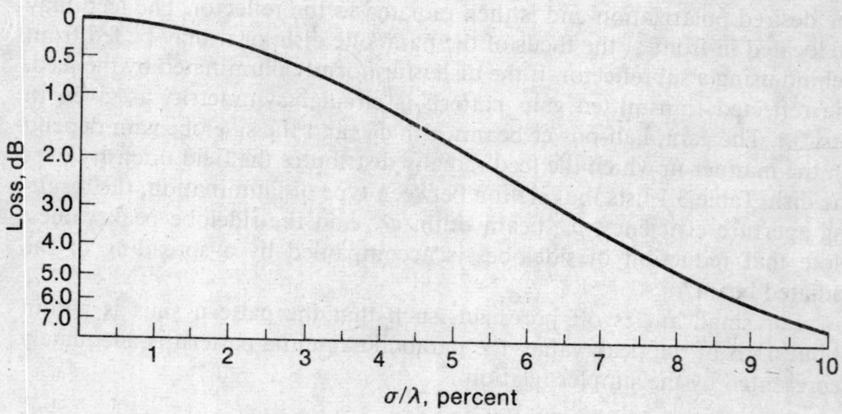

Figure 3.6. Surface roughness loss in reflector antennas (σ = rms surface roughness).

target location. Pointing errors to geostationary satellites are usually about 0.1–0.5 degree, depending on the antenna pointing and tracking capabilities, and slightly higher for orbiting satellites. The presence of a pointing error means that the power to the receiver is determined by the antenna gain on the skirts of the pattern, rather than by the peak gain g. For a parabolic antenna with pointing error ϕ_e, (3.2.3) shows that

$$g(\phi_e) = ge^{-2.76(\phi_e/\phi_b)^2} \tag{3.2.5}$$

where g is the peak gain and ϕ_b the half power beamwidth. Equation (3.2.5) indicates that an exponential decrease in gain occurs for small pointing errors, as the pointing error increases relative to beamwidth. When narrow beams are used, a given pointing error therefore becomes more critical. Since beamwidth depends directly on the d/λ (diameter/wavelength) ratio, pointing-error losses increase exponentially with this product. Figure 3.7 plots $g(\phi_e)$ as a function of d/λ for several values of pointing errors. This pointing-error loss is added directly to surface roughness loss, L_r, in (3.2.4). Note that while roughness losses prevent use of high frequencies, pointing errors prevent use of narrow beams, and therefore constrain both frequency

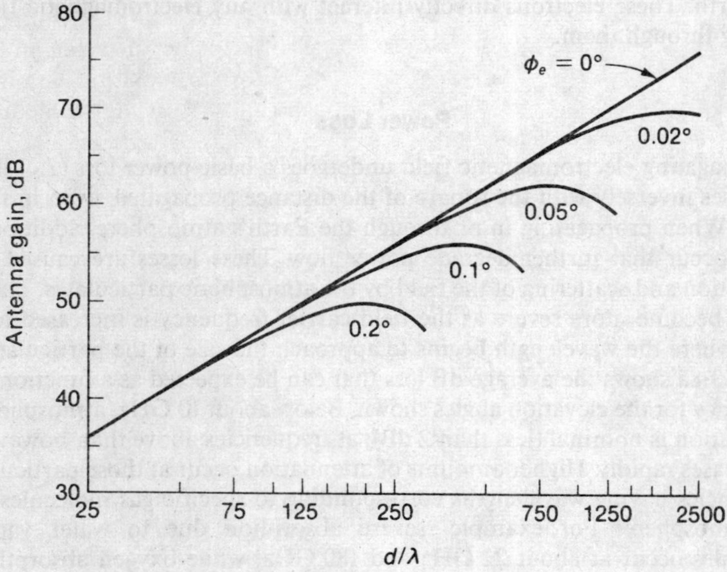

Figure 3.7. Pointing-error loss in antennas (ϕ_e = pointing error). Antenna efficiency = 55%.

and antenna size. For example, if no more than 1 dB of pointing loss can be tolerated, it is necessary that $(\phi_e/\phi_b) \leqslant 0.28$. From (3.2.2) this requires

$$\frac{d}{\lambda} \leqslant .41/\phi_e \tag{3.2.6}$$

where ϕ_e is in radians. Hence, link pointing error limits the useable d/λ ratio of the antenna.

3.3 ATMOSPHERIC LOSSES

The Earth is surrounded by a collection of gases, atoms, water droplets, pollutants, and so on captured by the Earth's gravity field, and extending to an altitude of about 400 miles. This constitutes the Earth's atmosphere. The heaviest concentration of these particulates is near the Earth, with particle density decreasing with altitude. The particles in the upper part of the atmosphere (**ionosphere**) absorb and reflect large quantities of radiated energy from the sun. The absorbed energy is then reradiated in all directions by the ionosphere. In addition, the absorbed energy ionizes the ionospheric atoms, producing bands of upper atmospheric free electrons that surround the Earth. These electrons directly interact with any electromagnetic field passing through them.

Power Loss

A propagating electromagnetic field undergoes a basic power loss (L_p) that increases inversely with the square of the distance propagated, even in free space. When propagating in or through the Earth's atmosphere, additional losses occur that further degrade power flow. These losses are caused by absorption and scattering of the field by the atmospheric particulates. These effects become more severe as the field carrier frequency is increased to a point where the wavelength begins to approach the size of the particulates. Figure 3.8a shows the average dB loss that can be expected as a function of frequency for the elevation angles shown. Below about 10 GHz, atmospheric attenuation is nominal (less than 2 dB); at frequencies above that, however, it increases rapidly. Higher amounts of attenuation occur at those particular frequencies having wavelengths corresponding to specific gas molecules in the atmosphere. For example, severe absorption due to water vapor molecules occur at about 22 GHz and 180 GHz, while oxygen absorption occurs at about 60 GHz and 118 GHz. This attenuation increase at the higher frequencies is the primary disadvantage of shifting operation to the higher frequency bands in satellite systems.

Since the density of particulates in the atmosphere decreases with

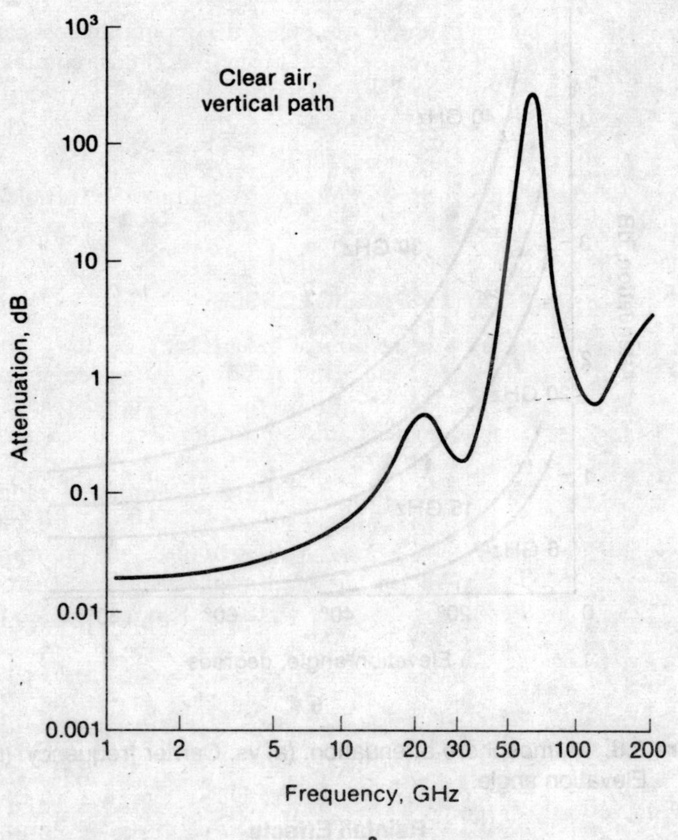

Figure 3.8. Atmosphere attenuation. (a) vs. Carrier frequency. (b) vs. Elevation angle.

distance above Earth, atmospheric attenuation is lower at the higher altitudes. This means the total attenuation expected in a satellite link will depend on both the link elevation angle and the slant range. Most severe attenuation occurs at angles close to the horizon, and decreases for vertical paths directly overhead. Figure 3.8b plots the atmospheric attenuation at various satellite frequency bands as a function of elevation angle measured from ground. From these curves, it is clear that it is preferable that satellites be viewed above a minimum elevation angle. Domestic satellite systems serving particular areas are usually designed to ensure that the satellite will be higher than some acceptable viewing angle.

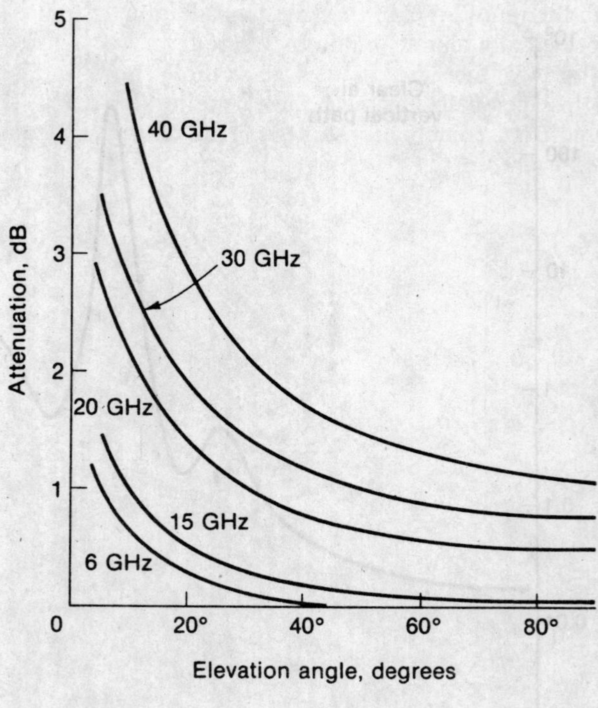

Figure 3.8. Atmosphere attenuation. (a) vs. Carrier frequency. (b) vs. Elevation angle.

Rainfall Effects

The most serious atmospheric effect in a satellite link is rainfall. Water droplets scatter and absorb impinging radiation, causing attenuation many times the clear air losses shown in Figure 3.8. Rain effects become most severe at wavelengths approaching the water drop size, which is dependent on the type of rainfall. In heavy rains raindrop size may approach a centimeter, and severe absorption may occur at frequencies as low as 10 GHz. Thus rainfall effects can become extremely severe at satellite frequencies at X-band and above.

If a satellite link is to be maintained during a rainfall, it is necessary that enough extra power (called **power margin**) be transmitted to overcome the maximum additional attenuation induced by the rain. Hence it is necessary to have an accurate assessment of expected rain loss when evaluating link parameters. The expected additional rain loss depends on the operating frequency, the amount of rainfall, and the path length of the propagation through the rain [2–7]. To evaluate this additional rain loss we first obtain the expected rainfall rate in millimeter/hour for the region of the communication link. We then use curves such as those shown in Figure 3.9a to read off dB loss per path length at the operating frequency. These curves are generated from combinations of empirical data and mathematical models

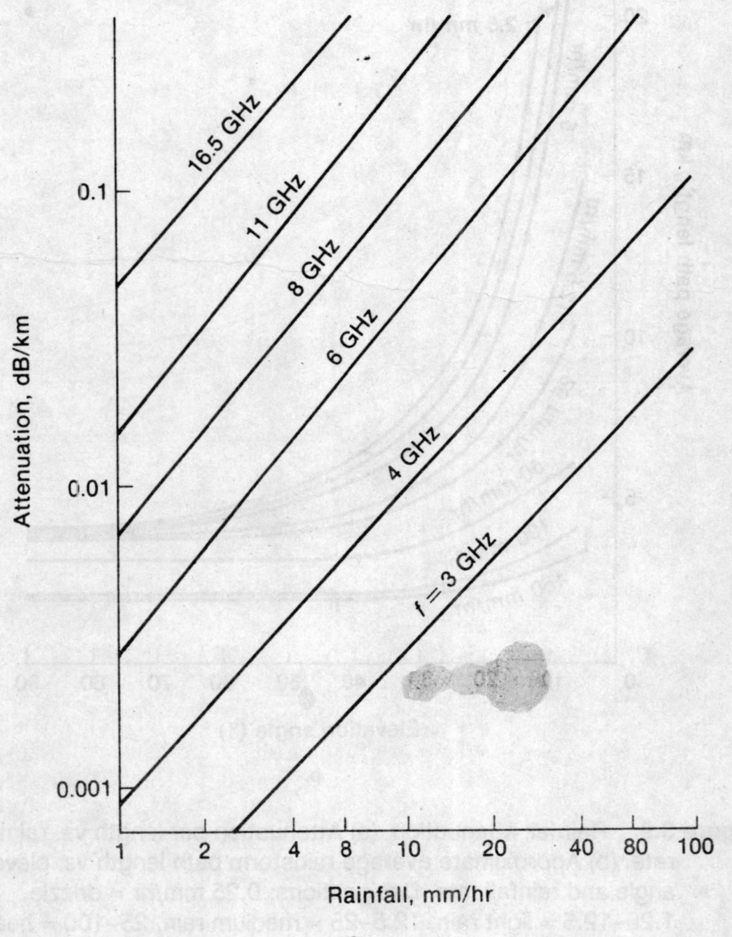

Figure 3.9. Rainfall attenuation. (a) Attenuation per length vs. rainfall rate. (b) Approximate average rainstorm path length vs. elevated angle and rainfall rate. Designations: 0.25 mm/hr = drizzle, 1.25–12.5 = light rain, 12.5–25 = medium rain, 25–100 = heavy rain, >100 = tropical downpour.

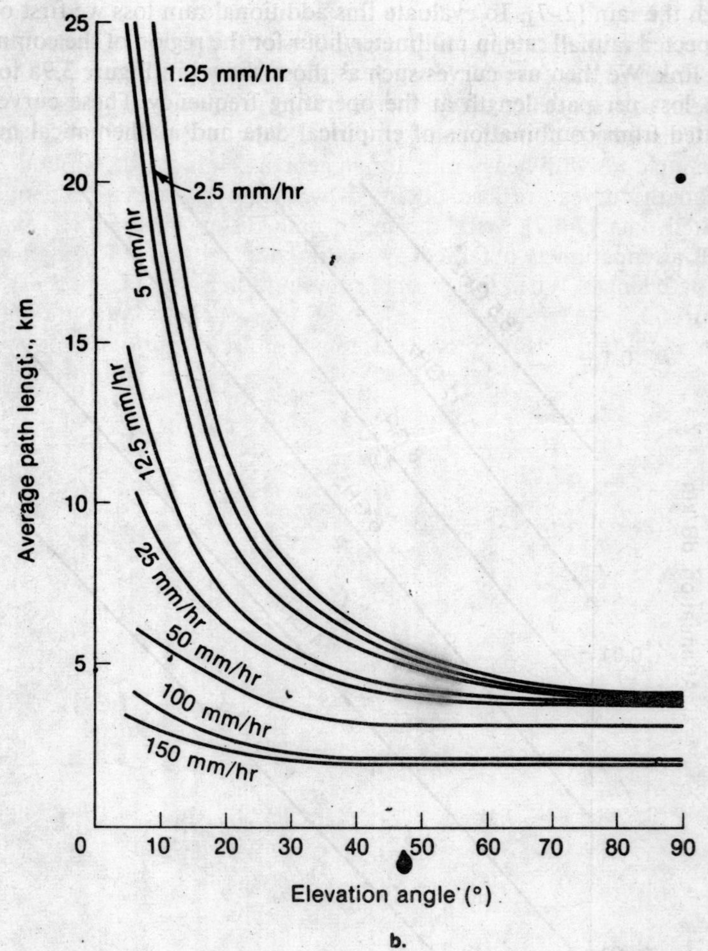

Figure 3.9. Rainfall attenuation. (a) Attenuation per length vs. rainfall rate. (b) Approximate average rainstorm path length vs. elevated angle and rainfall rate. Designations: 0.25 mm/hr = drizzle, 1.25–12.5 = light rain, 12.5–25 = medium rain, 25–100 = heavy rain, >100 = tropical downpour.

that fit the data. The rainfall attenuation model commonly used [2] is of the form

$$\text{dB loss/length} = ar^b \tag{3.3.1}$$

where r is the rainfall note, and a and b are frequency-dependent coefficients obtained via curve-fitting and extrapolation (e.g., see Problem 3.7). The mean path length of the rain is then determined for the given elevation angle. This length also depends on rainfall rate, as shown in Figure 3.9b, since rainclouds with heavy rain are, in general, closer to the ground. These path length curves are also obtained by fitting mathematical models to measured data [2,6,7]. With the mean path distance estimated, expected rainfall attenuation is obtained by multiplying the rain dB/length by the mean path length. When this rainfall computation is carried out for the data in Figures 3.9, we see that even at C-band frequencies, a heavy rainfall can add an additional 5 dB or more of attenuation to the path loss.

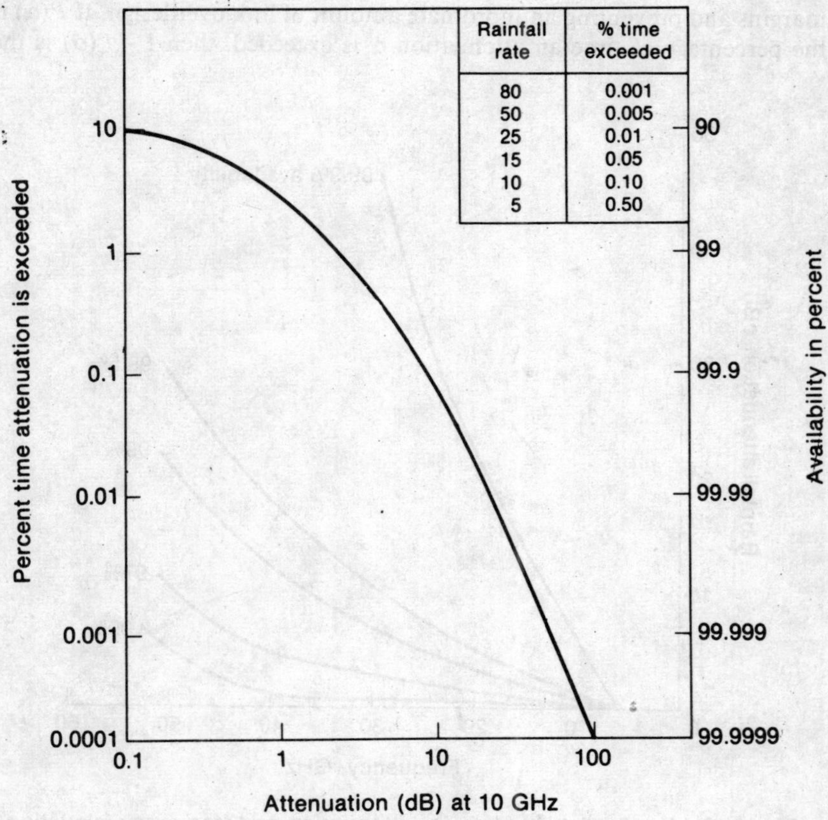

Figure 3.10. Attenuation distribution at 10 GHz and 30° elevation angle.

Rainfall attenuation computed as just described is actually a conditional attenuation dependent on the rainfall rate selected. Since the latter is itself a statistical phenomenon, it is often more meaningful to take into account the probability that a given rainfall rate will be exceeded. Data on such probabilities are usually available for most regions of the world. When these probabilities are taken into account we compute rain attenuation statistics similar to that shown in Figure 3.10. This shows, for a particular region, the expected percent of time that a given rainfall attenuation level will be exceeded. Since Figure 3.9 allows us to convert rainfall rate to expected attenuation at specific frequencies, these rainfall probabilities allow us to associate a probability with a given attenuation being exceeded at that frequency and elevation angle.

Curves of this type are much more meaningful for allowing safe design margins and preventing an inordinate amount of link overdesign. If $P(\alpha)$ is the percentage of time an attenuation α is exceeded, then $1 - P(\alpha)$ is the

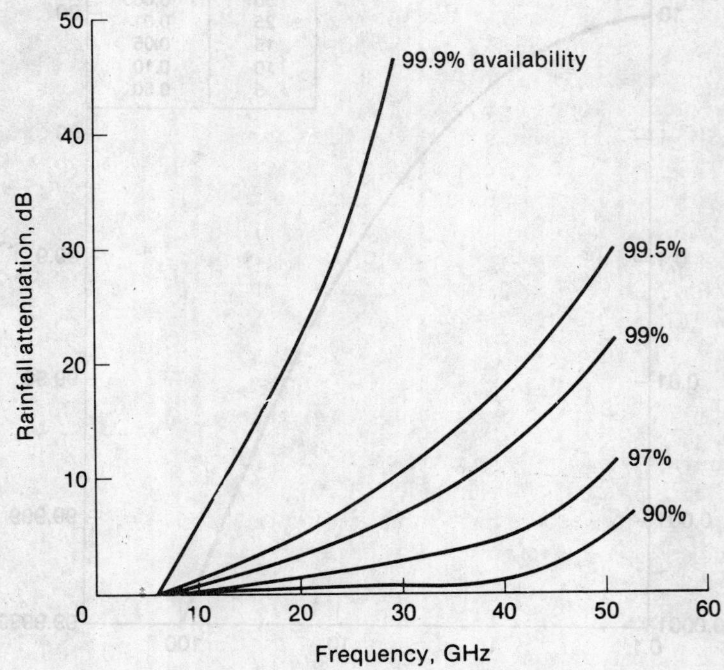

Figure 3.11. Availability data for attenuation and frequency (elevation angle = 30°).

percent **availability** of the link with an attenuation less than α. The value $P(\alpha)$ is often called the percent **outage** time of the link, with an attenuation exceeding α. Repeated conversions of this type will generate a crossplot of link availability with respect to a given rain attenuation level and frequency. Such a curve is shown in Figure 3.11, using the data of Figures 3.9 and 3.10. This shows us, for example, that if a 30 GHz link at an elevation angle of 30° can withstand a rain attenuation of 10 dB, it will be available 99.5% of the time, or, equivalently, it will have an outage 0.5% of the time (about 45 hours a year). If the elevation angle decreases, the link will be available for less time.

3.4 RECEIVER NOISE

In addition to receiving the impinging field from a transmitting source, a receiving antenna also collects other forms of electromagnetic energy that may be present. This other radiation appears as interference, or noise, that tends to mask the desired field propagating from the transmitter. The primary cause of these unwanted fields is background radiation from galactic and cosmic sources in the sky and atmospheric reradiation, and radio frequency interference (RFI) from other transmitters and emitters. In addition to this noise collected by the receiving antenna, noise can be generated directly within the electronics of the receiver immediately following the antenna. The contributions from all these sources of interference combine to define a total noise level for the receiving system. This noise sets the minimal required power from the desired transmitter for achieving reliable communications. That is, even before any field processing is performed, it is necessary for the receiving antenna to collect enough transmitter power (P_r in Section 3.1) to overcome the total noise occurring at the receiver.

Noise Temperature

The amount of receiver noise present is defined by a receiver noise temperature T°_{eq}. The parameter T°_{eq} is an effective equivalent temperature that an external noise source would have to have to produce the same amount of receiver noise. This equivalent temperature is written as

$$T^\circ_{eq} = T^\circ_b + (F - 1)290^\circ \qquad (3.4.1)$$

where T°_b is the background noise temperature accounting for contributions collected by the antenna (from galactic and sky noise) and F is the **noise figure** of the receiver. This latter accounts for the contribution due to receiver electronics. A noise source with a temperature T°_{eq} produces an effective noise spectrum level of

$$N_0 = kT^\circ_{eq} \text{ watts/Hz} \tag{3.4.2}$$

at the antenna input, where k is Boltzmann's constant:

$$\begin{aligned} k &= 1.379 \times 10^{-23} \text{ w/°K-Hz} \\ &= -228.6 \text{ dBw/°K-Hz} \end{aligned} \tag{3.4.3}$$

From the spectral level in (3.4.2), the total noise power entering the receiver over a bandwidth B_{RF} is then

$$P_n = kT^\circ_{eq} B_{RF} \tag{3.4.4}$$

Here, B_{RF} typically represents the RF bandwidth of the receiving system. Hence a computation of total receiver noise can be obtained from knowledge of the T°_{eq} of the receiver.

The value of T°_b depends on the specific characteristics of the actual noise background observed by the receiving antenna. For example, an earth-based antenna facing skyward would see the galactic noise sources (stars, planets, moon, etc.) in the antenna beamwidth, along with the reradiation effects of the sun's noise energy by the atmosphere. On the other hand, a satellite-based antenna, looking back toward Earth, would see primarily the reradiation noise emissions of the Earth itself. These latter would appear as a uniform bright spot encompassing the Earth, set against the blackness of the outer universe. When viewed from outer space, the Earth has a reradiation temperature of about 300° K. Thus, the background noise effects may be significantly different for the two cases.

Background noise temperatures for earth-based antennas also depend indirectly on frequency, since they are primarily a combination of reflected galactic noise and reradiated atmospheric noise, both of which are themselves frequency-dependent. Figure 3.12 shows a typical sky background noise temperature T°_b, showing the galactic noise decreasing with frequency, and the atmospheric reradiated noise increasing with both frequency and elevation angle. The combination of the two produces a minimum **noise window** in the range of about 1–10 GHz. This is a primary reason why the bulk of microwave terrestrial and satellite communication systems (specifically C-band and X-band satellite links) have evolved in this range. It should be pointed out that rainfall may alter the effective sky background temperature slightly, since it introduces more scatterers (raindrops) to the antenna input. In general, rainfall rates below about 10 mm/hr cause no appreciable increase in T°_b, but may add an additional 10°–50° in severe rainstorms.

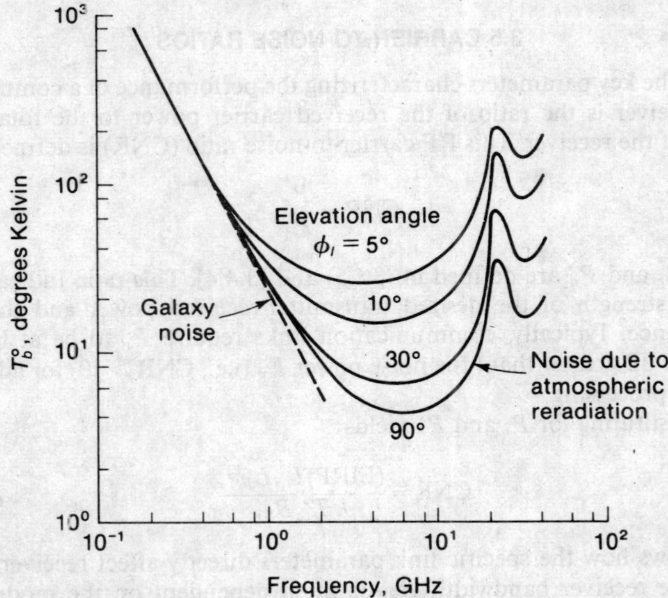

Figure 3.12. Background noise temperature for earth-based receivers.

Noise Figure

Internal circuit noise is accounted for in T_{eq}° by specifying the receiver noise figure F, which depends on the specific electronic circuitry following the antenna. Noise figure for an electronic system is defined as

$$F = \frac{\text{Total system output noise power}}{\text{Output system noise power due to system input noise at 290°K}} \tag{3.4.5}$$

When defined in this way, $(F - 1)290°$ is the temperature of an equivalent noise source at the system input that will produce the same contribution to the system output noise as the internal noise of the system itself. For an antenna system, this equivalent circuit temperature adds directly to the background noise collected by the antenna, producing the combined equivalent noise T_{eq}° in (3.4.1). Explicit formulas for noise figure for typical receiver front ends will be given in Chapter 4, when specific satellite circuits are considered.

3.5 CARRIER-TO-NOISE RATIOS

One of the key parameters characterizing the performance of a communication receiver is the ratio of the received carrier power to the total noise power of the receiver. This RF carrier-to-noise ratio (CNR) is defined by

$$\mathrm{CNR} = \frac{P_r}{P_n} \tag{3.5.1}$$

where P_r and P_n are defined in (3.1.5) and (3.4.4). This ratio indicates the relative strength of the desired transmitter-received power and the total interference. Typically, communication links require P_r to be at least 10 times (10 dB greater than) the noise power P_n (i.e., CNR $\geqslant$ 10) for adequate receiver processing.

Substituting for P_r and P_n yields

$$\mathrm{CNR} = \frac{(\mathrm{EIRP})L_p L_a g_r}{k T^\circ_{\mathrm{eq}} B_{\mathrm{RF}}} \tag{3.5.2}$$

This shows how the specific link parameters directly affect receiver CNR. Since the receiver bandwidth B_{RF} is often dependent on the modulation format, we often isolate the RF link power parameters by normalizing out bandwidth dependence. We therefore define instead RF carrier-to-noise level ratio,

$$\left(\frac{C}{N_0}\right) = \frac{(\mathrm{EIRP})L_p L_a g_r}{k T^\circ_{\mathrm{eq}}} \tag{3.5.3}$$

which does not depend on B_{RF}. In digital systems the C/N_0 ratio allows us to compute directly the receiver bit energy-to-noise level ratio as

$$\frac{E_b}{N_0} = \left(\frac{C}{N_0}\right) T_b \tag{3.5.4}$$

where T_b is the bit time. Thus, from knowledge of the link C/N_0, which depends only on the RF link parameters, we can directly compute either analog CNR by dividing in bandwidth, or digital E_b/N_0 by multiplying in bit times.

It is often convenient to factor (3.5.3) as

$$\left(\frac{C}{N_0}\right) = \left[\frac{\mathrm{EIRP}}{k}\right][L_p L_a]\left[\frac{g_r}{T^\circ_{\mathrm{eq}}}\right] \tag{3.5.5}$$

The first bracket contains only transmitter parameters, the second bracket contains propagation parameters, and the last receiver parameters. Thus (3.5.5) separates out the contribution of each subsystem to the total C/N_0. This interpretation is interesting in that it shows, for example, that in terms of C/N_0 the only effect of the receiving system is through the ratio g_r/T°_{eq} (i.e., the ratio of the receiver antenna gain to its equivalent noise temperature). It in fact shows that as far as the receiver is concerned, performance can be maintained with a lower receiver gain (smaller antenna) if T°_{eq} can be suitably reduced. Hence there is a direct trade-off of receiver antenna size and receiver noise temperature in achieving a desired performance. Receiver temperature can be controlled by careful control of the antenna background (orbit selection, elevation angles, etc.) and receiver electronics (lower noise figure). Since antenna size directly impacts overall receiver cost and construction, this type of receiver noise quality–antenna size trade-off is often desirable. This is especially true when many receivers (earth stations) are to be used. Figure 3.13 plots the value of g/T° for a given frequency–antenna size product at various values of noise temperature T°_{eq}.

Conversely, use of a high-gain antenna allows a noisier receiver to be employed; such a receiver will generally dominate the noise contribution from the background. This makes the performance of the system less sensitive to parameters influencing the background contribution, such as field of view, rainfall, and so on. That is, small changes in T°_b will not affect T°_{eq}, and therefore C/N_0, if the second term dominates in (3.4.1).

One must be careful, however, of overemphasizing the g/T° parameter in attempting to improve satellite performance, since it often leads to serious misconceptions. For example, at a glance Figure 3.13 implies that g/T° can be improved by using a higher carrier frequency with a given antenna size, since this directly increases receiving antenna gain. However, we recall from (3.1.6) that propagation loss also increases as f^2, so that with a fixed-transmitter EIRP in (3.5.5), C/N_0 does not directly depend on carrier frequency. (In fact, it may be reduced since the atmospheric losses L_a generally increase with f). This can be made more obvious by reinserting (3.1.6) and (3.2.1) to rewrite (3.5.3):

$$\left(\frac{C}{N_0}\right) = \left[\frac{(\text{EIRP})L_a}{kT^\circ_{eq}}\right]\left[\frac{A_r}{z^2}\right] \tag{3.5.6}$$

For a fixed transmitting EIRP and T°_{eq}, C/N_0 is independent of frequency, and depends only on propagation path length and receiving area. The apparent dependence on frequency appears in L_p only if we choose to write A_r in terms of receiving gain, g_r. Thus, selecting a higher frequency band will not directly aid the receiving system.

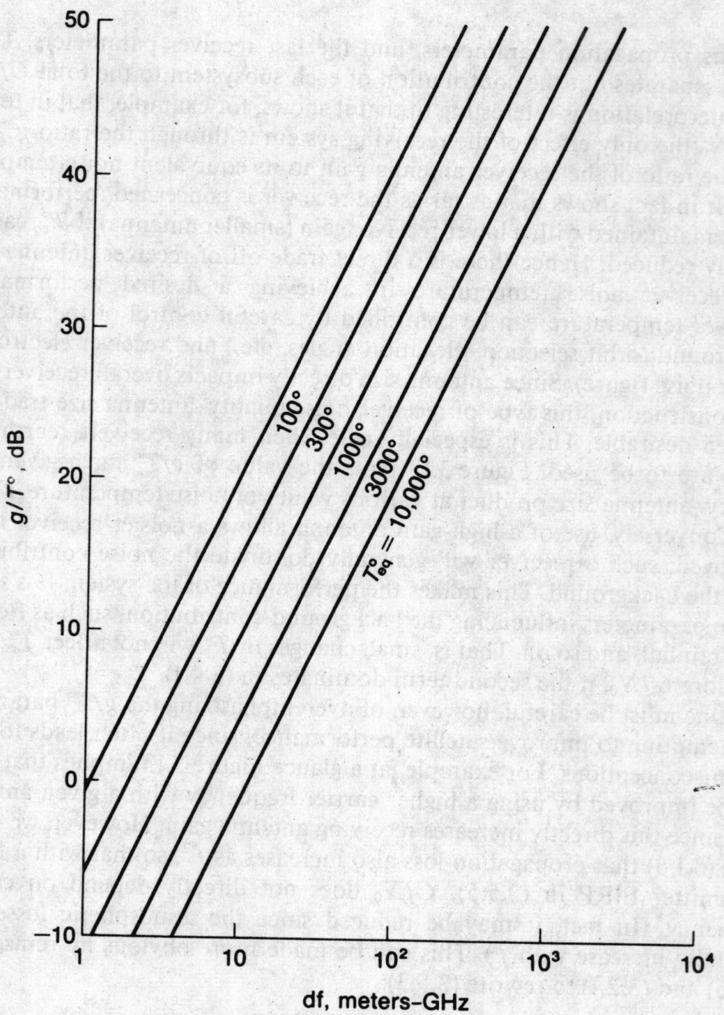

Figure 3.13. Receiver g/T° values (d = meters, f = GHz, T°_{eq} = degrees Kelvin).

3.6 SATELLITE LINK ANALYSIS

The CNR link budgets of the preceding section can now be directly applied to the analysis of specific satellite links.

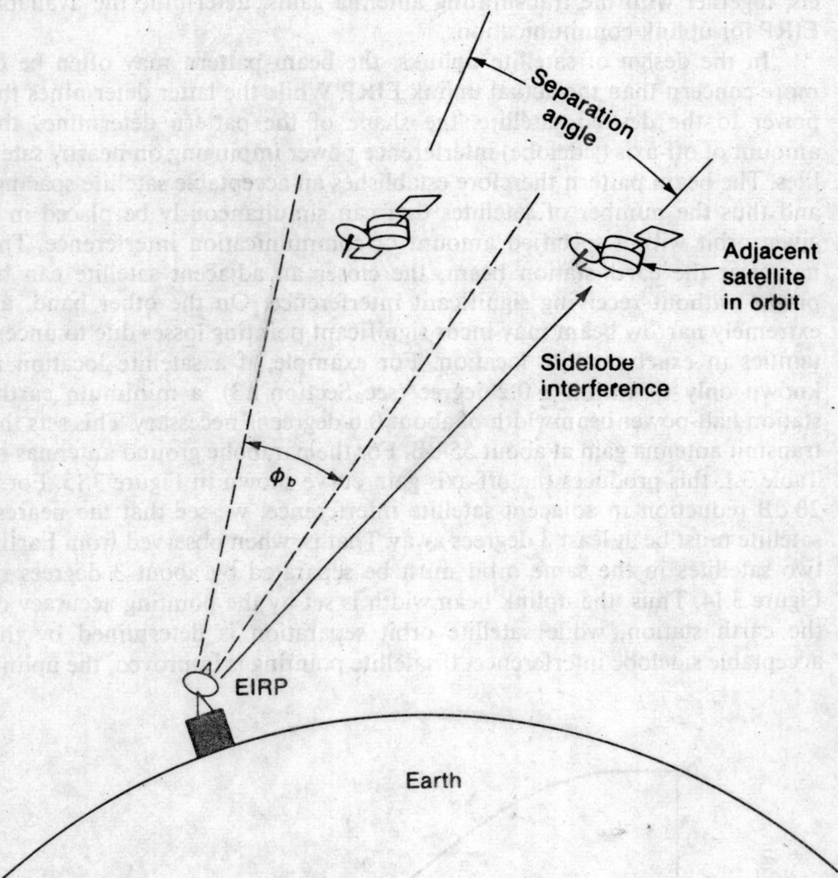

Figure 3.14. Satellite uplink.

Satellite Uplink

Figure 3.14 sketches a simplified earth station–satellite uplink. Transmitter power for earth stations is generally provided by high-powered amplifiers, such as TWTs and Klystrons. Since the amplifier and transmitting antenna are located on the ground, size and weight are not prime considerations, and fairly high transmitter EIRP levels can be achieved. Earth-based power outputs of 40–60 dBw are readily available at frequency bands up through K-band, using cavity-coupled TWTA or Klystrons [8, 9]. These power levels, together with the transmitting antenna gains, determine the available EIRP for uplink communications.

In the design of satellite uplinks, the beam pattern may often be of more concern than the actual uplink EIRP. While the latter determines the power to the desired satellite, the shape of the pattern determines the amount of off-axis (sidelobe) interference power impinging on nearby satellites. The beam pattern therefore establishes an acceptable satellite spacing, and thus the number of satellites that can simultaneously be placed in a given orbit with a specified amount of communication interference. The narrower the earth-station beam, the closer an adjacent satellite can be placed without receiving significant interference. On the other hand, an extremely narrow beam may incur significant pointing losses due to uncertainties in exact satellite location. For example, if a satellite location is known only to within ± 0.2 degree (see Section 1.3), a minimum earth-station half-power beamwidth of about 0.6 degree is necessary. This sets the transmit antenna gain at about 55 dB. For the parabolic ground antennas in Table 3.1, this produces the off-axis gain curve shown in Figure 3.15. For a 20 dB reduction in adjacent satellite interference, we see that the nearest satellite must be at least 3 degrees away. That is, when observed from Earth, two satellites in the same orbit must be separated by about 3 degrees in Figure 3.14. Thus, the uplink beamwidth is set by the pointing accuracy of the earth station, while satellite orbit separation is determined by the acceptable sidelobe interference. If satellite pointing is improved, the uplink

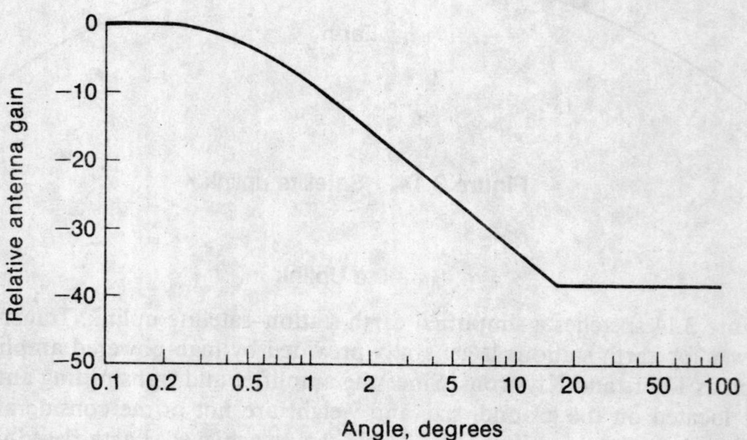

Figure 3.15. Uplink earth-station antenna pattern. Angle measured from boresight.

beamwidth can be narrowed, allowing closer satellite spacing in the same orbit. This would increase the total number of satellites placed in a common orbit, such as the synchronous orbit.

With the half-power beamwidth set, a higher carrier frequency will permit smaller earth stations. Figure 3.16 shows the relation between earth-

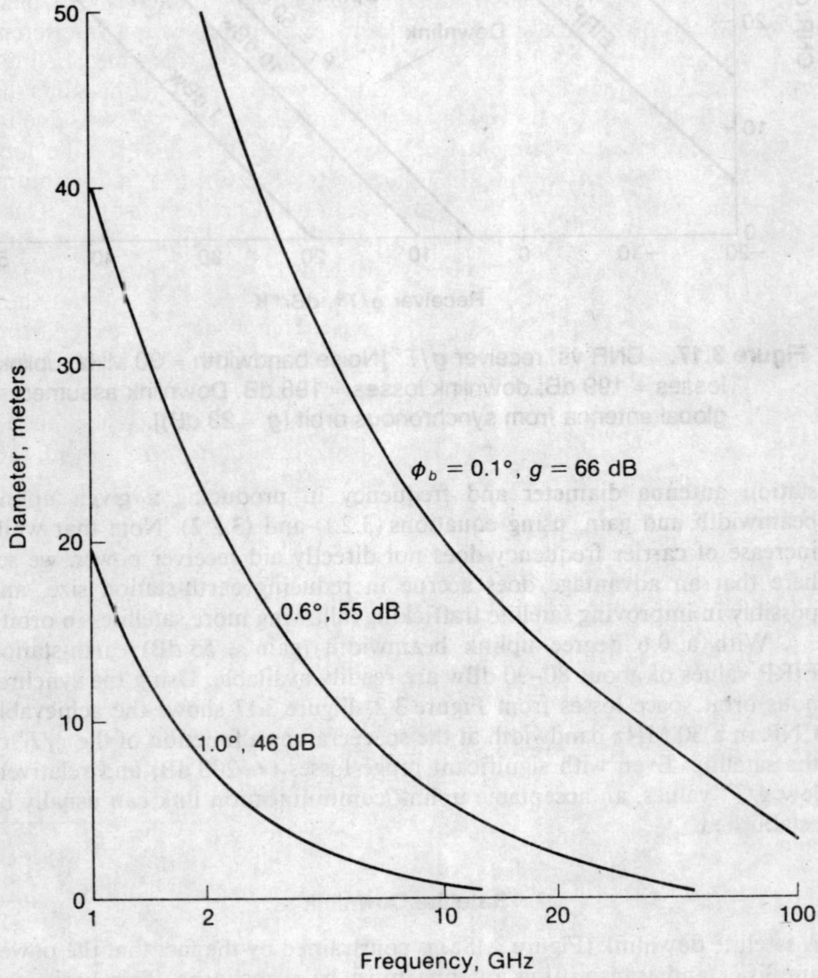

Figure 3.16. Earth-station antenna size vs. frequency (ϕ_b = half-power beamwidth, g = gain, $p_a = 1$).

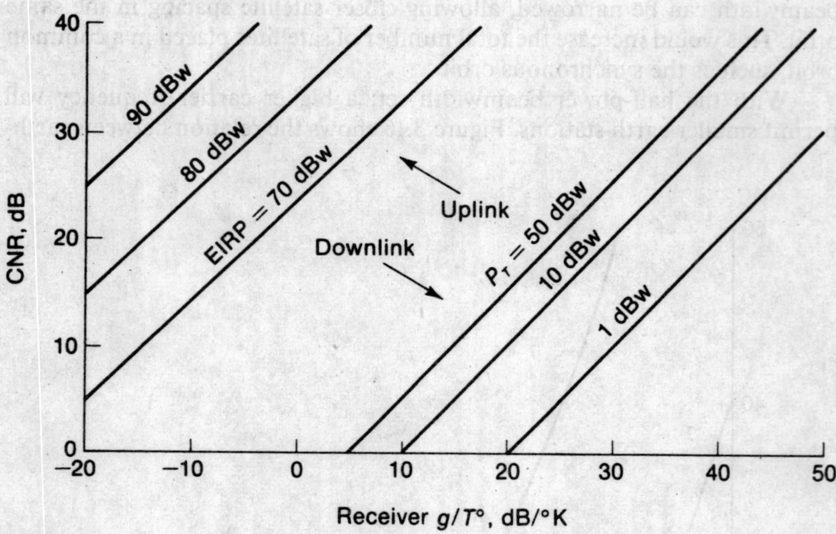

Figure 3.17. CNR vs. receiver $g/T°$ [Noise bandwidth = 30 MHz; uplink losses = 199 dB; downlink losses = 196 dB. Downlink assumes global antenna from synchronous orbit (g = 23 dB)].

station antenna diameter and frequency in producing a given uplink beamwidth and gain, using equations (3.2.1) and (3.2.2). Note that while increase of carrier frequency does not directly aid receiver power, we see here that an advantage does accrue in reducing earth-station size, and possibly in improving satellite trafficking (allowing more satellites in orbit).

With a 0.6 degree uplink beamwidth (gain $\approx$ 55 dB) earth-station EIRP values of about 80–90 dBw are readily available. Using the synchronous orbit space losses from Figure 3.2, Figure 3.17 shows the achievable CNR in a 30 MHz bandwidth at the spaçecraft as a function of the $g/T°$ of the satellite. Even with significant range losses ($\approx$ 200 dB) and relatively low $g/T°$ values, an acceptable uplink communication link can usually be established.

Satellite Downlink

A satellite downlink (Figure 3.18a) is constrained by the fact that the power amplifier and transmitting antenna must be spaceborne. This limits the power amplifiers to the efficient, lightweight devices discussed in Section 1.4, with limited output power capabilities that are dependent on the carrier frequency (see Figure 3.18b). The spacecraft antenna, while similarly

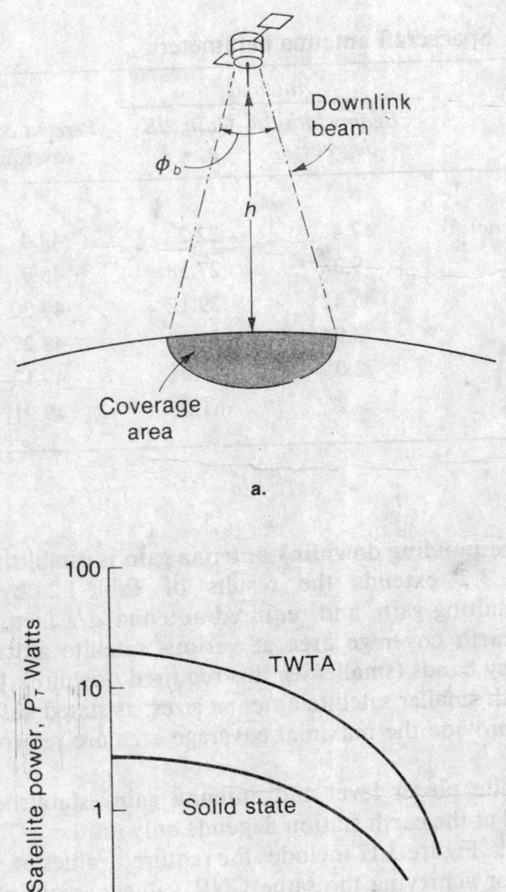

Figure 3.18. Satellite downlink. (a) Model. (b) Spacecraft power sources.

limited in size, must use beam patterns that provide the required coverage area on Earth. Recall that the maximum coverage area for a specified minimal viewing elevation angle depends only on the satellite altitude. Hence the satellite downlink beamwidth for maximal coverage area is automatically selected as soon as the satellite orbit altitude is selected. This also

Table 3.2. Spacecraft antenna parameters.

Altitude, miles	Antenna: Beamwidth, degrees	Antenna: Gain, dB $\rho_a = 1$	Percent earth coverage	d/λ
10,000				
19,360 (sync)	17.4°	22.2	42.4	4.18
2 × sync	9.38°	27.58	45.9	7.75
3 × sync	6.42°	29.12	47.20	11.33
5 × sync	3.94°	35.12	48.27	18.46
10 × sync	2.0°	41.01	49.12	36.38
100 × sync	.2°	61.05	49.91	363.8

means the corresponding downlink antenna gain is established by the orbit altitude. Table 3.2 extends the results of Table 1.2 by showing the beamwidth, resulting gain, and required antenna d/λ factor for achieving the maximal earth coverage area at various satellite altitudes. By using higher frequency bands (smaller λ), this required downlink beamwidth can be achieved with smaller satellite antenna sizes, as stated before. Spacecraft antennas that provide the maximal coverage area are referred to as **global antennas**.

With satellite power level and antenna gain established, the carrier power collected at the earth station depends only on the g/T° factor, just as for the downlink. Figure 3.17 includes the required values of g/T° needed in the downlink for achieving the same CNR values, assuming synchronous orbit and global satellite antennas. It is evident that relatively large earth station g/T° is needed to overcome the smaller EIRP of the satellite. This means small earth stations will be severely limited in their ability to receive large bandwidth carriers.

Although use of higher carrier frequencies allows smaller satellite antennas, care must again be used in accounting for its effect in downlink analysis, as discussed in Section 3.5. It will produce higher earth-station g/T° values, but it will not increase CNR due to the increased downlink space loss. To emphasize this point, let us rewrite the CNR formula in (3.5.6), with satellite beamwidth $\phi_b^2 \cong (4\pi/g_t)$ inserted, as

$$\mathrm{CNR}_d = \frac{P_T A_r}{\phi_b^2 z^2 k T^\circ_{\mathrm{eq}} B_{\mathrm{RF}}} \tag{3.6.1}$$

With the terms in the denominator fixed by the link, we see that downlink CNR depends only on available satellite power P_T and on receiver collecting area A_r. Note that neither satellite EIRP nor receiver gain directly affect downlink quality. The choice of frequency band is, of course, important in determining available P_T (Figure 3.18b), and in determining atmospheric losses. A secondary consideration in frequency band selection is the possible advantage that may be attained by allowing wider RF bandwidths, as in the example in the next section.

Direct Home TV Broadcasting

A special type of satellite downlink is the direct broadcasting of television from satellite to home from synchronous orbit (Figure 3.19). These systems have the added complexity of requiring relatively small rooftop antennas, large RF bandwidths, and fairly high demodulated SNR for the commercial TV receivers. In addition, the amplitude modulation (AM) formats of the commercial terrestrial TV system must be matched to the constant envelope FM transmissions of the satellite. Although this requires a carrier-waveform converter (FM to AM) as additional external home circuitry, it allows increases in AM CNR to be made through the FM improvement operation at the expense of downlink bandwidth. By increasing the FM deviation of

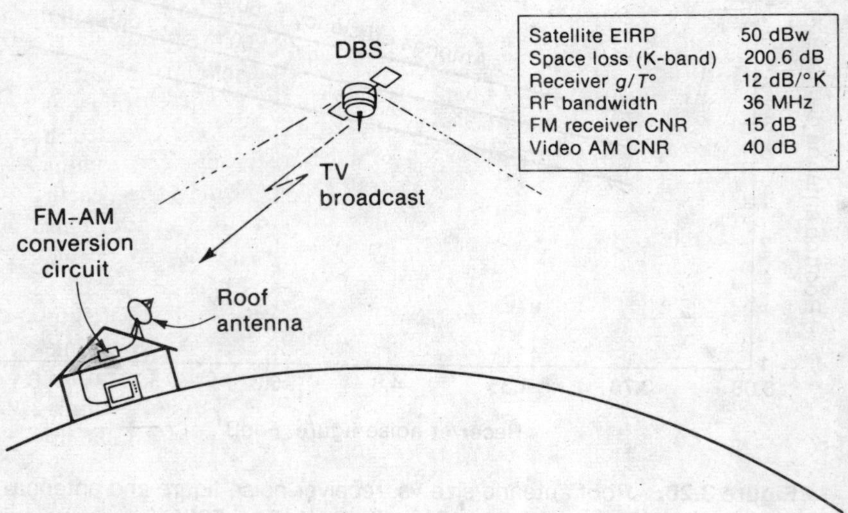

Figure 3.19. Direct broadcast video link.

the video carrier in the satellite uplink, improved AM CNR is achievable at the home receiver after satellite retransmission. This can be converted to reduced FM CNR at the rooftop antenna. This now produces a direct advantage to increasing carrier frequency band, since a wider FM bandwidth will be available for this trade-off. For this reason direct home video broadcasting is primarily designed for K-band operation. Satellites used for this type of video transmission are referred to as **direct broadcast satellites (DBS)**.

A link budget for a downlink home broadcast system at 12 GHz is included in Figure 3.19. By using an RF bandwidth of 36 MHz, an FM improvement of 26 dB allows an AM CNR of 40 dB to be achieved with a satellite downlink EIRP of 50 dBw and a rooftop receiver (g/T°) of 12 dB/°K. To achieve the last, careful control of the noise figure and efficiency of the rooftop antenna and front-end electronics is needed. Figure 3.20 plots the required roof antenna dish diameter as a function of receiver noise figure F and antenna efficiency to achieve this g/T° at 12 GHz. To limit antenna size to about a 1-meter, 60% dish, a receiver noise figure of about 4.5 dB is needed in the front-end electronics. Hence the success of direct video broadcasting is inherently related to the development of low-cost, low-noise electronics [10–12].

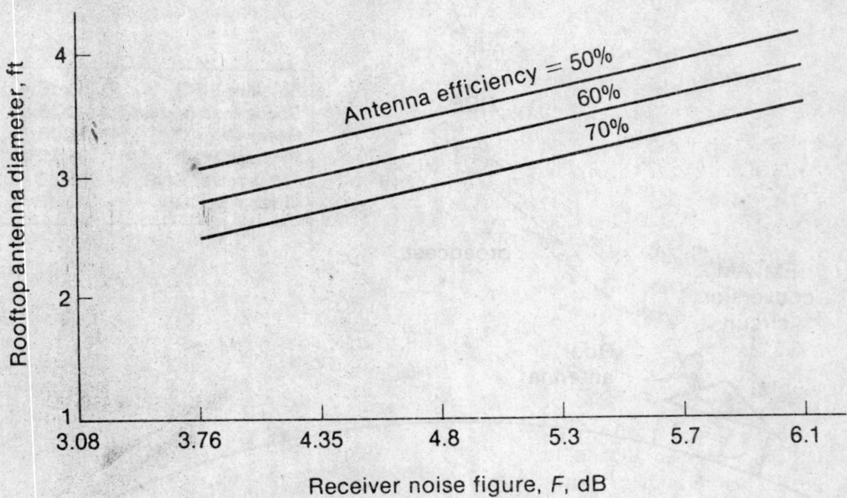

Figure 3.20. Roof antenna size vs. receiver noise figure and antenna efficiency to achieve $g/T^{\circ} = 12$ dB/°K ($T_b^{\circ} = 50$°K, frequency = 12 GHz).

Up-Down Link Analysis (Ideal Amplifier)

In transponding satellites, the primary function of the spacecraft is to relay the uplink carrier into a downlink. The circuit details of such relay satellites will be considered in Chapter 4. In this section we analyze a transponder channel as a combined uplink–downlink, where we model the satellite simply as an ideal linear power amplifier. We neglect the frequency translation between uplink and downlink, and simply convert the former to the latter through an amplifier with power gain G (Figure 3.21). This represents the most basic, idealized, repeater link that can be constructed. The uplink power is composed of a signal term from the uplink earth station, P_{us}, and the noise power collected at the satellite front end, P_{un}. The downlink power P_T is composed of an amplified signal and noise power term

$$P_T = GP_{us} + GP_{un} \tag{3.6.2}$$

Let L represent the combined total power gain (or loss) in the downlink, including antenna gains and channel losses. From (3.1.5):

$$L = g_t L_a L_p g_r \tag{3.6.3}$$

The received downlink carrier power is then

$$P_{rs} = GP_{us} L \tag{3.6.4}$$

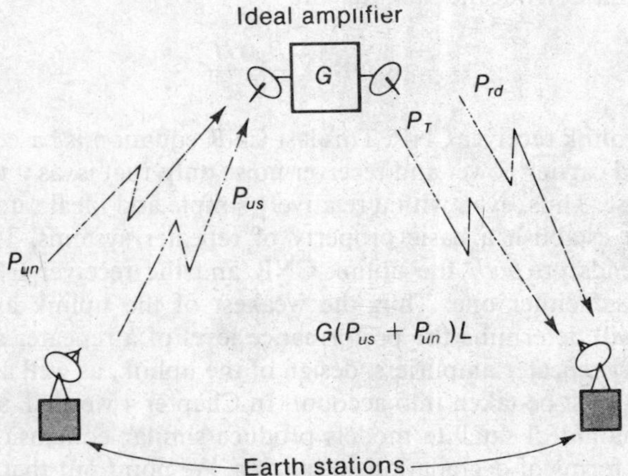

Figure 3.21. Combined up-down link, with ideal satellite amplifier.

The retransmitted uplink noise appearing at the downlink receiver is

$$P_{rn} = GP_{un}L \tag{3.6.5}$$

In addition, a noise power $P_{rd} = kT_d^\circ B_d$ appears at the downlink receiver due to its noise temperature T_d° and bandwidth B_d. Hence the combined CNR at the downlink receiver is

$$\begin{aligned} \mathrm{CNR}_d &= \frac{P_{rs}}{P_{rn} + P_{rd}} \\ &= \frac{P_{us}}{P_{un} + (P_{rd}/GL)} \end{aligned} \tag{3.6.6}$$

Dividing by P_{un}, we have

$$\begin{aligned} \mathrm{CNR}_d &= \frac{P_{us}/P_{un}}{1 + (P_{rd}/P_{rn})} \\ &= \frac{(\mathrm{CNR}_u)(\mathrm{CNR}_r)}{\mathrm{CNR}_u + \mathrm{CNR}_r} \end{aligned} \tag{3.6.7}$$

where we have denoted

$$\mathrm{CNR}_u \triangleq \frac{P_{us}}{P_{un}} \tag{3.6.8}$$

as the uplink CNR at the satellite, and

$$\mathrm{CNR}_r \triangleq \frac{P_{us}GL}{P_{rd}} \tag{3.6.9}$$

as the downlink receiver CNR. This last CNR equation is based on satellite-transmitted carrier power and receiver noise only, that is, as if there were no uplink noise. Thus, even with a relatively simple and ideal satellite repeater model, we establish a basic property of repeater systems. The downlink CNR depends on *both* the uplink CNR and the receiver CNR, and can never exceed either one. Thus the weakest of the uplink and downlink channels will determine the performance level of a repeater system. Even with perfect repeater amplifiers, design of the uplink, as well as the satellite downlink, must be taken into account. In Chapter 4 we shall see that more practical, nonideal satellite models produce similar conclusions, but with additional forms of degradations occurring. We point out that by inverting CNR_d we can rewrite (3.6.7) as

$$(\mathrm{CNR}_d)^{-1} = (\mathrm{CNR}_u)^{-1} + (\mathrm{CNR}_r)^{-1} \tag{3.6.10}$$

This is sometimes more convenient to use in computing CNR_d in repeater analyses.

For a transponded digital link, the downlink CNR_d can be converted to E_b/N_0 to determine bit-error probability for the linear amplifier satellite. This requires replacing B_r by $1/T_b$, and writing

$$\left(\frac{E_b}{N_0}\right)_d = \frac{(E_b/N_0)_u(E_b/N_0)_r}{(E_b/N_0)_u + (E_b/N_0)_r} \tag{3.6.11}$$

where $(E_b/N_0)_u$ and $(E_b/N_0)_r$ are obtained from (3.6.8) and (3.6.9) by taking the noise bandwidth as $1/T_b$ Hz.

The resulting bit-error probability, PE, for a phase coherent BPSK link in Table 2.3 is then

$$\text{PE} = Q\left[\left(\frac{2E_b}{N_0}\right)_d^{1/2}\right] \tag{3.6.12}$$

where $Q(x)$ is the Gaussian tail integration in Table 2.3. Note again that digital performance depends on both uplink and downlink CNR. Figure 3.22 plots PE in (3.6.12) for both these parameters, showing how the weaker of the two links determines the overall PE performance.

Satellite Crosslinks

Satellite systems often require communication between two satellites via a crosslink. A crosslink between two orbiting satellites is referred to as an **intersatellite link (ISL)**. As a communication link, an intersatellite link has the disadvantage that both transmitter and receiver are spaceborne, limiting operation to both low P_T and low g/T° values. To compensate in long links, it is necessary to increase EIRP by resorting to narrow transmit beams for higher power concentration. With satellite antenna size constrained, the narrow beams are usually achieved by resorting to higher carrier frequencies. Hence satellite crosslinks are typically designed for K-band (20–30 GHz) or EHF (60 GHz) frequencies. The emerging possibilities of optical (laser) crosslinks are considered in Chapter 9.

Consider the crosslink model in Figure 3.23. Two satellites at altitude h are separated by angle ϕ_s as shown. The transmitting satellite has transmission power P_T available, and we assume both satellites use antennas of diameter d. The receiving satellite has noise temperature T°_{eq}. The propagation distance between the satellites is given by

$$z = 2(h + r_E)\sin\phi_s \tag{3.6.13}$$

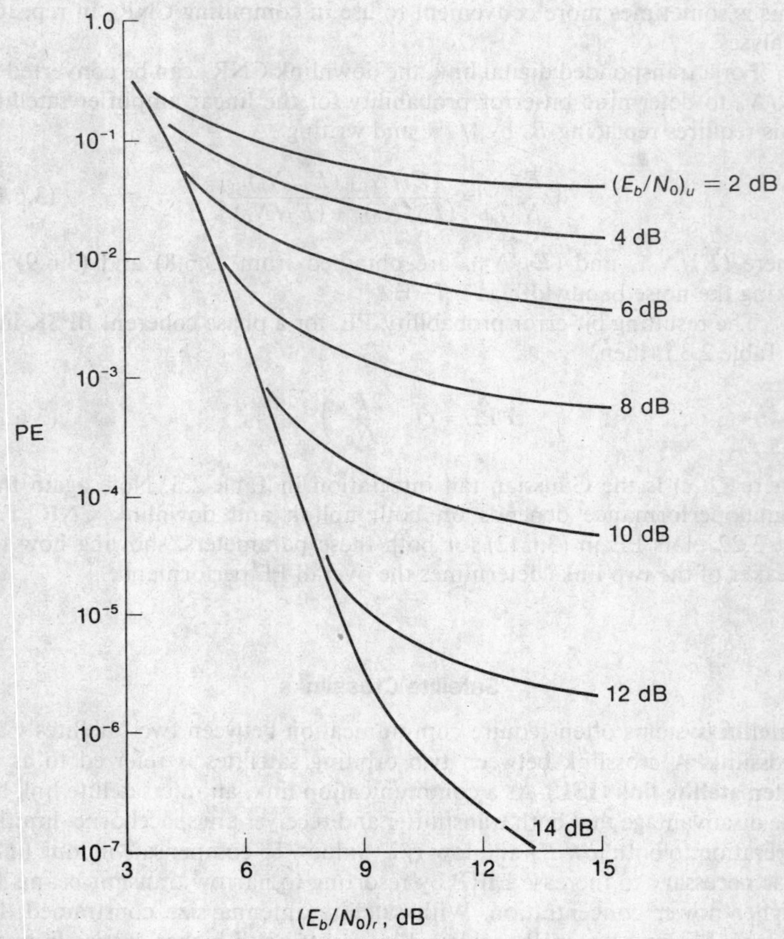

Figure 3.22. Bit-error probability, PE, for a BPSK up-down link. $(E_b/N_0)_u$ refers to uplink, $(E_b/N_0)_r$ to downlink.

where r_E is the Earth's radius. The maximum line-of-sight distance occurs when

$$z_{\max} = 2[(h + r_E)^2 - r_E^2]^{1/2} \tag{3.6.14}$$

which, for $h >> r_E$, is approximately $2h$. We assume first that both satellite locations are known exactly by each, and each is perfectly stabilized, so that

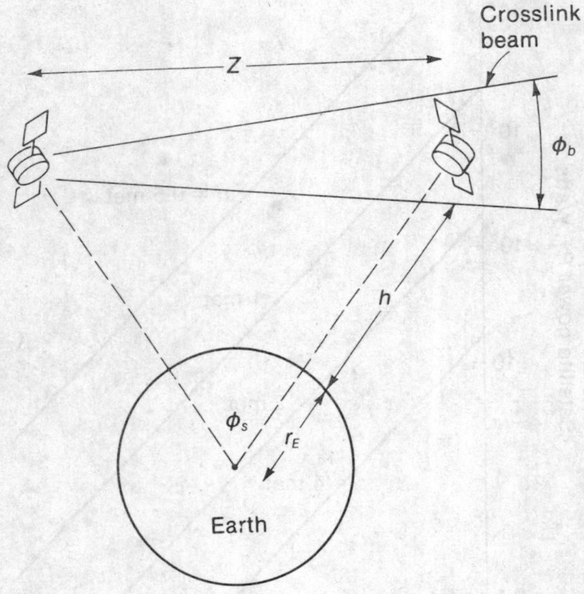

Figure 3.23. Satellite crosslink model.

each satellite uses antenna beamwidths ϕ_b pointed exactly at each other. The CNR delivered to the receiving satellite over the crosslink, using (3.6.1), is then

$$\text{CNR} = \frac{P_T(\pi d^2/4)}{\phi_b^2 z^2 k T_{\text{eq}}^{\circ} B_{\text{RF}}} \tag{3.6.15}$$

The crosslink transmitting beamwidth ϕ_b is related to the carrier frequency through (3.2.2). Assuming $\rho_a = 1$, we substitute $\phi_b \cong \lambda/d$, and (3.6.15) can be simplified to

$$\text{CNR} = 0.71(10^9)P_T\left[\frac{f^2 d^4}{x^2 T_{\text{eq}}^{\circ} B_{\text{RF}}}\right] \tag{3.6.16}$$

where P_T is in watts, f in GHz, d in meters, and x is the crosslink range in multiples of the geosynchronous altitude ($z = x \cdot 3.5 \cdot 10^4$ km). We see that CNR increases as the fourth power of the antenna diameters. Hence the most efficient way to improve a crosslink is to increase antenna size.

With antenna selected, CNR can be increased only by lowering front-

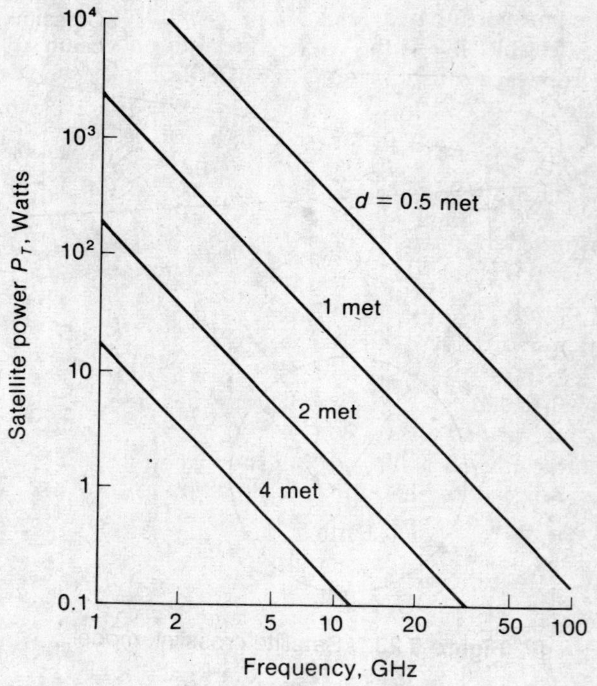

Figure 3.24. Crosslink parameter trade-offs for CNR = 10 dB, $T^{\circ}_{eq} = 3000$ (F = 10 dB), B = 100 MHz, $Z = 3.5 \times 10^7$ meters.

end temperature, increasing transmitter power, or increasing carrier frequency. Figure 3.24 shows how these parameters can be traded off in achieving a CNR of 10 dB over a crosslink path with $x = 1$ and a bandwidth of 100 MHz. With 2-meter antennas at X-band, the link can be established with a transmitter power of 2 watts with a receiver noise temperature of $T^{\circ}_{eq} = 3000°$. If we reduce the antennas to 1 meter, we will need to operate at $f = 40$ GHz for the same transmitter power.

Equation (3.6.16) shows that the system improves by using higher frequency bands. This is a direct result of a more concentrated beamwidth. The limitation of extremely narrow crosslink beams, however, is the pointing error that exists due to the relative uncertainty of the location of each satellite with respect to each other, and to the satellite attitude error (the inability of a satellite to properly orient itself so as to point exactly in a desired direction). These errors are invariably much larger than those encountered in earth-based links where ground control of tracking and pointing is feasible. If r is the relative location uncertainty distance when observed from each satellite, and if the attitude error is ϕ_a, the total uncertainty angle is

$$\phi_e = \left(\frac{r}{z} + \phi_a\right) \tag{3.6.17}$$

The transmitted beamwidth must be wide enough to encompass these pointing errors. This restricts $\phi_b \geqslant \phi_e$, and f can be increased only as long as

$$f \leqslant \frac{0.3}{\phi_e d} \tag{3.6.18}$$

Figure 3.25 shows the relation between maximum frequency and pointing error for various antenna sizes in a satellite crosslink. Typically, the satellite uncertainty is about 100 km, producing at maximum geosynchronous cross-range $r/z \cong 100/70 \times 10^4 \cong 0.0014$ radian. Attitude errors however are usually in the range 0.01–0.002 radian and therefore are usually the

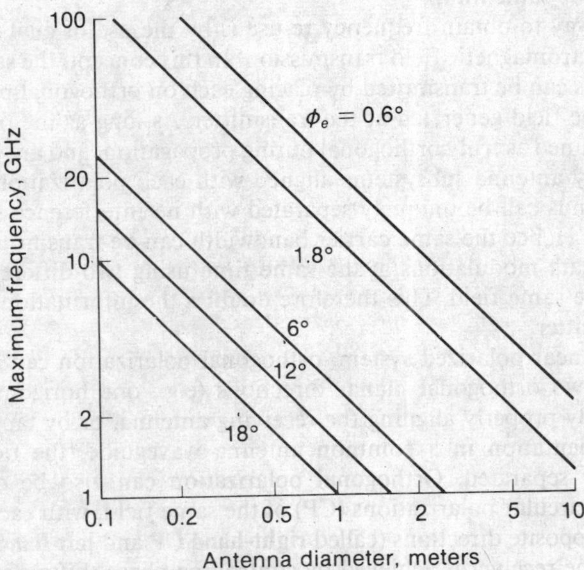

Figure 3.25. Maximum carrier frequency vs. pointing error and antenna size in satellite crosslinks.

prime contributor to total pointing error. Figures 3.24 and 3.25 taken together show the interesting fact that satellite pointing errors eventually limit the available CNR of the link by dictating carrier frequency and antenna size. Although this is basically true for any communication link, it becomes particularly important in the crosslink, where pointing errors tend to be compounded.

3.7 FREQUENCY RE-USE BY DUAL POLARIZATION

The satellite links considered in Section 3.6 were assumed to transmit a fixed-carrier bandwidth with an electromagnetic field having the prescribed power level with a specific field polarization. Since bandwidth preservation is vital in satellite links, it would be extremely beneficial to be able to transmit additional carrier waveforms occupying the same bands using the same link. The concept of using the same frequency band to transmit separate carriers is referred to as **frequency re-use**. Frequency re-use increases the information capacity of the link without increasing link bandwidth. To accomplish this, it is necessary to maintain separability of the carriers even though they occupy the same frequency band and propagate over the same link.

One way to obtain frequency re-use is by the use of **dual polarization** during electromagnetic field transmission. In this concept, the same band of frequencies can be transmitted by placing each on orthogonal polarizations of the same field generated at the transmitter. As long as the polarizations are maintained as truly orthogonal during propagation, and are individually received by antenna subsystems aligned with each polarization, the information bands can be uniquely separated with no interference from any of the others. Hence the same carrier bandwidth can be transmitted with two different data modulations at the same time using two different polarizations of the same field. This therefore doubles the information capacity of the transmitter.

In a linear polarized system, orthogonal polarization can be obtained by using two orthogonal planar directions (e.g., one horizontal and one vertical). By properly aligning the receiving antenna, or by tapping off the desired orientation in a common antenna waveguide, the fields can be adequately separated. Orthogonal polarization can also be obtained by using two circular polarizations (CP) of the same field, with each phased to rotate in opposite directions (called **right-hand CP** and **left-hand CP**). Separation at the receiver is achieved by controlling phase shifters inserted into the antenna waveguide. The phase shifter is designed so that one field is rotated in the guide in such a way that its field components cancel, while the other field components add.

Depolarization

A problem with dual-polarized satellite downlinks is that the atmosphere, in addition to producing attenuation effects, also may affect the orthogonality of the two polarizations. This would cause an inherent cross-coupling of one channel into the other at the same frequency band, producing interference and cross talk in that channel, even with perfectly aligned receiving systems. This latter effect is referred to as **depolarization**, and is strongly dependent on the nature of the atmosphere and on the field wavelength. Atmospheric depolarization is basically negligible below about 10 GHz, and dual polarization is therefore commonly used in C-band satellite systems. However, depolarization significantly increases at higher carrier frequencies, especially when high water content is present in the atmosphere. This makes the feasibility of using dual polarization for frequency re-use in the 10–30 GHz range somewhat questionable.

Depolarization is formally defined as the fraction of power in one channel that is cross-coupled into the other. Depolarization is therefore a number less than 1, and can be expressed in units of negative decibels. The more negative the dB value, the less the cross-coupling. The reciprocal of depolarization (the dB value without the negative sign) is a measure of the channel **isolation**. The higher the isolation, the less the cross-coupled power.

Depolarization is caused primarily by nonspherical water droplets that affect the orthogonal polarizations of the impinging field by different amounts. The result is differential attenuation and differential phase shifts between the orthogonal field components in space, thereby altering the spatial alignments of these components. The amount of these differential effects depends on the amount of water and ice in the atmosphere, and therefore becomes most severe during rain and snow. In particular, depolarization depends on rainfall rate and extent (path length), raindrop size, raindrop orientation (rain **canting angle**), and on carrier wavelength. Since falling rain tends to have a fixed average canting angle, depolarization will depend on the field polarization orientation relative to this angle, and therefore will be more severe for some orientations than for others. A linear polarized field has minimum depolarization if it is horizontal or vertical relative to the canting angle. A CP field has a depolarization corresponding to the worst case angle of a linearly polarized field. Figure 3.26 shows some reported worst case depolarizations of either a linear or CP field, as a function of rainfall rate and carrier frequency for a 5 km atmospheric path. Results are obtained from both theoretical models [13–15], and from projecting measured K-band data [16–20].

The simplest procedure to use to account for depolarization in a dual polarization link is to determine its effect on receiver CNR. This can then be converted to performance reduction in either analog demodulation or

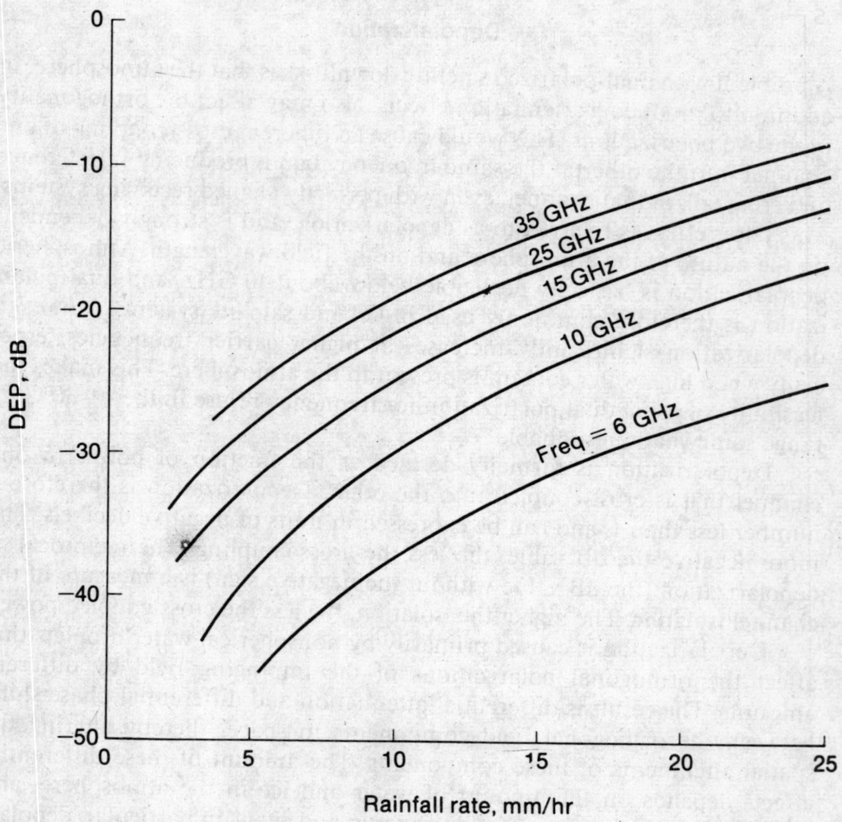

Figure 3.26. Depolarization vs. rainfall rate and frequency. Worst case polarization, 5 km rain path.

digital decoding, using the results of Chapter 2. If we assume that any cross-coupled power due to depolarization appears as additive noise at the receiver, then CNR can be computed by extending the results of the previous sections. From (3.5.1) the CNR with depolarization DEP becomes

$$\text{CNR}_{dp} = \frac{P_r}{P_n + P_r(\text{DEP})} \tag{3.7.1}$$

where P_r is received power per polarization mode. Defining CNR = P_r/P_n as the CNR without depolarization,

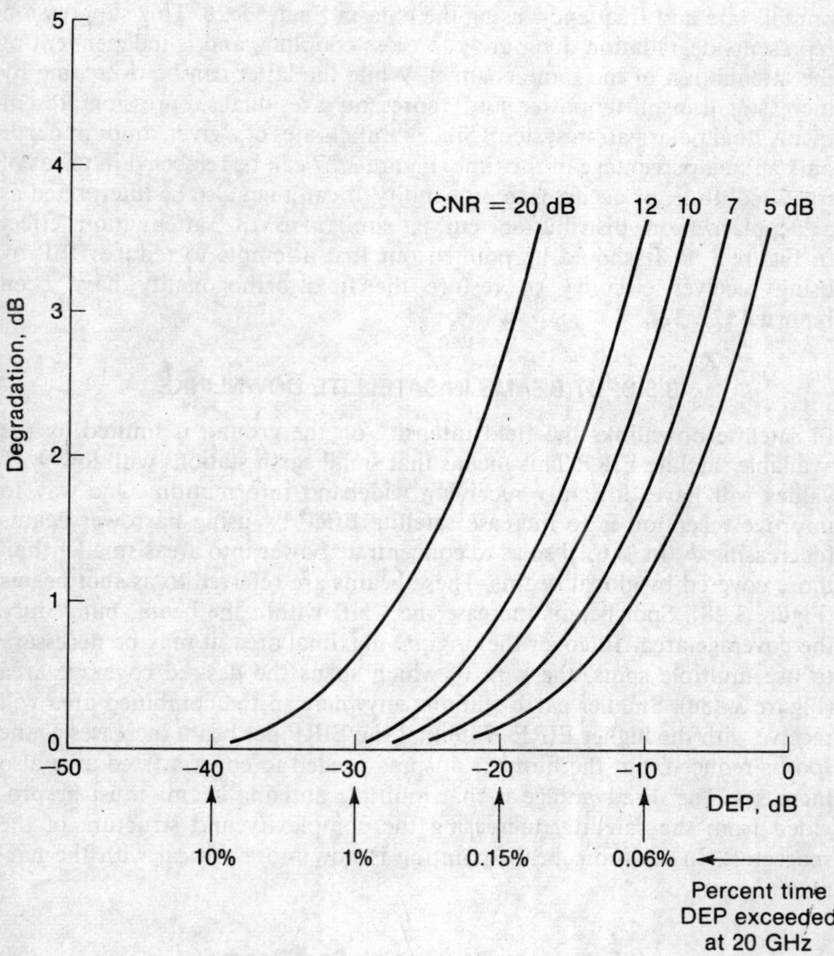

Figure 3.27. Depolarization degradation in CNR. Percent time based on rainrate occurrence and DEP at 20 GHz.

$$CNR_{dp} = CNR\left[\frac{1}{1 + (CNR)DEP}\right] \tag{3.7.2}$$

The bracket appears as a suppression effect on CNR, dependent on the value of DEP. Figure 3.27 plots this DEP suppression as a function of rainfall rate and frequency, using the data in Figure 3.26. This suppression represents degradation due purely to cross-coupling, and is independent of the attenuation of the same channel. While the latter can be overcome by increasing transmitter power, DEP represents a residual suppression present in any dual polarization system. Since rainfall rates of a given amount occur only a fixed percentage of the time, Figure 3.27 can be relabeled in terms of fractional time, or occurrence probability. It can then also be interpreted as a depolarization distribution curve, similar to the attenuation effect in Figure 3.10. It should be pointed out that attempts to reduce DEP by using receiver circuitry to restore the field orthogonality have been reported [21, 22].

3.8 SPOT BEAMS IN SATELLITE DOWNLINKS

In satellite downlinks the field intensity on the ground is limited by the available satellite EIRP. This means that small earth stations with low g/T° values will have difficulty receiving wideband information. One way to improve reception is to increase satellite EIRP by using narrower beams [decreasing ϕ_b in (3.6.1)] so as to concentrate power into areas smaller than those covered by global beams. These beams are referred to as **spot beams** (Figure 3.28). Spot beams increase the CNR within the beam, but reduce the coverage area. To cover the original maximal area, it may be necessary to use multiple spots, the sum of which spans the desired coverage area (Figure 3.28c). Smaller earth stations anywhere in the combined area will receive with the higher EIRP. Note that the EIRP per beam increases as the spot is reduced, but the number of spots needed to cover a fixed area also increases. The disadvantage is that multiple antenna beams must be provided from the satellite, increasing the complexity and structure of the spacecraft. In addition, beam pointing is now more critical with the narrower beams.

Frequency Re-use with Spot Beams

Spot beams also can be used as a form of frequency re-use to increase the system information capabilities. Suppose different information is to be sent to different points within the coverage area, and each point is within a different spot beam area. A global beam will send the same carrier to all points. However, spot beams can be used to send the separate information simultaneously to each point. One modulated carrier is sent in one beam and another modulated carrier, at the same frequency, is sent in the other. Thus the total amount of information relayed can be increased. Roughly, if we have M beams, then theoretically M times the amount of information

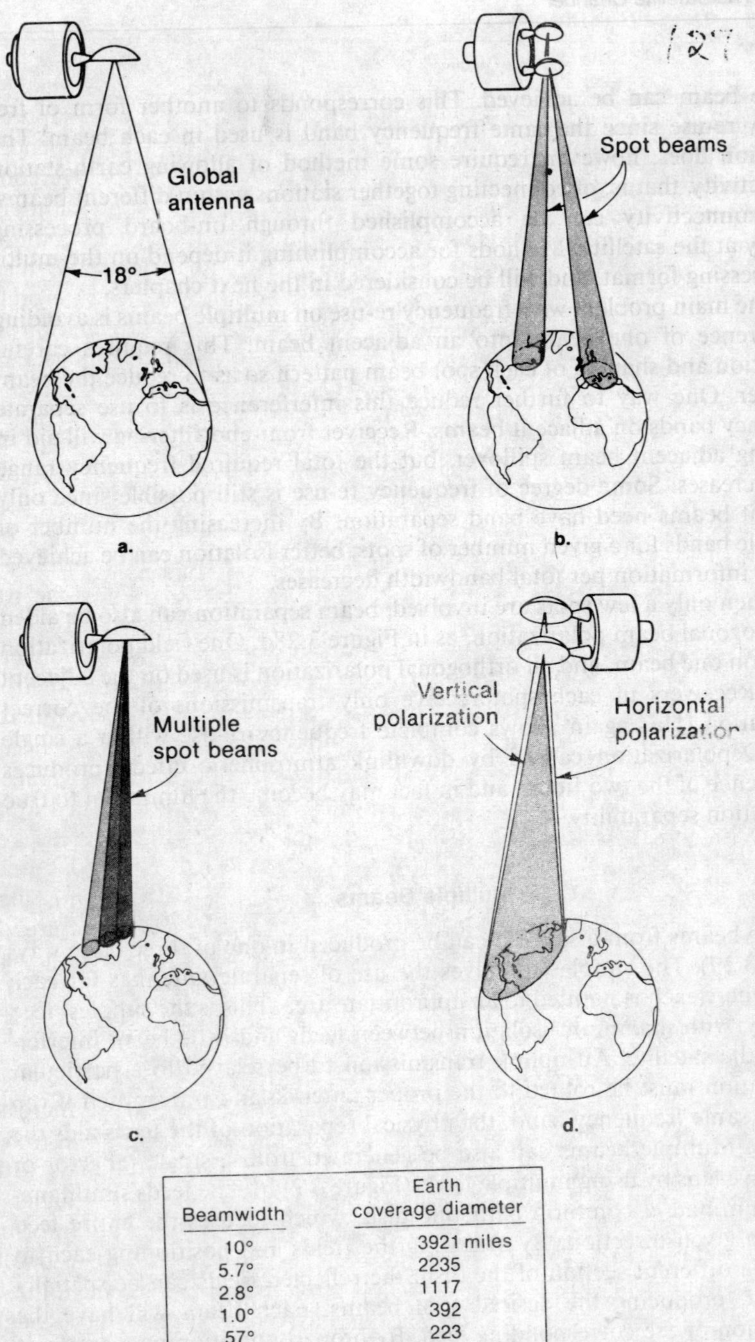

Beamwidth	Earth coverage diameter
10°	3921 miles
5.7°	2235
2.8°	1117
1.0°	392
.57°	223

Figure 3.28. Antenna beams. (a) Global. (b) Dual spots. (c) Multiple spots. (d) Dual polarized spot beams.

of one beam can be achieved. This corresponds to another form of frequency re-use since the same frequency band is used in each beam. The operation does, however, require some method of allowing earth-station connectivity, that is, of connecting together stations within different beams. This connectivity can be accomplished through on-board processing directly at the satellite. Methods for accomplishing it depend on the multiple-accessing format, and will be considered in the next chapters.

The main problem with frequency re-use on multiple beams is avoiding interference of one beam into an adjacent beam. This requires careful separation and shaping of each spot beam pattern so as to reduce the beam spillover. One way to further reduce this interference is to use separate frequency bands on adjacent beams. Receiver front-end filtering will aid in reducing adjacent beam spillover, but the total required frequency range now increases. Some degree of frequency re-use is still possible since only adjacent beams need have band separation. By increasing the number of available bands for a given number of spots, better isolation can be achieved but the information per total bandwidth decreases.

When only a few spots are involved, beam separation can also be aided by orthogonal beam polarization, as in Figure 3.28d. One field polarization is used on one beam, and an orthogonal polarization is used on the adjacent beam. Receivers in each spot receive only transmissions of the correct polarization. This again allows complete frequency re-use within a single band. Depolarization caused by downlink atmospheric effects produces interference of the two fields, and in fact may become the limitation to true polarization separability.

Multiple Beams

Multiple beams from a satellite can be produced in one of three basic ways (Figure 3.29). The simplest involves the use of separate antennas for each beam, where each is pointed to an appropriate area. This is the simplest feed assembly, with maximum isolation between feeds and little beam interference at the satellite. An uplink transmission to be relayed to a particular earth station must be routed to the proper antenna and transmitted. Even with the same frequency band, the physical separation of the feeds aids the isolation. Multiple beams can also be generated from a single reflector or microwave lens by using multiple feeds (Figure 3.29b). The feeds simultaneously illuminate a common parabolic dish, which focuses the entire feed field in a given direction. By offsetting the fields and positioning each to point to a different section of the dish, the reflected fields can be spatially separated, producing the desired spot beams. Each beam will have the polarization of the corresponding feed. By properly positioning a group of

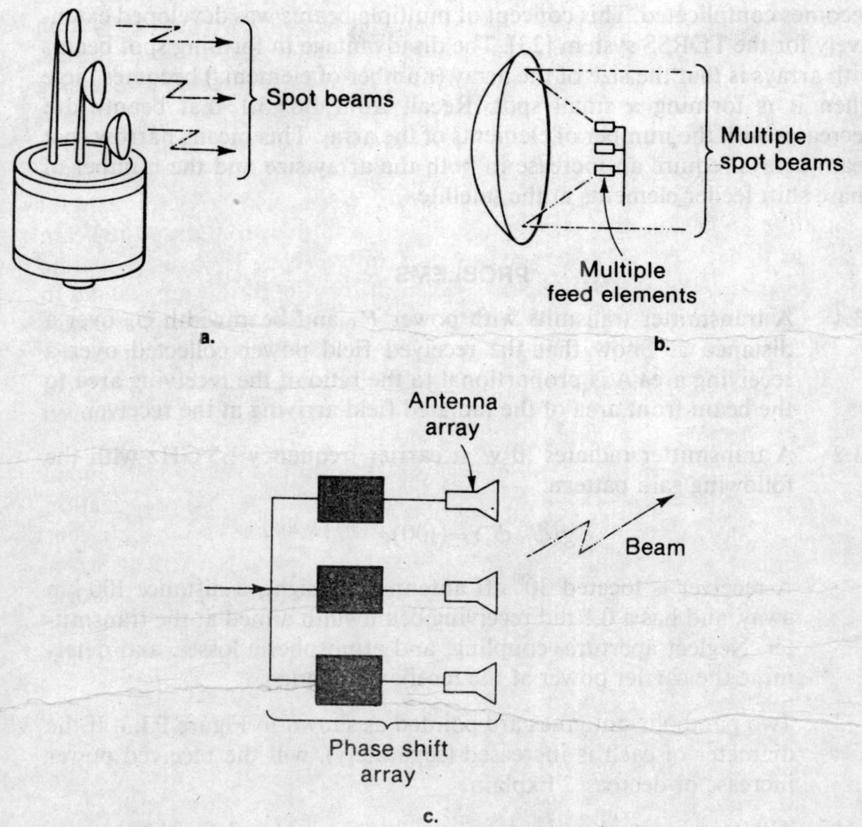

Figure 3.29. Multiple beam antennas. (a) Separate antennas. (b) Multiple feed, single reflector. (c) Array.

feeds so as to slightly overlap their spots, downlink earth patterns can be formed that match the contours of specific countries or continents.

A third method for producing multiple beams is by phased antenna arrays. By properly phasing a modulated carrier the field can be transmitted in a given direction (Figure 3.29c). Spot patterns can be formed by phasing all carriers of a given band into a single spot. A separate frequency band can be separately phased to form another spot. A set of M spots is formed by M sets of phase shifter banks feeding a common antenna (horn, dipole, helix) array, with each bank producing the proper array shift for that bank. Only a single antenna array is used, but the feed (phase shifters) mechanism becomes complicated. This concept of multiple beams was developed extensively for the TDRSS system [23]. The disadvantage in forming spot beams with arrays is that the size of the array (number of elements) becomes large when it is forming a small spot. Recall from Box 3.1 that beamwidth decreases with the number of elements of the array. This means narrow spot beam arrays require an increase in both the array size and the number of phase shift feeder elements at the satellite.

PROBLEMS

3.1 A transmitter transmits with power P_T and beamwidth ϕ_b over a distance z. Show that the received field power collected over a receiving area A is proportional to the ratio of the receiving area to the beam front area of the radiated field arriving at the receiver.

3.2 A transmitter radiates 10 w at carrier frequency 1.5 GHz with the following gain pattern:

$$g(\phi_l, \phi_z) = (100)e^{-(\phi_l^2 + \phi_z^2)/2(15^\circ)}$$

A receiver is located 30° off antenna boresight, a distance 100 km away, and has a 0.1 rad receiving beamwidth aimed at the transmitter. Neglect aperture, coupling, and atmospheric losses, and determine the carrier power at the receiving antenna.

.3 Two parabolic antennas are pointed as shown in Figure P3.3. If the diameter of each is increased (separately), will the received power increase or decrease? Explain.

.4 The gain function $g(\phi_l, \phi_z)$ of an antenna is also defined by

$$g(\phi_l, \phi_z) = \frac{\text{Power radiated per unit solid angle in direction } (\phi_l, \phi_z)}{P_T/4\pi}$$

where P_T is the total radiated power. (a) Show that g always integrates over a sphere to a constant for any pattern. (b) The noise temperature T_b° of an antenna is defined as

$$T_b^\circ = \frac{1}{4\pi} \int_{\text{sphere}} T(\phi_l, \phi_z) g(\phi_l, \phi_z) d\Omega$$

where $T(\phi_l, \phi_z)$ is the noise temperature of the background in the direction (ϕ_l, ϕ_z). Show that if the background has constant temperature T_s°, then $T_b^\circ = T_s^\circ$.

3.5 An FM system is operated within the following RF parameters:

Transmitter power = 1 Kw	Rain attenuation = 0.2 dB/mile
Range 500 miles	Free space loss = 150 dB
Tr. ant. gain = 60 dB	Sky background = 50°K
RF bandwidth = 0.2 MHz	Rec. noise fig. = 3 dB
Basebandwidth = 10 KHz	Rec. ant. gain = 10 dB

What is the achievable baseband SNR_d at the receiver after FM demodulation?

3.6 A communication station on Earth is to transmit to the moon at 5 GHz. (a) Design a transmitting antenna so that the transmission from Earth just covers the moon. Assume an antenna efficiency of 50%. The distance to the moon is 200,000 mi and its diameter is 0.27 that of the Earth's. (b) What is the resulting antenna gain?

3.7 Given Table P3.7, showing values of a and b coefficients in (3.3.1) as a function of frequency [from References 2, 6]. Plot dB/km curves as a function of rain rate for frequencies 1 GHz, 10 GHz, and 30 GHz, and compare to Figure 3.9.

3.8 The attenuation distribution curve in Figure 3.10 is convex. In some models the curve is shown concave. Explain how the shape of the curve will influence conclusions concerning link availability–link margin trade-offs.

Table P3.7

Frequency (GHz)	$a(f)$, $\frac{\text{dB}}{\text{mm/hr}}$	$b(f)$, exponent
1	.00015	.95
4	.00080	1.17
6	.00250	1.28
10	.0125	1.18
15	.0357	1.12
20	.0699	1.10
30	.170	1.075
40	.325	.99
60	.650	.84
80	.875	.753

Figure P3.3

3.9 Show that if a device has a noise figure F, defined in (3.4.5), then $(F - 1)290°$ is the temperature of an equivalent noise source that must be added at the input of the device to produce the same output noise power. [*Hint*: Divide the output noise into a part due to input noise and a part due to internal noise.]

3.10 Show that the number of satellites that can be placed in geosynchronous orbit with no more than 20 dB sidelobe interference from the ground is $n \approx (20)fd$, where f is frequency in GHz and d is antenna diameter in meters.

3.11 Sketch a curve of required antenna size needed from geosynchronous orbit at frequency 10 GHz to provide a given spot size on Earth.

3.12 Given the uplink-downlink satellite system in Figure 3.21. The carrier is transmitted to the satellite, amplified, and retransmitted. Determine the received CNR at the ground receiver, using the following parameters:

Uplink EIRP = 90 dB	Satellite $g/T°$ = −40 dB
Uplink loss = −200 dB	Satellite bandwidth = 1 MHz
Satellite gain, G = 100 dB	Downlink loss = −190 dB
Satellite NF, F = 5 dB	Receiver $g/T°$ = 50 dB
Uplink sky temp = 300°	Receiver bandwidth = 1 MHz

REFERENCES

1. R. Ruze, "Effect of Surface Error Tolerance on Efficiency and Gain of Parabolic Antennas," *Proceedings of the IEEE*, vol. 54 (April 1966).

2. L. Ippolito et al., "Propagation Handbook for Satellite Systems Design," *NASA Reference Publication* 1082, December 1981; 1083, June 1983.

3. R. Engelbrecht, "The Effect of Rain on Satellite Communications," *RCA Review*, June 1979.

4. D. Hogg, and T. Chu, "The Role of Rain in Satellite Communications," *Proceedings of the IEEE*, (September 1975).

5. S. Calo, L. Schiff, and H. Staras, "Effects of Rain on Multiple Access Transmission via Satellite," *Proc. of the Inter. Conf. on Comm.*, Toronto, 1978, pp. 30.1.1–30.1.6.

6. R.K. Crane, "Prediction of the Effect of Rain on Satellite Communication Systems," *Proceedings of the IEEE*, vol. 65 (March 1977), pp. 456–474.

7. R.G. Medhurst, "Rainfall Attenuation of Centimeter Waves," *IEEE*

Trans. on Antennas and Propagation, vol. AP-13 (July 1965), pp. 550–563.

8. D. Angelakos, and T. Everhart, *Microwave Communications* (New York: McGraw-Hill, 1968).

9. H. Reich, *Microwave Theory and Techniques* (Princeton, N.J.: Van Nostrand, 1953).

10. W. Pritchard, and C. Kase, "Getting Set for Direct Broadcast Satellites," *IEEE Spectrum*, August 1981.

11. R. Douville, "A 12 GHz Low Cost Earth Terminal for Direct TV Reception," *IEEE Trans. MIT*, vol. MTT-25 (December 1977).

12. Y. Konishi, "12 GHZ FM Receiver for Satellite Broadcasting," *IEEE Trans. on MIT*, vol. MIT-26 (October 1978).

13. T. Oguchi, "Attenuation and Phase Rotation of Radio Waves Due to Rain," *Journal of Radio Science*, vol. 8, no. 1 (January 1973), pp. 31–38.

14. M. Saunders, "Cross-Polarization at 18 and 30 GHz Due to Rain," *IEEE Trans. on Antenna Propagation*, vol. AP-19, no. 10.

15. J. Morrison, M. Cross, and T. Chu, "Rain Induced DA and DPS at Microwave Frequencies," *BSTJ*, vol. 52, no. 4 (April 1973), pp. 579–604.

16. R. Semplak, "Measurements of Depolarization by Rain for LP and CP at 18 GHz," *BSTJ*, vol. 53, no. 2 (1974).

17. D. Cox, and H. Arnold, "Results from 19-28 GHz Comstar Satellite Propagation Experiment at Crawford Hill," *Proceedings of the IEEE*, vol. 70, no. 5, (May 1982), pp. 458–488.

18. D. Arnold et al., "Measurements of Prediction of the Polarization Dependent Properties of Rain and Ice Depolarization," *IEEE Trans. on Comm.*, vol. COM-29 (May 1981), pp. 710–716.

19. P. Gale, and J. Mon, "Effect of Ice Induced Cross-Polarization on Earth-Space Links," *Inter. Comm. Conference (ICC) Proceedings*, Philadelphia, June 1982, Paper 6H.2.1.

20. D. Arnold et al., "Rain Attenuation at 10-30 GHz Along Earth Space Paths," *IEEE Trans. on Comm.*, vol. COM-29 (May 1981), pp. 716–721.

21. T. Chu, "Restoring the Orthogonality of Two Polarizations in Radio Communications," Part 1, *BSTJ*, vol. 50 (November 1971); Part II, *BSTJ*, vol. 52 (March 1972).

22. D. DiFonza, W. Trachtman, and A. Williams, "Adaptive Polarization Control for Satellite Frequency Re-Use Systems," *Comsat Technical Review*, vol. 6, no. 2 (Fall 1976).

23. W. M. Holmes, "NASA's Tracking and Data Relay Satellite System, TDRSS," *IEEE Comm. Society Magazine*, vol. 16, no. 5 (September 1978), pp. 13–21.

4

The Satellite Transponder

In Chapter 3 we concentrated on the basic power flow and power budget equations for various links of a satellite system. In this and the next chapters we focus on the detailed characteristics of the waveshapes of a carrier and noise as they are processed in a satellite transponder. Waveform characteristics become important when investigating distortion and suppression effects imposed by the satellite hardware, or when seeking methods to further improve an existing system. The entire question of satellite system optimization requires an accurate waveform model in order to understand the exact manner by which system anomalies are introduced. In this chapter we concentrate on the basic single-channel transponder, in which a single uplink carrier is processed for downlink transmission.

4.1 THE TRANSPONDER MODEL

A satellite transponder receives and retransmits the RF carrier. A simplified diagram was shown back in Figure 1.4 to indicate the basic block structure. A more detailed diagram is shown here in Figure 4.1. The RF front end receives and amplifies the uplink carrier, while filtering off as much receiver noise as possible. The received carrier is then processed so as to prepare the retransmitted waveform for the return link. Carrier processing involves either some form of direct spectral translation or some form of remodulation. In spectral translation, the entire uplink spectrum is simply shifted in frequency to the desired downlink frequency. In remodulation processors, the uplink waveforms are demodulated at the satellite, and then remodulated onto the downlink carrier. Remodulation processors involve more complex circuitry, but provide for changeover of the modulation format between uplink and downlink. This restructuring of the downlink can provide advantages in decoding, power concentration (e.g., spot beams), and interference rejection.

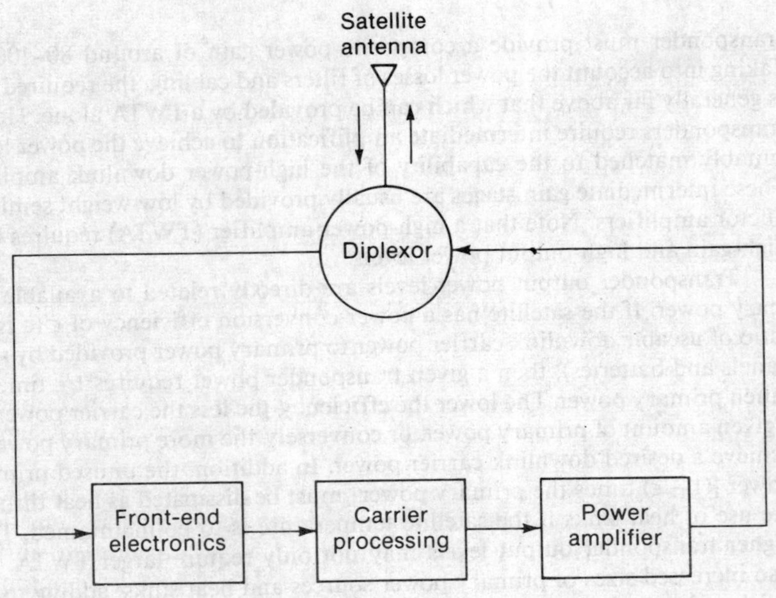

Figure 4.1. Transponder block diagram.

While the earlier transponder diagram showed a separate antenna for uplink receiving and downlink transmission, the same antenna can actually be used for both. This is possible since the uplink and downlink frequency bands are separated. A diplexor is used in the front end to allow simultaneous transmission and reception. The diplexor is a two-way microwave gate that permits received carrier signals from the antenna and transmitted carrier signals to the antenna to be independently coupled into and out of the antenna cabling. The carriers, being at different frequency bands, can flow in the same cabling and antenna feeds without interfering.

After front-end filtering and signal processing, the downlink carrier is power-amplified to provide the required power level for the downlink receiver. As discussed in Section 1.3 this power amplification is generally provided by traveling wave tube amplifiers (TWTA). These amplifiers may be preceded by stages of preamplification that set operating points for the TWTA. If we interpret the transponder as an ideal "amplifier in the sky," the entire transponder must provide the required overall gain needed to multiply the uplink power level to that of the downlink. Since uplink carrier power levels will be on the order of fractions of a microwatt (see Section 3.6), and since downlink power values of watts are needed, a typical transponder must provide a composite power gain of around 80–100 dB. Taking into account the power losses of filters and cabling, the required gain is generally far above that which can be provided by a TWTA alone. Hence, transponders require intermediate amplification to achieve the power levels suitably matched to the capability of the high-power downlink amplifier. These intermediate gain stages are usually provided by low-weight semiconductor amplifiers. Note that a high-power amplifier (TWTA) requires both high-gain and high-output power levels.

Transponder output power levels are directly related to available primary power. If the satellite has a power conversion efficiency of ϵ (ϵ is the ratio of useable downlink carrier power to primary power provided by solar panels and batteries), then a given transponder power requires $1/\epsilon$ times as much primary power. The lower the efficiency, the less the carrier power for a given amount of primary power, or conversely, the more primary power to achieve a desired downlink carrier power. In addition, the unused primary power [$(1 - \epsilon)$ times the primary power] must be dissipated as heat through the use of heat sinks if the satellite temperature is to be maintained. Thus higher transponder output levels may not only require larger TWTA, but also increased sizes of primary power sources and heat sinks, adding to the weight of the satellite. If the primary power of the satellite is limited by weight or cost, the efficiency parameter ϵ then becomes a critical design parameter, often dictating the transponder downlink capabilities.

4.2 THE SATELLITE FRONT END

Front-end electronics in satellite transponders are usually implemented as shown in Figure 4.2. The receiving antenna is coupled through cabling, usually to a diplexor or power splitter and followed by stages of RF filtering and amplifiers. The cabling, diplexors, and power splitters are lossy elements, while the filters and amplifiers determine bandwidth and power gain values.

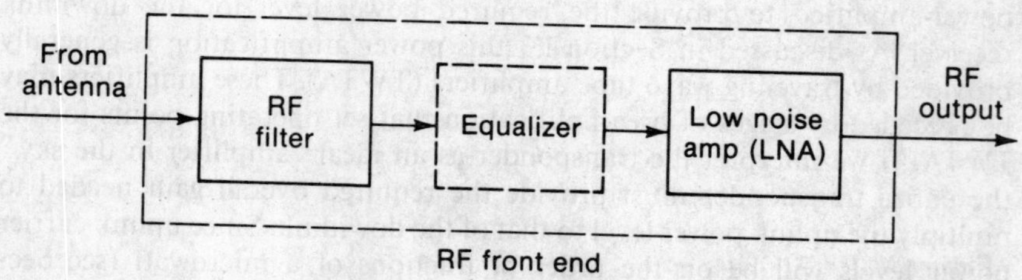

Figure 4.2. Front-end model.

Front-End Noise

The satellite front end establishes the uplink carrier signal and noise levels for the transponder. As stated in Section 3.4 front-end noise is contributed from two basic sources: antenna noise, determined by the background temperature, T_b°, and the front-end circuit noise, determined by the noise figure F. These parameters set the front-end spectral level as

$$N_0 = kT_{eq}^\circ \tag{4.2.1}$$

where k is Boltzmann's constant and

$$T_{eq}^\circ = T_b^\circ + (F - 1)290^\circ \tag{4.2.2}$$

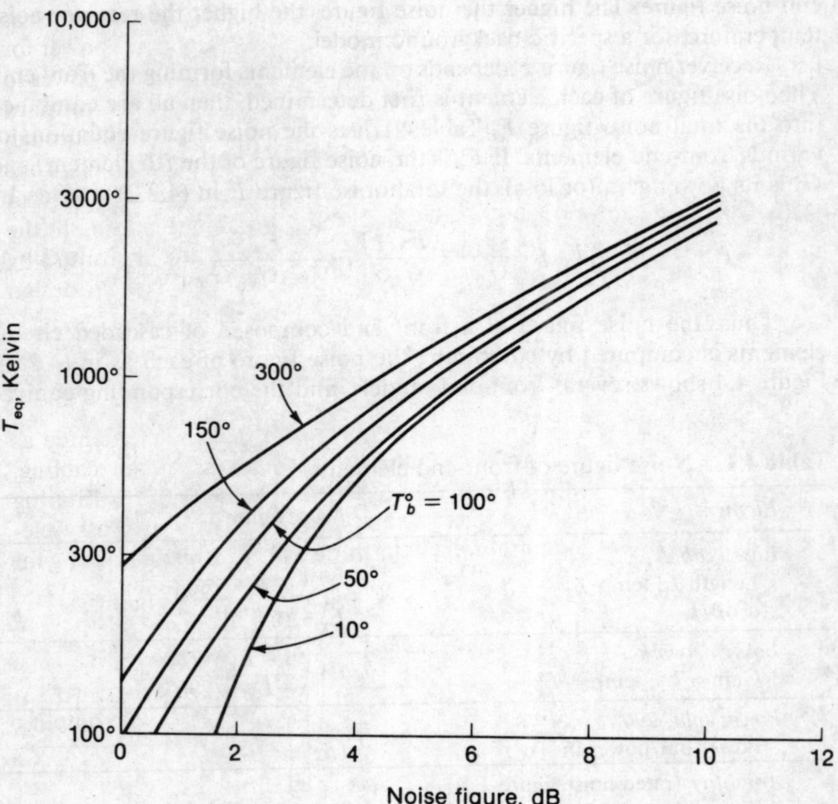

Figure 4.3. Equivalent receiver front-end noise temperature (T_b° = background temperature).

Background noise temperature T_b° was discussed earlier in Section 3.4. An earth-based antenna sees the sky and galactic background from all directions, producing the approximate T_b° values shown in Figure 3.12. A satellite looking down at the Earth sees the illuminated Earth at a uniform reradiation temperature of about 300° K, surrounded by the galactic noise of outer space. A global spacecraft antenna will see the Earth in its mainlobe, and the lower level galactic noise in its sidelobes. The antenna averaging will then tend to lower the combined background temperature. A satellite spot beam sees the illuminated Earth in its entire pattern, and therefore will have a background temperature closer to 300° K. When these background models are inserted into (4.2.2), the equivalent receiver temperature T_{eq}° plots shown in Figure 4.3 are derived, as a function of the receiver front-end noise figure. The higher the noise figure, the higher the receiver noise temperature, for a specific background model.

Receiver noise figure F depends on the elements forming the front end. The noise figure of each element is first determined, then all are combined into the total noise figure F. Table 4.1 lists the noise figure equations of various front-end elements. If F_i is the noise figure of the ith element, and G_i is its power gain (or loss), the total noise figure F in (4.2.2) is given by

$$F = F_1 + \frac{F_2 - 1}{G_1} + \frac{F_3 - 1}{G_1 G_2} \cdots \frac{F_N - 1}{G_1 G_2 \cdot G_{N-1}} \tag{4.2.3}$$

Thus, the noise figure of a front end composed of cascaded circuit elements is computed by combining the noise figure of each as in (4.2.3). Figure 4.4 shows several front-end models, and the corresponding equiva-

Table 4.1. Noise figure of front-end elements.

Element	*Noise figure*
Lossy cable Length L, temp T_g° α dB/L	$1 + \left(\frac{1 - L_g}{L_g}\right)\frac{T_g^\circ}{290^\circ}$ $L_g = 10^{-0.1(\alpha L)}$
Lossy network Gain = L_g, temp = T_g°	$1 + \left(\frac{1 - L_g}{L_g}\right)\frac{T_g^\circ}{290^\circ}$
Power split, 290° Power out/power in = α	$1/\alpha$
Amplifier (rated noise figure F_a) Lossy network (L_g) + amplifier at 290°	F_a/L_g

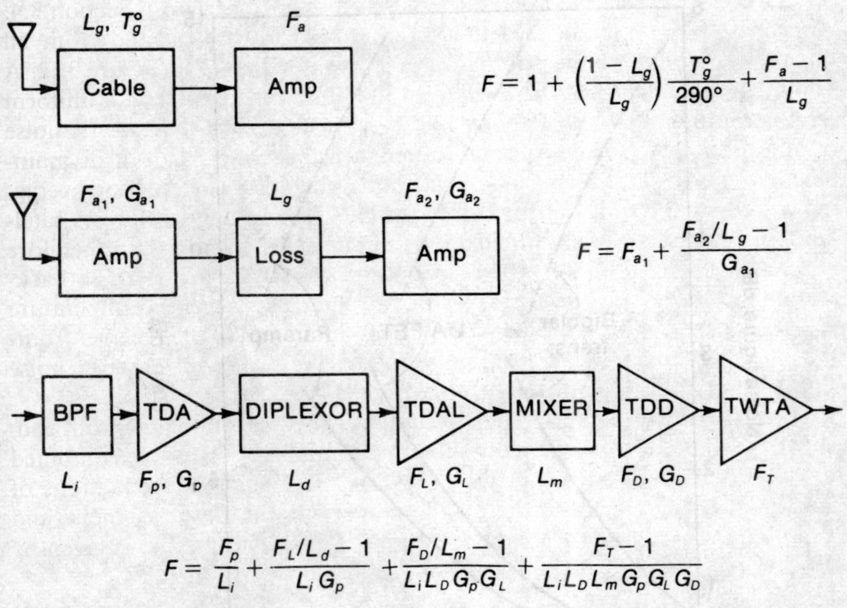

Figure 4.4. Front-end models and corresponding noise figures, F.

lent noise figure, obtained by computing F in (4.2.3). Table 4.1 and Figure 4.4 indicate the following points: When the front end uses an RF preamplifier immediately after the antenna, its noise figure determines the entire front-end noise figure if its gain is suitably high. Thus a basic requirement in preamplifier design is for high-gain, **low-noise amplifiers (LNA)** for this purpose. Figure 4.5 plots some preamplifier noise figures and gain values as a function of carrier frequency. Solid state microwave amplifiers, such as **tunnel diode amplifiers (TDA)**, with their inherent low noise contributions and moderately high power gains are almost universally used for C-band and K-band satellite front ends. Unfortunately, TDA have decreasing gain values at the higher microwave frequencies (> 10 GHz), and it is expected that TDA will be rapidly replaced by newer technological advances in LNA design, such as field-effect transistors (FET), for K-band satellites [1].

Equation (4.2.3) also shows that front-end elements further down the cascade contribute less to overall noise figure since they are divided down by the gain up to that point. Hence, noisy, high-gain preamplifiers are placed further back in the front-end stages. Also, lossy elements (devices with power gains less than 1) preceding an amplifier effectively increase the amplifier noise figure by the reciprocal of the element loss. Hence, an LNA

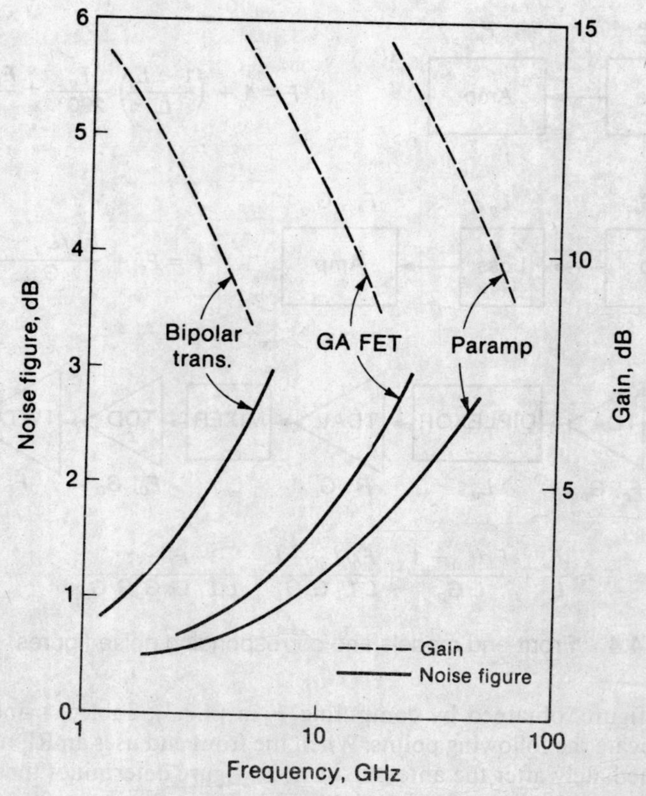

Figure 4.5. Noise figures and gain for typical front-end satellite amplifiers.

should be placed as close to the antenna terminals as possible, prior to any significant coupling losses. Cable losses leading from antenna to amplifier increase the effective receiver noise and should be minimized. Typically, spacecraft front-end noise figures are about 5–10 dB, producing receiver noise temperatures in Figure 4.3 of about 1000°–3000° K. An earth-based station can generally use extensive cooling to lower its front-end noise figure to the 2–5 dB range. Hence earth-station noise temperatures are more typically about 50°–800° K.

Front-End Filters

While background and noise figure set the spectral level of the receiver noise, the amount of noise power entering the front end depends on the noise bandwidth of the front-end filtering. This noise bandwidth depends on the type of filtering used, its spectral width, and its actual spectral shape [2]. If $H(\omega)$ is the combined filter transfer function of the front end, its noise

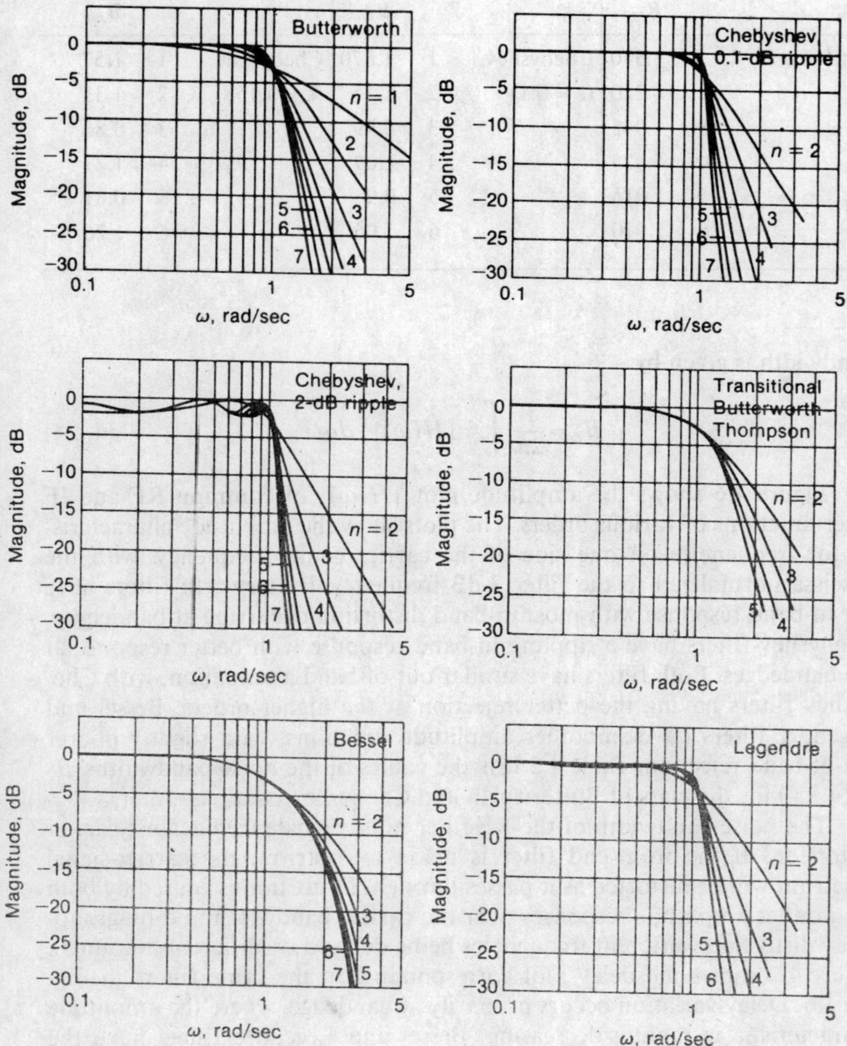

Figure 4.6. Amplitude characteristics of front-end bandpass filters, (n = order of filter).

Table 4.2. Bandpass filter noise bandwidths relative to 3-dB frequency for Butterworth and Chebyshev filters.

Filter	*Order*	$\frac{B_c}{B_{3dB}}$	*Filter*	*Order*	$\frac{B_c}{B_{3dB}}$	*Filter*	*Order*	$\frac{B_c}{B_{3dB}}$
Butterworth	1	1.570	Chebyshev	1	1.570	Chebyshev	1	1.57
	2	1.220	($\epsilon = 0.1$)	2	1.15	($\epsilon = 0.158$)	2	1.33
	3	1.045		3	0.99		3	0.86
	4	1.025		4	1.07		4	1.27
	5	1.015		5	0.96		5	0.81
	6	1.010		6	1.06		6	1.26

bandwidth is given by

$$B_c = \frac{1}{2\pi} \int_{-\infty}^{\infty} |H(\omega)|^2 \, d\omega \tag{4.2.4}$$

Figure 4.6 shows the amplitude plot $|H(\omega)|$ of common RF and IF filter functions of various orders. The plots show the amplitude characteristic for frequencies on one side of the carrier center frequency, with the abscissa normalized to the filter 3-dB frequency. Butterworth filters have flat in-band response with most in-band distortion occurring at bandedges. Chebyshev filters have a rippling in-band response with better response at the bandedges. Both filters have similar out-of-band attenuation, with Chebyshev filters having the better rejection at the higher orders. Bessel and Legendre filters have smoother amplitude functions, with slightly poorer out-of-band rejection. Table 4.2 lists the values of the noise bandwidths B_c in (4.2.4) for the class of Butterworth and Chebyshev bandpass filters.

The noise bandwidth of the RF filter must be balanced against carrier distortion. If the front-end filter is made too narrow, the carrier-signal spectrum will be distorted as it passes through. Distortion is caused by both the nonflat amplitude responses over the carrier bandwidth and by group-delay distortion (different frequencies being delayed by different amounts). Figure 4.7 shows the delay plot corresponding to the same filters in Figure 4.6. Delay variation occurs primarily at bandedge, where the amplitude characteristic is rapidly decreasing. Bessel and Legendre filters have the better delay characteristics and are the preferable filter when delay distortion is critical (usually where in-band response is more important than out-of-band noise rejection). The amount of tolerable distortion caused by

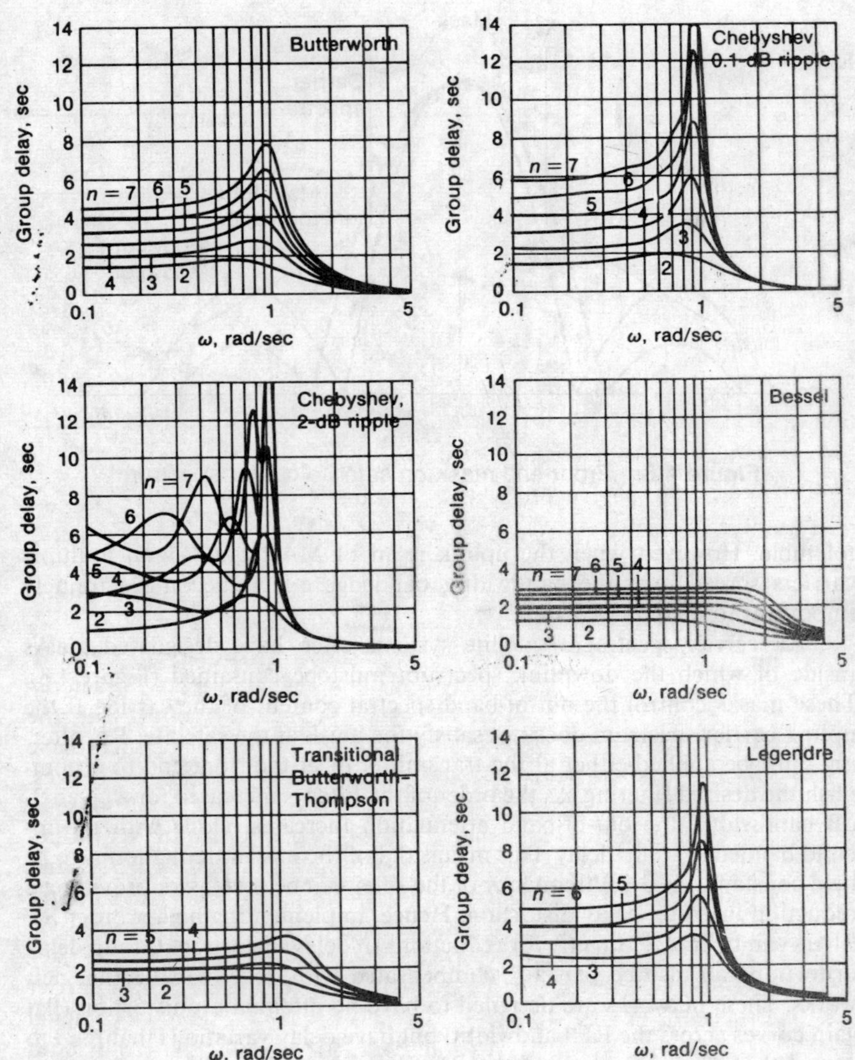

Figure 4.7. Group-delay characteristics of filters in Figure 4.6.

amplitude and group delay depends on the properties of the signal spectrum. If the uplink spectrum is that of a single wideband modulated carrier, with center frequency in the middle of the RF bandwidth, bandedge effects may not be that significant and some degree of band limiting may be

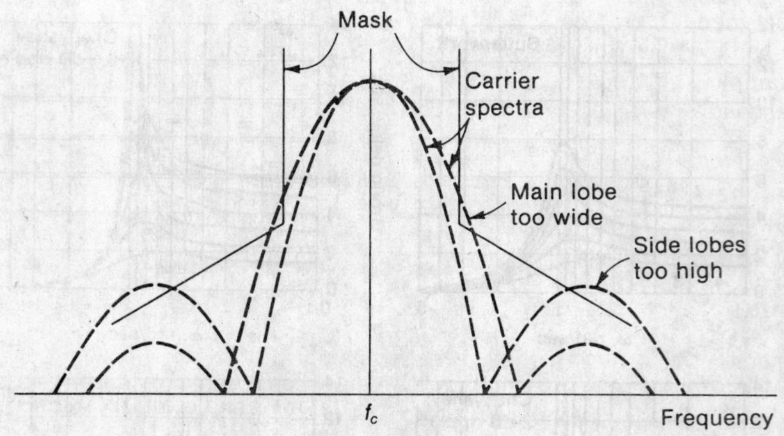

Figure 4.8. Front-end mask on satellite carrier spectrum.

tolerable. However, when the uplink is an FDMA format, with multiple carriers spread over the bandwidth, bandedge effects become extremely important to the outer carriers.

RF carrier spectra in satellite systems often have designated masks inside of which the downlink spectrum must be contained (Figure 4.8). These masks control the out-of-band spectral content of the carrier. If the uplink carrier spectrum does not satisfy the mask at the satellite, RF filtering must be applied either at the transmitter or at the front end to accomplish the desired filtering. As the order of the filter is increased for a given 3-dB bandwidth, the out-of-band attenuation increases, along with the in-band bandedge group delay. This means that if the mask attenuation is to be held constant, the 3-dB frequency of the filter can be increased, providing a reduction in group delay distortion. Hence, implementing higher order RF filters can be traded directly for reductions in delay distortion. Group delay distortion can also be partially compensated with delay **equalization** networks. These networks are designed to have no attenuation distortion (flat gain curves across the RF bandwidth) but have delay variations that tend to cancel the delay distortion of the RF filters. Usually a filter is first constructed to satisfy the mask, then an equalizer is added to correct the delay distortion.

Satellite filters must be designed to be lightweight while achieving the desired mask, noise rejection, and equalization. With the high satellite frequencies involved, RF filters are typically constructed as microwave waveguide filters [2–9]. Such integrated circuits allow better packaging and lower weight, and require less power. Increased use is also being made of dual-mode filters using cavity coupling. Such filters have center frequency-to-bandwidth ratios of about 10^4 at C-band and about 10^3 at K-bands. For example, satellites at C-band typically have carrier filters with RF bandwidths of about 36 MHz.

Front-End Waveforms

Bandpass Gaussian noise appearing in the RF front end can be represented by the mathematical expression

$$n_{RF}(t) = \tilde{n}_c(t) \cos(\omega_c t + \psi) - \tilde{n}_s(t) \sin(\omega_c t + \psi) \qquad (4.2.5)$$

where ψ is an arbitrary phase angle and $\tilde{n}_c(t)$ and $\tilde{n}_s(t)$ are random quadrature noise components. These quadrature components are each low-pass noise processes whose power spectrum is obtained by shifting the one-sided bandpass spectrum to the origin, as shown in Figure 4.9. Note that the one-sided spectral level of the bandpass noise becomes the two-sided spectral level of the noise components. When the spectrum of the bandpass RF noise is symmetric about the center frequency, ω_c, the noise components $\tilde{n}_c(t)$ and $n_s(t)$ are statistically independent processes, and their cross-correlation is everywhere zero. Also if $n_{RF}(t)$ is a Gaussian noise process, $\tilde{n}_c(t)$ and $\tilde{n}_s(t)$ are each also Gaussian processes, and (4.2.5) is an exact statistical model for the RF noise.

The effect of additive bandpass noise on a carrier waveform in the satellite front end is to modify the waveform. Consider a general carrier

$$c(t) = a(t) \cos(\omega_c t + \theta(t) + \psi) \qquad (4.2.6)$$

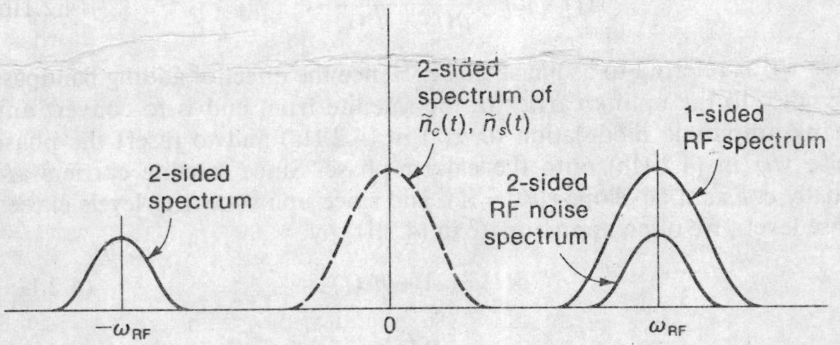

Figure 4.9. Front-end noise spectral models (—RF bandpass noise spectrum; ---- low-pass noise component spectra).

similar to the carrier forms discussed in Section 2.1. The addition of the noise waveform in (4.2.5) produces the combined waveform

$$\begin{aligned} x(t) &= c(t) + n(t) \\ &= a(t)\cos(\omega_c t + \theta(t) + \psi) + \tilde{n}_c(t)\cos(\omega_c t + \psi) \\ &\quad - \tilde{n}_s(t)\sin(\omega_c t + \psi) \end{aligned} \tag{4.2.7}$$

Trigonometrically expanding produces

$$\begin{aligned} x(t) = [a(t) + n_c(t)]\cos(\omega_c t + \theta(t) + \psi) \\ - n_s(t)\sin(\omega_c t + \theta(t) + \psi) \end{aligned} \tag{4.2.8}$$

where

$$\begin{aligned} n_c(t) &= \tilde{n}_c(t)\cos\theta(t) + \tilde{n}_s(t)\sin\theta(t) \\ n_s(t) &= \tilde{n}_c(t)\sin\theta(t) - \tilde{n}_s(t)\cos\theta(t) \end{aligned} \tag{4.2.9}$$

The noise components $n_c(t)$ and $n_s(t)$ are formed from combinations of the quadrature components $\tilde{n}_c(t)$ and $\tilde{n}_s(t)$. It can be shown [10] that $n_c(t)$ and $n_s(t)$ are also Gaussian for *any* $\theta(t)$, and will essentially have the same spectra as $\tilde{n}_c(t)$ and $\tilde{n}_s(t)$ as long as the RF bandwidth is larger than that of the modulation $\theta(t)$. Equation (4.2.8) can be rewritten as

$$x(t) = \alpha(t)\cos(\omega_c t + \theta(t) + \psi + v(t)) \tag{4.2.10}$$

where

$$\alpha(t) = [(a(t) + n_c(t))^2 + n_s^2(t)]^{1/2} \tag{4.2.11a}$$

$$v(t) = \tan^{-1}\frac{n_s(t)}{a(t) + n_c(t)} \tag{4.2.11b}$$

Here $v(t)$ is referred to as **phase noise**. Hence the effect of adding bandpass RF noise to the uplink carrier in the satellite front end is to convert any uplink amplitude modulation to $\alpha(t)$ in (4.2.11a) and to insert the phase noise $v(t)$ in (4.2.11b) onto the carrier phase. Since satellite carriers are usually constant envelope ($a(t) = A$), and since uplink carrier levels exceed noise levels, we often approximate in (4.2.11) by

$$\alpha(t) \approx A + n_c(t) \tag{4.2.12a}$$

$$v(t) \approx \frac{n_s(t)}{A} \tag{4.2.12b}$$

The amplitude is therefore corrupted primarily by $n_c(t)$, which is often referred to as **amplitude noise**, or **in-phase noise**. The phase is affected primarily by $n_s(t)$, which is referred to as **quadrature noise**. Having somewhat precise mathematical forms for the front-end waveforms will be extremely beneficial in subsequent processing analysis.

4.3 RF FILTERING OF DIGITAL CARRIERS

The effect of excessive RF filtering on carriers modulated with digital data is extremely important in maintaining digital performance. This filtering may occur either at the transmitter or at the satellite. To examine this effect in detail, let a digital carrier at the input to an RF filter be the generalized constant envelope quadrature carrier

$$c(t) = A[m_c(t) \cos(\omega_c t + \psi) + m_s(t) \sin(\omega_c t + \psi)] \tag{4.3.1}$$

introduced in Chapter 2. Here A is the carrier amplitude, and $m_c(t)$ and $m_s(t)$ are the quadrature data-modulated waveforms. From (2.3.12) this carrier has the spectrum

$$S_c(\omega) = \frac{A^2}{4}[S_{m_c}(\omega) + S_{m_s}(\omega)]_{\omega \pm \omega_c} \tag{4.3.2}$$

depending on the individual spectral densities of the quadrature modulation. The effect of a bandpass RF filter $H_{RF}(\omega)$ is to produce a filtered spectrum

$$S_y(\omega) = S_c(\omega)\,|H_{RF}(\omega)|^2 \tag{4.3.3}$$

at the filter output. The output carrier waveform can be determined by first writing

$$c(t) = A \text{ Real}\{m_c(t)e^{j(\omega_c t+\psi)}\} + A \text{ Im}\{m_s(t)e^{j(\omega_c t+\psi)}\} \tag{4.3.4}$$

where Real $[\cdot]$ and Im $[\cdot]$ refer to real and imaginary parts. The filter output waveform is then

$$\begin{aligned} y(t) = A \text{ Real}&\left\{\int_{-\infty}^{\infty} m_c(t-z)e^{j(\omega_c(t-z)+\psi)}h_{RF}(z)dz\right\} \\ + A \text{ Im}&\left\{\int_{-\infty}^{\infty} m_s(t-z)e^{j(\omega_c(t-z)+\psi)}h_{RF}(z)dz\right\} \end{aligned} \tag{4.3.5}$$

where $h_{\text{RF}}(t)$ is the bandpass filter impulse response. This means

$$\begin{aligned} y(t) &= A \text{ Real}\left\{ e^{j(\omega_c t+\psi)} \int_{-\infty}^{\infty} m_c(t-z)e^{-j\omega_c z} h_{\text{RF}}(z)dz \right\} \\ &\quad + A \text{ Im}\left\{ e^{j(\omega_c t+\psi)} \int_{-\infty}^{\infty} m_s(t-z)e^{-j\omega_c z} h_{\text{RF}}(z)dz \right\} \end{aligned} \tag{4.3.6}$$

The integrals are complex and correspond to the filtering of each *m(t)* by a filter whose impulse response is $\tilde{h}_{\text{RF}}(t) = e^{-j\omega_c t} h_{\text{RF}}(t)$. By Fourier transforming, $\tilde{h}_{\text{RF}}(t)$ corresponds to an equivalent filter function

$$\begin{aligned} \tilde{H}_{\text{RF}}(\omega) &= \int_{-\infty}^{\infty} h_{\text{RF}}(t)e^{-j\omega_c t} e^{-j\omega t} dt \\ &= H_{\text{RF}}(\omega + \omega_c) \end{aligned} \tag{4.3.7}$$

The latter is simply the low-pass filter function obtained by shifting the bandpass RF filter function centered at ω_c to $\omega = 0$. Hence (4.3.6) becomes

$$\begin{aligned} y(t) &= A \text{ Real}\{\tilde{m}_c(t)e^{j(\omega_c t+\psi)}\} \\ &\quad + A \text{ Im}\{\tilde{m}_s(t)e^{j(\omega_c t+\psi)}\} \end{aligned} \tag{4.3.8}$$

where $\tilde{m}_c(t)$ and $\tilde{m}_s(t)$ are the filtered versions of $m_c(t)$ and $m_s(t)$, each having transform

$$\begin{aligned} \tilde{M}_c(\omega) &= M_c(\omega)\tilde{H}_{\text{RF}}(\omega) \\ \tilde{M}_s(\omega) &= M_s(\omega)\tilde{H}_{\text{RF}}(\omega) \end{aligned} \tag{4.3.9}$$

The filtered carrier spectrum is then

$$\tilde{S}_c(\omega) = \frac{A^2}{4}[\,|M_c(\omega)\tilde{H}_{\text{RF}}(\omega)|^2 + |M_s(\omega)\tilde{H}_{\text{RF}}(\omega)|^2]_{\omega\pm\omega_c} \tag{4.3.10}$$

Equation (4.3.10) shows that the filtered carrier spectrum in (4.3.3) is equivalent to the filtering of the data modulation by a shifted RF filter. Hence the details of RF carrier spectra can be determined by examining the low-pass data filtering. Figure 4.10a shows filtered QPSK spectra corresponding to Chebyshev filtering of a QPSK carrier for several values of filter bandwidth and order. The reduction in out-of-band carrier power is apparent, although main-hump spectral reduction can also occur if the filter is too narrow.

Excessive filtering in trying to reduce spectral tails and noise, however, may produce distortions on the quadrature data. Let *m(t)*, prior to the

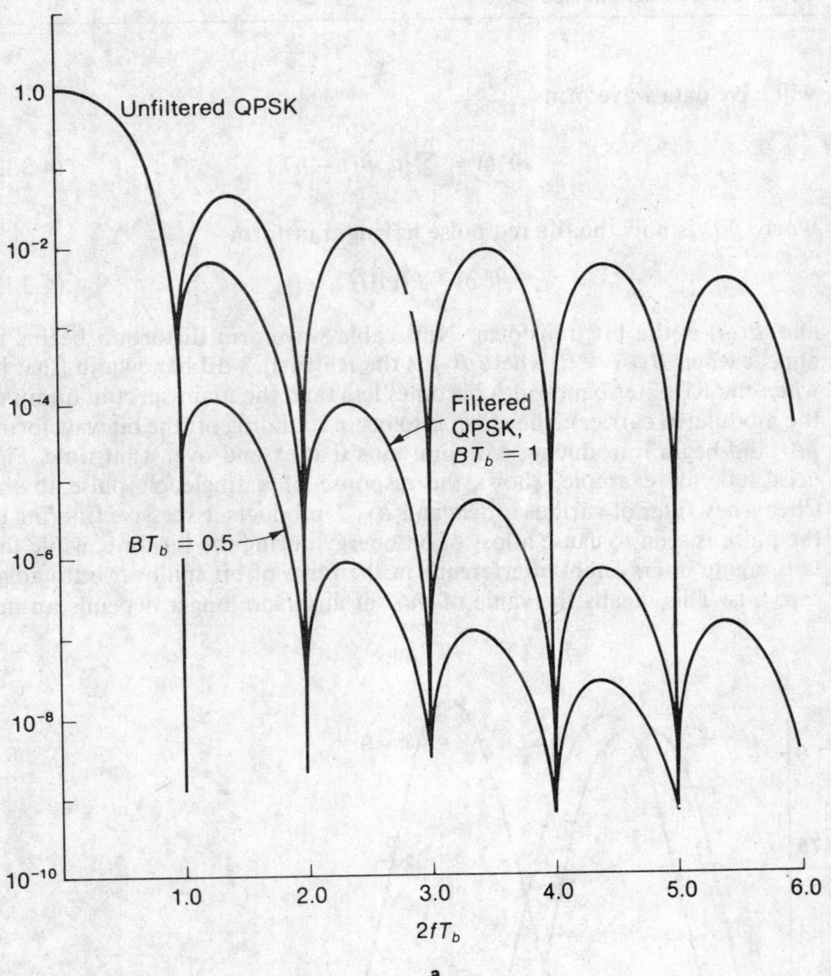

Figure 4.10. Bandpass-filtered QPSK carriers, Butterworth filters. (a) Spectrum. (b) Pulse time response. (n = order of filter, $BT_b = 0.5$)

filtering, be written as the NRZ waveform

$$m(t) = \sum_{n=-\infty}^{\infty} a_n p(t - nT) \tag{4.3.11}$$

where $p(t) = 1$, $0 \leqslant t \leqslant T$, $a_n = \pm 1$, and T is a bit time for BPSK and a symbol time for QPSK. Equation (4.3.9) shows that the RF-filtered carrier will have data waveforms

$$\tilde{m}(t) = \sum_{n=-\infty}^{\infty} a_n \tilde{p}(t - nT) \tag{4.3.12}$$

where $\tilde{p}(t)$ is now the filtered pulse having transform

$$\tilde{P}(\omega) = P(\omega)\tilde{H}_{RF}(\omega) \tag{4.3.13}$$

and $P(\omega)$ is the bit transform. Noticeable waveform distortion begins to appear when $B_{RF}T \lessapprox 2$, where B_{RF} is the RF filter 3-dB bandwidth (that is, when the RF filter bandwidth becomes less than the main spectral hump of the modulated carrier). The effect is to begin rounding off the bit waveforms $p(t)$ and begin introducing temporal tails that extend over a bit time. Figure 4.10b, for example, shows the response of a single bit pulse to the Chebyshev filter of various orders and $B_{RF}T$ products. Excessive filtering of the pulse is seen to cause a loss of bit energy during the bit time, while the tails create **intersymbol interference** in the form of bit spillover onto adjacent bits. This means the value of $\tilde{m}(t)$ at any t no longer depends on the

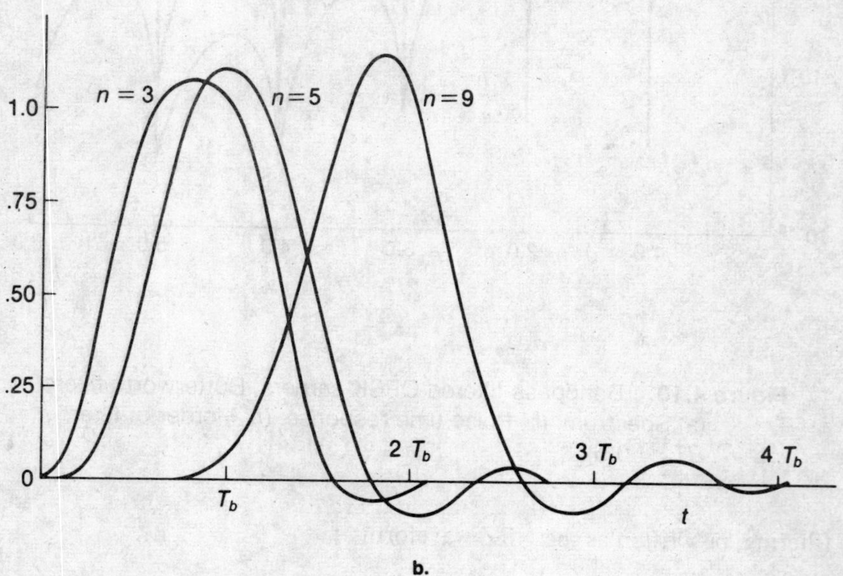

Figure 4.10. Bandpass-filtered QPSK carriers, Butterworth filters. (a) Spectrum. (b) Pulse time response. (n = order of filter, $BT_b = 0.5$)

present a_n but rather exhibits the intersymbol effect of other $\{a_n\}$ through the overlaps of $\tilde{p}(t)$.

Bit distortion means that even if the transponder retransmitted the filtered carrier directly to the decoder without further distortion, the effect of waveshape on bit decoding must still be considered. This topic is examined in Section A.2 of Appendix A. Figure 4.11a exhibits results derived in the section, showing the resulting degradation to PE caused by decreasing values of $B_{RF}T$. Figure 4.11b replots the same data by showing the effective increase in carrier power needed to overcome the combined bit energy loss and intersymbol interference in order to maintain a bit-error probability of

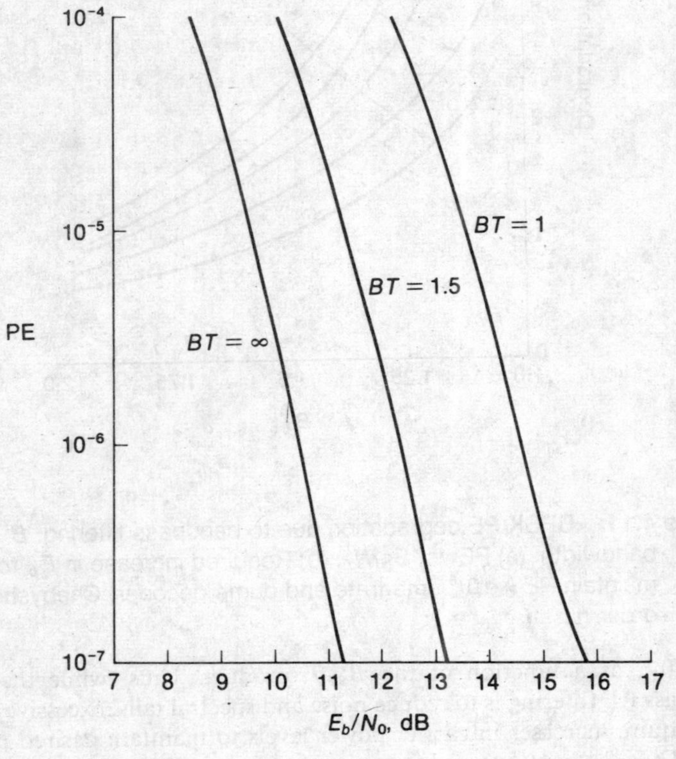

Figure 4.11. BPSK PE degradation due to bandpass filtering, B = 3-dB bandwidth. (a) PE vs. E_b/N_0. (b) Required increase in E_b to maintain PE = 10^{-6}. Integrate and dump decoder, Chebyshev filter, order n.

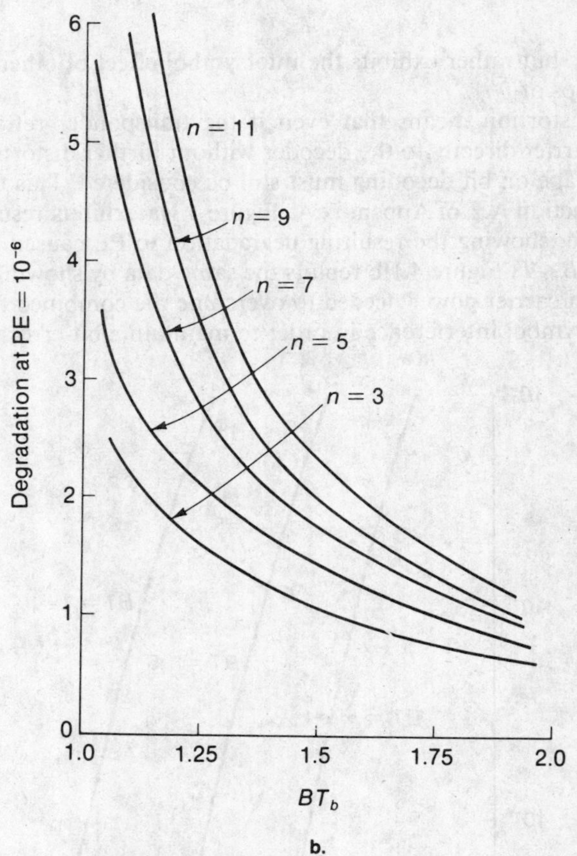

Figure 4.11. BPSK PE degradation due to bandpass filtering, B = 3-dB bandwidth. (a) PE vs. E_b/N_0. (b) Required increase in E_b to maintain PE = 10^{-6}. Integrate and dump decoder, Chebyshev filter, order n.

PE = 10^{-6}, as a function of the $B_{RF}T$ product. Thus, while the role of bandpass RF filtering is to reduce noise and spectral tails, excessive filtering will require increases in carrier power levels to maintain desired performance. Thus the communication engineer must carefully evaluate the trade-off in reduced front-end bandwidth (increased throughput in bits per sec per Hz) for decreased decoding performance.

Another important effect of narrow filtering is the possibility of creating a nonconstant envelope carrier from one that was originally constant envelope. At any t the envelope of $c(t)$ in (4.3.1), using (2.3.11) is $A[p_c^2(t) + p_s^2(t)]^{1/2}$, designed to be a constant at all t. However, $\tilde{c}(t)$ in (4.3.8) will have the envelope

$$|\tilde{c}(t)| = A[\tilde{m}_c^2(t) + \tilde{m}_s^2(t)]^{1/2}$$
$$= A\left[\left[\sum_{n=-\infty}^{\infty} a_n \tilde{p}(t - nT)\right]^2 + \left[\sum_{n=-\infty}^{\infty} b_n \tilde{p}(t - nT)\right]^2\right]^{1/2} \quad (4.3.14)$$

This envelope is no longer constant, due to both the distortion in $\tilde{p}(t)$ and the intersymbol effect. Hence, excessive RF filtering can be detrimental to subsequent system processing designed for constant envelope carriers.

The effect of RF filtering on constant envelope phase modulated carriers is more difficult to determine. If we write the general PM carrier as

$$c(t) = \text{Real}\{Ae^{j\theta(t)}e^{j(\omega_c t + \psi)}\} \quad (4.3.15)$$

where $\theta(t)$ represents the phase modulation, then the RF-filtered version, corresponding to (4.3.6), becomes

$$\tilde{c}(t) = A \text{ Real}\left\{e^{j(\omega_c t + \psi)} \int_{-\infty}^{\infty} e^{j\theta(t-z)}\, \tilde{h}_{\text{RF}}(z)dz\right\} \quad (4.3.16)$$

This contains in the integral the effective filtering by the low-pass filter $\tilde{H}_{\text{RF}}(\omega)$ on the complex modulation

$$m(t) = e^{j\theta(t)} \quad (4.3.17)$$

The waveform $m(t)$ is known to have a correlation function related to the second characteristic function of the process $\theta(t)$ [10, Chapter 2], and a power spectrum related to sums of repeated convolutions of the spectra of $\theta(t)$. Since convolutions spread the spectra of the modulation, the effect of filtering is to tend to reduce the significance of the higher order convolutions. The spectrum of the filtered carrier in (4.3.16) is therefore dominated by the first few terms of the convolved spectrum of $\theta(t)$. Hence, we often approximate the filtered phase modulation carrier spectrum as

$$S_{\tilde{c}}(\omega) = \frac{A^2}{4}[[S_\theta(\omega) + S_\theta(\omega) \otimes S_\theta(\omega)]\tilde{H}_{\text{RF}}(\omega)]_{\omega \pm \omega_c} \quad (4.3.18)$$

where $\otimes$ denotes spectral convolution. Thus, to a first-order approximation, $S_{\tilde{c}}(\omega)$ appears as a filtered version of the modulation spectra, plus the result of filtering the convolved modulation spectrum, all shifted to the carrier frequency.

4.4 SATELLITE SIGNAL PROCESSING

Satellite signal processing generates the microwave carrier for the return link. This carrier can be achieved by direct frequency translation or by carrier remodulation. Subsystems that accomplish these operations are shown in Figure 4.12. Figure 4.12a shows a direct RF-to-RF conversion using a single mixer system. Figure 4.12b shows a double conversion from RF to an intermediate lower IF, then back up to RF using a single mixing oscillator. This system has the advantage of allowing carrier filtering and amplification to be performed at the lower IF frequency band rather than at the higher RF band. In addition, RF–IF–RF systems allow uplink command carriers to be more easily removed (or new telemetry carriers inserted) at the satellite before return retransmission. Note that frequency translators of either type always cause all uplink noise to be similarly translated, and, therefore, directly superimposed onto the return spectra, as we assumed in Chapter 3. When the transponder merely frequency translates the uplink carrier to the downlink, the satellite appears to be simply "bending" the earth-station uplink into the receiving downlink. For this reason, frequency-translating satellite links are often referred to as **bent pipes**.

Remodulating processors involve a stage of modulation that generates the return carrier. This is accomplished by (1) translating the uplink RF spectrum down to a low IF band, and then modulating the entire IF onto the return RF, as shown in Figure 4.12c; or (2) directly demodulating the uplink carrier to baseband, and remodulating the baseband onto the return carrier, as in Figure 4.12d. With digitally modulated carriers, baseband demodulation can involve baseband decoding of the information bits, followed by digital remodulation. Remodulation removes uplink noise and interference from the return modulation, while facilitating uplink on-board digital processing and return link bit insertion. In the following sections we analyze the effect of a single uplink carrier processed in the transponder by each of these processing systems.

RF–RF Translation

Let the uplink front-end waveform be written as

$$x(t) = c_u(t) + n_u(t) \tag{4.4.1}$$

where $c_u(t)$ is an uplink carrier of the form

$$c_u(t) = \sqrt{2P_c}\cos(\omega_u t + \theta_u(t) + \psi) \tag{4.4.2}$$

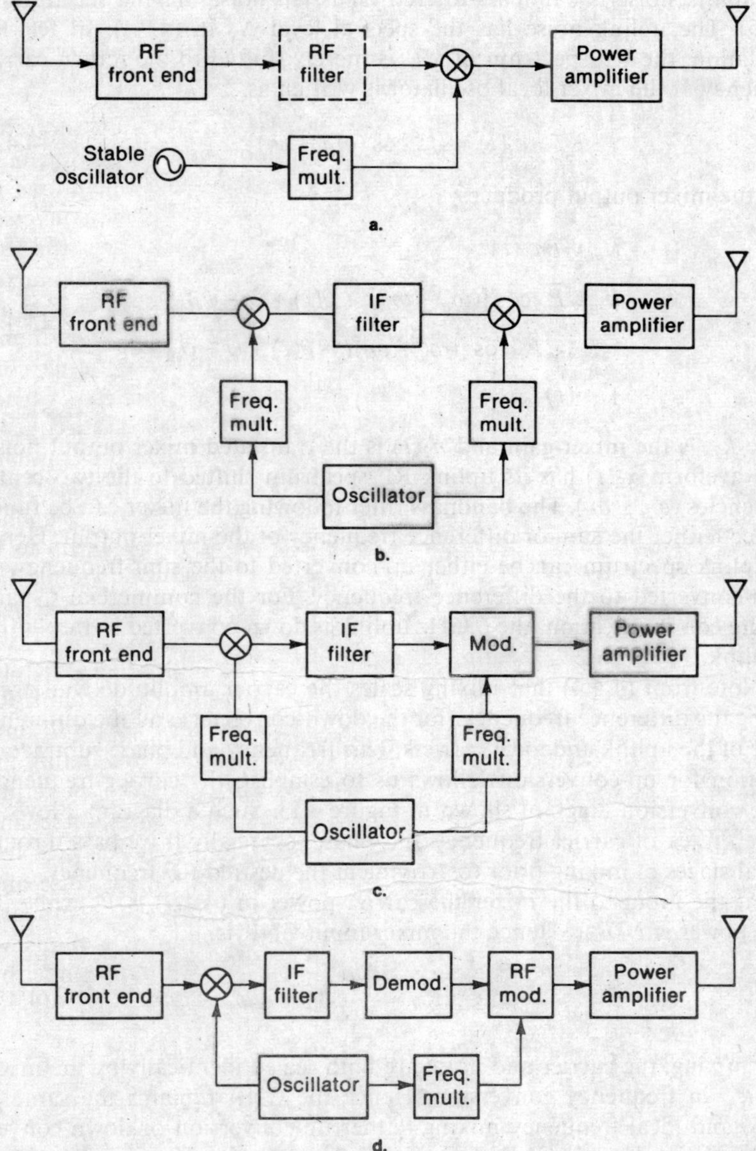

Figure 4.12. Satellite processing models. (a) RF–RF translation. (b) RF–IF–RF translation. (c) IF remodulation. (d) Demodulation–remodulation.

The uplink noise is bandpass-filtered Gaussian noise, having the form of (4.2.5). The uplink noise has the spectral level N_0 in (4.2.1). In RF–RF translation, the RF spectrum of *x(t)* is merely shifted to the return carrier frequency. If the mixer local oscillator is written as

$$c_l(t) = \sqrt{2}\cos(\omega_l t + \psi_l) \tag{4.4.3}$$

then the mixer output produces

$$\begin{aligned} x_2(t) &= k_m x(t) c_l(t) \\ &= k_m \sqrt{P_c}\cos[(\omega_u - \omega_l)t + \theta(t) + \psi - \psi_l] \\ &\quad + k_m \sqrt{P_c}\cos[(\omega_u + \omega_l)t + \theta(t) + \psi + \psi_l] \\ &\quad + n_2(t) \end{aligned} \tag{4.4.4}$$

where k_m is the mixer gain and $n_2(t)$ is the translated mixer output noise. The waveform $x_2(t)$ has its uplink RF spectrum shifted to the two center frequencies $(\omega_u \pm \omega_l)$. The bandpass filter following the mixer can be tuned to select either the sum or difference frequency of the mixer output. Hence the uplink spectrum can be either up-converted to the sum frequency, or down-converted to the difference frequency. For the commercial C-band satellite communication, the 6 GHz uplink is down-converted to the 4 GHz downlink.

Note from (4.4.4) that mixing scales the carrier amplitude while generating the difference frequency (for the down-converter) and the difference phase of the uplink and local carriers. This frequency and phase subtraction (addition for up-conversion) allows us to establish the carrier frequency-phase conversion diagram shown in Figure 4.13. Such a diagram allows us to keep track of carrier frequency and phase, especially if we pass through several stages of mixing prior to arriving at the desired RF frequency.

At the input to the mixer the carrier power in (4.4.2) is P_c while the noise power is $N_0 B_{\mathrm{RF}}$. Hence the mixer input CNR is

$$\mathrm{CNR}_u = \frac{P_c}{N_0 B_{\mathrm{RF}}} \tag{4.4.5}$$

After mixing, the carrier and noise are both scaled identically by the mixer gain k_m in frequency conversion. Hence the CNR remains the same as (4.4.5) and ideal frequency mixing (either up-conversion or down-conversion) does not degrade CNR. This means the analysis of Section 3.6, where earth station CNR_d was computed for an ideal amplifier as

$$(\mathrm{CNR}_d)^{-1} = (\mathrm{CNR}_u)^{-1} + (\mathrm{CNR}_r)^{-1} \tag{4.4.6}$$

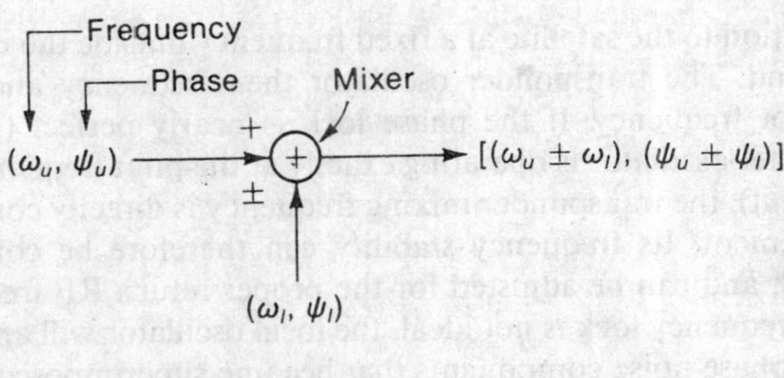

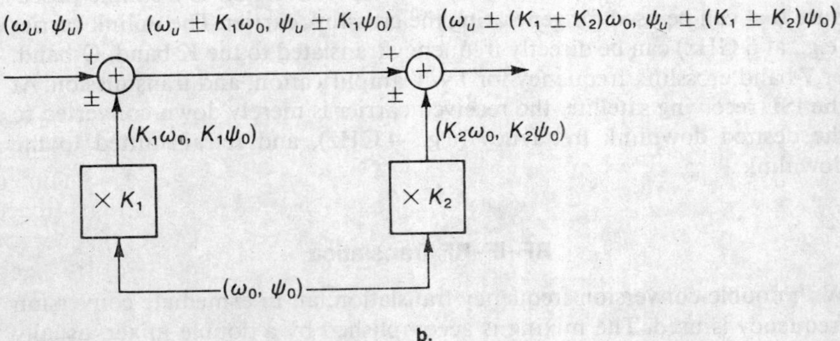

Figure 4.13. Frequency phase model for mixing. (a) Single mixer. (b) Multiple mixing.

is still valid, and CNR_u can be referred to either before or after frequency translation. In other words, ideal transponder frequency conversion does not affect downlink receiver CNR.

It is important to recognize the importance of the stability of the satellite master oscillator in the frequency and phase shifting of the RF translation operation. Offsets in the oscillator frequency produce offsets in the downlink carrier frequency. Phase variations on the local oscillator, such as phase noise variations, are transferred directly to the translated RF carrier. These effects become subtly important, since they can cause phase and frequency errors to permeate the entire system. For this reason an extremely stable master oscillator is usually selected for transponder translation.

To aid the frequency stability of the satellite oscillator, a pilot carrier is often used. The pilot is an unmodulated RF carrier transmitted from a control earth station to the satellite at a fixed frequency outside the modulation spectral band. The transponder oscillator then frequency and phase locks to the pilot frequency. If the phase lock is nearly perfect (i.e., the transponder master oscillator is operating exactly at the pilot frequency or a fixed multiple of it), the transponder mixing frequency is directly connected to the earth segment. Its frequency stability can therefore be controlled from the ground, and can be adjusted for the proper return RF frequency. When the pilot frequency lock is not ideal, the local oscillator will appear to have additional phase noise components that become superimposed on the translated RF carrier. This topic is discussed in detail in Chapter 8.

For intersatellite links (ISL), RF–RF up-conversion is a simple procedure that can be used for generating the crosslink carrier. The uplink carrier (e.g., at 6 GHz) can be directly frequency translated to the K-band, Q-band, or V-band crosslink frequency for TWT amplification, and transmission. At the ISL receiving satellite, the received carrier is merely down-converted to the desired downlink frequency (e.g., 4 GHz), and retransmitted to the downlink.

RF–IF–RF Translation

With double-conversion frequency translation, an intermediate conversion frequency is used. The mixing is accomplished by a double mixer, usually driven by a common master oscillator, as was shown in Figure 4.12b. The oscillator frequency is simultaneously multiplied to each mixing frequency, the first to down-convert to IF and the second to up-convert back to RF. The translation can be analyzed by applying the results of Figure 4.13a to both stages, as in Figure 4.13b. We assume that the frequency conversions from the master frequency f_0 to the desired conversion frequencies is obtained by a frequency multiplier, which simultaneously multiplies up (or divides down) by the same factor both the oscillator frequency and phase. Examination of Figure 4.13b shows that if the translator input signal is that given in (4.4.2), the RF signal after double conversion has the form

$$x_3(t) = \sqrt{P_c}\,k_{m_1}k_{m_2}\cos\,[\omega_3 t + \theta(t) + \psi_u - (g_1 + g_2)\psi_0] + n_3(t) \qquad (4.4.7)$$

where $\omega_3 = \omega_u - (g_1 + g_2)\omega_0$ is the desired return RF carrier frequency. The noise $n_3(t)$ has the RF front-end noise spectrum filtered by the IF bandpass filter and shifted to ω_3, with its spectral level scaled by $(k_{m_1}k_{m_2})^2$. Just as in RF–RF mixing, the sequence of mixing operations ideally preserves CNR during its operation. Note that the carrier portion of (4.4.7) can be written with the phase $\omega_3 t + \theta(t) + \psi_u + [(\omega_3 - \omega_1)/\omega_0]\phi_0]$. Thus the phase inserted by the local oscillator appears to have been multiplied up by the frequency-conversion difference normalized by the oscillator frequency. Hence it is only the total frequency *difference* of the translation that is important to the phase insertion, and not the number of translation stages.

IF Remodulation

Satellite processing using IF remodulation was shown in Figure 4.12c. The uplink is translated to IF, and the entire IF is modulated onto a downlink carrier. Since the IF bandwidth will be expanded into the RF bandwidth by the modulation, this conversion technique has application only if the uplink IF bandwidth is much smaller than that available in the downlink. The system, however, has the advantage that the noise spectrum in the satellite uplink is not retransmitted directly into the downlink. Instead, the uplink noise is effectively modulated onto the downlink carrier along with the desired signal. To analyze the processing, consider again the single uplink carrier in (4.4.2) containing the phase modulation $\theta(t) = \Delta_u m(t)$. The uplink RF is translated to IF, generating the IF signal

$$x_{\rm IF}(t) = A_{\rm IF} \sin\left[\omega_{\rm IF} t + \theta(t) + \psi_{\rm IF}\right] + n_{\rm IF}(t) \tag{4.4.8}$$

The above waveform has a CNR of

$$\mathrm{CNR}_u = \frac{A_{\rm IF}^2/2}{N_{0u} B_{\rm IF}} \tag{4.4.9}$$

where $B_{\rm IF}$ is the IF noise bandwidth. The IF signal has its amplitude adjusted to generate the desired phase index Δ_d for the downlink. This is equivalent to multiplying $x_{\rm IF}(t)$ by $\Delta_d/A_{\rm IF}$. The downlink-modulating waveform is then the bandpass signal

$$\begin{aligned} x_d(t) &= \left(\frac{\Delta_d}{A_{\rm IF}}\right) x_{\rm IF}(t) \\ &= \Delta_d \sin\left[\omega_{\rm IF} t + \Delta_u m(t) + \psi_{\rm IF}\right] + \left(\frac{\Delta_d}{A_{\rm IF}}\right) n_{\rm IF}(t) \end{aligned} \tag{4.4.10}$$

After transponder amplification the downlink carrier then becomes

$$c_d(t) = \sqrt{2P_T} \sin\left[\omega_d t + x_d(t)\right] \tag{4.4.11}$$

where P_T is the available satellite downlink power. Note that (4.4.11) contains no noise added to the downlink carrier. Instead, the IF noise is contained within the modulation and will appear only following downlink phase demodulation. The carrier in (4.4.11) will be received on the ground with power $P_T L$ with L given in (3.6.3). The downlink CNR is then

$$\mathrm{CNR}_d = \frac{P_T L}{N_{0d} B_c} \tag{4.4.12}$$

where N_{0d} is the receiver noise level of the downlink receiver. If this threshold is high enough to satisfy the receiver, the downlink carrier can be phase demodulated, producing the recovered baseband

$$x_d(t) = \Delta_d \sin\left(\omega_{\mathrm{IF}} t + \theta(t)\right) + \left(\frac{\Delta_d}{A_{\mathrm{IF}}}\right) n_{\mathrm{IF}}(t) + \frac{n_d(t)}{\sqrt{2 P_T L}} \tag{4.4.13}$$

where $n_d(t)$ is the downlink noise, having power $N_{0d} B_{\mathrm{IF}}$. The total modulation interfering noise in (4.4.13) can be interpreted as having been caused by an equivalent downlink receiver noise of spectral level

$$N_{0d}\left[1 + \Delta_d^2 \frac{2 N_{0u} P_T L}{A_{\mathrm{IF}}^2 N_{0d}}\right] = N_{0d}\left[1 + \Delta_d^2 \left(\frac{\mathrm{CNR}_u}{\mathrm{CNR}_d}\right)\right] \tag{4.4.14}$$

where the CNR are given in (4.4.9) and (4.4.12). Hence the receiver demodulated noise level is effectively increased by the uplink IF noise during demodulation, with the increase dependent on the ratio of the uplink CNR to the downlink CNR. We note, however, that the uplink noise does not alter the CNR in (4.4.12) required for establishing the receiver demodulation threshold. Contrast this result with the case of RF–RF conversion in (4.4.6) in which uplink noise directly reduced CNR_d.

IF remodulation methods have also been suggested for intersatellite links (ISL). Instead of simply up-converting the uplink carrier directly to the crosslink frequency, the uplink carrier is instead down-converted to an IF frequency (MHz), remodulated back onto the uplink carrier via FM, and up-converted to the crosslink frequency (20–60 GHz). At the ISL receiving satellite, the crosslink carrier is down-converted to RF, demodulated to regenerate the IF carrier, and the latter is up-converted to the downlink frequency. This method provides a higher downlink CNR than simple RF–RF ISL conversion with the same ISL CNR, since it has the advantage of the SNR_d improvement during FM demodulation. Conversely, the ISL can be operated with a smaller CNR (smaller antennas and TWT power) for the same downlink CNR, at the expense of inserting the additional mod-demod equipment. This reduction in crosslink CNR is particularly significant in considering antenna size, since we recall from (3.6.16) that crosslink CNR varies as the *fourth power* of antenna diameter.

Demodulation–Modulation Conversion

In satellite processing using demodulation and remodulation, the uplink is demodulated to baseband, and the entire baseband is remodulated onto a downlink carrier. Since demodulation is used, this conversion has primary application to the case when a single uplink carrier is involved (unless a separate satellite demodulator was provided for each uplink carrier). This processing format allows for (1) uplink commands transmitted with the carrier modulation to be recovered during the demodulation, and (2) satellite telemetry to be inserted into the baseband for downlink modulation. As with IF modulation, the system also has the advantage that the uplink noise spectrum is not retransmitted directly in the downlink.

Analysis of baseband remodulation is carried out in a manner similar to that of IF remodulation, except that demodulated waveforms are involved. If the uplink CNR in (4.4.9) is sufficiently high, the IF carrier can be ideally phase demodulated in the satellite generating the baseband waveform

$$x(t) = \Delta_u m(t) + \frac{n_u(t)}{A_u} \tag{4.4.15}$$

Here $n_u(t)$ is the uplink quadrature noise in the modulation bandwidth of $m(t)$. The baseband signal $x(t)$ now has its amplitude adjusted to generate a new phase index, Δ_d, for the downlink. The downlink carrier is then formed as in (4.4.11) with

$$x_d(t) = \Delta_d m(t) + \left(\frac{\Delta_d}{\Delta_u}\right)\frac{n_u(t)}{A_u} \tag{4.4.16}$$

After downlink phase demodulation, the equivalent receiver noise spectral level then becomes

$$N_{0d}\left[1 + \left(\frac{\Delta_d}{\Delta_u}\right)^2 \frac{\text{CNR}_u}{\text{CNR}_d}\right] \tag{4.4.17}$$

which is similar to (4.4.14).

When digital modulation is used, the transponder demodulation can be reinterpreted as bit decoding. Remodulation corresponds to encoding these decoded bits back onto the RF return carrier. This means a given source bit, in traveling through the transponder to the specific earth station, undergoes two stages of decoding in cascade. This may be diagrammed as shown in Figure 4.14. A given bit will be decoded correctly at the end if two correct decodings occurred, or if two incorrect decodings occurred. Let PE_1 denote

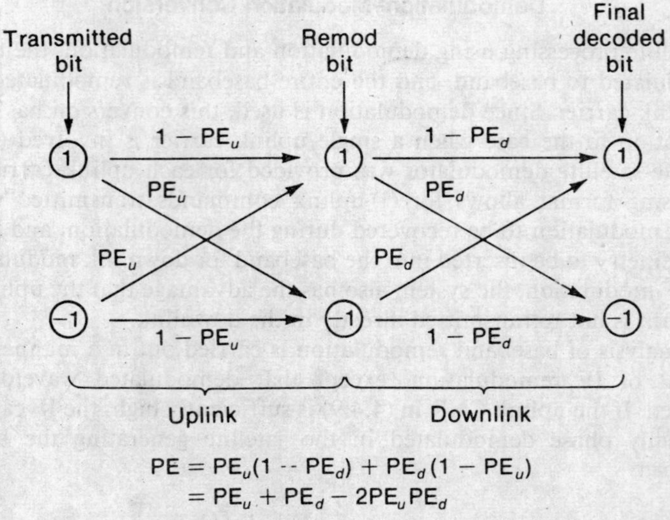

Figure 4.14. Cascaded binary-decoding stages, corresponding to demod-remod digital transponders.

the probability of a bit error during the uplink decoding, and let PE_2 be that for the downlink decoding. The average bit-error probability is then

$$\begin{aligned} PE &= (1 - PE_1)PE_2 + PE_1(1 - PE_2) \\ &= PE_1 + PE_2 - 2PE_1PE_2 \end{aligned} \tag{4.4.18}$$

If both links have been designed for small PE ($PE_1, PE_2 \leqslant 10^{-1}$), the last term will be negligible compared to the sum. This means the overall PE for the transponder link is the sum of the individual link error probabilities. The weakest link (largest PE_i) will therefore determine the overall PE, and there is no advantage in having one digital link significantly better than the other in terms of error probability.

As an example, consider a BPSK uplink and downlink, operating with an uplink $(E_b/N_0)_u$ and a downlink $(E_b/N_0)_r$, each calculated by the methods of Section 3.5. We wish to operate the overall transponder remodulation link with an error probability PE. Figure 4.15 shows the uplink-downlink E_b/N_0 combinations needed to produce a specified PE of $10^{-3} - 10^{-6}$ for the cascaded demod-remod link. Also included is the required E_b/N_0 values for the same PE using a linear amplifying up-down link,

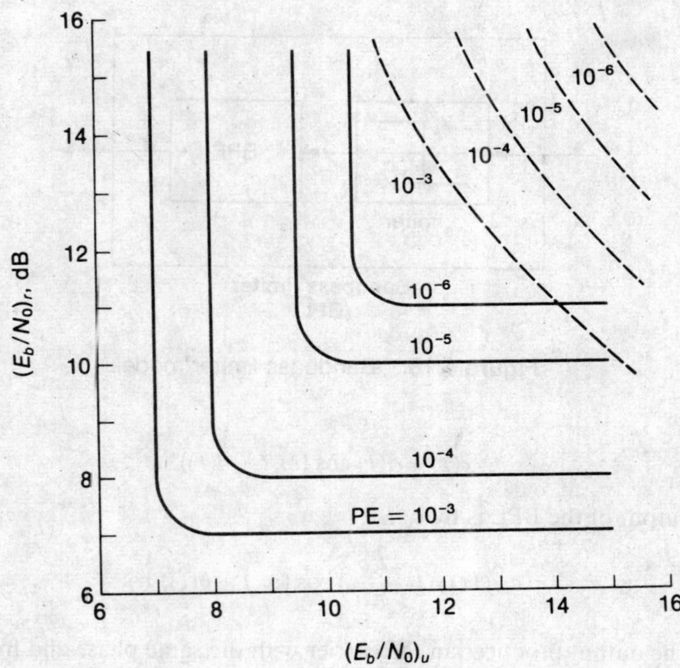

Figure 4.15. Required values of uplink E_b/N_0 and downlink E_b/N_0 to achieve a given PE (—= demod-remod system; ---- = ideal frequency translation).

obtained from Figure 3.22. The result shows clearly the advantage of inserting decoding-encoding hardware at the satellite. Curves of this type are useful for performing initial system design and sizing the hardware for satellite and earth station.

4.5 TRANSPONDER LIMITING

Often transponder signal processing includes hard limiting following frequency conversion. The ideal hard-limiter is a nonlinear gain device having the input-output characteristics shown in Figure 4.16. Hard-limiters are usually followed by bandpass filters tuned to the input carrier frequency, and the combined limiter-filter is referred to as a **bandpass limiter (BPL)**. Let us again write the combined RF carrier and noise at the BPL input as

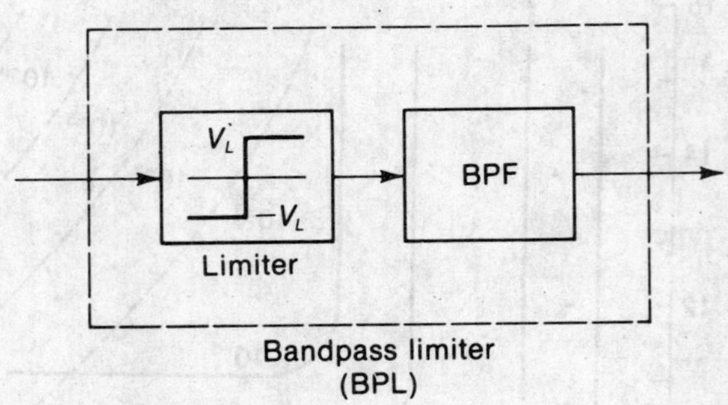

Figure 4.16. Bandpass limiter model.

$$x(t) = \alpha(t) \cos(\omega_c t + \theta(t)) \tag{4.5.1}$$

The output of the BPL is then

$$y(t) = \left(\frac{4V_L}{\pi}\right) \cos(\omega_c t + \theta(t)) \tag{4.5.2}$$

The output produces an RF carrier with the same phase and frequency modulation as the input but with a constant amplitude level. The BPL eliminates amplitude modulation, while preserving angle modulation. It is obvious that transponders with BPL are designed for constant envelope carriers. Note that the power at the output of a bandpass limiter is always given by

$$P_L = \frac{1}{2}\left(\frac{4V_L}{\pi}\right)^2 = \frac{8V_L^2}{\pi^2} \tag{4.5.3}$$

Since the limiter level V_L can be preset, the power of the BPL output can be accurately adjusted. Hence, a BPL serves as a simple power and amplitude control device. They are usually placed in transponders to prevent large amplitude swings and to set power levels for the remaining circuitry.

When the input to the BPL is the sum of an angle-modulated carrier plus additive receiver noise, it is often desirable to know the extent by which the carrier waveform has been preserved in passing through the BPL. This is difficult to determine from (4.5.3), since the limiter output noise is incorporated entirely into the phase noise of the carrier. However, it is shown in Appendix D that the carrier power at the BPL output is given by

$$P_{co} = \left(\frac{2V_L^2}{\pi}\right) \text{CNR}_i e^{-\text{CNR}_i} \left[I_0\left(\frac{\text{CNR}_i}{2}\right) + I_1\left(\frac{\text{CNR}_i}{2}\right) \right]^2 \tag{4.5.4}$$

where $I_0(x)$ and $I_1(x)$ are imaginary Bessel functions of order 0 and 1, respectively, and CNR_i is the input CNR of the BPL,

$$\mathrm{CNR}_i = \frac{P_c}{N_0 B_{\mathrm{RF}}} \tag{4.5.5}$$

Since the total power at the output of the BPL is P_L in (4.5.3), it follows that the noise must constitute the difference. Hence the BPL output noise power is

$$P_{no} = P_L - P_{co} \tag{4.5.6}$$

The resulting bandpass limiter output CNR is then

$$\begin{aligned}\mathrm{CNR}_{\mathrm{BPL}} &= \frac{P_{co}}{P_{no}} \\ &= \frac{P_{co}/P_L}{1-(P_{co}/P_L)}\end{aligned} \tag{4.5.7}$$

From (4.5.4)

$$\frac{P_{co}}{P_L} = \left(\frac{\pi}{4}\right)(\mathrm{CNR}_i)e^{-\mathrm{CNR}_i}\left[I_0\left(\frac{\mathrm{CNR}_i}{2}\right) + I_1\left(\frac{\mathrm{CNR}_i}{2}\right)\right]^2 \tag{4.5.8}$$

A plot of the normalized ratio

$$\Gamma = \frac{\mathrm{CNR}_{\mathrm{BPL}}}{\mathrm{CNR}_i} \tag{4.5.9}$$

is shown in Figure 4.17 as a function of CNR_i. The result shows the way in which the CNR is altered in passing through a BPL. Note that the effect of the BPL is to cause an increase in the CNR if the ratio is large but to cause a slight degradation (by about 2 dB) if the input CNR is low. Whereas pure frequency translation did not alter the CNR, we find that bandpass limiting does. This means that in retransmitting the limiter output by a linear power amplifier, the ground receiver CNR_d in (4.4.6) is instead

$$\begin{aligned}\mathrm{CNR}_d &= \frac{(\Gamma\mathrm{CNR}_u)(\mathrm{CNR}_r)}{\Gamma\mathrm{CNR}_u + \mathrm{CNR}_r} \\ &= [(\Gamma\mathrm{CNR}_u)^{-1} + (\mathrm{CNR}_r)^{-1}]^{-1}\end{aligned} \tag{4.5.10}$$

with Γ dependent on CNR through Figure 4.17. Hence, limiting modifies the effect of uplink CNR on the downlink receiver.

Since the CNR is altered in passing through the limiter, we can inter-

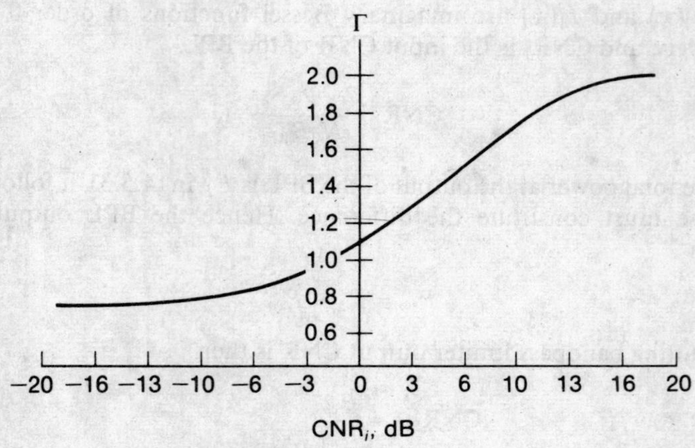

Figure 4.17. Output/Input CNR ratio vs. input CNR for BPL ($\Gamma = \mathrm{CNR_{BL}}/\mathrm{CNR}_i$.

pret limiting as effectively modifying the input carrier and noise powers at the output. Hence we denote α_s^2 and α_n^2 as the limiter carrier and noise *suppression* factors, defined by

$$\begin{aligned} P_{co} &= \alpha_s^2 P_c \\ P_{no} &= \alpha_n^2 (N_0 B_{\mathrm{RF}}) \end{aligned} \tag{4.5.11}$$

Since $\mathrm{CNR_{BL}} = P_{co}/P_{no}$, it follows that

$$\mathrm{CNR_{BL}} = \left(\frac{\alpha_s^2}{\alpha_n^2}\right)\mathrm{CNR} \tag{4.5.12}$$

This therefore defines the suppression factor ratio as

$$\frac{\alpha_s^2}{\alpha_n^2} = \Gamma \tag{4.5.13}$$

Thus Figure 4.17 actually plots the ratio of the carrier and noise factors given in (4.5.11). This means the suppression factors themselves depend on the input CNR$_i$. To determine the individual suppression values, we use (4.5.6) and (4.5.11) to write

$$\alpha_s^2 P_c + \alpha_n^2 (N_0 B_{\mathrm{RF}}) = P_L \tag{4.5.14}$$

Substituting from (4.5.13) and solving for the limiter output carrier power $\alpha_s^2 P_c$ defines the suppression factor as

$$\alpha_s^2 P_c = P_L \left[\frac{\text{CNR}_{\text{BL}}}{1 + \text{CNR}_{\text{BL}}} \right] \tag{4.5.15a}$$

Similarly we obtain the noise suppression factor with

$$\alpha_n^2 (N_0 B_{\text{RF}}) = P_L \left[\frac{1}{1 + \text{CNR}_{\text{BL}}} \right] \tag{4.5.15b}$$

Thus the α_s^2 and α_n^2 power suppression factors in passing through a limiter are such that they divide the available BPL output power P_L in accordance with the ratios in (4.5.15).

An equally important consideration with BPL is the effect of the limiting on the spectrum of the carrier. Let us consider a filtered quadrature carrier as in (4.3.8) at the BPL input,

$$\tilde{c}(t) = A\,\tilde{m}_c(t) \cos(\omega_c t + \psi) + A\,\tilde{m}_s(t) \sin(\omega_c t + \psi) \tag{4.5.16}$$

The output of the BPL is given by (4.5.2) where

$$\theta(t) = \tan^{-1}\left[\frac{\tilde{m}_s(t)}{\tilde{m}_c(t)} \right] \tag{4.5.17}$$

If we write (4.5.2) as a quadrature carrier

$$y(t) = f_c(t) \cos(\omega_c t + \psi) + f_s(t) \sin(\omega_c t + \psi) \tag{4.5.18}$$

it is evident that

$$[f_c^2(t) + f_s^2(t)]^{1/2} = 4V_L/\pi \tag{4.5.19}$$

and

$$\frac{\tilde{m}_s(t)}{\tilde{m}_c(t)} = \frac{f_s(t)}{f_c(t)} \tag{4.5.20}$$

Solution of these equations requires

$$f_c(t) \triangleq \frac{\tilde{m}_c(t)}{[\tilde{m}_c^2(t) + \tilde{m}_s^2(t)]^{1/2}} \tag{4.5.21a}$$

$$f_s(t) = \frac{\tilde{m}_s(t)}{[\tilde{m}_c^2(t) + \tilde{m}_s^2(t)]^{1/2}} \tag{4.5.21b}$$

We see that the BPL has converted the filtered quadrature carrier with components $\tilde{m}_c(t)$ and $\tilde{m}_s(t)$ into the new components in (4.5.21). In particular, the limiting has introduced coupling between the QPSK components, since both $f_c(t)$ and $f_s(t)$ depend on both data bit sequences. For example, in an offset QPSK format, if $\tilde{m}_s(t)$ changes bit sign during a bit time of $m_c(t)$, it is clear that $f_s(t)$ changes bit sign also. However, since $\tilde{m}_s(t)$ passes through zero during the bit change, $f(t)$ in (4.5.21a) must undergo a temporary transition to the value 1 during the bit change. Hence $f(t)$ develops blips in its waveform at the transitions of the quadrature bit changes, that is, during the middle of its own bit patterns (Figure 4.18). In QPSK, bit changes occur simultaneously when they occur, and the blips are effectively superimposed on each bit transition. We see that hard limiting has caused independent bit changes in the quadrature channels to be effectively coupled into other channels as waveform perturbations. These perturbations tend to increase the bandwidth of the limited carrier.

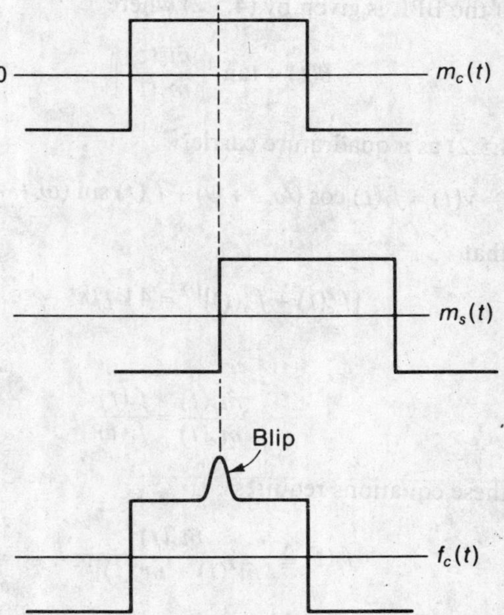

Figure 4.18. Blip development in QPSK with limiting.

The spectrum of the limited carrier $y(t)$ in (4.5.18) can be computed as in (4.3.2). This leads to

$$S_y(\omega) = \frac{1}{T}[\,|F_c(\omega)|^2 + |F_s(\omega)|^2]_{\omega \pm \omega_c} \tag{4.5.22}$$

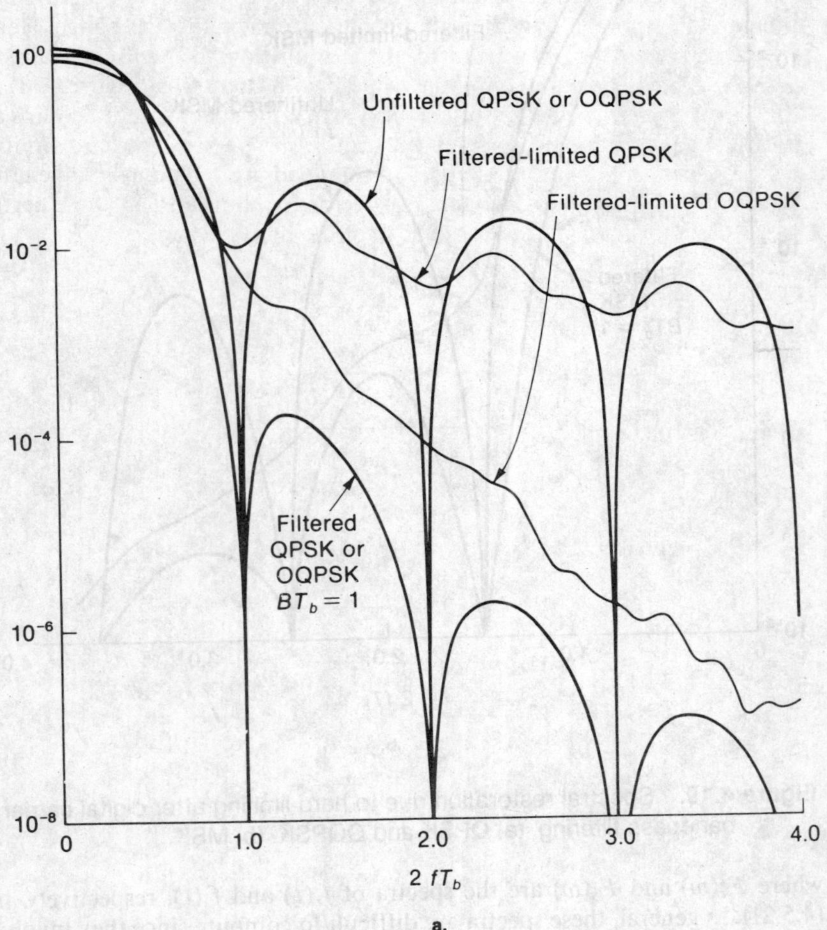

Figure 4.19. Spectral restoration due to hard limiting after digital carrier bandpass filtering. (a) QPSK and OQPSK. (b) MSK.

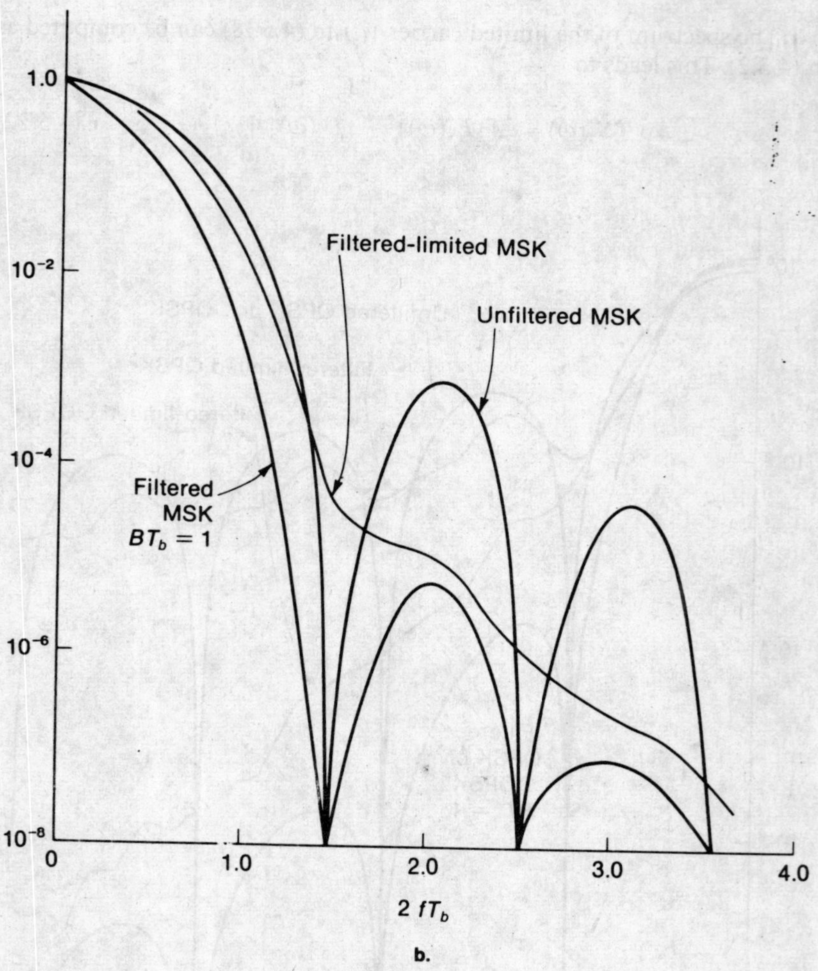

Figure 4.19. Spectral restoration due to hard limiting after digital carrier bandpass filtering. (a) QPSK and OQPSK. (b) MSK.

where $F_c(\omega)$ and $F_s(\omega)$ are the spectra of $f_c(t)$ and $f_s(t)$, respectively, in (4.5.21). In general, these spectra are difficult to compute since they involve ratios of time functions and two different data sequences, and are usually evaluated by simulation or numerical transform techniques. Figure 4.19 shows published [11] spectral results indicating the effect of hard limiting on the filtered forms of QPSK, OQPSK, and MSK carrier waveforms. We see that while filtering successfully reduces the spreading of the tails (as we discussed in Section 4.3), the hard limiting tends to restore the tails to prefiltered values. The result is that the limited carrier in the transponder may no longer satisfy spectral masks for which the filtered carrier was designed.

From Figure 4.19 we see that standard QPSK has the higher degree of tail restoration, while offsetting tends to reduce the amount of this regeneration, as exhibited by the OQPSK and MSK systems. This can possibly be attributed to the fact that filtered offset carriers, such as MSK, tend to retain a more constant envelope [the denominators in (4.5.21) are nearly constant] so that $f_c(t)$ and $f_s(t)$ are simply scaled versions of the corresponding prelimited components. In this case the hard-limited carrier retains the spectra of the filtered offset carrier in spite of the limiting. The reduced tail regeneration of offset carriers has been found to occur also in other types of bit waveforms, such as raised cosine pulses [12, 13].

Note that MSK, which has a slightly wider main hump spectrum than QPSK (see Figure 2.14), may often be filtered to reduce this main lobe in attempting to satisfy a satellite mask. We see from Figure 4.19 that while limiting only partly restores the tails, it restores almost fully the mainlobe. This may now violate the required mask, even though the tail reduction may be satisfactory.

4.6 NONLINEAR SATELLITE AMPLIFIERS

The traveling wave tube amplifier (TWTA) is the commonly used power amplifier for satellites. TWTAs achieve their power gain by using the input microwave carrier to phase-control resonant waves in a cavity so as to produce wave reinforcement. An output from the resonant cavity or tube, then, is an amplified, phase replica of the input carrier. Such mechanisms achieve the significantly large power gains needed for the satellite transponder links. Since TWTAs amplify phase-modulated carriers, they are intended primarily for constant amplitude carriers. Variations in input carrier amplitudes during amplification produce an additional unintentional phase modulation that appears as phase interference on the amplified carrier. This effect will be examined later in the section.

For constant amplitude input carriers there is a direct gain conversion to the output amplitude. As the amplitude of the input carrier is increased, the output amplitude is also increased until a saturation effect occurs within the cavity. This is exhibited by the input-output power curve of the TWTA, which is typically of the form shown in Figure 4.20a. As the input power is increased, a direct linear gain occurs in output power until the output power

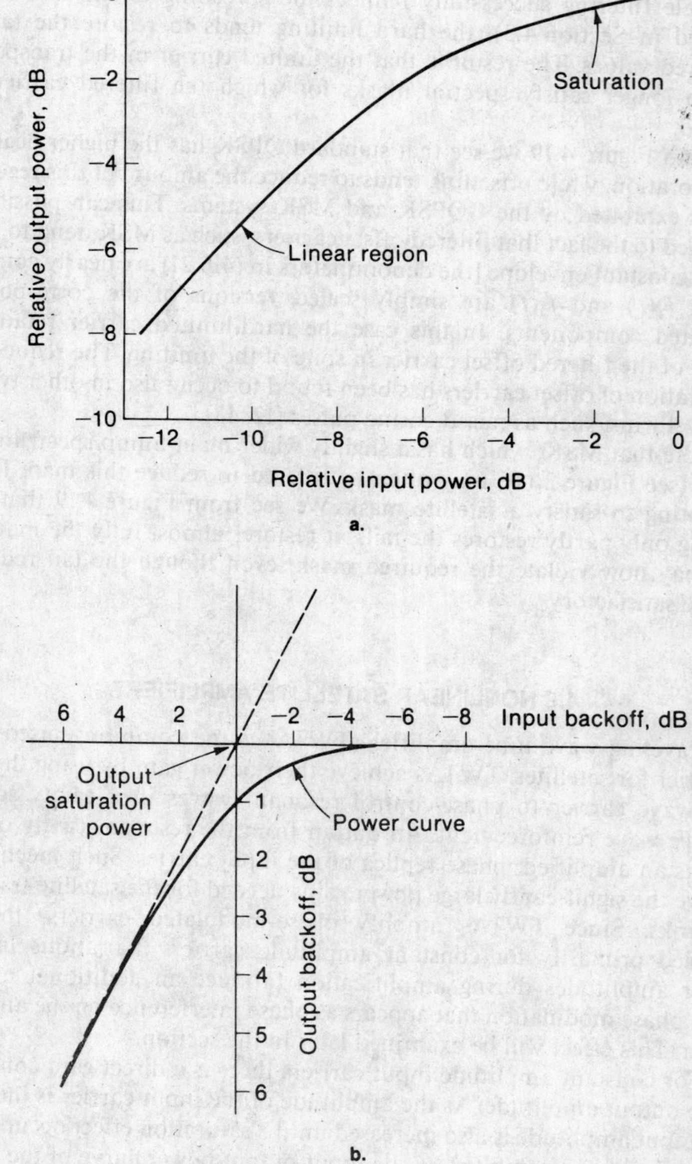

Figure 4.20. TWTA power-gain characteristic. (a) Normalized power. (b) Standardized for backoff definitions.

saturates, as shown, and further increase in input power no longer produces larger outputs. Achievement of this maximum output power is therefore accompanied by a nonlinear amplification within the amplifier as the saturation condition is approached. When only a single input carrier is involved, this saturation causes no carrier distortion, but only a limitation to its output power. When the TWTA input corresponds to multiple carriers, however, as in an FDMA format, this nonlinearity of the saturation effect becomes extremely important, as will be discussed in Chapter 5.

The drive power at which the output power saturation occurs is called the **input saturation power**. The ratio of input saturation power to desired drive power is called the amplifier **input backoff**. Increasing input backoff (decreasing input drive power) produces less output power but improves the linearity of the device, since the degree of nonlinearity is reduced. The **output saturation power** of the amplifier is the maximum total power available from the amplifier. **Output backoff** is the ratio of the maximum output (saturation) power to actual output power. Output backoff obviously depends on input backoff, that is, where the drive power is operated. Increasing input backoff lowers the output power and increases the output backoff.

Since the actual input power at which saturation occurs may be difficult to specify exactly, backoff definitions are sometimes defined relative to a standardized power curve as shown in Figure 4.20b. The 0 dB value of input backoff is specified at the point where the output power is 1 dB below saturation. This means that full output saturation will often occur at a negative dB value of input backoff.

Proper input control of the operating drive power of an amplifier is important in TWTA operation. Power control for the TWTA is often obtained by a BPL–amplifier combination, similar to that shown in Figure 4.21. Since the limiter produces fixed-output power levels, proper gain

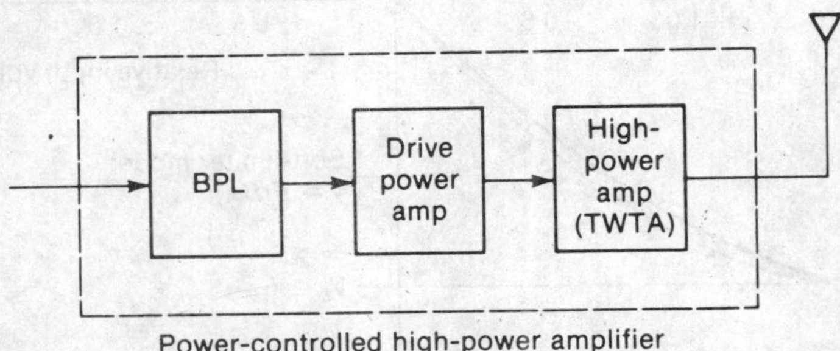

Figure 4.21. Power-controlled TWTA subsystem.

adjustment of the drive amplifier can carefully set the TWTA input to desired input backoff. This backoff setting can be extremely critical in satellite operation for achieving satisfactory downlink performance.

AM/AM Conversion

For constant amplitude carriers, carrier power is simply one-half the square of the amplitude. Hence, a TWTA power curve can be simply square-rooted to obtain the corresponding input-output amplitude curve. Figure 4.22 shows amplitude characteristics corresponding to TWTA power curves. This amplitude curve is often called the **AM/AM conversion** characteristics of the TWTA. When the input backoff is high, operation occurs on the linear part of the amplitude characteristic. For less backoff, the TWTA operation enters into the nonlinear region. For strong input drive powers, the amplifier is almost always in the saturated region, and the AM/AM conversion can be considered to have a hard-limiter characteristic, as shown. For intermediate operation, the characteristic is referred to as a **soft-limiter**

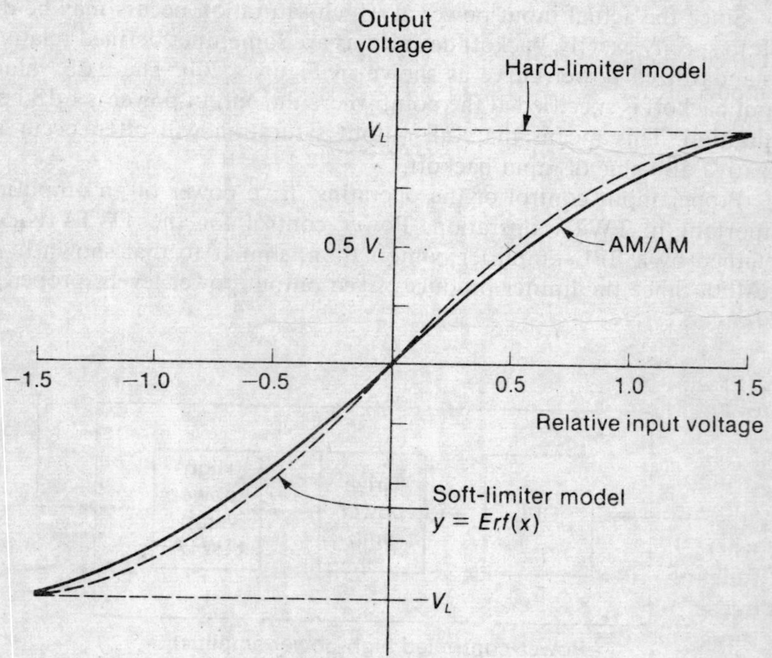

Figure 4.22. AM/AM conversion characteristics of TWTA.

curve, which accounts for the conversion between linear and hard-limiting operation.

Several mathematical forms for the TWTA AM/AM curve have been proposed. The most convenient is

$$\begin{aligned} g(\alpha) &= V_L \operatorname{Erf}\left(\frac{\alpha}{b}\right) \qquad \alpha \geqslant 0 \\ &= -V_L \operatorname{Erf}\left(\frac{|\alpha|}{b}\right) \qquad \alpha \leqslant 0 \end{aligned} \tag{4.6.1}$$

where α is the input carrier amplitude and $\operatorname{Erf}(x)$ is the function

$$\operatorname{Erf}(x) = \frac{2}{\sqrt{\pi}} \int_0^x e^{-u^2} du \tag{4.6.2}$$

The parameter b defines the input saturation voltage, and the corresponding input saturation power is then $b^2/2$. The input backoff is then

$$\beta_i = \frac{b^2/2}{\alpha^2/2} = \left(\frac{b}{\alpha}\right)^2 \tag{4.6.3}$$

Other functional models for AM/AM conversion have been suggested for modeling tunnel diode amplifiers that tend to be more nonlinear then TWTA. An example is [12, 14]:

$$\log_{10} g(\alpha) = \begin{cases} 0.39\left[\cos\left(1.9 \log_{10}\left(\dfrac{\alpha}{0.35}\right)\right) - 1\right] & \alpha > 0.35 \\ \log_{10} \alpha & \alpha \leqslant 0.35 \end{cases} \tag{4.6.4}$$

Athough more accurate in representing TDA AM/AM conversion, these functions tend to be analytically unwieldy.

Analysis of the nonlinear gain in (4.6.1) is carried out in detail in Appendix D. The amplifier output carrier power, when the input is a carrier of amplitude A_1, is shown to be

$$P_T = P_{sat} \int_0^\infty z^{-1} J_1(Az) e^{-b^2 z^2/2} dz \tag{4.6.5}$$

where P_{sat} is the output saturation power and $J_1(x)$ is the first-order Bessel function. Increasing input backoff (reducing A relative to b) reduces the output power since the amplifier is operated further from saturation. This can be seen by writing (4.6.5) in terms of β_i in (4.6.3) as

$$P_T = P_{sat} \int_0^\infty u^{-1} J_1(u) e^{-\beta_i^2 u^2/2} du \tag{4.6.6}$$

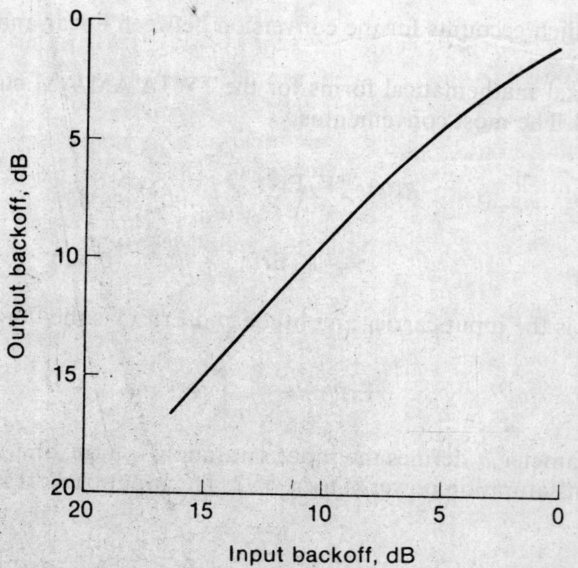

Figure 4.23. Output backoff vs. input backoff for Erf(x) soft-limiting characteristics.

The output backoff is then

$$\beta_o = \frac{P_{\text{sat}}}{P_T} \tag{4.6.7}$$

Equation (4.6.7) is plotted in Figure 4.23 in terms of input backoff β_i for a single carrier input. This figure demonstrates how increasing input backoff to improve satellite linearity also reduces the available downlink carrier power for satellite retransmission.

AM/PM Conversion

TWTAs are designed to operate with constant-amplitude input carriers to achieve cavity gain. Variations in input amplitude produce an unintentional phase modulation on the amplified carrier, referred to as **AM/PM conversion**. AM/PM conversion is a form of carrier distortion in which envelope variations on the total multiple-carrier waveform being amplified are converted into phase variations on each individual carrier. These phase variations appear as additive waveform interference in angle-modulated carriers.

Although the possibility of this conversion exists theoretically in any nonlinear device, its presence in cavity amplifiers is physically caused by the amplification mechanism of the cavity device itself. Envelope variations on the cavity field being amplified cause a variable retardation on the field in the cavity. This time-varying retardation appears as a phase delay variation, or a phase modulation—in synchronism with the envelope variations—on the cavity field. The resulting amplifier output waveform then has an additive phase modulation proportional to the envelope variation.

When the envelope variations are due to thermal noise, the additive phase variation appears as added random phase noise interference. When the envelope variation is due to baseband modulation (either intentional or not), the AM/PM of the nonlinear power amplifier may cause the modulated information to be coupled into the carrier as a form of intelligible crosstalk.

To examine AM/PM conversion analytically, again consider the amplifier input to be the general carrier waveform

$$x(t) = (A + \Delta(t)) \cos (\omega_c t + \theta(t)) \tag{4.6.8}$$

where $\Delta(t)$ represents amplitude variations around a fixed level A. AM/PM conversion of the amplifier causes the amplifier output carrier to have phase

$$\Omega(t) = \omega_c t + \theta(t) + \Phi(\Delta(t)) \tag{4.6.9}$$

where $\Phi(\Delta)$ is called the AM/PM conversion function. A typical plot of $\Phi(\Delta)$ is shown in Figure 4.24a, showing the manner in which the phase is coupled in. The actual form of this function depends on the particular characteristics of the amplifier tube itself. An accurate mathematical model for $\Phi(\Delta)$ is

$$\Phi(\Delta) = k_1[1 - e^{-k_2\Delta^2}] + k_3\Delta^2 \tag{4.6.10}$$

where the constants are selected for best overall fit to the true characteristic [12, 14].

A simpler model, valid for small levels of input amplitude variation, is to assume $\Phi(\Delta)$ is linear with respect to amplitude variations around the selected bias amplitude A in (4.6.8). We can then write

$$\Phi(\Delta(t)) = \eta\Delta(t) \tag{4.6.11}$$

The coefficient η is often called the **AM/PM conversion coefficient** of the amplifier. Its value depends on the degree of nonlinearity of the amplifier operation, which in turn depends on the input backoff through the amplitude A in (4.6.11). Figure 4.24b shows a plot of measured values of η vs.

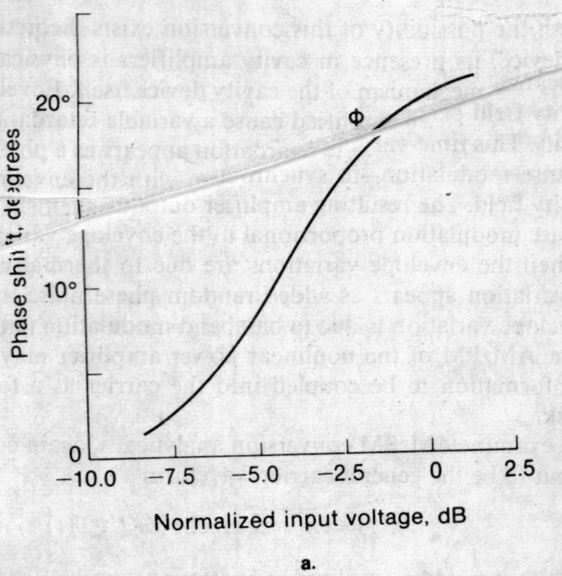

a.

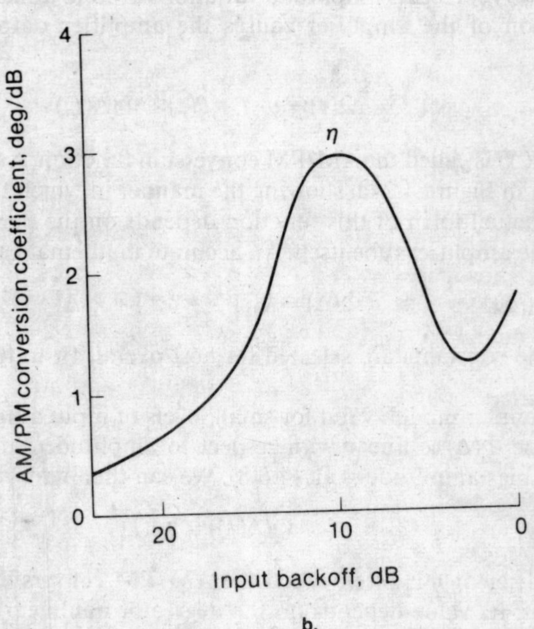

b.

Figure 4.24. AM/PM phase conversion function. (a) $\Phi(\Delta)$ (b) η coefficient vs. input backoff.

input backoff. When receiver noise is added to the uplink carrier, as in (4.2.10), and the envelope is written as in (4.2.12), we can see from (4.6.9) that an additional phase noise is coupled into the downlink carrier by the amplifier nonlinearity. Thus AM/PM noise is due to the uplink in-phase noise, and produces a phase noise of power $\eta^2 P_{nu}$, where P_{nu} is the satellite uplink noise power.

Nonlinear Amplifier Model

The combined AM/AM and AM/PM phenomena of the TWTA allow us to formulate a somewhat general nonlinear power amplifier model. If the input is again written as the general RF bandpass waveform

$$\begin{aligned} x(t) &= \alpha(t)\cos(\omega_{\mathrm{RF}}t + \theta(t) + \psi) \\ \alpha(t) &= A + \Delta(t) \end{aligned} \tag{4.6.12}$$

the output amplified carrier in the same band is then

$$\begin{aligned} y(t) &= g(\alpha(t))\cos(\omega_{\mathrm{RF}}t + \theta(t) + \phi(\alpha(t)) \\ \phi(\alpha(t)) &\triangleq \Phi(\alpha(t) - A) \end{aligned} \tag{4.6.13}$$

where again g and Φ are the AM/AM and AM/PM conversion functions. We now note that (4.6.13) is equivalent to

$$y(t) = \mathrm{Real}\{g(\alpha(t))e^{j\phi(\alpha(t))}e^{j\omega_{\mathrm{RF}}t + j\theta(t)}\} \tag{4.6.14}$$

Hence, the nonlinear amplifier can be represented by the complex gain, which effectively multiplies the complex input carrier to produce the output carrier, as shown in Figure 4.25a. Thus, AM/AM and AM/PM effects in power amplifiers convert the ideal gain (gain = constant) model to a complex gain model with amplitudes and phase dependent on the conversion effects.

The model extends to cascaded nonlinear amplifiers (Figure 4.25b). If the amplifiers have conversion functions $[g_1(\alpha), \phi_1(\alpha)]$ and $[g_2(\alpha), \phi_2(\alpha)]$, respectively, the overall AM/AM and AM/PM becomes

$$g(\alpha) = g_2(g_1(\alpha)) \tag{4.6.15a}$$

$$\phi(\alpha) = \phi_2(g_1(\alpha)) + \phi_1(\alpha) \tag{4.6.15b}$$

This model applies if a bandpass nonlinearity or a nonlinear amplifier precedes the TWTA. Note that if $\alpha(t) = V$ (the carrier waveform has been hard-limited prior to the TWTA), then the output also has a constant

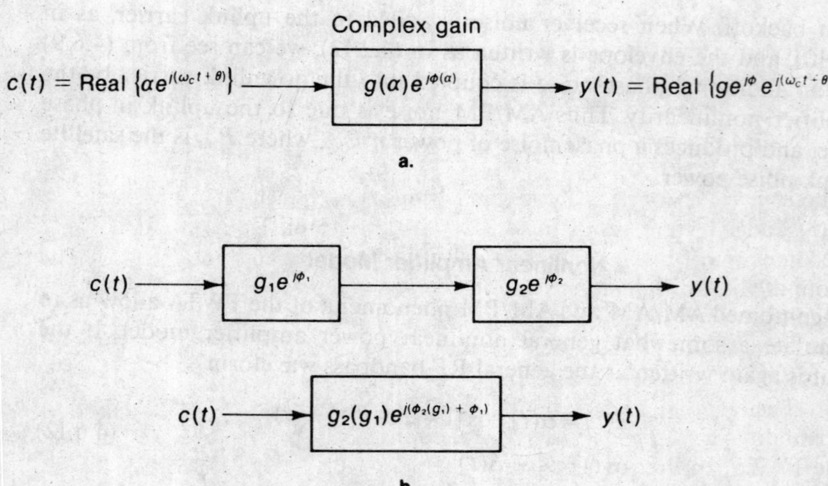

Figure 4.25. Nonlinear amplifier model. (a) Single nonlinearity. (b) Cascaded nonlinearities.

envelope, whether it is driven into saturation or not, and the AM/PM effect disappears. This shows why, when a single carrier is to be amplified in the transponder, it is advantageous to hard-limit immediately preceding TWTA amplification and to amplify into saturation for maximum power output. When multiple carriers are involved, however, the design procedure may be significantly different. Note also that the cascade of a BPL and a TWTA can always be replaced by a single BPL, with limiting level adjusted to the TWTA output amplitude, and no AM/PM effect. We point out that if a separate drive amplifier is inserted between the BPL and TWTA, the TWTA input is no longer constant envelope due to the insertion of drive amplifier noise. The TWTA must then be analyzed instead as the nonlinear amplification of a nonconstant carrier passing through the model in Figure 4.25.

The nonlinear TWTA operation also means that the spectral spreading of the limiting on filtered carriers may be present in the amplified carriers as well. Hence spectral tails removed by RF filtering, either at the earth-station transmitter or the transponder front end, may be restored for the downlink transmission after TWTA transponding. If the transponder contains a BPL followed by the TWTA, the spectral spreading is identical to that in Figure 4.19. If no limiting is involved, and the TWTA is backed-off, the amplifier, or the cascade of amplifiers, must be treated as a soft-limiter with an AM/AM characteristic $g(\alpha)$. The effect is to modify the hard-limited quadrature carrier in (4.5.18) to

$$\begin{aligned} c(t) = g[(\tilde{m}_c^2(t) + \tilde{m}_s^2(t))^{1/2}]\{f_c(t)\cos(\omega_c t + \psi) \\ + f_s(t)\sin(\omega_c t + \psi)\} \end{aligned} \tag{4.6.16}$$

where $\tilde{m}_c(t)$ and $\tilde{m}_s(t)$ are the soft-limiter filtered input components, and $f_c(t)$ and $f_s(t)$ are given in (4.5.21). As the amplifier is backed off, $g(\alpha)$ becomes more linear, and the quadrature components in (4.6.16) convert from the hard-limited components $f(t)$ to the filtered components $\tilde{m}(t)$. The degree of spectral regeneration in satellite downlink carriers is often important, and should be accurately accounted for in system design where spectral tails are of significant interest.

The fact that cascaded nonlinearities combine as in (4.6.15) suggests the possibility of purposely inserting a nonlinearity to compensate for that of the TWTA. In this way, the suppression and intermodulation effects of the amplifier alone will not occur in the cascaded combination, thereby serving as a practical means to combat the TWT nonlinearity. This procedure involves the insertion of a nonlinear device, placed either before or after the TWTA, so that the overall combination has a linear gain and no significant AM/PM effects. This requires that in (4.6.15) we have

$$\begin{aligned} g_2(g_1(\alpha)) &= k\alpha \\ \phi_2(g_1(\alpha)) &= -\phi_1(\alpha) + \psi \end{aligned} \tag{4.6.17}$$

where k and ψ are an arbitrary gain and phase angle, respectively. The difficulty is in producing the exact compensating nonlinearity, which in itself must have inherent AM/PM conversion [see Problem 4.8].

4.7 EFFECT OF NONLINEAR AMPLIFICATION ON DIGITAL CARRIERS

Nonlinear operation of the TWTA during satellite transponding of a digital carrier must be accounted for in the eventual ground decoding. Consider the simplified nonlinear satellite model in Figure 4.26. We write the uplink carrier in the general quadrature form

$$c_u(t) = A_u m_c(t)\cos(\omega_u t + \psi) + A_u m_s(t)\sin(\omega_u t + \psi) \tag{4.7.1}$$

In the presence of additive uplink noise, the combined carrier at the amplifier input is

$$\begin{aligned} x(t) &= c_u(t) + n_u(t) \\ &= \alpha_1(t)\cos(\omega_u t + \theta(t) + \psi + v_1(t)) \end{aligned} \tag{4.7.2}$$

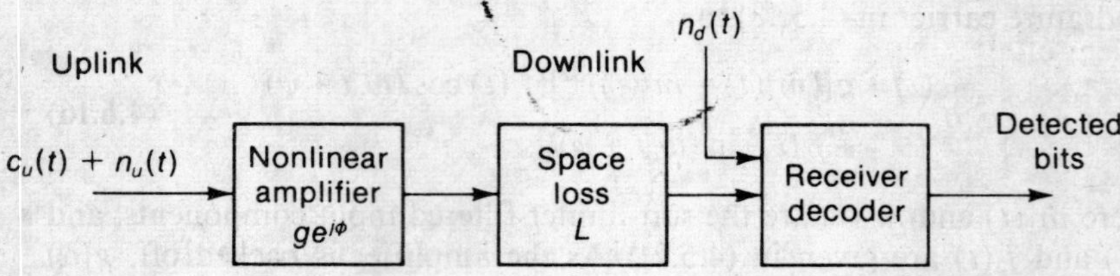

Figure 4.26. Nonlinear up-down link model.

where $\cos\theta(t) = m_c(t)$, $\sin\theta(t) = m_s(t)$, and $\alpha_1(t)$ and $v_1(t)$ are the uplink amplitude and phase-noise waveforms at the amplifier input. After nonlinear amplification, using the model of the Figure 4.26, and retransmission, we obtain the downlink received signal

$$y(t) = Lg(\alpha_1(t))\cos(\omega_d t + \theta(t) + \psi + v_1(t) + \phi(\alpha_1(t))) + n_d(t) \tag{4.7.3}$$

where $n_d(t)$ is the added downlink noise. Expanding out the first term, and using the quadrature noise expansion for the downlink noise, produces

$$\begin{aligned} z(t) = Lg(\alpha_1(t))[&\cos\theta\cos(\omega_d t + v_1 + \phi(\alpha_1) + \psi) \\ &- \sin\theta\sin(\omega_d t + v_1 + \phi(\alpha_1) + \psi)] \\ &+ n_{dc}(t)\cos(\omega_d t + \psi) - n_{ds}(t)\sin(\omega_d t + \psi) \end{aligned} \tag{4.7.4}$$

Further expansion yields

$$\begin{aligned} z(t) = {}&[F_c(t)m_c(t) + F_s(t)m_s(t) + n_{dc}(t)]\cos(\omega_d t + \psi) \\ &- [F_c(t)m_s(t) + F_s(t)m_c(t) + n_{ds}(t)]\sin(\omega_d t + \psi) \end{aligned} \tag{4.7.5}$$

where

$$F_c(t) = Lg(\alpha_1(t))\cos[v_1(t) + \phi(\alpha_1(t))] \tag{4.7.6a}$$

$$F_s(t) = Lg(\alpha_1(t))\sin[v_1(t) + \phi(\alpha_1(t))] \tag{4.7.6b}$$

We see that the effect of the nonlinear amplification with complex gain $g(\alpha)\exp(j\phi(\alpha))$ is to cause both distortion and interference in each quadrature component. For example, in the cosine component, the data waveform $m_c(t)$ is multipled by the distortion term $F_c(t)$, while the quadrature data $m_s(t)$ is coupled in through $F_s(t)$. A similar result holds for the sine component. The waveforms $F_c(t)$ and $F_s(t)$ are each random waveforms, dependent on the uplink amplitude and phase noise, and on the AM/AM and AM/PM conversion of the TWTA.

The operation of the quadrature decoder (see Appendix A, Section A.3) is to produce the decoder components

$$I(t) = F_c(t)m_c(t) + F_s(t)m_s(t) + n_{dc}(t) \tag{4.7.7a}$$

$$Q(t) = F_c(t)m_s(t) + F_s(t)m_c(t) + n_{ds}(t) \tag{4.7.7b}$$

These are used for decoding each bit stream separately. The effect on performance by the nonlinearity depends on the modulation format ($m_c(t)$ and $m_s(t)$), the type of decoding (sample or match filter), and the form of the nonlinearity.

For BPSK ($m_s(t) = 0$, $m_c(t) = \pm 1$) with bit time T_b and sample decoding, the bit-error probability follows as

$$\mathrm{PE} = \mathcal{E}_{\alpha_1, v_1}\left[Q\left(\frac{Lg(\alpha_1)\cos(v_1 + \phi(\alpha_1))}{\sqrt{N_{0d}/T_b}}\right)\right] \tag{4.7.8}$$

where N_{0d} is the receiver decoder noise level, and the average is taken over the random variables $\alpha_1(t)$ and $v_1(t)$ at the bit sampling time. These amplitude and phase variables at any t of a noisy carrier are known to have the joint probability density

$$p(\alpha, v) = \frac{\alpha}{2\pi\sqrt{P_{nu}}} \exp -\left[\frac{\alpha^2 + A_u^2 - 2\alpha A_u \cos v}{2P_{nu}}\right] \tag{4.7.9}$$

where P_{nu} is the uplink noise power and A_u is the uplink carrier amplitude. Hence, (4.7.8) is

$$\mathrm{PE} = \int_0^{\infty}\int_0^{2\pi} Q\left(\frac{Lg(\alpha)\cos[v + \phi(\alpha)]}{\sqrt{2N_{0d}/T_b}}\right) P(\alpha, v)\,dv\,d\alpha \tag{4.7.10}$$

In general, evaluation of (4.7.10) requires simulation or numerical techniques. Some simulation results were reported in [15]. For the special case of a hard-limiter, $g(\alpha) = \sqrt{P_T}$, $\phi(\alpha) = 0$, and (4.7.10) evaluates [see details in Appendix A, Section A.9] to the somewhat complicated form:

$$\mathrm{PE} = \frac{1}{2} - \frac{1}{\pi}\sum_{k=0}^{\infty}(-1)^k\left[\frac{\Gamma(k+\frac{1}{2})\Gamma(k+\frac{3}{2})}{[(2k+1)!]^2}\right]\rho_1^{2k+1}\rho_2^{2k+1} \cdot {}_1F_1\left(k+\frac{1}{2}, 2k+2, -\rho_1^2\right){}_1F_1\left(k+\frac{1}{2}, 2k+2, -\rho_2^2\right) \tag{4.7.11}$$

where $\Gamma(x)$ is the Gamma Function, ${}_1F_1$ is the confluent hypergeometric series [16], and

$$\rho_1^2 = \frac{A_u^2/2}{P_{nu}} = \left(\frac{E_b}{N_0}\right)_u \quad \rho_2^2 = \frac{LP_T}{N_{0d}/T_b} = \left(\frac{E_b}{N_0}\right)_r \tag{4.7.12}$$

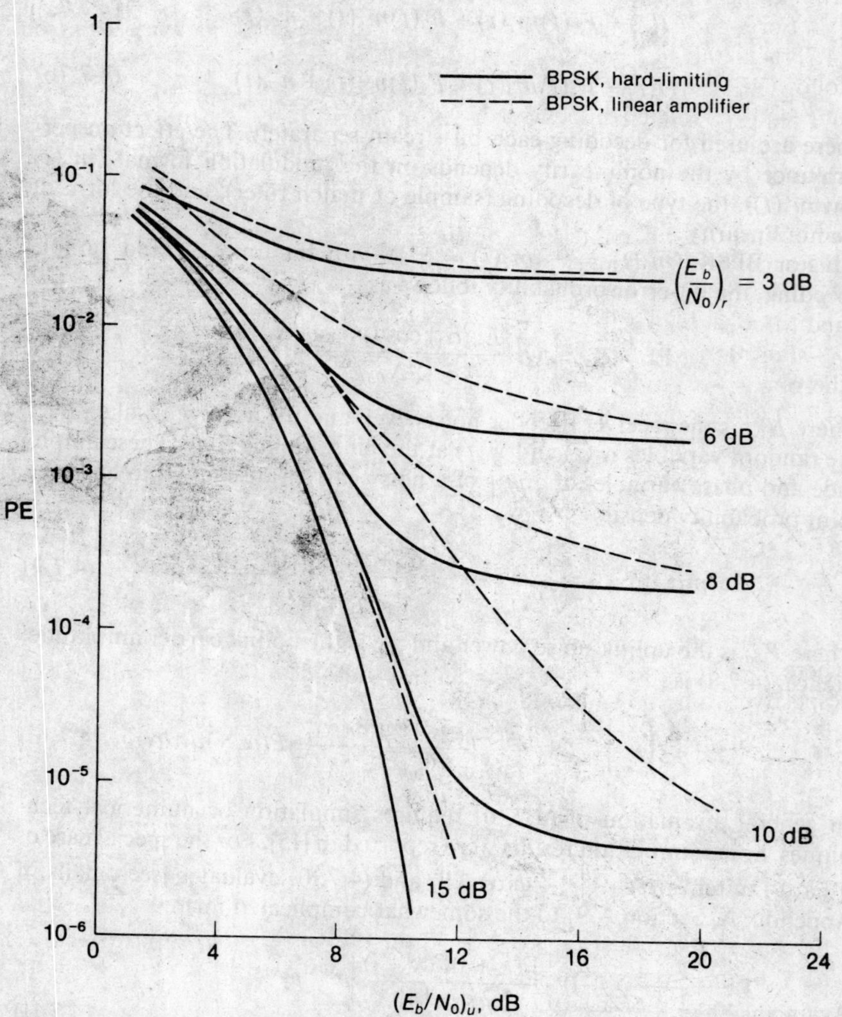

Figure 4.27. BPSK PE vs. uplink and downlink E_b/N_0 for hard-limiting and linear satellite channel.

Note that ρ_1 and ρ_2 correspond to the uplink (amplifier input) and downlink (decoder input) CNR, respectively. Equation (4.7.11) is plotted in Figure 4.27, showing the BPSK PE as a function of ρ_1^2 and ρ_2^2. Also shown is the PE for a linear amplifier [Equation (3.6.12)] for the same ρ_1 and ρ_2. Note that the hard-limited performance for BPSK is not significantly different from a linear amplifier with the same power levels.

For quadrature modulation ($m_s(t) \neq 0$) we must evaluate PE from (4.7.5), taking into account the interference term. However, we note the following: If MSK is used with sample decoding, and if the sample is taken in each decoding channel at the peak of the in-phase bit, then the quadrature data bit is passing through zero. This means the coupling term is zero in spite of the nonlinearity, and the PE is identical to (4.7.11). Hence, MSK with bit-sampling decoding performs identically the same as BPSK for the same nonlinear channel. For QPSK and OQPSK the quadrature term introduces interference that cannot be eliminated by choice of bit-sampling time. We therefore expect QPSK and OQPSK to perform more poorly than BPSK and MSK with nonlinear transponders.

For the case of QPSK we note that $m_s(t)$ will have either the same or the opposite bit sign as $m_c(t)$. This means that at sampling time *I(t)* in (4.7.7) will be either

$$I = F_c + F_s + n_{dc} \tag{4.7.13}$$

or

$$I = F_c - F_s + n_{dc}$$

where F_c, F_s, and n_{dc} are the sample values of $F_c(t)$, $F_s(t)$, and $n_{dc}(t)$, respectively. The bit-error probability on either quadrature channel is then

$$\text{PE} = \mathscr{E}_{\alpha_1, v_1}\left\{\frac{1}{2}Q\left(\frac{Lg(\alpha)\sin(v_1 + \phi(\alpha) + \pi/4)}{\sqrt{2N_{0d}/T_b}}\right)\right. \tag{4.7.14}$$
$$\left. + \frac{1}{2}Q\left(\frac{Lg(\alpha)\sin(\pi - v_1 - \phi(\alpha))}{\sqrt{2P_{0d}/T_b}}\right)\right\}$$

Again, evaluation requires numerical integration to complete the averaging. For the case of a hard-limiter, (4.7.14) evaluates in a similar way to (4.7.11), producing instead

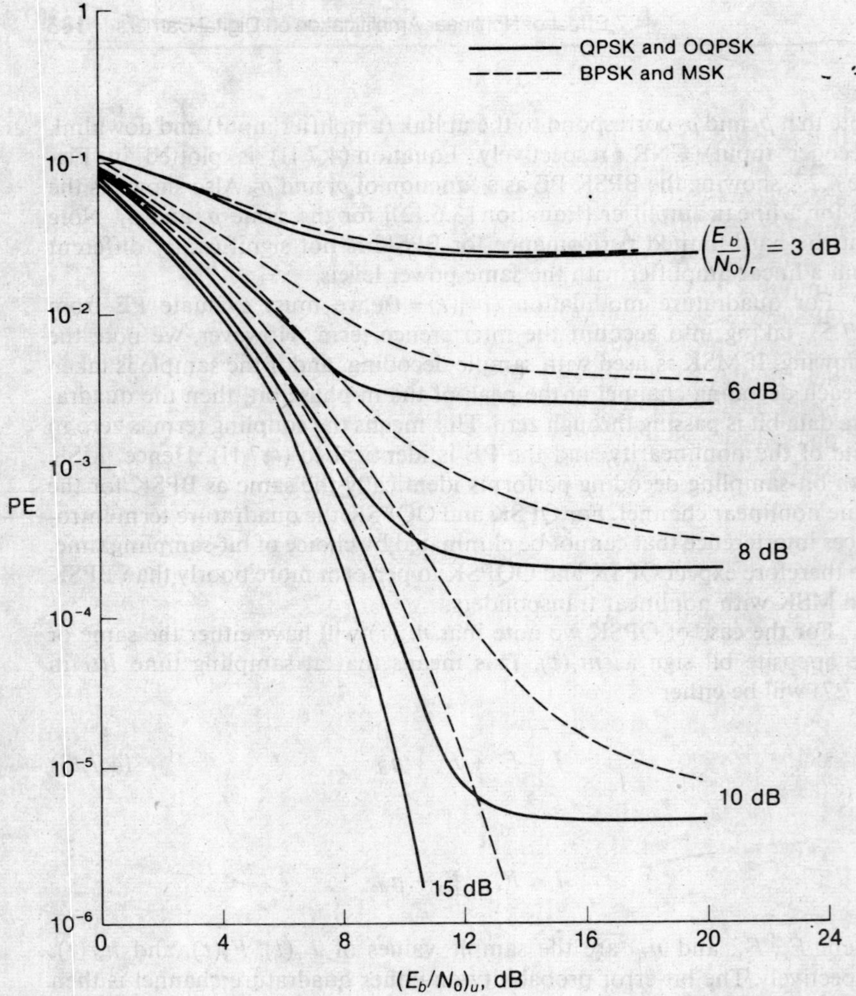

Figure 4.28. BPSK, QPSK, and MSK PE for hard-limiting satellite channel.

$$\text{PE} = \frac{1}{2} - \frac{1}{\pi}\sum_{k=0}^{\prime}(-1)^k\left[\frac{\Gamma(k+\frac{1}{2})\Gamma(k+\frac{3}{2})}{[(2k+1)!]^2}\right](\rho_1\rho_2)^{2k+1} \tag{4.7.15}$$

$$\cdot {}_1F_1(k+1, 2k+2, -\rho_1^2)\,{}_1F_1\left(k+\frac{1}{2}, 2k+1, -\rho_2^2\right)\cos\left(\frac{(2k+1)\pi}{4}\right)$$

with ρ_1^2 and ρ_2^2 given in (4.7.13). Equation (4.7.15) is plotted in Figure 4.28. Also included is the previous result for BPSK from Figure 4.27. It is evident that satellite hard limiting is more destructive to QPSK than to BPSK. This can be directly attributable to the fact that the quadrature channel interference occurs with QPSK, but is not present with BPSK or with MSK using mid-bit sampling. OQPSK also has transitions at mid-bit times, but the rectangular form of the bits produces an interference similar to (4.7.13) at sampling times. Hence OQPSK should perform identically the same as QPSK with hard-limiting satellite amplifiers.

Error probabilities for MPSK systems with nonlinear amplifiers can be determined by similar analysis. Since we encode information onto the phase angles of the uplink carrier, decoding is achieved by detecting these phase angles on the downlink receiver carrier. If the uplink carrier is written as in (4.7.2), the nonlinear amplified carrier has the phase angle

$$\Omega(t) = \omega_c t + \theta + \psi(t) \tag{4.7.16}$$

where θ is the uplink phase modulation (a multiple of $2\pi/M$ radians) and ψ is the combined random-phase error due to both uplink and downlink noise and AM/PM conversion. Hence

$$\psi(t) = v_u(t) + v_d(t) + \phi(\alpha_u(t)) \tag{4.7.17}$$

Phase decoding is achieved by determining which of the M phases of θ is being received during each block time. An error will occur if ψ in (4.7.16) (assumed to be constant during each block time) causes the received phase to differ by more than $\pm 2\pi/2M$ radians from the transmitted θ. Hence the probability of an MPSK word error is

$$\text{PWE} = 1 - \int_{-\pi/M}^{\pi/M} p(\psi)\,d\psi \tag{4.7.18}$$

where $p(\psi)$ is the probability density of ψ in (4.7.17) at any t. Since v_d is a sample of phase noise, its density is obtained from a joint density similar to (4.7.9), conditioned on v_u and α_u, by integrating out the amplitude variable. The density $p(\psi)$ then follows by averaging out v_u and α_u, again using the uplink joint density in (4.7.9). Results of this computation have been carried out [15] for a general AM/PM conversion $\phi(\alpha)$.

For the case of a hard-limiting amplifier, (4.7.18) evaluates for any M to

$$\text{PWE} = \frac{M-1}{M} - \frac{2}{\pi}\sum_{k=0}^{\infty} \frac{\sin\left(\frac{k\pi}{M}\right)}{k}\left[\frac{\Gamma\left(\frac{k}{2}+1\right)}{\Gamma(k+1)}\right]^2 (\rho_1\rho_2)^k \cdot {}_1F_1\left(\frac{k}{2}, k+1, -\rho_1^2\right){}_1F_1\left(\frac{k}{2}, k+1, -\rho_2^2\right) \tag{4.7.19}$$

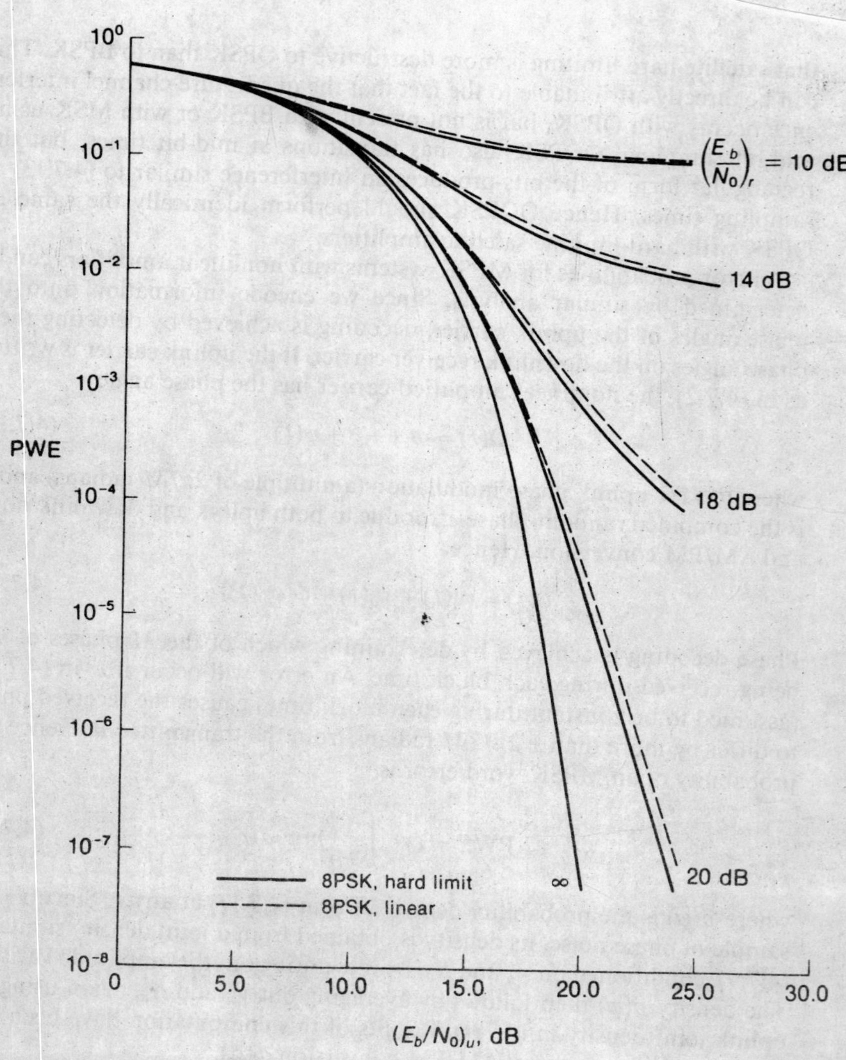

Figure 4.29. 8 PSK word-error probabilities for hard-limiting satellite channel. Comparison to linear up-down link 8 PSK.

where again ρ_1^2 and ρ_2^2 are the uplink and downlink SNR. Equation (4.7.19) is plotted in Figure 4.29 for the case $M = 8$. Since decoding is based on phase angles, the effect of hard limiting is minimal, and the nonlinear MPSK system performs almost identically the same as a linear system.

PROBLEMS

4.1 The front end of an RF receiver is shown in Figure P4.1. How much power gain G must the tunnel diode have to produce a front-end noise figure of 10 dB?

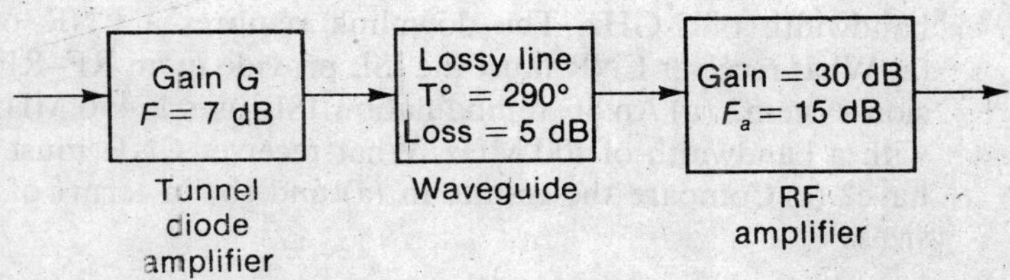

Figure P4.1

4.2 Given the parallel combination of two devices with noise figures F_1, F_2 and power gains G_1, G_2. Determine the overall noise figure, using the definition in (3.4.5).

4.3 A low-pass Butterworth filter has the transfer function

$$H(\omega) = \frac{1}{1 + j\left(\frac{\omega}{2\pi f_3}\right)^n}$$

where f_3 is the half-power frequency. Compute its noise bandwidth. [*Hint*: $\int_0^\infty (1 + x^q)^{-1}\,dx = (\pi/q)/\sin(\pi/q)$]

4.4 (a) Show that the correlation function of $n_{RF}(t)$ in (4.2.5) is given by

$$R_{n_{RF}}(\tau) = R_{cc}(\tau)\cos\omega\tau - R_{cs}(\tau)\sin\omega\tau$$

where $R_{cc}(\tau) = \overline{\tilde{n}_c(t)\tilde{n}_c(t+\tau)} = R_{ss}(\tau)$, and $R_{cs}(\tau) = \overline{\tilde{n}_c(t)\tilde{n}_s(t+\tau)} = R_{sc}(-\tau)$. (b) Compute the spectral density of $n_{RF}(t)$, using the spectrum of $\tilde{n}_c(t)$ and $\tilde{n}_s(t)$ in Figure 4.9 and assuming $R_{cs}(\tau) = 0$.

4.5 *Frequency noise* is defined as the derivative of phase noise $v(t)$ in (4.2.12b). Show that the power spectral density of frequency noise is quadratic in frequency when the phase noise has a flat spectrum. [*Hint*: Use the fact that dv/dt is the output of a filter whose input is $v(t)$ and whose transfer function is $H(s) = s$.]

4.6 The carrier-plus-noise waveform into a hard-limiter amplifier has CNR = 3 dB. The amplifier output power is 10 watts. Estimate how much power is in the output carrier and in the output noise at the amplifier output. Repeat for CNR = 10 dB and −3 dB.

4.7 An ISL is operated with an FM carrier and has a total carrier bandwidth of 2 GHz. The downlink requires a CNR of 40 dB. (a) What receiver CNR must the ISL provide in an RF–RF conversion system? (b) An IF remodulation ISL uses a 450 MHz carrier with a bandwidth of 100 MHz. What receiver CNR must this ISL have? (c) Compare the results in (a) and (b) in terms of antenna sizes.

4.8 A TWTA has the AM/AM gain function $g_1(\alpha)$ and AM/PM function $\phi_1(\alpha)$. Show that the required corrective nonlinearity to be inserted after the TWTA to linearize its gain and phase is given by $g_2(\alpha) = kg_1^{-1}(\alpha)$ and $\phi_2(\alpha) = -\phi_1(g_1^{-1}(\alpha)) + \psi$. (b) Is the same nonlinearity used before the TWTA for linear operation?

REFERENCES

1. R. Strauss, "Communications Satellite Receiver and Transmitter Technology," in *Satellite Communications*, ed. H. Van Trees (New York: IEEE Press, 1979), Section 4.3 (4 papers).

2. G.C. Terms, and S.K. Mitra, *Modern Filter Theory and Design* (New York, Wiley, 1973).

3. A.E. Williams, and A.E. Atia, "Dual Mode Canonical Waveguide Filters," *IEEE Trans. on Microwave Theory and Techniques*, vol. MTT-25 (Dec. 1977), pp. 1021–1026.

4. J.D. Rhodes, "The Design and Synthesis of a Class of Microwave Band Pass Linear Phase Filters," *IEEE Trans. on Microwave Theory and Techniques*, vol. MTT-17 (April 1969).

5. A.E. Atia, A.E. Williams, and R.W. Newcomb, "Narrow-Band Multiple-Coupled Cavity Synthesis," *IEEE Trans. Circuits Syst.*, vol. CAS-21 (Sept. 1974), pp. 649–654.

6. A.E. Atia, "Computer-Aided Design of Waveguide Multiplexers," *IEEE Trans. on Microwave Theory and Techniques*, vol. MTT-22 (March 1976), pp. 332–336.

7. R.M. Kurzrok, "General Four-Resonator Filters in Waveguide," *IEEE Trans. MTT*, vol. MTT-16, (1966), pp. 46–47.

8. G.L. Matthaei, L. Young, and E.M.T. Jones, *Microwave Filters*,

Impedance Matching Networks and Coupling Structures (New York: McGraw-Hill, 1964).

9. C.M. Kudsia, and V. O'Donovan, *Microwave Filters for Communications Systems* (Dedham, MA: Artech House, 1974).

10. R. Gagliardi, *Introduction to Communication Engineering* (New York: Wiley, 1978), chapter 3.

11. D. Morais, and K. Feher, "The Effects of Filtering and Limiting on the Performance of QPSK and MSK Systems," *IEEE Trans. on Comm.*, vol. COM-28 (December 1980).

12. D. Divsalar, and M. Simon, "The Power Spectral Density of Digital Modulations Transmitted over Nonlinear Channels," *IEEE Trans. on Comm.*, vol. COM-26 (May 1982).

13. D. Divsalar, and M. Simon, "Performance of Overlapped Raised Cosine Modulation over Nonlinear Channels," *Proceedings of the ICC*, Denver, Colorado, June 1981.

14. R. Forsey, V. Gooding, P. McLane, and L. Campbell, "M-ary PSK Transmission Via a Coherent 2-link Channel with AM-AM and AM-PM Nonlinearities," *IEEE Trans. on Comm.*, vol. Com-26 (January 1978), pp. 116–123.

15. P. Jain et al., "Detection of Signals Transmitted Through Nonlinear Repeaters," *Proc. of the NTC* (December 1977). Also in *Satellite Communications*, ed. H. Van Trees (New York: IEEE Press, 1979).

16. M. Abomonitz, and I. Stegun, *Handbook of Mathematical Functions* (Washington, D.C.: National Bureau of Standards, 1965).

5

Frequency-Division Multiple Access

In Chapter 4 we analyzed a single channel transponder with a single uplink carrier. We now extend the discussion to transponders designed for multiple carriers. Recall that when multiple carriers are used in satellite communications, it is necessary that a multiple-accessing format be established over the system. This format allows distinct separation of the uplink transmissions in passing through the satellite processor. In Section 1.6 three of the most common multiple-access formats were described. Each format has its own specific characteristics, advantages, and disadvantages. Satellite anomalies, such as nonlinear amplification and power division, will therefore have widely different effects on system performance for each method. Hence, it is necessary to carry out separate analysis procedures to assess (and therefore design) analytically satellite systems of each type. In this and the next two chapters we present comparisons of the accessing formats described in that section. Our basic objective is to describe the relationship, analytically and graphically, between key system parameters of the link and the established performance criterion, such as SNR and bit-error probability, of the system receivers. In this chapter we concentrate on *frequency-division multiple accessing (FDMA)* systems.

5.1 THE FDMA SYSTEM

The basic model of an FDMA satellite system is shown in Figure 5.1a. A set of earth stations transmit uplink carriers to be relayed simultaneously by the satellite to various downlink earth stations. Each uplink carrier is assigned a frequency band within the available RF bandwidth of the satellite (Figure 5.1b). In the basic satellite transponder, the entire RF frequency spectrum appearing at the satellite input is frequency-translated to form the downlink. A receiving station receives a particular uplink station by tuning to, and filtering off, the proper band in the downlink spectrum. Each carrier can be independently modulated, either analog or digital, from all others.

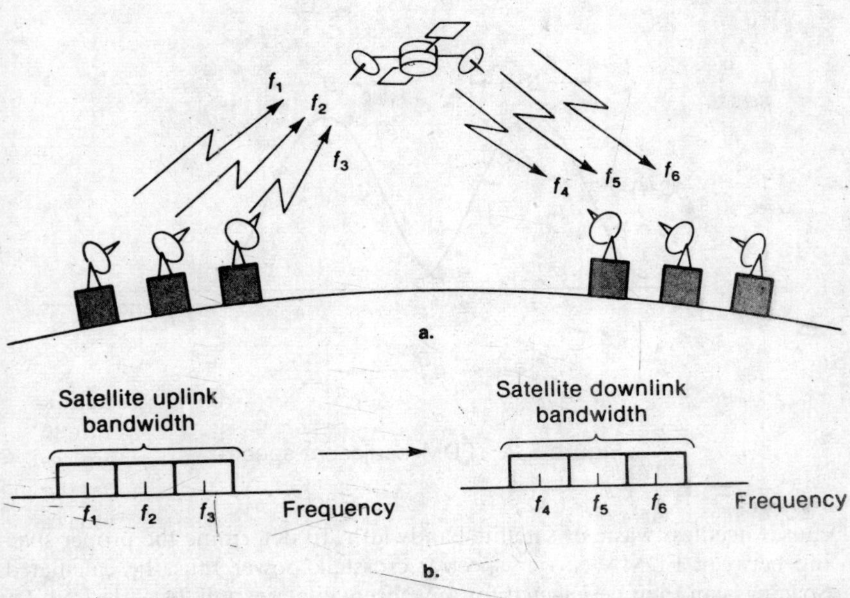

Figure 5.1. FDMA system model. (a) Block diagram. (b) Frequency plan.

With digital carriers, only synchronization between the desired carrier and the receiving station must be established without regard to other carriers at other frequency bands. FDMA represents the simplest form of multiple accessing, and the required system technology and hardware are almost all readily available in today's communication market.

Each uplink carrier may originate from a separate earth station, or several carriers may be transmitted from a particular station. Frequency band selection may be fixed or assigned. In **fixed frequency** operation each carrier is assigned a dedicated frequency band for the uplink, and no other carrier utilizes that band. In **demand-assignment multiple access** (DAMA) frequency bands are shared by several carriers, with a particular band assigned at time of need, depending on availability. DAMA systems can serve a greater number of carriers if the usage time of each is relatively low, but may require more complex ground routing hardware [1].

Individual carrier spectra in an FDMA system must be sufficiently separated from each other both to allow filtering off of the carriers at the downlink stations and to prevent carrier crosstalk (frequencies of one carrier spectrum falling into the band of another carrier, as shown in Figure 5.2). This is why spectral tails associated with digital carriers was discussed in detail in Sections 2.4 and 4.3. However, excessive separation

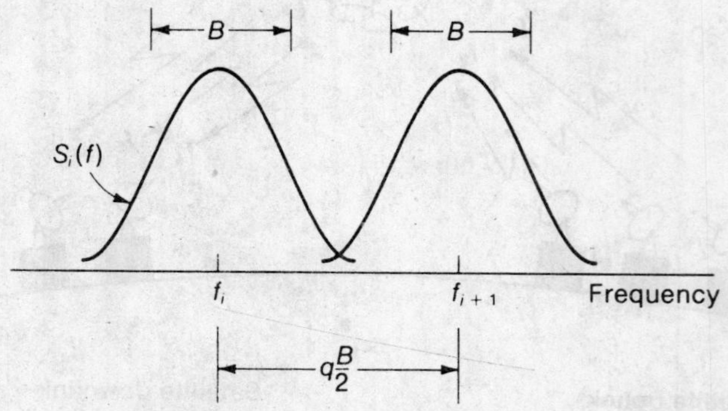

Figure 5.2. FDMA adjacent spectra.

causes needless waste of satellite bandwidth. To determine the proper spacing between FDMA carrier spectra, crosstalk power must be calculated. Spacings can then be selected for any acceptable crosstalk level desired. Let the ith carrier have a center frequency ω_i, and a one-sided power spectrum given by $S_i(\omega)$. The power of the carrier, referred to the satellite uplink receiver, is then

$$P_i = \frac{1}{2\pi}\int_{-\infty}^{\infty} \hat{S}_i(x)dx \tag{5.1.1}$$

Note that P_i includes the uplink station EIRP, uplink space losses, satellite antenna, and front-end gains. The spectrum $S_i(\omega)$ is assumed to occupy a 3-dB carrier spectral bandwidth of B Hz about ω_i. With the aid of Figure 5.2, we see that the fractional crosstalk power of the ith carrier falling into the adjacent carrier bandwidth is then

$$C_i = \frac{2}{2\pi P_i}\int_{\pi B(q-1)}^{\pi B(q+1)} S_i(\omega_i + x)dx \tag{5.1.2}$$

where the carrier center frequency spacing is denoted qB/2. Equation (5.1.2) is plotted in Figure 5.3 for the case of a Butterworth-shaped carrier spectrum

$$S_i(\omega) = \frac{P_i\left(\dfrac{\mu}{\pi B}\right)\sin(\pi/2\mu)}{1 + \left(\dfrac{\omega - \omega_i}{2\pi B}\right)^{2\mu}} \tag{5.1.3}$$

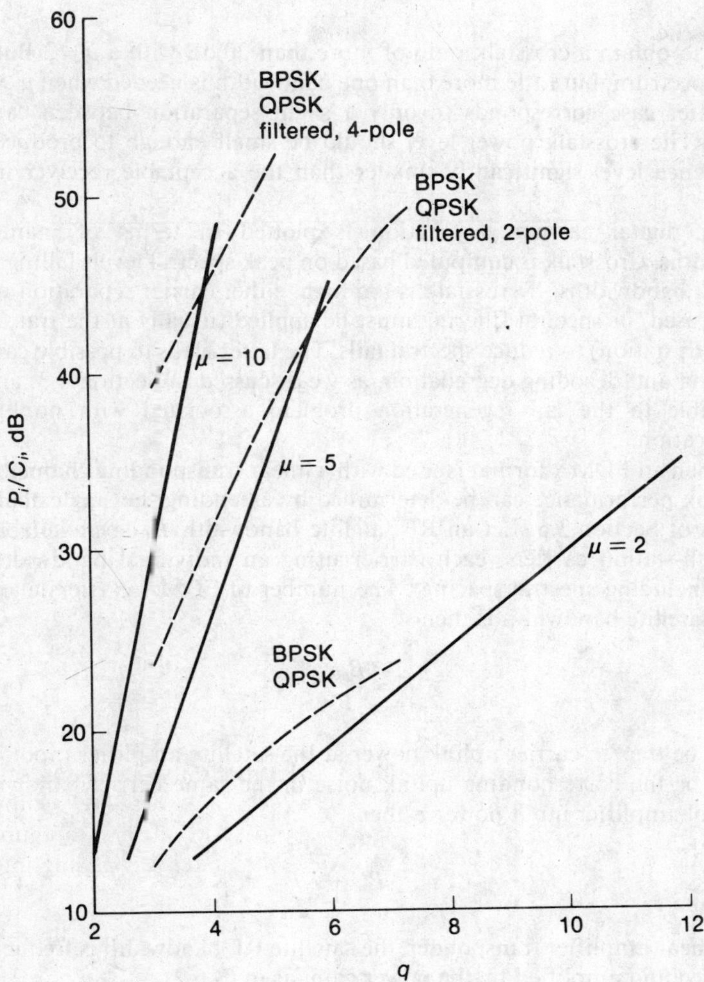

Figure 5.3. Signal to crosstalk ratio for adjacent carriers (—Butterworth spectra, fall-off rate μ ---- Digital carriers).

where the bandwidths and power of both adjacent carriers are assumed equal. Also included is the corresponding result for several types of digital carrier using the spectral information from Figure 2.7. The result shows the carrier-to-crosstalk power ratio, as a function of the spacing between center frequencies. Note that a spacing of approximately three bandwidths is needed to obtain a crosstalk ratio of more than 20 dB with a $\mu = 2$ Butterworth spectrum, but little more than one bandwidth is needed when $\mu \geqslant 10$. This latter case corresponds to only a slight separation between carrier spectra. The crosstalk power level should be small enough to produce an interference level significantly smaller than the acceptable receiver noise level.

For digital carriers, separation is plotted in terms of mainlobe bandwidths. Crosstalk is computed based on peak spectral levels falling into adjacent bandwidths. If crosstalk is too high, either carrier separation must be increased, or spectral filtering must be applied (usually at the transmitting earth station) to reduce spectral tails. The latter leads to possible carrier distortion and decoding degradation, as we discussed in Section 4.3, and is susceptible to the tail regeneration problem associated with nonlinear amplification.

When an FDMA format is used with a linear transponding channel, the downlink performance can be determined by extending the single channel analysis of Section 3.6. Let an RF satellite bandwidth B_{RF} be available to the earth-station carriers, each carrier using an individual bandwidth of B Hz (including spectral spacing). The number of FDMA carriers allowed by the satellite bandwidth is then

$$K = \frac{B_{RF}}{B} \tag{5.1.4}$$

Let P_{ui} be the ith carrier uplink power at the satellite amplifier input, and let P_{un} be the corresponding uplink noise in the same carrier bandwidth. The total amplifier input power is then

$$P_u = \sum_{i=1}^{K} P_{ui} + KP_{un} \tag{5.1.5}$$

For a linear amplifier transponder, the satellite RF bandwidth is frequency-translated and amplified by the power gain, as in (3.6.2),

$$G = \frac{P_T}{P_u} = \frac{P_T}{\sum_{i=1}^{K} P_{ui} + KP_{un}} \tag{5.1.6}$$

The downlink receiver power of the ith carrier after amplifying and downlink transmission is then

$$P_{di} = LGP_{ui} = LP_T\left[\frac{P_{ui}}{\sum_{i=1}^{K} P_{ui} + KP_{un}}\right] \tag{5.1.7}$$

where L is again the combined downlink power losses and gains from satellite amplifier output to earth-station receiver input. Note that the power robbing on the downlink carrier that was caused in the single carrier case only by the noise (Section 3.6) is now increased by the additional power robbing of the other carriers.

The total receiver noise is the sum of the transponded uplink noise and the receiver noise. Hence the downlink CNR of a single carrier in its own bandwidth B is then

$$\mathrm{CNR}_d = \frac{P_{di}}{LGP_{un} + N_{0d}B} \tag{5.1.8}$$

where N_{0d} is the receiver noise spectral level. We again rewrite this as

$$(\mathrm{CNR}_d)^{-1} = (\mathrm{CNR}_u)^{-1} + (\mathrm{CNR}_r)^{-1} \tag{5.1.9}$$

where

$$\mathrm{CNR}_u = \frac{P_{di}}{LGP_{un}} = \frac{P_{ui}}{P_{un}} \tag{5.1.10}$$

$$\mathrm{CNR}_r = \frac{P_{di}}{N_{0d}B} = \frac{P_T L}{N_{0d}B}\left(\frac{P_{ui}}{P_u}\right) \tag{5.1.11}$$

Here CNR_u is the uplink CNR of a single carrier. The receiver CNR_r is that which the satellite power P_T can produce at the receiver, reduced by the power-robbing loss of the uplink. If the system is power-balanced (all carriers have some uplink power) and if the uplink CNR_u is high ($\mathrm{CNR}_u >> 1$), then $\mathrm{CNR}_r \approx P_T L / K N_{0d} B$. That is, the available satellite P_T is equally divided among the FDMA downlink carriers. If we solve (5.1.9) for P_T, we can compute the required satellite power to support an FDMA system with K carriers. This yields

$$P_T = \frac{KN_{0d}B}{L}\left[\frac{\mathrm{CNR}_d}{1 - (\mathrm{CNR}_d/\mathrm{CNR}_u)}\right] \tag{5.1.12}$$

With a specified value of CNR_d and CNR_u we see that P_T increases linearly with the number of carriers. Equation (5.1.12) is plotted in Figure 5.4. Also superimposed is the relation between the satellite bandwidth and the number of carriers in (5.1.4). This figure can also be used to balance the number of carriers allowed by the satellite power against that allowed by the satellite bandwidth. By entering the ordinate at the proper value of P_T and B_{RF}, we can read off the number of FDMA carriers that can be separately supported by each. The smaller of the two then determines the available FDMA system

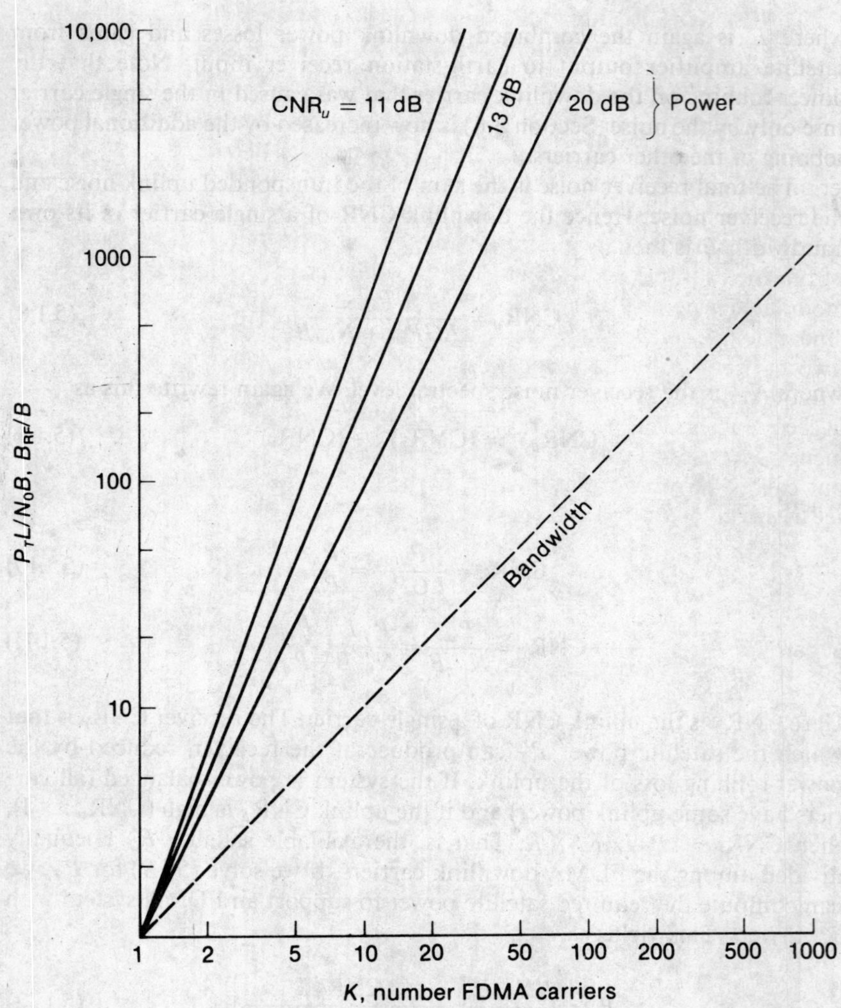

Figure 5.4. Required satellite power and satellite bandwidth to support K FDMA carriers; linear channel.

capacity. Hence an FDMA system may be either power-limited or bandwidth-limited, in terms of the number of carriers that can be simultaneously supported.

5.2 NONLINEAR AMPLIFICATION WITH MULTIPLE FDMA CARRIERS

Nonlinear transponder effects, discussed in Section 4.6 for a single carrier, become even more important when an FDMA format is used. As multiple carriers pass through a transponder, the nonlinear effects of limiters and power amplifiers cause intermodulation products (beats) among these carriers. These beat terms produce additional frequency components at the nonlinear output that can interfere with the desired carriers. This can be seen from the example depicted in Figure 5.5. Suppose two frequency tones (unmodulated carriers) are to be simultaneously passed into the general nonlinear device shown. The inherent nonlinearity of the device will cause the two carriers to beat together, producing cross-products that generate new frequency components at all the multiple combinations of the two input frequencies. The output of the device will therefore have the output frequency spectrum similar to that shown. The amplitude of the individual output carrier terms will depend on the degree of the nonlinearity. If the device is highly nonlinear, there will be many such terms of significant

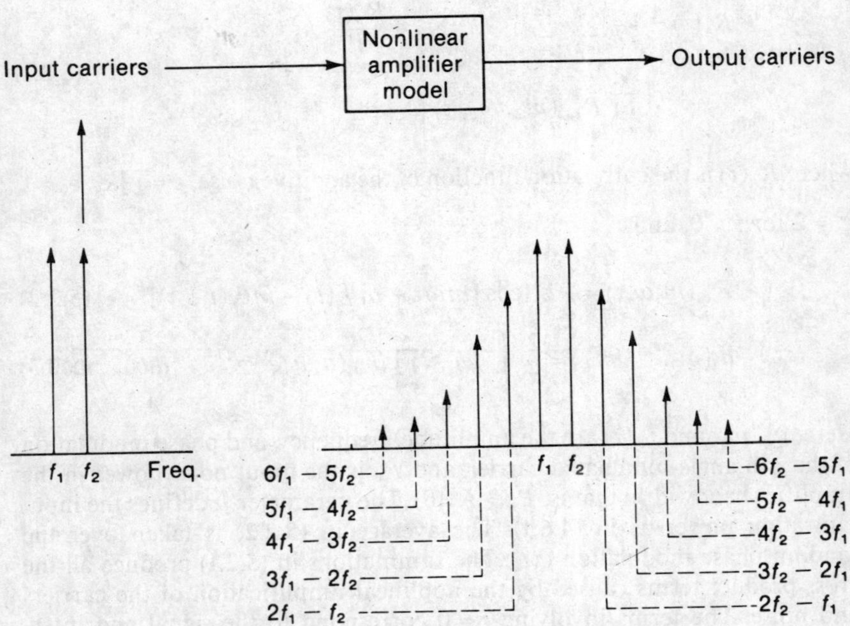

Figure 5.5. Intermodulation generation in nonlinear devices.

amplitude, possibly dominating the two desired frequencies. For a weak nonlinearity (i.e., a device that is nearly linear), the amplitude of the additional beat frequency terms will be reduced, and only the two input carriers will dominate. When the input tones correspond to modulated carriers, the output cross-product terms involve convolutions of the carrier spectra of the input, centered at all the beat frequencies previously shown. The combined beat terms now appear as intermodulation noise distributed over the entire frequency band. This intermodulation noise must be included in assessing FDMA performance. In order to do this, however, it is first necessary to derive a somewhat rigorous nonlinearity model that will analytically account for the intermodulation terms. This model must allow for extension to multiple FDMA carriers and to general types of amplifier nonlinearities. This is developed in this section.

A mathematical analysis of nonlinear processing is discussed in Appendix D. It is shown that the autocorrelation function of the output of the nonlinear power amplifier in (4.6.1), resulting from an input of K angle-modulated carriers and additive Gaussian noise, is given by (D.23), rewritten here as,

$$R_y(\tau) = V_L^2 \sum_{i=0}^{\infty} \sum_{m_K=-\infty}^{\infty} \cdots \sum_{m_1=-\infty}^{\infty} \epsilon \frac{R_n^i(\tau)}{i!} h_i^2(m_1,\ldots,m_K) \cdot \left[\prod_{q=1}^{K} R_{cq}(m_q, \omega_q, \tau)\right] \tag{5.2.1}$$

where $R_n(\tau)$ is the correlation function of the additive noise, $\epsilon = \prod_{i=0}^{K} \epsilon_i$, $\epsilon_0 = 1$, $\epsilon_i = 2$ for $i > 0$, and

$$R_{cq}(m,\omega,\tau) = \frac{1}{2} \mathcal{E} \{\cos [m\omega\tau + m\theta_q(t) - m\theta_q(t+\tau)]\} \tag{5.2.2}$$

$$h_i(m_1,\ldots,m_K) = \frac{2}{\pi} \int_{-\infty}^{\infty} u^{i-1} \prod_{q=1}^{K} J_{m_q}(a_q u) e^{-(P_n+b^2)u^2/2} du \tag{5.2.3}$$

Here, a_q, ω_q, and $\theta_q(t)$ are the amplitude, frequency, and phase modulation of the qth angle-modulated carrier, and P_n is the input noise power in the amplifier bandwidth; that is, $P_n = R_n(0)$. The parameter b defines the input saturation power as in (4.6.1). The average in (5.2.2) is taken over the random phase modulation $\theta(t)$. The summations in (5.2.1) produce all the cross-product terms caused by the nonlinear amplification of the carriers and noise. The terms involving $i = 0$ correspond to the signal and intermodulation terms only. The terms for $i > 0$ produce the noise-signal cross terms. The total amplifier output power is obtained from (5.2.1) by setting $\tau = 0$. Hence

$$P_0 = V_L^2 \sum_{i=0}^{\infty} \sum_{m_K=-\infty}^{\infty} \cdots \sum_{m_1=-\infty}^{\infty} \left(\frac{\epsilon}{2}\right) \frac{P_n^i}{i!} h_i^2(m_1, \ldots, m_K) \tag{5.2.4}$$

Equation (5.2.4) indicates the manner in which the various output terms contribute to the total amplifier intermodulation. For example, the jth carrier will have an output power component P_{cj} corresponding to the terms with $i = 0$, $m_q = 0$, $q \neq j$, $|m_j| = 1$. There are two such terms (for $m_j = \pm 1$) and for each $\epsilon = 2$. Hence,

$$P_{cj} = \frac{8V_L^2}{\pi^2} \left[\int_0^{\infty} u^{-1} J_1(a_j u) \prod_{\substack{q=1 \\ q \neq j}}^{K} J_0(a_q u) e^{-(P_n + b^2)u^2/2} du \right]^2 \tag{5.2.5}$$

The preceding can be evaluated for each particular carrier. Contributions from intermodulation and noise cross-product terms can be evaluated from (5.2.4) in a similar manner. In the following section we examine such terms for specific power amplifier models.

Hard-Limiting Amplifiers

Consider first the case where the amplifier is operated in saturation so that a hard-limiter model can be used. This can be accounted for by letting $b = 0$ in the previous equations. The output power contributions can be determined by evaluating (5.2.5) under this condition. For a single input carrier, $K = 1$, the output power is that of a single bandpass hard-limiter, with level V_L, and represents the maximum output carrier power of the amplifier. In Section 4.6, this was called the saturated output power, and was given as

$$P_{\text{sat}} = \frac{8V_L^2}{\pi^2} \tag{5.2.6}$$

For the case of two carriers ($K = 2$), with amplitudes a_1 and a_2, respectively, the power in each output carrier, normalized to the available saturation power in (5.2.6) is then

$$\begin{aligned} \frac{P_{c1}}{P_{\text{sat}}} &= h_0^2(1,0) = \left[\int_0^{\infty} J_1(a_1 u) J_0(a_2 u) e^{-P_n u^2/2} \, du/u \right]^2 \\ \frac{P_{c2}}{P_{\text{sat}}} &= h_0^2(0,1) = \left[\int_0^{\infty} J_1(a_2 u) J_0(a_1 u) e^{-P_n u^2/2} \, du/u \right]^2 \end{aligned} \tag{5.2.7}$$

The ratio of these output carrier powers is then

$$\frac{P_{c1}}{P_{c2}} = \frac{h_0^2(1,0)}{h_0^2(0,1)} \tag{5.2.8}$$

and the total normalized output carrier power, $P_T(2)$, is

$$\frac{P_T(2)}{P_{\text{sat}}} = \frac{P_{c1} + P_{c2}}{P_{\text{sat}}} = h_0^2(1,0) + h_0^2(0,1) \tag{5.2.9}$$

Equations (5.2.8) and (5.2.9) are plotted in Figure 5.6 as a function of the input carrier power ratio $(a_1/a_2)^2$, for the noiseless case, $P_n^2 = 0$. The result

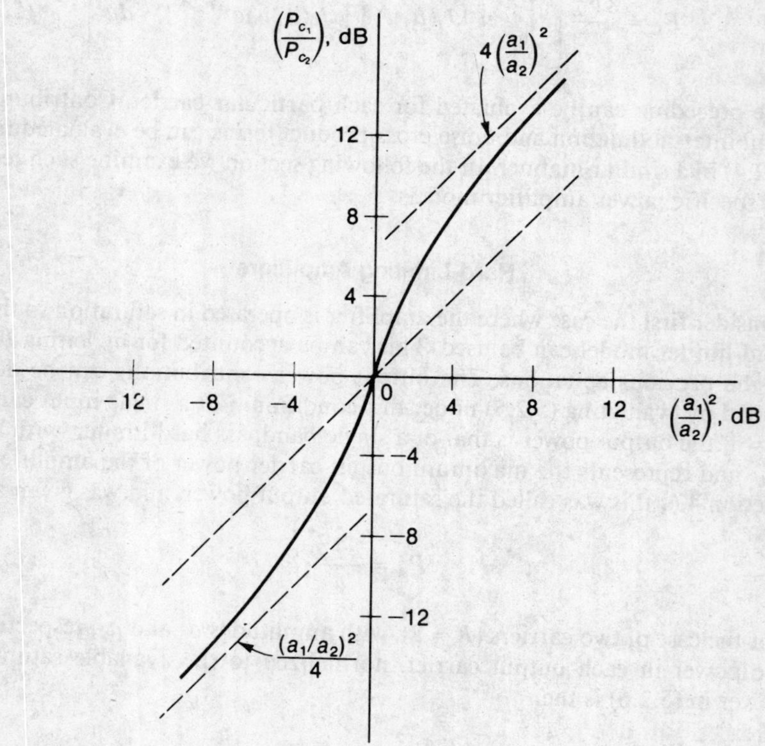

Figure 5.6. Two-carrier power suppression with hard-limiting nonlinearities [(a_1, a_2) = input carrier amplitudes; P_{c_1}, P_{c_2} = output carrier power].

shows that the total output carrier power is less than the single carrier saturation power, the difference being the power lost to intermodulation. The curve also exhibits the interesting fact that the output carrier power ratio is not equal to that of the input but instead has the stronger input carrier even stronger at the output. That is, the stronger carrier tends to suppress the weaker carrier during hard-limiting amplification. We see that this suppression approaches a factor of 4 (i.e., the output ratio is 6 dB larger than the input ratio). This effect is referred to as **carrier suppression**, and illustrates the disadvantage of having strong and weak carriers simultaneously amplified in a saturating amplifier.

Similar studies for larger numbers of carriers, with and without noise, have been reported, making use of computerized versions of (5.2.7) [2–4]. Shaft [2] has examined in detail the case of three and four carriers, and a portion of his results are shown in Figure 5.7 for four carriers. The curves exhibit the carrier suppression effect of the stronger carriers on the weaker carriers, for various combinations of input power distributions, in the noiseless case. With one strong carrier a maximum of about 5.5 dB suppression of a weaker carrier occurs, whereas only about 1 dB occurs for three strong carriers. In the case of two strong carriers, the stronger signals are actually suppressed relative to the weaker ones during amplification. (Apparently, the two strong signals destructively interfere with each other, allowing the weaker signal to obtain a larger portion of the available output power.) Note that the 1 dB suppression with multiple carriers is similar to the effect of strong noise on a single carrier for the BPL, as discussed in Section 4.5. Hence, the combination of many carriers appears as an additive noise to a single carrier, as far as hard-limiting suppression is concerned. The effect of input noise is shown in Figure 5.7d, indicating the manner in which the noise increases the suppression effect by causing power loss to the noise-carrier cross-product terms.

The total normalized output carrier power for K equal amplitude carriers is obtained from (5.2.5) as

$$\frac{P_T(K)}{P_{\text{sat}}} = K\, h_0^2(1, 0, \ldots, 0) = K\left[\int_0^\infty J_1(au)\, J_0^{K-1}(au) e^{-P_n u^2/2} du/u\right]^2 \qquad (5.2.10)$$

The result is plotted in Figure 5.8 as a function of K for CNR = $(a^2/2P_n)$ of 20 dB. The curve shows the hard-limited total power loss as more carriers are simultaneously amplified. Note that the largest loss occurs during an increase from one to two carriers, and the output power tends to remain relatively constant with K for values beyond about 5. We emphasize that this is the total amplifier power available to all carriers, and therefore each amplified carrier will obtain $1/K$ of this power level.

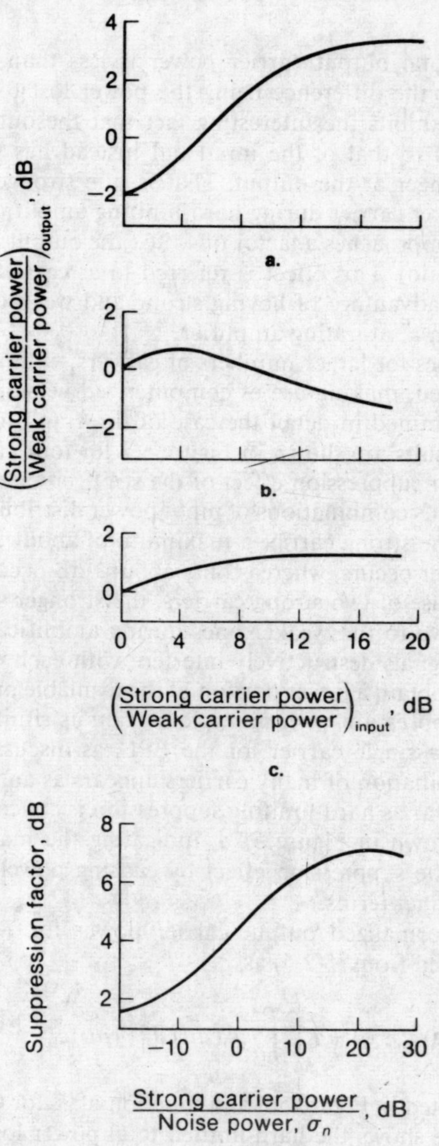

Figure 5.7. Four-carrier power suppression with hard-limiting nonlinearities (from Reference 2). (a) One strong, 3 weak. (b) 2 strong, 2 weak. (c) One weak, 3 strong. (d) One carrier plus noise.

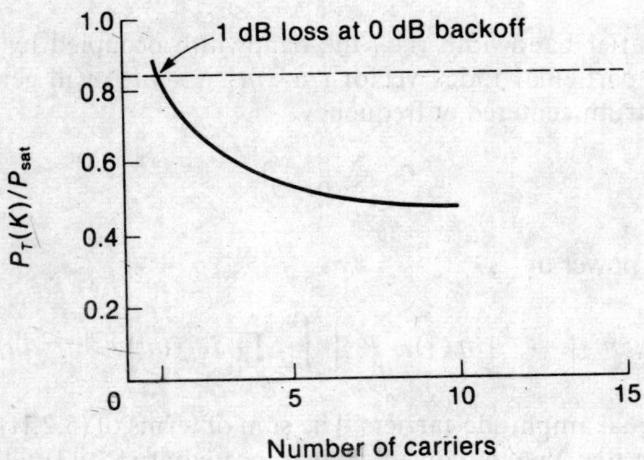

Figure 5.8. Decrease in total available output carrier power vs. number of carriers; hard-limiting nonlinear amplifier.

The remaining terms of (5.2.4), other than the carrier terms, constitute the intermodulation terms of the amplified output. The important terms, however, are only those whose frequencies fall within the satellite input bandwidth, since the remaining ones will be filtered in the downlink RF bandpass filtering. To determine these interfering terms it is necessary to compute the spectral distribution of the amplifier output. This can be obtained by Fourier transforming the output correlation in (5.2.1) with $i = 0$. Hence,

$$S_y(\omega) = \sum_{m_K=0}^{\infty} \cdots \sum_{m_1=0}^{\infty} \epsilon h_0^2(m_1, \ldots, m_K)\,[S_{c_1}(m_1, \omega_1, \omega) \otimes S_{c_2}(m_2, \omega_2, \omega) \cdots \otimes S_{c_K}(m_K, \omega_K, \omega)] \tag{5.2.11}$$

where ⊗ denotes frequency convolution and

$$S_{c_q}(m_q, \omega_q, \omega) = \int_{-\infty}^{\infty} R_c(m_q, \omega_q, \tau) e^{-j\omega\tau} d\tau \tag{5.2.12}$$

Here $S_c\,(m_q,\omega_q,\omega)$ is simply the power spectrum of the qth modulated carrier whose phase argument has been multiplied by m_q. The Kth order convolution of such spectrum, summed over all combinations of $\{m_q\}$, produces the total amplifier output spectrum. The interfering intermodulation terms are those components whose convolution produces frequencies in the amplifier bandwidth (i.e., the bandwidth occupied by the K input carriers). A particular index vector $(m_1, m_2, \cdots m_K)$ will generate a convolved spectrum centered at frequency

$$\sum_{q=1}^{K} m_q \omega_q \tag{5.2.13}$$

with a total power of

$$h_0^2(|m_1|,|m_2|,\cdots,|m_K|) = P_{\text{sat}}\left[\int_0^{\infty} \prod_{q=1}^{K} J_{m_q}(au)e^{-P_n u^2/2}\,du/u\right]^2 \tag{5.2.14}$$

assuming equal amplitude carriers. The sum of terms of (5.2.11) for all index vectors such that the convolved spectra located at (5.2.13) falls within the amplifier bandwidth will generate the total interfering intermodulation spectrum. The value of such a sum will depend on the location of the carrier frequencies ω_q in (5.2.13), and its computation theoretically requires a search over all possible index vectors. However, since Bessel functions decrease quite rapidly with their index, it would be expected that only interfering intermodulation terms with the smaller $|m_q|$ values will contribute most significantly to the in-band interference.

The **order** of a particular intermodulation term is defined as

$$\text{Order} = \sum_{q=1}^{K} |m_q| \tag{5.2.15}$$

With the condition of (5.2.13) and $i = 0$, we see that the order of the intermodulation is always odd, with the lowest order being 3. The most significant interference would be derived from terms corresponding to the lower orders, if such intermodulation terms fall in-band. If the carrier frequencies are equally spaced over the amplifier bandwidth, as shown in Figure 5.9, then it is evident that third-order intermodulation terms of the form $\omega_i + \omega_q - \omega_k$ and $2\omega_i - \omega_q$ can always be found in-band. For equal amplitude carriers, each intermodulation term of the former type will have power level

$$h_0^2(1,1,1,0,\ldots,0) = P_{\text{sat}}\left[\int_0^{\infty} J_1^3(au)\, J_0^{K-3}(au)e^{-P_n u^2/2}\,du/u\right]^2 \tag{5.2.16}$$

while those of the latter type have power of

$$h_0^2(2,1,0,\ldots,0) = P_{\text{sat}}\left[\int_0^{\infty} J_2(au)\, J_1(au)\, J_0^{K-3}(au)e^{-P_n u^2/2}\,du/u\right]^2 \tag{5.2.17}$$

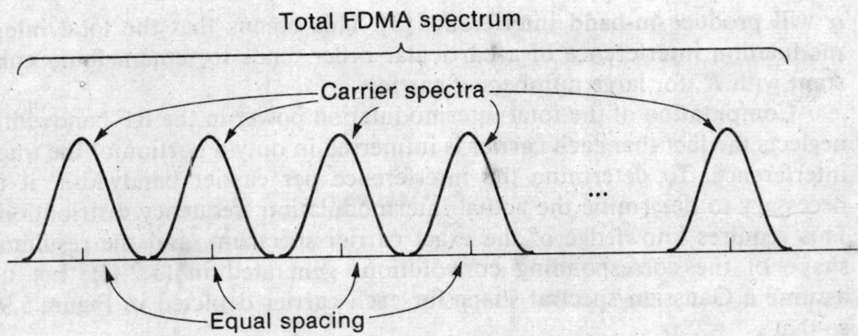

Figure 5.9. FDMA spectra.

Equations (5.2.16) and (5.2.17) are plotted in Figure 5.10 as a function of K, for two values of P_n. Terms corresponding to fifth and seventh orders are included for comparison. Note that the intermodulation power of a particular term decreases approximately as $1/\alpha$, where α is the order. The total intermodulation power of a particular order requires an accumulation of all such terms of each type that produce in-band interference. In general, for equally spaced carriers and large K, approximately α combinations of order

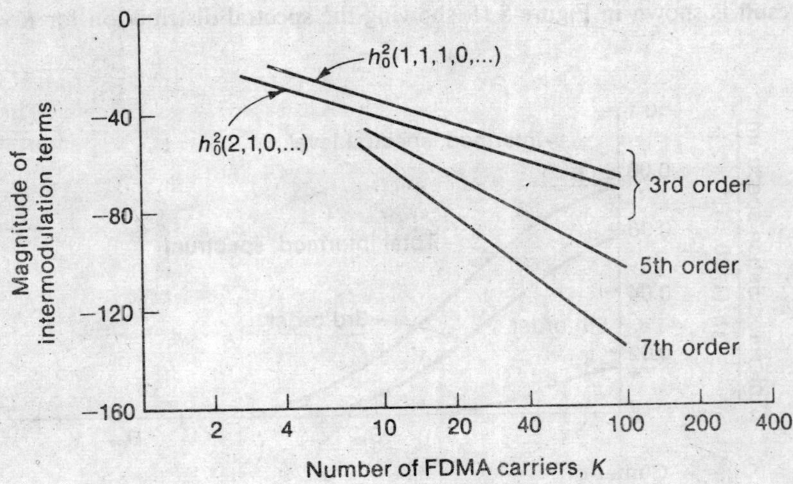

Figure 5.10. Magnitude of intermodulation terms vs. number of FDMA carriers; hard-limiting nonlinearity.

α will produce in-band interference [3]. This means that the total intermodulation interference of a particular order tends to remain fairly constant with K, for large numbers of carriers.

Computation of the total intermodulation power in the RF bandwidth neglects the fact that each carrier is immersed in only a portion of the total interference. To determine the interference per carrier bandwidth, it is necessary to determine the actual intermodulation frequency distribution. This requires knowledge of the exact carrier spectrum, and the resultant shape of the corresponding convolutions generated in (5.2.11). Let us assume a Gaussian spectral shape for each carrier depicted in Figure 5.9, so that

$$G_{c_q}(1, \omega_q, \omega) = \frac{e^{-(\omega-\omega_q)^2/2\tilde{B}_c}}{\sqrt{2\pi B_c}} \tag{5.2.18}$$

where B_c is the carrier bandwidth (measured between spectral inflection points) in Hz. Convolution of such spectra regenerate a Gaussian spectrum centered at (5.2.13) with bandwidth

$$2[|m_1|^2 + |m_2|^2, \ldots, |m_K|^2]^{1/2} B_c \tag{5.2.19}$$

and amplitude given by $h_0(|m_1|, \ldots, |m_K|)$ in (5.2.14). The resulting intermodulation spectrum is obtained by summing over all such orders (i.e., all values of each m_q) and superimposing the convolved spectra. A typical result is shown in Figure 5.11, showing the spectral distribution for $K = 20$

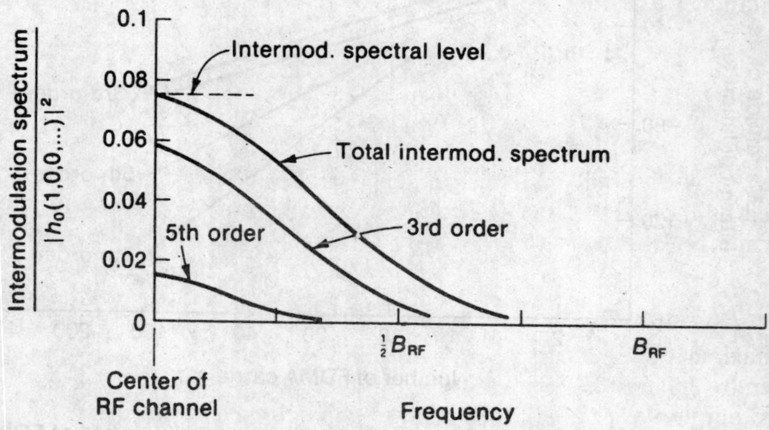

Figure 5.11. Intermodulation spectral distribution over FDMA bandwidth hard-limiting nonlinearity, Gaussian shaped carrier spectra.

carriers, with the spectral values normalized to the power of a single carrier. Note that the intermodulation tends to be concentrated in the center of the RF bandwidth, so that center carriers receive the most intermodulation interference. Note also the predominance of the third- and fifth-order intermodulation interference. The peak value of the intermodulation spectrum is often defined as the **intermodulation spectral level**.

Studies have been performed to determine if intermodulation levels can be reduced by separating the individual FDMA carrier spectra so as to lessen the possibility and degree of spectral overlap. The studies have shown that if uneven spacing of the carrier spectra is used and if the overall RF bandwidth is extended, spectral locations can be found such that all possible intermodulation terms of a given order and type will not overlap any carrier spectrum [5, 6]. However, these methods are extremely wasteful of RF bandwidth, and the total required bandwidth is much larger than that occupied by the sum of the carrier bandwidths. This is because wide spacings must be inserted between the spectra in order to achieve significant intermodulation reduction.

Soft-Limiting Amplifiers

When the input power is not strong enough to force operation into saturation, the actual soft-limiting characteristics of the amplifier must be taken into account. If the amplifier nonlinearity is modeled as in (4.6.1), then our previous equation (5.2.3) must be examined with $b \neq 0$ in order to determine power loss and intermodulation interference. Recall from (4.6.3) that the parameter b defines the input saturation power and the input backoff as

$$\text{input } P_{\text{sat}} = b^2/2 \tag{5.2.20}$$

$$\beta_i = \frac{b^2/2}{P_{in}} \tag{5.2.21}$$

where P_{in} is the total input power. The amplifier output backoff, β_o, is defined as the ratio of the maximum achievable output power with the given number of carriers to that actually obtained. Hence,

$$\beta_o = \frac{\max P_T(K)}{P_T(K)} \tag{5.2.22}$$

The maximal power occurs when the amplifier is driven into saturation and is given by the hard-limiting result in (5.2.10) when $P_n = 0$. The actual soft-limited output power obtained with K equal amplitude carriers is

$$P_T(K) = KP_{\text{sat}}\left[\int_0^{\infty} J_1(au)\, J_0^{K-1}(au) e^{-(P_n+b^2)u^2/2} du/u\right]^2 \tag{5.2.23}$$

Using (5.2.21), and the fact that $P_u = (Ka^2/2) + P_n$, this can be rewritten directly in terms of the input backoff as

$$P_T(K) = KP_{\text{sat}}\left[\int_0^{\gamma} J_1(u)\, J_0^{k-1}(u)\, e^{-K\beta_i u^2/2} du/u\right]^2 \qquad (5.2.24)$$

Equation (5.2.24) is plotted in Figure 5.12 as a function of input backoff for several values of K. The asymptotic upper bound is the hard-limited result of (5.2.6) and is reached only if the amplifier is driven well into saturation. We see, therefore, that the output backoff parameter in (5.2.22) is a function of both the input backoff and the number of carriers, and depends explicitly on the amplifier characteristic. It is obvious that output backoff increases with input backoff for all values of K, and that the two can be related through the power characteristic for a given value of K.

Besides increasing output backoff, increasing the input backoff forces the amplifier to operate more in its linear region, reducing the effective nonlinearity and associated intermodulation. A particular intermodulation

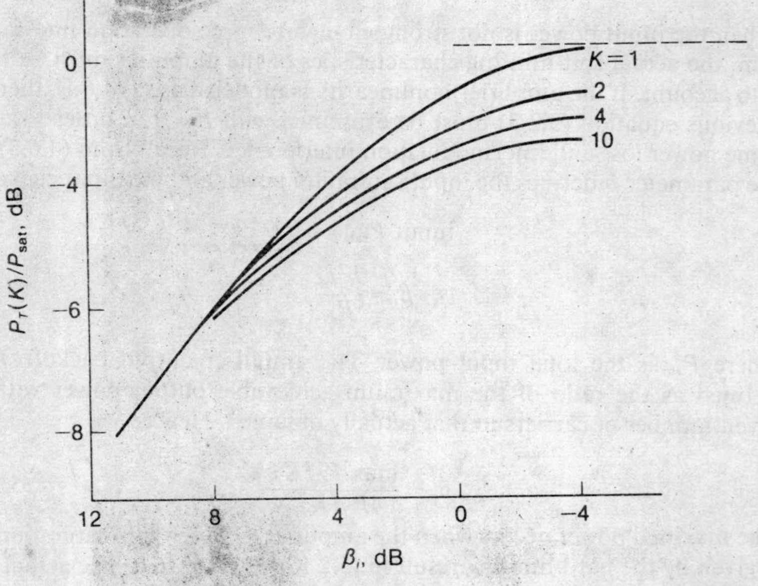

Figure 5.12. Output backoff vs. input backoff for various numbers of FDMA carriers; soft limiting.

term will now have a power contribution of

$$P_{\text{sat}}\left[\int_0^{\infty}\prod_{q=1}^{K} J_{|m_q|}(au)e^{-b^2u^2/2}\,du/u\right]^2$$
$$= P_{\text{sat}}\left[\int_0^{\infty}\prod_{q=1}^{K} J_{|m_q|}(v)\,e^{-K\beta_i v^2/4}\,dv/v\right]^2 \qquad (5.2.25)$$

Using the same Gaussian carrier spectra of Figure 5.9, the resultant intermodulation spectrum, similar to that in Figure 5.11, can be computed for a given value of K and various degress of input backoff. Figure 5.13 shows a plot of the carrier power–to–intermodulation power ratio of the center channel as a function of the input backoff for several values of K. The curve shows the decrease in the intermodulation interference as backoff is

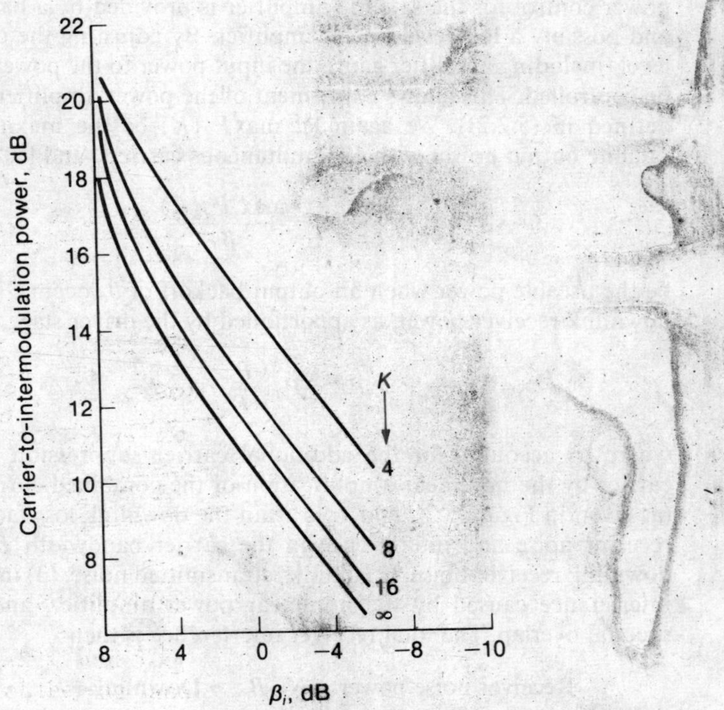

Figure 5.13. Carrier-to-intermodulation power ratio vs. input backoff; center FDMA channel assumed (peak intermodulation).

increased and the amplifier is operated more as a linear amplifier. Thus, a natural trade-off exists in satellite systems between decreasing downlink carrier power levels and reducing the accompanying intermodulation interference. Analysis of the various design alternatives must be made to assess these trade-off directions. This we do in the next section.

5.3 FDMA NONLINEAR ANALYSIS

Carrier-to-Noise Ratios

In Section 5.1 we computed carrier CNR_d for an FDMA system operating with a linear amplifying transponder. In this section we extend these results to include the nonlinear amplifier. We again assume K equal bandwidth uplink carriers, and a total uplink power as in (5.1.5). Assume the driver power control for the satellite amplifier is provided by a bandpass limiter, and possibly a low-level linear amplifier. By adjusting the output limiting level (including amplifier gain), the input power to the power amplifier can be controlled. This allows adjustment of the power amplifier input backoff defined in (5.2.21). We again let $\max P_T(K)$ be the maximum available satellite output power with K simultaneous carriers, and let

$$P_T = \frac{\max P_T(K)}{\beta_o} \tag{5.3.1}$$

be the useable power when an output backoff of β_o occurs. The ith carrier downlink receiver power, as apportioned by the driver stage, is then

$$P_{di} = P_T\left(\frac{P_{ui}}{P_u}\right)\alpha_s^2 L \tag{5.3.2}$$

where α_s^2 accounts for the additional carrier suppression imposed on a carrier by the nonlinear amplification of the combined carriers plus noise (as given in Figure 5.7), and L is again the downlink loss factor. Downlink receiver noise and interference in the carrier bandwidth B is due to (1) downlink receiver noise, (2) uplink retransmitted noise, (3) intermodulation interference caused by the nonlinear power amplifier, and (4) crosstalk spectral overlap. The total receiver interference is then

$$\begin{aligned} \text{Receiver noise power} &= N_{0d}B \quad \leftarrow \text{Downlink} \\ &\quad + P_T\left(\frac{P_{un}}{P_u}\right)\alpha_n^2 L \quad \leftarrow \text{Uplink} \end{aligned} \tag{5.3.3}$$

$$+ N_{0I}BL \leftarrow \text{Intermodulation}$$

$$+ c_i P_{di} \leftarrow \text{Crosstalk}$$

where

α_n^2 = Noise suppression factor of the nonlinear amplifier
N_{0d} = Receiver noise level
P_{un} = Uplink noise power in bandwidth B
N_{0I} = Intermodulation noise spectral level at the satellite amplifier output
c_i = Fraction of carrier power falling into adjacent carrier bandwidths

The resulting downlink receiver carrier power–to–total interference ratio, CNR_d, for the ith carrier is then the ratio of (5.3.2) to (5.3.3):

$$\text{CNR}_d = \frac{P_T\left(\dfrac{P_{ui}}{P_u}\right)\alpha_s^2 L}{N_{0d}B + P_T\left(\dfrac{P_{un}}{P_u}\right)\alpha_n^2 L + N_{0I}LB + c_i P_T\left(\dfrac{P_{ui}}{P_u}\right)\alpha_s^2 L} \tag{5.3.4}$$

This represents the downlink receiver CNR_d of a *particular* FDMA carrier. As such it represents the extension of the single carrier result in (4.5.10) to the general multiple carrier, nonlinear transponder case. To emphasize this, we divide through by the numerator to obtain

$$(\text{CNR}_d)^{-1} = (\Gamma\text{CNR}_u)^{-1} + (\text{CNR}_r)^{-1} + (\text{CNR}_I)^{-1} + (\text{CNR}_c)^{-1} \tag{5.3.5}$$

where

$\text{CNR}_u = \text{P}_{ui}/\text{P}_{ni}$ = Uplink carrier CNR at the satellite limiter input
$\text{CNR}_r = P_{di}/N_{0d}B$ = Downlink carrier CNR due to available satellite power
$\text{CNR}_I = (P_T(K)/K)/N_{0I}B$ = Carrier-to-intermodulation ratio
$\text{CNR}_c = 1/c_i$ = Carrier-to-crosstalk ratio
$\Gamma = \dfrac{\alpha_s^2}{\alpha_n^2}$ = Nonlinear suppression of the satellite limiter

Equation (5.3.5) extends (4.5.10) by inserting the backoff suppression (via $P_T(K)$), intermodulation (via N_{0I}), and crosstalk (via c_i) effects for multiple carriers. The first two effects are both dependent on the input backoff (operating drive power) of the nonlinear power amplifier. When uplink and downlink power levels are sufficient, and crosstalk is negligible, downlink CNR is determined primarily by the intermodulation, and we can approximate:

$$\text{CNR}_d \approx \text{CNR}_I = \frac{(\max P_T)/K\beta_0}{N_{0I}B} \tag{5.3.6}$$

The numerator term of CNR_I decreases with input backoff (see Figure 5.12.) while the intermodulation level N_{0I} is likewise reduced with backoff (Figure 5.13). When these results are superimposed, the ratio of the two behaves as shown in Figure 5.14. As backoff increases, the intermodulation decreases, increasing CNR_I; eventually, however, the available satellite power will decrease, producing a backoff point at which CNR_I is maximized. Plots of this type are most convenient for locating optimal backoff operating points in FDMA systems. We emphasize that the desired opera-

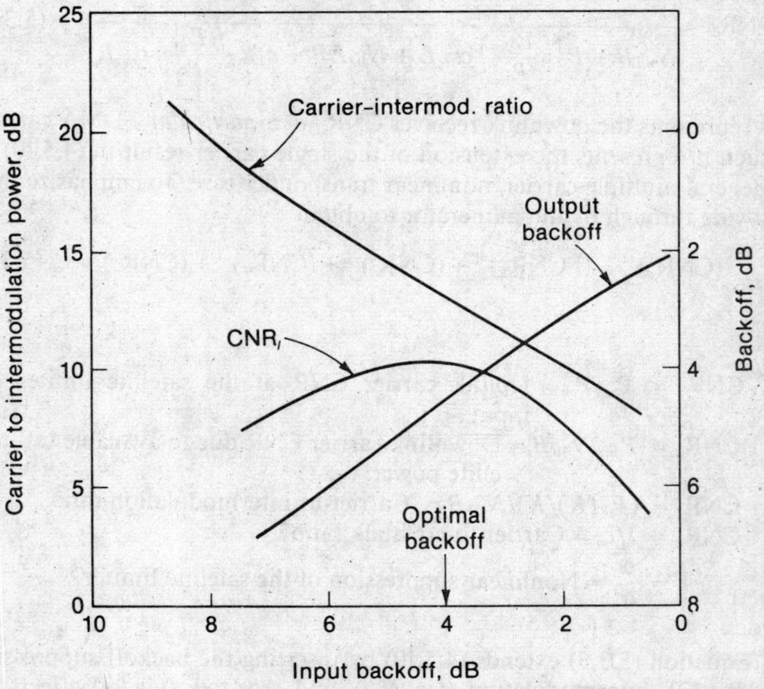

Figure 5.14. CNR_I vs. input backoff ($K = 10$ FDMA carriers).

ting backoff is strongly dependent on the shape of the backoff curves in Figures 5.12 and 5.13, and therefore will vary with the particular power amplifier involved.

For digital carriers, decoding performance can be determined by computing E_b/N_0 for that carrier channel. This can be obtained by replacing bandwidth B by bit time T_b^{-1} in (5.3.4). That is,

$$\left(\frac{E_b}{N_0}\right) = \text{CNR}_d \Big|_{B = 1/T_b} \tag{5.3.7}$$

Note that the resulting error-probability performance now depends on the four CNR in (5.3.5), and each must be evaluated to determine the combined CNR_d in order to plot PE performance curves.

Required Satellite Power

Again, as we did in Section 5.1, we can determine the amount of satellite power required to support an FDMA system with K carriers. Letting $P_T = P_T(K)$ and solving for P_T in (5.3.4) yields

$$P_T = \frac{\beta_o}{L}\left[\frac{N_{0d}B(P_{ui}/P_u)\text{CNR}_d}{\alpha_s^2 - \text{CNR}_d\left[\dfrac{P_{un}}{P_{ui}} + \dfrac{N_{0I}B}{P_{ui}} + c_i\right]}\right] \tag{5.3.8}$$

Note again that P_T depends on the amplifier output backoff and the intermodulation level N_{0I}, both of which depend on the input drive level, that is, β_i. Equation (5.3.8) yields the required amplifier power, P_T, at the satellite in order for the ith carrier downlink to operate with the given CNR_d. This must be evaluated separately for each carrier of the system. To guarantee that every carrier achieves its desired CNR_d during operation, it is necessary that P_T correspond to the maximum value of all P_T computed from (5.3.8).

As an example, consider the case where $P_{ui} = P$ (equal uplink carrier power); $P/P_{un} >> 1$ (high uplink carrier CNR_u); and there is negligible crosstalk ($c_i = 0$). Under these conditions, (5.3.8) simplifies to

$$P_T = \frac{\beta_o \, \text{CNR}_d(N_{0d}B)K/L}{1 - \text{CNR}_d(\text{CNR}_I)^{-1}} \tag{5.3.9}$$

where α_s^2 is taken as 1. Equation (5.3.9) is plotted in Figure 5.15 as a function of desired CNR_d for several values of the parameter CNR_I. We see that the required P_T increases linearly with CNR_d as long as $(\text{CNR})_d/\text{CNR}_I << 1$. However, the required power increases more rapidly as $\text{CNR}_d \to \text{CNR}_I$, and it becomes infinite at the value $\text{CNR}_d = \text{CNR}_I$. This simply means the

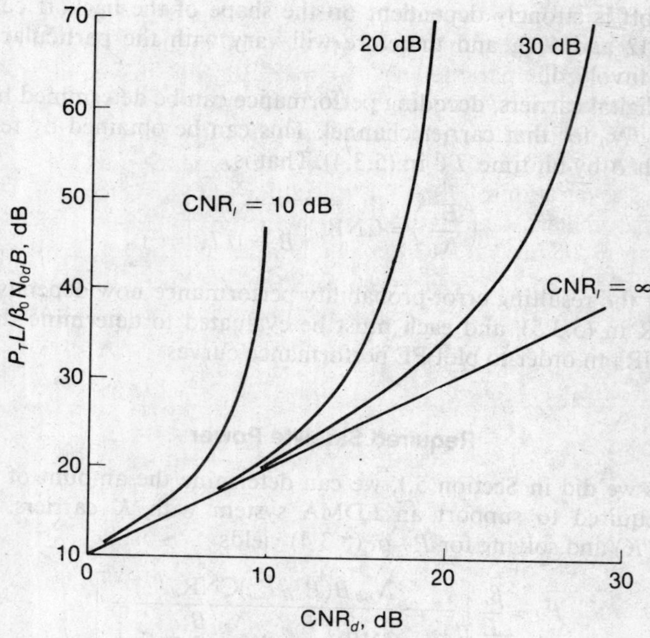

Figure 5.15. Required satellite power to achieve CNR_d in an FDMA channel, with specified carrier to intermodulation ratio ($K = 10$ carriers, $CNR_u >> 1$).

desired CNR_d becomes more difficult to maintain as it approaches the intermodulation ratio CNR_I. The entire allowed interference is being provided by the intermodulation alone, and additional noise interference cannot be tolerated. The inclusion of crosstalk into (5.3.9) would decrease further the denominator and cause the asymptotic increase to occur at a lower value of CNR_d.

Number of Carriers

In Figure 5.15 the number K of uplink carriers was considered a fixed parameter. Another aspect of design is to determine the number of carriers that can be supported in a nonlinear FDMA satellite system. As we saw in Section 5.1, this number is determined by either the available satellite bandwidth or the available satellite power P_T. The number of FDMA carriers permitted by the nonlinear satellite power can be obtained from

(5.3.8) [or (5.3.9) if the stated conditions are satisfied]. However, we see that K directly affects the numerator in (5.3.9) and indirectly affects the denominator through the parameter N_{0I}. (Recall that the degree of intermodulation in a given bandwidth depends on the number of carriers appearing in the satellite bandwidth.) As K increases, CNR_I decreases, and a larger value of P_T is required over that predicted by the numerator in (5.3.9). The result produces a variation of P_T, with K similar to that sketched in Figure 5.16 for the parameters stated. Also included are the bandwidth and linear power curves from Figure 5.4. We see that the satellite nonlinearity eventually causes a more rapid increase in P_T with the number of carriers. Conversely, when operating with a fixed satellite power, fewer FDMA carriers can be

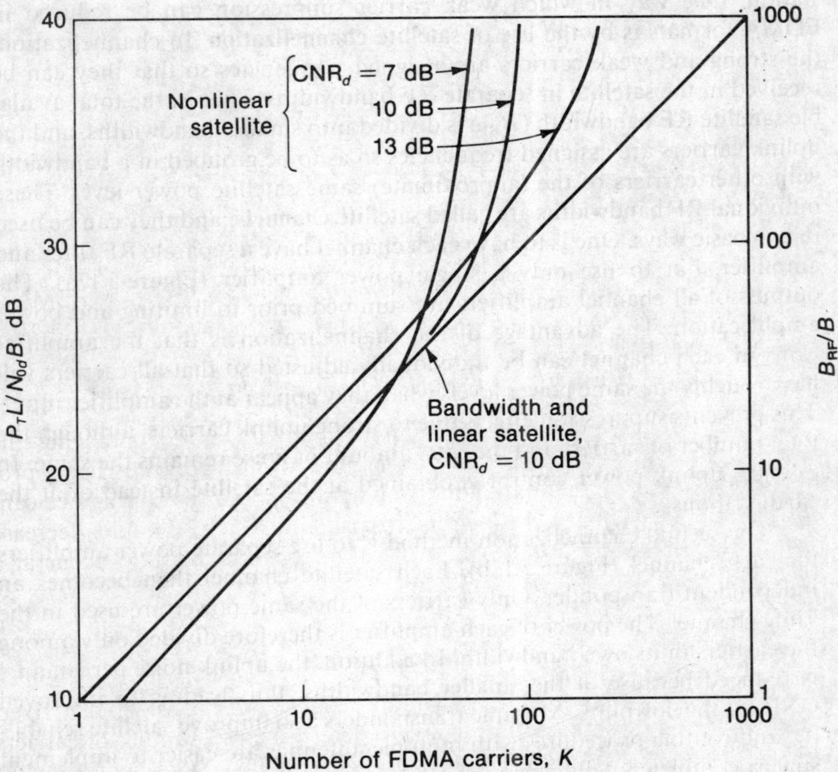

Figure 5.16. Required satellite power and bandwidth to support K FDMA carriers; linear and nonlinear satellite.

supported than when a linear satellite amplifier is used. Again, the actual number of carriers permitted will be the smaller of the number allowed by the power P_T and the number allowed by the satellite bandwidth.

5.4 FDMA CHANNELIZATION

We have found that when dealing with an FDMA system using nonlinear satellite amplifiers, the available satellite power in the downlink must be divided among all carriers. Furthermore, strong carriers tend to suppress weak carriers in the downlink. This means that when a mixture of both strong and weak carriers are to use the satellite simultaneously, we must ensure that the weaker carriers can maintain a communication link, especially if it is to be transmitted to a relatively small (small $g/T°$) receiving station. One way in which weak carrier suppression can be reduced in FDMA formats is by the use of satellite **channelization**. In channelization, the strong and weak carriers are assigned frequencies so that they can be received in the satellite in separate RF bandwidths. That is, the total available satellite RF bandwidth (B_{RF}) is divided into smaller bandwidths, and the uplink carriers are assigned frequencies so as to be grouped in a bandwidth with other carriers of the (approximate) same satellite power level. These individual RF bandwidths are called satellite **channels**, and they can be used in two basic ways. One is to have each channel have a separate RF filter and amplifier, but to use only a single power amplifier (Figure 5.17a). The outputs of all channel amplifiers are summed prior to limiting and power amplification. The advantage of the channelization is that the amplifier gains in each channel can be individually adjusted so that all carriers will have roughly the same power levels when they appear at the amplifier input. This prevents suppression effects due to strong uplink carriers, although the total number of carriers and the total amount of noise remains the same. In essence, uplink power control is obtained at the satellite instead of at the earth stations.

The second channelization method is to use separate power amplifiers for each channel (Figure 5.17b). Each satellite channel then becomes an independent transponder. Only carriers of the same power are used in the same channel. The power of each amplifier is therefore divided only among the carriers in its own bandwidth. In addition, the uplink noise per channel is reduced because of the smaller bandwidths, thus leading to improved CNR for the downlink. Multiple transponders also improve satellite reliability, and routing procedures with multiple antennas are easier to implement since a complete satellite channel can be assigned (fixed or by command) to a particular downlink antenna (see Section 5.6). These advantages are achieved, of course, at the expense of a more complex satellite, since the weight not only of the additional power amplifiers and filters must be included, but also that of the supporting auxiliary primary power. The advantages of the increased number of independent transponders must be carefully weighed against the additional satellite cost.

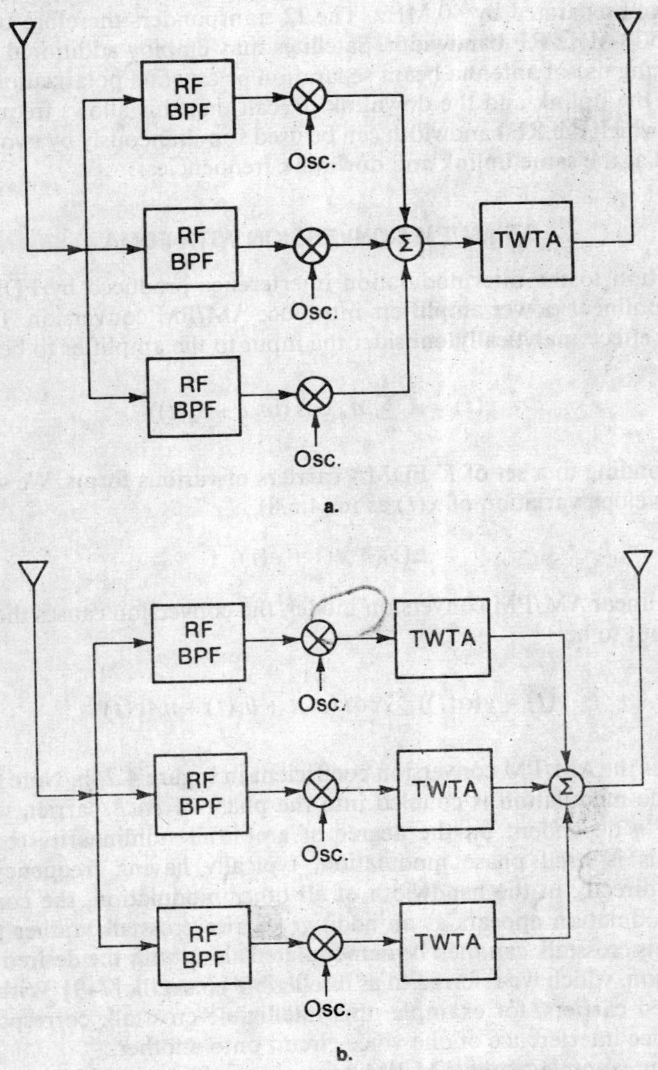

Figure 5.17. Channelized satellite. (a) Single TWTA. (b) Multiple TWTA.

The use of increasing numbers of satellite transponders is an obvious trend in modern satellite design (see Table 1.1). Figure 5.18a shows the processing block diagram for the 12-transponder Intelsat satellite. The uplink and downlink RF bandwidth is divided, as shown in Figure 5.18b. Each individual transponder has a 36-MHz bandwidth, with each channel center frequency separated by 40 MHz. The 12 transponders therefore utilize the entire 500-MHz RF bandwidth. Satellites may employ additional channels by making use of antenna beam separation or antenna polarization separation in the uplink and the downlink. Recall that this allows frequency reuse, in which the RF bandwidth can be used simultaneously by two separate carriers at the same uplink and downlink frequencies.

5.5 AM/PM CONVERSION WITH FDMA

In addition to the intermodulation interference produced by FDMA carriers, nonlinear power amplifiers introduce AM/PM conversion. To examine this effect analytically, consider the input to the amplifier to be

$$x(t) = A \sum_{q=1}^{K} a_q \cos(\omega_q t + \theta_q(t)) \tag{5.5.1}$$

corresponding to a set of K FDMA carriers of various forms. We write the total envelope variation of $x(t)$ as in (4.6.8),

$$\alpha(t) = A(1 + e(t)) \tag{5.5.2}$$

Using a linear AM/PM conversion model, the conversion causes the amplifier output to be

$$y(t) = g(\alpha(t)) \sum_{q=1}^{K} \cos(\omega_q t + \theta_q(t) + \eta A e(t)) \tag{5.5.3}$$

where η is the AM/PM conversion coefficient in Figure 4.24b. Note that the amplitude modulation is coupled into the phase of *each* carrier, with the value of η dependent on the degree of amplifier nonlinearity (backoff). Since this is itself phase modulation, typically having frequency components directly in the bandwidth of all other modulation, the converted phase modulation appears as an additive carrier crosstalk, rather than as noise. This crosstalk can then be demodulated along with the desired carrier modulation, which we referred to as **intelligible crosstalk** [7–9]. With voice-modulated carriers, for example, this intelligible crosstalk corresponds to direct voice interference of one voice circuit onto another.

As an example of the AM/PM conversion effect, consider the simpli-

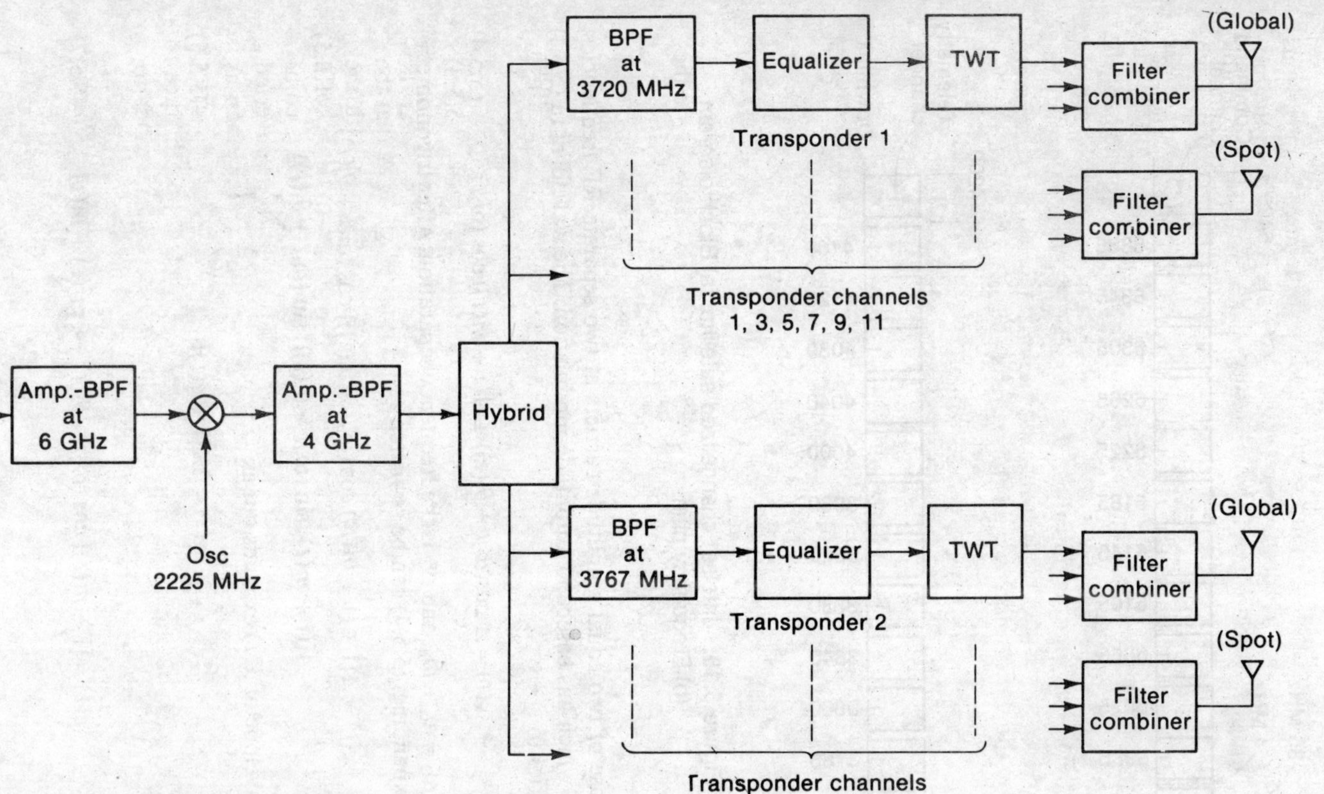

Figure 5.18. Intelsat channelized satellite. (a) Block diagram. (b) Frequency plan.

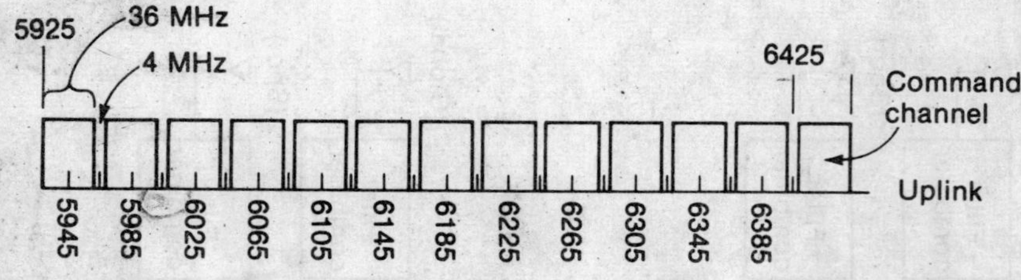

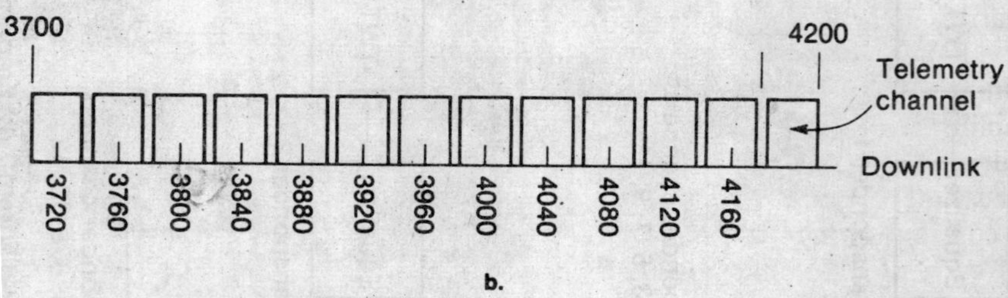

b.

Figure 5.18. Intelsat channelized satellite. (a) Block diagram. (b) Frequency plan.

fied case of two equal amplitude carriers at two separate RF frequencies, one of which has baseband amplitude modulation. The waveform in (5.5.1) simplifies to

$$x(t) = A\cos(\omega\ t + \theta_1(t)) + A(1 + m(t))\cos(\omega_2 t) \tag{5.5.4}$$

where $\omega_2 = \omega_1 + \omega_d$, and ω_d is the frequency separation. After trigonometrically expanding, (5.5.4) can be rewritten as

$$\begin{aligned} x(t) = {} & A[1 + (1 + m(t))\cos(\omega_d t - \theta_1(t))]\cos(\omega_1 t + \theta_1(t)) \\ & + A[(1 + m(t))\sin(\omega_d t - \theta_1(t))]\sin(\omega_1 t + \theta_1(t)) \end{aligned} \tag{5.5.5}$$

The envelope of $x(t)$ expands out as

$$\alpha(t) = 2A[1 + e(t)] \tag{5.5.6}$$

where

$$e(t) = [1 + m(t)]\cos(\omega_d t - \theta_1(t) + \frac{1}{2}m^2(t) + m(t) \tag{5.5.7}$$

The amplifier output in (5.5.3) is then

$$\begin{aligned} y(t) &= g(\alpha(t)) \cos(\omega_1 t + \theta_1(t) + 2A\eta e(t)) \\ &\quad + g(\alpha(t)) \cos(\omega_2 t + 2A\eta e(t)) \end{aligned} \tag{5.5.8}$$

Since $e(t)$ has a component due to the modulation $m(t)$, $e(t)$ in (5.5.8) introduces intelligible crosstalk onto the phase of the angle modulated carrier, the strength of which depends on the coefficient η. It is for precisely this reason that amplitude-modulated carriers are usually not used in multiple-carrier FDMA satellite systems having TWT amplification.

Often the undesired amplitude modulation $m(t)$ in (5.5.4) appears unintentionally. In FDMA formats with channelization, FM carriers of the uplink are filtered and combined for downlink amplification. During the filtering, if the RF filters are somewhat narrow, the filter gain characteristics cause the FM to be converted to undesired AM. For example if $|H_c(\omega)|$ has a constant slope of V_ω volts/rps (called the filter **gain slope**) in the vicinity of carrier center frequency, then an FM carrier with frequency variation $\Delta_\omega m(t)$ produces an amplitude variation on this carrier of

$$e(t) = V_\omega \Delta_\omega m(t) \tag{5.5.9}$$

This envelope variation is then coupled into the phase of all other channelized carriers using the same transponder. Hence, the frequency modulation of one carrier is transferred to all other carriers through the filter gain slope and amplifier AM/PM effect. The strength of this FM crosstalk depends on the filter gain slope and the AM/PM coefficient. The former is reduced by better control of the filter functions, while the latter is reduced by backing off the amplifier.

5.6 SATELLITE-SWITCHED FDMA

A channelized FDMA format is particularly suited for operation with multiple spot beams. Consider the multiple-beam model in Figure 5.19. Each spot beam illuminates a particular set of earth stations, and within each beam FDMA is used. The frequency separation of the carriers in each uplink beam can be used to channelize each beam, with a separate carrier filter at the satellite for each carrier within a beam. An uplink carrier designated for a downlink earth station is then routed to the particular spot beam covering that station. Hence, each uplink channel filter output must be switched to the proper downlink beam channel. Since all uplinks must be switched simultaneously, an onboard switching matrix is needed to provide all possible routing directions. This switching can be suitably provided by a

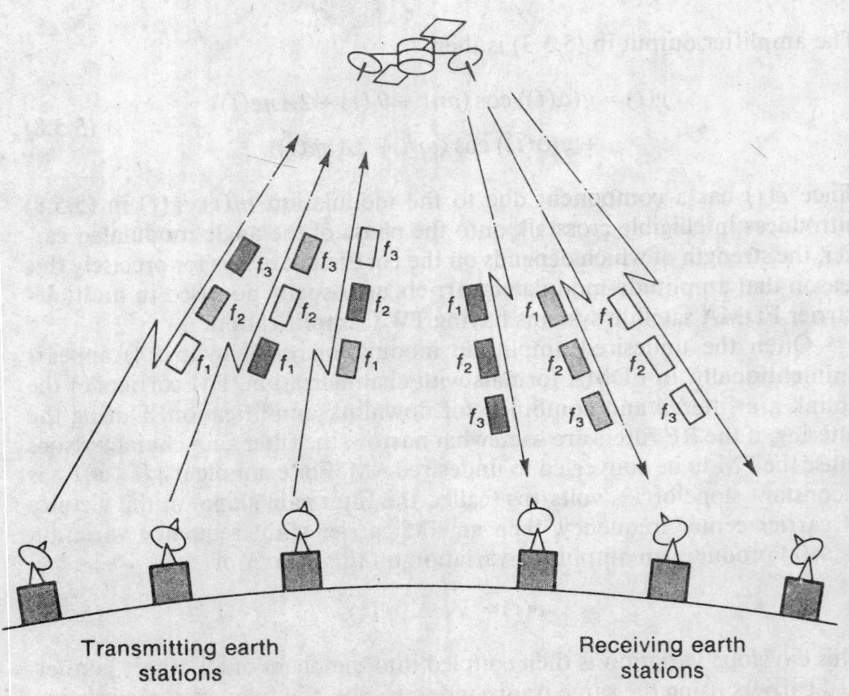

Figure 5.19. Satellite-switched FDMA model.

microwave diode gate matrix that allows signal flow in only specified directions. An FDMA satellite system of this type is referred to as **satellite-switched FDMA (SS-FDMA).**

Figure 5.20 shows a simplified channelized diode switch matrix implementation for a three-beam SS-FDMA satellite. Each beam uses the same frequency bands, and an uplink carrier to be routed to a particular downlink spot beam is assigned a specific frequency band in each uplink beam. This band is different for every uplink beam. The uplink beams are then channelized, and each band filtered off. The diode switch matrix connects each band to a different downlink. In other uplink beams, the same bands are switched to different downlinks. In this way, the same frequency bands from different beams are never superimposed on the same downlink. An uplink earth station need only select the appropriate band for the desired downlink earth-station beam. Thus, at any one time each uplink in any beam has connectivity to any downlink earth station in any beam.

Note that the system utilizes complete frequency re-use, with the same bands being used in each uplink beam. In addition, channelization of the

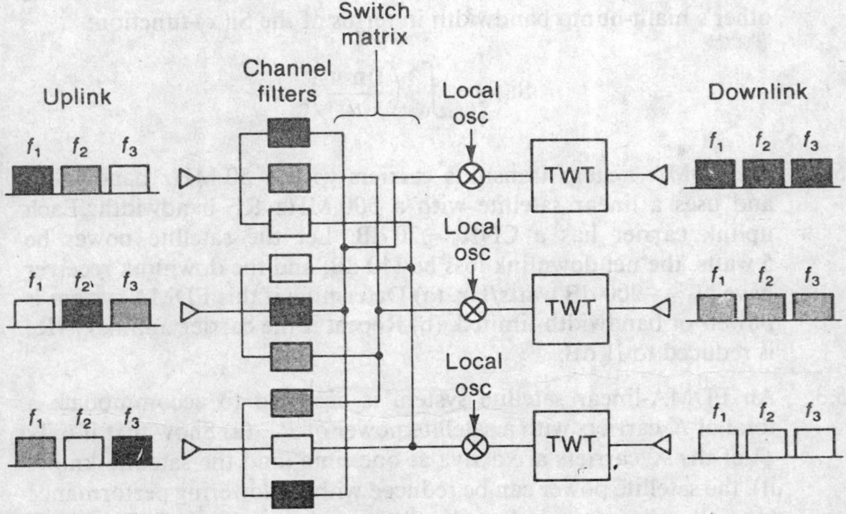

Figure 5.20. SS-FDMA satellite block diagram.

uplinks in SS-FDMA allows the filters to include gain adjustment as well, providing power control over the downlink carriers in the same beam. This reduces suppression effects on weaker carriers being routed to the same beam as stronger carriers.

A basic disadvantage with SS-FDMA is that the routing must be incorporated a priori; that is, the switch matrix is "hardwired in." Thus, the frequency distribution pattern is then fixed for that matrix, and traffic patterns cannot be altered. (We shall find this is not the case with TDMA systems.) In addition, care must be used to prevent the same frequency band in two different beams from appearing in the same downlink and causing crosstalk. Preventing this crosstalk interference requires a significant isolation from the channel filters, and negligible leakage in the diode matrix. Isolation as high as 60 dB is possible with microwave switches. Another disadvantage is that the number of filters increases directly with the product of the number of one-way beams and frequency bands. Hence, if 3 bands are used with 4 uplink and downlink beams, a total of 12 carrier filters is required in the satellite.

PROBLEMS

5.1 Given two adjacent BPSK carriers, each with power P, data rate R bps, and carrier frequency separation Δf Hz. Derive an expression for the crosstalk interference of one carrier spectrum onto the other's main-hump bandwidth in terms of the Si(x) function:

$$\mathrm{Si}(x) = \int_0^x \left(\frac{\sin u}{u}\right)^2 du$$

5.2 An FDMA system transmits carriers with a 50 MHz bandwidth, and uses a linear satellite with a 500 MHz RF bandwidth. Each uplink carrier has a $\mathrm{CNR}_u = 20$ dB. Let the satellite power be 5 watts, the net downlink loss be 140 dB, and the downlink receiver have $N_0 = -200$ dB watts/Hz. (a) Determine if this FDMA system is power- or bandwidth-limited. (b) Repeat if the carrier uplink CNR_u is reduced to 11 dB.

5.3 An FDMA-linear satellite system is designed to accommodate a total of K carriers with a satellite power of P_T. (a) Show that if only Q of the K carriers are active at one time (and the satellite knows it), the satellite power can be reduced without lowering performance (i.e., all active downlinks will still have the required CNR_d). (b) If each carrier has a 60% activity time, determine the reduction in average satellite power P_T if Q can be continuously monitored.

5.4 Given K equally spaced carrier spectral lines at frequency f_i, $i = 1, 2, \ldots, K$. (a) Determine the number of intermodulation lines of the form $f_i + f_j - f_m$ that will fall on top of the rth line. (b) Show that for the middle line ($r = K/2$) and high K, this number is approximately $3K^2/8$.

5.5 A TWTA saturates with an input power of 8 milliwatts and has the intermodulation performance of Figure 5.13. If a 16 carrier FDMA system is operated through this amplifier, what will be the carrier-to-intermodulation ratio if the total input power is maintained at 2 milliwatts?

5.6 Consider the FDMA system in Problem 5.2 with the same bandwidths, downlink losses, and N_0, except that a nonlinear TWTA is used. The required CNR_d is 13 dB. Using Figure 5.16, what is the required value of satellite power P_T to operate with the maximum number of carriers?

5.7 An FDMA repeater is to be channelized as in Figure 5.17a. Consider the following simple 5-carrier system with a linear satellite amplifier:

Carrier	P_{uc}(mw)	P_{sd}(w)
1	10	10
2	10	5
3	20	10
4	20	2
5	20	4

Here P_{uc} is the uplink power, and P_{sd} is the required satellite downlink power for each carrier. (a) What is the minimum value of P_T that can satisfy all downlinks? (b) What P_T is needed for a single transponder (no channelization)? (c) Repeat (b) for a 2- and 3-channel transponder. (d) How many channels are needed to achieve the minimum P_T in (a)?

5.8 Consider a filter function $|H(\omega)| = \omega^n$, operating with an FM carrier at its input. The carrier has frequency ω_0 rps and frequency modulation $\Delta_\omega m(t)$ rps. The filter is followed by an amplifier with AM/PM coefficient η rad/volt. By expanding around ω_0, show that the AM/PM power varies at $(\eta n)^2$.

5.9 In nonlinear FDMA, optimal backoff points for maximizing CNR_d depend on the parameter Q, the number of carrier signals passing through the satellite at any one time, as in Problem 5.3. Devise a satellite block diagram (onboard equipment) that will optimally adapt an FDMA satellite for optimal operation, as the number of active carriers change in time.

REFERENCES

1. "Demand Assignment," in *Satellite Communications*, ed. H. Van Trees (New York: IEEE Press, 1979), section 3.6.5.

2. P. Shaft, "Limiting of Signals and Its Effect on Communication," *IEEE Trans. Comm. Tech*., vol. COM-13 (December 1965), pp. 504–512.

3. J. Sevy, "The Effect of FM Signals Through a Hard Limiting TWT," *IEEE Trans. Comm. Tech.*, vol. COM-14 (October 1966), pp. 568–578.

4. T. Spoor, "Intermodulation Noise in FDMA Communications Through a Hard Limiter," *IEEE Trans. Comm. Tech*., vol. Com-15 (August 1967), pp. 557–565.

5. W. Babcock, "Intermodulation Interference in Radio Systems," *BSTJ* (January 1953), pp. 63–69.

6. R. Westcott, "Investigation of Multiple FDMA Carriers Through a

Satellite TWT Operating Near Saturation," *Proc. IEEE*, vol. 114, no. 6 (June 1967), pp. 726–740.

7. R. Chapman, and J. Millard, "Intelligible Crosstalk with FM Carriers Through AM-PM Conversion," *IEEE Trans. Comm. Syst.*, vol. CS-12 (June 1964), pp. 160–166.

8. J. Bryson, "Intelligible Crosstalk in FM Systems with AM-PM Conversion," *IEEE Trans. Comm. Tech.*, vol. Com-19 (June 1971), pp. 366–368.

9. G. Stette, "Intelligible Crosstalk in Nonlinear Amplifiers: Calculation of AM-PM Transfer," *IEEE Trans. Comm.*, vol. 52 (February 1975), pp. 256–268.

6
Time-Division Multiple Access

In multiple accessing through a satellite, uplink carriers can be separated in time rather than in frequency. Instead of assigning a frequency band to each uplink, we assign a specific time interval, and a given station transmits only during its allotted interval. This type of operation is referred to as *time-division multiple access (TDMA)*. As we shall see, TDMA theoretically avoids the problem of many carriers trying to pass through the satellite at the same time, thereby avoiding the intermodulation problem of FDMA. However, while FDMA involves relatively simple frequency tuning for accessing, and providing essentially independent channel on-off operation, TDMA requires communication concepts that are relatively new. To accommodate many users, TDMA time intervals must necessarily be short, requiring burst-type transmissions, and the time intervals of all users must be properly and accurately synchronized, requiring several levels of timing control. The required high-speed hardware for these operations is relatively new and, in many cases, is still under development.

Experimental TDMA systems were first reported in 1965 [1]. These early systems proved that time-interleaved, short-interval communications were in fact technically feasible. Later systems [2-7] established that advanced operational TDMA concepts, such as high-accuracy, fast-acquisition synchronization, and high-capacity data formats, were both possible and advantageous. In this chapter we examine TDMA satellite communications.

6.1 THE TDMA SYSTEM

In time-division multiple-accessing systems, each uplink earth station is assigned a prescribed time interval in which to relay through the satellite. During its interval, a particular station has exclusive use of the satellite, and its uplink transmission alone is processed by the satellite for the downlink.

This means each carrier can use the same carrier frequency and make use of the entire satellite bandwidth during its interval. Since no other carrier uses the satellite during this time interval, no intermodulation or carrier suppression occurs, and the satellite amplifier can be operated in saturation so as to achieve maximal output power. Thus TDMA downlinks always operate at full saturation power of the satellite. However, the entire TDMA system must have all earth stations properly synchronized in time so that each can transmit through the satellite only during its prescribed interval, without interfering with the intervals of other stations. This time synchronization between satellite and all earth stations is called **network synchronization**. A downlink earth station, wishing to receive the transmissions from a particular uplink, must gate in to the satellite signal during the proper time interval. This means that all earth stations, whether transmitting or receiving, must be part of the synchronized network.

Since there may be many users of the TDMA satellite, each wishing to establish a communication link in approximately real time, the total transmission time must be shared by all users. Thus, the time intervals of each station must be relatively short, and repeated at regular epochs. This type of short-burst, periodic operation is most conducive to digital operation, where each station transmits bursts of data bits during its intervals. However, TDMA systems using digital transmissions require that all receiving stations must obtain decoder synchronization in each interval, in addition to the required network synchronization for slot timing. For phase-coherent decoding, decoder synchronization requires establishing both a coherent phase reference and a coherent bit timing clock before any bits can be decoded within a slot. Also, word sync may be needed to separate the digital words occurring during a slot. This hierarchy of decoding synchronization must be established at the very beginning of each slot if the subsequent slot bits are to be decoded. Furthermore, since each slot contains data from a different source, synchronization must be separately established for each slot being received. In fact, even when receiving from the same station, synchronization must generally be reestablished from one periodic burst to the next. Hence digital communications with TDMA has an inherent requirement for rapid synchronization in order to perform successfully. The technology for short-burst communications is rather new, and of course, will be closely linked to the development of high-speed digital processing hardware.

TDMA Formats

A TDMA satellite system is shown in Figure 6.1a. Each uplink station is assigned one of a contiguous set of time slots, and the group of all such time

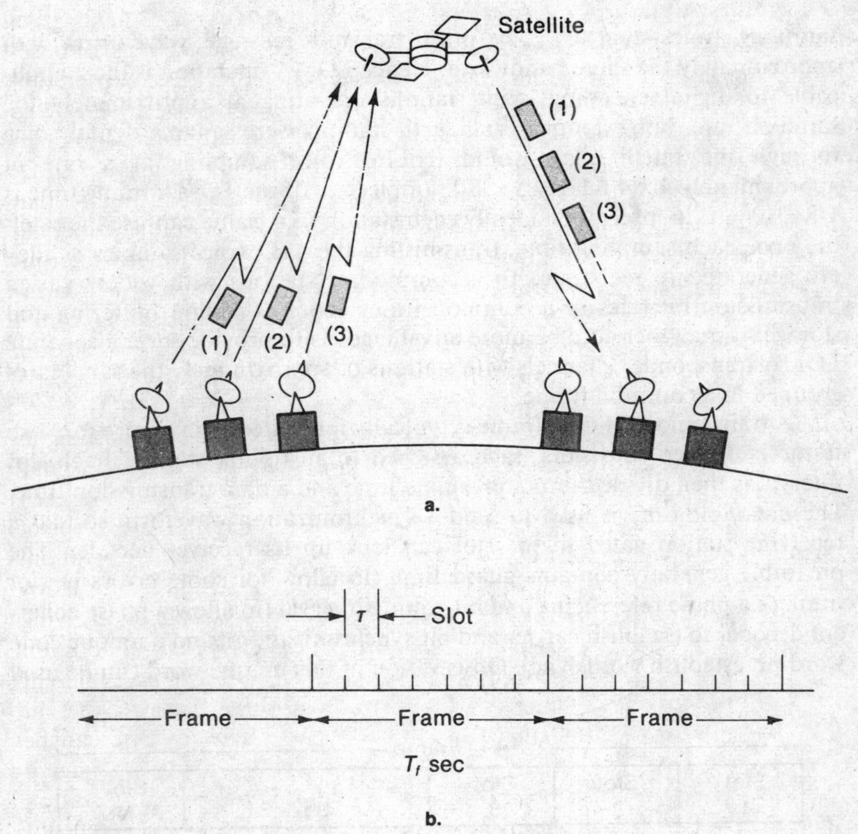

Figure 6.1. TDMA satellite system. (a) System model. (b) Time-frame structure.

slots forms a transponder time frame (Figure 6.1b). We assume a single transponder operating at the satellite. During each successive frame, each transmitting station has its own specific slot. Hence, if slots are τ sec, a given station uses the satellite τ sec during each T_f sec frame. The station transmits bursts of data bits during its τ-sec transmission time, while using the remaining frame time to generate the next set of data bits. If the frame time corresponds exactly to the sampling time of the earth-station message, then the bit transmissions during the τ-sec intervals would correspond to the real-time transmission of a quantization word. For this to be true for all stations of the network simultaneously, all stations must use the same sampling times—that is, they must transmit message waveforms with approximately the same bandwidth. Hence TDMA operation is most applicable to digital encoding, with stations operating at approximately the same bit rate. For example, if all earth-stations were sending digital voice through the satellite, all would require voice sampling at a rate of approximately 2×4 KHz $= 8 \times 10^3$ samples/sec. If the TDMA frame time is $1/8 \times 10^3 = 0.16$ msec, then ideally each station in a frame can use the satellite once each sampling time, transmitting the A–D voice samples as they are generated in real time. To accommodate stations with widely varied transmission bit rates in a common frame requires station buffering and storage. It may therefore be more advantageous to provide several separate TDMA transponder channels with stations of approximately the same rates grouped in a common frame.

A transponder TDMA frame is typically formatted as in Figure 6.2. The frame is divided into slots, each assigned to an uplink station. Each slot interval is then divided into a **preamble** time and a data transmission time. The preamble time is used to send a synchronization waveform so that a receiving station gated to the slot can lock up its receiver decoder. The preamble generally contains guard time (to allow for some errors in slot timing), a phase referencing and bit-timing interval (to allow a phase coherent decoder to establish carrier and bit synchronization), and a unique code word (to establish word sync). Observation of this unique word can be used

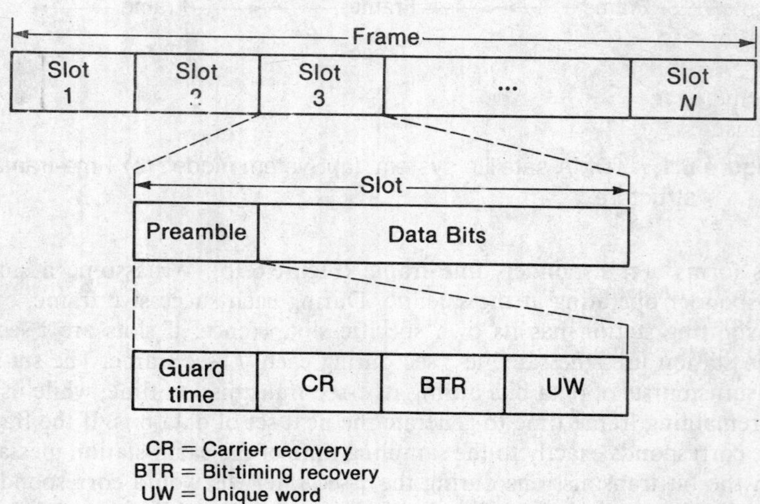

Figure 6.2. Frame formatting in TDMA.

to set the word markers for the data transmission during the remainder of that slot interval. Each frame slot can be formatted in this way. Any station can be received by gating in at the proper slot time, referred to the earth-station time axis. The latter must be separately referenced by each earth station to the satellite time axis through network synchronization. All transmitting stations use the same carrier frequency, so that every receiving station has (approximately) frequency synchronization throughout a frame. Thus, the preamb'e time is needed primarily to adjust to the phase and bit timing of a given station, which can possibly drift from one frame to the next.

Preambles

In general, preamble time should be long enough to establish reliable synchronization, but should be short compared to the data transmission time. The ratio of preamble time to total slot time is sometimes called the **preamble efficiency**, or **overhead**. We often measure these times in numbers of bits or symbols and write this efficiency as

$$\eta_p = \frac{\text{Number of preamble symbols}}{\text{Total number of symbols per slot}} \tag{6.1.1}$$

Typically, TDMA systems are designed with overhead efficiencies of about 10% or less.

Assume that a preamble requires a total of P transmitted bits for sync, including guard-time, carrier referencing, bit timing, and unique word transmission. For a preamble efficiency of η_p in (6.1.1), a total of D data bits must be sent in each slot, where

$$D = \left(\frac{1-\eta_p}{\eta_p}\right)P \tag{6.1.2}$$

Let the data to be transmitted during a slot correspond to transmissions from digital sources producing b bits/slot and operating at a rate of R_c bits/sec. This requires that the frame time be

$$T_f = \frac{b}{R_c} \text{ sec} \tag{6.1.3}$$

For example, a digital voice source operating at 64 Kbps, sending 4 bits in each burst, would require a frame time of $T_f = 4/64 \times 10^3 = 0.063$ msec, while 8-bit bursts would require 0.125 msec and 16-bit bursts, 0.25 msec. Thus we see that frame times in TDMA voice formats are usually relatively short, which of course complicates the slot synchronization operation. Increasing the number of bits per burst lengthens the frame time, but as the frame is lengthened, more time elapses between bursts from a given station, allowing more drift time to produce larger station oscillator phase shifts. Hence shorter frames tend to produce better burst-to-burst sync coherency. Note that b refers to the number of bits per burst from a single source (we refer to this as a single channel) while D in (6.1.2) refers to the total number of data during the entire slot.

Assume the satellite channel has an RF capability of sending bits at a rate R_{RF} bps, based on the satellite bandwidth and power levels. This means the slot time τ must be long enough to allow $D+P$ bits. Hence $R_{RF}\tau = D + P$, or

$$\tau = \frac{D+P}{R_{RF}} \text{sec} \tag{6.1.4}$$

The number of slots in a frame is then

$$Q = \frac{T_f}{\tau} = \frac{bR_{RF}}{R_c(D+P)} \tag{6.1.5}$$

The total number of data channels (i.e., separate sources operating at b bits/burst and rate R_c bps) that can be accommodated in the TDMA frame is then

$$\begin{aligned} K &= \frac{QP}{b} \\ &= \frac{D}{R_c\tau} \\ &= \frac{\left(R_{RF} - \dfrac{P}{\tau}\right)}{R_c} \end{aligned} \tag{6.1.6}$$

Note that a TDMA frame can generally support many more channels than the number of slots, since D is generally much larger than b. Equation (6.1.6) is plotted in Figure 6.3, showing the number of TDMA channels that can be supported by particular satellite bit rates, for different preamble efficiencies.

As an example, suppose a QPSK TDMA system requires a total preamble of 40 QPSK symbols (in the next section we consider how to estimate the required preamble length) and is to operate with a 10% preamble efficiency. Sampled voice transmissions at a rate of 64 Kbps and 8 bits/burst

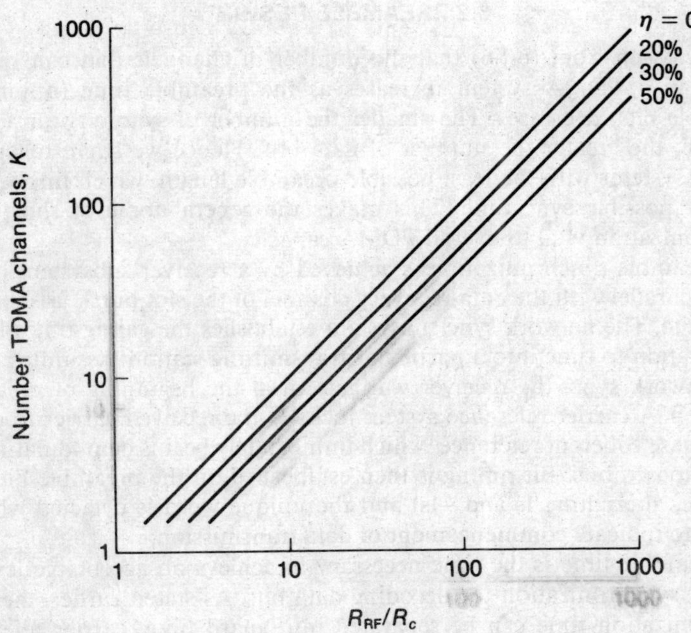

Figure 6.3: Number TDMA channels vs. RF bandwidth and frame efficiency.

are to be transmitted over a TDMA satellite with an RF bit rate of 60 Mbps. The total number of QPSK data bits per slot should be 40/0.1 = 400 symbols = 800 bits. The required frame length must then be $8/6.4 \times 10^3$ = 0.12 msec. The slots are $(800 + 80)/60 \times 10^6$ = 14.6 μsec long. This means each frame has $Q = 0.12 \times 10^{-3}/\ 14.6 \times 10^{-6} \approx 9$ slots per frame, and a total of

$$K = \frac{(800)9}{(64 \times 10^3)(0.12 \times 10^{-3})} \approx 937 \qquad (6.1.7)$$

voice channels can be sent each frame. Each slot can therefore be divided into $937/9 \approx 117$ separate voice channels that are serially multiplexed and modulated onto the station carrier for that slot. With the same frame format, a single earth station can alternatively send data at a combined rate of 800/0.12 msec = 6.7 Mbps through the TDMA link.

6.2 PREAMBLE DESIGN

We have seen from (6.1.6) that the number of channels that can be supported in a TDMA system increases as the preamble time (number of preamble bits) decreases. The smaller the number of sync bits for a given slot size, the greater the number of data bits. Hence we strive to operate TDMA systems with the least possible preamble length, which implies that shortest possible sync time. This makes the general topic of short-burst synchronization vital to overall TDMA capacity.

Preamble synchronization is achieved by a receiver subsystem operating in parallel with the data recovery channel of the slot burst, as shown in Figure 6.4. The network sync subsystem establishes the gating times for an earth station to tune into a particular transmitting station. Assuming accurate network sync, the receiver will gate in at the beginning of preamble reception. A carrier reference system locks to the received carrier to establish a phase coherent reference, which immediately begins demodulating the superimposed bits. Bit timing is then established on the preamble bits (for example, alternating 1s and −1s) and the unique word is detected when it arrives to indicate commencement of data transmission.

Preamble time is the time necessary to achieve an acceptable level of receiver synchronization for decoding data bits. As stated earlier, the total synchronization time can be separated into guard time, carrier reference and bit sync time, and unique word recovery time. We investigate each of these separately.

Guard Time

The required guard time is set by the accuracy of the network sync clocks (to be discussed in Section 6.4). These clocks set the overall slot timing of

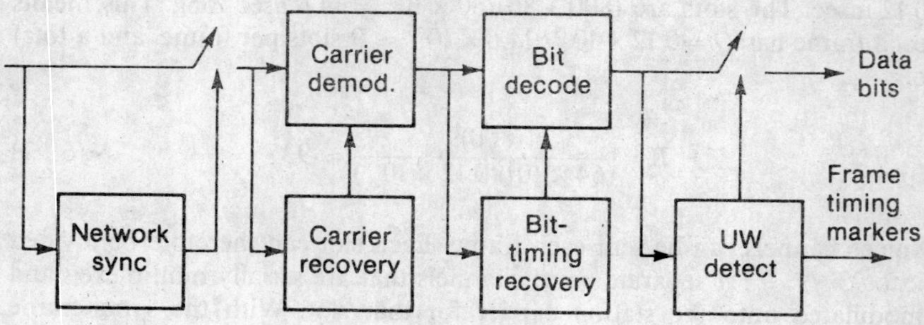

Figure 6.4. Preamble synchronization subsystem.

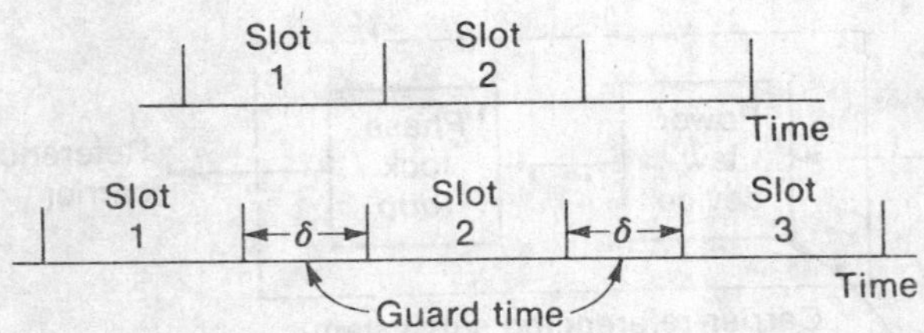

Figure 6.5. Slot timing and guard spacing.

the earth stations, and errors in this timing will tend to offset the slot gate time (Figure 6.5). By allowing some guard time between slots, these errors will not significantly degrade TDMA operation. If there is an inherent rms network timing error e_τ, then guard time should be about $\pm$ 10 times e_τ in order to fully compensate. Hence guard time is generally taken as

$$\delta = 20 e_\tau \tag{6.2.1}$$

Expressed in data bit times,

$$\frac{\delta}{T_b} = 20\left(\frac{e_\tau}{T_b}\right) \tag{6.2.2}$$

Since e_τ can generally be maintained within a fraction of a bit, guard times of only one or two bits are usually all that is needed.

Carrier Reference Time

At the beginning of a slot, the carrier burst from the satellite is received at the earth station with a known frequency but an arbitrary phase offset. Phase reference is achieved by phase locking a local reference to the received reference burst during the preamble. The referencing time is therefore the time needed to achieve phase pull-in. The theory of referencing loops operating with typical digital formats is discussed in Appendix B. For BPSK or QPSK carriers, reference systems are usually power law devices (squaring or fourth-order loops) followed by tracking loops, as shown in Figure 6.6. The power law device removes the modulation, and the loop locks to the resultant carrier phase. Phase lock is essentially achieved when the phase error between the unmodulated carrier and the local carrier is reduced to about 5°–10°. The time to reduce an initial phase error of ϕ_0 to these values depends on the loop transient time, which is related to the loop

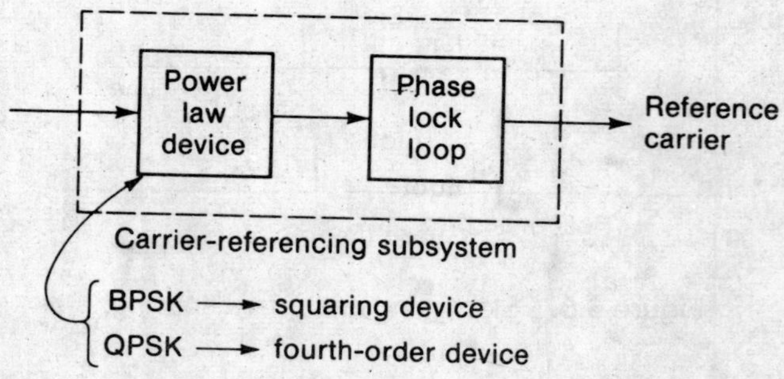

Figure 6.6. Carrier-recovery subsystem. Power law device depends on data modulation format.

natural frequency ω_n and **damping factor** ζ. These parameters are related to the **loop noise bandwidth** B_L by

$$B_L = \frac{\omega_n}{8\zeta}(1 + 4\zeta^2) \tag{6.2.3}$$

The **loop response time** (time to reduce an offset to about 10% of its initial value) is about $0.5/\omega_n$. Hence

$$\text{Loop response time} \approx \frac{(1 + 4\zeta^2)}{16\zeta B_L} \tag{6.2.4}$$

For loop damping of $\zeta = 0.707$ (a common value for trading off steady-state and noise-bandwidth values), $B_L = 0.53\omega_n$, and when converted to bits, (6.2.4) becomes

$$\begin{bmatrix} \text{Loop response time} \\ \text{in numbers of} \\ \text{bits} \end{bmatrix} \approx \frac{0.26}{B_L T_b} \tag{6.2.5}$$

Equation (6.2.5) is plotted in Figure 6.7, showing the number of bits that must generally be allowed for carrier referencing. For example, if $B_L T_b = 0.01$, then the response time will be about 26 bit times. However, while increasing B_L reduces response time, it also increases the loop noise bandwidth, which makes it more difficult to maintain loop lock-up. To examine this lock-up effect, it is necessary to determine the loop carrier-to-noise ratio CNR_L produced from the retransmission through the satellite. The latter can be computed via the analyses in Chapter 4, since the satellite

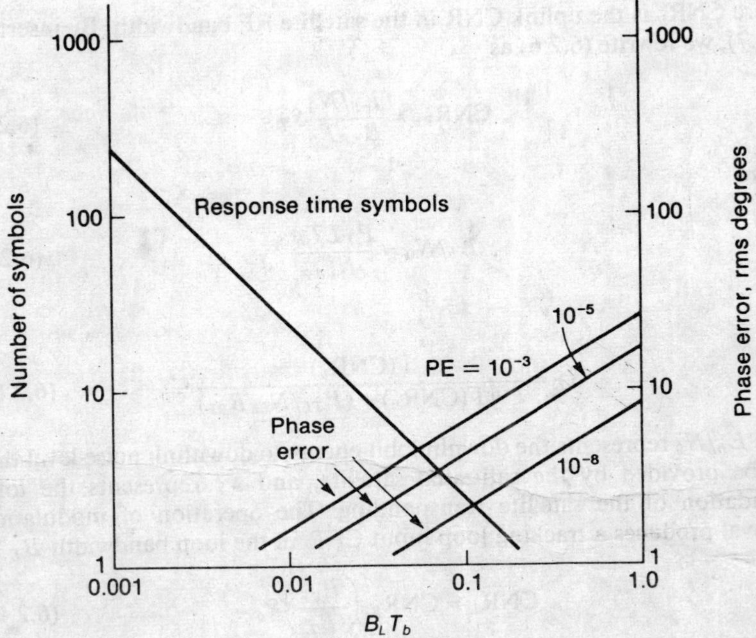

Figure 6.7. Carrier-referencing performance: number of symbols to pull in and resulting rms phase error.

acts as a single carrier, hard-limiting transponder during each slot time. After uplink-downlink retransmission we can use (4.5.10) to compute the downlink CNR in the RF bandwidth as

$$\text{CNR}_{\text{RF}} = \frac{P_T \alpha_s^2 L}{[\alpha_n^2 P_T L + N_{0d}] B_{\text{RF}}} \tag{6.2.6}$$

where P_T is the saturation power, and α_s^2, α_n^2 are the signal and noise suppression factors of a hard-limiting TWT (from (4.5.15)).

$$\alpha_s^2 = \frac{\Gamma(\text{CNR}_u)}{1 + \Gamma(\text{CNR}_u)} \tag{6.2.7a}$$

$$\alpha_n^2 = \frac{1}{1 + \Gamma(\text{CNR}_u)} \tag{6.2.7b}$$

where CNR_u is the uplink CNR in the satellite RF bandwidth. By inserting (6.2.7), we rewrite (6.2.6) as

$$\mathrm{CNR_{RF}} = \frac{E_b/N_0}{B_{\mathrm{RF}} T_b} \mathcal{S}_T \tag{6.2.8}$$

where

$$E_b/N_0 = \frac{P_T L T_b}{N_{0d}} \tag{6.2.9}$$

and

$$\mathcal{S}_T = \frac{\Gamma(\mathrm{CNR}_u)}{1 + \Gamma(\mathrm{CNR}_u) + (P_{TL}/N_{0d} B_{\mathrm{RF}})} \tag{6.2.10}$$

Here E_b/N_0 represents the downlink bit energy to downlink noise level that can be provided by the saturated satellite, and $\mathcal{S}_T$ represents the total degradation of the satellite transponding. The operation of modulation removal produces a tracking loop input CNR in the loop bandwidth B_L of

$$\mathrm{CNR}_L = \mathrm{CNR_{RF}} \left(\frac{B_{\mathrm{RF}}}{B_L} \right) \mathcal{S}_q \tag{6.2.11}$$

where $\mathcal{S}_q$ is the squaring loss (see Appendix B),

$$\mathcal{S}_q = \left[1 + \frac{2}{\mathrm{CNR_{RF}}} \right]^{-1} \quad \text{for BPSK} \tag{6.2.12a}$$

$$= \left[1 + \frac{4.5}{\mathrm{CNR_{RF}}} + \frac{6}{(\mathrm{CNR_{RF}})^2} + \frac{1.5}{(\mathrm{CNR_{RF}})^3} \right]^{-1} \quad \text{for QPSK} \tag{6.2.12b}$$

Rewriting,

$$\mathrm{CNR}_L = \frac{E_b/N_0}{B_L T_b} \mathcal{S}_T \mathcal{S}_q \tag{6.2.13}$$

The rms loop phase error, which should be maintained at no larger than about 5° for minimal decoding degradation, is then given by

$$\begin{aligned} \sigma_\phi &= \left(\frac{1}{\mathrm{CNR}_L} \right)^{1/2} \\ &= \left[\frac{B_L T_b}{(E_b/N_0) \mathcal{S}_T \mathcal{S}_q} \right]^{1/2} \end{aligned} \tag{6.2.14}$$

Thus, increasing loop bandwidth B_L shortens acquisition time, but it also increases loop noise, which can degrade phase lock-in if the phase error caused by the noise becomes too excessive. Figure 6.7 also plots (6.2.14) for various values of BPSK bit-error probability [which sets the value of the denominator in (6.2.14)]. Plots of this type allow a proper balance to be obtained for both acquisition time and loop phase error.

A serious problem that arises with short-burst phase referencing with phase lock loops is loop **hang-up**. If the initial phase offset that is to be

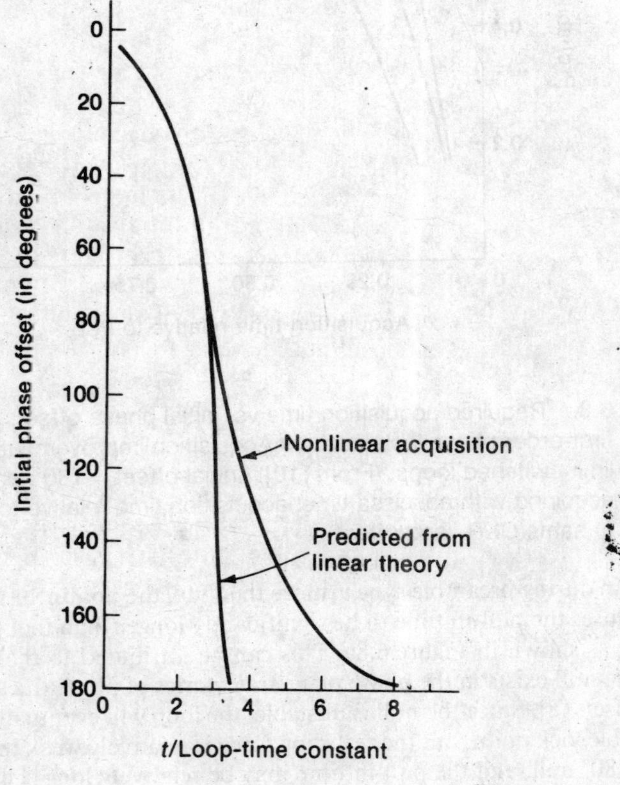

Figure 6.8. Required acquisition time vs. initial phase offset. (a) With first-order phase lock loop. (b) Acquisition improvement with limit-switched loops. (From [10]) (Initial offset = 180°; probability of acquiring with abscissa time; acquisition time relative to that of PLL at same CNR_L and offset).

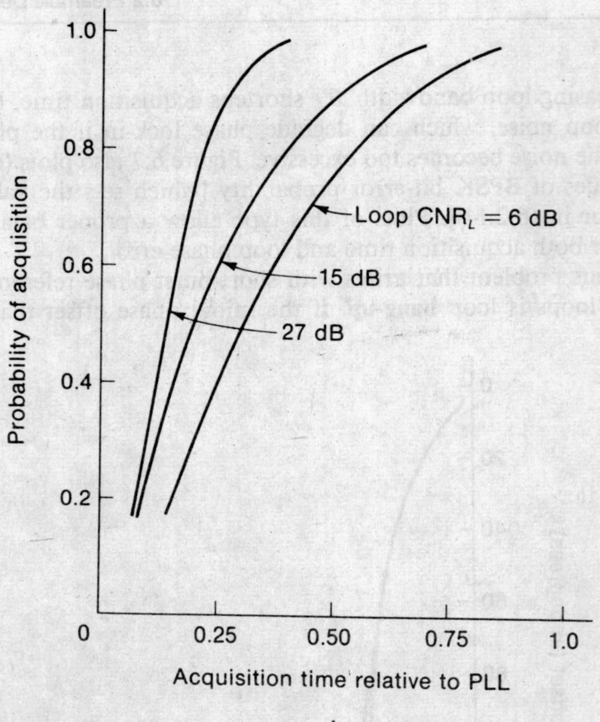

Figure 6.8. Required acquisition time vs. initial phase offset. (a) With first-order phase lock loop. (b) Acquisition improvement with limit-switched loops. (From [10]) (Initial offset = 180°; probability of acquiring with abscissa time; acquisition time relative to that of PLL at same CNR$_L$ and offset).

pulled in during preamble sync is more than 90°, the nonlinear nature of the loop causes the pull-in time to be significantly longer than that predicted by (6.2.5), as shown in Figure 6.8a. This can be attributed to the fact that an unstable null exists in the phase plane trajectories of phase tracking loops at 180° offsets [8]. Since the null is unstable, the loop will eventually slide away to a stable lock point, but the restoring force is relatively weak in the vicinity of the 180° null, and the pull-in time may be relatively long. This slow pull-in will be extremely detrimental to the short-burst phase referencing needed in TDMA operation.

Several alternative schemes have been suggested for avoiding hang-up. One is to modify the standard phase lock loop to aid pull-in when the initial phase offset is large. Gardner [8, 9] suggests inserting an additional restoring voltage of the proper polarity when the phase offset is greater than 90° (Figure 6.9a). This requires a logic circuit to determine polarity and time of

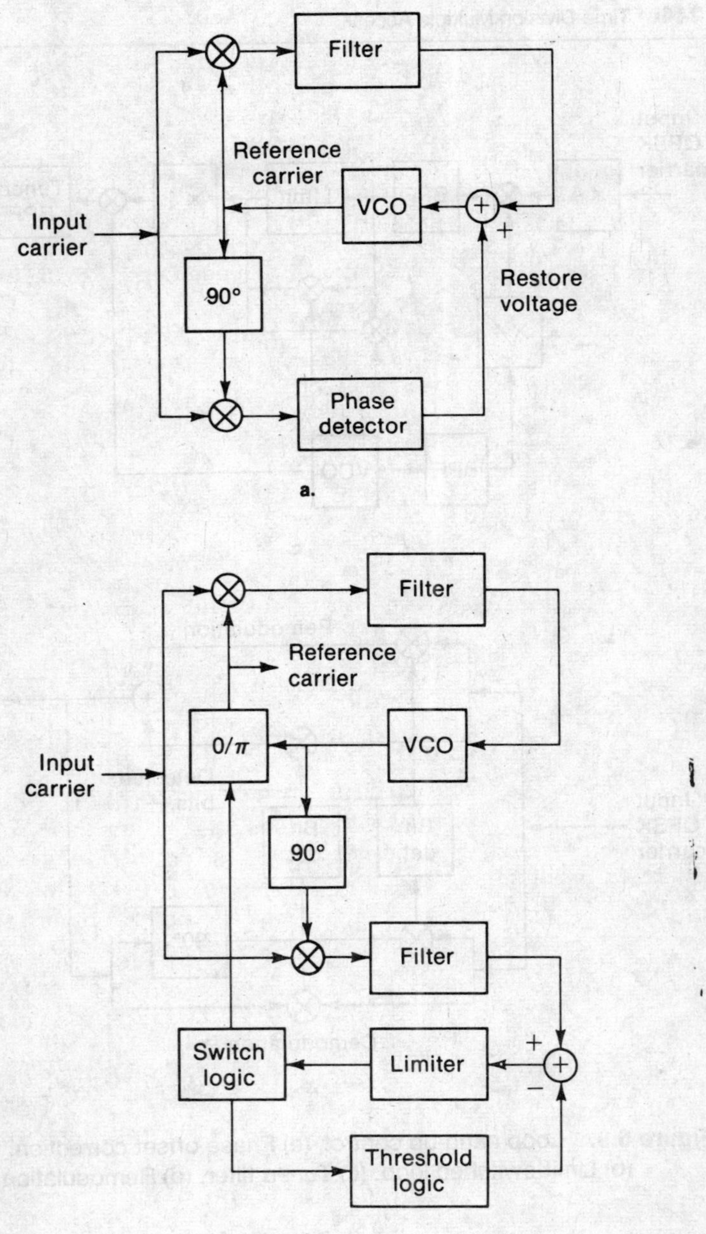

Figure 6.9. Loop hang-up control. (a) Phase offset correction. (b) Limit-switched loop. (c) Tuned filter. (d) Remodulation scheme.

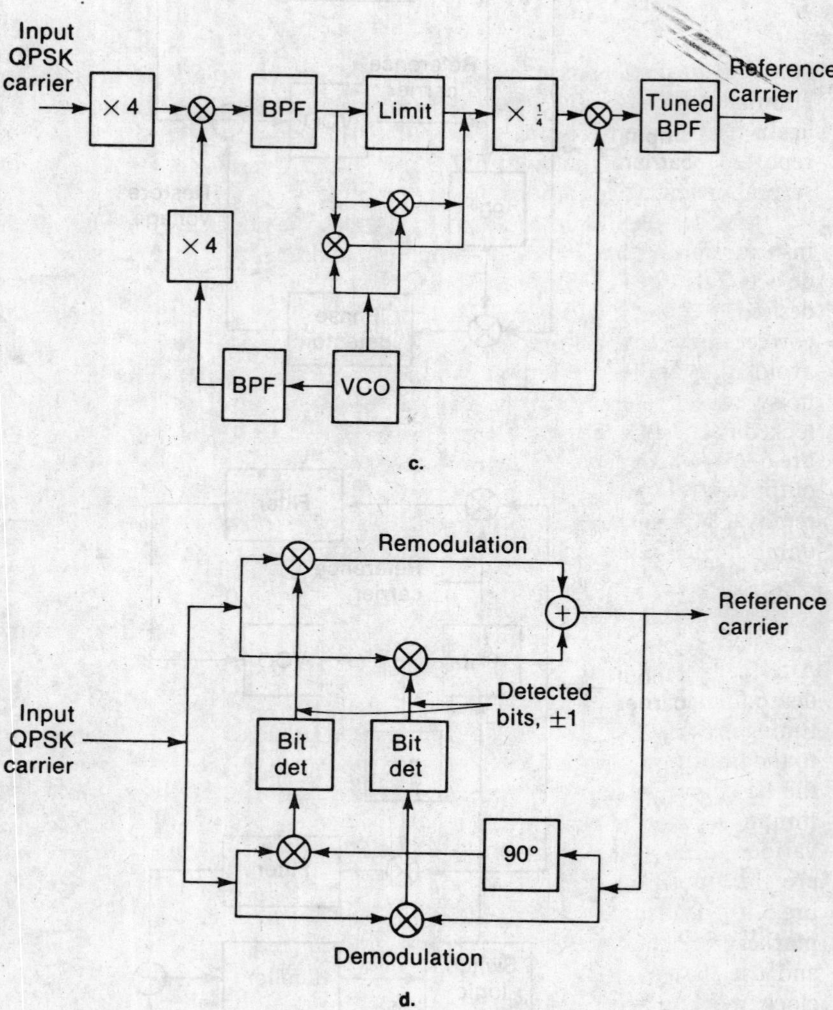

Figure 6.9. Loop hang-up control. (a) Phase offset correction. (b) Limit-switched loop. (c) Tuned filter. (d) Remodulation scheme.

voltage insertion, and therefore needs high CNR to ensure correct decisioning. A variation of this concept is the *limit-switched loop* in Figure 6.9b proposed by Taylor et al. [10]. Instead of applying an external voltage, the loop VCO is internally shifted by 180° when a large offset is detected. This converts unstable phase offsets near 180° to stable offsets near 0°, and eliminates hang-up. The loop is basically a decision-directed loop, which again uses phase decisions to modify error signals. Figure 6.8b shows the reported results of hang-up reduction by limit-switched operation under several operating conditions.

Another technique to avoid hang-up is to not use a loop at all, but instead simply use a narrow-band tuned filter following the power law device (Figure 6.9c). Since the power law device output is generally at the desired frequency, and if the CNR is sufficiently high, a tuned filter at the correct frequency will produce a reasonably accurate carrier reference. This avoids the nonlinear loop operation at large offset angles, but generates a noisy carrier reference instead of the relatively clean reference of a phase locked VCO. An alternative to this is the remodulation scheme (Figure 6.9d), which replaces the power law operation by bit estimators whose outputs are used to remodulate back onto a carrier for data modulation removal. A tracking filter then reproduces the carrier reference from the unmodulated reference.

Bit Timing

After carrier referencing is achieved, the phase modulated carrier can be demodulated to baseband, but the data bit cannot be decoded until bit timing is achieved. Bit timing is obtained by locking a decoder timing block to the transition points in the baseband waveform. A transition occurs when the baseband waveform changes sign at the end of each data symbol. Bit timing is achieved by a symbol synchronizer subsystem that can take on various forms (see Appendix B, Section B.6) The most common methods are the transition tracking loop and the filter-square synchronizer (Figure 6.10). Transition trackers measure the timing error between local clock markers and the measured transition times of the demodulated baseband, and use the error to pull the local clock into synchronization. The local clock markers then time the subsequent bit decoder, as was shown in Figure 6.4. Variations in the form of the symbol synchronizer loops differ primarily in the way in which the transition errors are measured, and in the way the bit modulation is removed. Filter-square synchronizers use a baseband nonlinear operation to generate an unmodulated tone at the bit-rate frequency. A phase lock loop can then be locked to that tone, producing timing markers in phase with the transitions. The design of the prefilter and the square (usually accomplished by a delay and multiply circuit) are the key aspect of bit synchronizer implementation [11].

The number of bit times needed to achieve adequate bit timing depends on the number of symbol transitions that must be observed for accurate

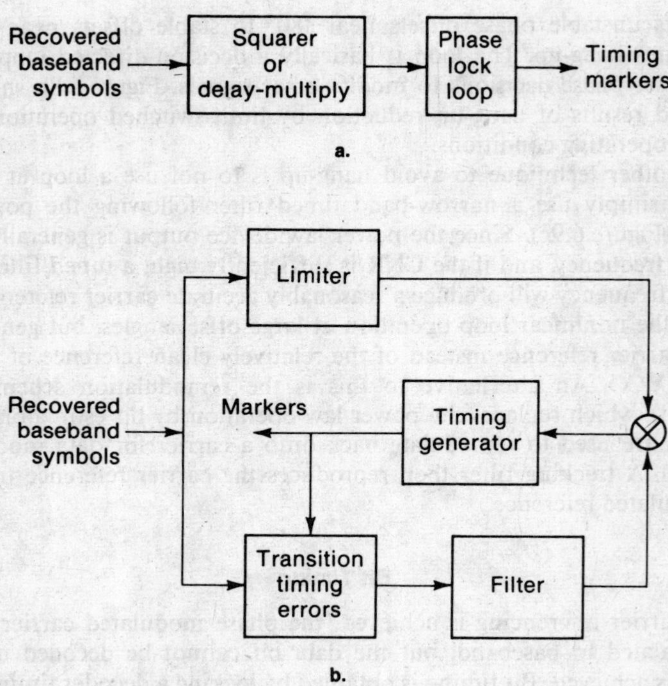

Figure 6.10. Bit-timing subsystems. (a) Squaring system. (b) Transition tracking.

local clock control. Since each symbol transition is measured in noise, increasing the number of symbols accumulated prior to timing adjustment reduces the effective timing error variance. The rms timing error per symbol time of a symbol-synchronizing loop is given by

$$e_t = \frac{1}{[m(E_b/N_0)\mathcal{S}_T\mathcal{S}_q]^{1/2}} \tag{6.2.15}$$

where m is the number of symbols accumulated, $\mathcal{S}_T$ is again the transponder loss, and $\mathcal{S}_q$ is the squaring loss, depending on whether a transition tracking loop or filter-squarer is used [see equation (B.4.8) and (B.4.17) of Appendix B]. Figure 6.11 shows how bit-timing rms error is reduced as the number of accumulations is increased, for several values of desired bit error probability. Bit timing errors should be no larger than about 10% of the bit period in order to avoid significant decoding degradation. Figure 6.11 can be used to determine the necessary number of symbols m needed to achieve

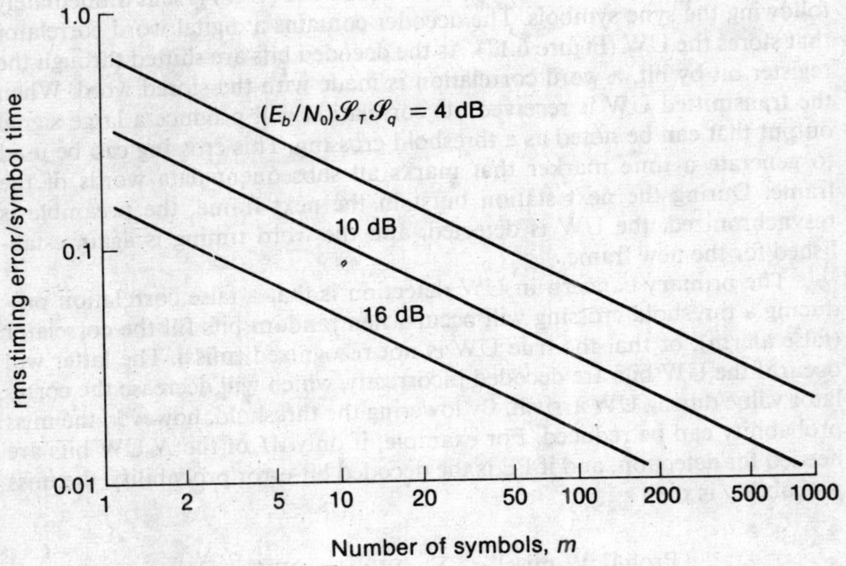

Figure 6.11. Bit-timing rms error vs. number of symbols accumulated (E_b = baseband symbol energy).

this value. It should be remembered that for BPSK carriers, a symbol corresponds to a bit, and a symbol transition can occur every bit time. In QPSK a symbol time corresponds to two bit times, and the number of symbols is half the number of bits.

A problem that occurs with symbol synchronization via transition tracking is that an abnormally long sequence of like bits will have no transition, and the loop will essentially "float" with no error updates during this time. During preamble lock-up this can be avoided by intentionally using bit patterns with many transitions (e.g., alternating ls and –ls). During a TDMA data burst, however, transitions cannot be guaranteed unless alternating sync symbols are purposely inserted periodically in place of data bits. The problem is entirely avoided by use of Manchester baseband signals (Section 2.3), which have guaranteed transitions at the middle of each symbol for any bit sequence.

Unique Word Detection

After obtaining both phase referencing and bit timing, subsequent carrier bits can now be decoded. To mark the data words in the frame, and to signal the beginning of data transmission, a **unique word (UW)** is sent immediately following the sync symbols. The decoder contains a digital word correlator that stores the UW (Figure 6.12). As the decoded bits are shifted through the register bit by bit, a word correlation is made with the stored word. When the transmitted UW is received, its correlation will produce a large signal output that can be noted as a threshold crossing. This crossing can be used to generate a time marker that marks all subsequent data words of the frame. During the next station burst in the next frame, the preamble is resynchronized, the UW is detected, and the word timing is again established for the new frame.

The primary concern in UW detection is that a false correlation producing a threshold crossing will occur when random bits fill the correlator (false alarm), or that the true UW is not recognized (miss). The latter will occur if the UW bits are decoded incorrectly, which will decrease the correlator value during UW arrival. By lowering the threshold, however, the miss probability can be reduced. For example, if only M of the N UW bits are needed for detection, and if PE is the decoded bit-error probability, the miss probability is then

$$\text{Prob [UW miss]} = \sum_{i=N-M}^{N} (\text{PE})^i(1-\text{PE})^{N-i}\binom{N}{i} \tag{6.2.16}$$

On the other hand, decreasing M to lower the miss probability will increase

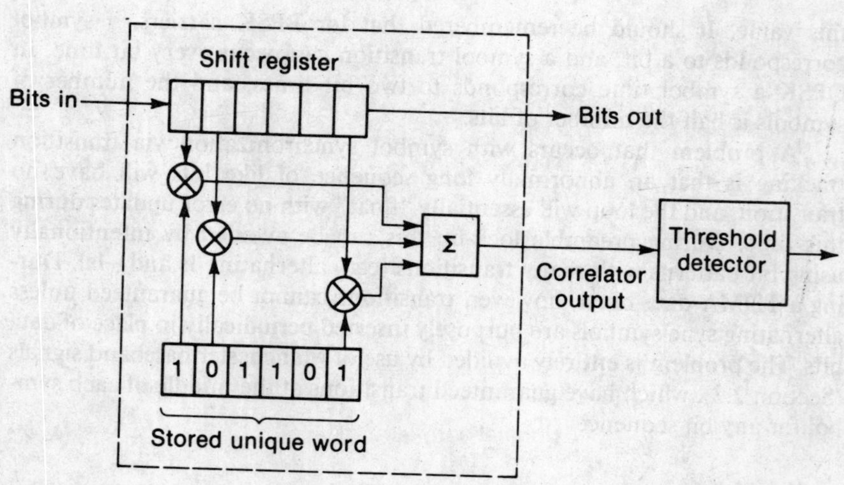

Figure 6.12. Unique word detector.

the probability of a false alarm. The probability that a random set of bits in the correlator will match M bits or more of the N bit UW is

$$\text{Prob [UW false alarm]} = \frac{1}{2^N}\sum_{i=M}^{N}\binom{N}{i} \tag{6.2.17}$$

If we assume M is selected as a fixed fraction of the word length N, then increasing N decreases both the false alarm and miss probabilities of UW detection. Figure 6.13 plots (6.2.16) and (6.2.17) as a function of word length N. Of course, increasing UW length adds to the preamble length.

False alarm probabilities also can be reduced by the use of **forward**

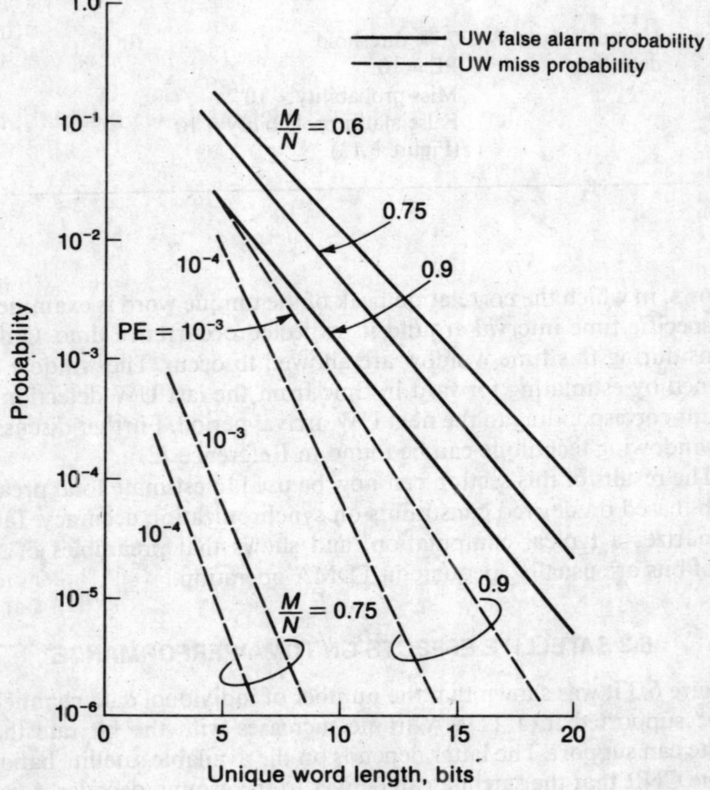

Figure 6.13. Miss and false alarm probabilities for unique word (UW) detection vs. word length.

Table 6.1. Preamble length computation.

Sync operation	*Constraints*	*Number bits*
Carrier referencing	$B_L T_b = 0.01$ PE = 10^{-3} phase error = 2° (Figure 6.7)	20
Bit timing	10% accuracy $E_b/N_0 = 10$ dB (Figure 6.11)	10 symbols = 10 bits BPSK = 20 bits QPSK
Unique word detection	75% threshold PE = 10^{-3} Miss probability = 10^{-4} False alarm probability = 10^{-4} (Figure 6.13)	10

windows, in which the correlation peak of the unique word is examined only in a specific time interval around its expected occurrence time. Only false alarms during this time window are allowed to occur. The window can be obtained by estimating forward in time from the last UW detection by an amount corresponding to the next UW arrival period. Further discussion of this windowing technique can be found in Reference 12.

The results of this section can now be used to estimate total preamable length, based on desired constraints on synchronization accuracy. Table 6.1 summarizes a typical computation, and shows that preambles of several tens of bits are usually adequate in TDMA operation.

6.3 SATELLITE EFFECTS ON TDMA PERFORMANCE

In Figure 6.3 it was shown that the number of individual data channels that can be supported in a TDMA frame increases with the bit rate that the satellite can support. The latter depends on the available satellite bandwidth and the CNR that the satellite can deliver to the ground decoder. A satellite RF bandwidth B_{RF} will allow a bit rate

$$R_{\mathrm{RF}} = \eta_T B_{\mathrm{RF}} \tag{6.3.1}$$

where η_T is the satellite channel throughput, which depends on the encoding format of the TDMA carriers, as was discussed in Section 2.8. The bit rate permitted by the power level of the satellite depends on the receiver decoder E_b/N_0 and on the desired bit-error probability PE.

The receiver downlink CNR, after transponding through the satellite, is again obtained as in (6.2.8). Substituting with (6.2.9), the decoder E_b/N_0 is then

$$\frac{E_b}{N_0} = \left(\frac{P_T L T_b}{N_{0d}}\right) \mathscr{S}_T \tag{6.3.2}$$

with $\mathscr{S}_T$ given in (6.2.10). The allowable RF bit rate produced by the satellite is then

$$R_{\text{RF}} = \frac{P_T L \mathscr{S}_T}{\gamma N_{0d}} \tag{6.3.3}$$

where γ is the value of E_b/N_0 required to achieve the desired PE. The bit rate that can be supported by the satellite is the smaller of (6.3.1) and (6.3.3). This can then be converted to allowable number of channels using Figure 6.3.

Suppose we wish to send K QPSK digital carriers, each with bit rates of R_c bps through the TDMA system. Neglecting overhead bits, the required RF bandwidth is

$$B_{\text{RF}} = K R_c \tag{6.3.4}$$

If the desired PE is 10^{-5}, we require a decoder $E_b/N_0 = \gamma = 10$ dB. We wish to determine the required satellite power P_T that will support the K channels. Assume a given CNR_u, and assume that limiter suppression effects in the satellite are negligible ($\Gamma = 1$). Solving (6.3.3) yields

$$P_T \mathscr{S}_T = K R_c N_{0d} \gamma / L \tag{6.3.5}$$

Equations (6.3.4) and (6.3.5) are plotted in Figure 6.14 for several values of PE and CNR_u. As the satellite power is increased, the number K of channels operating at R_c bps and PE increases. Eventually a point is reached when the number of channels is limited by the uplink CNR_u rather than the satellite power. At the same time, the satellite bandwidth only permits a fixed number of channels. Thus, the overall system capability is determined by the smaller number of allowable channels determined by each of these constraints.

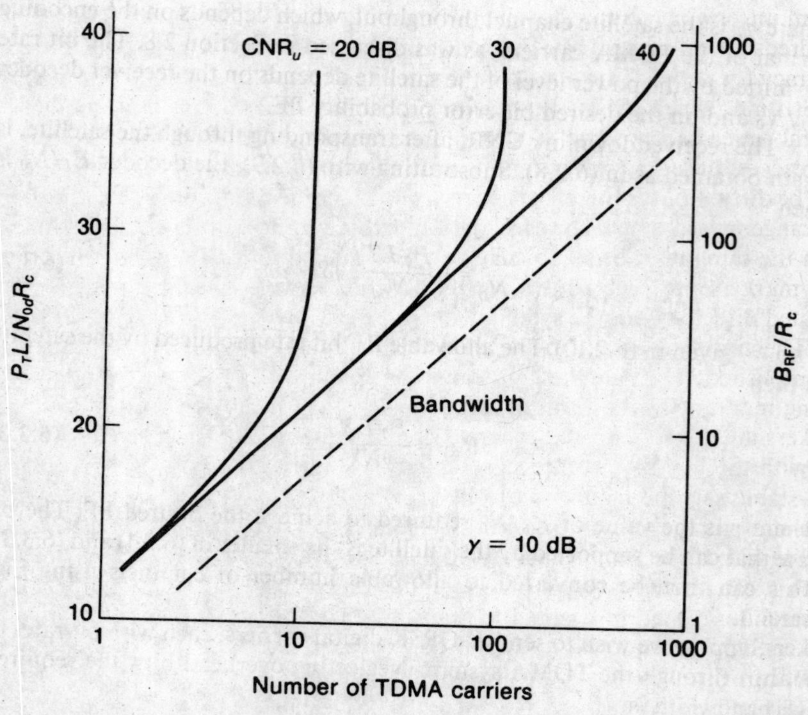

Figure 6.14. Required satellite power and RF bandwidth to support K TDMA channels.

6.4 NETWORK SYNCHRONIZATION

Network synchronization is achieved by clocking together all the transmitting and receiving stations of the TDMA system. Theoretically, if each transmitting station knew its range to the satellite precisely, network synchronization could be achieved by a single ground master clock used to time all earth stations. Accurate timing could be obtained from the master clock to each station using terrestrial links, and each station could be assigned a satellite time slot beginning at a fixed-time epoch relative to the master clock. Each station then need only adjust its uplink transmission so as to arrive at the satellite at exactly the correct time interval. The earth station would merely compensate in the uplink for the time delay due to its range to the satellite. This is referred to as **open loop timing**. In practice, however, range values to a satellite cannot be determined precisely due to inherent uncertainty in satellite location. Recall from Equation (1.4.9) that a typical

40 km uncertainty in satellite slant range will cause a timing uncertainty of hundreds of microseconds in transmission time. Unfortunately, timing accuracy for network sync must be maintained to within a small fraction of a slot time, which from the previous examples, may be on the order of several microseconds. In addition, maintaining common clocks with microsecond accuracy over remote earth stations for long periods of time may be difficult. It is therefore necessary to combine a common, simultaneous range measurement for each station with a timing marker transmission from the satellite in order to achieve the desired timing. The synchronization markers are sent in the downlink, and network synchronization is initiated directly from the satellite.

The timing diagram in Figure 6.15 illustrates how this can be easily accomplished. The satellite transmits continually a periodic sequence of timing markers (in the form of some convenient waveform). These timing markers must be sent over a separate satellite bandwidth, and cannot interfere with the TDMA channels. The markers can be self-generated on-board by a stable satellite clock, or can be relayed through the satellite from an earth-station clock. Each transmitting station is assigned a time slot at the satellite with respect to the marker points; that is, a station is assigned a time length t_s after each marker initiation, indicating where its time slot begins at the satellite. A station wishing to transmit first sends up its own ranging markers, which are retransmitted by the satellite and received back at the transmitting station, along with the satellite markers. By measuring the total two-way transmit time, t_r, of its range signal, a transmitting station can then adjust its own uplink transmission so it arrives exactly in its own time slot. From Figure 6.15 we can easily establish that, after receiving the satellite markers, a station must wait t_a sec before transmitting, where

$$t_a = \begin{cases} t_s - t_r & \text{if} \quad t_s > t_r \\ t_s - t_r + T_f & \text{if} \quad t_s < t_r \end{cases} \tag{6.4.1}$$

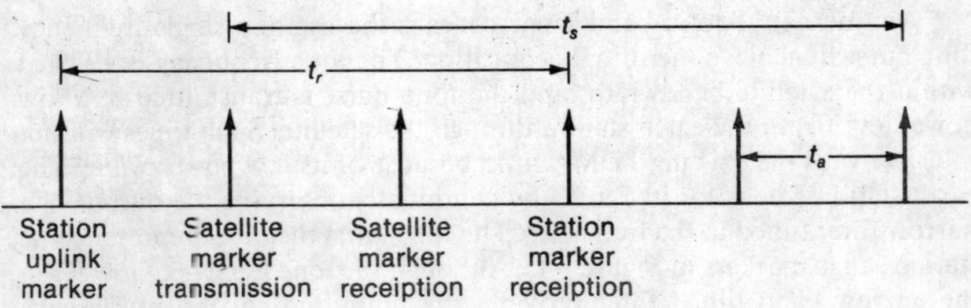

Figure 6.15. Timing diagram for TDMA network synchronization.

This now allows the earth station to acquire the correct slot, and transmission of the slot burst can begin. By monitoring the return time of the unique word of its own burst preamble (relative to the received timing marker of the satellite), closed-loop control of the slot timing can be maintained.

In effect, the earth station replaces the ranging signal by the preamble word, and adjusts uplink burst transmission so that the returned sync word falls exactly in the proper slot position t_s sec after marker reception. Since the satellite may drift slowly, the return preamble measurement must be continually updated to provide station-keeping, and maintain the transmitting station synchronized within the network. This discussion points out a basic disadvantage of this type of TDMA operation. The necessity for continual network synchronization requires that each transmitting station have the capability of receiving its own transmissions. This can occur only with global downlink antennas, and requires all transmitting stations to have reception capability also. Note, however, that a receiving earth station does not require a ranging operation, but only the ability to receive the satellite markers. If it wishes to recover the transmission from a station using a time slot t_s sec after marker generation, it need only adjust to the time slot beginning t_s sec after marker reception.

The role of the ranging signal is only to aid in the initial acquisition of the slot [i.e., in the initial estimate of the parameter t_a in (6.4.1)]. While the preamble unique word can be used to maintain slot timing, it cannot be used for the initial acquisition. This is due to the fact that without some a priori indication of slot location, transmission of the preamble burst from an earth station would directly interfere with other slots. For this reason, the ranging operation is generally performed in an adjacent satellite band so as not to interfere with the TDMA channels (e.g., ranging through a TT&C subsystem). An alternative that avoids use of other bands is use of low-level range codes that are spread over the entire satellite bandwidth. If the power level of the range code is low enough, it will not interfere with any TDMA slot, and its length can be correlated up to provide accurate range markers. However, each station would then have to have its own recognizable range code.

An alternative to in-band range codes is the use of a single-frequency tone burst to achieve the initial acquisition. The tone frequency is selected within the satellite bandwidth, and the tone burst is transmitted at a low power level from the earth station through the satellite. Such tones will not interfere with the existing TDMA links because of its low power value. The earth station listens for its return by continually observing the output of a narrow filter tuned to the frequency. The tone burst therefore represents the station range markers in Figure 6.15. Although the tone burst is of low level, the narrow band tuned filter provides the noise and carrier interference reduction that allows detection of the burst arrival.

The accuracy to which the network timing must be maintained is directly determined by the selection of the size of the station slot time τ in Figure 6.1. Inaccuracies in network timing will cause station transmissions to fall into adjacent time slots, causing station crosstalk. To prevent this, time guard bands at the end of each time slot must be provided, as shown in Figure 6.5.

Synchronization Subsystem

The network synchronization operations require a synchronization subsystem at the earth station similar to that shown in Figure 6.16. The satellite generates timing markers in the form of digital words that are broadcast continuously from the satellite to all earth stations. These marker words, for example, can be transmitted as BPSK modulation on a separate downlink carrier, usually located in a satellite band outside the TDMA band. These markers are produced at the TDMA frame rate, and correspond to a fixed word size. They can be produced from a satellite clock, or can be trans-

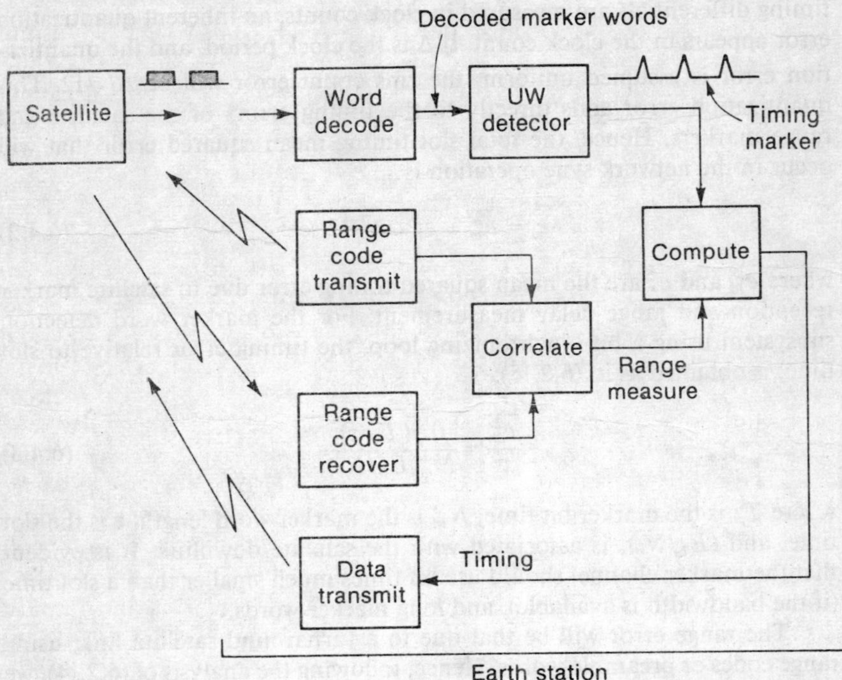

Figure 6.16. Earth-station network, synchronization subsystem.

ponded from an earth-control station. At the earth station the marker bits are decoded and correlated with stored marker words, as in unique word detection. When the decoded marker bits fill the receiver correlator, a timing marker is produced, corresponding to the time points t_s in Figure 6.15. Since the satellite marker channel must operate at low bit-error probability, the primary effect of the marker detection is bit-timing errors, which cause timing offsets in the satellite marker location.

Simultaneous with the marker reception is the range measurement via round-trip transmissions through the satellite and back, using either a range code (see Appendix C) or burst preamble. The timing markers and range markers are then used to adjust the subsequent uplink burst transmissions for the TDMA data link. The time differential measurement is usually made by starting a digital clock counter with the satellite markers, and stopping the count with the returned range marker. The number of counted clock ticks is then a numerical indication of the required uplink adjustment. Since the TDMA slot bursts are generally timed by a digital clock as well, the numerical clock count can be easily converted to fractional TDMA slot delays or advances by deleting or inserting clock cycles. However, when timing differentials are measured in clock counts, an inherent quantization error appears in the clock count. If Δ is the clock period, and the quantization error is assumed uniform, the rms count error will be $\Delta/\sqrt{12}$. This quantization error adds directly to the timing errors of the satellite and range markers. Hence, the total slot timing mean squared error that will occur in the network sync operation is

$$\overline{e_\tau^2} = \overline{e_m^2} + \overline{e_r^2} + \Delta^2/12 \text{ sec}^2 \tag{6.4.2}$$

where $\overline{e_m^2}$ and $\overline{e_r^2}$ are the mean squared timing error due to satellite marker reception and range delay measurement. For the marker word detection subsystem using a bit-synchronizing loop, the timing error relative to slot time, is obtained as in (6.2.15):

$$\frac{\overline{e_m^2}}{\tau^2} = \frac{0.5(T_b/\tau)^2}{N_m(E_b/N_0)_s} \tag{6.4.3}$$

where T_b is the marker bit time, N_m is the marker word length, τ is the slot time, and $(E_b/N_0)_s$ is associated with the satellite downlink. It is evident that the marker channel should use bit times much smaller than a slot time (if the bandwidth is available), and long marker words.

The range error will be that due to a turnaround satellite link, using range codes or preamble words. Hence, following the analysis of (6.2.14), we have

$$\frac{\overline{e_r^2}}{\tau^2} = \left(\frac{T_c}{\tau}\right)^2 \left(\frac{1}{N_c(E_c/N_0)\mathcal{S}_T}\right) \qquad \text{Range code} \qquad (6.4.4a)$$

$$= \left(\frac{T_b}{\tau}\right)^2 \left(\frac{1}{N_m(E_b/N_0)\mathcal{S}_T}\right) \qquad \text{Preamble word} \qquad (6.4.4b)$$

where E_b and E_c are the bit and code chip energies, N_c and N_m are the number of code and marker symbols, and T_c and T_b are the code chip or bit times. Figure 6.17 plots $\overline{e_\tau^2}$ in (6.4.2), using (6.4.3) and (6.4.4), as a function of downlink E_b/N_0 and several clock rates. Note that operation with network sync errors well below a fraction of a slot time is quite feasible. Further discussions of TDMA synchronization methods can be found in reference [13].

6.5 SS-TDMA

The advantage of spot beams in satellite links was pointed out in Section 3.6. It is therefore natural to extend the spot beam advantage to TDMA

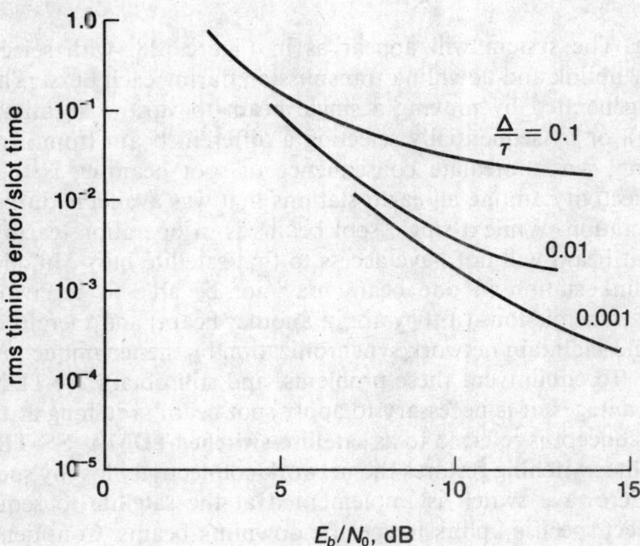

Figure 6.17. Timing error (rms) vs. downlink E_b/N_0 and clocking rates. Assumes $e_M = e_r$, $T_b/\tau\sqrt{N_M} = 0.001$.

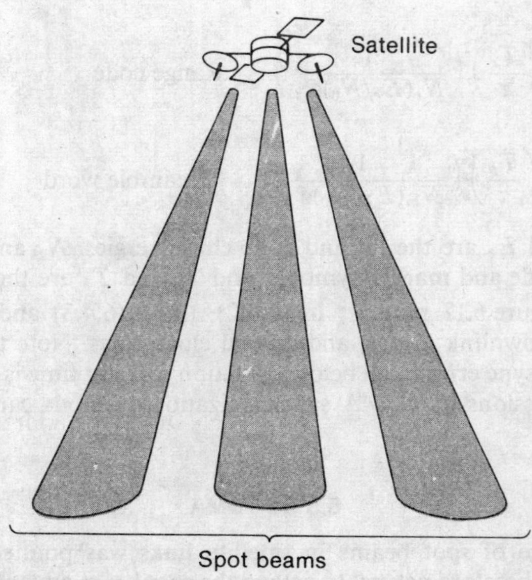

Figure 6.18. TDMA spot beam model.

operation. The system will appear as in Figure 6.18, with selected spot beams for uplink and downlink transmission during each burst. The beams must be generated by moving a single beam to various locations (**beam switching**), or by sequentially selecting a different beam from a multiple-beam array. An immediate consequence of spot beaming is the loss of interconnectivity among all earth stations that was available during global beam operation. While a single spot beams is in operation, earth stations not in that beam will not have access to that satellite burst. In addition, a given uplink station in one beam may not be able to receive its own downlink transmissions (if they are in another beam) and therefore cannot acquire and maintain network synchronization by the technique previously described. To circumvent these problems, and still obtain the TDMA spot beam advantages, it is necessary to apply spot beam switching at the satellite. This concept is referred to as **satellite-switched TDMA (SS-TDMA)**.

Satellite switching restores the network connectivity lost by spot beaming. A microwave switch is implemented at the satellite to sequentially interconnect specific uplink to specific downlink beams. Consider the diagram in Figure 6.19a. A diode switch matrix (as in SS-FDMA) establishes the necessary connections of uplink spots to downlink spots. During the first switching "window" of the frame, uplink spot 1 is interconnected to

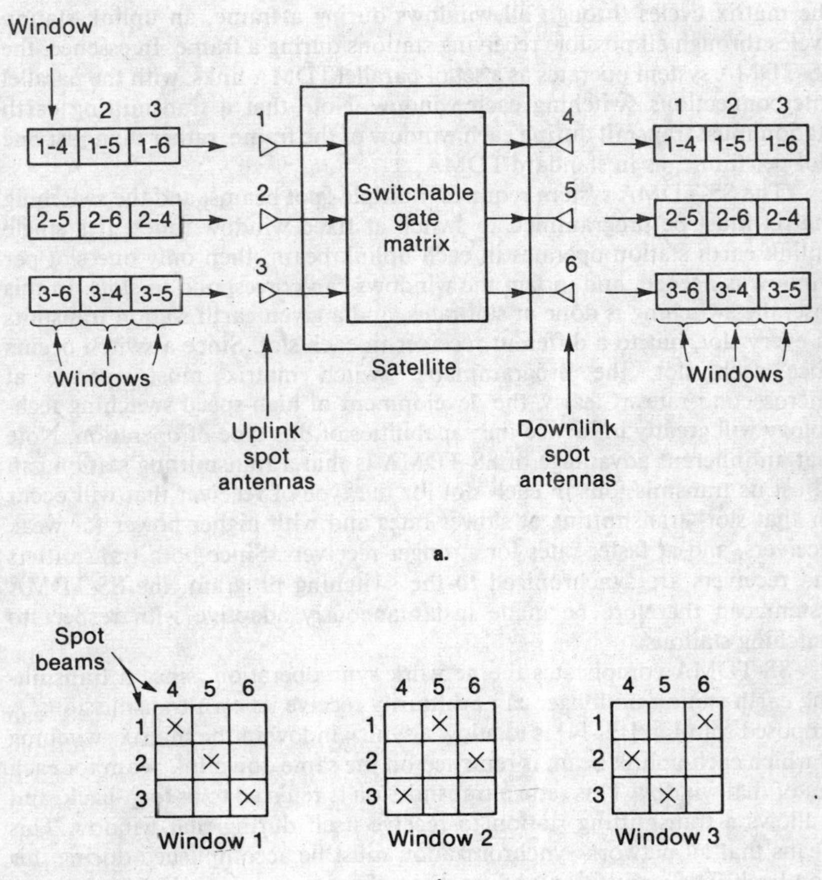

Figure 6.19. SS-TDMA system. (a) Block diagram. (b) Switching matrix.

downlink spot 4, uplink spot 2 is interconnected to downlink spot 5, and so on, as indicated by the matrix in Figure 6.19b. Frame slots of earth stations in the uplink spots (divided among the number of stations in that spot) are therefore available during that window to receiving stations in the interconnected downlink spot. During the second window the matrix switch is reconnected so that uplink spot 1 is interconnected to downlink spot 5, uplink 2 to downlink 6, and so on. Thus, during the second window a different set of earth stations has connectivity to a given uplink station. If the matrix cycles through all windows during a frame, an uplink station cycles through all possible receiving stations during a frame. In essence, the SS-TDMA system operates as a set of parallel TDMA links, with the parallel interconnections switching each window. Note that a transmitting earth station must transmit during each window of the frame, rather than just one slot per frame, as in standard TDMA.

The SS-TDMA system requires multiple-spot beams, and the switching matrix must be programmed to switch at fixed window times. If a single uplink earth station operates in each uplink beam, then only one slot per window is needed, and in fact the windows can correspond to slots. In this case, the switching is done at slot rates, and a given earth station transmits in every slot, but to a different receiver in each slot. Since a switch occurs once each slot, the programmable switch matrix must operate at microsecond rates. Clearly, the development of high-speed switching technology will greatly influence the capabilities of this type of operation. Note that an inherent advantage of SS-TDMA is that a transmitting station can adjust its transmissions in each slot for the type of receiver that will occur for that slot—transmitting at slower rates and with higher power for weak receivers, and at faster rates for stronger receivers. Since both transmitters and receivers are synchronized to the switching program, the SS-TDMA system can therefore be made instantaneously adaptive with respect to matching stations.

SS-TDMA complicates the network sync operation, since a transmitting earth station no longer can arbitrarily receive its own transmissions. A proposed solution [12–14] is to allow a sync window in the matrix switching in which each uplink beam is returned on the same downlink beam for each slot of that window. This return transmission is referred to as **loop-back**, and it allows a transmitting station to receive itself during that window. This means that all network synchronization must be accomplished during this loop-back. The acquisition and tracking of the network timing must therefore be modified from that discussed in Section 6.4 when global antennas were available (a transmitter could receive any of its transmissions at any time). With loop-back, a transmitting station has only one slot per frame to receive itself. When first entering the network it must determine where this slot is. Since the satellite provides no markers, this can only be accomplished by randomly transmitting a slot burst at a fixed point per frame, and listening for its return. The satellite matrix switch acts as a gate, which returns the uplink only for the loop-back slot. During all other slots, the gate is open and nothing is received (see Figure 6.20).

If the transmitter receives no return from its initial transmissions, it must move to another slot position and repeat. The station therefore searches throughout a frame until loop-back provides a return. This means the uplink is arriving at the satellite when the switch-gate is closed. This lost

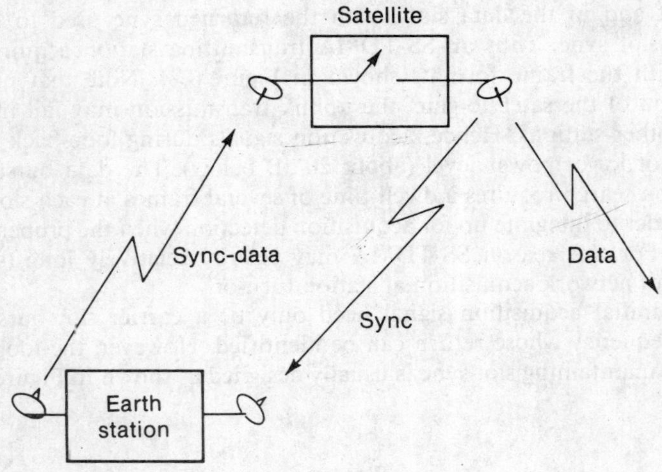

Figure 6.20. Satellite gating model for slot synchronization with loop-back.

transmission point in the frame identifies the loop-back slot of the sync window. By counting down to the next window, the station has acquired network synchronization, and its data burst transmission can begin. To maintain slot sync, the station continues to transmit in both the sync loop-

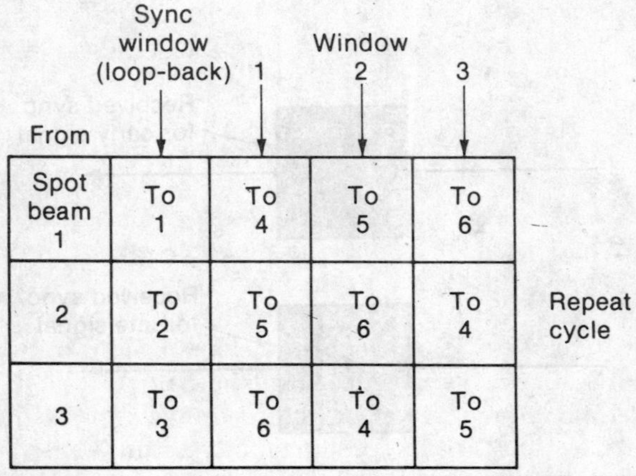

Figure 6.21. SS-TDMA frame formats with sync window.

back slot and in the data slots, with the returned sync used to update network slot sync. Thus an SS-TDMA transmitting station acquires and tracks with the frame formats shown in Figure 6.21. Note that prior to acquisition of the satellite gate, the uplink transmission may fall into the slots of other stations. Hence, acquisition signals during loop-back search must be of lower power level (about 20 dB below). The data bursts, and acquisition search requires a dwell-time of several frames at each slot position in order to integrate up for acquisition detection when the proper slot is selected. For this reason SS-TDMA may require relatively long (several seconds) of network acquisition at station turn-on.

The initial acquisition signal need only be a carrier slot burst at a known frequency whose return can be identified. However, the loop-back signal for maintaining slot sync is usually designed as shown in Figure 6.22.

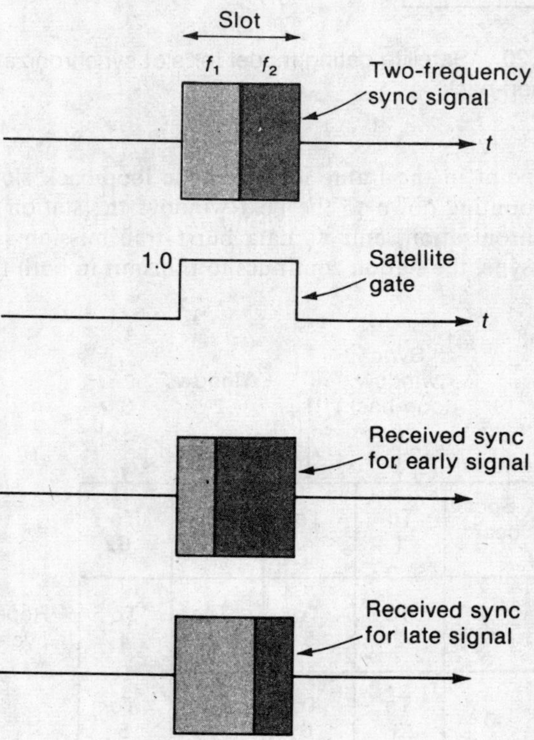

Figure 6.22. SS-TDMA slot sync using two-frequency transmission; frequency time length depends on sync error.

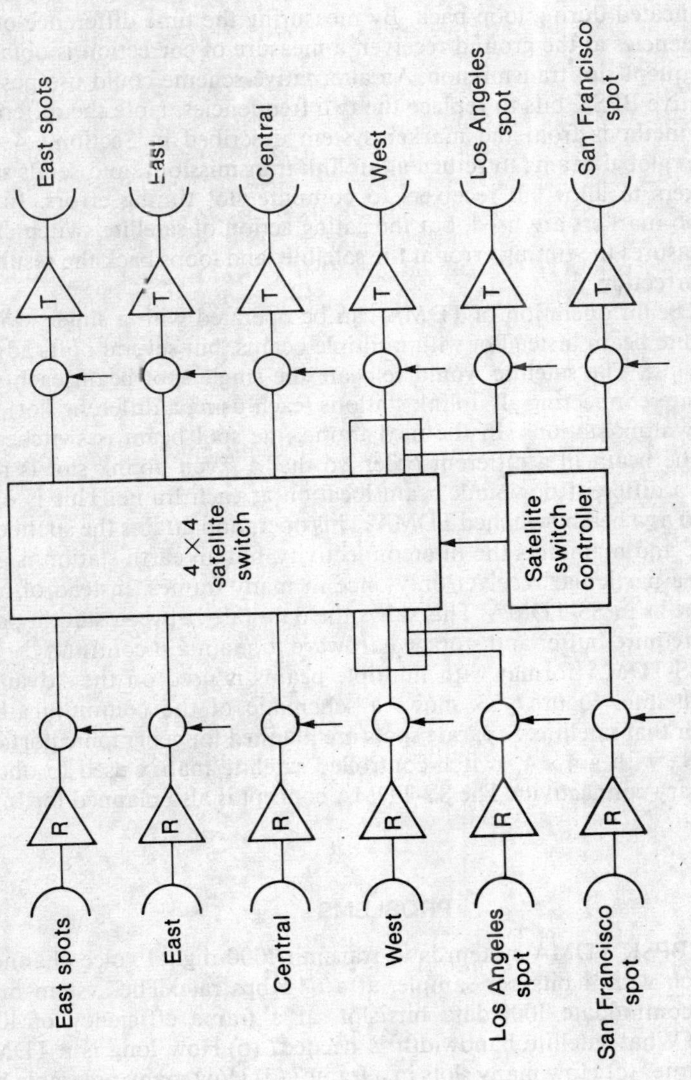

Figure 6.23. An example: Westar SS-TDMA block diagram.

The transmitted signal for the sync slot is divided into equal bursts of two different frequencies. As the sync signal passes through the gate in Figure 6.20, an early or late arrival will have either the beginning or end of the burst truncated during loop-back. By measuring the time difference of the two frequencies at the ground receiver, a measure of correction is obtained for subsequent slot transmission. An alternative scheme could use positive and negative BPSK bits to replace the two frequencies. Note the difference in these methods from the marker system described in Section 6.4. The latter uses global beams to return all uplink transmissions, and sends satellite markers to allow all receivers to compute slot timing errors. In SS-TDMA no markers are used, but the gating action of satellite switch effectively measures the timing error at the satellite, and loops back the result for timing correction.

Spot beam operation of TDMA can be operated with a single switchable satellite beam instead of with multiple beams, but several of its advantages are lost. The satellite would relocate the single spot beam each slot, thereby interconnecting all uplink stations (each using a different slot) to a set of downlink stations. In the next frame, the spot beam is switched to relocate the beam in a different order, so that a given uplink slot is redirected to a different downlink beam location at each frame. This is often referred to as a beam-switched TDMA. This operation attains the spot beam advantage and maintains the interconnectivity, but an earth station is connected to a particular receiver only once in many frames, instead of once each frame as in SS-TDMA. This slows the data rate between station pairs, and may require buffer and storage hardware to maintain continuity.

An SS-TDMA format with multiple beams is used on the Advanced Westar Satellite. Figure 6.23 shows a schematic of the communications payload for that satellite. Separate spots are planned for geographic portions of the U.S., with a 4×4, switch-controlled satellite matrix used to obtain the necessary connectivity. The SS-TDMA concept is also planned for Intelsat VI.

PROBLEMS

6.1 A BPSK TDMA system is to transmit 1000 digital voice channels, each with 4 bits per sample, at a 64 Kbps rate. The system must accommodate 1000 data bits/slot, at a frame efficiency of 10%. (a) What satellite bandwidth is needed? (b) How long is a TDMA frame? (c) How many slots in a frame? (d) How many preamble bits can be used?

6.2 (a) Derive equations (6.2.16) and (6.2.17) for unique word detection. (b) Recompute the false alarm probability, assuming a window is used that observes the expected correlation peak to within $\pm q$ bits around its true arrival time.

6.3 A TDMA system requires timing to occur within 5% of a slot time. Plot a curve showing the available slot length vs. satellite location uncertainty. [*Hint*: Recall equation (1.4.9)].

6.4 A TDMA sync system uses 1 millisecond slots, and the satellite transmits 10-bit marker words of bit length 5×10^{-4} seconds, with $(E_b/N_0)_s = 10$ dB. Assume no range timing error. What timing clock frequency is needed to ensure an rms timing error of no more than 5% of a slot time?

6.5 A TDMA slot acquisition system uses a frequency burst of 20 μsec to determine its range. The satellite has a 500 MHz bandwidth and can produce a carrier downlink $\text{CNR}_{\text{RF}} = 10$ dB. How much lower in power can the frequency burst be, relative to a TDMA carrier, to produce the same CNR in its filter bandwidth?

REFERENCES

1. T. Sekimoto, and J.G. Puento, "A Satellite Time-Division Multiple Access Experiment," *IEEE Trans. on Comm. Tech.*, vol. COM-16 (August 1968), pp. 581–588.

2. W.G. Schmidt, O.G. Gabbard, E.R. Cacciamani, W.G. Maillet, and W.W. Wu, "MAT-1:INTELSAT's Experimental 700-Channel TDMA/DA System," *Proceedings of the 1969 INTELSAT/IEE Conference on Digital Satellite Communications*, London, England, pp. 428–440.

3. W. Maillet, "INTELSAT's 50 Mbits/s TDMA-2 System," *Proceedings of the 1972 International Conference on Digital Satellite Communications*, Paris, France, 1972.

4. K. Nosaka, "TTT System—50 Mbps PCM/TDMA System with Time Preassignment and TASI Features," *Proceedings of the 1969 INTELSAT/IEE International Conference on Digital Satellite Communications*, London, England, pp. 83–94.

5. A. Ogawa, I. Muratani, M. Okawa, and K. Nosaka, "Analysis and Satellite Field Test Results of PSK Model for PCM/TDMA System," *Proceedings of International Colloquim on Space and Communications*, Paris, France, 1971.

6. R.K. Kwan, "A TDMA Application in the Telesat Satellite Systems," *Proceedings of NTC*, 1973.

7. See "Special Issue on Satellite Communications," *IEEE Trans. on Comm.*, vol. COM-27 (October 1979), pp. 1381–1423.

8. F. Gardner, "Hang up in Phase Lock Loops," *IEEE Trans. on Comm.* (October 1977).

9. ———, "Clock Recovery for QPSK-TDMA Receivers," *Proc. of the ICC*, Paper 43B, Minneapolis, June 1974.

10. D. Taylor, S. Tang, and S. Marivz, "The Limit Switched Loop–A PLL For Burst Mode Operation," *IEEE Trans. on Comm.*, vol. COM-30 (February 1982).

11. R.D. McCallister, and M. Simon, "Cross Spectrum Symbol Synchronization," *Proceedings of the NTC*, Houston, 1981.

12. J. Camponella, and D. Shaefer, "TDMA Synchronization," in *Digital Communications–Satellite Earth Station Engineering*, by K. Feher (Englewood Cliffs, N.J.: Prentice-Hall, 1983), chapter 8.

13. P. Nuspl, K. Brown, W. Steenaart, and B. Ghicopoulis, "Synchronization Methods for TDMA," *Proceedings of the IEEE*, vol. 65 (March 1977).

14. C. Carter, "Survey of Synchronization Techniques for a SS-TDMA System," *IEEE Trans. on Comm.*, vol. COM-28 (August 1980).

7 Code-Division Multiple Access

In *code-division multiple access (CDMA)* satellite systems, uplink stations are identified by uniquely separable address codes embedded within the carrier waveform. Each uplink station uses the entire satellite bandwidth and transmits through the satellite whenever desired, with all active stations superimposing their waveforms on the downlink. Thus no frequency or time separation is required. Carrier separation is achieved at an earth station by identifying the carrier with the proper address. These addresses are usually in the form of periodic binary sequences that either modulate the carrier directly or change the frequency state of the carrier. Address identification is accomplished by carrier correlation operations. CDMA carrier crosstalk occurs only in the inability to correlate out the undesired addresses while properly synchronizing to the correct address for decoding. As in TDMA, CDMA carriers have the use of the entire satellite bandwidth for their total activity period, and CDMA has the advantage that no controlled uplink transmission time is required, and no uniformity over station bit rates is imposed. However, system performance depends quite heavily on the ability to recognize addresses, which often becomes difficult if the number of stations in the system is large.

Digital addresses are obtained from code generators that produce periodic sequences of binary symbols. A station's address generator continually cycles through its address sequence, which is superimposed on the carrier along with the data. If the address is modulated directly on the carrier, the format is referred to as **direct sequence CDMA (DS-CDMA)**. If the digital address is used to continually change the frequency of the carrier, the system is referred to as **frequency hopped CDMA (FH-CDMA)**. Superimposing addresses on modulated uplink carriers generally produces a larger carrier bandwidth than that which will be generated by the modulation alone. This spreading of the carrier spectrum has caused CDMA systems to be referred to also as **spread-spectrum multiple access (SSMA) systems**.

Spreading of the carrier spectrum has an important application in military satellite systems since it produces inherent antijam advantages (see Section 7.4). For this reason the designation SSMA is generally used in conjunction with military systems, while CDMA is usually reserved for commercial usage.

7.1 DIRECT-SEQUENCE CDMA SYSTEMS

A digital version of a direct sequence CDMA link is shown in Figure 7.1a. The ith uplink station has assigned to it a digital address code, $q_i(t)$, the latter a periodic binary sequence with binary symbols (chips) of width w sec, and code length k (i.e., k chips per period). Each earth station has its own such address code. Digital information bits are transmitted by superimposing the bits onto the address code. If the ith station is to transmit the binary data waveform $d_i(t)$ ($d_i(t) = \pm 1$), it forms the binary sequence

$$m_i(t) = d_i(t)q_i(t) \tag{7.1.1}$$

If T_b is the bit time of $d_i(t)$, then T_b may correspond to either a full period of $q_i(t)$, or to a fraction of a period. That is,

$$T_b \leqslant kw \tag{7.1.2}$$

If each T_b is exactly one address code period, then each data bit is effectively used to modulate the polarity of each code period. If T_b is less than one code period, then the data bits are modulating the polarity of a portion of a code period. Figure 7.1b shows an example of these situations for a particular address code and data sequence. In either case the address code $q_i(t)$ is serving as a subcarrier for the source data. The binary sequence in (7.1.1) is then PSK directly onto the station RF carrier located at the center frequency of the satellite uplink RF bandwidth. Since each station can use the entire satellite bandwidth, and since (7.1.1) has a code chip rate of $1/w$ chips per sec, each BPSK carrier will utilize a RF bandwidth of approximately

$$B_{\mathrm{RF}} = 2/w \text{ Hz} \tag{7.1.3}$$

Conversely, the available satellite RF bandwidth determines the minimum chip width, while the code period k determines its relation to the bit times. Each station forms its PSK carrier in exactly the same way, each using the same RF carrier frequency and RF bandwidth, but each with its own address code $q_i(t)$. At the satellite, the frequency spectra of all active carriers are superimposed in the RF bandwidth.

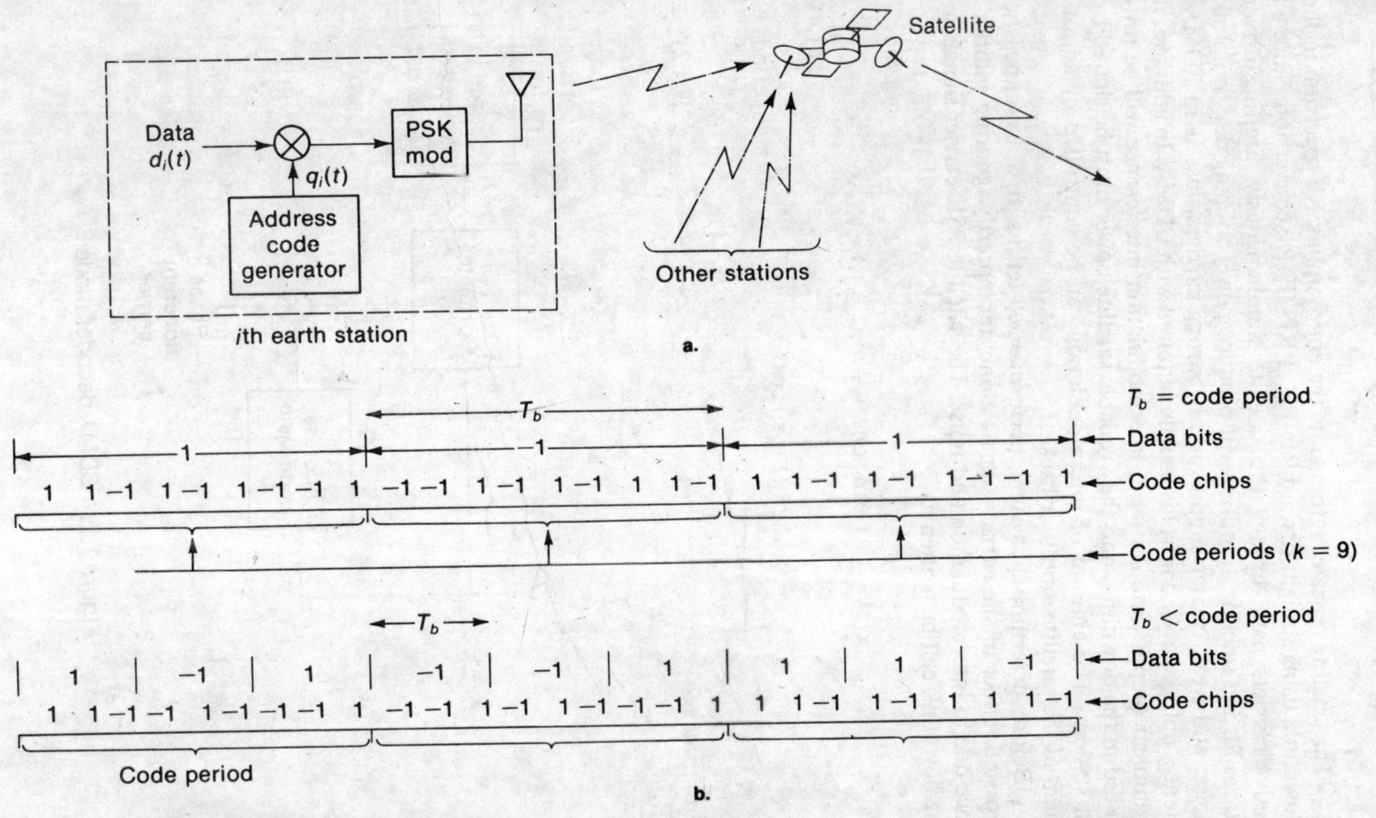

Figure 7.1. CDMA system. (a) Block diagram. (b) Bit and code period alignments.

The satellite repeater retransmits the entire uplink RF spectrum in the downlink, using straightforward RF–RF or RF–IF–RF conversion. Since all active carriers pass through the satellite simultaneously, limiting driver stages for the satellite amplifier will produce power robbing due to uplink noise, and weak carrier suppression by strong carriers, just as in FDMA. Hence, uplink power control is usually required with CDMA. In addition, if nonlinear amplification is used, intermodulation interference will be produced in the downlink, and the available satellite power must be shared by all stations. The amount of intermodulation can be controlled by adjustment of the satellite amplifier backoff.

Before determining system performance, let us first examine the crosstalk effect of the carrier signals alone, temporarily ignoring interference due to intermodulation and noise. The satellite PSK carrier signals in the downlink can be written as

$$\begin{aligned} x(t) &= \sum_{i=1}^{K} A_i \sin\left[\omega_c t + \frac{\pi}{2} m_i(t-\tau_i) + \psi_i\right] \\ &= \sum_{i=1}^{K} A_i m_i(t-\tau_i) \cos(\omega_c t + \psi_i) \end{aligned} \tag{7.1.4}$$

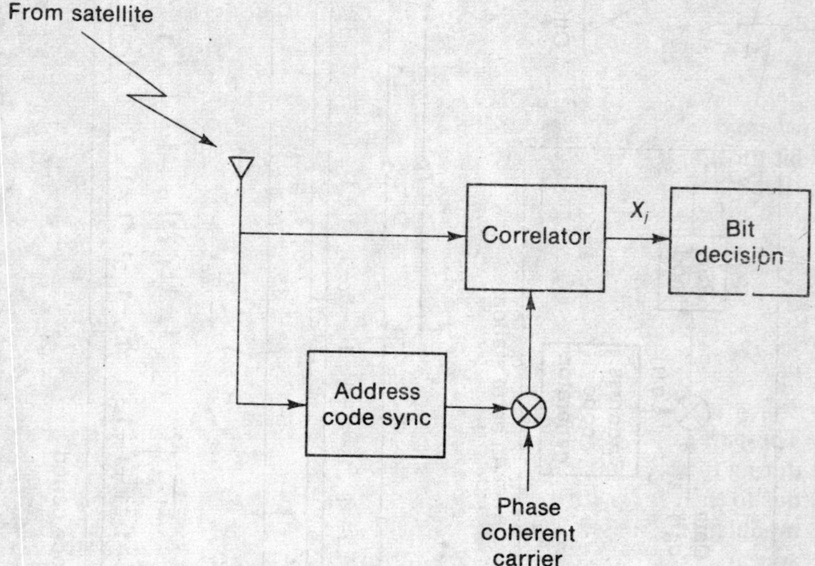

Figure 7.2. CDMA decoder model.

where the sum is over all active carriers and where $\{\tau_i\}$ and $[\psi_i]$ account for the different time shifts and phase shifts in passing through the satellite. At a particular earth receiving station, a correlating decoder is used to recover the message bits of a particular uplink station, as shown in Figure 7.2. A receiver decoding the jth uplink therefore would generate the coherent coded reference

$$r_j(t) = 2q_j(t - \tau_j)\cos(\omega_c t + \psi_j) \tag{7.1.5}$$

Note that the generation of this receiver reference signal requires a time-referenced code and a phase coherent RF carrier. Time and phase coherency of this type requires a combined phase locking, code locking loop, as will be discussed in Section 7.5. In order to maintain the required address code synchronism, the code locking subsystem must first acquire, then accurately track, the received address code. It does this by operating its own address code generator (identical to that of the transmitting station to be decoded) in time sync with the arriving address.

Assuming perfect code acquisition and lock-up, a decoder for the jth uplink correlates over a bit period the received waveform in (7.1.4) with the coded reference in (7.1.5), generating

$$\begin{aligned} x_j &= \frac{1}{T_b}\int_{\tau_j}^{\tau_j+T_b} r_j(t)\,x(t)\,dt \\ &= d_j A_j + C_j \end{aligned} \tag{7.1.6}$$

where $d_j = \pm 1$ is the desired data bit being received during the jth decoding bit time, and

$$C_j = \sum_{\substack{i=1 \\ i \neq j}}^{K} A_i \cos[\psi_i - \psi_j]\gamma_{ij}(\tilde{\tau}_i) \tag{7.1.7}$$

$$\gamma_{ij}(\tilde{\tau}_i) = \frac{1}{T_b}\int_0^{T_b} m_i(t - \tilde{T}_i)q_j(t)\,dt \tag{7.1.8}$$

$$\tilde{\tau}_i = \tau_i - \tau_j$$

The parameter C_j is the carrier crosstalk term arising in the jth decoder during the bit interval $(0, T_b)$, and is composed of a crosstalk contribution due to each active carrier in the downlink. The effect of each depends on the modulated address code cross-correlation $\gamma_{ij}(\tilde{\tau}_i)$ in (7.1.8). The crosstalk C_j appears as an effective data-dependent interference term that adds to, or subtracts from, the desired correlation value $d_j A_j$ in (7.1.6). Note that the value of C_j depends on (1) the data bits $\{d_i(t)\}$ being sent in the various uplinks, (2) the properties of the addressing sequences during the bit correlation, and (3) on the amplitudes of the interfering stations. The latter is important since an interfering earth station may arrive with more power than the desired station, resulting in a significant cross-correlation contribution even though the code correlation γ_{ij} is minimal. This is the so-called **near-far problem** in CDMA, which arises when a near transmitter (shorter propagation distance) produces more receiver power than a desired transmitter located further away, even though both stations transmit with the same power. In satellite relay systems the near-far effect may not be that significant, since overall propagation distances through satellites tend to be comparable. The primary effect of a power imbalance is the power robbing produced in the satellite amplification.

An accurate assessment of CDMA interference requires a careful examination of (7.1.7), and depends on the specific properties of the address codes and on the specific manner in which they are used. Two modes of operation are discussed in the following sections.

Synchronized DS-CDMA

In synchronized CDMA, the system is operated with the bit intervals of each uplink station in time alignment at the satellite. That is, when the uplink PSK carriers arrive at the satellite, the code periods of each must overlap exactly. This requires that all stations have the same code period, and therefore they must all operate at the same code rate. In addition, if they all make full use of the available RF bandwidth, they will have the same number of code symbols per code length. The entire uplink system must have network synchronization just as in TDMA, in order to ensure the synchronized arrival times. With the entire system so synchronized, we can consider $\tilde{\tau}_i = 0$ in (7.1.8). The crosstalk parameter C_j simplifies to

$$C_j = \sum_{\substack{i=1 \\ i \neq j}}^{K} d_i A_i \gamma_{ij} \tag{7.1.9}$$

where d_i is the data bit of the ith carrier, and

$$\gamma_{ij} = \frac{1}{T_b} \int_0^{T_b} q_i(t) q_j(t) dt \tag{7.1.10}$$

is the code cross-correlation of the ith and jth address during the time interval $(0, T_b)$. The ability to evaluate (7.1.10) will depend on the relative lengths of the address code period and the bit intervals. If the code period exactly equals a bit interval, then γ_{ij} in (7.1.10) will be the same over every bit interval, and will depend on the full period cross-correlation of the code address waveform. If the binary symbols of the address codes form a binary orthogonal code set, then $\gamma_{ij} = 0$, and

$$C_j = 0 \qquad \text{for all } j \tag{7.1.11}$$

and no station interference occurs. Each decoder correlates out the undesired stations by using the orthogonality of the address codes. Such CDMA systems are sometimes called **orthogonal-coded** multiple-access systems. Note that orthogonal CDMA systems completely eliminate the near-far problem. Orthogonal-coded operation, however, induces specific limitations on the overall system capacity. Since all addresses have the same code length k, only k distinct orthogonal addresses can be generated. The total number of uplink stations that can be used in the orthogonal CDMA uplink network is therefore limited to $K \leqslant k = T_b/w$. From (7.1.3) this is equivalent to

$$K \leqslant \frac{1}{2}\left(\frac{B_{\mathrm{RF}}}{R_b}\right) \tag{7.1.12}$$

where $R_b = 1/T_b$ is the data bit rate. Hence, the maximum number of orthogonal CDMA users is limited by the ratio of the satellite bandwidth to the bit rate. We shall find that this ratio is a key parameter in CDMA analysis. Note that any binary orthogonal code set of length k symbols can be used to form the station addresses. However, it is imperative that each carrier bit time be exactly synchronized with its specific code period, since orthogonal code words may not be orthogonal when shifted relative to each other.

When the system is code-synchronized but not perfectly orthogonal, $\gamma_{ij} \neq 0$ in (7.1.10) and crosstalk occurs between carriers. To determine the effect of nonorthogonality, we must evaluate the variable C_j, which is dependent on the random data bits $\{d_i\}$ being sent from each station. Note that C_j has a form much like that of intersymbol interference, except that simultaneous bits from other stations are involved rather than previous bits from the same station. Since the data bits from each station are equally likely and independent, we can establish that, after averaging over the data bits, C_j will have the moments:

$$\text{Mean } C_j = 0 \tag{7.1.13a}$$

$$\text{Variance } C_j = \overline{C_j^2} = \sum_{\substack{i=1 \\ i \neq j}}^{K} A_i^2 \gamma_{ij}^2 \tag{7.1.13b}$$

Thus, the mean squared value of the address code interference C_j increases directly with the set of address code cross-correlations $\{\gamma_{ij}\}$.

For long-length codes (multiple data bits per each code period), the codes being correlated in any bit interval will involve only a portion of the total code period, and will be different in each bit interval. Each code crosstalk parameter γ_{ij}, therefore, corresponds to address cross-correlation over a fraction of its full period. Such a correlation is referred to as a **partial cross-correlation**. Thus, in selecting code sequences for long-length addresses in CDMA operation, attention must be given to all possible partial cross-correlations in assessing crosstalk effects [1–3]. In this regard, an interesting result is that of Welch [4] who showed that when partial cross-correlations involve ν code symbols and K separate carriers, the maximum value of all γ_{ij} must be greater than $[(K-1)/\nu K-1]^{1/2}$. For large K and ν, this implies that the worst case effect decreases as $1/\nu^{1/2}$, and can be reduced only by increasing the partial correlation length. In this case, performance can often be estimated by replacing γ_{ij} in (7.1.13b) by maximum partial cross-correlation values, rather than full code cross-correlations.

Nonsynchronized CDMA

In nonsynchronized CDMA no attempt is made to synchronize or align the bit intervals, and the various uplink carriers operate independently with no overall network timing. This is the more common format for DS-CDMA. Each active station simply transmits its modulated addressed carrier through the satellite into the downlink. A ground receiver must again obtain phase, bit, and code coherency with the desired uplink transmission in order to detect coherently, in the presence of the undesired carriers, the bits of the desired addressed carrier. The crosstalk during decoding is given by (7.1.8), where $\{\tilde{\tau}_i\}$ must now be considered a set of random, independent time shifts occurring between the various uplink carriers as they arrive at the satellite. This means that the crosstalk parameter C_j again evolves as a random disturbance, only now due to both the random data bits and the random time shifts. We proceed by assuming all carriers use the same bit time, T_b. In this case, during a decoding interval of the jth carrier, the ith carrier arrives with relative delay $\tilde{\tau}_i$. This means we can write

$$\begin{aligned} d_i(t-\tilde{\tau}_i) &= d_{i1} \qquad 0 \leqslant t \leqslant \tilde{\tau}_i \\ &= d_{i0} \qquad \tilde{\tau}_i \leqslant t \leqslant T_b \end{aligned} \tag{7.1.14}$$

where d_{i1} and d_{i0} are the previous and present bits, respectively, of the ith carrier during $(0, T_b)$ (see Figure 7.3). Because of the equal bit-rate assump-

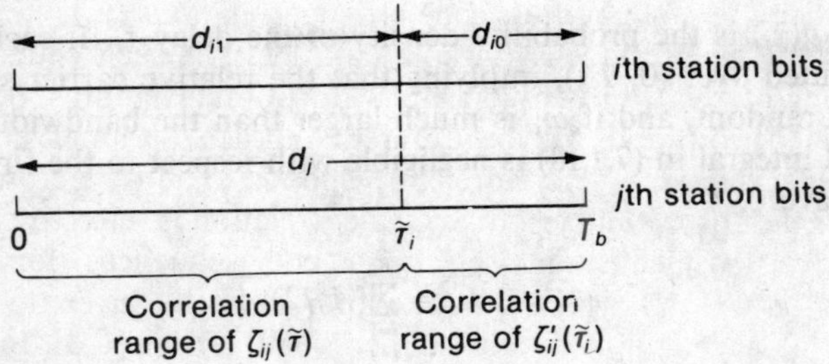

Figure 7.3. Bit alignment in nonsynchronized CDMA.

tion, only two separate bits can cause crosstalk interference. This means the crosstalk parameter C_j, conditioned on the data bits and the set of random shifts $\{\tilde{\tau}_i\}$, is again given by (7.1.8), only now with

$$\gamma_{ij}(\tilde{\tau}_i) = d_{i1}\zeta_{ij}(\tilde{\tau}_i) + d_{i0}\zeta'_{ij}(\tilde{\tau}_i) \tag{7.1.15}$$

where

$$\zeta_{ij}(\tilde{\tau}_i) = \frac{1}{T_b}\int_0^{\tilde{\tau}_i} q_i(t-\tilde{\tau}_i)q_j(t)\,dt \tag{7.1.16a}$$

$$\zeta'_{ij}(\tilde{\tau}_i) = \frac{1}{T_b}\int_{\tilde{\tau}_i}^{T_b} q_i(t-\tilde{\tau}_i)q_j(t)\,dt \tag{7.1.16b}$$

The terms ζ_{ij} and ζ'_{ij} are again partial cross-correlations of the address codes, each involving integrations over only a portion of the T_b sec interval (Figure 7.3). Averaging over the data bits shows that the mean of $C_j = 0$, while the mean squared value follows as

$$\overline{C_j^2} = \sum_{\substack{i=1\\i\neq j}}^{K} A_i^2 \mathscr{E}[\cos^2(\omega_c\tilde{\tau}_i)\gamma_{ij}^2(\tilde{\tau}_i)] \tag{7.1.17}$$

Substituting from (7.1.15), and averaging over the data bits, yields

$$\begin{aligned}\mathscr{E}[\cos_3(\omega_c\tilde{\tau}_i)\gamma_{ij}(\tilde{\tau}_i)] &= \int_{-\infty}^{\infty} \cos^2(\omega_c\tilde{\tau}_i)[\zeta_{ij}^2(\tilde{\tau}_i) + \zeta_{ij}'^2(\tilde{\tau}_i)]p(\tilde{\tau}_i)\,d\tau_i \\ &= \frac{1}{2}\int_{-\infty}^{\infty} [\zeta_{ij}^2(\tau) + \zeta_{ij}'^2(\tau)]p(\tau)\,d\tau \\ &\quad + \frac{1}{2}\int_{-\infty}^{\infty} \cos(2\omega_c\tau)[\zeta_{ij}^2(\tau) + \zeta_{ij}'^2(\tau)]p(\tau)\,d\tau\end{aligned} \tag{7.1.18}$$

where $p(\tilde{\tau}_i)$ is the probability density of the delay $\tilde{\tau}_i$. If each is uniformly distributed over $(0, T_b)$, implying that the relative carrier shifts are completely random, and if ω_c is much larger than the bandwidth of $q_i(t)$, the second integral in (7.1.18) is negligible with respect to the first integral. We then have

$$\overline{C_j^2} = \sum_{\substack{i=1 \\ i \neq j}}^{K} (A_i^2/2)\overline{\gamma_{ij}^2} \tag{7.1.19}$$

where now

$$\overline{\gamma_{ij}^2} = \frac{1}{T_b}\int_0^{T_b} [\zeta_{ij}^2(\tau) + \zeta_{ij}'^2(\tau)]\,d\tau \tag{7.1.20}$$

We see that $\overline{\gamma_{ij}^2}$ plays the same role in the nonsynchronous case as the code cross-correlation parameter γ_{ij}^2 in the synchronized case. Note that nonsynchronous performance depends on the squared integrated partial cross-correlation functions in (7.1.16). It is this complexity that makes the nonsynchronous case difficult to analyze. Investigation of maximum partial correlation values alone can be extremely misleading here, since it is the *integrated squared* value that is of prime importance. The interested reader is referred to References [5–8] for further discussions on the properites of $\overline{\gamma_{ij}^2}$, including some useful bounds for estimating (7.1.19).

7.2 PERFORMANCE OF DS-CDMA SATELLITE SYSTEMS

The effect of code cross-correlation from interfering stations during CDMA receiver decoding is to add an interference term to the desired correlator output during bit decoding, as was shown in (7.1.6). To these correlation terms must be added the noise interference terms due to correlating with the noise and intermodulation occurring during the satellite retransmission. If we denote the total downlink interference waveform as $n(t)$, then the decoder output due to correlating with $n(t)$ over a bit term is

$$n_j = \frac{1}{T_b}\int_0^{T_b} n(t)r_j(t)\,dt \tag{7.2.1}$$

where $r_j(t)$ is the synchronized addressed carrier waveform in (7.1.5). If the total interference is taken as a zero mean white Gaussian process, with spectral level N_{0T} due to the up and down link noise and the level of the intermodulation spectrum, then n_j is a zero mean Gaussian variable with variance

$$\text{Var}(n_j) = N_{0T}/2T_b \tag{7.2.2}$$

The bit correlator output used for downlink bit decisioning is then

$$y_j = d_j A_j + C_j + n_j \tag{7.2.3}$$

In the following sections, y_j and the subsequent bit decisioning is examined separately for the several modes of address operation discussed in section 7.1.

Orthogonal CDMA Systems

When an orthogonal CDMA system is operated (i.e., (7.1.11) is true), the decoder interference comes from only the system noise and intermodulation term n_j. This interference has spectral level

$$\begin{aligned} N_{0T} = N_{0d} & \quad \leftarrow \text{Downlink receiver noise} \\ + P_T L\left(\frac{N_{0u}}{P_u}\right)\alpha_n^2 & \quad \leftarrow \text{Retrans. uplink noise} \\ + N_{0I} & \quad \leftarrow \text{Intermodulation noise} \end{aligned} \tag{7.2.4}$$

where all parameters are defined in (5.3.3). The downlink carrier amplitudes $\{A_i\}$ are evaluated from the inherent power division at the satellite, and therefore

$$P_i = A_i^2/2 = P_T L\left(\frac{\Gamma P_i}{P_u}\right)\alpha_s^2 \tag{7.2.5}$$

The decoding bit energy-to-noise level for the jth carrier, when orthogonal codes are used, is then

$$\begin{aligned} \left(\frac{E_b}{N_0}\right)_{or} &= \frac{P_j T_b}{N_{0T}} \\ &= \frac{P_T L T_b\left(\frac{\Gamma P_j}{P_u}\right)}{N_{0d} + P_T L\left(\frac{N_{0u}}{P_u}\right) + N_{0I} L} \end{aligned} \tag{7.2.6}$$

After substituting (7.2.4) and (7.2.5) into (7.2.6), it is convenient to rewrite more compactly as

$$\left(\frac{E_b}{N_0}\right)_{or} = [\mathrm{CNR}_u^{-1} + \mathrm{CNR}_d^{-1} + \mathrm{CNR}_I^{-1}]^{-1} \tag{7.2.7}$$

where the CNR terms are defined in Section 5.3. Equation (7.2.7) is identical in form to the FDMA result in (5.3.5) when no spectral crosstalk occurs, and when $B = 1/T_b$. Hence, orthogonal CDMA performs similarly to FDMA, and Figures 5.14 and 5.15 can be used directly to determine satellite power, with $(E_b/N_0)_{or}$ interpreted as CNR_d. The resulting carrier bit-error probability can then be obtained from $(E_b/N_0)_{or}$ using standard PE curves. It should be noted, however, that the intermodulation in CDMA is due to the nonlinear amplification of overlapping carrier spectra. This is in contrast to the case in FDMA where the carrier spectra are contiguous. Nevertheless, intermodulation spectra for the two cases have been observed to be quite similar, and intermodulation effects for the FDMA case are often used in CDMA analysis as well. Note also that the number of users (number of active stations) enters into (7.2.7) only through its effect on the intermodulation level N_{0I}. Furthermore, the near-far problem does not appear in the cross-correlation effect in an orthogonal system, and the only concern of unequal station powers is its effect on power robbing at the satellite.

The previous analysis was based on the assumption that the predominate intermodulation effect is to produce a noise-type interference. From the discussion in Chapter 5, this assumption is essentially valid if there are many approximately equal power carriers passing through the satellite, or if the uplink noise (which mixes with the carriers) is relatively significant. However, these are situations that could cause a few dominant direct sequence carriers to mix in the satellite nonlinearity to produce intermodulation terms that are not noiselike but retain the structure of the addressed carrier. This effect may, in fact, be more severe than the code cross-correlation of other carriers. Consider two equal powered, addressed carriers:

$$\begin{aligned} c_1(t) &= A d_1(t) q_1(t) \cos(\omega_c t + \psi_1) \\ c_2(t) &= A d_2(t) q_2(t) \cos(\omega_c t + \psi_2) \end{aligned} \tag{7.2.8}$$

In passing through a hard-limiting nonlinear amplifier, a third-order intermodulation will be generated having the form

$$\begin{aligned} [3^{rd} \text{ order term}] &= h_3 d_1(t) q_1(t) [d_2(t) q_2(t)]^2 \cos(\omega_c t + \psi_3) \\ &= h_3 d_1(t) q_1(t) \cos(\omega_c t + \psi_3) \end{aligned} \tag{7.2.9}$$

where h_3 is the third-order harmonic amplitude. This intermodulation term is therefore identical in form (but out of phase) with the carrier that will be decoded in the $c_1(t)$ channel. Subsequent address correlation with $q_1(t)$ will, however, correlate with the intermodulation in (7.2.9) as well, and produce an interference that will not correlate out as the other codes. Furthermore, there may be several of these terms, as well as possible fifth- and seventh-order intermodulation terms with the same effect. An interesting study of these effects was reported in [9–11].

Nonorthogonal CDMA Systems

For a nonorthogonal, or nonsynchronized, CDMA system, the effect of C_j in (7.2.3) must be considered. Formally, C_j is a random variable dependent on the data sequences and random delays. To determine bit-error probability for a particular receiver decoder, we must proceed by treating station cross-correlation as intersymbol interference. The bit-error probability for the jth receiver must then be obtained by averaging over all possible bit sequences and code delays of all interfering stations. Although the resulting PE_j will then represent the exact bit-error probability for a particular receiver, its computation may become quite lengthy if the number of interfering carriers is large. This is due to the fact that the number of possible data vectors that must be averaged grows exponentially with the number of carriers, K. This computation can be circumvented, however, when K is large, since we can model C_j as an additive Gaussian crosstalk variable that simply adds to the Gaussian interference of the downlink carrier. Justification and conditions for the validity of this Gaussian assumption were studied in depth in References [12–14]. Using (7.1.13b) we can establish that C_j has a zero mean, and a variance given by

$$\overline{C_j^2} = \sum_{\substack{i=1 \\ i \neq j}}^{K} \gamma_{ij}^2 P_i \tag{7.2.10}$$

with P_i given in (7.2.5), and γ_{ij}^2 has one of the forms in either (7.1.10) or (7.1.20). We can interpret (7.2.10) as an interference power spread over the satellite bandwidth. Hence, the decoder E_b/N_0 is now modified from (7.2.6) to

$$\left(\frac{E_b}{N_0}\right) = \frac{P_j T_b}{N_{0T} + (\overline{C_j^2}/B_{\mathrm{RF}})} \tag{7.2.11}$$

This can be rewritten in the form of (7.2.7) as

$$\left(\frac{E_b}{N_0}\right) = [\text{CNR}_u^{-1} + \text{CNR}_d^{-1} + \text{CNR}_I^{-1} + \text{CNR}_c^{-1}]^{-1} \tag{7.2.12}$$

where the cross-correlation CNR_c is now defined as

$$\text{CNR}_c = \frac{P_j T_b B_{\text{RF}}}{\overline{C_j^2}} \tag{7.2.13}$$

In this interpretation, address cross-correlation simply adds an auxiliary CNR_c term to the overall satellite CNR result. We can instead rewrite (7.2.11) as

$$\left(\frac{E_b}{N_0}\right) = \frac{(E_b/N_0)_{or}}{1 + \left(\frac{E_b}{N_0}\right)_{or}\left[\frac{\overline{C_j^2}/P_j}{B_{\text{RF}} T_b}\right]} \tag{7.2.14}$$

This relates the (E_b/N_0) of the nonorthogonal CDMA system to that which would occur if the system were truly orthogonal (i.e., no station cross-correlation). The latter system depends only on the intermodulation and power division that occurs in passing through the satellite with the addressed carriers. Note that the operating E_b/N_0 with nonorthogonal carriers is always less than that with the same number of orthogonal carriers, due to the denominator in (7.2.14). Thus a nonorthogonal CDMA system must be designed with higher power levels than an orthogonal system if it is to have the same performance.

To further examine the cross-correlation effect, consider the simplified case where

$$\begin{aligned} P_i &= P \quad \text{(Equal carrier power)} \\ \gamma_{ij} &= \gamma \quad \text{(Equal address correlation)} \\ \left.\begin{aligned} \frac{N_{0u} B_{\text{RF}}}{P_u} &= 0 \\ \alpha_s^2 &= 1 \end{aligned}\right\} &\quad \text{High uplink CNR} \end{aligned} \tag{7.2.15}$$

Under these conditions,

$$\begin{aligned} \frac{P_i}{P_u} &= \frac{1}{K} \\ \overline{C_j^2} &= (K-1)\gamma^2 P \end{aligned} \tag{7.2.16}$$

Therefore,

$$\left(\frac{E_b}{N_0}\right) = \frac{LP_T/K}{N_{0T} + [LP(K-1)\gamma^2/B_{RF}]}$$
$$= \frac{(E_b/N_0)_{or}}{1 + (E_b/N_0)_{or}[(K-1)\gamma^2/B_{RF}]} \tag{7.2.17}$$

where $(E_b/N_0)_{or} = LP_T/KN_{0T}$. Equation (7.2.17) can be solved for the required satellite power P_T needed to achieve a desired (E_b/N_0) of Υ. Hence

$$P_T = \frac{1}{L}\left[\frac{(\Upsilon N_{0T}/T_b)K}{1 - \Upsilon[(K-1)\gamma^2/B_{RF}T_b]}\right] \tag{7.2.18}$$

Equation (7.2.18) is plotted in Figure 7.4, showing a normalized P_T as a function of number of stations K for several values of cross-correlation γ^2 and $B_{RF}T_b$, with $\Upsilon = 10$ dB. When $\gamma = 0$ (orthogonal CDMA), K is limited by either the available satellite power or the RF bandwidth, as shown, with both increasing linearly with K. However, we see that the build-up of interference with γ^2 will ultimately limit the number of CDMA users. In fact, an infinite satellite power is required in (7.2.18) if K is larger than

$$K_{\max} = \frac{B_{RF}T_b}{\Upsilon\gamma^2} \tag{7.2.19}$$

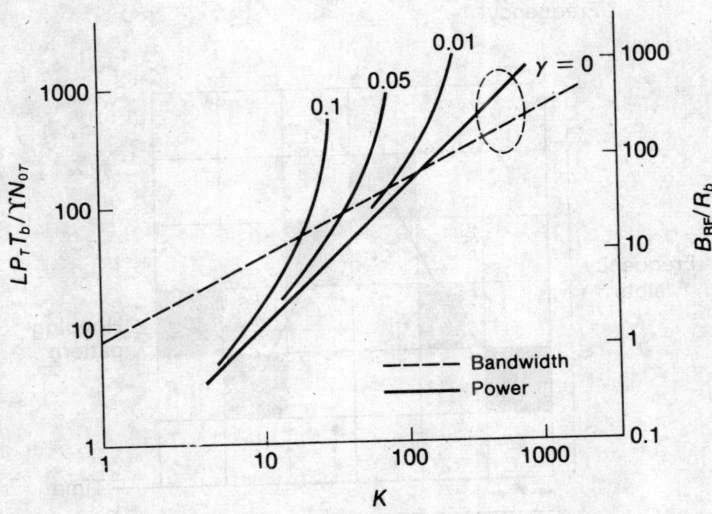

Figure 7.4. Required satellite power (normalized) and bandwidth to support K CDMA carriers.

Generally, we desire $\Upsilon(K-1)\gamma^2/B_{RF}T_b < 0.1$ in (7.2.18), which restricts the useable K to about one-tenth of the right side of (7.2.19). For $\Upsilon = 10$ dB and $\gamma^2 = 0.1$, this limits K to about $B_{RF}T_b/10$, which is about one-tenth the capacity of the orthogonal system in (7.1.12). Cross-correlation values for large sets of address codes can be decreased by increasing the number of code symbols per bit interval, but this leads directly to an increase in the code rate and RF bandwidth. We again see that design of CDMA systems for large numbers of users is intimately related to finding large sets of binary codes with low cross-correlation values. Analytical studies in this problem area have been reported [15–21].

7.3 FREQUENCY-HOPPED CDMA

The alternative to direct sequence CDMA is to use the digital sequence to produce frequency hopping. In this mode the available satellite bandwidth is partioned into frequency bands, and the transmission time partitioned into time slots, as shown in Figure 7.5. A hopping pattern in this frequency-time matrix is defined as a sequence of specific frequency bands, one for each time slot, as shown. A transmitter assigned a particular hopping pattern jumps from one band to the next according to the pattern, readjusting

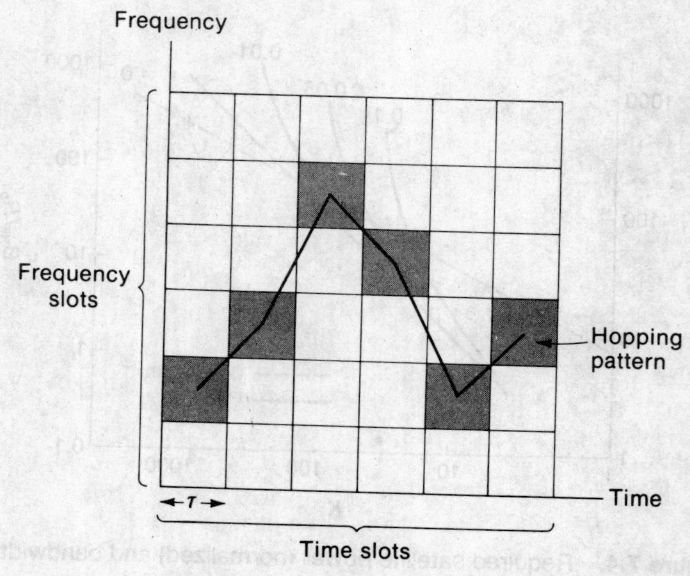

Figure 7.5. Frequency-time hopping diagram.

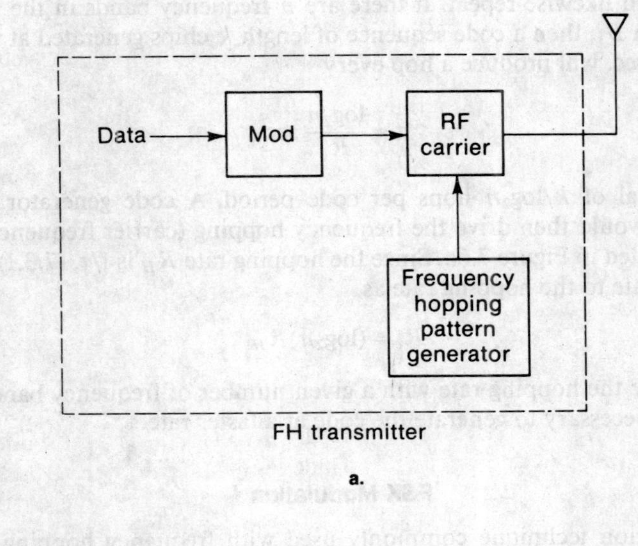

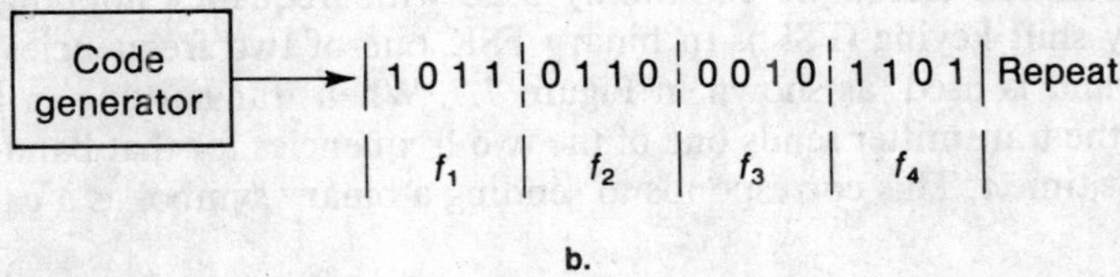

Figure 7.6. Frequency-hopping system. (a) Transmitter. (b) Code generator sequence. ($\{f_i\}$ = frequencies)

its carrier frequency from one time slot to the next. Such a frequency hopping transmitter is shown in Figure 7.6a. During each band transmission, the transmitter sends some form of modulated carrier that occupies only the designated band. Thus, a station with a hopping pattern appears to utilize the entire satellite bandwidth when observed over a long time although transmitting only within a specified band at any one time. In a military environment, it is often further required that the hopping patterns appear random, so that future values of the pattern cannot be predicted.

Hopping patterns can be obtained from periodic binary sequences similar to the address codes. If such a sequence is partitioned into blocks, each block can designate a particular frequency band in the frequency-time matrix (Figure 7.6b). Thus a particular binary sequence specifies a specific hopping pattern, and as the code sequence periodically repeats, the hopping pattern will likewise repeat. If there are n frequency bands in the satellite bandwidth B_s, then a code sequence of length k chips generated at the rate R_c chips/sec, will produce a hop every

$$\tau = \frac{\log_2 n}{R_c} \text{ sec} \tag{7.3.1}$$

with a total of $k/\log_2 n$ hops per code period. A code generator of this sequence would then drive the frequency hopping (carrier frequency shifting) indicated in Figure 7.6a. Since the hopping rate R_H is $1/\tau$, (7.3.1) relates the code rate to the hopping rate as

$$R_c = (\log_2 n) R_H \tag{7.3.2}$$

To increase the hopping rate with a given number of frequency bands, it is therefore necessary to generate the code at a faster rate.

FSK Modulation

A modulation technique commonly used with frequency hopping is frequency shift keying (FSK). In binary FSK one of two frequencies within each band is used, as shown in Figure 7.7. When transmitting in a given band, the transmitter sends one of the two frequencies for that band during the slot time τ. This corresponds to sending a binary symbol as a carrier of

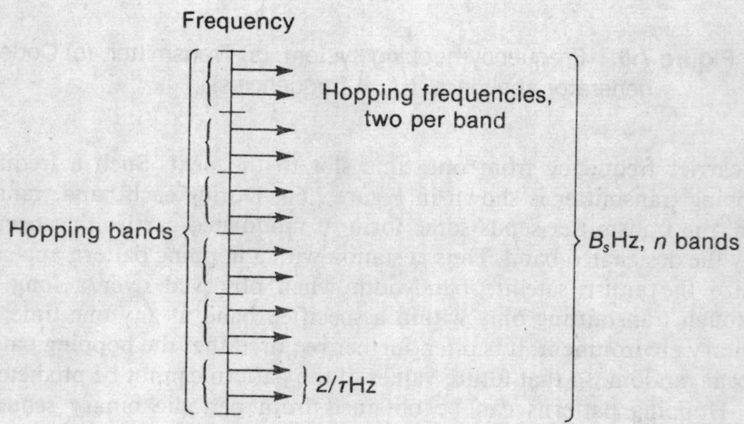

Figure 7.7. Binary-encoded FSK with frequency hopping. Frequency diagram.

fixed frequency for τ sec, producing a transmitter carrier of bandwidth of approximately $2/\tau$ Hz around each frequency. Hence the FSK frequencies must be separated by $2/\tau$ Hz to guarantee sufficient separation during decoding. A satellite bandwidth B_s would then support

$$n = \frac{1}{2}\left(\frac{B_s}{2/\tau}\right) = \frac{B_s\tau}{4} \tag{7.3.3}$$

hopping bands. If the hopping time τ corresponds to a bit time, then the hopping system is producing one bit per hop, or equivalently, operating at one hop per bit. This is usually referred to as *slow* frequency hopping. If a bit time is several hop times (i.e., a sequence of hops represents each data bit), then the transmitter is hopping several times per bit, and is called *fast* frequency hopping.

An obvious extension is M-ary FSK when one of M distinct frequencies is used in each band. In this case the transmitter, as it hops from band to band according to the hopping pattern, would send $\log_2 M$ bits per hop. With n frequency bands the required satellite bandwidth is

$$\begin{aligned} B_s &= nM(2/\tau) \\ &= 2nMR_H \end{aligned} \tag{7.3.4}$$

The corresponding bit rate is then

$$R_b = (\log_2 M)R_H \tag{7.3.5}$$

Hence (7.3.5) relates the bit rate and hopping rate through the modulation parameter M (the number of FSK frequencies per channel), while (7.3.4) relates bandwidth, hopping rate, and the number of hopping frequencies.

A receiver for a frequency hopped FSK carrier is shown in Figure 7.8. In order to decode, the receiver must have a synchronized version of the hopping pattern. This is achieved by running an identical code sequence generator in time synchronism with the code sequence producing the hopping pattern of the received carrier. It hops its local carrier frequency in synchronism with the received carrier, so that only the modulation frequency (FSK shift in each band) appears as a difference frequency. A bank of filters tuned to each possible FSK frequency then noncoherently decodes the symbol modulation in each time slot. An advantage of noncoherent FSK is that only slot timing is needed for decoding, precluding the necessity of achieving FSK phase coherency. Note that with synchronized patterns, each transmitted frequency band is individually mixed to baseband, and the same noncoherent FSK decoder can be used successively during each slot. In effect, the synchronized local pattern removes the hopping from the

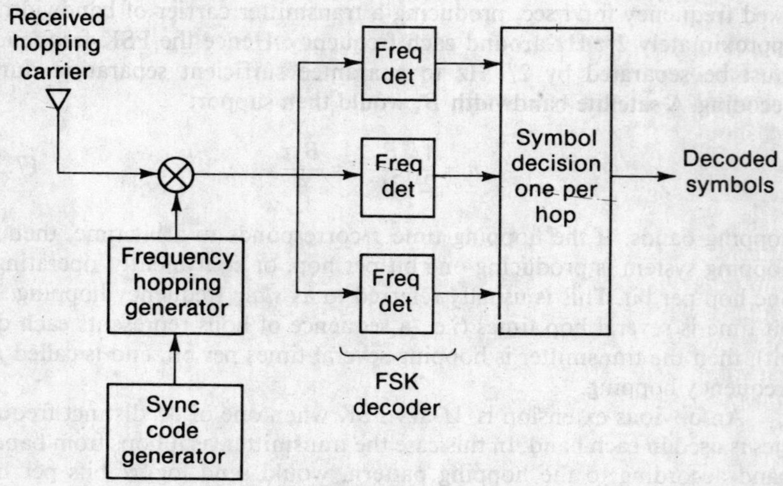

Figure 7.8. Receiver for frequency hopped carrier.

received carrier, and we say the received carrier has been **dehopped**.

In FSK frequency hopped systems, severe constraints are placed on the frequency generators at both the transmitter and receiver in Figures 7.6 and 7.8. Since the frequencies are commanded to hop over the entire RF bandwidth, the frequency generators must have the capability of changing frequency both accurately and rapidly over an extremely wide frequency band. The accuracy is necessary because any unresolved frequency offset of the dehopped carrier will lead directly to FSK decoding errors, since the data frequency will be misaligned with the FSK-tuned filters by the same offset. Frequency accuracy is directly related to the frequency resolution capability of the frequency generators, that is, how close its frequency can be set to a prescribed value. In addition, the hop settling time (time to hop from one frequency to another) must be short, since FSK performance will be degraded by the decoding time lost during the hop transition. If an FSK word time (hopping period) is T_w seconds long, and the settling time is ϵ seconds, then the FSK decoding energy in Figure 2.29 is reduced by the factor $(1 - \epsilon/T_w)^2$. For example, a hop settling time of 10% of the hop period will produce a 0.91 dB energy degradation. Hence frequency hopping systems with high hop rates place severe settling time conditions on the frequency generators. These combined range–accuracy–settling time constraints will strongly influence the overall frequency generator design—a topic to be considered in Chapter 8.

Hopping Patterns

A complete frequency hopped CDMA satellite system is obtained by assigning each transmitting station a different hopping pattern. Each active station operates by generating its own pattern, encoding the data symbols at each hop, and accessing through the satellite whenever desired. A station receives a transmission by hopping in sync with the desired station, and decoding each symbol after dehopping. In effect, the hopping pattern is playing the role of an address, with all interfering stations having different patterns. The latter will be rejected if they hop into other bands at each slot. If no other station hopped into the same band at the same slot, the system would be truly orthogonal, and no station interference would exist. If there are n frequency bands per slot, there can be at most $K \leqslant n$ distinct patterns that will never overlap. Hence the number of orthogonal, frequency hopped CDMA users is, from (7.3.3) and (7.3.2)

$$K \leqslant n = \frac{B_s \tau}{4M} \qquad (7.3.6)$$

$$= 2^{R_c/R_H}$$

The number of orthogonal users therefore increases linearly with the satellite bandwidth. or equivalently, increases *exponentially* with the code rate generating the hopping. Recall that the number of orthogonal users in DS-CDMA increased only linearly with code rate [see (7.1.3)]. Hence, when code rate is the limiting factor, frequency hopping has a decided capacity advantage over direct sequence modulation.

If more than n user stations are involved, they cannot be assigned patterns without some overlap occurring. If the patterns are selected without regard to the patterns of other stations, then it can be assumed that during any slot time, locations of all stations are randomly distributed in frequency. In an FSK system, receiver performance can be estimated by taking into account the chance of a pattern overlap. If no other active station overlaps a given station operating in a particular band, the error probability for that time slot is that of a standard noncoherent FSK link with the noise level N_{0T} in (7.2.4). This clear (no interference) symbol-error probability is obtained from Table 2.4 as

$$\mathrm{PSE}_0 = 1 - e^{-\rho^2/2} \sum_{q=0}^{M-1} (-1)^q \binom{M-1}{q} \frac{\exp[(\rho^2/2)/1+q]}{1+q} \qquad (7.3.7)$$

where $\rho^2 = E_s/N_{0T}$, and E_s is the carrier energy per slot. If another carrier overlaps during that band, its modulation may either aid or hinder the FSK decoding in that band. Assuming a hindrance will always cause a bit error, the frequency hopped symbol error probability is then

$$\mathrm{PSE} = \left(\frac{M-1}{M}\right)P_H + (1 - P_H)\mathrm{PSE}_0 \tag{7.3.8}$$

where P_H is the probability that another carrier hops into the same band. For K active carriers and n bands,

$$P_H = 1 - \left(1 - \frac{1}{n}\right)^{K-1} \tag{7.3.9}$$

As the number of users increases, $P_H \to 1$ and PSE increases from PSE_0 to $(M-1)/M$, essentially destroying the data link. As a rule of thumb, $\mathrm{PSE} \lesssim 2\,\mathrm{PSE}_0$ when $P_H \leqslant \mathrm{PSE}_0$, which requires

$$K \lesssim n\mathrm{PSE}_0 \tag{7.3.10}$$

Hence, the number of users employing randomly selected hopping patterns is considerably less than the number of possible orthogonal pattern users.

7.4 ANTIJAM ADVANTAGES OF SPECTRAL SPREADING

The use of either direct sequence modulation or frequency hopping allows station addressing and reduced interference in a CDMA format. However, the resulting spectral spreading associated with these methods also affords some defensive advantages against intentional jamming of the system by an external source. For this reason spread-spectrum communications play an important role in data links operating in a military environment.

To see the inherent advantages of spectral spreading in a jamming situation, consider the system in Figure 7.9a. We assume a communication link between two stations, with the presence of an external source intentionally transmitting noise into the receiver to attempt to destroy the link. We initially neglect both receiver noise and the interference effect of other stations, and omit the presence of a satellite relay. Hence, the only form of interference at the receiver is due to the jamming signal alone. Refer to the spectral diagram in Figure 7.9b. The transmitter uses a DS-CDMA modulated carrier in which a data rate R_b is spread to occupy a carrier bandwidth of B_s Hz. The jammer produces a noise spectrum of width B_j Hz and power P_j at the receiver input. If $B_j = B_s$, we say the jammer is **broadband**. When $B_j < B_s$ we refer to the jammer as being **partial band**.

Under these assumptions the received waveform is

$$x(t) = Ad(t)q(t)\cos(\omega_c t + \psi) + j(t) \tag{7.4.1}$$

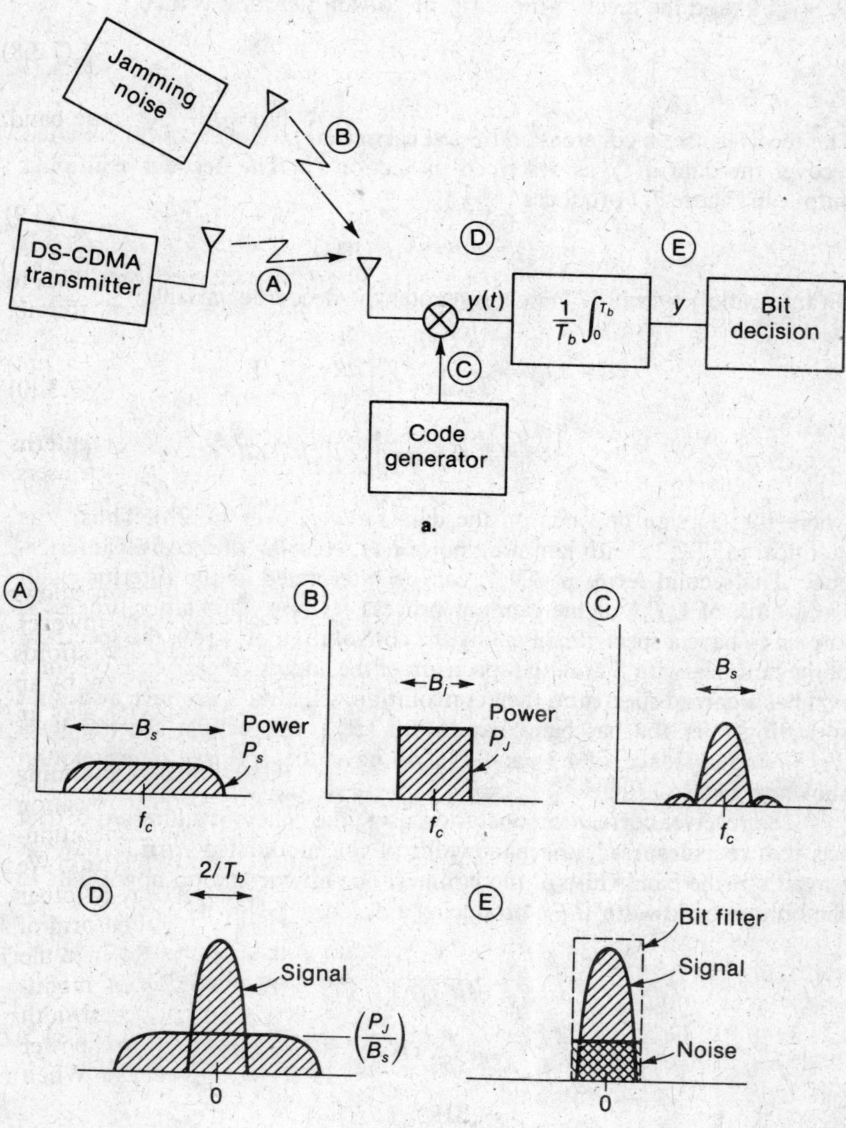

Figure 7.9. CDMA system with jamming. (a) Block diagram. (b) Signal spectra.

where $j(t)$ is the jamming noise. The received carrier therefore has power $P_c = A^2/2$, and the receiver-input-signal–to–jammer ratic is then

$$\text{SJR}_{in} = \frac{P_c}{P_J} \tag{7.4.2}$$

The receiver uses a coherent addressed carrier $r(t) = 2q(t)\cos(\omega_c t + \psi)$ to recover the data $d(t)$, as described in Section 7.1. The decoder multiplier output in Figure 7.9 produces

$$y(t) = Ad(t) + j(t)r(t) \tag{7.4.3}$$

Bit integration over $(0, T_b)$ now generates the decoding variable

$$\begin{aligned} y &= \frac{1}{T_b}\int_0^{T_b} y(t)dt \\ &= \pm A + \frac{1}{T_b}\int_0^{T_b} j(t)r(t)dt \end{aligned} \tag{7.4.4}$$

where the (±) sign depends on the data bit $d(t)$ over $(0, T_b)$. Thus, y is identical to (7.2.3), with jamming noise $j(t)$ replacing the receiver interference. The second term in (7.4.4) can be interpreted as the filtering (with bandwidth of $1/T_b$) of the random process $j(t)r(t)$. This latter process is known to have a spectrum given by the convolution of $S_j(\omega)$, the spectrum of the jammer, with $S_r(\omega)$, the spectrum of the addressed carrier, $r(t)$. Since $r(t)$ has a spread spectrum, then convolution will always produce a spectral spreading over the baseband bandwidth $(B_s + B_j)$, with a spectral level P_J/B_s w/Hz. Hence (7.4.3) and (7.4.4) have the spectral interpretation shown in Figure 7.9b.

The receiver correlation operation using the coherent addressed carrier has reduced (**despread**) the bandwidth of the modulated carrier, but has spread out the bandwidth of the jammer. The bit correlation now filters to the bit rate bandwidth $1/T_b$, producing a decoding SNR of

$$\begin{aligned} \frac{E_b}{N_0} &= \frac{P_c}{(P_J/B_s)(1/T_b)} \\ &= \left(\frac{P_c}{P_J}\right) B_s T_b \\ &= (\text{SJR})_{\text{in}}\,(B_s/R_b) \end{aligned} \tag{7.4.5}$$

Thus, the spreading and despreading with the addressed carriers has produced a gain in SNR by the factor B_s/R_b. This gain is often referred to as the **processing gain** of the spread-spectrum system,

$$PG \triangleq \frac{B_s}{R_b} \tag{7.4.6}$$

The gain depends only on the ratio of the spread carrier bandwidth relative to the data rate. Hence the more the carrier is spectrally spread, the larger is the effective processing gain, and the lower the input SJR can be in achieving a desired E_b/N_0. Figure 7.10a shows the required value of P_J/P_c needed to achieve the stated bit-error probabilities for different processing gains. Figure 7.10b shows the required bandwidth B_s needed to achieve a specified PG at different bit rates. Processing gain therefore acts to overcome a strong power advantage that a jammer may have over a transmitter. By substituting $R_b = 1/T_b$, we see PG $= B_sT_b$, and the processing gain is actually the bandwidth–bit time product of the link. This is the same product that

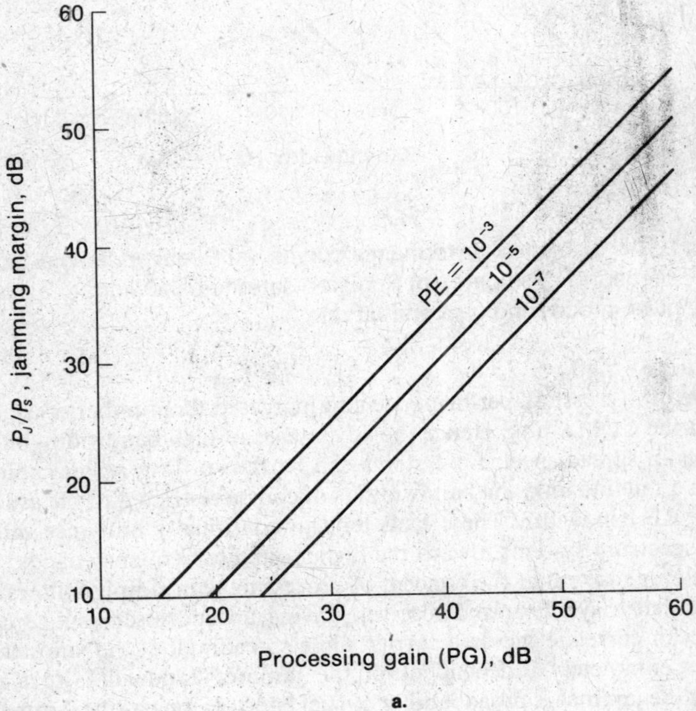

Figure 7.10. Jamming performance curves. (a) Required jammer power needed to overcome. (b) Required satellite bandwidth to achieve given processing gain and bit rate.

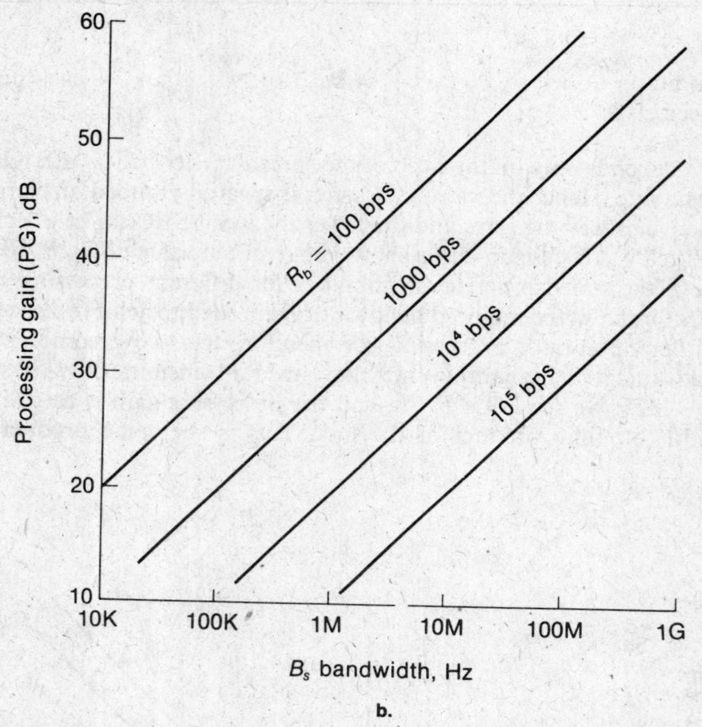

Figure 7.10. Jamming performance curves. (a) Required jammer power needed to overcome. (b) Required satellite bandwidth to achieve given processing gain and bit rate.

improved the crosstalk performance and increased the number of available users in the CDMA link. Hence the advantages of high bandwidth–bit time products in spread-spectrum systems can be shown from several points of view. In a satellite link, the bandwidth is of course restricted to the available satellite RF bandwidth. These facts tend to continually influence military spread-spectrum systems toward the higher satellite frequency bands.

We emphasize that the concept of processing gain simply follows from the fact that a synchronized receiver, having an addressed replica of the carrier, can correlate the data carrier while spreading out the jammer. The result is completely independent of the jammer bandwidth—that is, of whether the jammer is broadband or partial band, as long as the jammer has finite power.

It is common to define P_j/P_c in Figure 7.10a as the **jamming margin**, which in decibels is

$$(\text{JM})_{\text{dB}} = (\text{PG})_{\text{dB}} - \left(\frac{E_b}{N_0}\right)_{\text{dB}} \tag{7.4.7}$$

This margin indicates how much stronger in power the jammer can be relative to the transmitter, referred to the receiver input, while achieving a desired (E_b/N_0). The latter is dependent on the desired bit-error probability and the modulation format. Jamming margin can be increased by either increasing processing gain (spreading the carrier bandwidth or reducing bit rate) or by reducing the required E_b/N_0 (via coding). However, E_b/N_0 reduction through coding can only produce several dB of margin improvement (recall Figure 2.20), whereas processing gain increases continually with available RF bandwidth.

Satellite Jamming

In a satellite system, the jammer may have the opportunity to jam the satellite instead of the receiving earth station (Figure 7.11). By transmitting strong, broadband noise up to the satellite, the jammer can control the limiting power suppression that occurs in the satellite processing. In effect, the jammer power P_J replaces the uplink noise power in our earlier analysis. If we assume limiter suppression models as in (4.5.9), the downlink SNR

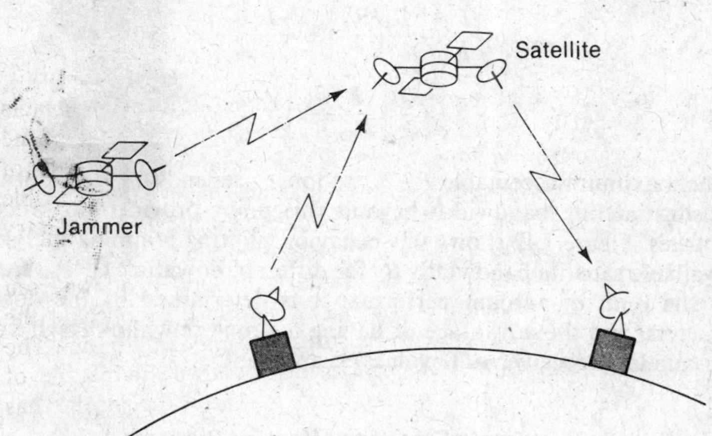

Figure 7.11. Jamming of a satellite.

in a bandwidth B_s is, from (3.6.6),

$$\mathrm{SNR}_d = \frac{\left(\frac{P_c}{P_c + P_J}\right) P_T L}{P_T L \left(\frac{P_J}{P_c + P_J}\right) + N_{0d} B_s} \tag{7.4.8}$$

If $P_J/P_c >> 1$, this is

$$\mathrm{SNR}_d \simeq \left(\frac{P_c}{P_J}\right)\left[\frac{\mathrm{CNR}_d}{\mathrm{CNR}_d + 1}\right] \tag{7.4.9}$$

where $\mathrm{CNR}_d = P_T L / N_{0d} \mathrm{B}_s$. If we solve for the required jamming margin to achieve a specified despread SNR of Y, we have

$$\frac{P_J}{P_c} = \left(\frac{PG}{\mathrm{Y}}\right)\left[\frac{\mathrm{CNR}_d}{\mathrm{CNR}_d + 1}\right] \tag{7.4.10}$$

This is the maximum uplink $(\mathrm{SJR})^{-1}$ that can be tolerated in achieving the Y performance. If the downlink is strong ($\mathrm{CNR}_d >> 1$), (7.4.10) simply states that the uplink determines downlink performance, and the entire link has the full advantage of the receiver processing gain. However, as the bandwidth is increased, the downlink is eventually weakened, and the bracketed term begins to reduce the effective receiver PG. In fact, when $\mathrm{CNR}_d << 1$,

$$\begin{aligned} \frac{P_J}{P_c} &= \frac{B_s/R_b}{\mathrm{Y}}\left[\frac{P_T L}{N_{0d} B_s}\right] \\ &= \frac{1}{\mathrm{Y}}\left[\frac{P_T L}{N_{0d} R_b}\right] \end{aligned} \tag{7.4.11}$$

and the maximum acceptable P_J/P_c no longer depends on B_s. Continually increasing satellite bandwidth beyond this point provides no processing advantages. Figure 7.12 shows this behavior, plotting jamming margin versus available satellite bandwidth B_s for different downlink CNR values. In effect the limit of antijam performance is determined by the downlink parameters, and the advantage of having a strong downlink (high satellite power and large receiver $g/\mathrm{T}°$ values) is apparent.

Jamming in Frequency-Hopped Systems

In frequency hopping the jamming effect is slightly different. In fact, it may be advantageous for the jammer to concentrate his power rather than oper-

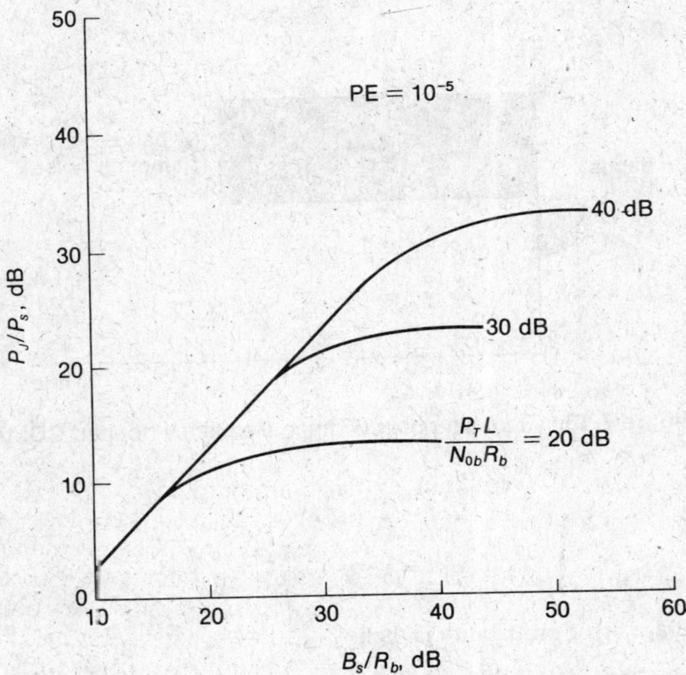

Figure 7.12. Jamming margin vs. satellite bandwidth and downlink CNR.

ate broadband. Suppose, for example, the transmitter uses a frequency hopped, binary FSK system, and assume the jammer concentrates his available power over q FSK bandwidths, Figure 7.13. (The jammer may actually change the q bands from one time slot to the next, so the jammed bands cannot be known in advance.) The jammer, therefore, introduces an effective noise level of $P_J\tau/q$ W/Hz over these bands. If the frequency hopped carrier is not in these bands, decoding is achieved with the PE associated with the receiver thermal noise. For the binary FSK case we write this as

$$\mathrm{PE}_T = \frac{1}{2}e^{-E_b/N_{0T}} \tag{7.4.12}$$

If the jammer overlaps the carrier band, it adds its noise level to the thermal noise level, and now

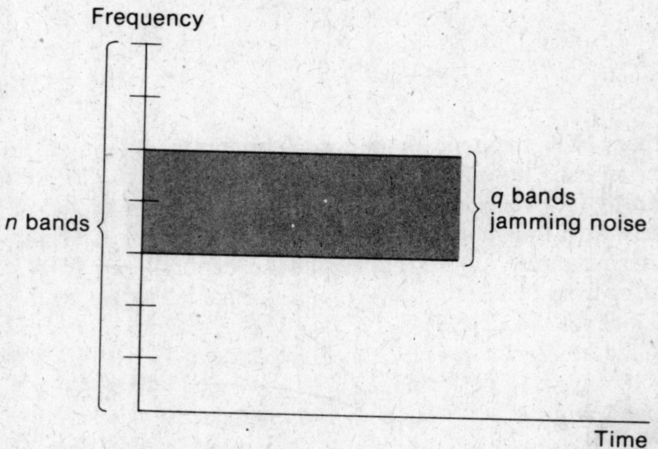

Figure 7.13. Jamming bandwidth in frequency hopped CDMA.

$$\mathrm{PE}_J = \frac{1}{2} e^{-[E_b/N_{0T}+(P_J\tau/q)]}$$
$$= \frac{1}{2}\exp - \left[\frac{N_{0T}}{E_b} + \frac{P_J}{qP_c}\right]^{-1} \quad (7.4.13)$$

The average error probability is then

$$\mathrm{PE} = P_H(\mathrm{PE}_J) + (1 - P_H)\mathrm{PE}_T \quad (7.4.14)$$

where now P_H is the probability that the carrier band is jammed. Assuming the jammer randomly selects his q bands,

$$P_H = \frac{q}{n} \quad (7.4.15)$$

By increasing q (jamming over a wider bandwidth), the probability of overlapping is increased, but the jammer dilutes his power over the jammed bands. To see this trade-off, let the thermal noise be neglected so that (7.4.14) is approximately

$$\mathrm{PE} \approx \left(\frac{q}{n}\right) e^{-q(P_c/P_J)} \quad (7.4.16)$$

A simple calculation shows that the largest PE (best jamming strategy) occurs for the choice

$$\frac{q}{n} = \frac{1}{nP_c/P_J} \quad (7.4.17)$$

for which

$$PE \approx \frac{e^{-1}}{nP_c/P_J} \tag{7.4.18}$$

Thus, in a binary FSK, frequency hopping system, optimal jammer strategy would use partial band jamming, with the fraction of total bandwidth to be jammed given by (7.4.17). This produces an error probability that at best varies inversely with transmitter power (instead of exponentially, as when combating thermal noise alone). Note that the denominator in (7.4.18), after substituting from (7.3.3), is directly proportional to the processing gain defined in (7.4.6) for the DS-SSMA system. We see that in frequency hopping as well, the ability to increase the link bandwidth–bit time product leads directly to improved performance.

Partial band jamming in frequency hopping can be combated by the use of fast-frequency hopping (multiple hops per bit), which increases the chance of some portion of the bit being received in a band without jamming. (However, the receiver processing necessary to take advantage of this also increases in complexity.) The jammer has other options as well, such as sweep frequency jamming, repeat-back jamming, and so on, to further combat these alternatives. A complete discussion of jamming and antijamming strategies is outside the scope of our discussion here, and the reader is referred to discussions on these subjects in References [22–25].

7.5 CODE ACQUISITION AND TRACKING

We have shown that multiple accessing and spectral spreading can be achieved by using digital codes to either encode directly or generate frequency hopping patterns. To decode in either format, however, it is necessary to have at the receiver a time-coherent replica of the same code sequence in order to despread the address or dehop the frequency pattern. This code synchronization is obtained by a code-locking subsystem operating in parallel with the data decoding channel, as we showed in Figure 7.2. A local version of the code is generated at the receiver, using the identical code generator. Initially, however, the local code is out of alignment with the received code from the transmitter, and it is necessary to bring the two codes into synchronization before data can be decoded. This synchronization is accomplished by an acquisition operation that basically applies a search-and-test aligning procedure. When an indication appears that the codes are nearly aligned, a tracking subsystem is activated to maintain the code synchronization throughout the subsequent data transmissions. The specific implementation of the acquisition and tracking subsystems depends on the addressing format used.

DS-CDMA Acquisition and Tracking

When direct sequence addressing is used, the acquisition subsystem appears as in Figure 7.14. The output code sequence from the receiver code generator is multiplied with the received modulated carrier. The mixer output is then bandpass filtered, envelope detected, and integrated for a fixed interval T_{in}. The voltage value of the integrator output serves as an indication of whether the two codes are in alignment or not. If it is concluded that the codes are not aligned, the local code sequence can be delayed or advanced, and another correlation measurement is performed. This testing can be repeated until code alignment is indicated.

The fact that the integrated envelope voltages serve as an indicator of code alignment can be shown as follows. Assume the received addressed carrier $c(t)$ arrives with an δ-sec code offset relative to the local code $q(t)$. Thus, neglecting interfering carriers,

$$c(t) = Ad(t + \delta)q(t + \delta) \cos(\omega_c t + \psi) \tag{7.5.1}$$

where $d(t)$ is the data waveform. The multiplier in Figure 7.14 multiplies $c(t)$ by the local code. The bandpass filter is centered at ω_c and is wide enough to pass the data $d(t)$, but not the code $q(t)$. Hence the filter output is

$$\text{BPF output} = A\,\overline{q(t)q(t + \delta)}\; d(t + \delta) \cos(\omega_c t + \psi) \tag{7.5.2}$$

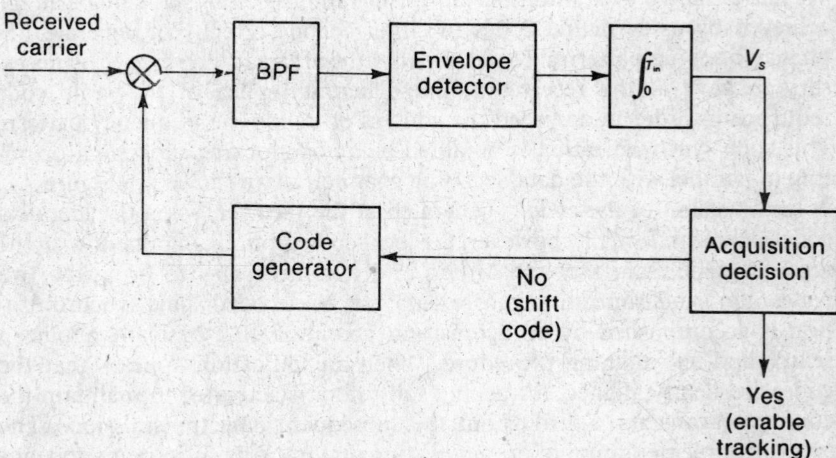

Figure 7.14. CDMA noncoherent code acquisition subsystem.

where the overbar denotes the averaging effect of the BPF on the code. The output of the envelope detector is then

$$\begin{bmatrix}\text{Envelope detector} \\ \text{output}\end{bmatrix} = \begin{bmatrix}\text{Envelope of} \\ \text{BPF output}\end{bmatrix} = |A\overline{q(t)q(t+\delta)}| \tag{7.5.3}$$

where we have used the fact that the envelope of the PSK carrier is unity. The envelope detector output is then integrated to produce the voltage v_s. If we take the integration time to be an integer multiple of a code period T_c, we have $T_{in} = \eta T_c$, and

$$v_s = \left(\frac{AT_c}{2}\right)\eta |R_q(\delta)| \tag{7.5.4}$$

where we have written

$$\overline{q(t)q(t+\delta)} \triangleq R_q(\delta) = \frac{1}{T_c}\int_0^{T_c} q(t)q(t+\delta)dt \tag{7.5.5}$$

The function $R_q(\delta)$ is the periodic autocorrelation function of the code. Thus the integrator voltage reading is directly related to the code correlation function evaluated at the offset δ. It is desirable to have this voltage v_s low when the codes are out of alignment, and high when the codes are perfectly aligned. This requires that the code autocorrelation function be (ideally) zero for $\delta \neq 0$, and maximum when $\delta = 0$. Such a function would allow observations of the voltages v_s to directly indicate when the codes are aligned. Note that this autocorrelation condition places an additional requirement on the codes selected for addressing in the CDMA format. We have previously found that address codes should be long (many chips per data bit for high processing gain) and that sets of codes should exhibit low pairwise cross-correlation, or partial cross-correlation, with other address codes. We now see that the acquisition operation further constrains the autocorrelation properties of each address code as well. Note that the correlation values v_s are generated without knowledge of the carrier phase ψ and independent of the specific data $d(t)$ being sent. This is referred to as **noncoherent** code acquisition.

Code Generation. The desired code autocorrelation for $R_q(\delta)$ can be adequately approximated by the correlation function of codes generated from digital **feedback shift registers**. Such a code generator is shown in Fig-

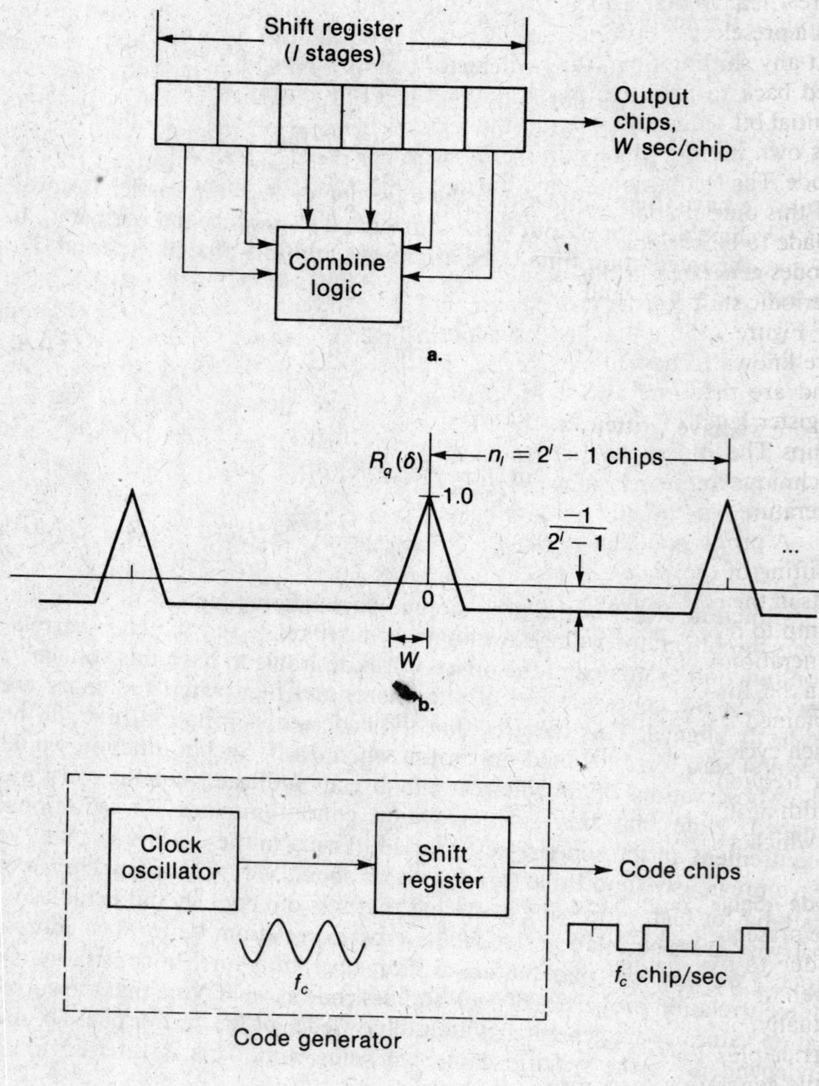

Figure 7.15. Shift register code generator. (a) Block diagram. (b) Code correlation function. (c) Clock-driven shift register for code generation.

ure 7.15a. Digital sequences are shifted through the register one bit at a time at a preselected shifting rate. The register output bits form the address code. At any shifting time, the contents of the register are binary combined and fed back to form the next input bit to the register. Once started with an initial bit sequence stored in the register, the device continually regenerates its own inputs, while shifting bits through the register to form the output code. The feedback logic and the initial bit sequence determine the structure of this output code. With properly designed logic, the output codes can be made to be periodic, and the register acts as a free-running code oscillator. Codes generated in this manner are called **shift register codes**. The class of periodic shift register codes having the desired binary waveform correlation of Figure 7.15b are called **pseudo-random noise (PRN)** codes. PRN codes are known to have the longest period associated with a given register size, and are therefore also called **maximal length** shift register codes. If the register length is l stages, the PRN code will have a period of $n_l = 2^l - 1$ chips. The underlying mathematical structure of shift register codes, and the technique for determining proper feedback logic are well documented in the literature [26–28] and will not be considered here.

A property of shift register codes well suited to acquisition is that time shifting of the code can be easily implemented by externally changing the bits in the register at any time shift. Changing these bits causes the output to jump to a new position in the code period, which then continues periodic generation from that point on. Thus, within one shift time the output code can be forced to skip ahead in its cycle. Practical code generators are obtained by driving the shift register with a clock oscillator, Figure 7.15c. Each cycle of the clock provides the register shifting rate, so that an oscillator frequency of f_c would produce a code rate of f_c chips/sec, and a chip width of $w = 1/f_c$ sec. Hence code rates are determined by the maximal rate at which a shift register can be driven.

Code Acquisition. The code correlation voltages in (7.5.4) are observed in the presence of additive noise arriving with the addressed carrier. The noise is due to the satellite downlink, and therefore will have the spectral level given in (7.2.4), neglecting station interference. The correlation integral will actually produce an output dependent on the envelope of a combined carrier plus noise waveform, instead of simply the signal term in (7.5.4), while generating these noisy envelope values. The code acquisition system must decide when true acquisition has been achieved. There are two basic procedures for deciding the correct code position from these noisy voltage observations. One method is called **maximum-likelihood (ML) acquisition**, and involves an observation of the correlation of all code positions in a period, selecting the position with the maximum voltage for acquisition. The second method, called **threshold acquisition**, selects the first position whose voltage exceeds a fixed threshold value as the acquisition position. Note that in maximum-likelihood acquisition every code position is examined, and a decision is always made after completing the entire examination. In threshold acquisition, code positions are continually examined until a threshold crossing occurs.

In ML acquisition, incorrect acquisition occurs if an incorrect position voltage exceeds the correct one. As such, the effect is similar to that occurring in an M-ary noncoherent orthogonal decoder. In this case, word decisions are also based on maximal envelope samples, where all incorrect words have a zero signal voltage. (For shift register codes, the assumption is that the codes are long enough that the offset code correlation values in Figure 7.15b can be considered zero.) The probability of incorrect ML acquisition is therefore given by the word-error probability of a corresponding noncoherent orthogonal M-ary system where M is equal to the number of possible code positions, that is, the code length n_l. Such curves were shown in Figure 2.29 as a function of the word energy and noise spectral level. For the acquisition case, the energy corresponds to the integrated carrier envelope energy collected in the T_{in} sec integrator,

$$\left(\frac{E}{N_0}\right) = \frac{(A^2/2)T_{in}}{N_{0T}} = \eta(E_c/N_{0T}) \tag{7.5.6}$$

where η is the number of code periods in T_{in}, and E_c is the carrier energy in a code period. Making the change of variable allows us to replot noncoherent word-error curves as equivalent acquisition probability curves, as shown in Figure 7.16. The curves relate the ML acquisition probability, the integrated acquisition energy, and the code length. With fixed acquisition carrier power, Figure 7.16 serves as a basis for determining the required envelope integration time. If E_c is not satisfactory for the desired acquisition probability, we must integrate over more periods in the correlation detector in order to integrate up the acquisition power to the desired energy value. This means we spend more time examining a code shift position. Since each position must be examined, the total acquisition time to perform the ML test is then

$$T_{acq} = n_l T_{in} = n_l \eta T_c \tag{7.5.7}$$

Hence, acquisition time depends directly on the code length. We see the

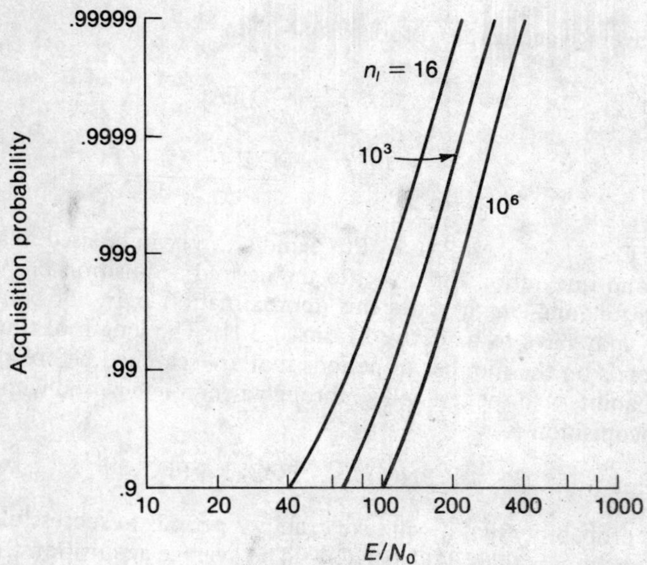

Figure 7.16. Maximum likelihood code acquisition probability vs. integrated code energy (n_l = code length, $E = A^2 T_{in}/2$).

obvious trade-off of long-length address codes (many chips per bit) versus the disadvantage of increased acquisition time.

For threshold acquisition with a threshold value of Υ volts, a false threshold crossing will occur with envelope samples with probability

$$\text{PFC} = Q(0, \Upsilon) \tag{7.5.8}$$

where $Q(a, b)$ is defined in (A.8.5). A correct threshold crossing occurs with probability

$$\text{PCC} = Q\left(\frac{E}{N_0}, \Upsilon\right) \tag{7.5.9}$$

with E/N_0 given in (7.5.6). If the jth code position is correct, and the acquisition code search begins with the first, correct acquisition will occur with probability

$$\text{PAC}_j = \text{PCC}\,(1 - \text{PFC})^{j-1} \quad . \tag{7.5.10}$$

The average acquisition probability is then

$$\begin{aligned} \text{PAC} &= \frac{1}{n_l}\sum_{j=1}^{n_l}\text{PAC}_j \\ &= \frac{\text{PCC}}{n_l}\left[\frac{1-(1-\text{PFC})^{n_l}}{\text{PFC}}\right] \end{aligned} \tag{7.5.11}$$

If PFC << $1/n_l$, then PAC $\approx$ PCC, and (7.5.9) can be used to adjust threshold and integration time, T_{in}, to the desired acquisition probability. However, for long-length codes this approximation may not be accurate, and PAC may have to be derived from (7.5.11). The length of time for the test depends on the number of periods that are searched before acquiring. The probability that the test will go through a complete period without reporting an acquisition is

$$\text{PNC} = (1-\text{PCC})(1-\text{PFC})^{n_l-1} \tag{7.5.12}$$

The probability that it will take exactly i periods to successfully acquire the jth position is then $\text{PAC}_j\,(\text{PNC})^{i-1}$. The average acquisition time is then

$$\begin{aligned} T_{\text{acq}} &= \frac{1}{n_l}\sum_{j=1}^{n_l}\sum_{i=1}^{\infty} T_{\text{in}}((i-1)n_l+j)\text{PAC}_j(\text{PNC})^{i-1} \\ &= (n_l T_{\text{in}})\frac{1}{n_l}\sum_{j=1}^{n_l}\text{PAC}_j\sum_{i=1}^{\infty} i(\text{PNC})^i + T_{\text{in}}\sum_{i=1}^{\infty}(\text{PNC})^{i-1}\left(\frac{1}{n_l}\sum_{j=1}^{n_l} j\text{PAC}_j\right) \\ &= T_{\text{in}}\left[n_l\text{PAC}\left(\frac{\text{PNC}}{(1-\text{PNC})^2}\right)+\frac{\text{PCC}}{1-\text{PNC}}\sum_{j=1}^{n_j}\text{J}(1-\text{PNC})^{i-1}\right] \end{aligned} \tag{7.5.13}$$

When PFC << $1/n_l$, PAC $\approx$ PCC $\approx$ 1 – PNC, and

$$T_{\text{acq}} \approx T_{\text{in}}\left[\frac{n_l(1-\text{PAC})}{\text{PAC}}+\frac{n_l}{2}\right] \tag{7.5.14}$$

Thus, on the average, approximately one-half the code chips will be searched before acquisition. We see therefore that threshold testing also has an acquisition time dependent on the code length. However, it must be remembered that T_{acq} is an average time, and individual acquisition operations may run considerably longer.

Since coded acquisition with shift register codes may have an abnormally long acquisition time, there has been interest in finding modifications that can reduce that time. One method is to use **preacquisition detection** of the code chips. Recall that shift register codes are generated at the register output by a binary sequence, passing through the register. If the register had

l stages, then each l chip subsequence of the address code must have been a binary sequence in the register at one time. Furthermore, if we observed any l consecutive chips of the code and loaded them in order into an identical register, the feedback chip generated at the next register shift time must be the $(l + 1)$st chip of the code. This immediately suggests an acquisition aid in which we first attempt to determine l consecutive chips of the incoming address code. If these l chips are determined correctly, and loaded into the receiver register, the sequence of chips generated from the feedback logic from then on will exactly match the incoming code. Hence, no code position search is required and acquisition is immediately achieved.

The method, however, requires the correct detection of l consecutive input address chips. That is, we must treat the received addressed carrier as a modulated PSK carrier, and perform binary detection. Since this detection requires carrier phase referencing, we must first construct a squaring or *Costas loop* to remove the address modulation. The phase referenced carrier can then be used for address code detection, and the decisions used to load the receiver shift register. When loaded, the register is then switched into the code acquisition loop of Figure 7.14. If the l address chips were all correctly decoded, the loop is immediately in time synchronism. If an error was made, the two codes are not aligned (which is so indicated by the correlation detection). The detection of l new chips must then be repeated. The task of correctly decoding l successive code chips, however, may not be trivial. This is because the energy used for the code chip decisioning is that of only a single chip in the entire code. If the code has length n_l then only $1/n_l$ of the available code energy is used for this decoding. That is, if E_{cc} is the code chip energy, $E_{cc} = E_c/n_l$, which produces an (E_{cc}/N_{0T}) that is n_l times smaller than E_c/N_0. Unless the acquisition energy is large, this reduction with long codes will produce such a poor chip detection probability that the l chip detection may have to be repeated many times. In such cases the usefulness of the predetection operation is suspect, and must be carefully evaluated.

Code Tracking. Once code acquisition has been accomplished (local and received codes brought into alignment), the received code must be continually tracked to maintain the synchronization. A code-tracking loop for discrete sequences is shown in Figure 7.17a. It contains two parallel branches of a multiplier, bandpass filter, and envelope detector. (One branch can be that used in the acquisition operation, so that initiation of tracking requires only the insertion of the second branch.) The two-branch system in Figure 7.17 is referred to as a **delay-locked loop** [29]. A delay-locked tracking loop uses the local code to generate error voltages $e(t)$ that are fed back to correct any timing offsets of the local code generator as they arise. Timing-error voltages are obtained by using the local code to generate

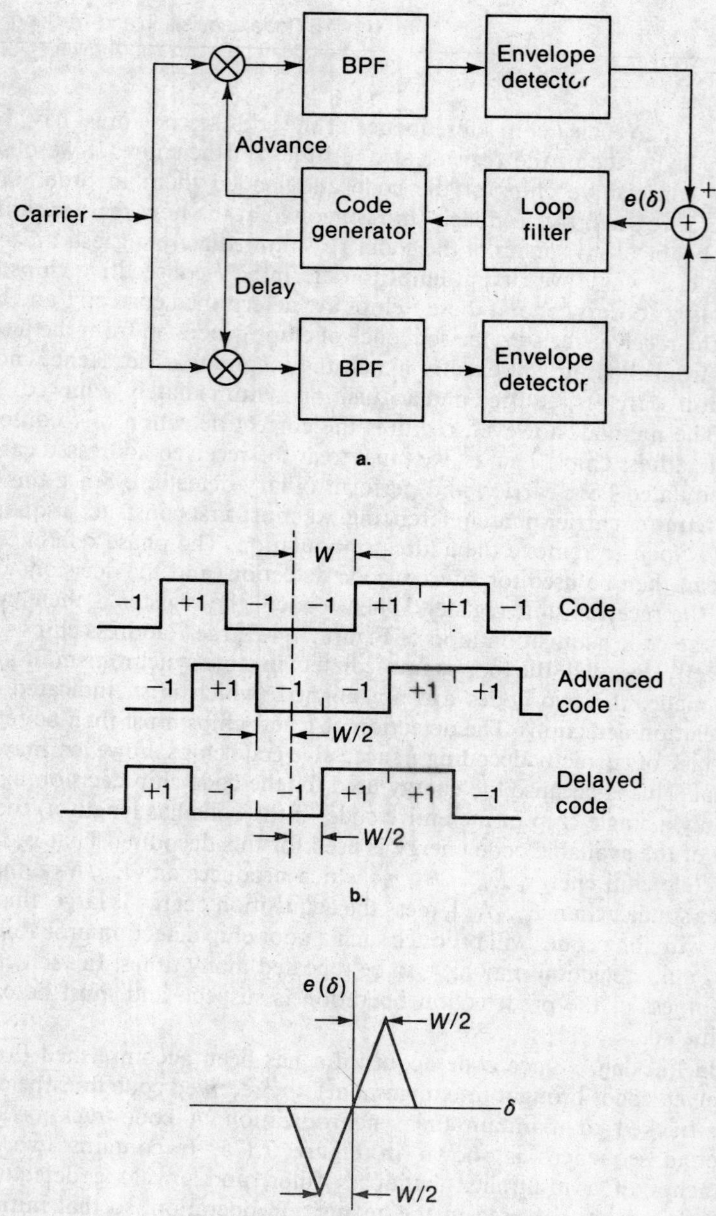

Figure 7.17. Delay-locked code-tracking subsystem. (a) Block diagram. (b) Advanced and delayed code alignment. (c) Code-error voltage vs. timing offset.

two offset sequences advanced and delayed by one-half chip (see Figure 7.17b). With shift register codes, these are obtained from different taps within the same register. Thus if $q(t)$ is the local code, the sequences $q(t+\frac{w}{2})$ and $q(t-\frac{w}{2})$ are simultaneously generated from the register. These offset codes are each separately multiplied with the input in the two channels of the delay-locked loop. The multiplied outputs are then bandpass filtered and envelope detected to produce output voltages that are subtracted to form the correction signal for code timing adjustment. Again, each BPF passes the data bits but averages the code product, which is then envelope detected. Following the discussion in (7.5.3), the advanced code channel output is

$$\begin{aligned} V_a &= \text{envelope of}\left[A\overline{q(t+\delta)\, q\left(t+\frac{w}{2}\right)} d(t+\delta)\cos(\omega_c t+\psi)\right] \\ &= A\left| R_q\left(\delta-\frac{w}{2}\right)\right| \end{aligned} \tag{7.5.15}$$

where $R_q(\delta)$ is defined in (7.5.5). Similarly, the delayed code channel produces

$$V_d = A\left| R_q\left(\delta+\frac{w}{2}\right)\right| \tag{7.5.16}$$

The output of the subtractor therefore is the correction voltage

$$\begin{aligned} e(\delta) &= V_d - V_a \\ &= A\left| R_q\left(\delta+\frac{w}{2}\right)\right| - A\left| R_q\left(\delta-\frac{w}{2}\right)\right| \end{aligned} \tag{7.5.17}$$

for any offset δ.

This function is plotted in Figure 7.17c for the code correlation functions of Figure 7.15b. We see that whether δ is positive or negative, a voltage proportional to δ is produced having the proper sign to adjust correctly the local code timing to reduce δ. This is accomplished by using $e(\delta)$ to adjust the code clock that drives the code register (slow it down or speed it up). Note that a proportional correction voltage is generated only if $|\delta| < w/2$; that is, only if we are within a half chip time of code lock. This is why an initial acquisition procedure is necessary to first align the codes to within this accuracy. The delay-locked loop then operates to continually correct for subsequent timing errors. For this reason code acquisition is often called *course* synchronization, while code tracking is referred to as *fine* synchronization. Note that due to the envelope detection the delay-locked loop achieves code tracking noncoherently, that is, without knowledge of the carrier phase or frequency (as long as the multiplier outputs pass through the BPF).

The acquisition system in Figure 7.14 and the delay-locked loop in Figure 7.17a can be combined to form the total DS-CDMA acquisition and tracking subsystem shown in Figure 7.18. When the tracking error is zero the local code generator (without the offsets) is exactly in phase with the received code and can therefore be used to despread the received carrier. Thus, in the data channel in Figure 7.18, we use the fact that $q(t) \cdot q(t) = q^2(t) = 1$ to form the product

$$[d(t)q(t)\cos(\omega_c t + \psi)]q(t) = d(t)\cos(\omega_c t + \psi) \tag{7.5.18}$$

The despread PSK carrier can now be processed in a standard PSK decoder for data recovery.

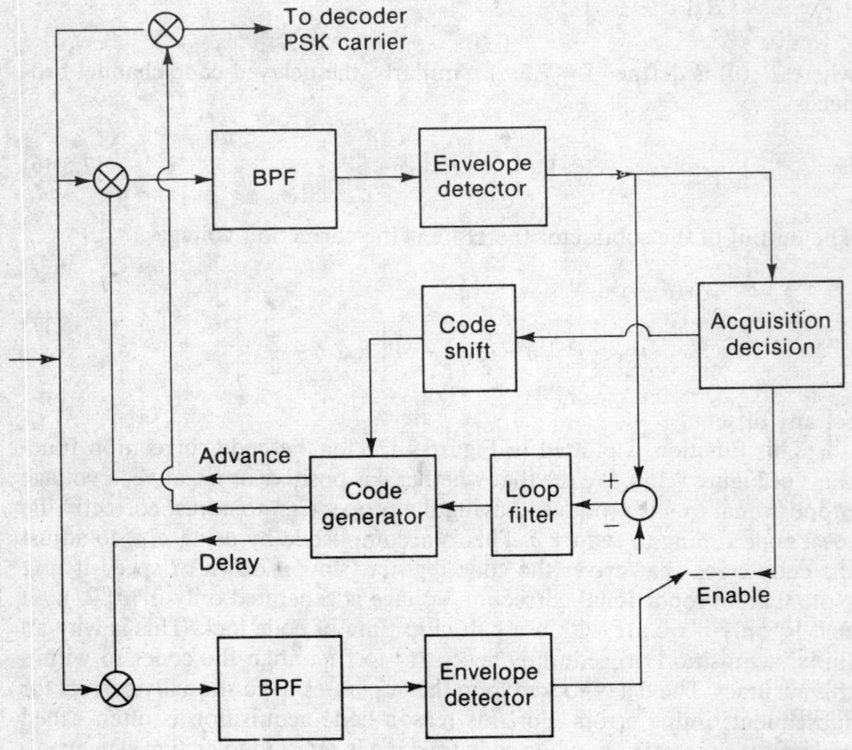

Figure 7.18. Combined code acquisition and tracking subsystem.

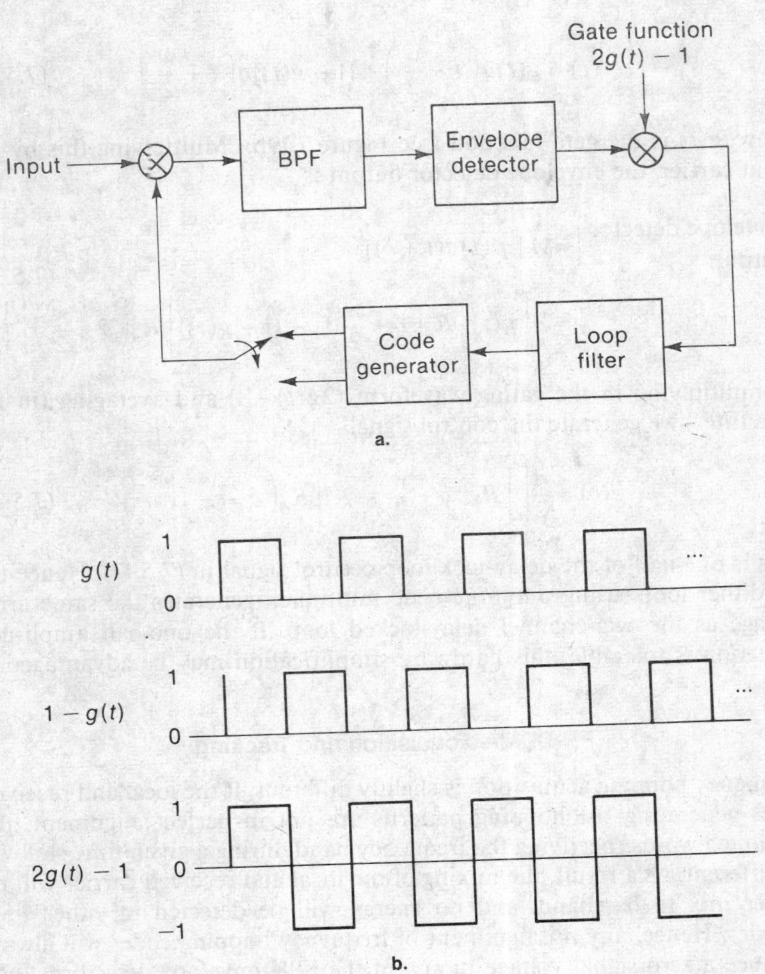

Figure 7.19. Tau-dither code-tracking loop. (a) Block diagram. (b) Gating functions.

An alternative to the two-channel delay-locked loop is to use a **tau-dither loop** [30]. This loop uses only a single channel to perform serially the advanced and delayed multiplication, as shown in Figure 7.19. Although the same code offsets are generated, only one is used at a time with a single multiplier channel. This is accomplished by gating in each offset code over separate periodic intervals. In effect we generate the gated local code

$$q'(t) = g(t)q\left(t - \frac{w}{2}\right) + [1 - g(t)]q\left(t + \frac{w}{2}\right) \tag{7.5.19}$$

where $g(t)$ is the gate function (see Figure 7.19b). Multiplying this by the input carrier, the envelope detector output is

$$\begin{aligned}\begin{bmatrix}\text{Envelope detector}\\ \text{output}\end{bmatrix} &= A\,|\overline{q'(t)q(t+\delta)}| \\ &= A\left[g(t)\left|R_q\left(\delta + \frac{w}{2}\right)\right| + (1 - g(t))\left|R_q\left(\delta - \frac{w}{2}\right)\right|\right]\end{aligned} \tag{7.5.20}$$

By multiplying in the gating waveform $(2g(t) - 1)$ and averaging (in the loop filter) we generate the control signal

$$e(\delta) = \frac{A}{2}\left[\left|R_q\left(\delta + \frac{w}{2}\right)\right| - \left|R_q\left(\delta - \frac{w}{2}\right)\right|\right] \tag{7.5.21}$$

This is one-half of the delay-lock loop control signal in (7.5.17). Hence the tau-dither loop, using only one code multiplier, generates the same error voltage as the two-channel delay-locked loop. If the one-half amplitude reduction is tolerable, this hardware simplification may be advantageous.

FH-CDMA Acquisition and Tracking

Frequency hopping acquisition is slightly different. If the local and received codes generating the hopping patterns are not in perfect alignment, the partioned words specifying the frequency band during a given time slot will be different. As a result, the mixing of the local and received carrier will no longer mix to baseband, and no energy will be detected in either FSK decoder. Hence, any misalignment of frequency hopping codes will always produce a zero signal voltage in any of the FSK envelope detectors. Only when the codes are perfectly aligned, and the carrier frequencies are hopping in synchronism, will signal energy be continually observed in the decoder. Acquisition is therefore achieved by mixing the local and received carriers as they hop, and observing FSK decoder energy for a fixed integration time. The local code can then be shifted one chip at a time (shifting the local hopping pattern) until decoding energy is observed at one position.

Frequency hopped acquisition performance is governed by FSK decoder variables, which also correspond to envelope samples, as in noncoherent DS-CDMA acquisition. Hence the decoding SNR is again given by (7.5.6), except that E_c is now the carrier energy per slot time, and the integer η here indicates the number of slot times (number of hops) over which the decoder energy is integrated. Acquisition probabilities can be computed using either the maximum-likelihood or threshold procedures discussed earlier.

Tracking in frequency hopped systems is obtained via the system diagram in Figure 7.20a. Again, acquisition is used to bring the hopping patterns in near alignment, and the tracking subsystem is used to remove any residual offsets and hold the patterns aligned. As in direct sequence tracking, the frequency hopped tracking operates by generating a correction voltage to adjust the timing of the local code generator that drives the local hopping pattern. This correction voltage is obtained using the fact that if the hopping patterns are offset by δ sec ($|\delta|$ less than a chip time) there will be a δ-sec interval in each slot time when the frequencies of the hopping patterns are not aligned (see Figure 7.20b). During this δ-sec interval no signal energy appears in the FSK decoder. This δ-sec interval will be either at the front end or rear end of the slot time, depending on whether the local pattern is early or late. By multiplying the energy detector output in each slot time by the periodic square wave in Figure 7.20a and integrating, we generate a correction voltage with the proper sign and magnitude for timing control. If $\delta = 0$ (codes perfectly aligned), the square wave clock causes the product to contain equal positive and negative areas, and the integrator output sums to zero. If a δ-sec interval of zero voltage arises (codes not perfectly aligned), a portion of the product area will cancel, reducing the integrator value by an amount proportional to δ. Whether the zero area subtracts from the positive or negative area depends on whether the δ-sec interval is at the beginning or ending of the slot. Hence a filtered correction voltage $e(t)$ in Figure 7.20a will be proportional to δ with the proper sign for continually correcting the local code.

While the tracking subsystems for either discrete sequence or frequency hopped CDMA operate to keep any offset δ small, it should be pointed out that even a relatively small offset can seriously degrade data decoding. For example, consider again (7.5.18) when the codes used for despreading or dehopping are slightly offset. The signal portion of the data decoder waveform is now given by

$$A[\overline{q(t)q(t+\delta)}]d(t)\cos(\omega_c t + \psi) = AR_q(\delta)d(t)\cos(\omega_c t + \psi) \qquad (7.5.22)$$

Hence the effective PSK amplitude is reduced by the value $R_q(\delta)$ of the code correlation function. If the latter function falls off rapidly, a relatively small value of δ can produce a significant amplitude degradation. For example, with the correlation function of Figure 7.15b, an offset of $\delta = 0.2w$ produces $R_q(\delta) = 0.8$, and the decoding power is reduced by 0.64. Hence only a 20% of a chip offset in timing can cause a 1.93 dB loss in decoding E_b/N_0.

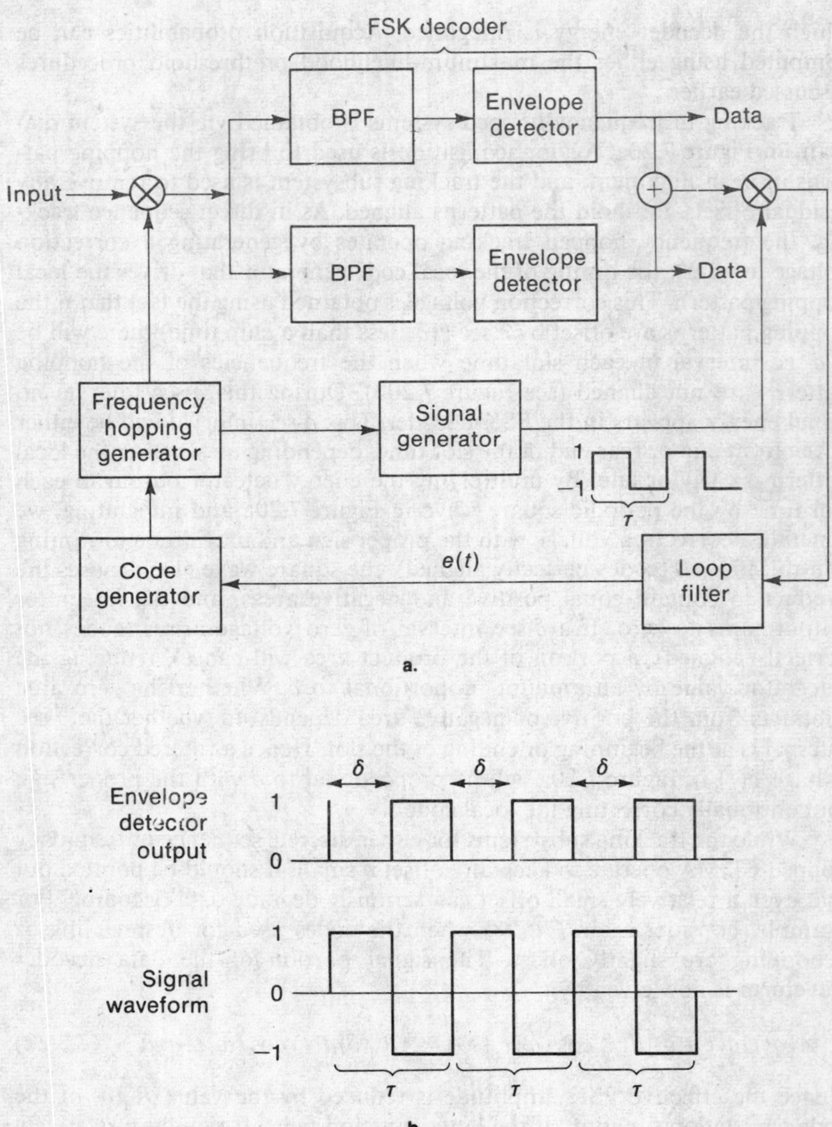

Figure 7.20. Frequency hopping CDMA acquisition and tracking system. (a) Block diagram. (b) Waveforms.

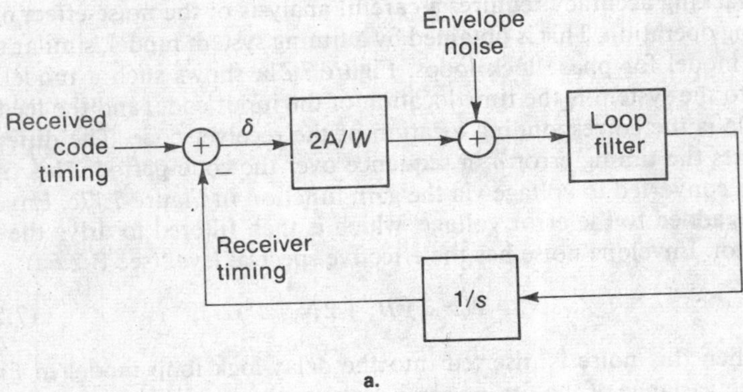

a.

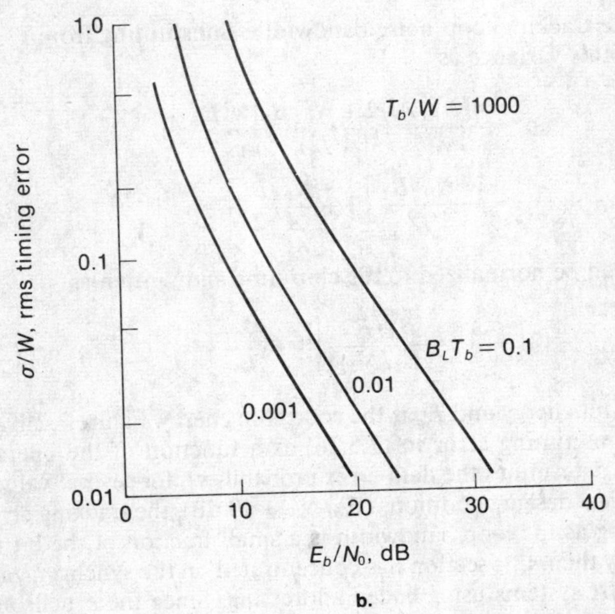

b.

Figure 7.21. Code-tracking loop analysis. (a) Timing block diagram. (b) rms loop-timing error due to noise. Equation: $\sigma^2/w^2 = [(B_L/R_b)/E_b/N_0]\,[1 + (T_b/w)/(E_b/N_0)]$.

Tracking accuracy requires a careful analysis of the noise effect on the tracking operation. This is obtained by a timing system model, similar to the phase model for phase lock loops. Figure 7.21a shows such a model. The input to the system is the time location of the input code, and the feedback variable is the corresponding location of the receiver code. The difference generates the timing error δ in sequence over the code period. This timing error is converted to voltage via the gain function in Figure 7.17c. Envelope noise is added to the error voltage, which is then filtered to drive the local generator. Envelope noise has the effective spectral level (see B.2.6a)

$$N_0 = 2(N_{0T})^2 B_s + 2N_{0T}A^2/2 \tag{7.5.23}$$

When this noise is inserted into the delay-lock loop model in Figure 7.21, the variance of the timing error δ due to the noise is

$$\sigma^2 = \frac{w^2 N_0 2B_L}{4(A^2/2)^2} \tag{7.5.24}$$

where B_L is the tracking loop noise bandwidth. Substituting from (7.5.23) we can rewrite this variance as

$$\begin{aligned}\sigma^2 &= \frac{4[N_{0T}A^2/2 + N_{0T}^2 B_s]w^2 B_L}{4(A^2/2)^2} \\ &= \frac{w^2 N_{0T} B_L}{A^2/2}\left[1 + \frac{N_{0T}B_s}{A^2/2}\right]\end{aligned} \tag{7.5.25}$$

This variance can be normalized to the chip time and written as

$$\left(\frac{\sigma}{w}\right)^2 = \frac{B_L/R_b}{(E_b/N_{0T})}\left[1 + \frac{N_{0T}}{E_c}\right] \tag{7.5.26}$$

where E_b is the bit energy and E_c is the code chip energy. Figure 7.21b plots the fractional rms timing error in (7.5.26) as a function of the operating (E_b/N_0) (which determines the data-error probability), for several values of B_L/R_b. For typical design conditions ($E_b/N_0 \approx 10$ dB), the tracking error is negligible as long as the loop bandwidth is a small fraction of the bit rate.

In summary then, this section has concentrated on the synchronization aspects of CDMA systems using coded addressing. Since the synchronization accuracy is of ultimate importance in link performance, these subsystems were examined in detail to demonstrate both their complexity and their feasibility with modern hardware. The continual development in high-speed code processing will obviously directly impact CDMA performance, both for commercial and military applications.

PROBLEMS

7.1 Given two periodic, binary-coded (±1) NRZ waveforms $m_1(t)$ and $m_2(t)$, with chip period τ sec and n chips per period. Show that the cross-correlation of these waveforms becomes

$$\gamma = \frac{1}{n\tau}\int_0^{n\tau} m_1(t)m_2(t)\,dt$$

$$= \frac{1}{n}\,[(\text{number of matching symbols}) - (\text{number of mismatched symbols})]$$

where the matching refers to corresponding symbols of the same chip period.

7.2 Given the two periodic code sequences:

Code 1:	1	−1	1	1	−1	−1	1	1	(one period)
Code 2:	−1	1	1	−1	−1	−1	−1	1	

(a) Compute the *periodic* cross-correlation of the sequences at each chip shift time. [*Hint*: Use the results of Problem 7.1.] (b) Without shifting, compute the *partial* cross-correlations of length three.

7.3 Define a binary, square 2 × 2 matrix H_1 as

$$H_1 = \begin{bmatrix} 1 & -1 \\ 1 & 1 \end{bmatrix}$$

Define its nth order extension as

$$H_n = \begin{bmatrix} H_{n-1} & \hat{H}_{n-1} \\ H_{n-1} & H_{n-1} \end{bmatrix}$$

where $\hat{H}_{n-1}$ is obtained by changing the signs of H_{n-1}. Show that the rows of H_n, for any n, represent a set of n orthogonal binary sequences.

7.4 An acquisition waveform in FH systems is composed of a specific sequence of frequency bursts, $\mathbf{F} = \{f_i\}$, where each f_i is one of a set of n frequencies. Acquisition is achieved by frequency correlating the input waveform with the expected frequency sequence **F**. Good acquisition requires high correlation only when the true **F** completely arrives, and zero correlation at all other times.

Assume during each burst two identical frequencies will correlate to one, while two different frequencies correlate to zero. Show that the desired correlation property is satisfied if and only if no two f_i of **F** are identical. What does this mean about the length of **F**?

7.5 An *array* is a matrix of cells, with dots in some cells. A *Costas Array* is a square array with only one dot in any row or column, and having the property that any shift of the array horizontally and/or vertically will produce no more than one dot overlap with the original array.

Explain how the solution of this mathematical problem has direct application to the acquisition problem of a frequency hopping system. [*Hint*: Observe Figure 7.5.]

7.6 An FH FSK system uses a frequency bandwidth of 160 MHz, and transmits 3-bit words at 1000 hops per second. The decoding FSK $E_b/N_0 = 7$ dB. (a) How many separate carriers can be supported? (b) What will be the symbol-error probability, PSE?

7.7 A DS-CDMA system is to operate with PE = 10^{-5} and transmit a carrier data rate of 10^4 bps through a satellite with a 10 MHz bandwidth. A jammer can deliver a power of 10^{-6} watts to the receiver. How much power must the carrier provide at the receiver to operate the system, assuming the full satellite bandwidth is used?

7.8 Consider the shift register in Figure P7.8. Start with all zeros in the register, and shift in one bit from the left. Compute the output sequence from the register as the bits are clocked through.

7.9 A FH system hops over a 50 KHz bandwidth. The frequency generator is simply an oscillator that is swept at a rate of 50 MHz/sec.

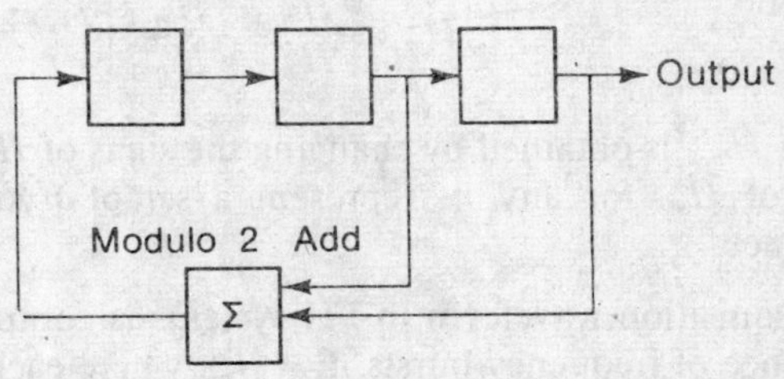

Figure P7.8

What is the worst case decoding energy degradation that can be expected in a system that hops at 150 hops per second?

7.10 In **pulse-addressed multiple accessing (PAMA)**, a station pair uses a τ-sec burst of PSK carrier modulation placed in a specific location in a T sec data frame. The burst locations are selected randomly by each station pair, and any station transmits when desired, without knowledge of other station pairs. (a) Show that the mean square cross-correlation for any station pair is $(\tau/3T)$. (b) For equal amplitude carriers, show that the maximum number of users is $K \leqslant 3T/\tau$.

In **slotted PAMA**, only specific τ-sec slots can be used. Assume the T-sec frame is divided into T/τ disjoint slots, and each station pair selects its slot randomly. Show that the probability that r of k users will lie in the same slot is

$$P(r) = \binom{k}{r}\left(\frac{1}{\mu}\right)^r\left(\frac{\mu-1}{\mu}\right)^{k-r}$$

where $\mu = T/\tau$.

REFERENCES

1. R. Gold, "Maximal Recursive Sequence with Multi-valued Cross correlation," *IEEE Trans. Inf. Theory*, vol. IT-14 (January 1968), pp. 154–156.

2. T. Kasami, and L. Lin, "Coding for a Multiple Access Channel," *IEEE Trans. Inf. Theory*, vol. IT-22 (March 1976), pp. 123–132.

3. M. Pursley, "The Role of Coding in Multiple Access Satellite Communication Systems," University of Illinois Report R-724, Coordinated Science Lab., April 1976.

4. L. Welch, "Lower Bounds on the Maximum-Cross Correlation of Signals," *IEEE Trans. Inf. Theory*, vol. IT-20 (May 1974), pp. 397–399.

5. D. V. Sarwate, and M. B. Pursley, "Crosscorrelation Properties of Pseudorandom and Related Sequences," *Proc. IEEE*, vol. 68 (May 1980), pp. 593–619.

6. M. Pursley, "Performance Evaluation for Phase-Coded Spread Spectrum Multiple-Access—Part I: System Analysis," *IEEE Trans. on Comm.*, vol. COM-25 (August 1977), pp. 795–799.

7. M. B. Pursley, and H. F. A. Roefs, "Numerical Evaluation of Correla-

tion Parameters for Optimal Phases of Binary Shift-Register Sequences," *IEEE Trans. Comm.*, vol. COM-27 (October 1979), pp. 1597–1604.

8. See Section on "Coded Division Multiple Access" in *IEEE Trans. on Comm.*, vol. COM-30 (May 1982).

9. D. Anderson, and P. Wintz, "Analysis of Spread Spectrum System with a Hard Limiter," *IEEE Trans. on Comm. Tech.* (April 1969).

10. H. Kochevar, "Spread Spectrum Multiple Access Experiment Through a Satellite," *IEEE Trans. on Comm.* (August 1977).

11. H. Baer, "Interference Effects of Hard Limiters in PN Spread Spectrum Systems," *IEEE Trans. on Comm.*, vol. COM-30 (May 1982).

12. N. E. Bekir, "Bounds on the Distribution of Partial Correlation for PN and Gold Sequences," Ph.D. dissertation, Department of Electrical Engineering, University of Southern California, Los Angeles, January 1978.

13. K. Yao, "Error Probability of Asynchronous Spread Spectrum Multiple-Access Communication Systems," *IEEE Trans. Comm.*, vol. COM-25 (August 1977), pp. 803–809.

14. C. Weber, G. Huth, and B. Batson, "Performance Considerations of CDMA Systems," *IEEE Trans. on Vehicle Tech.*, vol. VT-30 (February 1981).

15. R. Frank, and S. Zadoff, "Phase Shift Codes with Good Periodic Correlation Proportion Properties," *IEEE Trans. Info. Theory*, vol. IT-8 (October 1962), pp. 381–382.

16. R. Heimiller, "Codes with Good Period Correlations," *IEEE Trans. Info. Theory*, vol. IT-7 (October 1961), pp. 254–256.

17. D. Chu, "Polyphase Codes With Good Correlation Properties," *IEEE Trans. Info. Theory*, vol. IT-18 (July 1972), pp. 531–540.

18. R. Gold, "Optimal Binary Sequences for Spread Spectrum Multiplexing," *IEEE Trans. Info. Theory*, vol. IT-13 (October 1967), pp. 619–621.

19. N. Mohanty, "Multiple Frank-Heimiller Signals for Multiple Access System," *IEEE Trans. on Aerospace Electronic Systems*, vol. AES-11 (July 1975).

20. K. Schneider, and R. Orr, "Aperiodic Correlation Constraints on Binary Sequences," *IEEE Trans. on Info. Theory* (January 1975).

21. G. Turyn, "Sequences with Small Correlation," in *Error Correcting Codes*, ed. H. Mann (New York: Wiley, 1968).

22. "Special Issue on Spread Spectrum Communications," *IEEE Trans. on Comm.*, vol. COM-25 (August 1977) and vol. COM-30 (May 1982).

23. S. Houston, "Tone and Noise Jamming of Spread Spectrum FSK and DPSK Systems," *Proc. of the IEEE Aerospace and Electronic Conference*, Dayton, Ohio, 1975.

24. R. Pettit, *ECM and ECCM Techniques For Digital Communications* (Belmont, Calif.: Lifetime Learning, 1982).

25. P. Kullstam, "Spread Spectrum Performance in Arbitrary Interference," *IEEE Trans. on Comm.*, vol. COM-25 (August 1977).

26. S. Golomb, *Shift Register Sequences*, (San Francisco: Holden-Day, 1967).

27. S. Golomb, et al. *Digital Communications with Space Applications* (Englewood Cliffs, N.J.: Prentice-Hall, 1964).

28. J. Lee, and D. Smith, "Families of Shift Register Sequences with Impulse Correlation Registers," *IEEE Trans. on Info. Theory*, vol. IT-20 (March 1974).

29. J. Spilker, *Digital Communication by Satellite*, (Englewood Cliffs, N.J.: Prentice-Hall, 1977).

30. H. Hartmann, "Analysis of a Dithering Loop for Code Tracking," *IEEE Trans. on Aerospace and Electronic Systems*, vol. AES-10 (January 1974).

8

Phase Coherency in Satellite Systems

In previous chapters we have pointed out the advantages of having a phase coherent carrier reference at the receiver. This reference can be used to coherently decode data modulated carriers to achieve maximal decoding performance. In addition, if a frequency measurement is to be made on the received carrier, as in doppler tracking subsystems, the measurement can be made on the coherent reference instead of the noisy received carrier. Coherent references are obtained by some form of phase locking system that forms a local oscillator to track the phase of the received carrier. A measure of the degree of phase coherence in such systems is the instantaneous phase difference between the two carriers when referred to the same frequency. When this phase difference is small (i.e., the carriers are close in phase) they are said to be **phase locked**, or **phase coherent**.

In a communication link the ability to maintain phase coherency is affected by system noise and inherent instabilities in the oscillators generating the carrier. It is therefore necessary to understand how these anomalies affect phase coherency, and how they may be combated by improved system design. In satellite systems the phase referencing problem is further compounded by the existence of the satellite transponder between the transmitter and receiver. The transponder can add additional oscillator instability, as well as additional noise, to the carrier being transponded to the receiver. In this chapter, we present a basic phase coherency analysis that has general application to all types of satellite links. The basic objective is to indicate procedures for establishing useable phase error models, and to point out some intricacies and philosophies of satellite phase coherency analysis that must be considered for candidate satellite systems.

8.1 CARRIER PHASE NOISE

The basis of the phase coherency problem associated with any type of communication link is the total **phase instability** superimposed on the RF data carriers when they arrive at their receiver destination. The greater this carrier instability, the harder it is to establish phase-coherent references at the receiver. By phase instability, we refer to the aggregate phase variation (both deterministic and random) of the carrier other than the portion due to the modulation or to doppler frequency shifts. In particular we include random phase variations (phase noise) and random phase offsets (i.e., constant phase shifts) due to differential phase effects, such as medium dispersion and device delay. The primary sources of phase noise are the system oscillators, which generate the link carriers and mixing frequencies, and the additive thermal noise, which is directly converted to phase noise by amplitude limiting, power amplification, and carrier extraction. Secondary sources of phase noise are excess noise in multipliers, mixers, and distributed amplifiers. These latter sources generally contribute significantly lesser (but not always negligible) amounts of phase noise relative to the oscillators themselves.

In previous modeling of carrier waveforms, the carrier phase has been written as $(\omega_c t + \psi)$, where ω_c is the frequency and ψ was considered a fixed phase angle to be tracked. In reality RF carriers are generated from electronic or solid state oscillators formed from resonant circuits or tuned cavities. These resonances inherently contain vibration or internal thermal noise, which cause the carrier phase to vary randomly in time. Hence the carrier phase ψ should instead be written as a phase noise process $\psi(t)$. It is this phase noise that contributes primarily to carrier phase instability. Figure 8.1 shows how phase noise $\psi(t)$ alters the phase angle variation of an ideal oscillator with a fixed frequency ω_c. Any system attempting to establish phase coherency with this carrier must track these instantaneous phase noise variations in order to remain phase coherent.

Oscillators generated from atomic resonances (cesium, rubidium, hydrogen) and solid-state cavities (quartz crystals) are the more stable frequency sources, but are basically untunable, producing harmonic outputs only at specific frequencies. Because of their stability, these oscillators are often used as **frequency standards**, or **reference frequencies**, for generating all other frequencies in a transmitter or receiver. Their fixed-frequency outputs are converted to the desired RF or microwave carriers used in the communication link.

Tunable oscillators are generally constructed from electronic tuned circuits, whose resonant frequency can be easily shifted. Such oscillators are significantly less stable than the reference oscillators, due to the tuning

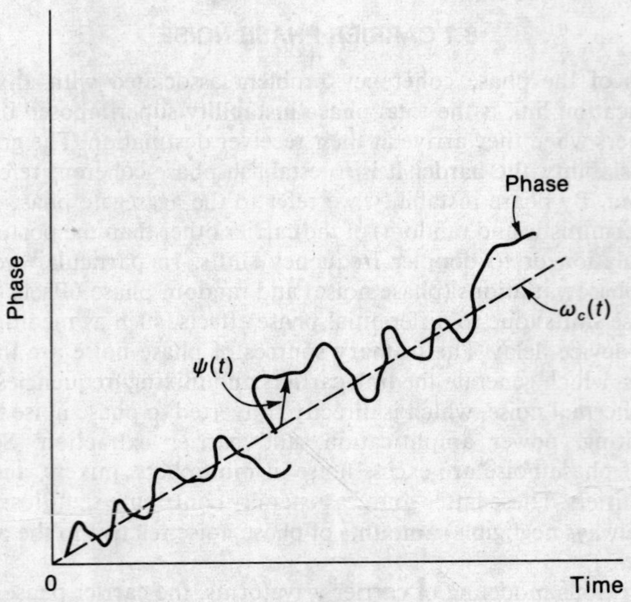

Figure 8.1. Phase variation on oscillators (ω_c = carrier frequency; $\psi(t)$ = phase instability).

circuit thermal noise that is converted internally to phase noise. Tunable oscillators are used primarily as **voltage controlled oscillators (VCO),** where instantaneous control of output frequency and phase is required.

Phase-Noise Spectra

Oscillator phase noise, being a random process, is generally described by its spectral density. Some oscillator phase-noise spectra are shown in Figure 8.2. Here a 5 MHz cesium reference oscillator spectrum [1], a quartz crystal oscillator spectrum, and a typical voltage-controlled oscillator (VCO) spectrum are illustrated. Cesium and quartz references are commonly used as earth-station transmitter oscillators in satellite systems. Hence, understanding their phase noise contribution is mandatory. A VCO is used in tracking and carrier referencing loops, and is inherently more noisy. As is typical of most oscillators [2], low-frequency phase noise (below about 1–10 Hz) tends to dominate, due to the inverse frequency flicker effect, with a fairly rapid spectral rise occurring at the extremely low frequencies. For this reason it is especially important to keep track of this low-

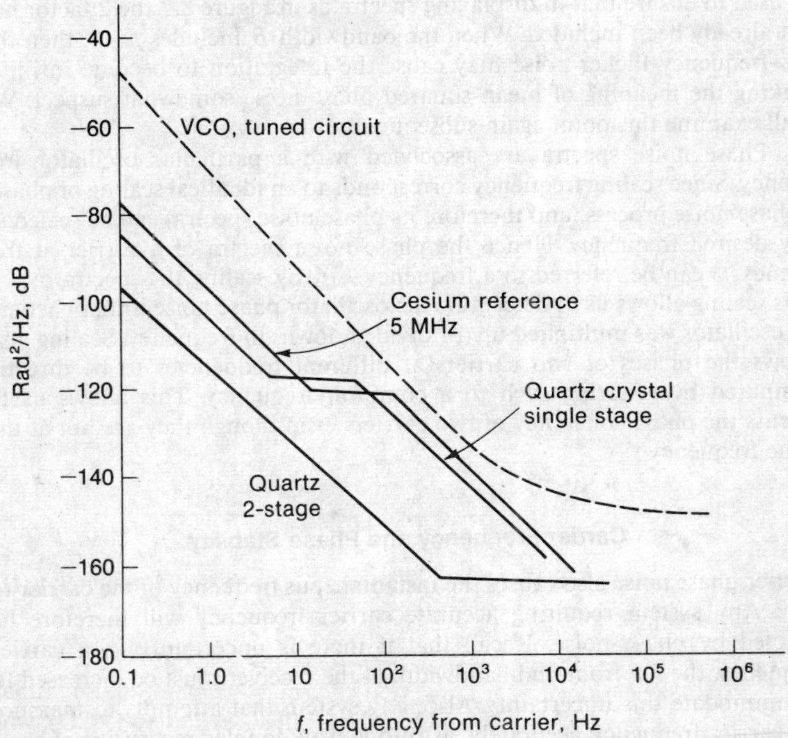

Figure 8.2. Oscillator phase-noise spectra. Frequency *f* measured from oscillator carrier frequency. All oscillators at 5 MHz.

frequency phase noise throughout the system. At the higher frequencies, the usual spectral flattening and roll-off occurs, governed by the noise characteristics of the oscillator tuning cavity. This roll-off can be enhanced by the use of narrow bandpass-tuned crystal filters immediately following the oscillators. By this technique, most oscillator phase noise above about 10 KHz is generally rendered negligible. Figure 8-2 shows a one-sided spectrum in rad^2 per Hz, plotted in terms of frequency f from the oscillator center frequency.

The ordinate in Figure 8.2 may sometimes be labeled instead in terms of power levels relative to the carrier power, or it may be plotted in decibels below carrier power. To determine mean squared phase noise in a bandwidth B, the phase noise spectrum in rad^2/Hz must be integrated over B, and multiplied by 2 to account for the two-sided bandwidth. Care must be used to ensure that in displaying spectra as in Figure 8.2 the 2 factor has not already been included. When the bandwidth B includes $f = 0$, then the low-frequency flicker noise may cause the integration to become infinite, making the meaning of mean squared phase noise somewhat suspect. We shall examine this point again subsequently.

Phase noise spectra are associated with a particular oscillator frequency. Since scaling frequency corresponds to an identical scaling of phase, a phase noise process (and therefore its phase noise spectra) can be scaled to any desired frequency. Hence the phase noise spectra of a carrier at frequency f_0 can be referred to a frequency $k_1 f_0$ by scaling the spectra by k_1^2. This scaling allows us to determine the oscillator phase noise if that particular oscillator was multiplied up (or divided down) in frequency. Scaling also allows the phases of two carriers at different frequencies to be directly compared by referring each to a common frequency. This allows us to discuss the phase coherency of two carriers even though they are not at the same frequency.

Carrier Frequency and Phase Stability

Carrier phase noise also causes the instantaneous frequency of the carrier to vary. Any system requiring accurate carrier frequency will therefore be affected by phase noise. Recall that if there is uncertainty in a carrier frequency, the RF front-end bandwidth at the receiver must be increased to accommodate this uncertainty. Also, any system that attempts to measure the carrier frequency accurately, as in one-way doppler measuring subsystems, must be concerned with frequency errors due to phase noise. If the carrier is written as $\cos[\theta(t)]$, then the carrier frequency is formally defined as

$$f(t) = \frac{\theta(t+T) - \theta(t)}{2\pi T} \text{Hz} \tag{8.1.1}$$

where T is the frequency measuring time. For an ideal oscillator, $\theta(t) = 2\pi f_c t + \psi$, and (8.1.1) always produce

$$\begin{aligned} f(t) &= \frac{[2\pi f_c(t+T) + \psi] - [2\pi f_c t + \psi]}{2\pi T} \\ &= f_c \end{aligned} \tag{8.1.2}$$

for any T. That is, the change in phase is constant for any T, and the oscillator has a single fixed frequency for all t. When phase noise $\psi(t)$ is present, the frequency instead becomes

$$f(t) = f_c + \left[\frac{\psi(t+T) - \psi(t)}{2\pi T}\right] \tag{8.1.3}$$

The bracketed term represents a random variation from the ideal frequency f_c that statistically depends on measuring time T. An important parameter is the rms frequency error from f_c for a given T, denoted

$$\sigma(T) = \frac{[D_\psi(T)]^{1/2}}{2\pi T} \tag{8.1.4}$$

where

$$D_\psi(T) = E[\psi(t+T) - \psi(t)]^2 \tag{8.1.5}$$

Here $D_\psi(T)$ is the mean squared phase noise difference over an interval T, and is often called the **accumulated phase noise** over T, or sometimes simply the **structure function** [3] of the phase noise. Thus, the rms frequency offset in (8.1.4) is directly related to the accumulated phase noise, and is said to be an indication of the **frequency stability** of the oscillator. The latter is formally defined as the parameter

$$\frac{\sigma(T)}{f_c} \triangleq \frac{[D_\psi(T)]^{1/2}}{2\pi f_c T} \tag{8.1.6}$$

and is simply the ratio of the rms frequency offset to the oscillator design frequency f_c. For example, an oscillator with a frequency stability of 10^{-6} (often stated as being stable to within one part in a million) can be expected to have an instantaneous frequency within $\pm\, 10^{-6} f_c$ Hz around f_c. For a 1-MHz oscillator this means its frequency will generally be no more than 1 Hz away. However, it should be emphasized that frequency stability is actually dependent on measuring time T.

The frequency stability of an oscillator can be obtained directly from its phase noise spectrum $S_\psi(\omega)$. Noting that the transform of $\psi(t+T) - \psi(t)$ is given by $\Psi(\omega)\,[e^{j\omega T} - 1]$, the mean squared value in (8.1.5) can equivalently be written as

$$D_\psi(T) = \frac{1}{2\pi}\int_{-\infty}^{\infty} S_\psi(\omega)\,|\,e^{j\omega T} - 1\,|^2 d\omega \tag{8 1.7}$$

Since $|\,e^{j\omega T} - 1\,|^2 = 4\sin^2(\omega T/2)$, this is

$$D_\psi(T) = \frac{4}{\pi}\int_0^{\infty} S_\psi(\omega)\sin^2\left(\frac{\omega T}{2}\right) d\omega \tag{8.1.8}$$

The frequency stability in (8.1.6) is then

$$\frac{\sigma(T)}{f_c} = \frac{1}{\pi f_c T}\left[\frac{1}{\pi}\int_0^\infty S_\psi(\omega)\sin^2\left(\frac{\omega T}{2}\right)d\omega\right]^{1/2} \tag{8.1.9}$$

Hence the frequency stability of an oscillator can be obtained by integrating its phase noise spectra as in the preceding. In general, the longer the T, the more stable the oscillator due to the division by T in (8.1.9). That is, the longer the time interval over which frequency is measured, the closer the measured frequency will be to the true frequency. In doppler measuring systems, however, T is usually dictated by the required doppler updating time, which may be confined to specific intervals. Figure 8.3 plots oscillator frequency stability as a function of T for some common reference oscillators. Note that as $\omega \to 0$ the integrand in (8.1.9) behaves as does $\omega^2 S_\psi(\omega)$ due to the $\sin^2$ term. This offsets the $1/\omega^n$ flicker effect of the phase noise

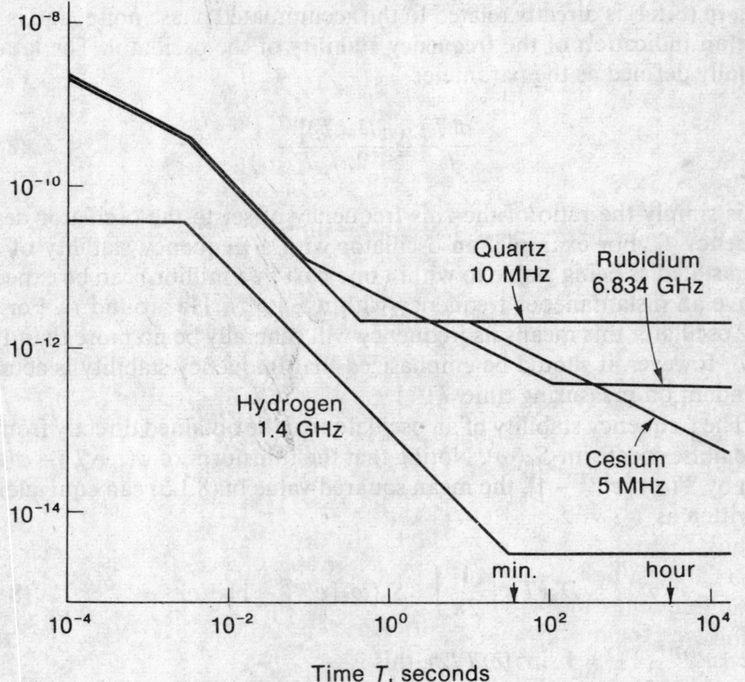

Figure 8.3. Frequency stability vs. frequency measurement time for common frequency sources.

spectrum and will make the integral converge (as long as the low-frequency spectrum increases more slowly than $1/\omega^3$). Thus frequency stability of an oscillator may exist even though the integral of the phase noise spectra may not.

A stability parameter closely related to the frequency stability is the **frequency differential** stability of a carrier. This is a measure of how much the frequency changes over a specific time period. Formally the frequency differential over a time period τ is defined as

$$\Delta f(\tau) = f(t+\tau) - f(t) \tag{8.1.10}$$

where $f(t)$ is given in (8.1.3) and corresponds to a frequency measurement over a prescribed T-sec interval. Frequency differential is important in two-way doppler measurement systems, in which a carrier is transmitted to a moving transponder and returned to the transmitter. A measurement of the frequency difference between the transmitted and returned carrier frequency then indicates the doppler offset caused by the transponder. Any inherent frequency differential error in the oscillator itself produces an error in this measurement. The rms frequency differential stability of a carrier is therefore defined as*

$$\frac{\sigma_{\Delta f}(\tau)}{f_c} = \frac{[D_{\Delta f}(\tau)]^{1/2}}{f_c} \tag{8.1.11}$$

where $D_{\Delta f}(\tau)$ is now the mean squared value of $\Delta f(\tau)$ in (8.1.10). This also can be obtained directly from the phase noise spectra of the returned carrier. Since

$$\Delta f(\tau) = \frac{\psi(t+\tau+T) - \psi(t+\tau)}{T} - \frac{\psi(t+T) - \psi(t)}{T} \tag{8.1.12}$$

its mean squared value follows as

$$D_{\Delta f}(\tau) = \frac{2}{\pi T}\int_0^\infty S_\psi(\omega)\sin^2\left(\frac{\omega\tau}{2}\right)\sin^2\left(\frac{\omega T}{2}\right)d\omega \tag{8.1.13}$$

Thus, frequency differential stability is also obtained by direct integration of the carrier phase noise spectrum. Note that the result depends on both T (the frequency measurement time) and τ (the frequency differential time). However, the mean squared differential error now increases with τ, and the

*The nomenclature used here is not standard, and often leads to confusion in the literature. In some places (8.1.6) is called a *phase stability* parameter while (8.1.11) refers to *frequency stability*. In other references, frequency stability refers directly to (8.1.6).

rms frequency differential error is larger as the frequency measurements are made further apart. In the two-way doppler system, τ will correspond to the round-trip transit time of the transponded carrier.

8.2 FREQUENCY GENERATORS, MULTIPLIERS AND SYNTHESIZERS

The RF and microwave carriers used in the transmitters, satellites, and receivers, are obtained from frequency generators. In these devices, oscillators from reference frequency sources are converted to the desired carrier frequencies through some type of frequency conversion mechanism. The most common conversion methods are described here.

Digital Frequency Generators

A **digital frequency generator (DFG)** is obtained by storing in memory a sequence of numerical values of one period of a sine wave. These numbers are then continually read out in sequence at a prescribed clock rate driven by the reference frequency. This produces the discrete values of a repetitive sine wave, which are then converted to an analog waveform, forming the output carrier, as shown in Figure 8.4a. By altering the read-out clock rate, and reading out only selected sine wave values, the output frequency can be controlled over a desired range (see Problem 8.3). The maximum frequency

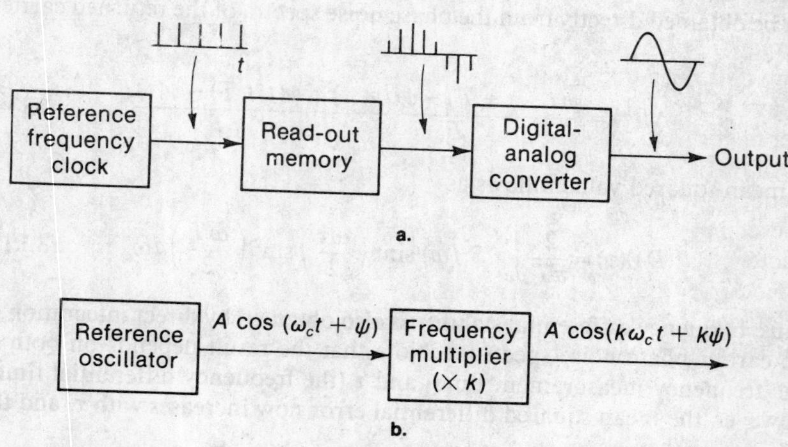

Figure 8.4. Frequency multiplication. (a) Digital frequency generator. (b) Nonlinear multiplying device.

of a DFG is limited by the digital bit rate that can be processed, and by the storage capacity of the digital memory. Any phase noise on the reference source is directly converted to the analog output carrier.

Frequency Multipliers

A **frequency multiplier** simply multiplies up the carrier reference frequency by a fixed frequency multiplication factor, as shown in Figure 8.4b. However, the phase noise of the reference is likewise multiplied up as well. Frequency multiplication is obtained by nonlinear harmonic generation, and is generally restricted to relatively low (2 or 3) multiplication factors, due to the distortion and inherent low amplitudes of higher harmonics. Higher factors, of course, can be obtained by cascading several low factor multipliers.

Frequency Synthesizers

Digital frequency generators and multipliers are limited in both the output frequency range and the maximum output frequency that they can produce from a fixed reference source. These limitations can be partly overcome by **frequency synthesizers** (Figure 8.5a). In such devices, an RF VCO is frequency divided to phase lock to the frequency standard via a tracking loop. This produces an RF carrier phase locked to the multiplied reference, achieving the desired frequency conversion with the frequency stability of the reference. Such a system requires only a frequency divider, which is significantly easier to implement than high-factor frequency multipliers.

Frequency division is obtained by a digital counter that counts down the zero crossings of its input frequency and emits a synchronous sine wave having zero crossings at some submultiple of the input crossings. If the divider factor is k_1, then an output zero crossing is produced once every k_1 cycles of the input frequency, producing a synchronized output sine wave at frequency $1/k_1$ of the input. Divider factors from two to several thousand can be achieved in this way, provided the counting circuit can operate satisfactorily at the frequency of the input. The synthesizer loop in Figure 8.5a then forces the divided frequency to phase lock to the reference. If the reference frequency is f_r, then the synthesizer will phase lock at a VCO output frequency f_o satisfying

$$f_o = k_1 f_r \tag{8.2.1}$$

Hence, setting the divider factor controls the VCO output frequency. Since divide-counters are easily and quickly readjusted, synthesizer output frequencies can be commanded over a fairly wide frequency range.

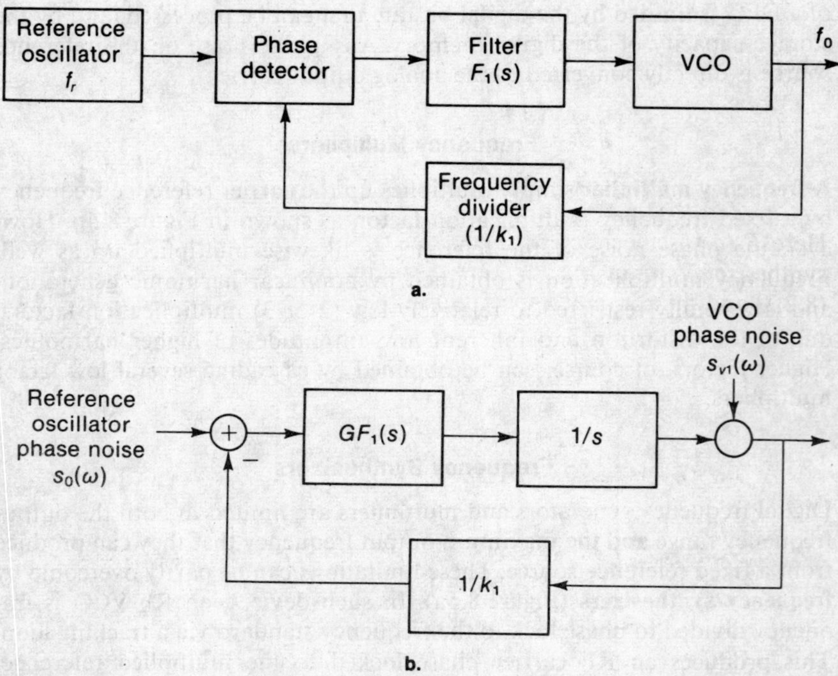

Figure 8.5. Frequency synthesizer. (a) Block diagram. (b) Equivalent phase noise diagram.

The phase noise of a synthesizer output carrier is generated in a different manner than for a direct frequency multiplier. In addition to the reference phase noise, the phase noise of the synthesized VCO is superimposed on that of the filtered multiplied reference. This can be seen by tracing the phase throughout the synthesizer loop, using the linear phase lock model developed in Section B.1 of Appendix B. The synthesizer phase model is shown in Figure 8.5b, and shows how the phase noises of the reference oscillator and VCO contribute to the resulting RF carrier phase at the synthesizer output. The synthesizer loop is described by its closed-loop gain function

$$H_1(s) = \frac{GF_1(s)/k_1 s}{1 + GF_1(s)/k_1 s} \tag{8.2.2}$$

where $F_1(s)$ is the synthesizer loop filter and k_1 is the frequency divider factor. Note that this factor, along with the total loop component gain G, define the closed-loop gain G/k_1. Straightforward analysis in Figure 8.5b shows that the output RF carrier phase noise spectra is given by

$$S_\psi(\omega) = S_r(\omega) + S_1(\omega) \tag{8.2.3}$$

where

$$S_r(\omega) = k_1^2 S_0(\omega) |H_1(\omega)|^2 \tag{8.2.4a}$$

$$S_1(\omega) = S_{v1}(\omega) |1 - H_1(\omega)|^2 \tag{8.2.4b}$$

Here $S_0(\omega)$ is the reference spectrum and $S_{v1}(\omega)$ is the spectrum of the synthesizer VCO at the RF carrier frequency. The component spectra in (8.2.3) and the combined spectrum in (8.2.2) are sketched in Figure 8.6 for

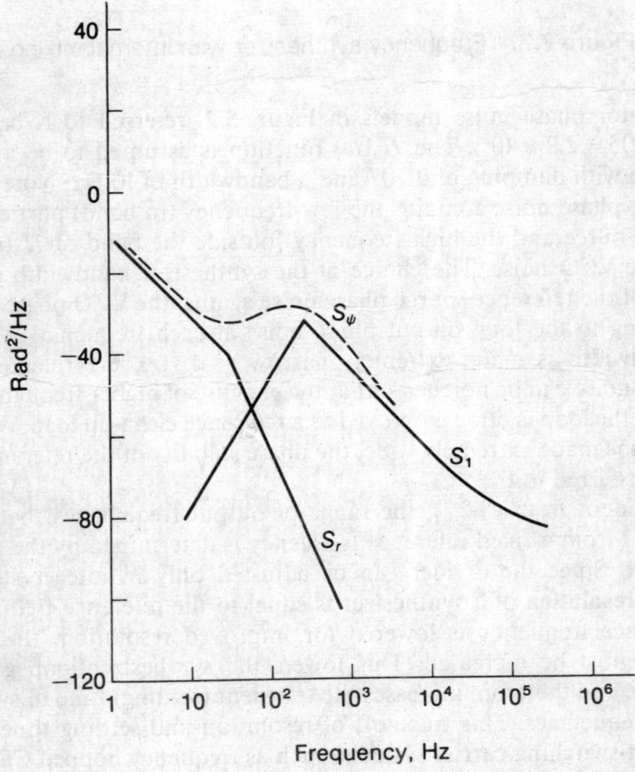

Figure 8.6. Combined frequency synthesizer output phase noise spectra $S_\psi(\omega)$: $S_1(\omega)$ due to VCO: $S_r(\omega)$ due to reference oscillator.

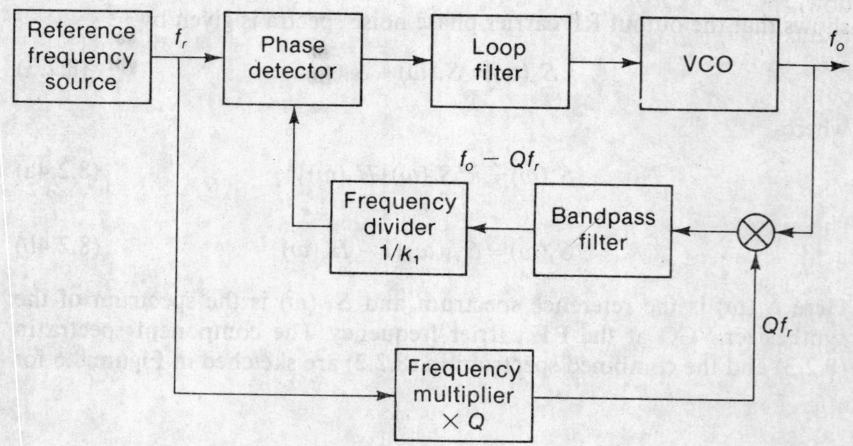

Figure 8.7. Frequency synthesizer with internal mixing

the oscillator phase noise models in Figure 8.2, referred to K-band (i.e., $k_1 = 14/.005 = 2.2 \times 10^3$). The $H_1(\omega)$ function is assumed to be a second-order loop with damping of 0.707 and a bandwidth of 10 Hz. Note that the RF carrier phase noise contains the low-frequency (in band) portion of the reference source and the high-frequency [outside the band of $H_1(\omega)$] portion of the VCO noise. The choice of the synthesizer bandwidth allows a trade-off of the reference source phase noise against the VCO phase noise in contributing to the total output phase noise at each frequency. When the loop bandwidth is made extremely narrow ($\leqslant 1$ Hz), the reference low-frequency noise can be notched out at the expense of higher frequency VCO noise, and the loop is often employed as a reference **clean-up loop**. When the bandwidth is made extremely wide, the phase stability of the reference is, in effect, transferred to the VCO.

As evident from (8.2.1), the range of output frequencies that can be synthesized from a fixed reference frequency is determined by the range of the divider. Since the divider can be adjusted only in integer steps, the **frequency resolution** of a synthesizer is equal to the reference frequency. If the reference frequency is lowered for improved resolution, the divider factor k_1 must be increased. This lowers the synthesizer loop gain and bandwidth, and therefore increases the transient (settling) time in switching between frequencies. This trade-off of resolution and settling time can be vital in fast-switching carrier systems, such as frequency hopped CDMA.

If the required output frequency is exceptionally high (say K-band or above), the divide-counter may not be operable at the VCO frequency. This problem can be avoided by inserting a bandpass mixer in the loop to mix down the VCO output prior to dividing, as shown in Figure 8.7. This also reduces the required divider factor, if the reference frequency multiplication used to perform the mixing is high enough. Referring to Figure 8.7, the output frequency f_o is now related to the reference frequency by $f_r = (f_o - Qf_r)/k_1$, or,

$$f_o = (k_1 + Q)f_r \tag{8.2.5}$$

The multiplication factor Q used for mixing therefore adds to the division factor k_1 in converting f_r to f_o. Note that if Q is made a fraction (divider), (8.2.5) shows that the frequency resolution of the synthesizer is improved (can be adjusted to $1/Q$ of the reference frequency), but the role of the mixer bandpass filter is now more critical. It must separate out the sum and difference mixing frequencies that are now fairly close together. Only the difference frequency is used for the divided reference. Further discussion of synthesizer circuitry can be found in References 3–6.

If more than one RF carrier is to be formed, all can be generated from the same reference with separate synthesizers (Figure 8.8). Note that while the reference phase noise would be common to all carriers, each synthesizer VCO would produce an independent noise contribution to each carrier formed. For this reason, the phase noise having spectrum $S_r(\omega)$ in (8.2.3a) is often referred to as forward **coherent** phase noise, while each VCO contribution is called **noncoherent** phase noise. The latter follows since it is statisti-

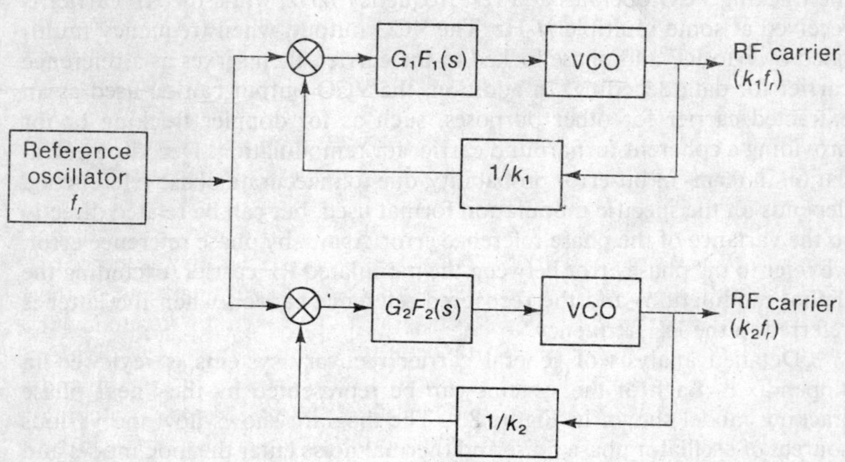

Figure 8.8. Multiple-carrier frequency generation from a common reference oscillator.

cally noncoherent with the VCO noise in all other forward carriers generated from separate synthesizers. By controlling the bandwidth of the synthesizer function $H_1(\omega)$, the frequency range over which the satellite uplink carriers are phase-coherent and noncoherent can be adjusted. We emphasize that a measurement of the synthesizer output carrier phase noise will yield only the combined spectra, and the degree of coherency involved in suppressed. As we will see, it may be necessary to place separate specifications on both the coherent and noncoherent contributors to the carrier phase in order to satisfy phase stability requirements at various points in the satellite link.

8.3 PHASE ERRORS IN CARRIER REFERENCING

Carrier referencing is achieved by phase-tracking systems that force a local receiver VCO to track the phase of the input carrier. The form of the tracking subsystem depends on the manner in which the carrier has been modulated. (Recall that the referencing system must track the phase of the carrier but not the phase modulation.) If no modulation is present (pure carrier is received), phase referencing can be achieved by a standard phase lock loop. With BPSK carriers, a carrier reference is extracted with either a Costas or squaring loop (Section B.2). For QPSK, carrier recovery is achieved by a modified form of Costas crossover loop, or by a fourth-power loop (Section B.3). In all these carrier recovery subsystems, a tracking loop is used to force a VCO to phase track the incoming RF carrier. Generally, the tracking VCO operates at a rest frequency f_0Hz, while the RF carrier is received at some multiple rf_0Hz. The VCO output, when frequency multiplied by r to RF and phase locked to the carrier, then serves as a reference carrier for data decoding. In addition, the VCO output can be used as an extracted carrier for other purposes, such as for doppler tracking or for providing a coherent turnaround carrier for remodulation. Decoding degradation in terms of bit-error probability, due to inaccurate phase referencing, depends on the specific modulation format used, but can be related directly to the variance of the phase reference error. Again, by phase reference error, we refer to the phase error between the modulated RF carrier (excluding the digital modulation) and the recovered reference carrier, when the latter is referred to the RF frequency.

Detailed analysis of general carrier recovery systems is reviewed in Appendix B. Each of the systems can be represented by the linear phase tracking model shown in Figure 8.9. The diagram shows how the various sources of oscillator phase noise and thermal noise enter the loop model and contribute to the total phase. The only difference in the model for various referencing systems is the effective amplitude and the spectral level of the noise entering the loop. The table in Figure 8.9 lists these values for

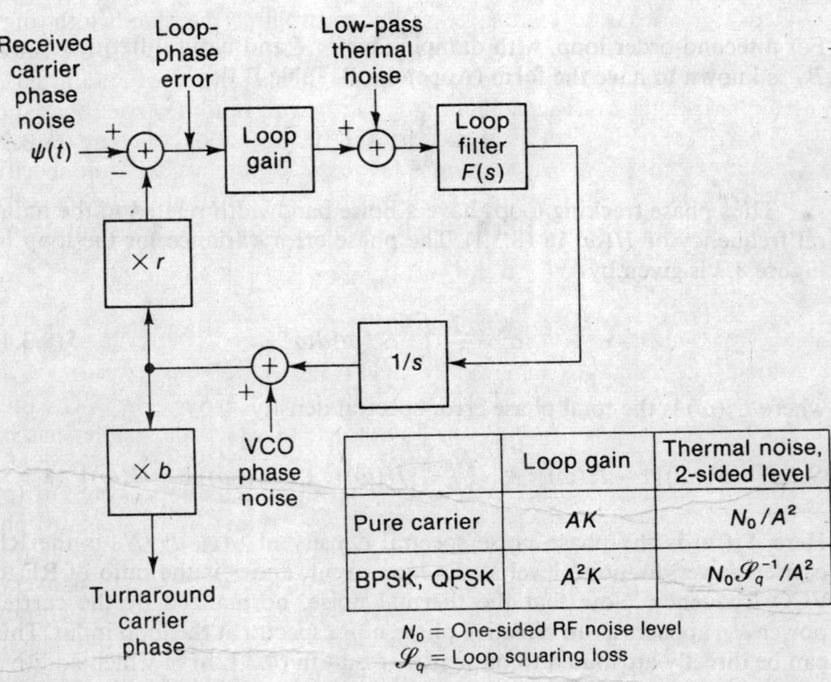

	Loop gain	Thermal noise, 2-sided level
Pure carrier	AK	N_0/A^2
BPSK, QPSK	A^2K	$N_0\mathcal{S}_q^{-1}/A^2$

N_0 = One-sided RF noise level
$\mathcal{S}_q$ = Loop squaring loss

Figure 8.9. Phase noise model of receiver carrier recovery subsystem.

the systems previously described. Assume the modulated RF carrier arrives with a detuned (offset) frequency of Ω Hz relative to rf_0, and contains phase noise $\psi(t)$. It is phase tracked in a carrier recovery subsystem in the presence of thermal noise of effective one-sided level N_0 W/Hz. The loop VCO will be driven to a steady-state frequency of $f_0 + (\Omega/r)$ Hz, and will have a phase noise variation produced by the equivalent loop in Figure 8.9. In this equivalent loop, the RF carrier phase noise $\psi(t)$, the thermal noise with appropriate spectral level, and the inherent phase noise of the VCO appear as input processes. The loop has the closed loop gain function

$$H(\omega) = \frac{KF(\omega)/j\omega}{1 + KF(\omega)/j\omega} \tag{8.3.1}$$

where $F(\omega)$ is the loop filter and K is the total closed loop gain. The loop has a closed loop noise bandwidth defined by

$$B_L = \frac{1}{2\pi}\int_0^\infty |H(\omega)|^2 d\omega \tag{8.3.2}$$

For a second-order loop, with damping factor ξ and natural frequency ω_n, B_L is known to have the form (Appendix B, Table B.1):

$$B_L = \frac{\omega_n}{8\xi}(1 + 4\xi^2) \tag{8.3.3}$$

Thus phase tracking loops have a noise bandwidth related to the natural frequency of $H(\omega)$ in (8.3.1). The phase error variance for the loop in Figure 8.7 is given by

$$\sigma_e^2 = \frac{2}{2\pi}\int_0^\infty S_e(\omega)d\omega \tag{8.3.4}$$

where $S_e(\omega)$ is the total phase error spectral density

$$S_e(\omega) = S_\psi(\omega)|1 - H(\omega)|^2 + \left(\frac{N_0}{2P_c}\right)|H(\omega)|^2 + r^2 S_v(\omega)|1 - H(\omega)|^2 \tag{8.3.5}$$

Here $S_\psi(\omega)$ is the phase noise spectral density of $\psi(t)$, P_c/N_0 is the RF carrier power–to–noise level at the loop input, and r is the ratio of RF to VCO frequency. Note that the thermal noise, normalized by the carrier power P_c, appears as an effective phase noise spectra at the loop input. This can be directly attributed to our earlier result in (4.2.12b) in which additive thermal noise is coupled into the carrier as carrier phase noise with the same spectra. For a pure-carrier tracking loop, P_c is the power in the carrier spectral line. For modulated carriers, P_c is the total power in the carrier. The spectrum $S_v(\omega)$ is the phase noise spectrum of the loop VCO at its rest frequency f_0. Correspondingly, the phase noise spectra on the extracted carrier, obtained by frequency multiplying the VCO by b to the desired extraction frequency, is

$$S_x(\omega) = \left(\frac{b}{r}\right)^2\left[S_\psi(\omega) + \frac{N_0}{2P_c}\right]|H(\omega)|^2 + b^2 S_v(\omega)|1 - H(\omega)|^2 \tag{8.3.6}$$

where

$$\frac{b}{r} = \frac{\text{Extracted carrier frequency}}{\text{RF input frequency}} \tag{8.3.7}$$

Note that only carrier phase noise outside the loop bandwidth, and thermal noise inside the loop bandwidth contribute to the reference error variance, while both phase and thermal noise inside the loop bandwidth, are translated to the extracted carrier. In particular, since $H(0) = 1$, dc phase shifts (either random or deterministic phase offsets) included in $\psi(t)$ never affect phase error but do get directly superimposed onto the extracted carrier. Since the VCO frequency is offset from f_0 by Ω/r, the extracted carrier will be offset from frequency bf_0 by $\Omega(b/r)$. The parameter b/r in (8.3.7) is often called the **turnaround ratio** of the recovery loop. Note that the VCO phase noise is always high pass filtered in contributing to either phase error or extracted carrier phase.

Figure 8.10 sketches the spectrum $S_v(\omega)|1-H(\omega)|^2$ for a VCO with spectrum $S_v(\omega)$ as in Figure 8.2, when a second-order loop is used with a B_L of 400 Hz and a damping of 0.707. Note that the effective high pass filtering of the loop greatly reduces the low-frequency VCO phase noise. The loop frequency multiplication factor r acts to multiply up the VCO noise, but divides down the in-band RF phase noise in carrier extraction. These factors are pointed out, since it is the interplay of these specific parameters that will often dictate potential phase-coherency problems in phase locked satellite systems. Equations (8.3.5) and (8.3.6) demonstrate an inherent

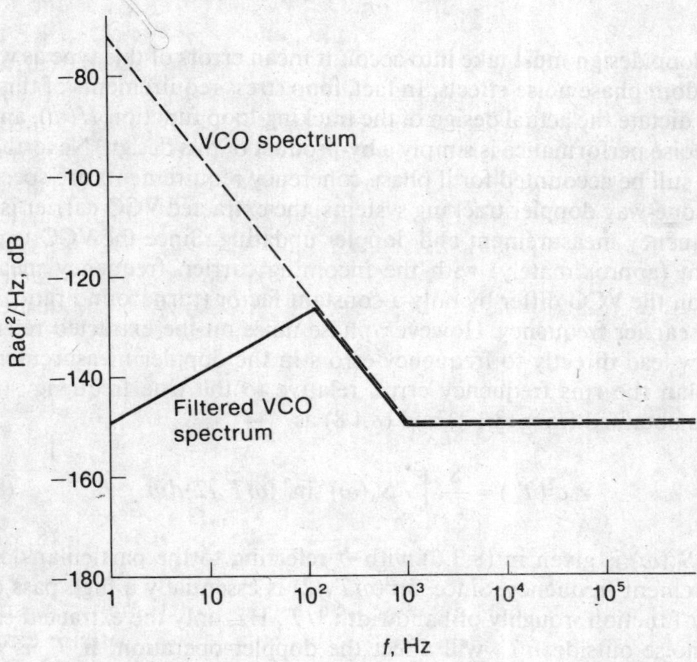

Figure 8.10. Filtered VCO phase noise spectra. Second-order loop, B_L = 400 Hz, loop damping = 0.707.

aspect of the phase coherency problem, which is that a different portion of the carrier spectra $S_\psi(\omega)$ affects the phase referencing operation from that which affects operations performed on extracted carriers (such as doppler tracking). To satisfy decoding specifications, $H(\omega)$ should be wide enough to reduce the excessive low-frequency oscillator noise in $\psi(t)$, but, on the other hand, this then increases the phase noise in the extracted carrier.

In addition to phase noise effects, tracking loops may also develop phase errors due to tracking of the carrier frequency dynamics (doppler rates, frequency changes, pull-in and sweep variations, etc.). These effects tend to produce a mean phase error (sometimes called *loop stress*) that depends on the specific loop parameters. The most serious of these is the mean phase error caused by a loop attempting to track a linear frequency change in the received carrier (e.g., due to a doppler rate). If the frequency rate of change is $\dot{f}$ Hz/sec, the mean tracking phase error of a second-order loop with natural frequency ω_n is [3, chapter 4]

$$m_e = \frac{\dot{f}}{\omega_n^2} \text{ radians} \tag{8.3.8}$$

Hence loop design must take into account mean errors of this type as well as the random phase noise effects. In fact, loop stress requirements of this type usually dictate the actual design of the tracking-loop function $H(\omega)$, and the phase noise performance is simply a by-product of this design. Nevertheless, it must still be accounted for if phase coherency requirements are specified.

In one-way doppler tracking systems, the extracted VCO carrier is used for frequency measurement and doppler updating. Since the VCO is phase coherent (approximately) with the incoming carrier, frequency measurements on the VCO differ by only a constant factor (turnaround ratio) from the RF carrier frequency. However, phase noise on the extracted reference will now lead directly to frequency errors in the doppler measurement. In particular, the rms frequency error, relative to the true frequency of the VCO, is obtained from (8.1.4) and (8.1.8) as

$$\sigma^2(T_s) = \frac{8}{T_s}\int_0^\infty S_x(\omega)\sin^2(\omega T_s/2)\,d\omega \tag{8.3.9}$$

where $S_x(\omega)$ is given in (8.3.6) with b referring to the particular doppler measurement frequency. Since $\sin^2(\omega T_s/2)$ is essentially a high pass comb transfer function, roughly of bandwidth $1/T_s$ Hz, only the extracted carrier phase noise outside $1/T_s$ will affect the doppler operation. If T_s is much greater than 1 sec, much of the low-frequency phase noise (below about 1 Hz) in $S_x(\omega)$ will be included. In general, then, doppler specifications are generally low-frequency phase noise specifications, while phase error performance translates to more of a high-frequency condition. For this reason it is extremely important to know the various phase noise contributors to $\psi(t)$, and their individual phase noise spectra. Hence phase coherency analysis reduces to accurate predictions of phase noise effects, which requires generation of fairly reliable source spectral data. This becomes particularly complicated in satellite systems, where a multitude of oscillators may be interconnected through various combinations of tracking loops and frequency conversions. In the following section we extend the results of this section to some of these satellite systems.

8.4 SATELLITE-LINK PHASE COHERENCY

The phase-coherency problem for a forward satellite-link (earth station through satellite to user or earth station) can be described by the simplified diagram in Figure 8.11. The diagram shows a single receiver and a relatively simple satellite conversion in order to illustrate the coherency problem. In FDMA and CDMA systems many parallel uplink carriers are being transmitted simultaneously, and the frequency conversions are much more complex, often involving elaborate programmable and commandable frequency mixing operations. Most of these complicated systems can often be reduced to some modified version of this diagram. In Figure 8.11 a frequency standard (e.g., cesium oscillator) acts as the earth-station reference source, generating a common reference frequency for all uplinks from that station. This frequency source is multiplied to RF, usually by a frequency synthesizer, as discussed in Section 8.2. The RF synthesized carriers are modulated according to the multiple-access format used and transmitted to the satellite, undergoing a forward transmission delay and additive uplink noise. At the satellite the uplink is frequency-mixed to the satellite forward (downlink) frequency and retransmitted to an earth station or user.

At the receiver the modulated carrier is processed according to the multiple-access format used. In TDMA downlinks, the carrier is time-gated, and passed to the data decoder. In FDMA the carriers are filtered in the proper bandpass filter prior to decoding. In CDMA, the carrier is despread or dehopped before decoding. In each case, the decoding that follows involves carrier referencing, from which the modulated carrier is coherently detected (this may not be used in frequency hopped CDMA systems). It is this receiver-carrier referencing that is now susceptible to all the sources of phase noise throughout the satellite link. Carrier references are obtained from carrier-tracking loops, as discussed in the previous section. Any frequency offset or phase noise on the RF carrier, after the multiple-access processing, will directly hinder the ability to establish the reference needed for coherent decoding or frequency measurements.

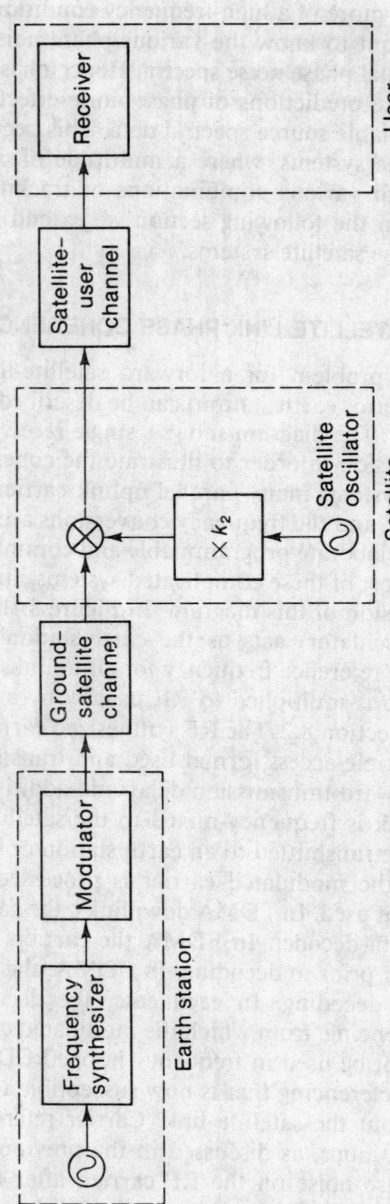

Figure 8.11. Simplified satellite oscillator model.

To analyze the satellite conversion effect we again impose the frequency-phase conversion models of Figure 4.13, noting that carrier phase processes add or subtract just as frequencies do in RF mixing (up-converting or down-converting). The phase noise model for the entire forward satellite link will take the form shown in Figure 8.12. The diagram shows the significant phase noise sources and the manner in which they contribute to the carrier phase $\psi(t)$ at the user receiver input. The exponentials account for the transmission delays τ_1 and τ_2 during propagation over the uplink and forward paths. By tracing the path from each source and applying linear filter analysis, this receiver input carrier phase noise spectrum is found to be

$$S_\psi(\omega) = k_1^2 S_{01}(\omega) |H_1(\omega)|^2 + S_{v1}(\omega) |1 - H_1(\omega)|^2 + \left(\frac{N_0}{P_c}\right)_u + k_2^2 S_{v2}(\omega) \tag{8.4.1}$$

Hence the S(ω) are the oscillator phase noise spectra, the $H_1(\omega)$ is the frequency synthesizer loop function in Figure 8.5b, and the k's are the frequency conversion factors. Subscripts 1 and 2 refer to the ground transmitter and satellite parameters, respectively. The ratio $(P_c/N_0)_u$ is the

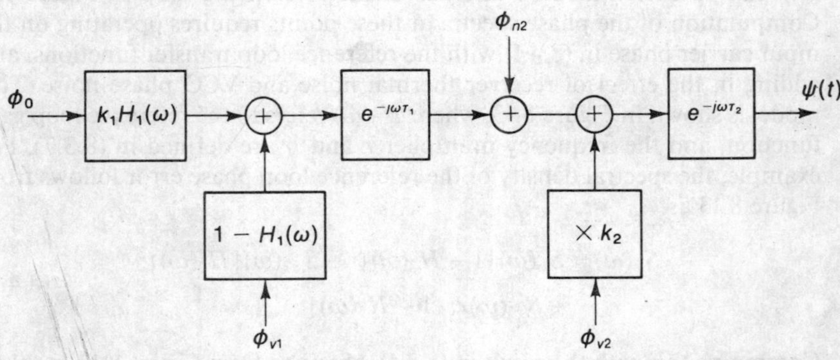

ϕ_0 = Reference oscillator phase noise
ϕ_{v1} = Earth-station synthesizer phase noise
$H_1(\omega)$ = Synthesizer loop function
τ_1, τ_2 = Uplink delay, downlink delay
ϕ_{n2} = Thermal noise at satellite
ϕ_{v2} = Satellite VCO phase noise

Figure 8.12. Equivalent phase noise diagram for satellite forward link in Figure 8.11 ($\psi(t)$ = total phase noise on carrier arriving at the user receiver).

uplink, carrier-to-noise level at the satellite input; $S_{v2}(\omega)$ is the satellite mixing oscillator phase noise spectrum; and

$$k_2 = \frac{\text{Satellite mixing frequency}}{\text{Satellite oscillator frequency}} \tag{8.4.2}$$

Thus the forward carrier phase noise at the receiver contains the transmitter reference source noise (multiplied to RF) and the satellite oscillator low-frequency phase noise, and the noncoherent high pass phase noise of the transmitter synthesizer. The satellite thermal noise effectively adds directly to the forward noncoherent phase noise and acts as a high-frequency noise "floor" out to the bandwidth of the carrier modulation. This phase noise bandwidth limitation is due to the bandpass filtering applied to the modulated carrier in the satellite and receiver RF front end. Although P_c/N_0 is generally fairly high for most earth stations, receiver thermal noise can nonetheless still become the dominant contributor to carrier phase noise at the upper ends of the carrier spectrum.

With the received carrier input phase noise defined, the phase error $e(t)$ of the receiver carrier referencing loop and any turnaround carrier phase $x(t)$ can be determined by analysis of the referencing loop in Figure 8.9. Computation of the phase spectra at these points requires operating on the input carrier phase in (8.4.1) with the reference loop transfer functions, and adding in the effect of receiver thermal noise and VCO phase noise. This model is shown in Figure 8.13, where $H_3(\omega)$ refers to the reference loop gain function, and the frequency multiplier r and b are defined in (8.3.7). For example, the spectral density of the reference loop phase error follows from Figure 8.13 as

$$\begin{aligned} S_e(\omega) &= S_\psi(\omega)|1 - H_3(\omega)|^2 + S_{n3}(\omega)|H_3(\omega)|^2 \\ &\quad + S_{v3}(\omega)r^2|1 - H_3(\omega)|^2 \end{aligned} \tag{8.4.3}$$

Combining this with the result in (8.4.1), obtained from Figure 8.12, we then have

$$\begin{aligned} S_e(\omega) &= k_1^2 S_0(\omega)|H(\omega)|^2|1 - H_3(\omega)|^2 + S_v(\omega)|1 - H_1(\omega)|^2|1 - H_3(\omega)|^2 \\ &\quad + \left[\left(\frac{N_0}{P_c}\right)_u + k_2^2 S_{v2}(\omega)\right]|1 - H_3(\omega)|^2 + \left(\frac{N_0}{P_c}\right)_d |H_3(\omega)|^2 \\ &\quad + r^2 S_{v3}(\omega)|1 - H_3(\omega)|^2 \end{aligned} \tag{8.4.4}$$

where the receiver phase noise $\phi_{n3}(t)$ is assumed to have the phase spectrum $(N_0/P_c)_d$. This corresponds to the total noise level–to–received carrier

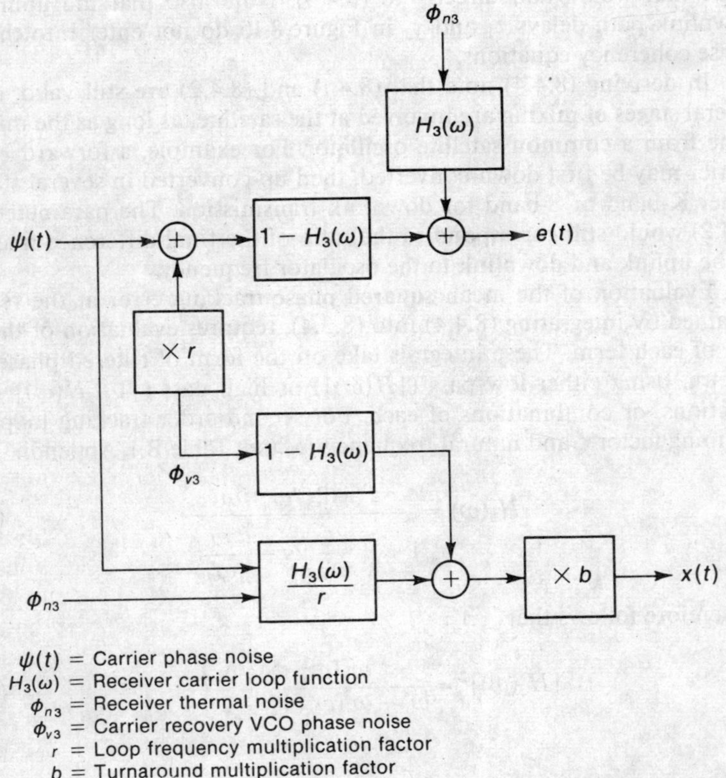

Figure 8.13. Phase-noise diagram for receiver carrier referencing loop.

power ratio of the forward (satellite-to-user) link. This latter contains the combined noise spectral level of the downlink receiver thermal noise, the intermodulation noise, and any crosstalk spectra (as in FDMA or CDMA) between carriers. It does not include, however, uplink noise, which acts to produce phase noise on the downlink carrier instead of thermal noise into the referencing loop. Note that all spectra are high pass filtered by the reference loop at the receiver, except for the receiver thermal noise. Receiver thermal noise may actually dictate the amount of phase reference error at the lower frequencies, while the satellite uplink noise may determine the high-frequency effects. The former may be of particular concern if satellite-receiver operating modes exist that involve low carrier power levels, which may prevent use of large referencing bandwidths.

We should point out that we have neglected multiplier and mixer excess noise that would add directly to (8.4.4). Note also that the uplink and downlink path delays τ_1 and τ_2 in Figure 8.10 do not enter into the final phase coherency equations.

In deriving (8.4.4) note that (8.4.1) and (8.4.2) are still valid, even if several stages of mixing are involved at the satellite, as long as the mixing is done from a common satellite oscillator. For example, a forward K-band carrier may be first down-converted, then up-converted in several stages to either K-band or S-band for downlink transmission. The parameter k_2 in (8.4.2) would still correspond to the ratio of the final difference frequency of the uplink and downlink to the oscillator frequency.

Evaluation of the mean squared phase tracking error at the receiver, obtained by integrating (8.4.4) into (8.3.4), requires evaluation of the integral of each term. These integrals take on the form of filtered phase noise spectra, using either low pass ($|H(\omega)|$) or high pass ($|1 - H(\omega)|^2$) filter functions, or combinations of each. For second-order tracking loops with damping factor ξ and natural frequency ω_n (see Table B.1, Appendix B),

$$H_3(\omega) = \frac{1 + (2\xi/\omega_n)j\omega}{1 + j\left(\dfrac{2\xi}{\omega_n}\right)\omega - \left(\dfrac{\omega}{\omega_n}\right)^2} \tag{8.4.5}$$

It therefore follows that

$$|H_3(\omega)|^2 = \frac{\omega_n^2[\omega_n^2 + 4\xi^2\omega^2]}{\omega^4 + \omega^2[\omega_n^2(4\xi^2 - 2)] + \omega_n^4} \tag{8.4.6}$$

and

$$|1 - H_3(\omega)|^2 = \frac{\omega^4}{\omega^4 + \omega^2[\omega_n^2(4\xi^2 - 2)] + \omega_n^4} \tag{8.4.7}$$

These functions, which may have different parameter values for the different loops, must be inserted into (8.4.4) and integrated to evaluate mean squared phase errors. In addition, an accurate model of each of the phase spectra $S(\omega)$ is required. It is common to model these spectra as

$$S(\omega) = \frac{S_3}{\omega^3} + \frac{S_2}{\omega^2} + \frac{S_1}{\omega} + S_0 \tag{8.4.8}$$

where the coefficients are selected for best fit to the true spectra. The first term represents the flicker noise; the second and third terms, the frequency noise conversion regions; and the last, the noise floor, which is assumed to exist out to some upper frequency ω_u. The contribution of each term in (8.4.8) to each integral in (8.4.4) can be separately evaluated and summed for each spectrum. These integrals, with the functions in (8.4.6), (8.4.7), and

Table 8.1. Tabulation of rms phase noise integrals.

k	$\frac{1}{2\pi}\int_{-\infty}^{\infty}\omega^{-k}\lvert 1-H(\omega)\rvert^2 d\omega$	$\frac{1}{2\pi}\int_{-\infty}^{\infty}\omega^{-k}\lvert H_1(\omega)\rvert^2\lvert 1-H_2(\omega)\rvert^2 d\omega$ $\left(\gamma = \frac{\omega_{n_1}}{\omega_{n_2}}\right)$	$\frac{1}{2\pi}\int_{-\infty}^{\infty}\omega^{-k}\lvert 1-H_1(\omega)\rvert^2\lvert 1-H_2(\omega)\rvert^2 d\omega$ $(\gamma = \omega_{n_1}/\omega_{n_2},\ \gamma_H = \omega_u/\omega_{n_2})$
3	$\frac{1}{4\omega_n^2}$	$\frac{\gamma^4}{4\omega_{n_1}^2(1-\gamma^4)}\left\{1-\gamma^2-\frac{2}{\pi}\ln\gamma^4\right\}$	$\frac{1}{\pi\omega_{n_1}^2}\left\{\frac{\gamma^4(1-\gamma^4)}{(1-\gamma^4)^2}-\frac{\gamma^2(1-\gamma^4)}{(1-\gamma^4)^2}\right\}$
2	$\frac{1}{2\sqrt{2}\omega_n}$	$\frac{\gamma^3(1-\gamma)(2+\gamma)}{2\sqrt{2}\omega_{n_1}(1-\gamma^4)}$	$\frac{1}{2\omega_{n_1}}\left\{\frac{\gamma^4}{1-\gamma^4}+2(1-\gamma^4)\right\}$
1	$\frac{1}{4\pi}\ln\left(1+\frac{\omega_u}{\omega_n}\right)$	$\frac{\gamma^2}{4(1-\gamma^4)}\left\{2(1-\gamma^2)-\frac{\gamma^2}{\pi}\ln\gamma^4\right\}$	$\frac{1}{4\pi}\left\{\left(\frac{\gamma^4}{1-\gamma^4}\right)\ln\left(\frac{1+(\gamma_H/\gamma)^4}{1+\gamma_H^4}\right)+\ln(1+\gamma_H^4)\right\}$
0	$\frac{\omega_n}{\pi}\left[\frac{\omega_u}{\omega_n}-\frac{1}{4\sqrt{2}}\ln\left(\frac{1+\left(\frac{\omega_u}{\omega_n}\right)+\left(\frac{\omega_u}{\omega_n}\right)^2}{1-\left(\frac{\omega_u}{\omega_n}\right)+\left(\frac{\omega_u}{\omega_n}\right)^2}\right)-\frac{1}{\sqrt{2}}\tan^{-1}\left(\frac{\omega_u}{\omega_n}\sqrt{2}\right)\right]$	$\frac{\gamma\omega_{n_1}}{2\sqrt{2}(1-\gamma^4)}[2+\gamma^2-3\gamma^3]$	$\frac{\omega_{n_1}}{\pi}\left\{\frac{\gamma_H}{\gamma}-\left(\frac{1-\gamma}{\sqrt{2}}\right)\ln\left(\frac{1+\gamma^2}{1-\gamma^2}\right)+2(1+\gamma)\tan^{-1}\left(\frac{2\gamma-\sqrt{2}}{2}\right)\right\}$

(8.4.8), require partial fraction expansion of the integrands in order to evaluate exactly.

When the tracking loops involved use a damping factor of $\xi = 0.707$ (critical damping), the integrals of the terms in (8.4.8) for the various filter combinations have been obtained in closed form. Using results published in References [7, 8], Table 8.1 summarizes these integrals. This allows rms phase error to be evaluated by merely inserting parameter values and summing.

8.5 PILOT-TONE FREQUENCY CORRECTIONS

Satellite oscillators are used to convert the uplink frequency to the proper downlink frequency. If the uplink frequency varies from its design value, due to possible frequency drifts of the transmitter carrier oscillators, the mixed downlink frequency may be offset from its desired value. In such cases, it is necessary to adjust the satellite oscillator to compensate for this uplink frequency drifting. One way to accomplish this is to transmit a pilot carrier (separate RF carrier obtained from the same source oscillator) to the satellite to adjust the mixing frequencies. Such a system is shown in Figure 8.14a. The pilot is transmitted up to the satellite in parallel with the modulated carrier. At the satellite the pilot carrier is separately phase tracked, and the extracted pilot is used to adjust the satellite mixing frequencies. Any drifts or variations in the transmitter frequencies appear on the pilot as well as on the modulated carriers. If the pilot frequency adjusts the satellite frequency, the mixed satellite downlink frequencies always occur at a fixed value. In effect, the pilot transfers uplink carrier frequency variations to the satellite.

The use of a pilot, however, alters the phase noise in the link, since it provides a secondary path from ground oscillator to the satellite. From a phase noise point of view, however, the phase noise diagram is altered to that shown in Figure 8.14b. The spectrum of the forward carrier phase noise $\psi(t)$ now becomes

$$\begin{aligned} S_\psi(\omega) = {} & S_r(\omega)\,|1 - r_2 H_2(\omega)|^2 + S_{1u}(\omega) + \left(\frac{N_0}{P_c}\right)_u \\ & + S_{v2}(\omega) k_2^2 |1 - H_2(\omega)|^2 \\ & + \left[\left(\frac{N_0}{P_c}\right)_p + S_{1p}(\omega)\right] |H_2(\omega)|^2 (k_2/q)^2 \end{aligned} \tag{8.5.1}$$

where $S_r(\omega)$ and $S_1(\omega)$ are spectra associated with the earth-station frequency synthesizer and are defined in (8.2.3). The thermal noise spectrum

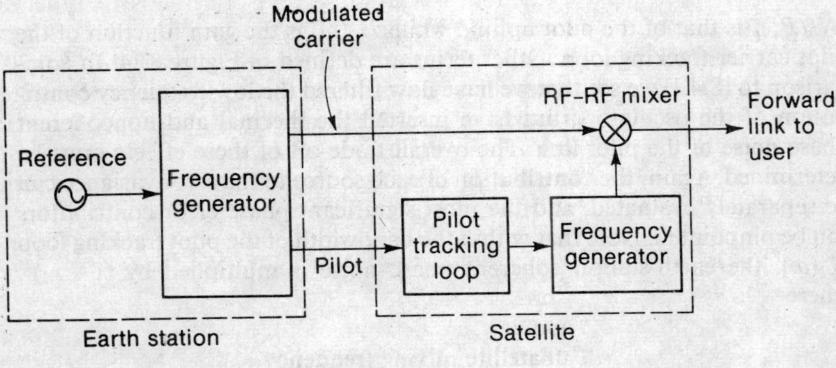

a.

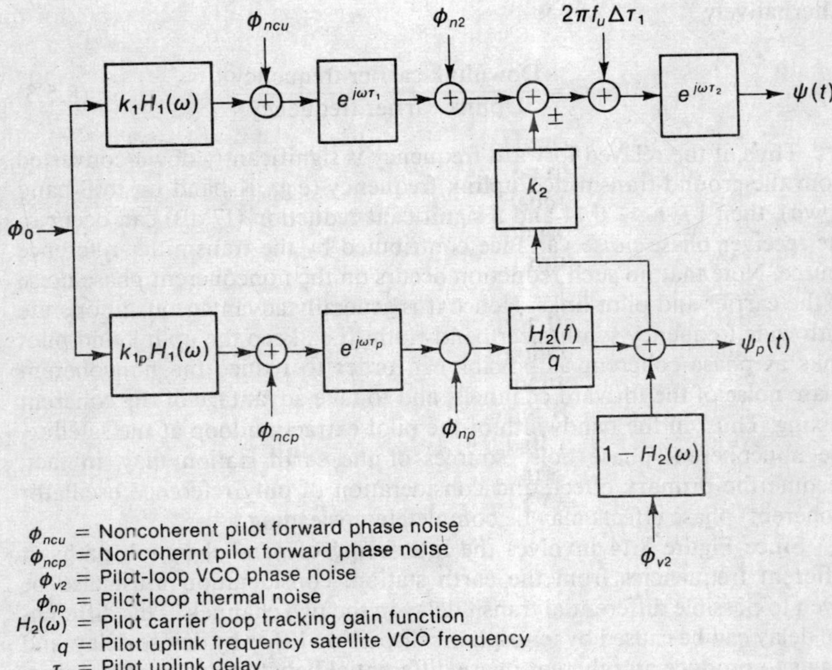

b.

Figure 8.14. Pilot-reference model. (a) Block diagram. (b) Phase-noise model.

$(N_0/P_c)_p$ is that of the pilot uplink, while $H_2(\omega)$ is the gain function of the pilot carrier tracking loop. Other terms are defined in Figure 8.14. In comparison to (8.4.1) we see that we have now filtered the low-frequency contribution of the oscillators, but have inserted the thermal and noncoherent phase noise of the pilot link. The overall trade-off of these effects must be determined. Again, the contribution of each source to the error variance can be separately evaluated, and the most significant phase error contributors can be pinpointed. Note that within the bandwidth of the pilot tracking loop $H_2(\omega)$, the earth-station coherent phase noise is multiplied by $(1 - r_2)^2$, where

$$r_2 = \frac{\text{Satellite mixing frequency}}{\text{Uplink carrier frequency}} \tag{8.5.2}$$

Alternatively,

$$1 - r_2 = \frac{\text{Downlink carrier frequency}}{\text{Uplink carrier frequency}} \tag{8.5.3}$$

Thus, if the relayed forward frequency is significantly down-converted from the ground-transmitted uplink frequency (e.g., K-band up to S-band down), then $1 - r_2 \approx 0.14$ and a significant reduction (17 dB) can occur in the receiver phase noise variance contributed by the transmitter reference source. Note that no such reduction occurs on the noncoherent phase noise of the carrier and pilot links. Hence it is generally advantageous to operate with wide frequency synthesizer bandwidths (i.e., keep the uplink and pilot links as phase coherent as possible) in order to reduce the noncoherent phase noise of the forward channels, and to take advantage of the coherent mixing. Thus, in the bandwidth of the pilot extraction loop at the satellite, the noncoherent phase noise sources of the earth station may, in fact, become the primary effect, and consideration of only reference oscillator (coherent) phase effects may be completely misleading.

Since Figure 8.14 involves the interfacing of parallel uplink paths at different frequencies from the earth station, consideration must also be given to possible differential transit delay in the two channels. This differential delay can be caused by ionospheric dispersion [9] or by device delay, and it acts to produce an inherent phase differential between two carriers transmitted over parallel links at approximately the same frequency. This phase differential, which is proportional to the differential delay $\Delta\tau_1$ and the forward carrier frequency f_u, is inserted as a constant phase shift of $2\pi f_u \Delta\tau_1$ radians on the satellite downlink carrier. Even though the differential delay may be extremely small (nanosec), the inserted phase offset may be significant when referred to K-band. Although a constant phase offset will not affect phase referencing error at the receiver, as stated earlier, it may become important as a bias phase on the extracted carrier $x(t)$ at the receiver when used for turnaround retransmission.

8.6 SATELLITE RETURN-LINK PHASE COHERENCY

In many cases a return communication link is established from the receiver back through the satellite to the transmitter (Figure 8.15). This establishes a two-way link between earth station and user (or between two earth stations), allowing data to be sent in both directions. The modulated carrier used in the return also has phase noise that must be derived in a similar manner as the forward link. However, the return phase coherency has added significance if, in addition to data transmission, frequency (two-way doppler) measurements for receiver tracking are to be carried out from the return carrier as well. This doppler tracking allows an earth station to track a moving user through a relay satellite. The frequency measurement must be made on the two-way round-trip frequency differential between the initial transmitted frequency at the forward transmitter and the returned extracted carrier. The latter is mixed with the transmitter source, and a frequency measurement is made on the beat frequency. An exact frequency measurement would indicate the doppler shift of the receiver, and would therefore determine exactly the receiver velocity (assuming the user is in motion). This operation requires that the receiver return carrier be a coherently turned around version of the forward carrier, and be coherently relayed back through the satellite. Coherent turnaround is obtained at the receiver by using the extracted reference carrier $x(t)$ in Figure 8.9 as the return carrier.

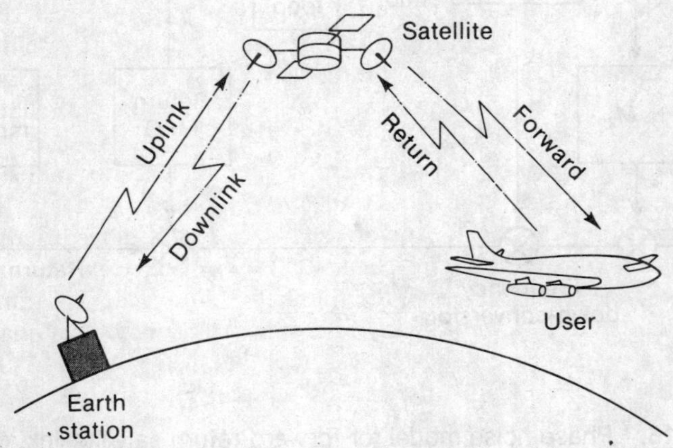

Figure 8.15. Earth–satellite–user link, forward and return.

Minimal phase degradation at the satellite can be obtained by using mixing frequencies generated from the same forward pilot tone, which theoretically is keeping the satellite phase coherent with the earth-station reference. The extraneous sources of phase noise (thermal, noncoherent, VCO, etc.), however, act to destroy this coherency and degrade the round-trip doppler operation. Figure 8.16a shows a block diagram of a typical coherent turnaround system. The extracted pilot tone drives the satellite **master frequency generators (MFG)** for providing all forward and return mixing. Since carriers and pilot tone are common to the forward and return paths, much of the phase noise of the forward link also appears on the return link. In particular, all the received forward phase noise is modulated back onto the return carrier.

The overall phase noise diagram of the return system is now shown in Figure 8.16b. The uplink carrier and pilot phase diagram is identical to that

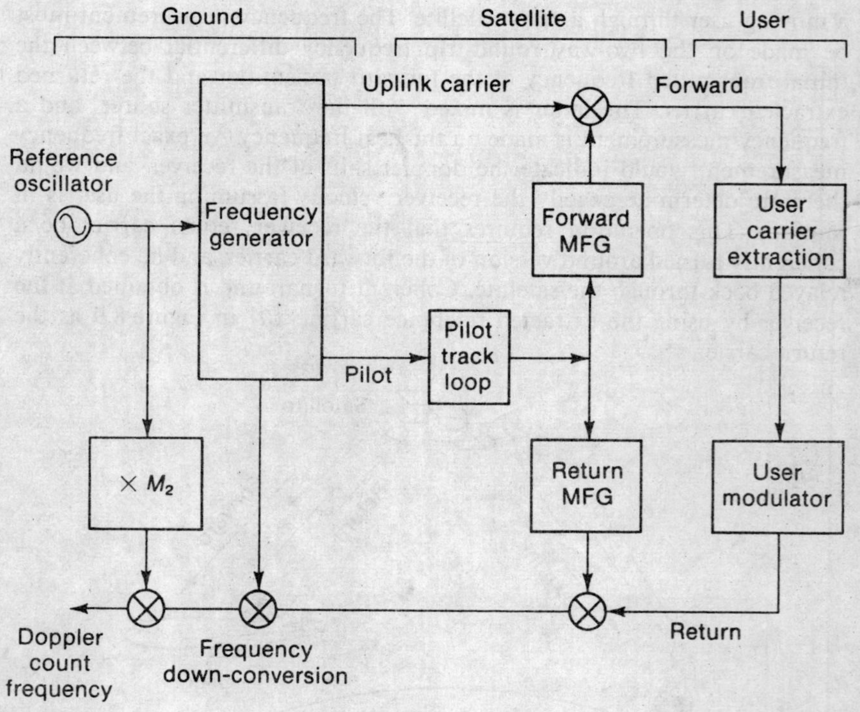

Figure 8.16. Phase-noise model for forward-return satellite link. (a) Block diagram. (b) Phase-noise model.

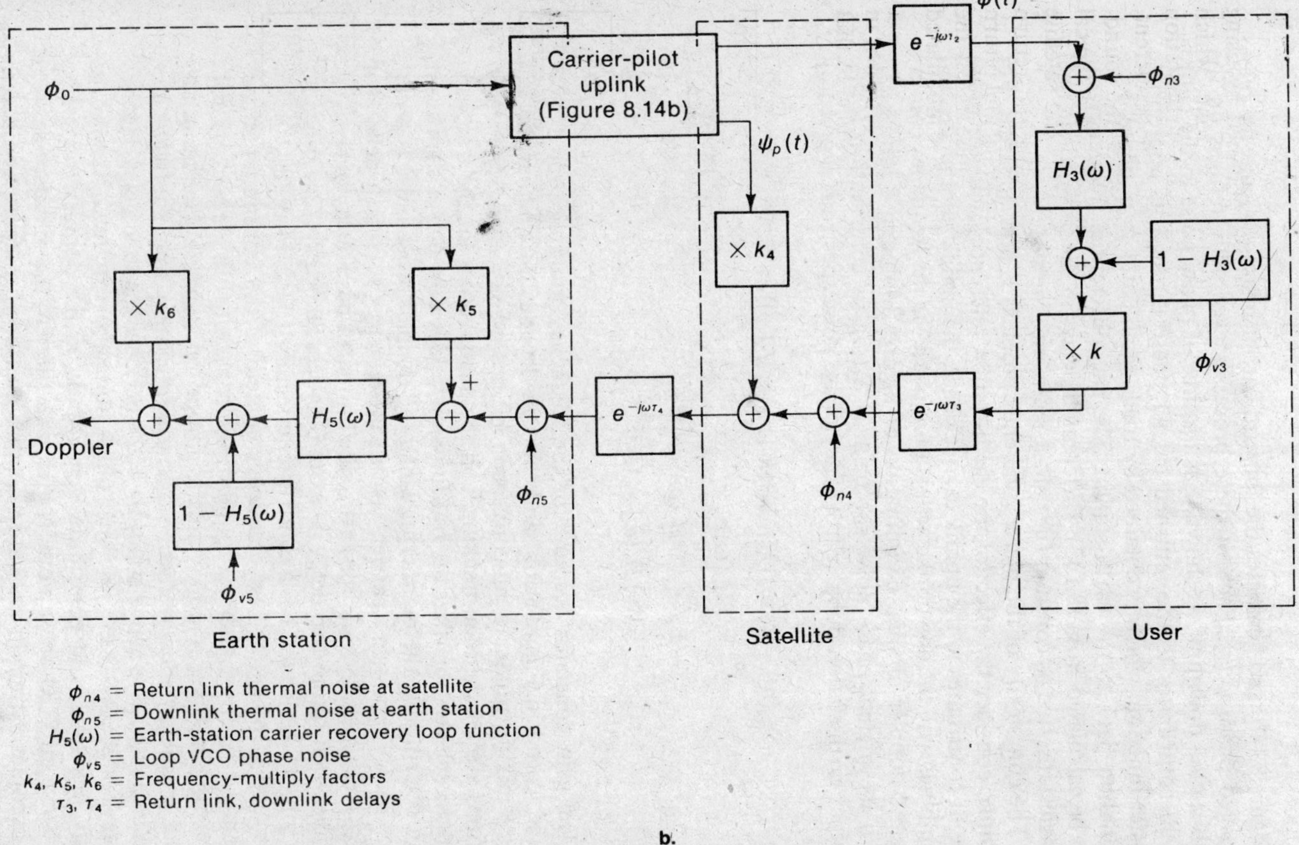

Figure 8.16. Phase-noise model for forward-return satellite link. (a) Block diagram. (b) Phase-noise model.

in Figure 8.14b, and generates the forward carrier phase $\psi(t)$ and the pilot extracted phase $\psi_p(t)$. Each of these processes eventually returns on the earth-station downlink, as shown. Each source of phase noise in the entire system contributes to the returned carrier phase through its appropriate transfer function, which is obtained by tracking all paths from phase noise origination back to the earth station. The rms differential frequency can then be calculated from (8.1.13). Differential delays in the forward channel are again inserted as constant (dc) phase shifts into the system.

The complexity of the phase coherency problem is now apparent. For example, consider the effect of the earth-station reference oscillator phase noise. It contributes to the uplink carrier phase, the uplink pilot phase, and recombines with the downlink earth-station phase via the frequency conversion and doppler mixing. Examination of Figures 8.14b and 8.16b reveals that if its original phase noise spectrum is $S_0(\omega)$, its contribution to the eventual earth-station doppler frequency phase noise spectrum is given by

$$
\begin{aligned}
S_{d0}(\omega) = S_0(\omega)\,|\,H_1(\omega)\,|\{k_1[1 - r_2H_2(\omega)]e^{-j\omega(\tau_1+\tau_2)} \\
\times JH_3(\omega)e^{-j\omega\tau_3} \\
\pm Le^{-j\omega\tau_1}H_2(\omega)\}e^{-j\omega\tau_4} \\
\pm M\,|\,H_4(\omega) - M_2\,|^2
\end{aligned}
\tag{8.6.1}
$$

The gain constants account for the frequency multiplication factors (see the legend in Figure 8.16b) and the sign depends on whether the frequency mixing produces up-conversion or down-conversion. The $H(\omega)$ functions are for the loop tracking, and the exponentials for the transmission path delays. Note that the transmission delays now play a significant role in determining the manner in which the doppler phase noise is generated. The round-trip carrier path introduces a total delay of $(\tau_1 + \tau_2 + \tau_3 + \tau_4)$ sec, while the earth–satellite–earth has a delay of $(\tau_1 + \tau_4)$. Typically, total round-trip delay is about 0.34 sec. Since $\exp(j2\pi f\tau)$ has no effect for $f << 1/\tau$, and it has a comb filter effect for $f >> 1/\tau$ (see (8.1.7)), the delays tend to make the high-frequency content of the transmitter source phase noise, returned after the round trip, incoherent with the source itself. As a result, the final mixing with the ground reference in generating the doppler frequency measurement superimposes, rather than subtracts, the reference phase noise above about $1/\tau$ Hz, where τ is the total delay. Hence, for delays of about 0.3 sec, reference phase noise above about 2 Hz may be actually increased, and contribute significantly to the doppler frequency error. Since all VCO phase noise is high pass filtered, the reference source noise becomes extremely critical in doppler measuring systems, and is the primary reason why only very phase stable (low phase noise) sources should be considered for station reference. This doppler condition also tends to change the role of the frequency synthesizer loop in Figure 8.5. We now see that by reducing the bandwidth of $H_1(s)$ in (8.2.2) we filter out most of the high-frequency noise on the reference source. We therefore have conflicting requirements on the synthesizer design in terms of forward and return doppler phase noise considerations. The former desires wide coherency bandwidths (at least as large as the pilot-loop bandwidth), while the latter prefers narrow coherency bands for reduction of high-frequency reference phase noise.

A filtering effect similar to (8.6.1) must be computed for each phase noise source in Figure 8.16. The combined phase noise spectrum then sums to form $S_x(\omega)$, which must be integrated in (8.1.8) to determine the actual doppler degradation. Again, this integration can be computed separately for each source, and the effect of each on doppler error can be separately catalogued.

In this chapter we have attempted to show how phase noise modeling techniques can be applied to satellite systems. These models are extremely convenient for assessing phase instability degradation on phase coherent data decoding and doppler measurements through the satellite. We first established the basic phase noise models for general carrier recovery systems, then extended to forward and return link analysis in a typical satellite system involving interconnected recovery subsystems. The advantage of such models is that they diagrammatically exhibit the manner in which various sources of phase noise originating throughout the system are amplified, filtered, and combined to generate the phase instability at various points in the system. From diagrams of this type, trade-off analysis can begin by direct computation of the cumulative effects of all sources on decoding and doppler tracking.

Although it is difficult to show specific numerical results here because of the many parameters (spectral shapes, loop filter functions, frequency allocations, mixing frequencies, carrier-to-noise levels, etc.) that must b defined, design techniques and procedures were illustrated for their applica tion. Most existing relay satellite systems allow for many more operationa modes than was considered here, so that actual implementation may b significantly more complicated than that presented. Nevertheless, the ger eral approach was intended to guide the reader through the methodology fo reducing these systems to analytically tractable models, and to show ho some initial interpretation of the phase noise problem can be gleaned fro the resulting equations, without resorting to extensive computatio Reports of extended phase noise applications to specific systems (Shutt and TDRSS) can be found in References [10–12].

PROBLEMS

8.1 Show that the *rms offset frequency* of an oscillator is the square root of the mean squared value of its phase noise spectrum. [*Hint*: Recall Problem 4.5.]

8.2 Given a sequence of phase values θ_i, $i = 1, 2, 3, \ldots, N$), of an oscillator. The **Allan Variance** is defined as

$$\mathrm{AV} = \frac{1}{N-3}\sum_{n=3}^{N}(\theta_n - \theta_{n-1})^2 - (\theta_{n-1} - \theta_{n-2})^2$$

Show that the AV is an estimate of the difference frequency stability of the oscillator.

8.3 Let N sequential values of a sine wave (taken at $360/N$ degrees apart) be stored in memory as k-bit words. These sample words are then read out at a clock rate f_s words/sec. (a) Plot out the sequence of sample values, carefully labeling the time axis, and connect the points to form a continuous sine wave. (b) Use the same read-out rate, but assume every other sample value is read out, and plot the sequence waveform on the same time axis. (c) Repeat for every fourth sample value. Show that the maximum and minimum frequency of the output sine wave is

$$\text{Minimum frequency} = f_s/2^k$$

$$\text{Maximum frequency} = f_s/4$$

8.4 Consider the frequency synthesizer in Figure 8.7, with $f_r = 5$ MHz, $k_1 = 1000$, and $Q = 1/1000$. (a) Plot on a single-frequency axis the spectral lines for f_r, f_o, and the mixing frequencies. (b) Explain the bandpass filtering problem after the mixer.

8.5 Revise the phase noise model of the standard frequency synthesizer in Figure 8.5b to include the mixer system in Figure 8.7.

8.6 A *fractional divider* can be obtained as follows. After each N input zero crossings, produce an output crossing. Do this for $M - 1$ output crossings. For the Mth, count one extra input crossing before producing the output crossing. Show that this will fractionally divide the input frequency.

8.7 Show that a differential delay between parallel paths of the same propagating waveform will effectively "filter" the waveform. Estimate the filter bandwidth.

REFERENCES

1. Hewlett-Packard Electronic System and Instrumentation Catalog, HP 5061A Option 004, 1977, p. 267.

2. R.M. Gagliardi, *Introduction to Communications Engineering*, (New York: Wiley, 1978), Appendix C.

3. W. Lindsey, and C. Chie, "Theory of Oscillator Instability Based on Structure Functions," *Proceedings of the IEEE*, vol. 64, no. 12, p. 197.

4. V. Kroupa "Noise Properties in PLL Systems" *IEEE Trans. on Comm.*, vol. COM-30, No. 10, pp. 2244-2253, October 1982.

5. J. Vanier and M. Teta, "Phase locked loops with Atomic Frequency Standards" *IEEE Trans. on Comm.*, vol. COM-30, No. 10, pp. 2355-2362, October, 1982.

6. U. Rohde, *Digital PLL Frequency Synthesizers*, Prentice Hall, Inc., Englewood Cliffs, N.J., 1983.

7. W. Lindsey, and K. Tu, "Phase Noise Effects on Space Shuttle Communication Link Performance," *IEEE Trans. on Comm.*, vol. COM-26 (November 1978), pp. 1532–1541.

8. W.C. Lindsey, and M.K. Simon, *Telecommunication Systems Enginering* (Englewood Cliffs, N.J.: Prentice-Hall, 1973), chapter 3.

9. J. Spilker, *Digital Communications by Satellite* (Englewood Cliffs, N.J.: Prentice-Hall, 1977), p. 131.

10. R. Gagliardi, K.T. Woo, Z. Ezzudin, and L. Yen, "Phase Noise Analysis of the TDRSS," *Proc. of the National Telemetry Conference*, Los Angeles, December 1977.

11. W. Lindsey, and W. Braun, "TDRSS Performance Evaluation For Shuttle Services Using Analytical Simulation," *IEEE Trans. on Comm.*, vol. COM-26 (November 1978), pp. 1723–1731.

12. R.M. Gagliardi, "Phase Referencing in the TDRSS," *Proc. of the International Telemetry Conf.*, Los Angeles, November 1978, Session 16.

9

Optical Satellite Communications

In Chapter 3 it was pointed out that intersatellite links (satellite crosslinks) generally require narrower beamwidths for increased power concentration. This additional power density is needed to compensate for the longer path lengths (perhaps twice the synchronous altitude) and the limitation of satellite payloads at both ends of the link. The latter limits both the transmitter EIRP and the receiver $g/T°$ values. Since antenna area cannot be arbitrarily increased with spaceborne vehicles, the better way to achieve narrower beams is to use a higher frequency. For example, by operating a satellite crosslink at 60 GHz (EHF) we achieve about a tenfold increase in frequency over a C-band link, resulting in about a 20-dB power increase with the same size antennas. A power gain of this amount can be used to effectively combat the longer links and the smaller transmitted power levels. Unfortunately, the source technology and the modulation hardware required at these higher frequency bands are still in the development stage.

The next possibility is to extend to optical frequencies, where the development of laser sources providing light wave beams has been advancing rapidly. With the availability of feasible light sources, and the existence of efficient optical modulators, communication links with optical beams are presently being given serious consideration in intersatellite links. Furthermore, laser operation (at frequencies of about 10^{14} Hz) provide a 10^5 factor over C-band frequencies, which theoretically can now produce about a 90-dB power advantage, as well as a 10^5 advantage in information bandwidth. Although the power advantage aids in overcoming the weaker link, a portion of this improvement can be used to reduce component size (and therefore spacecraft cost and weight). Hence optical transmitters and receiver packages are usually smaller and lighter than the equivalent RF or microwave subsystems.

The introduction of laser communications, however, requires some modification to the design, implementation, and analysis of the crosslinks. These modifications are caused by the different characteristics of optical devices as opposed to their RF counterpart. In particular, there are: (1) a different technology used for component and device development (quantum mechanical principles instead of electronics), (2) a laser source instead of electronic oscillators and amplifiers, (3) narrow light beamwidths (fractions of a degree) instead of antenna gain patterns of several degrees, (4) lensing systems for beam transmission and focusing, instead of RF antennas, and (5) photodetectors for light reception instead of the usual field-current conversion in RF reception. Although these differences primarily pertain to device description (all electromagnetic waves obey the same laws of radiation propagation, whether at RF or optical frequencies), they do tend to introduce new nomenclature, terminology, and parameters from those in RF links. These in turn alter link analysis and performance evaluation. In this chapter we attempt to reformulate satellite crosslink analysis for an optical communication link.

9.1 REVIEW OF OPTICAL BEAM TRANSMISSION AND RECEPTION

In an optical communication link a laser is used as the transmitting source, and optical fields are generated at carrier frequencies in the optical portion

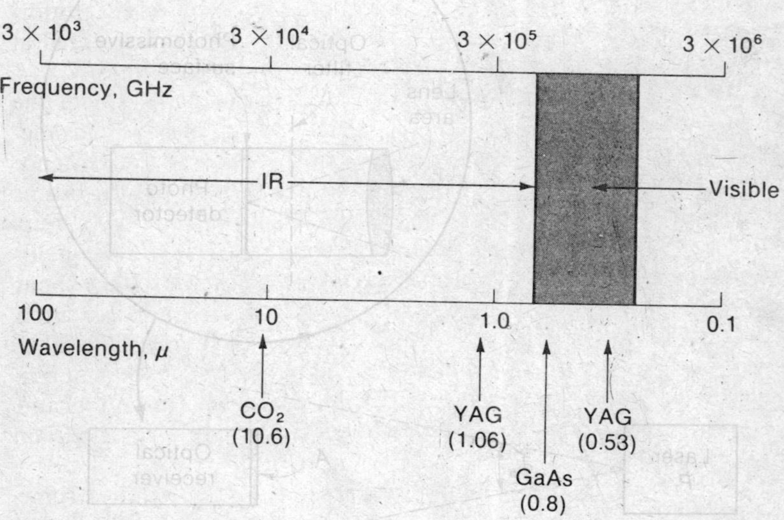

Figure 9.1. Upper end of the electromagnetic frequency chart (Wavelength = 3×10^8/frequency). Location of some optical sources shown.

of the frequency spectrum. Figure 9.1 shows this part of the electromagnetic spectrum (recall Figure 1.4) along with the corresponding wavelengths associated with each frequency. Note that an optical system operates at wavelengths on the order of microns (10^{-6} meters), which is several orders of magnitude smaller yet than those of millimeter waves (K-band). Since the atmosphere will have extreme deleterious effects at these wavelengths, optical links are usually designed to avoid propagation through the atmosphere. Thus a satellite crosslink, involving transmissions above the Earth's atmosphere, is a natural candidate for optical wavelength propagation. If the crosslink passes through the atmosphere, or involves an earth station or satellite in a low near-earth orbit, the atmosphere's effect on light waves must be carefully evaluated. This will be considered in Section 9.3.

A laser optical link model is shown in Figure 9.2. A laser source generates a light wave, which is focused into an optical beam and propagates a distance Z over a free-space path to a collecting area A_r. Focused laser

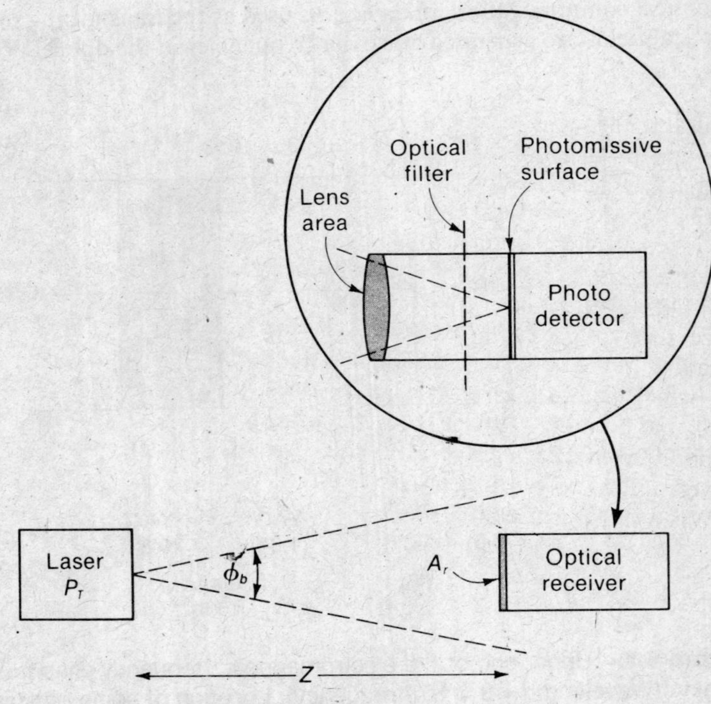

Figure 9.2. Laser link model.

beams are typically modeled as having circular symmetric beam patterns with beamwidth

$$\phi_b = \frac{\lambda}{d_t} \tag{9.1.1}$$

where λ is the wavelength of the laser light and d_t is the diameter of the transmitting optics of the laser. It is important to comprehend the order of the dimensions involved. In the visible optical range ($\lambda \approx 1\mu = 10^{-6}$ meters) a transmitting lens of only 6 inches (0.15 meter) will produce a beamwidth of about 10 microradians (recall 17.5 milliradian $\cong$ 1°). Hence a laser transmitter produces beamwidths several orders of magnitude narrower than beamwidths used in RF systems. In optical links, therefore, we deal with beamwidths measured in microradians or milliradians, instead of degrees.

The laser source power P_T is distributed over the beamfront at the distance Z. The optical power density incident over a collecting area A_r in Figure 9.2 is then computed as in an RF system. Hence the power collected over A_r is

$$P_r = \frac{P_T A_r}{\phi_b^2 Z^2} \tag{9.1.2}$$

A natural tendency is to attempt to rewrite (9.1.2) in terms of antenna gain values and propagation losses, as we did in earlier RF link analysis. This indeed can be done for the transmitting end by again defining $g_t \cong 4\pi/\phi_b^2$, as in (3.2.6). At optical wavelengths, this will produce extremely high values of g_t (e.g., a 6-inch optical transmitter will have a gain of 115.6 dB). Of course, this will be largely overcome by the corresponding large space loss ($L_P = (4\pi/\lambda Z)^2$) at these wavelengths. The introduction of gain values to replace receiving area A_r in (9.1.2) in the same way, however, can be misleading in the optical system. This is due to the fact that receiver field of view (which determines receiver gain) does *not* depend only on receiver area A_r but on other receiver focusing parameters as well. (We shall explore this point later.) For the present it is perhaps best to simply deal with received optical power directly, as in (9.1.2).

When (9.1.1) is used in (9.1.2), we have instead

$$P_r = \frac{P_T (d_t d_r)^2}{\lambda^2 Z^2} \tag{9.1.3}$$

which depends only on the squared product of the transmit and receive diameters. Figure 9.3 plots P_r as a function of optic size for a propagation length Z = 45,000 miles (twice synchronous range) at wavelength $\lambda = 1$

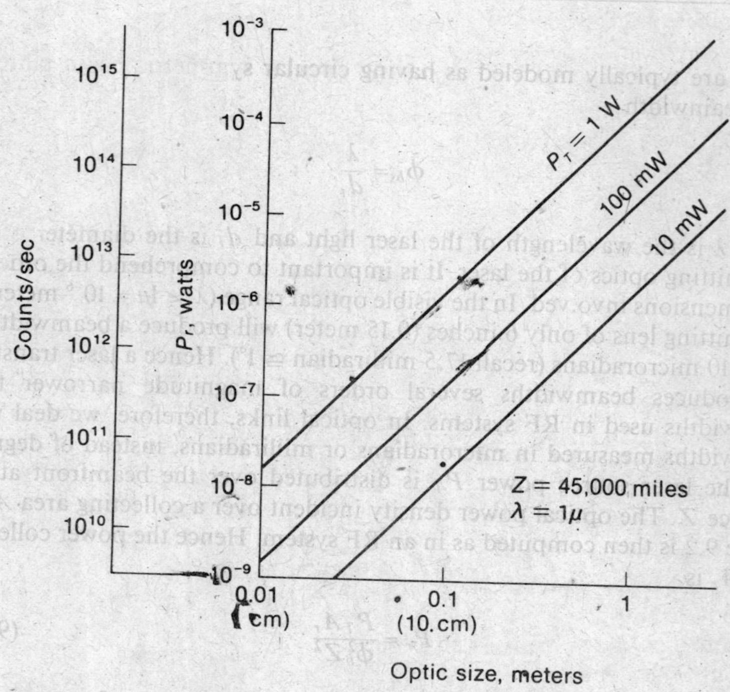

Figure 9.3. Received optical power vs. optic size. Transmit and receiver optics are the same size. P_T is the laser source power. Counts per sec refers to received photoelectron count rate, equation (9.1.4).

micron, and assuming identical transmit–receive optics. We see that power levels comparable to those received in RF links are obtainable with only milliwatts of source power and with optic diameters on the order of a foot or less. This significant reduction in source power values and optic sizes is a key driving force for continued interest in laser links.

In optical link analyses it is common to convert power values P_r to equivalent **photoelectron count rates**. This is accomplished by dividing P_r by the energy value hf_0, where h is Planck's constant ($h = 6.6 \times 10^{-34}$ watts/Hz) and f_0 is the optical frequency. Hence, we denote the number of received photoelectrons per sec (usually called simply counts per second), corresponding to P_r in (9.1.2), as

$$n_r = \frac{P_r}{hf_0} \tag{9.1.4}$$

The number of received counts per sec is, therefore, simply a normalization of received power. At optical frequencies (say $\lambda \cong 1$ micron), equation (9.1.4) becomes $n_r = (5.1)10^{18}P_r$, and it is evident that count rates are usually extremely large numbers (relative to the fractional watt values for P_r). Figure 9.3 is also labeled in counts per sec obtained by using this conversion factor at 1 micron.

Lasers

Laser sources [1–3] exist at specific wavelengths, depending on the material achieving the lasing. Materials of various types (gases, liquids, semiconductor, etc.) have been used to produce lasers. The material determines the physical properties, power conversion efficiency, and required auxiliary hardware of the laser. Box 9.1 summarizes the characteristics of common laser sources projected for use in space communication links. The lasers extend from high-powered, low-efficiency, bulky devices to the smaller, lightweight GaAs (gallium arsenide) solid-state diodes. The latter devices are inherently low powered (output power on the order of tens of milliwatts), and it is generally necessary to combine diodes into arrays to increase source power outputs.

When such **diode arrays** are used, the important parameter becomes the amount by which the combined beam spreads as elements are added to the array. Any beam spreading increases the divergence and dilutes beam power. Array beam spreading depends on the method used to combine the powers of the individual array elements. A perfect combiner adds the individual diode powers without increasing the transmitted beamwidth, thereby directly increasing P_r in (9.1.2). Diode stacking methods that multiply up the power per diode, but likewise spread the beam by the same factor, dilute the increased power, and P_r is not actually increased. It is expected that the development of improved array combining will continue to be vigorously pursued in optical communication technology.

Optical Filters

The receiver optical filter in Figure 9.2 limits the range of wavelengths that pass through it. It therefore plays the same role as an RF front-end filter, with its prime function being to reduce the amount of unwanted radiation entering the photodetector. The range of wavelengths around the laser wavelength allowed by the optical filter is called the **optical bandwidth**. The optical bandwidth in wavelengths, $\Delta\lambda$, around wavelength λ_0 is related to the

Box 9.1. Summary of laser sources.

Laser Type	Wavelength	Average Power Output	Efficiency	Characteristics
Nd–YAG (neodymium–yittrium aluminum garnet) crystal	1.06μ 0.532μ	0.5–1 w 100 Mw	0.5–1% 0.5–1%	• Requires elaborate modulation equipment • Requires diode or solar pumping • 10,000 life hours • Frequency doubling loses efficiency
GaAs (solid-state diode)	0.8-.9μ	40 Mw	5–10%	• Small, rugged, compact • Directly and easily modulated • Easily combined into arrays • Nanosec pulsing • 50,000 life hours, reliable
CO_2 (gas laser) carbon dioxide	10.6μ	1–2 w	10–15%	• In IR range (poor detectors) • Discharge tube • Modulation difficult • 20,000 life hours, existing technology
HeNe (helium neon)	0.63μ	10 Mw	1%	• Gas tube, power limited, inefficient • Requires external modulation • 50,000 life hours

optical bandwidth B_0 in Hz around the frequency f_0 corresponding to λ_0 by

$$\frac{\Delta\lambda}{\lambda_0} = \frac{B_0}{f_0} \tag{9.1.5}$$

Optical filters rely on wavelenth rejection within the filter media, and usually have their bandwidths stated in wavelengths [4, 5]. Typical optical filter bandwidths at 1 micron generally range from 10–100 angstroms (1 angstrom = 10^{-4} microns), corresponding to an equivalent frequency bandwidth of about $B_0 \approx 10^{11}$–10^{12} Hz (100–1000 GHz). Hence, front-end optical bandwidths are several orders larger than those encountered in microwave systems.

Photodetection

The primary element for receiving an optical field is a focusing lens and a photodetecting surface (Figure 9.4). In RF systems an antenna dish concentrates the impinging field at the feed point, which electronically converts the field at the feed directly to an electronic signal current. In optics, the focusing lens (or perhaps a series of lens and mirrors) likewise focuses the field onto the photodetector. However since the optical field is at such a high frequency, it cannot be directly detected. Instead the photodetector responds quantum mechanically by using the radiation to excite its photoemissive surface and produce a photoelectron (current) flow. The latter depends on the instantaneous **field intensity** over the detector surface (*field intensity* is the square of the field envelope; the integral of intensity over the detector area is the *detected field power*). Hence a photodetector detects the instantaneous field power (instead of the field itself) of the focused field on

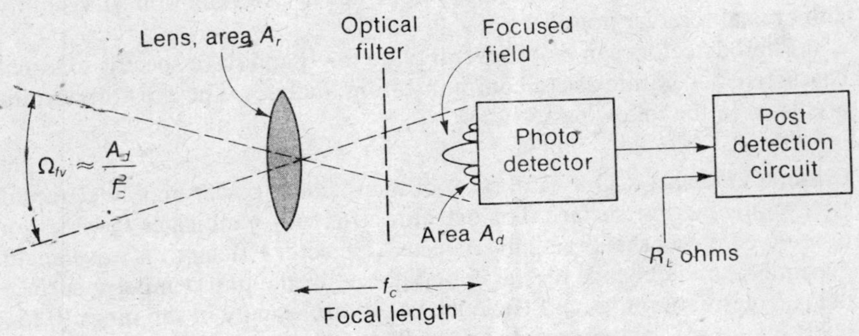

Figure 9.4. Optical receiver model.

the detector. This means that all modulation must be imposed on field power (called **intensity modulation**) or must be inserted in such a way that a power detector will recover it. The amount of field power focused onto the detector is equal to the amount of field power incident over the focusing lens. Hence photodetected power can be equivalently computed by determining receiving field power over the lens area, instead of by focused field power over the detector area. The former is obtained directly from (9.1.2) with A_r corresponding to the receiver lens aperture area. Hence, (9.1.2) is indeed valid for computing detector field power even though it does not explicitly involve the actual photodetecting area.

A photodetector will respond to all radiation focused on its photoemissive surface. This therefore defines the optical receiver field of view as the field arrival angles over which the lens will focus the impinging field onto the photodetector surface. From Figure 9.4 we see that this will depend on the detector area A_d and the optical focal length rather than on the size of the receiving lens. Recall that in RF systems, receiver field of view depended only on the size of the receiving antenna A_r, and was given as the **diffraction-limited** field of view, λ^2/A_r. Thus, optical systems have a field of view that can be adjusted independently of the receiver lens area. Typically the focal length in Figure 9.4 is set to approximately the aperture diameter ($f_c \approx \sqrt{A_r}$), and the optical field of view is generally stated as

$$\Omega_{fv} \cong \frac{A_d}{f_c^2} \approx \frac{A_d}{A_r} = \left(\frac{A_d}{\lambda^2}\right)\left(\frac{\lambda^2}{A_r}\right) \tag{9.1.6}$$

Since detector area is on the order of millimeters or centimeters, while λ is on the order of microns, we see that the optical field of view is usually many times larger than the diffraction limited field of view (λ^2/A_r) of the same aperture area. This point becomes important in assessing optical visibility and optical receiver noise.

Photodetectors can be of several types [6–9] and have specific external characteristics of interest to communication analyses. The most important are listed in the following sections.

Detector Efficiency. Only a portion of the incident power may be detected by a photoemissive surface. The detector efficiency η indicates the fraction of received power that is actually detected. Detector efficiency is wavelength dependent, and depends on the material used in the photoemissive surface (silicon, germanium, etc.). Efficiency values are usually in the range (0.15–0.90) for visible frequencies, but fall off rapidly at the higher wavelengths (lower frequencies). The detector efficiency allows us to convert received power P_r in (9.1.2) to effective detected power ηP_r. Likewise, by extending

(9.1.4), we denote

$$n_s = \left(\frac{\eta}{hf_0}\right)P_r \tag{9.1.7}$$

as the *detected* count rate of the optical receiver.

Gain. Photodetectors may be relatively simple photoemissive structures (e.g., PIN diodes) or may be designed as photomultipliers, such that a single emitted photoelectron from its primary surface due to incident radiation may eventually produce multiple photoelectrons at its output. This increases the output current flow for a given incident power, thereby achieving an effective gain during the detection process. This gain may be achieved by cascaded emissive surfaces (as in photomultiplier tubes) or by inherent avalanche mechanisms, as in **avalanche photodetectors (APD)**. Photomultiplication gain can be interpreted as either a multiplication of the number of electrons emitted during reception, or as an increase in the current output of the detector. Unfortunately, the multiplication factor achieved by the gain mechanisms is often random in nature, producing a random gain distributed about some mean gain $\overline{G}$. This causes a statistical dependence of the output current on this gain, and introduces an additional degree of randomness to the detector output model. The gain variance, σ_d^2, or photomultiplier **spread**, is an indication of the extent of this randomness. The photomultiplier **excess noise factor** is defined as

$$F \triangleq 1 + \frac{\sigma_d^2}{(\overline{G})^2} \tag{9.1.8}$$

Typically, vacuum tube photomultipliers have mean gains of approximately $\overline{G} = 10^4 - 10^6$, and excess noise factors between 1 and 2. An APD, being a smaller, lighter device, is limited to gains of about 50–300. Its excess noise factor increases with $\overline{G}$ and is usually in the range of 2 to 5 for the above gain values.

Responsivity. A parameter closely related to efficiency is the detector responsivity, labeled in amps/watt. The responsivity simply indicates how much current will be produced for a given power input. Responsivity values for detectors account not only for their efficiency factors, but also for any inherent photomultiplication mean gain. Formally, the responsivity u is given by

$$u = \frac{e\eta\overline{G}}{hf_0} \text{ amps/watt} \tag{9.1.9}$$

where e is the charge of an electron ($e = 1.97 \times 10^{-19}$ coulombs). Hence responsivity is also frequency-dependent, and indicates the average photodetecting capability of the device.

Bandwidth. The photodetector bandwidth determines the rate of power variation that can be detected. It therefore indicates the highest frequency at which the power can be varied and have the variation detected by the output current. As such, it constrains the maximum modulation bandwidth used with intensity modulation. Typical detector bandwidths are usually 1–10 GHz. This bandwidth should not be confused with the optical bandwidth of the receiver filter, defined in (9.1.5).

Optical Receiver Noise

An anomaly in optical detection is that a photodetector does not respond perfectly to impinging field power. This can be demonstrated as in Figure 9.5. If a fixed power field is focused onto a photodetector, then the output current should be constant at a value proportional to the input

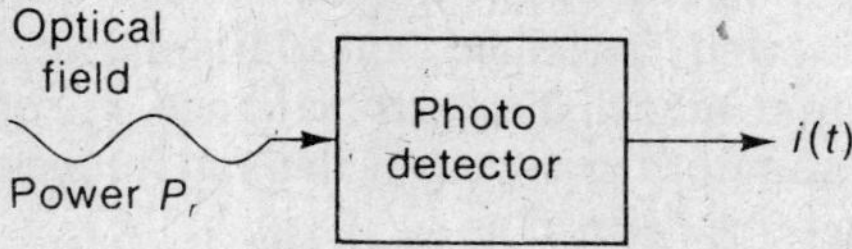

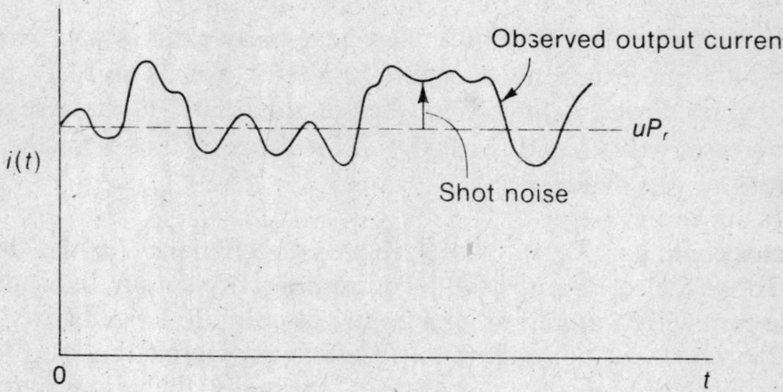

Figure 9.5. Photodetector output time function with constant input power.

power. In reality, however, the output current observed will appear as a random variation around that proportional value, as shown. This random variation around the true value is called detector **shot noise**, and is caused by the statistical nature of the emission of photoelectrons during radiation reception. As a noise process (i.e., the process obtained by subtracting the mean output value from the total output), shot noise has a flat spectral density with a level that depends on the input power value. Hence shot noise is stronger during the reception of high power levels, and weaker during weak power reception. This means that shot noise is in reality a nonstationary process when the input field power is time varying. And this fact obviously creates a degree of complication in any type of rigorous receiver study. For communication analysis we generally avoid this difficulty by simply treating shot noise as a stationary random process with a spectral level dependent on the average power collected over a time interval corresponding to roughly the reciprocal bandwidth of the processing subsystem. The actual shot noise spectral level is known to be [10]:

$$N_{sn}(\omega) = \overline{G}^2 F e u \overline{P} \text{ amps}^2/\text{Hz} \tag{9.1.10}$$

where $\overline{G}$, F, and u are the detector gain, noise factor, and responsivity parameters previously discussed; e is the electron charge; and $\overline{P}$ is the time-averaged mean received power.

In addition to shot noise, a photodetector produces **dark current**. Dark current is output current that appears even with no input radiation, and is caused by the random thermal emission of photoelectrons due to the inherent temperature of the device. Dark current is a random process, and must be considered an additional noise in the receiving operation. It also is described as a shot noise process, with a spectral level proportional to the average output dark current. Thus, its spectral level is [11]:

$$N_{dc}(\omega) = e I_{dc} \text{ amps}^2/\text{Hz} \tag{9.1.11}$$

where I_{dc} is the detector mean dark current. Typical detector dark current values are in the range 10^{-16}–10^{-12} amperes, and can be further reduced by detector cooling.

To the output detector current must be added the thermal noise current of the post detection circuitry. This introduces a noise current spectral level of [12]:

$$N_t(\omega) = \frac{4kT^{\circ}_{eq}}{R_L} \text{ amp}^2/\text{Hz} \tag{9.1.12}$$

where k is Boltzmann's constant, R_L is the impedance loading the photodetector, and T°_{eq} is its equivalent noise temperature (Figure 9.4). The last depends on the noise figure of the loading circuitry (amplifiers, networks, etc.). Note that the thermal noise spectrum is reduced by increasing the load impedance R_L, but this, in conjunction with output capacitance, may tend to reduce the bandwidth of the loading circuitry.

9.2 OPTICAL BACKGROUND-NOISE POWER

An optical receiver collects background noise just as with an RF antenna. However, the emission characteristics of background radiation at optical frequencies are much different than at the lower microwave frequencies. The amount of background power at frequency f impinging on an optical receiver of collecting area A_r is given by

$$P_b = H(f) B_0 \Omega_{fv} A_r \tag{9.2.1}$$

where $H(f)$ is the background **spectral radiance** function at frequency f, B_0 is the optical front-end bandwidth in Hz, and Ω_{fv} is the field of view of the receiver in steradians. Background radiance functions are obtained from blackbody radiation models, which depend on the equilibrium temperature of the actual background. The latter is composed of the contributions from all galactic sources in the field of view, including the solar (sunlit) sky.

To better understand the interpretation of (9.2.1) at optical frequencies, consider first its evaluation at RF frequencies. In this case the receiver has the diffraction limited field of view related to its area by $\Omega_{fv} = \lambda^2/A_r$, and (9.2.1) simplifies to

$$P_b = [N(f)\lambda^2] B_0 \qquad \text{RF frequencies} \tag{9.2.2}$$

The function in brackets is plotted in Figure 9.6. At the RF frequencies, $hf/kT^{\circ} << 1$, $N(f)\lambda^2 \approx kT^{\circ}$, where T° is the equivalent background temperature in degrees Kelvin, and (9.2.2) reduces to the RF background power used in Chapter 3. Thus Figure 9.6 plots the effective receiver background noise spectral level as a function of the operating carrier frequency. At the higher optical frequencies, the blackbody radiation spectrum falls off rapidly. Since the optical field of view Ω_{fv} is not directly related to receiving area, it is convenient to rewrite (9.2.1) as

$$\begin{aligned} P_b &= [N(f)\lambda^2] B_0 \Omega_{fv} A_r / \lambda^2 \\ &= [N(f)\lambda^2] B_0 D_s \end{aligned} \tag{9.2.3}$$

where

$$D_s = \frac{\Omega_{fv}}{\lambda^2/A} \tag{9.2.4}$$

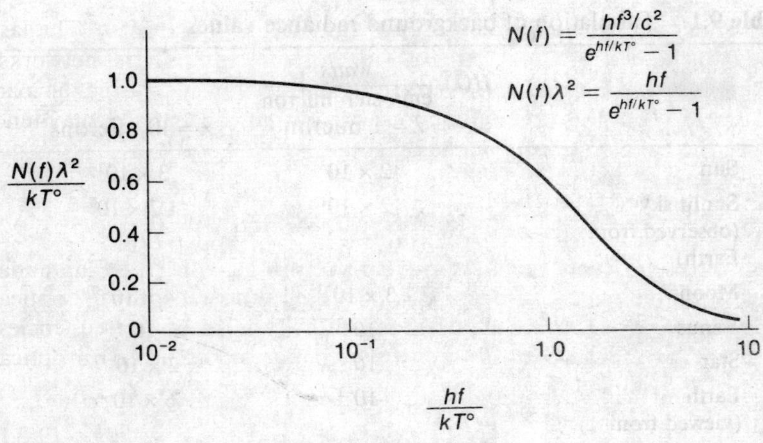

Figure 9.6. Blackbody radiation spectral level as a function of operating frequency.

Hence optical background power can be obtained by reading the spectral level at optical frequency f_0 from Figure 9.6, multiplying by the optical bandwidth B_0, and then additionally multiplying up by the factor D_s. The last factor is the ratio of the actual receiver field of view to the diffraction limited field of view and, as we pointed out in (9.1.6), is generally a large number. For example, an optical receiver with a 10-μrad field of view and 6-inch optics will have $D_s \cong 14{,}000$, The D_s factor simply accounts for the additional noise being collected with an optical field of view many times larger than the diffraction limited field of view.

It may appear at first glance from Figure 9.6 that optical receivers are less noisy than RF receivers. In fact, since they operate at even higher frequencies, it appears that the noise can actually be neglected. It must be remembered, however, that this applies only to background noise and, as we have found in Section 9.1, other sources of detector noise must also be taken into account. Furthermore, multiplication by a large optical bandwidth B_0 and a large D_s factor may counteract a relatively small spectral value.

To actually evaluate (9.2.3) requires an accurate plot of $N(f)\lambda^2$ for the true background temperature. Unfortunately, background data is generally available only in wavelength units [13, 14]. It is, therefore, more convenient to use (9.2.1) directly in wavelength notation rather than frequency. If we denote $H(\lambda)$ as the equivalent radiance plotted in wavelengths, and again denote $\Delta\lambda$ as the optical bandwidth in wavelengths, we can restate (9.2.1) as

$$P_b = H(\lambda)\Delta\lambda\Omega_{fv}A_r \tag{9.2.5}$$

Table 9.1. Tabulation of background radiance values.

	$H(\lambda)$, $\frac{\text{watts}}{\text{cm}^2\text{–ster–micron}}$ $\lambda = 1$ micron	$\lambda = 10$ microns
Sun	2×10^3	3×10^2
Sunlit sky (observed from Earth)	2×10^1	1.7×10^0
Moon	3×10^{-3}	4×10^{-5}
Venus	10^{-3}	10^{-4}
Star	10^{-9}	2×10^{-11}
Earth (viewed from sync orbit)	10^{-3}	6×10^{-5}

Table 9.1 lists values of $H(\lambda)$ at several wavelengths for common background sources. Total background power is obtained by multiplying the appropriate radiance values by the proper values of optical bandwidth, field of view, and receiver collecting area. Contributions from extended backgrounds (e.g., sky as viewed from Earth) increase continually with field of view, while localized sources (stars, planets, etc.) contribute only if they appear in the field of view. Their power contribution increases only until the receiver field of view encompasses the entire source, after which the power remains constant. Figure 9.7 plots typical background power levels as a function of receiver beamwidth for specific optical background noise sources. As in (9.1.4) background power can be converted to equivalent receiver background count rates as

$$n_b = \left(\frac{\eta}{hf_0}\right) P_b \tag{9.2.6}$$

where again h is Planck's constant and f_0 is the optical frequency. This is included in Figure 9.7.

When a transmitting laser field is received in addition to the background noise field, the photodetection operation must take into account the combined field. Thus, if $f_s(t)$ and $f_b(t)$ are laser and background fields at the receiver area A_r, a photodetector produces a current

$$i(t) = uA_r|f_s(t) + f_b(t)|^2 \tag{9.2.7}$$

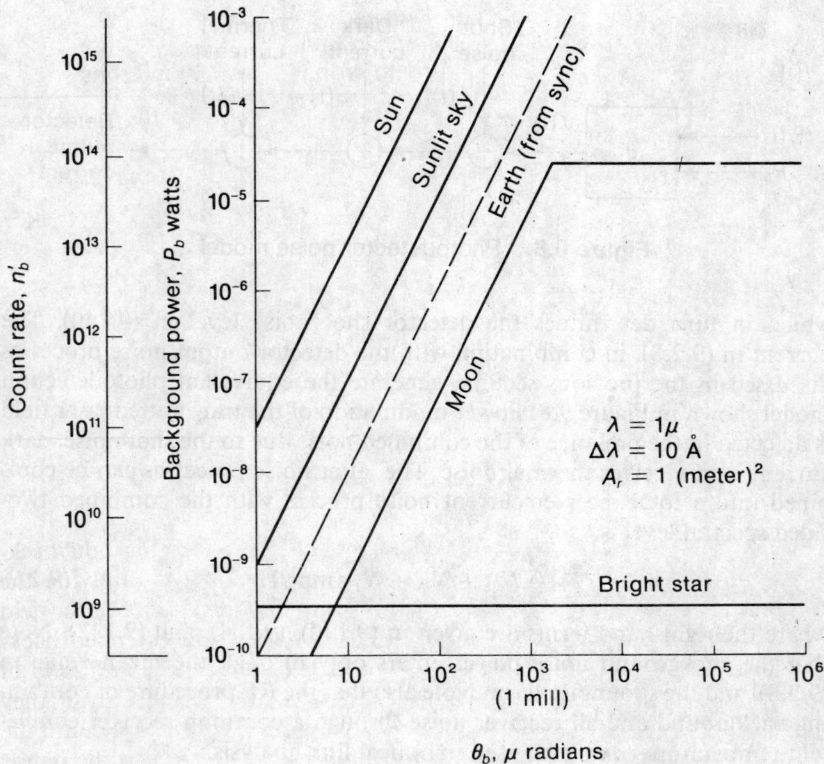

Figure 9.7. Background power and count rate due to stated sources.

where u is the photodetector responsivity in (9.1.9). When expanded out, $i(t)$ contains a term due to the laser intensity, a term due to the background intensity, and terms due to the field cross-product. The current in (9.2.7) has a mean value proportional to the average laser power [P_r in (9.1.3)] and the average background power [P_b in (9.2.5)]. In addition, the current contains the intensity modulation of the laser, and the random variation of both the background intensity and the cross-product term. The latter two processes have negligibly small spectra levels, and can be neglected (Reference [10], chapter 6). Hence the photodetected current in (9.2.7) is approximately

$$i(t) = uA_r|f_s(t)|^2 + uP_b \tag{9.2.8}$$

Thus the primary effect of the background is to add to the mean current,

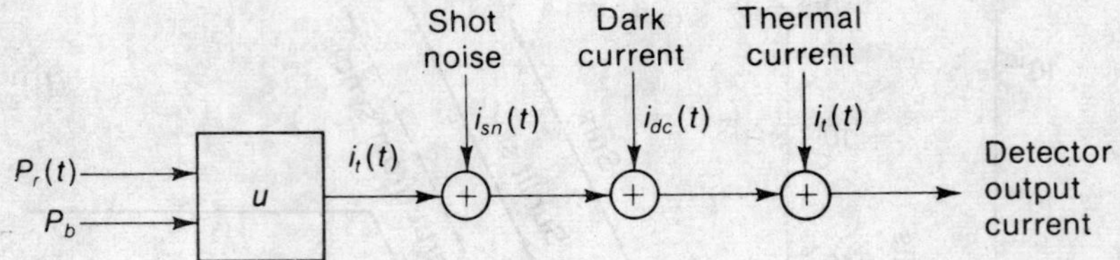

Figure 9.8. Photodetector noise model.

which in turn determines the detector shot noise level in (9.1.10). The current in (9.2.8), in combination with the detector output noise processes discussed in the previous section, generate the equivalent photodetection model shown in Figure 9.8. Power modulation of the transmitted laser field is detected in the presence of the combined noise due to the shot noise, dark current, and receiver thermal noise. The latter noise processes can be combined into a total receiver current noise process with the combined two-sided spectral level

$$N_0 \triangleq N_{sn} + N_{dc} + N_t \text{ amp}^2/\text{Hz} \tag{9.2.9}$$

where the right-hand terms are given in (9.1.10), (9.1.11), and (9.1.12). Note that the background noise power enters only through the mean value in (9.2.8), and the shot noise term. Note also that the RF procedure of combining background and all receiver noise through a common receiver equivalent temperature *cannot* be used in optical link analysis.

9.3 OPTICAL-LINK ANALYSIS

The optical receiver models of the previous sections can now be applied to the analyses of an optical communication link. Optical systems are of two basic types. In the standard system, the information waveform modulates the laser intensity, and the receiver is of the type previously described. It contains a focusing lens, a wavelength filter, and a photodetector that attempts to demodulate the field intensity (Figure 9.9a). Such a system is referred to as a **direct detection** link, and the models of the previous sections directly apply. An alternative system is one in which the receiver uses a local laser field to mix with the received field prior to photodetection (Figure 9.9b). The latter system is referred to as a **heterodyne** receiver. Since the local laser must be spatially aligned at the photodetector, the heterodyne system is often called a **coherent** (spatially) optical system. Because of the local laser, the modulation and demodulation procedures of the heterodyne

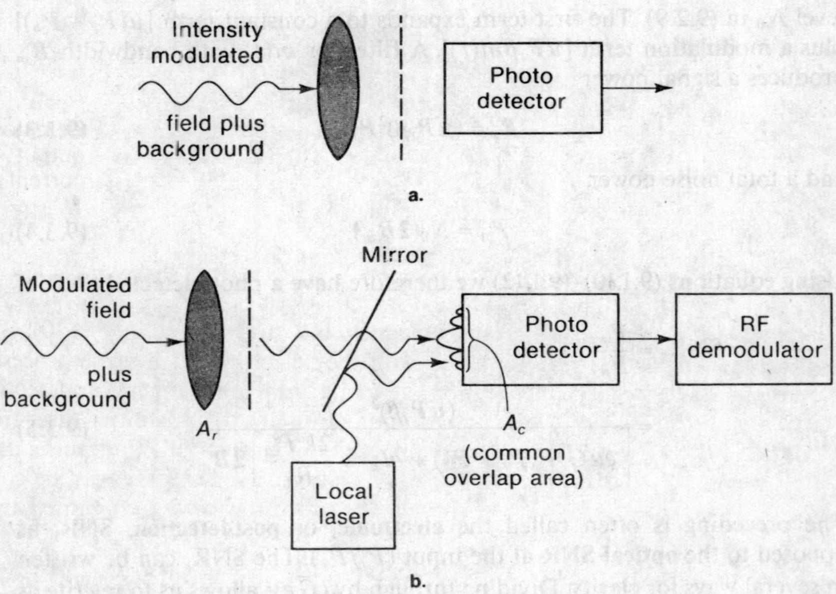

Figure 9.9. Optical receiver models. (a) Direct detection. (b) Heterodyne.

system are markedly different from the direct detection system. We examine each system in the next sections.

Direct Detection Systems

With intensity modulation, information waveform $m(t)$ is modulated onto the laser field by modulating the transmitted power. Hence we can write the received field power over the receiver lens area as

$$P_r(t) = P_r[1 + \beta m(t)] \tag{9.3.1}$$

where P_r is the average power in (9.1.2) and β is the intensity modulation index. We can assume $m(t)$ is normalized to unit amplitude and power P_m, requiring $\beta \leq 1$ to prevent overmodulation. After direct detection we generate the current process, from the model in Figure 9.8, as

$$i(t) = u[P_r(t) + P_b] + i_{sn}(t) + i_{dc}(t) + i_t(t) \tag{9.3.2}$$

The first term is the response to the impinging laser and background fields, and the remaining terms combine to a total noise with two-sided spectral level N_0 in (9.2.9). The first term expands to a constant term $[u(P_r + P_b)]$ plus a modulation term $[uP_r\beta m(t)]$. A filter for $m(t)$ with bandwidth B_m produces a signal power

$$P_s = (uP_r\beta)^2 P_m \tag{9.3.3}$$

and a total noise power

$$P_n = N_0(2B_m) \tag{9.3.4}$$

Using equations (9.1.10)–(9.1.12) we therefore have a photodetected SNR of

$$\begin{aligned} \text{SNR}_s &= \frac{P_s}{P_n} \\ &= \frac{(uP_r\beta)^2}{\left[eu\overline{G}^2F(P_r + P_b) + eI_{dc} + \dfrac{2kT^\circ_{\text{eq}}}{R_L}\right]2B_m} \end{aligned} \tag{9.3.5}$$

The preceding is often called the **electronic**, or **postdetection**, SNR, as opposed to the **optical** SNR at the input (P_r/P_b). The SNR_s can be written in several ways for clarity. Dividing through by $(\overline{G}e)^2$ allows us to rewrite as

$$\text{SNR}_s = \beta^2\left[\frac{(\eta P_r/hf_0)^2}{\left[(\eta/hf_0)F(P_r + P_b) + \dfrac{I_{dc}}{\overline{G}^2e} + \dfrac{2kT^\circ_{\text{eq}}}{\overline{G}^2e^2R_L}\right]2B_m}\right] \tag{9.3.6}$$

Note that the detected SNR_s is nonlinearly related to the optical power P_r, and depends on both P_r and P_b, and *not* simply on their ratio. That is, the electronic SNR is not a simple scaling of the optical SNR. This means that front-end optical losses (in the front-end mirrors, lens, and optical filters) must be correctly accounted for in computing both P_r and P_b. (In RF analysis, all front-end gains and losses cancel out since only their ratio is needed for performance evaluation.) Note further that both the dark current and thermal noise are reduced by the square of the photodetector mean gain. Hence high-gain photomultipliers aid in reducing the effect of postdetection noise, although the detector noise factor F also tends to increase with higher gain values.

To further simplify (9.3.6), we introduce the use of count rates, defined in (9.1.7) and (9.2.6), and write

$$\text{SNR}_s = \beta^2\left[\frac{n_s^2}{[F(n_s + n_b) + n_d + n_t]2B_m}\right] \tag{9.3.7}$$

where we have denoted

$$n_d \triangleq \frac{I_{dc}}{\overline{G}^2 e} = \begin{bmatrix} \text{Average number of} \\ \text{dark current photoelectrons} \\ \text{per second} \end{bmatrix} \tag{9.3.8}$$

$$n_t = \frac{2kT^{\circ}_{eq}}{\overline{G}^2 e^2 R_L} = \begin{bmatrix} \text{Average number of} \\ \text{thermal photoelectrons} \\ \text{per second} \end{bmatrix} \tag{9.3.9}$$

Hence SNR_s appears in a more compact form when written in terms of equivalent count rates instead of power values. The noise count rates n_{dc} and n_t are plotted in Figure 9.10. Note that thermal noise counts are usually more significant, and we again see the advantage of high photodetection gains in reducing these rates. It is convenient to rewrite (9.3.7) in the form

$$\text{SNR}_s = \beta^2\left(\frac{n_s}{2B_m}\right)\left[\frac{n_s}{n_s + (n_b + n_d + n_t)}\right] \tag{9.3.10}$$

Since n_s is a count rate, the term $(n_s/2B_m)$ can be interpreted as the number of signal counts in a time $1/2B_m$ seconds and is often referred to as the **quantum-limited** SNR for a bandwidth B_m. This connotation follows since $n_s/2B_m = \eta P_r/hf_0 2B_m$, and can be equivalently interpreted as a signal

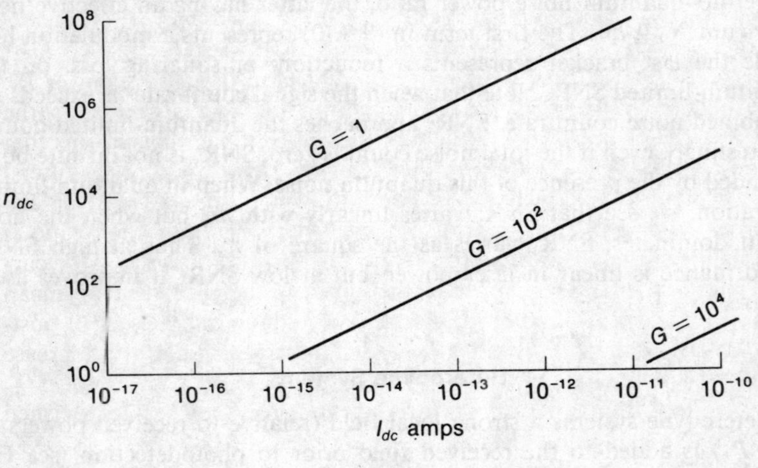

Figure 9.10. Count rates due to receiver noise. (a) Dark current. (b) Postdetection thermal noise.

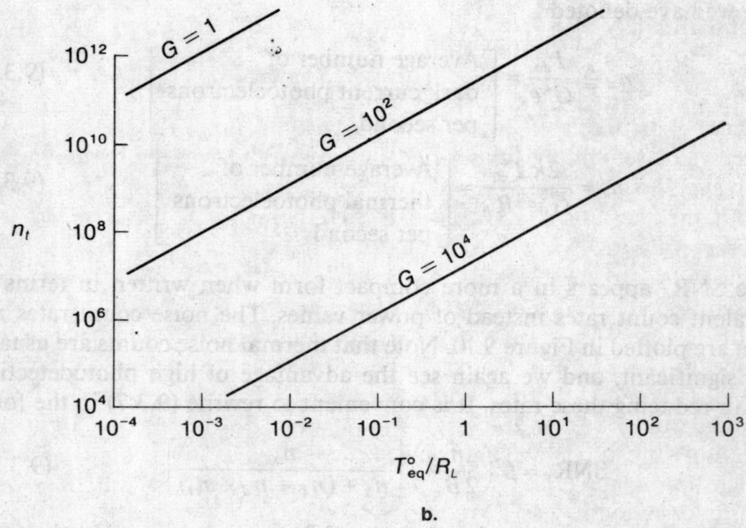

Figure 9.10. Count rates due to receiver noise. (a) Dark current. (b) Postdetection thermal noise.

power–to–quantum noise power ratio, the latter having an effective noise spectrum $N_0 \triangleq hf_0$. The first term in (9.3.10) represents a modulation loss, while the last bracket represents a reduction, or squaring loss, on this quantum-limited SNR. Note that when the signal count rate n_s exceeds the combined noise count rate, SNR_s approaches the quantum-limited bound. Interestingly, even if the total noise count is zero, SNR_s is not infinite but is bounded by the presence of this quantum noise. When in quantum-limited operation, we see that SNR_s varies linearly with n_s, but when the noise count dominates, SNR_s varies as the square of n_s. Thus at high SNR_s, performance is linear in laser power, but at low SNR_s it improves as its square.

Heterodyne Systems

In heterodyne systems a strong local field (relative to received powers P_r and P_b) is added to the received field prior to photodetection (see Figure 9.9b). The photodetector responds to the intensity of the combined field (laser plus background plus local field). Since the local laser power is much larger than the received field power, the photodetected response current is approximately

$$i(t) = uP_L + 2uf_s(t)f_L(t)A_r + 2uP_b(t)f_L(t)A_c \quad (9.3.11)$$

where P_L is the laser power over the detector area, $f_s(t)$ and $f_L(t)$ are the received laser and local laser fields, respectively, over the receiver area, and $P_b(t)$ is the background power collected over the detector area common to both the local and focused fields (A_c in Figure 9.9b). From (9.3.11) we observe the following facts of a heterodyne system: (1) The average current (and therefore the shot noise spectrum) is determined primarily by the local laser power P_L. (2) The laser signal field is detected only as a product term with the local laser field. This means modulation on the laser field must appear in such a form that it can be recovered only by mixing with the local field. This allows modulation formats of phase modulation (PM), frequency modulation (FM), or amplitude modulation (AM, instead of intensity modulation) directly on the laser optical carrier. By using the local laser field at a slight frequency offset from the received laser field, the mixing in (9.3.11) shifts the modulated laser carrier spectrum to a carrier spectrum at the difference frequency. When the difference frequency is set to an RF frequency, the modulated carrier can then be demodulated by standard RF methods. (3) The background noise spectrum at the laser frequency f_0 is shifted to the same RF frequency, and appears directly as additive noise during the RF demodulation. (4) The power of the background process $P_b(t)$ is related to the common detector area A_c and not necessarily the full area of the detector. Hence by focusing the local laser, the effective detector area can be reduced, producing an equivalent reduction in the receiver field of view (recall Figure 9.4). Heterodyne receivers therefore can be made to receive less background noise than direct detection receivers with the same areas.

Detected heterodyne SNR_s can be computed from (9.3.11). The received laser carrier power, after mixing to RF, is then (assuming the laser transmitter remains in the reduced field of view)

$$P_s = (2u)^2 P_L P_r \quad (9.3.12)$$

where P_r is the received power over the area A_r. The detected noise is due to the mixed background, the shot noise, and the detector output noises [$i_{dc}(t)$ and $i_t(t)$ in Figure 9.8]. Hence

$$\mathrm{SNR}_s = \frac{4u^2 P_L P_r}{\left[euP_l + 4euP_L N_b/2 + eI_{dc} + \dfrac{2kT^\circ_{\text{eq}}}{R_L}\right] 2B_c} \quad (9.3.13)$$

where B_c is the modulated carrier bandwidth at RF and $N_b = \eta N(f)\lambda^2/hf$. This can be rewritten as

$$\mathrm{SNR}_s = \frac{4(\eta/hf)P_r}{\left[1 + 2N_b + \dfrac{I_{dc}}{uP_L} + \dfrac{2kT^\circ_{eq}}{euP_L R_L}\right]2B_c}$$

$$= \frac{4n_s/2B_c}{1 + 2N_b + \left(\dfrac{n_d}{n_L}\right) + \dfrac{n_t}{n_L}} \tag{9.3.14}$$

where $n_L = \eta P_L/hf$ is the effective local laser count rate. This SNR_s is similar, but not identical, to the postdetection SNR_s of a direct detection system. In particular we note the following:

(1) The laser power P_L acts like detector gain in reducing the effect of postdetection noise. Hence high-gain photomultipliers are not needed in heterodyne receivers [for this reason F and G are taken as unity in (9.3.13)].

(2) Since N_b is the optical background spectral level (shifted to RF), only the background noise in the carrier bandwidth B_c (instead of the optical bandwidth B_0) affects SNR_s.

(3) Background noise again depends on D_s in (9.2.4), but the latter depends on the reduced field of view of the heterodyne mixing. This can be controlled by local laser focusing, provided P_r is not also reduced. Thus a heterodyne receiver can achieve spatial discrimination against background sources.

(4) The received laser power still depends on the receiver area A_r due to the mixing of the received and local fields at the detector. However, if these fields are not aligned [6], the receiver area is effectively reduced, and P_r is decreased. Hence a heterodyne system requires a more delicate receiver design. This fact alone may preclude its use for spaceborne satellite crosslink application.

Atmospheric Effects

If the satellite crosslink, or a satellite downlink, passes through the Earth's atmosphere, its effect must be carefully accounted for in optical link analysis. Because of the extremely small wavelengths, the disturbances to the propagating beam by atmospheric particulates are much more pronounced at optical frequencies. Even in clear air, the mixing of warm and cool atmospheric strata produce turbulence that can also interact with impinging light waves. These particulates and turbulences combine to cause beam absorption, scattering, and refocusing that can greatly reduce link capability.

The principal effects of the atmosphere in the optical range are: (1) attenuation, due to energy absorption; (2) beam spreading, due to scattering of light waves; (3) beam bending, due to refocusing of optical beams; and (4) beam break-up, due to loss of field coherence over the beam front. Beam attenuation loss is computed from atmospheric absorption coefficients (in dB/length) and multiplied by atmospheric path lengths. Absorption coefficients depend on elevation angle, type of atmosphere (clear, hazy, cloudy, etc.), and wavelength. Figure 9.11a shows the dependence on wavelength, exhibiting the various regions of deep absorptions and optical windows. Figure 9.11b shows the dependence on elevation angle for a downlink optical receiver. These figures show average attenuation losses for optical downlinks, and must be accounted for in system link margins. Losses will generally be significantly higher in rain, while uplinks may exhibit deep fades for short time periods. Attenuation losses directly affect both laser and background powers, effectively reducing P_r and P_b in both direct detection and heterodyne systems.

Atmospheric scattering causes the optical beam to spread, which further dilutes the beam power at the receiver (Figure 9.12). Typical atmospheric spreading has been measured to be about 10 μradians (the received downlink beam appears to be about 10 μradians larger). If the transmitted beam is initially much wider than this, the additional spreading

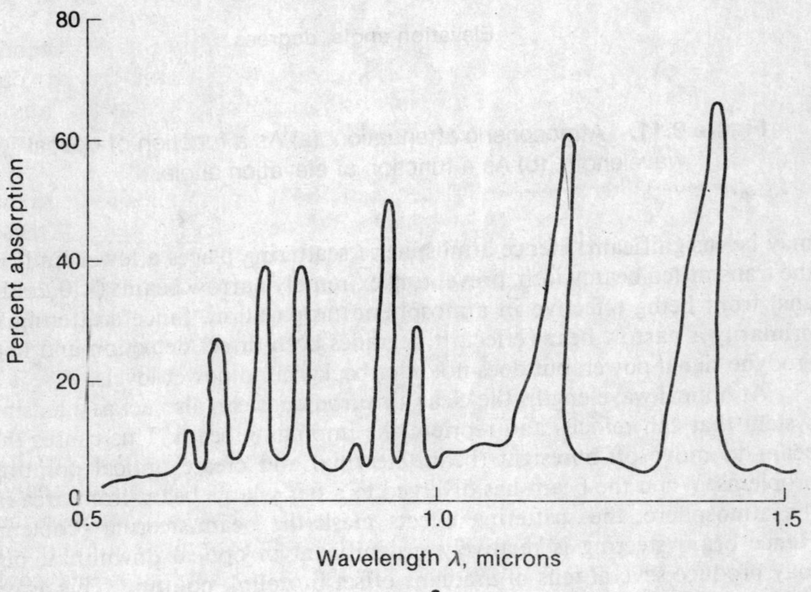

Figure 9.11. Atmospheric attenuation. (a) As a function of optical wavelength. (b) As a function of elevation angle.

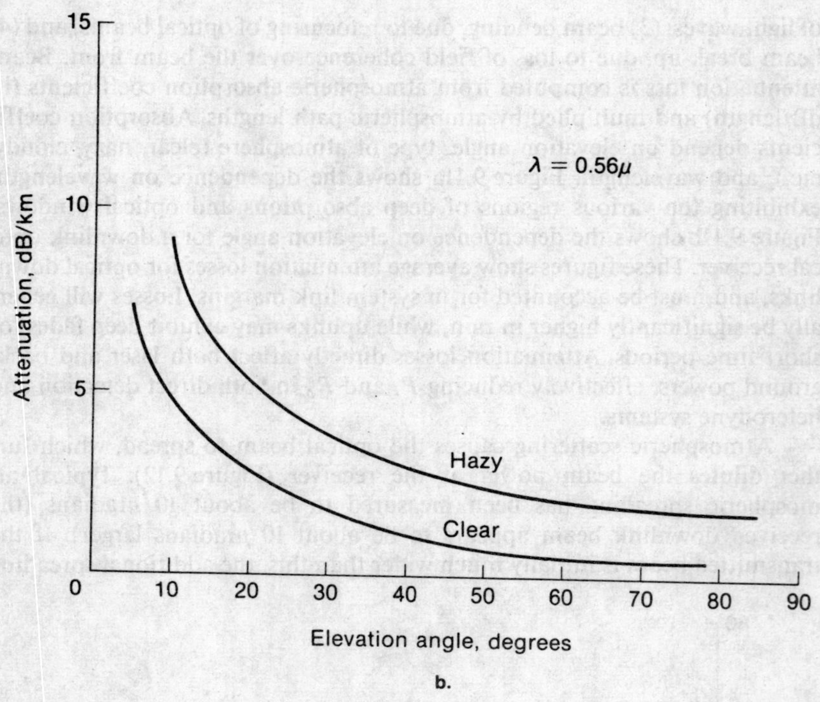

Figure 9.11. Atmospheric attenuation. (a) As a function of optical wavelength. (b) As a function of elevation angle.

may be insignificant. Hence atmospheric scattering places a lower limit to the transmitted beamwidth, preventing extremely narrow beams (<10 μradians) from being effective in atmospheric propagation. Since scattering is primarily a narrow beam effect, it degrades both direct detection and heterodyne signal power, but does not alter background power levels.

At optical wavelengths the clear air turbulence can also act as a lensing system that can refocus and reorient the impinging beam. This causes the beam to move off-boresight (beam steering) and create optical pointing problems. When the beam has diverged to a fairly large beam-front area in the atmosphere, the scattering effects mask the beam-steering problem. Hence beam steering is relatively insignificant in optical downlinks, but may produce several tens of μradians offset in uplink pointing. This again acts to defeat the advantages of narrow optical beam links. From a receiver point of view, atmospheric refocusing causes beam-wander, or variations in the expected beam arrival angle. In direct detection receivers, this forces an

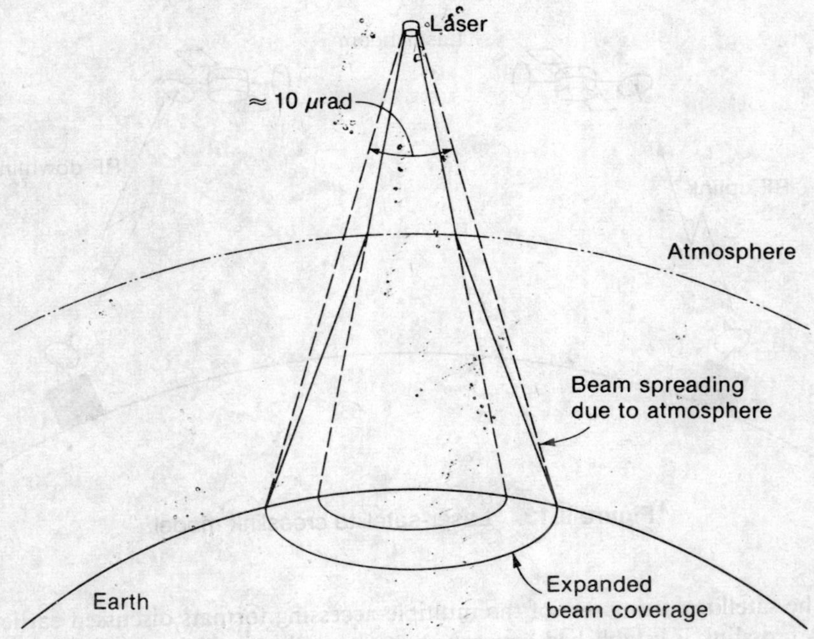

Figure 9.12. Optical beam spreading due to atmosphere.

increased field of view, while in heterodyne receivers it complicates the beam alignment problem.

The atmosphere also causes loss of beam-front coherence, so that two points on the beam front are no longer in phase. In a direct detection system, where only field power is detected, this effect may not be that serious. However, in a heterodyne system, where beam-front coherence is needed to achieve the local field mixing, beam break-up prevents heterodyning over large receiver areas. In effect, the coherence area of the beam front (area over which the beam front is optically phase coherent) limits the collecting area A_r in (9.3.11). In a clear-air atmosphere this coherence diameter may be on the order of a foot or more, but may be reduced to only several centimeters in severe turbulence [15, 16]. This means that even if a large collecting aperture is implemented, only a small portion of that area is effectively being used for beam reception in heterodyne systems.

9.4 LASER-CROSSLINK ANALYSIS

We can now analyze an actual laser crosslink. Consider the satellite system in Figure 9.13. An RF link is used for uplink and downlink transmission to

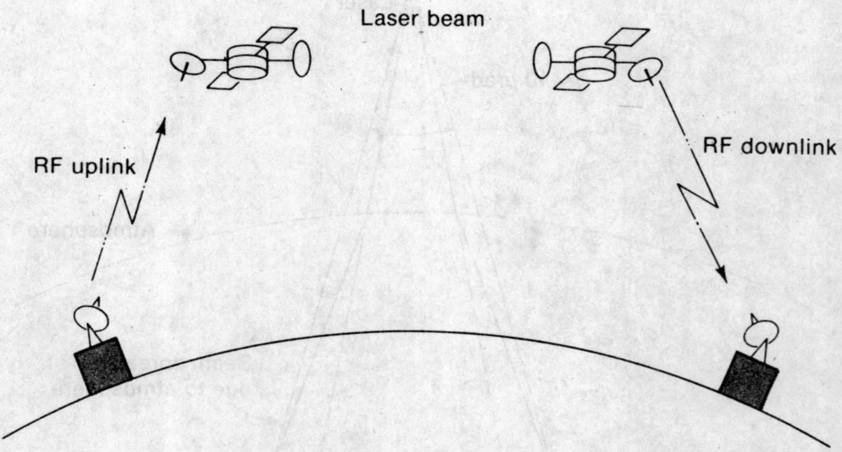

Figure 9.13. Laser-satellite crosslink model.

the satellites, using one of the multiple-accessing formats discussed earlier. A crosslink is established between the two satellites utilizing a direct detection optical link for waveform transmission. We assume a C-band RF carrier with a 500 MHz bandwidth for the uplinks. The uplink satellite uses a direct frequency translation in which the uplink carrier bandwidth is directly intensity-modulated onto the optical carrier for the crosslink. It must be assumed that the upper RF frequency at C-band is within the receiving photodetector bandwidth. If not, the uplink bandwidth must first be down-connected before laser modulation. We denote the satellite RF uplink waveform as

$$m(t) = c(t) + n_u(t) \tag{9.4.1}$$

where $c(t)$ is the RF uplink carrier and $n_u(t)$ is the uplink noise and interference. The laser power at the optical receiver is intensity-modulated as in (9.3.1)

$$P(t) = P_r[1 + \beta m(t)] \tag{9.4.2}$$

Here P_r is again the average power and β is the intensity modulation index ($\beta \leqslant 1$). The laser receiver at the receiving satellite therefore has the signal model shown in Figure 9.14. It detects a modulated signal as

$$u[\beta P_r m(t)] = u\beta P_r[c(t) + n_u(t)] \tag{9.4.3}$$

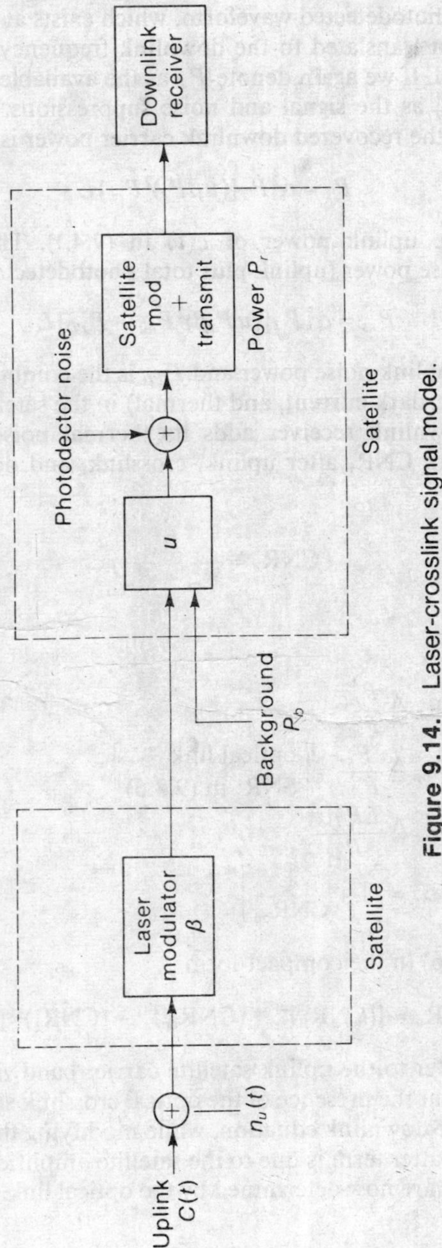

Figure 9.14. Laser-crosslink signal model.

The noise at the photodetector output is the combined noise processes in Figure 9.8. The photodetected waveform, which exists at the C-band uplink frequency, is then translated to the downlink frequency, power-amplified, and retransmitted. If we again denote P_T as the available downlink satellite power, α_s and α_n as the signal and noise suppressions, and L as the net downlink losses, the recovered downlink carrier power is

$$P_s = \alpha_s^2 P_T[(u\beta P_r)^2 P_{cu}]L \tag{9.4.4}$$

where P_{cu} is the uplink power of $c(t)$ in (9.4.1). The total downlink retransmitted noise power (uplink plus total photodetector noise) is

$$P_{ns} = \alpha_n^2 P_T[(uP_r\beta)^2 P_{nu} + P_{PD}]L \tag{9.4.5}$$

where P_{nu} is the uplink noise power and P_{PD} is the combined photodetector noise power (shot, dark current, and thermal) in the satellite bandwidth. In addition, the downlink receiver adds its thermal noise P_{nd}. Hence the resulting downlink CNR, after uplink, crosslink, and downlink transmission, is finally

$$\text{CNR}_d = \frac{P_s}{P_{ns} + P_{nd}} \tag{9.4.6}$$

Defining

$$\text{CNR}_u \triangleq \frac{P_{cu}}{P_{nu}} \tag{9.4.7a}$$

$$\text{CNR}_{\text{op}} \triangleq \frac{P_s}{P_{PD}} = \begin{bmatrix}\text{optical link} \\ \text{SNR}_s \text{ in } (9.3.5)\end{bmatrix} \tag{9.4.7b}$$

$$\text{CNR}_r \triangleq \frac{LP_T\alpha_s^2}{P_{nd}} \tag{9.4.7c}$$

$$\alpha_s^2 = \left[1 + \frac{1}{\text{CNR}_{\text{op}}}\right]^{-1} \tag{9.4.7d}$$

we can write (9.4.6) in the compact form

$$\text{CNR}_d = [(\text{CNR}_u)^{-1} + (\text{CNR}_{\text{op}})^{-1} + (\text{CNR}_r)^{-1}]^{-1} \tag{9.4.8}$$

where all CNR refer to the uplink satellite carrier bandwidth. Comparison to (3.6.3) shows that the presence of the optical crosslink simply adds a term to the basic uplink-downlink equation, while modifying the usual downlink CNR_r term. This latter term is due to the satellite amplifier carrier suppression effects, which are now determined by the optical link. We again see that

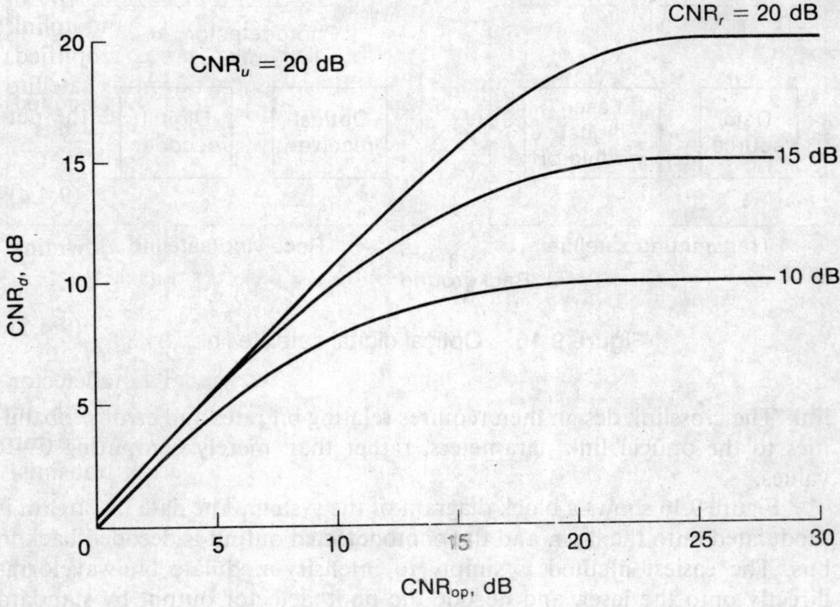

Figure 9.15. Downlink CNR degradation vs. optical crosslink CNR. CNR_r is the downlink RF CNR.

overall performance is determined by the weaker of the three links. The system is **transparent** to the optics if the optical CNR_{op} is maintained at a larger value than the individual RF uplink and downlink CNR in the satellite bandwidth. This fact is shown in Figure 9.15, in which the degradation caused by the optical link CNR_{op} (computed by the analysis of Section 9.3) on CNR_d for a specific uplink and several downlink CNR_r is plotted.

Digital Optical Crosslinks

In some cases it may be necessary to establish a laser crosslink to transmit digital data at a prescribed performance level, independent of the uplink and downlink. This may occur, for example, in a decode-encode system where data on the uplink is decoded at the satellite prior to retransmission on the crosslink. In other cases, the digital data may be generated directly at one satellite, and is to be transmitted to the other satellite via a direct optical

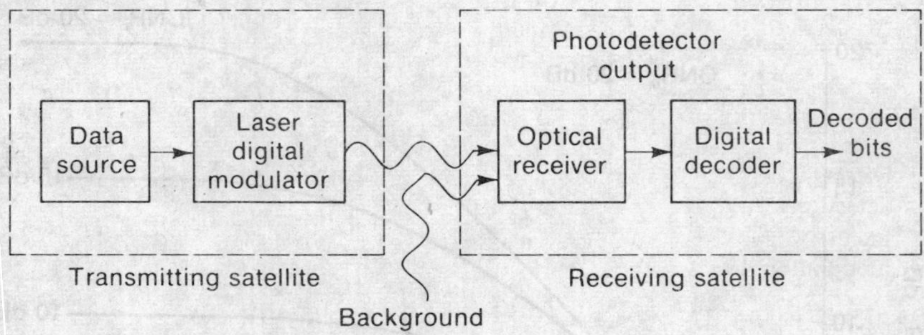

Figure 9.16. Optical digital satellite link.

link. The crosslink design then requires relating bit rates and error probabilities to the optical link parameters, rather than merely computing CNR values.

Figure 9.16 shows a block diagram of the system. The data bit stream is modulated onto the laser, and the photodetected output is decoded back to bits. The easiest method is simply to intensity-modulate bit waveforms directly onto the laser, and decode the photodetector output by standard baseband circuitry. The bit waveforms can be NRZ, Manchester, or BPSK, using a data subcarrier. NRZ systems utilize the least intensity bandwidth, while Manchester and subcarrier waveforms avoid the low-frequency (dc) optical interference. An alternative is phase (PSK) or frequency (FSK) modulating directly onto the optical carrier, using heterodyne detection with a local laser for decoding. Performance of all these sytems can be determined by using Gaussian* error probability curves, with an E_b/N_0 determined from the detected CNR derived in Section 9.3. Specifically, we evaluate the detected SNR_s at a bandwidth equal to the bit rate. Hence

$$\left(\frac{E_b}{N_0}\right) = \text{SNR}_s \Big|_{B_s = R_b = 1/T_b} \tag{9.4.9}$$

where R_b is the bit rate, T_b is the bit time, and SNR_s is obtained from either (9.3.7) or (9.3.14). Table 9.2 lists the resulting bit-error probability for sev-

*The use of Gaussian receiver statistics in computing error probabilities is only an approximation. Photodetected noise processes are shot noise processes [10] with counting statistics evolving as classes of Poisson processes [10]. It has been shown that these processes approach Gaussian statistics at high count values (number counts per bit $\gtrsim$ 50), and PE can be adequately approximated from Gaussian analysis. For further discussions of these models see Reference [10].

Table 9.2. Tabulation of digital error probabilities PE for continuous carrier modulation.

Signal Format		*PE*	E_b/N_0
Direct detection, intensity modulation	NRZ Manchester PSK	$Q\left(\sqrt{\frac{2E_b}{N_0}}\right)$	$\beta^2 \frac{K_s^2}{K_s + K_b + K_n}$ $K_s = n_s T_b$ $K_b = n_b T_b$ $K_n = (n_d + n_t) T_b$
	Noncoherent FSK	$\frac{1}{2} e^{-E_b/2N_0}$	
Heterodyne detection	PSK, FSK on optical carrier	$Q\left(\sqrt{\frac{2E_b}{N_0}}\right)$	$\frac{K_s}{1 + 2N_b + \frac{n_n}{uP_L}}$

eral encoding schemes. Hence performance can be estimated via standard Gaussian curves using the appropriate values of E_b/N_0. Note that the latter will depend primarily on the parameters:

$$\begin{aligned} K_s &\triangleq n_s T_b = \text{Number of signal counts in a bit time} \\ K_b &\triangleq n_b T_b = \text{Number of background noise counts per bit time} \\ K_n &\triangleq (n_d + n_t) T_b = \text{Number of effective detector noise counts per bit time} \end{aligned} \tag{9.4.10}$$

Thus, in laser-encoded digital systems, error probabilities can be determined directly from the number of detected signal and noise counts occurring in a bit time.

Pulsed-Laser Encoding

When either the background or receiver noise counts are high relative to the signal count, E_b/N_0 may be low, and performance for any of the schemes in Table 9.2 will be poor. This can often be improved by pulsing the laser, and

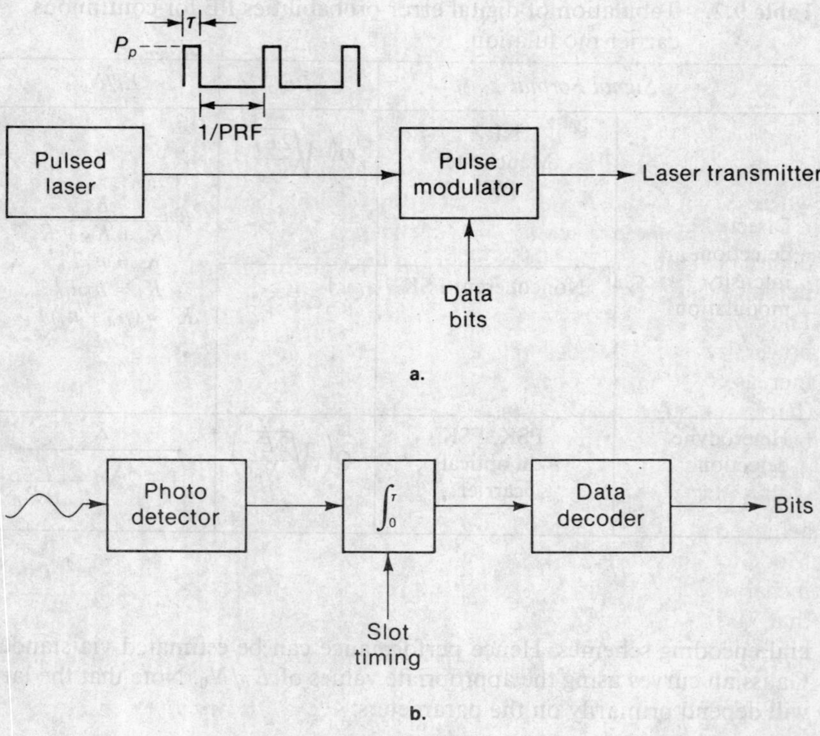

Figure 9.17. Pulsed-laser digital modulation system. (a) Pulsed transmitter. (b) Receiver decoder.

encoding the resulting light pulses (Figure 9.17a). The laser source is pulsed on and off at a prescribed **pulse repetition frequency (PRF)**, producing a light pulse with fixed pulse width (τ) and peak pulse power (P_p) every 1/PRF sec. The laser, therefore, operates at an average power P_r (referred to the receiver) satisfying

$$P_p\tau = P_r/\text{PRF} \tag{9.4.11}$$

At the receiver the pulsed laser field is photodetected (Figure 9.17b), and its output integrated over the τ-sec pulse time, producing a signal count $K_s = n_p\tau$, where n_p is the detected count rate produced during the peak power P_p. The detected pulse SNR after photodetection is now

$$\text{SNR}_s = \frac{K_s^2}{K_s + K_b + K_n}$$

$$= K_s\left[\frac{P_p}{P_p + P_b + P_n}\right] \tag{9.4.12}$$

where K_s, K_b, and K_n are detected pulse counts over a pulse time.

With average laser power constrained, SNR_s can be increased with higher peak power P_p. Hence, performance is improved by using higher and narrower laser pulses, while still maintaining the same average laser power. The noise terms in the bracket in (9.4.12) are now offset by the peak laser power, instead of by its average power. Note from (9.4.11) that peak power is increased by either decreasing PRF (slower pulse rate) or decreasing τ (narrower pulse width, with a corresponding increase in laser modulation bandwidth). The minimal value of τ is determined by the maximum photodetector bandwidth. The maximum value for P_p is determined by the largest peak power that the laser source can generate. Laser pulsing is achieved by two basic source modifications—**mode locking** and **Q-switching**. Mode locking allows laser pulses to be formed at a high PRF (hundreds of megapulses per second). Q-switching involves a cavity dumping procedure that allows extremely high pulses to be generated at a low PRF (tens of kilopulses per second).

With pulsed lasers, digital data is transmitted by encoding each of the individual pulses. In **on-off keying (OOK)** a laser pulse (or no pulse) is transmitted to represent each bit. In **quaternary encoding** the pulse, or a delayed version, is sent, with the pulse having one of two possible field polarizations. (At the receiver, two separate polarizers are needed to detect each possible polarization.) Hence two bits are sent with each laser pulse. In **pulse position modulation (PPM)** the laser pulse is delayed into one of M possible pulse locations during each pulse period. In this case $\log_2 M$ bits is sent with each pulse. In each system the corresponding error probability depends on the ability of the receiver to detect the true pulse states, which are related to the detected pulse counts. Table 9.3 lists the performance characteristics of each of these pulse-encoding formats. Note the data rate is directly related to PRF, while error probability depends on both signal and noise counts occurring in a pulse time τ.

The data rate R in Table 9.3 can also be written as

$$R = \frac{\text{Bits}}{\text{Signal count}} \cdot \frac{\text{Signal count}}{\text{Second}} \tag{9.4.13}$$

$$\triangleq \rho n_s$$

Table 9.3. Tabulation of pulsed laser formats.

Coding format	*PE*	*Rate (bits/sec)*	*Comments*
On-off keying	$\frac{1}{2}Q(\sqrt{2\mathrm{SNR}_1}) + \frac{1}{2}Q(\sqrt{2\mathrm{SNR}_0})$ $\mathrm{SNR}_1 = \frac{1}{4}\frac{(GK_s)^2}{GK_s + 2GK_b + 2K_n}$ $\mathrm{SNR}_0 = \frac{1}{4}\frac{(GK_s)^2}{2GK_b + 2K_n}$	PRF	• Threshold decode at each pulse time • Threshold = $GK_s/2$ • Perfectly synchronized pulse integrator • G = photodetector gain $K_s = n_s\tau$ $K_b = n_b\tau$ $K_n = (n_d + n_t)\tau$
Quarternary encoding	$\approx 3/2\ Q(\sqrt{2\ \mathrm{SNR}})$ $\mathrm{SNR} = \frac{(GK_s)^2}{GK_s + 2GK_b + 2K_n}$	2 PRF	• Requires polarization modulation and separation • Detect both polarization and pulse delay for decode
pulse position modulation	$\left(\frac{M/2}{M-1}\right)(M-1)\ Q(\sqrt{2\ \mathrm{SNR}})$ $\mathrm{SNR} = \frac{(GK_s)^2}{GK_s + 2GK_b + 2K_n}$	(log M) PRF	• Select maximum slot count per PPM frame • Decode log M bit word with each frame decision
Coded PPM (hard decision) • code length N • code rate γ • code distance d	$\left(\frac{M/2}{M-1}\right)(1-\gamma)\sum_{i=d}^{N}\binom{N}{i}P^i(1-P)^{N-i}$ $P = Q(\sqrt{2\ \mathrm{SNR}})$ $\mathrm{SNR} = \frac{(GK_s)^2}{GK_s + 2GK_b + 2K_n}$	γ(log M) PPF	• Decode PPM code symbol each frame • Decode sequence of code symbols as data word
Coded PPM (soft decision)	$\left(\frac{M/2}{M-1}\right)\left(\frac{d}{N}\right)\binom{N}{d}(M-1)\ Q(\sqrt{2\ \mathrm{SNR}})$ $\mathrm{SNR} = d\frac{(GK_s)^2}{GK_s + 2GK_b + 2K_n}$	γ(log M) PRF	• Accumulate slot counts over N frames • Decode code sequence after N frame accumulation

Here ρ is called the **quantum efficiency**, and has units of bits per detected photoelectron. The achieved efficiency depends on the encoding scheme and the desired bit-error probability of the receiver. Equation (9.4.13) separates the achievable data rate into a product of a term ρ depending on the encoding format, and a term n_s depending on the average laser power. The advantage of this interpretation is that it can be evaluated for all types of encoding—pulsed or intensity modulation. Figure 9.18 plots link bit-error

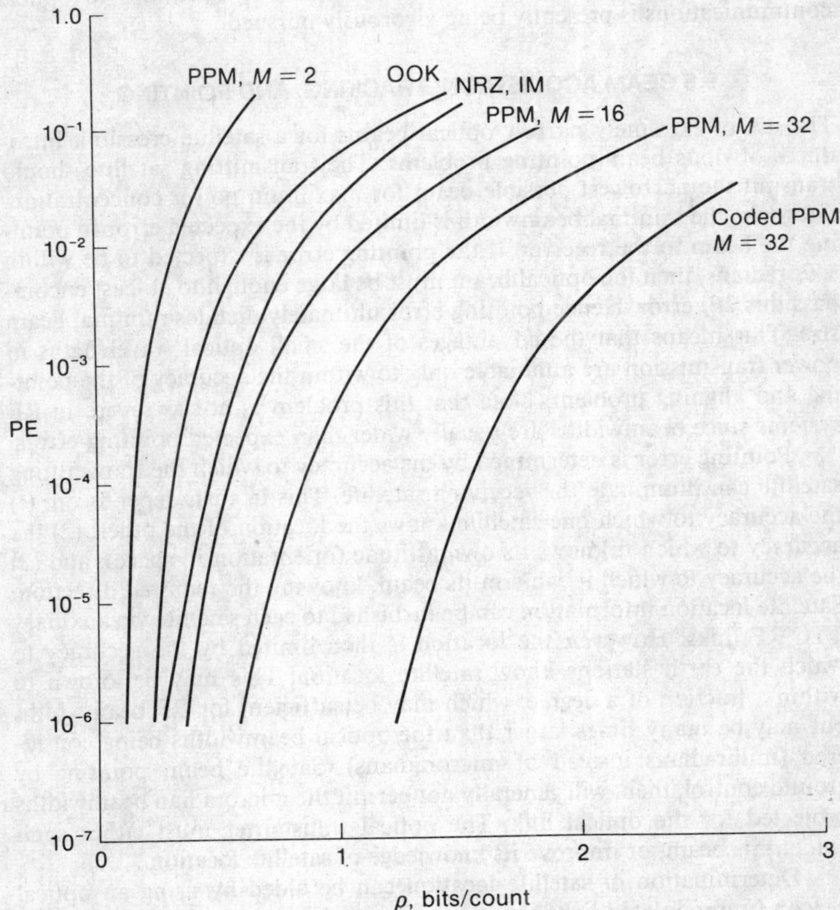

Figure 9.18. Bit-error probability vs. quantum efficiency for digital laser modulation.

probability as a function of ρ for several such formats. As ρ is increased, either by attempting to encode more bits or by reducing the signal count, the system error probability increases. In order to reduce PE at a fixed ρ it is necessary to increase the complexity of the encoding (and therefore the decoding). If a desired PE is to be achieved, one can read off the required ρ that must be attained by the stated formats. The resulting bit rate of the link follows from (9.4.13). In general, ρ will be limited to $\rho \leqslant 1$, in which case n_s in counts/sec is an immediate upper limit to the bit rate in bps. The development of improved pulse encoding and decoding hardware in optical communications is presently being vigorously pursued.

9.5 BEAM ACQUISITION, TRACKING, AND POINTING

The use of extremely narrow optical beams for a satellite crosslink introduces obvious beam-pointing problems. The transmitting satellite should transmit the narrowest possible beam for maximum power concentration. However, the minimal beamwidth is limited by the expected error in pointing the beam to the receiver. If the pointing error is expected to be within $\pm\,\theta_e$ radians, then the optical beam must be large enough to at least encompass this $2\theta_e$ error. Hence pointing error ultimately dictates minimal beam size. This means that the advantages of the small optical wavelengths in power transmission are attainable only to within the accuracy of the pointing and aligning problem. Note that this problem is not as severe in RF systems since beamwidths are usually wider than expected pointing errors.

Pointing error is determined by the accuracy to which the transmitting satellite can illuminate the receiving satellite. This in turn depends on: (1) the accuracy to which one satellite knows the location of the other; (2) the accuracy to which it knows its own attitude (orientation in space); and (3) the accuracy to which it can aim its beam, knowing the required direction. Satellite location information can be furnished to each satellite via auxiliary TTC RF links. However, the location is then limited by the accuracy to which the earth stations know satellite location. This may be known to within a fraction of a degree, which may be sufficient for RF beamwidths but may be many times larger than the optical beamwidths being considered (milliradians instead of microradians). Satellite beam pointing by ground control, then, will generally not permit the microradian beamwidths projected for the optical link. The optical transmitter must either **spoil** (widen) its beam, or improve its knowledge of satellite location.

Determination of satellite location can be aided by using an optical beacon (unmodulated light source) transmitted from the receiving satellite back to the transmitting satellite. The transmitting satellite first receives the beacon, then transmits its modulated laser beam back toward the beacon direction of arrival. The uncertainty in absolute satellite location by the earth station is therefore transferred to the smaller uncertainty in reading beacon arrival direction. As the satellites drift, or if the satellites are in relative motion (e.g., one may be synchronous and one may be in a low Earth orbit), the beacon must be continually tracked in time to provide updated position information. Note that the beacon can use a wider beam to ensure illumination of the other satellite, but its arrival angle can be measured to a resolution well within its original uncertainty angle.

When the beams are extremely narrow there exists the possibility that the receiving satellite may have moved out of the transmitter's beamwidth during the round-trip transmission time. It is then necessary that the transmitting satellite "point-ahead" from its measured beacon arrival direc-

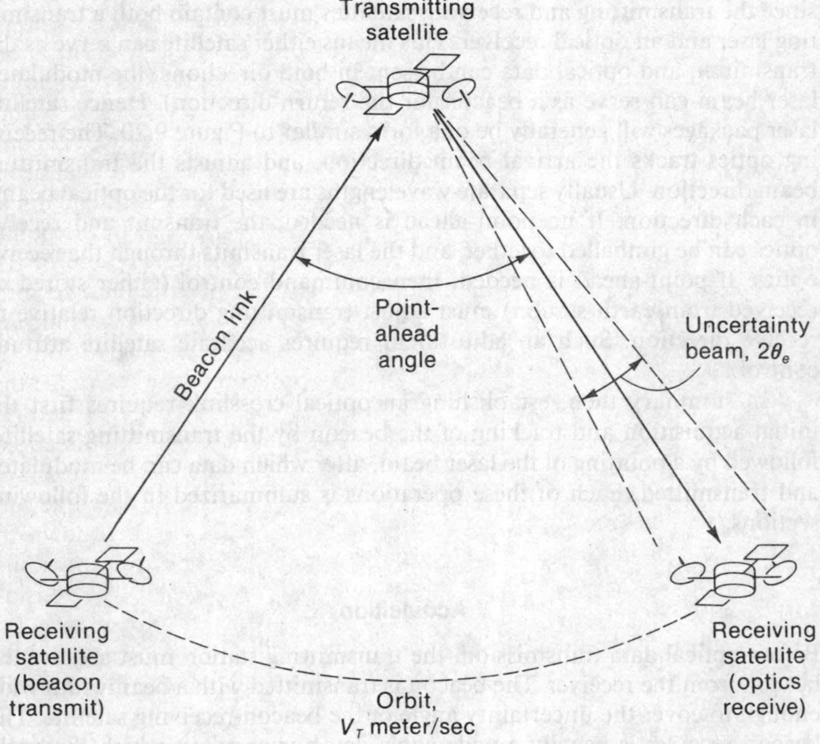

Figure 9.19. Required beam widths and point-ahead model for optical pointing.

tion (Figure 9.19). If the relative tangential velocity of the satellites is V_T meters/sec, then a point-ahead of

$$\alpha = \frac{V_T}{150}\,\mu radians \tag{9.5.1}$$

is required. If this exceeds one-half the beamwidth, then point-ahead must be used. This means the transmitting laser cannot transmit back through the same optics from which the beacon is received. Note that the point-ahead angle is independent of the satellite crosslink distance. For velocities at Earth-orbiting speeds ($V_T = 30$ km/s) point-ahead angles up to approximately 200 μrad may be expected. For beamwidths on the order of 10–100 μrad, the point-ahead angle may therefore be many multiples of the beamwidth.

The use of a beacon modifies the optical hardware on each satellite, since the transmitting and receiving satellites must contain both a transmitting laser and an optical receiver. This means either satellite can serve as the transmitter, and optical data can be sent in both directions (the modulated laser beam can serve as a beacon for the return direction). Hence satellite laser packages will generally be of a form similar to Figure 9.20. The receiving optics tracks the arrival beam direction, and adjusts the transmitting beam direction. Usually separate wavelengths are used for the optical beams in each direction. If no point-ahead is needed, the transmit and receive optics can be gimballed together, and the laser transmits through the receive optics. If point-ahead is needed, then command control (either stored or received from earth station) must adjust transmitting direction relative to receive direction. Such an adjustment requires accurate satellite attitude control.

In summary then, establishing an optical crosslink requires first the initial acquisition and tracking of the beacon by the transmitting satellite, followed by a pointing of the laser beam, after which data can be modulated and transmitted. Each of these operations is summarized in the following sections.

Acquisition

Before optical data transmission, the transmitting station must acquire the beacon from the receiver. The beacon is transmitted with a beamwidth wide enough to cover the uncertainty angle of the beacon-receiving satellite. The beacon receiver is usually a wide-angle detector array, in which the combined field of views of the array elements cover a portion of the uncertainty beamwidth of the beacon transmitter. The array field of view must then be

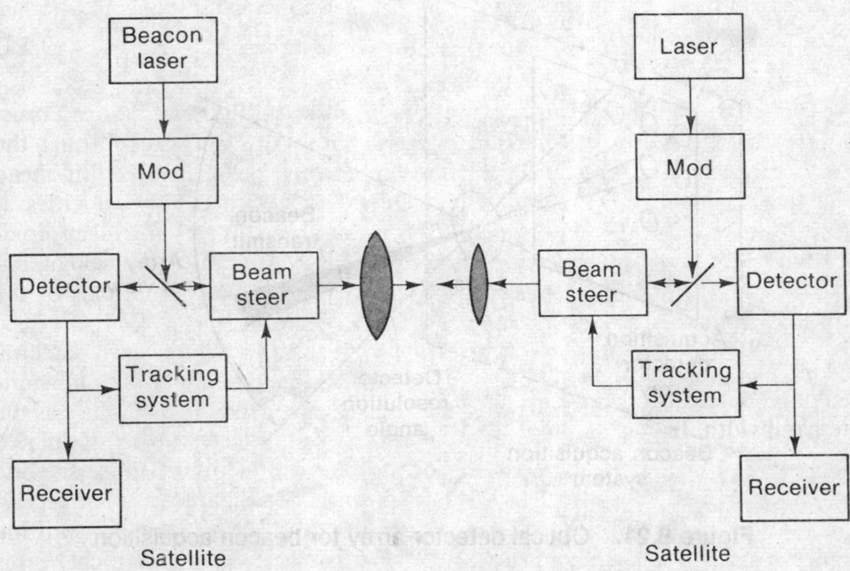

Figure 9.20. Optical transmitter and receiver block diagrams for optical satellites.

scanned to cover the total uncertainty angle. Detection of the array element illuminated by the laser beacon (see Figure 9.21) determines the beacon location to within the resolution angle of the element. The amount of beacon power impinging on the correct array detector can be computed from (9.1.2) with θ_b the beacon beamwidth and A_d the detector receiving area.

The amount of noise on each detector can be computed from the detection model in Figure 9.8. From these, the signal and noise count rates can be determined for each detector of the wide-angle array. This allows computation of acquisition probabilities, depending on the test used to decide which element of the array is being illuminated [see Reference 10, chapter 11]. As a rough rule of thumb, if n_s and n_n are the beacon and total noise count rates of the array elements, satisfactory acquisition requires

$$n_s \geqslant 10 n_n \tag{9.5.2a}$$

and

$$n_s T_{\text{in}} \cong 10 \tag{9.5.2b}$$

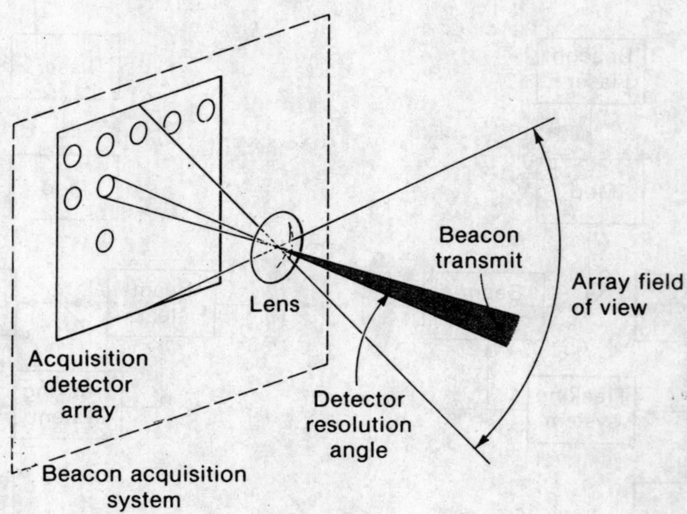

Figure 9.21. Optical detector array for beacon acquisition.

where T_{in} is the detector integration time. Equation (9.5.2a) requires the beacon power to sufficiently exceed the noise power, while (9.5.2b) sets the laser energy level for acquisition.

The parameter n_n depends on the detector field of view, and the latter relates the array size and array field of view. If θ_d is the detector beamwidth and if there are Q detectors in the array, the array field of view is $Q(\theta_d)^2$ steradians, and it will take $(\theta_u^2/Q\theta_d^2)$ scans to cover the uncertainty field of view. At each scan location, we must spend T_{in} sec observing each detector output. Hence the total acquisition time for a single coverage of the uncertainty region (neglecting beam propagation time) is

$$\begin{aligned} T_{acq} &= \left[\frac{\theta_u^2}{Q\theta_d^2}\right] QT_{in} \\ &= \left(\frac{\theta_u}{\theta_d}\right)^2 T_{in} \end{aligned} \tag{9.5.3}$$

Equations (9.5.2) and (9.5.3) relate power levels and acquisition time for an array detector. As the field of view of the elemental detectors are reduced, less noise is received and the beacon count rate needed to produce the desired acquisition probability decreases, but the acquisition time increases. Figure 9.22 plots required n_s and T_{acq} as a function of detector field of view,

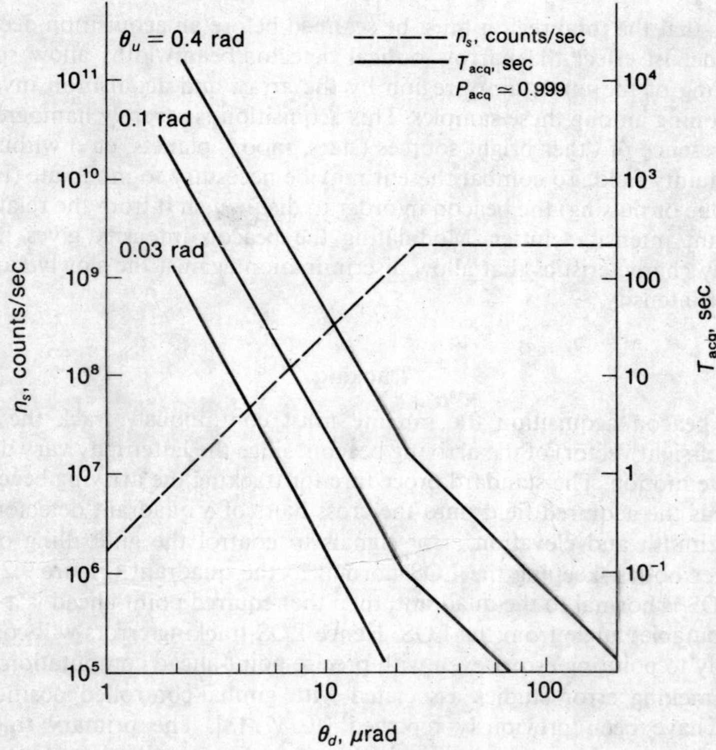

Figure 9.22. Required beacon count rate and acquisition time vs. array detector field of view.

for several uncertainty beam angles, exhibiting these effects. A background model based on the solar sky at a wavelength of 1 micron with a 10Å bandwidth optical filter was used. If it is assumed that the beacon count is known, Figure 9.22 is entered at the left ordinate, projected across the n_s curve, and the required detector viewing angle and resulting acquisition time for the given uncertainty are read off. Conversely, for a given detector view angle one can read vertically to determine the required beacon count and approximate acquisition time. Some methods have been suggested [10, chapter 11] for using arrays to reduce acquisition time at the expense of increased receiver processing.

The use of (9.5.2) is based on acquisition using comparison tests among the detector integrated counts from the entire uncertainty region. This means that the total region must be scanned before an acquisition decision is made. In effect the narrow optical detector beamwidths allow spatial sampling of the uncertainty region by the array, and acquisition involves decisioning among these samples. This acquisition is severely hampered by the presence of other bright sources (stars, moon, planets, etc.) within the uncertainty field. To combat these it may be necessary to modulate (intensity tone or pulsing) the beacon in order to distinguish it from the relatively constant intensity clutter. Modulating the beacon intensity gives it frequency characteristics that allow discrimination against the slowly varying clutter intensity.

Tracking

After beacon acquisition the satellite must continuously track the LOS (line-of-sight vector) of the arriving beacon, since the latter may vary due to relative motion. The standard procedure for tracking the arriving beacon is to focus the acquired field onto the cross hairs of a quadrant detector and use azimuth and elevation error signals to control the gimballing of the receiver optics, keeping the LOS normal to the quadrant (Figure 9.23). If the LOS is normal to the quadrant, then the required point-ahead is a fixed (computable) angle from the LOS. Hence LOS-tracking errors will convert directly to pointing errors even with precise point-ahead computation.

Tracking error studies associated with gimbal-controlled positioning loops have been previously reported [10, 17, 18]. The primary tracking errors are caused by motion of the LOS, noise, clutter, and internal mechanical vibrations. LOS motion should be minimal when both satellites are in synchronous orbits. If satellites are in near-earth orbits, the tracking loop bandwidth B_L must be large enough to cover the LOS rotation. If Ω_L is the angular rotation rate of the LOS in rad/sec, we require approximately

$$B_L \geqslant \Omega_L/4 \tag{9.5.4}$$

for accurate LOS tracking. The rms tracking error due to quadrant detector noise is given by

$$\theta_{\text{rms}} = \frac{1.4\lambda/d}{\sqrt{\text{SNR}_s}} \tag{9.5.5}$$

where λ is the optical beacon wavelength, d is the beacon receiver diameter, and SNR_s is the quadrant detector SNR given by

$$\text{SNR}_s = \left(\frac{16n_s}{3\pi B_L}\right)\left[\frac{n_s}{n_s + 4n_n}\right] \tag{9.5.6}$$

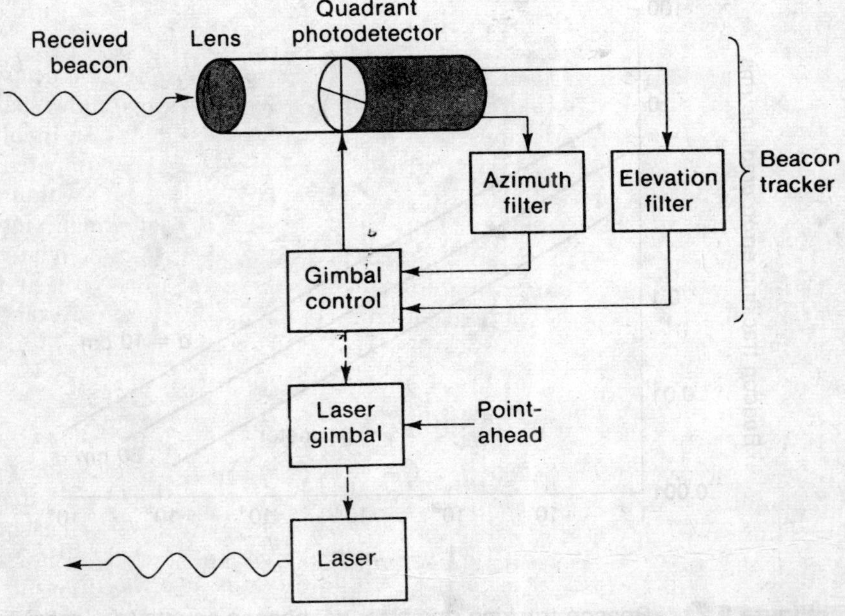

Figure 9.23. Optical beacon-tracking subsystem.

Here n_s is the beacon count rate and n_n is the total noise count per each quadrant detector. Figure 9.24 plots beacon-tracking error as a function of beacon count rate n_s for several diameters d and loop bandwidths B_L, assuming $n_s >> n_n$. Note that for $n_s = 10^5$ counts/sec, a 1 KHz bandwidth, negligible noise, and a 1-foot beacon receiver at 1 micron, an rms tracking error of roughly half a microradian, can be maintained.

Tracking errors due to internal vibrations can be reduced by ensuring that the tracking loop tracks out the vibrations. This requires the loop bandwidth B_L to exceed the significant frequencies of the vibration spectrum, the latter generally extending out to about 10 Hz. Hence internal vibrations place lower bounds on tracking-loop bandwidths. Bias error due to detector imbalance and background clutter may be the severest hindrance to accurate beam tracking. These effects add constant offsets to the loop-control signals that can steer the receiver from the LOS. Detector imbalance can often be compensated, although the imbalance is related to the detector gain and dark current, both of which are random and can change in time. Clutter effects can be the most severe. If clutter (light sources) appears in the beacon field of view, it can possibly capture the

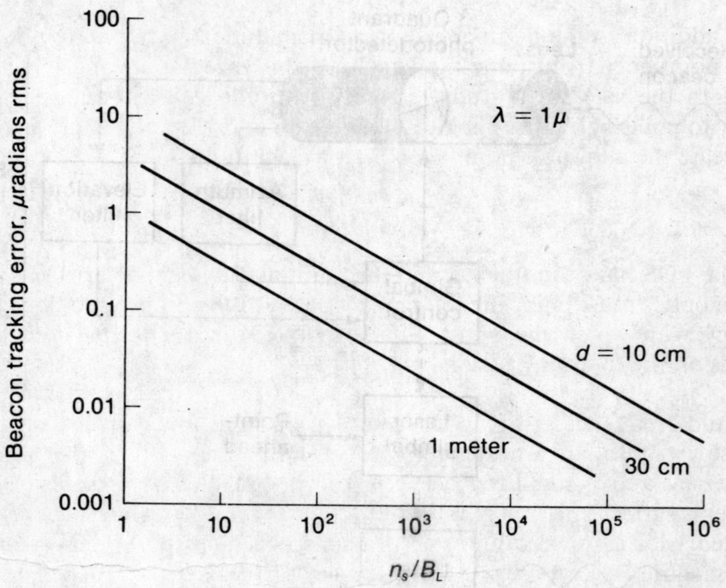

Figure 9.24. Beacon-tracking rms error vs. beacon counts (d = receive optics diameter, B_L = tracking loop bandwidth).

tracking operation. This again can be combated by either modulating the beacon or ensuring that the beacon count dominates over the clutter count.

Point-Ahead

If point-ahead is required, the satellite laser transmitter must point ahead by the proper angle and direction, with the former given by (9.5.1). It is expected that in typical system concepts the required point-ahead will be transmitted as commands from the earth station through the RF or microwave links. The point-ahead accuracy will therefore depend on how well the earth station can predict the instantaneous V_T and how accurately and how often it is transmitted to the satellite. If the satellite obtains V_T with a total error of ΔV_T meters/sec, then a pointing error of $\Delta\alpha = \Delta V_T/150$ μradians will occur. Operation with less than 1 microradian point-ahead angle error requires tangential velocity accuracy within 150 meters/sec. Present satellite capability in measuring V_T is well below 50 meters/sec, so the primary concern is the accuracy to which the true tangential velocity can be decoded at the satellite, considering quantization and data errors.

In addition to the point-ahead angle magnitude, the orientation angle of the point-ahead must be known. Since this orientation angle is with respect to the satellite attitude, errors in attitude control will translate directly to pointing errors. The overall effect of an orientation angle error is to decrease the allowable point-ahead error magnitude $\Delta\alpha$.

Pointing

After the LOS has been tracked and the point-ahead angle determined, the satellite optics must point the return data beam to the proper position. The accuracy with which the optics can be pointed in the desired direction depends on the following factors:

1. Attitude reference errors in the satellite. In order to point, the satellite must establish an attitude reference. This is generally accomplished either by a gyro-stabilized platform or via star and sun sensors. Gyro systems suffer from inherent drift effects that must be continually recalibrated. Star sensing requires separate star-tracking subsystems to align the satellite axis.
2. Mechanical and structural variations. Inherent vibrations, material stress, and component disturbances cause the axis of the spacecraft to become misaligned.
3. Boresight errors. The transmitting optics and gimbals produce errors in the ability to aim a narrow beam in the exact direction required. This problem is avoided if the received beacon and transmitted data use common optics, but must be considered when point-ahead is required.

Although the contributions of these error sources may be relatively small, the primary difficulty is that the errors are open-loop errors that cannot be corrected unless the entire pointing operation is closed around the satellite pair. This can be achieved by monitoring the received optical beam and transmitting pointing corrections to the other satellite. The vibration and boresight errors can generally be maintained below 1 microradian, and therefore the attitude control will be the dominant contributor to overall pointing accuracy.

PROBLEMS

9.1 The count rate n, defined in (9.1.4) actually refers to the number of **photons** collected from a quantum-mechanical field. (For this reason, an optical receiver is often called a **photon bucket**.) Prove that

$n_r T$ is the number of field photons occurring in a time period T. [*Hint*: The energy of a photon of frequency f_0 is hf_0.]

9.2 (a) Plot the gain and beamwidth of an optical ($\lambda = 1\mu$) antenna as a function of aperture diameter d. (b) Plot the propagation loss at the same λ as a function of distance.

9.3 In a properly designed lensing system with focal length f_c, the field imaged on the detector $f_d(x,y)$ is the two-dimensional Fourier transform of the field passing through the lens aperture, $f_l(x,y)$. That is,

$$f_d(x,y) = \int_{\text{plane}} f_l(u,v) \exp\left[-j\frac{2\pi}{\lambda f_c}(xu + yv) \right] du dv$$

Assume an arriving plane wave (field constant over an infinite plane), and a square lens aperture of width d. Compute the imaged field.

9.4 In certain optical detection models, the count detected over a time interval has a Poisson distribution, in which the probability that the count is n (an integer) is given by

$$P(n) = \frac{K^n}{n!} e^{-K}$$

where K is the mean interval count. Use this to write the Poisson error probability of an M-slot PPM system, assuming the pulsed slot has mean count $K_s + K_b$, and all other slots have mean count K_b. Pulse decoding is based on selecting the signal slot as that with the largest count.

9.5 Given a blackbody background at temperature 300° Kelvin. How much noise per Hz would be collected at wavelength of 0.5μ in an optical receiver area of 2 meters^2 and a 1-degree field of view? [*Hint*: Use Figure 9.6.)

9.6 The **noise equivalent power (NEP)** of an optical receiver is defined as the value of received power P_r such that $\sqrt{\text{SNR}_s} = 1$ in a 1 Hz noise bandwidth. Use (9.3.5) or (9.3.6) to derive an equation for the NEP of an optical receiver with shot noise, background noise, dark current, and thermal noise.

9.7 It is desired to send 10^5 bps with OOK encoding over a quantum-limited optical (1μ) channel from Jupiter (10^{10} km) and achieve a

PE = 10^{-4}. How many joules (watt-sec) are required from a source having a 6-inch transmitting lens, assuming the receiver uses a 2 $meter^2$ area?

9.8 A 4-bit PPM direct detection optical communication system is desired with a word-error probability of 10^{-4}, and has a background count energy of $K_b = 3$ in each slot. Approximately how many joules per pulse must be received to operate the system. (1 Joule = 1 watt-sec).

9.9 An optical PPM system uses a source of average power P and pulse repetition rate of r pulses per sec. Derive the equation for the peak pulse power in a system sending R bits per sec.

REFERENCES

1. J. Geusic, W. Bridges, and J. Pankove, "Coherent Optical Sources for Communications," *Proc. IEEE* (October 1970).

2. B. Lengyel, *Introduction to Laser Physics* (New York: Wiley, 1966).

3. I. Kaminow, and A. Siegman, *Laser Devices and Applications* (New York: IEEE Press, 1973).

4. W. Pratt, *Laser Communication Systems* (New York: Wiley, 1969), chapter 3.

5. M. Ross, *Laser Receivers* (New York: Wiley, 1966).

6. A. Yariv, *Quantum Electronics* 2d ed. (New York: Wiley, 1975).

7. W. Spicer, and F. Wooten, "Photoemission and Photomultipliers," *Proc. IEEE* (August 1963).

8. L. Anderson, and B. McMurty, "High Speed Photodetectors," *Proc. IEEE* (October 1966).

9. J. Jamieson, et al., *Infrared Physics and Engineering* (New York: McGraw-Hill, 1963).

10. R. Gagliardi, and S. Karp, *Optical Communications* (New York: Wiley, 1975), chapter 4.

11. P. Kruse, et al., *Elements of Infrared Technology* (New York: Wiley, 1962).

12. A. Van der Ziel, *Noise* (Englewood Cliffs, N.J.: Prentice-Hall, 1954).

13. N. Kapeika, and J. Bordogna, "Background Noise in Optical Systems," *Proc. IEEE* (October 1970).

14. T. Merrit, and F. Hall, "Blackbody Radiation," *Proc. IRE*, vol. 47–9 (September 1959).

15. D. L. Fried, "Atmospheric Noise in an Optical Heterodyne Receiver," *IEEE Trans. on Quantum Electronics*, AE-3, June 1967.

16. D. L. Fried, "Limiting Resolution Through the Atmosphere," *Journal Optical Soc.*, vol. 56–10 (October 1966).

17. R. Gagliardi and M. Sheikh, "Pointing Error Statistics in Optical Beam Tracking," *IEEE Trans. on Aerospace and Electronic Systems*, vol. AES-16, No. 5, September 1980, pp. 674-682.

18. R. Gagliardi, V. Vilnrotter, and S. Dolinar, "Optical Deep Space Communications via Relay Satellite," *Jet Propulsion Labratory Report*, JPL-81-40, August 1981.

A
Review of Digital Communications

This appendix is a detailed backup for some of the results presented in Chapter 2. The objective is to guide the interested reader through some of the mathematical steps leading to equations, figures, and tabulations presented in that chapter. Further detail can be found in the references given at the end of this appendix.

A.1 BASEBAND DIGITAL WAVEFORMS

Let a data modulated baseband waveform be written as

$$m(t) = \sum_{k=-\infty}^{\infty} d_k p(t - kT_b + \epsilon) \tag{A.1.1}$$

where $\{d_k\}$ is a sequence of independent, binary random variables, each ± 1 and equal likely, and ϵ is a uniformly distributed location variable over $(0, T_b)$. Define the waveform correlation as

$$R_m(\tau) = \mathcal{E}[m(t)m(t+\tau)] \tag{A.1.2}$$

where $\mathcal{E}$ is the expectation operator. It therefore follows that *m(t)* in (A.1.1) has the correlation

$$\begin{aligned} R_m(\tau) &= \sum_k \sum_q \mathcal{E}[d_k d_q] \mathcal{E}[p(t - kT_b + \epsilon) \times p(t + \tau - qT_b + \epsilon)] \\ &= \sum_k \frac{1}{T_b} \int_{t+kT_b}^{t+(k+1)T_b} p(u)p(u+\tau)du \\ &= R_{pp}(\tau) \end{aligned} \tag{A.1.3}$$

where

$$R_{pp}(\tau) \triangleq \frac{1}{T_b}\int_{-\infty}^{\infty} p(t)p(t+\tau)dt \tag{A.1.4}$$

The spectral density of *m(t)* is the Fourier transform of $R_m(\tau)$, and is then

$$\begin{aligned} S_m(\omega) &= \text{Fourier transform of } R_{pp}(\tau) \\ &= \frac{1}{T_b}|F_p(\omega)|^2 \end{aligned}$$

where

$$F_p(\omega) = \int_{-\infty}^{\infty} p(t)e^{-j\omega t}\,dt \tag{A.1.5}$$

Hence, the Fourier transform of the bit waveform in (A.1.5) determines the spectral density of the baseband sequence. Some specific examples of baseband waveforms are: (1) the NRZ waveform,

$$\begin{aligned} p(t) &= 1 \qquad 0 \leqslant t \leqslant T_b \\ &= 0 \qquad \text{elsewhere} \end{aligned} \tag{A.1.6}$$

for which the Fourier transform produces

$$|F_p(\omega)|^2 = T_b^2\left|\frac{\sin(\omega T_b/2)}{(\omega T_b/2)}\right|^2 \tag{A.1.7}$$

and (2) the Manchester waveform,

$$\begin{aligned} p(t) &= 1 \qquad 0 \leqslant t \leqslant T_b/2 \\ &= -1 \qquad T_b/2 \leqslant t \leqslant T_b \\ &= 0 \qquad \text{elsewhere} \end{aligned} \tag{A.1.8}$$

for which

$$\begin{aligned} F_p(\omega) &= \int_0^{T_b/2} e^{-j\omega t}\,dt - \int_{T_b/2}^{T_b} e^{-j\omega t}\,dt \\ &= \frac{2\sin(\omega T_b/2) - \sin(\omega T_b)}{\omega} + j\frac{2\cos(\omega T_b/2) - (1+\cos\omega T_b)}{\omega} \end{aligned} \tag{A.1.9}$$

Using

$$2 \sin^2 \omega T_b = 1 \cos 2\omega T_b$$
$$4 \sin^4(\omega T_b/2) = 1 - 2 \cos(\omega T_b/2) + \cos^2(\omega T_b/2)$$

allows us to write

$$F_p(\omega) = \frac{4}{\omega^2}[\sin^4(\omega T_b/4)] \tag{A.1.10}$$

These spectra are plotted in Figure 2.6 in Chapter 2.

A.2 BPSK SYSTEMS

BPSK carriers are obtained by modulating baseband sequences onto carriers. The waveform is then

$$c(t) = Am(t) \cos(\omega_c t + \psi) \tag{A.2.1}$$

where $m(t)$ is of the form of (A.1.1) and ψ is taken as a random phase, uniformly distributed over $(0, 2\pi)$. The carrier has correlation function

$$\begin{aligned} R_c(\tau) &= A^2 \mathscr{E}[m(t)m(t+\tau)]\mathscr{E}[\cos(\omega_c t + \psi) \cos[\omega_c(t+\tau) + \psi]] \\ &= \frac{A^2}{2} R_m(\tau) \cos(\omega_c \tau) \end{aligned} \tag{A.2.2}$$

Its spectral density is then

$$\begin{aligned} S_c(\omega) &= \frac{A^2}{2}[S_m(\omega) \otimes] \left[\frac{1}{2}\delta(\omega + \omega_c) + \frac{1}{2}\delta(\omega - \omega_c)\right] \\ &= \frac{A^2}{4}[S_m(\omega + \omega_c) + S_m(\omega - \omega_c)] \end{aligned} \tag{A.2.3}$$

where $\otimes$ denotes frequency convolution. Hence the BPSK carrier has a spectrum obtained by shifting the spectrum of $m(t)$ to $\pm \omega_c$.

Decoding of BPSK in the presence of Gaussian noise is achieved by coherent phase correlation, followed by bit integration (see Figure 2.16). Letting

$$r(t) = 2p(t) \cos(\omega_c t + \hat{\psi}) \tag{A.2.4}$$

be the local reference, the decoder therefore forms over each bit interval the decoding variable

$$z \triangleq \int_0^{T_b} [c(t) + n(t)]r(t)dt \tag{A.2.5}$$

where $n(t)$ is a white Gaussian noise process of one-sided spectral level N_0. Bit decisioning is then made on the sign of z. For the data sequence in (A.1.1), with $p(t)$ normalized to unit power, we have

$$z = Ad_0 T_b \cos \psi_e + A \sum_{k \neq 0} d_k r_{pp}(k) \cos \psi_e + n \tag{A.2.6}$$

where d_0 is the present bit, n is a Gaussian variable with variance $N_0 T_b/2$, ψ_e is the phase-reference error, and

$$r_{pp}(k) = \frac{1}{T_b} \int_0^{T_b} p(t)p(t - kT_b)dt \tag{A.2.7}$$

The first term is the data bit being decoded and the second term represents intersymbol interference (II) from other bits. If the data pulse $p(t)$ is restricted to a bit time [$p(t) = 0$, t outside $(0, T_b)$], we have $r_{pp}(k) = 0$, $k \neq 0$, and there is no II. The probability that a bit error will occur (z has the opposite sign from d_0) in the absence of II is then

$$\text{PE} = Q\left[\left(\frac{2E_b}{N_0}\right)^{1/2} \cos \psi_e\right] \tag{A.2.8}$$

where

$$\frac{E_b}{N_0} = \frac{(A^2/2)T_b}{N_0} \tag{A.2.9}$$

and

$$Q[x] = \frac{1}{2\pi} \int_x^{\infty} e^{-t^2/2} dt \tag{A.2.10}$$

The $Q(x)$ function is the well-known Gaussian tail integral [1], and is shown in Figure A.1 along with some often used approximations. When used in the form of (A.2.8) with $\psi_e = 0$, the BPSK curve in Figure 2.17 results.

If the phase error ψ_e is a random variable, then PE in (A.2.8) must be averaged over the statistics of ψ_e. Hence we formally write

$$\text{PE} = \int_{-\infty}^{\infty} \text{PE}(\psi_e) p(\psi_e) d\psi_e \tag{A.2.11}$$

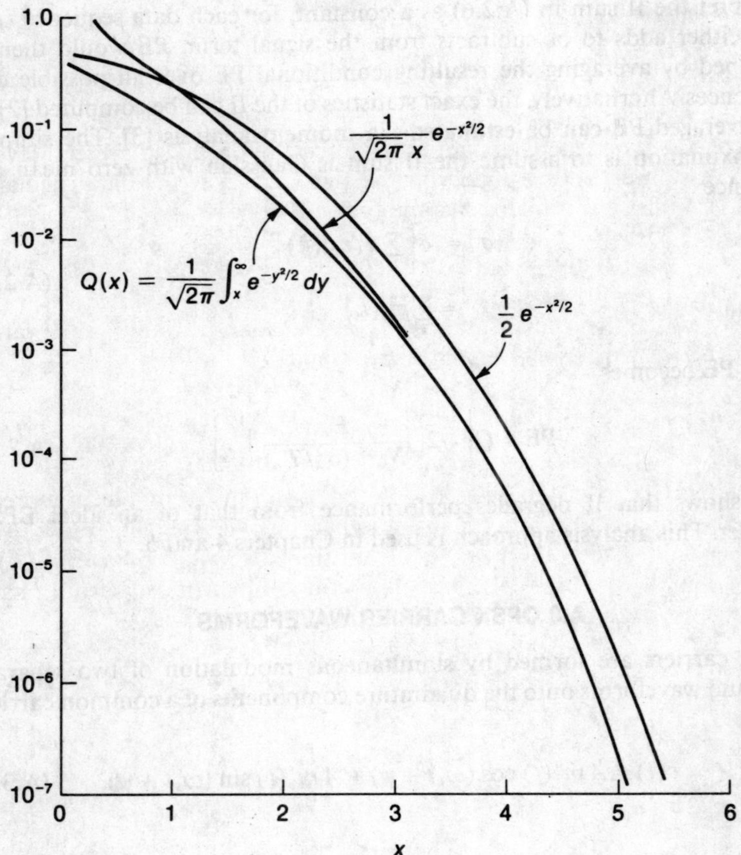

Figure A.1. Gaussian tail integral $Q(x)$ and some approximations.

For a Gaussian phase error having zero mean and variance σ_e^2, this becomes

$$\mathrm{PE} = \int_{-\infty}^{\infty} Q\left[\left(\frac{2E_b}{N_0}\right)^{1/2} \cos x\right] \frac{e^{-x^2/2\sigma_e^2}}{\sqrt{2\pi}\,\sigma_e} dx \tag{A.2.12}$$

The resulting integration is shown in Figure 2.19, for several σ_e values. The result shows how BPSK performance is degraded with nonperfect phase referencing.

If the system is phase coherent ($\psi_e = 0$) and II occurs, the statistics of the interference must be incorporated. Formally, it would be necessary to interpret the II sum in (A.2.6) as a constant, for each data sequence $\{d_k\}$, that either adds to or subtracts from the signal term. PE would then be obtained by averaging the resulting conditional PE over all possible data sequences. Alternatively, the exact statistics of the II can be computed [2], or the averaged PE can be estimated via moment analysis [3]. The simplest approximation is to assume the II sum is Gaussian with zero mean and variance

$$\begin{aligned}\sigma_I^2 &= \mathscr{E}\Big[\sum_k d_k r_{pp}(k)\Big]^2 \\ &= \sum_k r_{pp}^2(k)\end{aligned} \tag{A.2.13}$$

Then PE becomes

$$\mathrm{PE} = Q\left[\sqrt{2}\left(\frac{E_b}{N_0 + (\sigma_I^2/T_b)}\right)^{1/2}\right] \tag{A.2.14}$$

This shows that II degrades performance from that of an ideal BPSK decoder. This analysis approach is used in Chapters 4 and 5.

A.3 QPSK CARRIER WAVEFORMS

QPSK carriers are formed by simultaneous modulation of two separate baseband waveforms onto the quadrature components of a common carrier. Hence

$$c(t) = A\,m_c(t)\cos(\omega_c t + \psi) + A\,m_s(t)\sin(\omega_s t + \psi) \tag{A.3.1}$$

where

$$m_c(t) = \sum_k a_k p(t - kT_s) \tag{A.3.2a}$$

$$m_s(t) = \sum_k b_k q(t - kT_s) \tag{A.3.2b}$$

and a_k, b_k are ± 1. The correlation of $c(t)$ is then

$$\begin{aligned}R_c(\tau) &= \mathscr{E}[c(t)c(t+\tau)] \\ &= \frac{A^2}{2}\{R_{m_c}(\tau)\cos(\omega_c\tau) \\ &\quad + R_{m_s}(\tau)\cos(\omega_c\tau)\end{aligned}$$

$$+ \mathscr{E}[m_c(t)m_s(t+\tau)] \sin(\omega_c\tau)$$

$$+ \mathscr{E}[m_s(t)m_c(t+\tau)] \sin(\omega_c\tau)\} \tag{A.3.3}$$

If the data waveforms $m_c(t)$ and $m_s(t)$ contain uncorrelated data bits, this reduces to

$$R_c(\tau) = \frac{A^2}{2}[R_{m_c}(\tau) + R_{m_s}(\tau)] \cos(\omega_c\tau) \tag{A.3.4}$$

The corresponding spectral density is then

$$S_c(\omega) = \frac{A^2}{4}[S_{m_c}(\omega+\omega_c) + S_{m_s}(\omega+\omega_c)] + \frac{A^2}{4}[S_{m_c}(\omega-\omega_c) + S_{m_s}(\omega-\omega_c)] \tag{A.3.5}$$

Hence the QPSK carrier spectrum is the combined baseband spectra of each quadrature component superimposed at $\pm\,\omega_c$.

Decoding is achieved via the quadrature cross-correlator in Figure 2.16. The decoding voltages generated in each arm for a given symbol interval $(0, T_s)$ are

$$I = \int_0^{T_s} [c(t) + n(t)]p(t) \cos(\omega_c t + \hat{\psi})dt \tag{A.3.6a}$$

$$Q = \int_0^{T_s} [c(t) + n(t)]q(t) \sin(\omega_c t + \hat{\psi})dt \tag{A.3.6b}$$

Using the QPSK waveform in (A.3.2) and assuming that the bit waveforms *p(t)* and *q(t)* are each T_s seconds long and unit power, (A.3.6) becomes

$$I = AT_s\left(a_0 + \sum_{k\neq 0} a_k r_{pp}(k)\right) \cos\psi_e + AT_s\sum_k b_k r_{pq}(k) \sin\psi_e + n_c \tag{A.3.7a}$$

$$Q = AT_s\left(b_0 + \sum_{k\neq 0} b_k r_{eq}(k)\right) \cos\psi_e + AT_s\sum_k a_k r_{qp}(k) \sin\psi_e + n_s \tag{A.3.7b}$$

where now

$$r_{pq}(k) = \frac{1}{T_s}\int_0^{T_s} p(t)q(t - kT_s)dt \tag{A.3.8}$$

and n_c and n_s are independent Gaussian variables with the variance $N_0T_s/2$. In (A.3.7) the first term represents the present data symbol being decoded. The first summation represents II, the second summation represents quadrature channel interference, and the n terms are the noise interference. If the decoder is perfectly coherent ($\psi_e = 0$), the quadrature interference is zero, and both I and Q reduce to the BPSK decisioning variables in (A.2.6). Hence each quadrature channel can be separately decoded as a BPSK link, and the bit error probability of each is given in (A.2.8) or (A.2.14), with T_s replacing T_b. We point out that (A.3.7) is valid for any symbol waveform *p(t)* and *q(t)*, and therefore includes both OQPSK and MSK, described in Chapter 2.

If the phase error ψ_e is not zero, both II and quadrature channel interference must be included. It is no longer obvious that the bit integrator is the preferable decoder. A sampling decoder (phase coherent demodulation followed by a symbol sampler) would produce the decoding variable for I of

$$\begin{aligned} I &= AT_s\Big(a_0 + \sum_{k\neq 0} a_k p(k)\Big)\cos\psi_e \\ &\quad + AT_s\sum_k b_k q(k)\sin\psi_e + n_c \end{aligned} \tag{A.3.9}$$

where *p(k)* and *q(k)* are the quadrature samples of the waveforms $p(t - kT_s)$ and $q(t - kT_s)$. If the symbol waveform *q(t)* was designed such that all the samples *q(k)* during the present symbol sampling of *p(t)* were zero, no quadrature interference would occur. This can occur for both OQPSK and MSK, and shows the advantage of waveform shaping in QPSK decoding.

If *p(t)* and *q(t)* were restricted to one symbol time $(0, T_s)$, then (A.3.9) simplifies to

$$I = AT_s(a_0\cos\psi_e + b_0\sin\psi_e) + n_c \tag{A.3.10}$$

When $\psi_e \neq 0$, the quadrature channel symbol b_0 will either add to or subtract from the voltage of the correct symbol. The probability of error is then the average over these two possibilities. Hence

$$\text{PE} = \frac{1}{2}Q\left[\left(\frac{2E_b}{N_0}\right)^{1/2}(\cos\psi_e + \sin\psi_e)\right]$$

$$+\frac{1}{2}Q\left[\left(\frac{2E_b}{N_0}\right)^{1/2}(\cos\psi_e - \sin\psi_e)\right] \tag{A.3.11}$$

A given phase error ψ_e will always act to increase PE from the ideal case [4]. If the phase error ψ_e is random, PE must be further averaged over its probability density. In OQPSK, symbol transitions in the other channel occur at the midpoint of each symbol. If no transition occurs, PE is identical to the QPSK result in (A.3.11). When a transition occurs, the cross-coupled term involving $\sin\psi_e$ changes polarity at midpoint, and the integrated quadrature interference during the first half of the symbol is canceled by that during the second half. Hence no interference appears, and PE is identical to that of a BPSK link with the same phase error. Since a symbol transition occurs with probability one-half, the OQPSK PE is then the average of the PE for QPSK and BPSK with the same phase error ψ_e.

A.4 FSK

In frequency shift keyed systems, one of the two waveforms:

$$c(t) = A\cos[(\omega_c + \omega_d)t + \psi] \qquad t \in (0, T_b) \tag{A.4.1a}$$

or

$$c(t) = A\cos[(\omega_c - \omega_d)t + \psi] \qquad t \in (0, T_b) \tag{A.4.1b}$$

is transmitted, depending on the data bit. Each waveform occupies a bandwidth of $2/T_b$ Hz around each carrier frequency. Decoding is achieved using a two-channel decoder, one for each waveform in (A.4.1). In a coherent decoder, a phase coherent reference at each frequency is used to bit-correlate in each channel. The channel with the largest correlator output is selected as the transmitted bit. The correct channel correlates to

$$z_c = \frac{AT_b}{2} + n_c \tag{A.4.2a}$$

while the incorrect channel correlates to

$$z_{in} = n_s \tag{A.4.2b}$$

For Gaussian noise, the probability of deciding correctly is then

$$\mathrm{PE} = Q\left[\left(\frac{E_b}{N_0}\right)^{1/2}\right] \tag{A.4.3}$$

Note that E_b is effectively reduced by one-half from coherent BPSK. This result is plotted as coherent FSK in Figure 2.17.

If noncoherent FSK decoding is used (Figure 2.20), bit decisioning is based on the largest *envelope* sample in the two channels, and knowledge of carrier phase ψ is not required. The correct channel contains the bit tone in (A.4.1) plus Gaussian bandpass noise. Hence the BPF output is

$$y(t) = A\cos(\omega_0 t + \psi) + n_c(t)\cos(\omega_0 t + \psi) + n_s(t)\sin(\omega_0 t + \psi) \qquad \text{(A.4.4)}$$

where ω_0 is either $(\omega_c + \omega_d)$ or $(\omega_c - \omega_d)$ and $n_c(t)$ and $n_s(t)$ are the noise quadrature components in (3.2.5). The envelope of this waveform is

$$\alpha(t) = [(A + n_c(t))^2 + (n_s(t))^2]^{1/2} \qquad \text{(A.4.5)}$$

If the BPF bandwidth is matched to the bit time, a sample α_c of this envelope is known to have the probability density [5]

$$p(\alpha_c) = \frac{\alpha_c}{\rho^2} e^{-(\alpha_c^2+\rho^4)/2\rho^2} I_0(\alpha_c)\ \alpha_n \geq 0 \qquad \text{(A.4.6)}$$

where $I_0(x)$ is the imaginary Bessel function and

$$\rho^2 = \frac{2E_b}{N_0} = \frac{A^2 T_b}{N_0} \qquad \text{(A.4.7)}$$

If the frequency separation $2\omega_d$ is wide enough ($\omega_d >> 1/T_b$), the incorrect bandpass channel contains only noise, and a sample α_n of its envelope has density

$$p(\alpha_n) = \frac{\alpha_n}{\rho^2} e^{-\alpha_n^2/2\rho^2} \alpha_n \geq 0 \qquad \text{(A.4.8)}$$

The probability of a bit error is the probability that the incorrect envelope sample α_n will exceed the correct sample α_c. Using (A.4.6) and (A.4.8) this becomes

$$\begin{aligned} \text{PE} &= \int_0^\infty p(\alpha_c) \int_{\alpha_c}^\infty p(\alpha_n) d\alpha_n d\alpha_c \\ &= \frac{1}{2} e^{-\rho^2/4} \end{aligned} \qquad \text{(A.4.9)}$$

The result is plotted in Figure 2.17 as noncoherent FSK.

A.5 DPSK

Another method of decoding binary data without the need for a coherent reference is by the use of *differential* phase shift keying (DPSK). Here BPSK is used, but the previous bit waveform serves as the phase coherent reference for the present bit waveform. The bits are then decoded by the delay-and-correlate decoder shown in Figure 2.20. In DPSK, the present BPSK transmitted bit d_k is encoded according to the rule

$$d_k = d_{k-1} a_k \tag{A.5.1}$$

where a_k is the present data bit. The decoding variable for NRZ waveforms is then

$$z = \int_0^{T_b} [A d_0 p(t) \cos(\omega_c t + \psi) + n_0(t)] \cdot [A d_{-1} p(t) \cos(\omega_c t + \psi) + n_{-1}(t)] dt \tag{A.5.2}$$

where $n_0(t)$ and $n_{-1}(t)$ are the noise processes during the present and past bit intervals. Since $p(t) = 1$ for t in $(0, T_b)$, z expands as

$$z = \frac{A^2 T_b}{2}(d_0 d_{-1}) + n + \int_0^{T_b} n_0(t) n_{-1}(t) dt \tag{A.5.3}$$

where n is a Gaussian variable with variance $2A^2 N_0 T_b/4$. Since $d_0 d_{-1} = a_0$, from (A.5.1), the DPSK decoder has recovered the present bit without use of a phase-coherent reference. However, the decoding variable contains the noise–noise cross-product term due to the use of a noisy reference from the past bit, instead of a clean reference used in an ideal phase coherent decoder. The last term has variance

$$\sigma_{nn}^2 = N_0^2/4 \tag{A.5.4}$$

Hence the effective E_b/N_0 in (A.2.9) now becomes

$$\begin{aligned} \frac{E_b}{N_0} &= \frac{A^4 T_b^2/4}{(A^2 N_0 T_b/2) + (N_0^2/4)} \\ &= \frac{A^2 T_b/2N_0}{1 + (N_0/2A^2 T_b)} \end{aligned} \tag{A.5.5}$$

Thus E_b/N_0 is reduced from the ideal phase coherent case, unless $A^2 T_b/N_0 >> 1$. Note that the DPSK performance can be optimized by use of a two-channel parallel noncoherent decoder, each operating over two successive bits [6]. The upper bound DPSK performance for this decoder is included in Table 2.3 and Figure 2.17.

A.6 MPSK

In MPSK, a carrier with one of M distinct phase shifts $\theta_i = i(360°)/M$, $i = 0, 1, \ldots, M-1$, is transmitted. The modulated carrier therefore appears as

$$c(t) = A\cos(\omega_c t + \theta(t) + \psi) \tag{A.6.1}$$

where $\theta(t)$ shifts to one of the M phases θ_i every symbol time T_s. The spectrum of the MPSK carrier therefore corresponds to a BPSK carrier with symbol width T_s, and therefore occupies a main-hump bandwidth of $2/T_s$ Hz around ω_c.

Decoding is achieved by detecting the phase of the received noisy waveform and determining to which phase states θ_i the detected phase is closest. A phase detector requires a phase referenced carrier in order to distinguish the modulation phase θ_i from the carrier phase ψ. The probability of a symbol error is obtained by determining the probability that the detected phase is not closer to the true phase. For additive Gaussian noise this has been determined to be [7]

$$\begin{aligned} \text{PWE} &= \frac{M-1}{M} - \frac{1}{2}\,\text{Erf}\left[\left(\frac{E_w}{N_0}\right)^{1/2} \sin\left(\frac{\pi}{M}\right)\right] \\ &\quad - \frac{1}{\sqrt{\pi}}\int_0^{\sqrt{E/N_0}\sin(\pi/M)} e^{-y^2}\,\text{Erf}\left[y\cot\left(\frac{\pi}{M}\right)\right]dy \end{aligned} \tag{A.6.2}$$

where E_w is the word energy ($E_w = A^2 T_w/2$), and

$$\text{Erf}(x) = \frac{2}{\sqrt{\pi}}\int_0^x e^{-y^2}\,dy \tag{A.6.3}$$

For $M = 2$ and $M = 4$, (A.6.2) reduces to the previous BPSK and QPSK results. When $M >> 1$, the integral in (A.6.2) can be neglected, and PWE is adequately approximated by (2.7.3) in Chapter 2. The resulting word error probabilities are shown in Figure 2.27 for various M and E_w/N_0.

A.7 CORRELATION DETECTION OF ORTHOGONAL BPSK WAVEFORMS AND PHASE-SEQUENCE TRACKING

In Section 2.7, we considered the mapping of blocks of data bits into orthogonal sequences of BPSK carrier waveforms. Here we consider the decoding of these carriers.

Let a_i be a binary sequence $a_i = \{a_{iq}\}$, $a_{iq} = \pm 1$, of length ν. Let $c_i(t)$ be a BPSK carrier formed from this sequence as

$$c_i(t) = A \sum_{q=1}^{\nu} a_{iq} p(t - qT) \cos(\omega_c t + \psi) \qquad 0 \leqslant t \leqslant T_w = \nu T \qquad \text{(A.7.1)}$$

where $p(t)$ is the modulating waveform. Let a_j and $c_j(t)$, $j = 1, \ldots, M$ be a similar sequence and carrier formed in the same way, constituting a set of M such carriers. Let each carrier have energy E_w over $(0, T_w)$. Assume the ith carrier is transmitted, and received with additive white Gaussian noise $n(t)$, as in (A.2.5), forming

$$x(t) = c_i(t) + n(t) \qquad \text{(A.7.2)}$$

Consider a decoding bank of M phase coherent correlators, as shown in Figure 2.25b, each matched to one of the possible carriers $c_j(t)$. The jth correlator computes the correlation

$$\begin{aligned} y_j &= \int_0^{T_w} x(t) c_j(t)\,dt \\ &= \int_0^{T_w} c_i(t) c_j(t)\,dt + n \end{aligned} \qquad \text{(A.7.3)}$$

where n is a Gaussian random variable with variance $N_0 E_w/2$. Under the condition $\omega_c >> 2/T_w$, the first term integrates to

$$\frac{A^2}{2} \int_0^{T_w} \sum_{q=1}^{\nu} (a_{iq} a_{jq}) p^2(t - qT)\,dt = (E_w T/T_w) \sum_{q=1}^{\nu} a_{iq} a_{jq} \qquad \text{(A.7.4)}$$

Orthogonal sequences are those for which

$$\begin{aligned} \sum_{q=1}^{\nu} a_{iq} a_{jq} &= 0 \qquad i \neq j \\ &= \nu \qquad i = j \end{aligned} \qquad \text{(A.7.5)}$$

Orthogonal sequences of binary variables can be formed from Hadamard matrices [7], and M orthogonal sequences require a length $\nu \geqslant M$. With orthogonal sequences, y_j in (A.7.3) is a Gaussian variable with mean zero if $j \neq i$, and with mean E_w for $i = j$. The probability that the transmitted sequence is correctly decoded is the probability that y_i exceeds all other y_j. Thus if y_j has probability density $p_{y_j}(y)$, then the probability of decoding the sequence in error is then

$$\text{PWE} = 1 - \int_{-\infty}^{\infty} p_{y_i}(y) \left[\int_{-\infty}^{y} p_{y_j}(x)\,dx \right]^{M-1} dy \qquad \text{(A.7.6)}$$

When the Gaussian densities are substituted for each y_j, we obtain the entry in Table 2.4.

Now assume the bit sequence a_i phase modulates the carrier, with an arbitrary pulse shape $p(t)$, forming instead

$$c_i(t) = A\cos\left(\omega_c t + \psi + 2\pi\Delta_f \sum_{q=1}^{v} a_{iq} p(t - qT)\right) \tag{A.7.7}$$

The binary sequence now produces a carrier phase function that traces out a trajectory dependent on the bit sequence and waveform $p(t)$ (see Figure 2.12). Two different sequences therefore trace out two different trajectories.

Phase tracking decoding is obtained by attempting to determine which phase trajectory is being received during an interval $(0, T_w)$ by observing the noisy carrier. This is achieved by correlating the latter with a phase coherent carrier having each possible trajectory, and deciding which has the largest correlation. The jth correlator output now has the mean value

$$\begin{aligned} m_{ij} &= \int_0^{T_w} c_i(t)c_j(t)dt \\ &= E_w \int_0^{T_w} \cos\left[2\pi\Delta_f \sum_{q=1}^{v}(a_{iq} - a_{jq})p(t - qT)dt\right] \end{aligned} \tag{A.7.8}$$

Note that the mean signal again depends on the bit sequence, but it is effectively observed through the cosine function.

The probability of erring in decoding between the correct y_i and an incorrect y_j will depend on the *distance* between the carrier waveforms, given by

$$\begin{aligned} d_{ij}^2 &= \int_0^{T_w} (c_i(t) - c_j(t))^2 dt \\ &= 2(E_w - m_{ij}) \\ &= 2E_w\left[1 - \int_0^{T_w} \cos\left[2\pi\Delta_f \sum_q (a_{iq} - a_{jq})p(t - qT)dt\right]\right] \end{aligned} \tag{A.7.9}$$

Performance of the entire system (assuming all possible transmitted sequences) can be union bounded by

$$\text{PWE} \leq (M - 1)Q\left[\frac{d_{\min}E_w}{N_0}\right]^{1/2} \tag{A.7.10}$$

where $d_{\min}$ is the *minimum* distance d_{ij} over all i and j, $i \neq j$. Thus, performance bounds can be determined by estimating the $d_{\min}$ over all sequences in (A.7.9). For given phase functions $p(t)$ and deviations Δ_f, this generally requires numerical calculations or simulation. This was the procedure used in performance evaluation for CPFSK carriers reported in Chapter 2.

A.8 MFSK

In MFSK one of M distinct frequencies is used to transmit data words. Again, each transmitted word appears as a frequency burst of T_s seconds and therefore occupies a bandwidth of approximately $2/T_s$ Hz around each frequency. Noncoherent decoding is achieved by bandpass filtering at each frequency and sampling the envelope of each filter output. The transmitted frequency is decided by the one with the largest sample value. Following the discussion of binary FSK, the envelope sample value of the correct filter has the probability density in (A.4.6), while all other incorrect samples have the density in (A.4.8). The probability of a word error is then

$$\text{PWE} = 1 - \int_0^{\infty} p(\alpha_c)\left[\int_0^{\alpha_c} p(\alpha_n)\,d\alpha_n\right]^{M-1} d\alpha_c \tag{A.8.1}$$

In evaluating (A.8.1) we use the facts:

$$\begin{aligned}\left[\int_0^{\alpha_c} xe^{-x^2/2}dx\right]^{M-1} &= [1 - e^{-\alpha_c^2/2}]^{M-1}\\ &= \sum_{q=0}^{M-1}(-1)^q\binom{M-1}{q}e^{-q\alpha_c^2/2}\end{aligned} \tag{A.8.2}$$

and

$$\int_0^{\infty} ue^{-u^2(q+1)/2}I_0(pu)\,du = \frac{\exp\,[(p^2/2)/1+q]}{1+q} \tag{A.8.3}$$

When (A.8.2) and (A.8.3) are used in (A.8.1), PWE integrates to the function given in Table 2.4. This rather complicated function is straightforward to compute, and can be adequately approximated by (2.7.4).

A function closely related to PWE in (A.8.1) is the probability that a noncoherent envelope variable α_c or α_n will not exceed a level λ. This can be written as

$$\text{Prob}(\alpha_c < \lambda) = \int_0^{\lambda} p(\alpha_c)\,d\alpha_c \tag{A.8.4a}$$

and

$$\text{Prob}(\alpha_n > \lambda) = \int_{\lambda}^{\infty} p(\alpha_n)d\alpha_n \tag{A.8.4b}$$

These can be conveniently written in terms of the *Marcum Q function*, defined as

$$Q(a, b) \underline{\nabla} \int_{b}^{\infty} \exp\left[-\frac{a^2 + x^2}{2}\right] I_0(ax)xdx \tag{A.8.5}$$

From (A.4.6) and (A.4.8) it then follows that

$$\text{Prob}(\alpha_c < \lambda) = 1 - Q[\rho, \lambda] \tag{A.8.6a}$$

$$\text{Prob}(\alpha_n > \lambda) = Q[0, \lambda] \tag{A.8.6b}$$

The Q function in (A.8.5) has been tabulated [8], and recursive computational methods have been developed for its evaluation [9]. It occurs in noncoherent threshold detection, as when determining code acquisition probabilities in Chapter 7.

A.9 AVERAGE PE WITH PHASE NOISE

In satellite communications an important integral that arises (see Section 4.9) is the average error probability of a Gaussian BPSK decoding variable when the phase error corresponds to a sample of a bandpass noise process. Mathematically, this requires an average PE of the form

$$\text{PE} = \int_{-\infty}^{\infty} Q(a \cos v)p(v)dv \tag{A.9.1}$$

where $p(v)$ is the probability density of the phase noise sample. It is known [7] that a sample of the amplitude α and phase noise v of a bandpass process

$$\begin{aligned} c(t) &= A \cos(\omega_c t + \theta(t)) + n_c(t) \cos(\omega_c t + \psi) - n_s(t) \sin(\omega_c t + \psi) \\ &= \alpha(t) \cos(\omega_c t + \theta(t) + v(t)) \end{aligned} \tag{A.9.2}$$

has the joint density

$$p(\alpha, v) = \frac{\alpha}{2\pi\sigma^2} \exp\left[-\frac{\alpha^2 + A^2 - 2\alpha A \cos v}{z\sigma^2}\right] \tag{A.9.3}$$

where σ^2 is the bandpass noise power. The phase noise sample v therefore has the density

$$p(v) = \int_0^\infty p(\alpha, v)d\alpha$$

$$= e^{-\rho}\int_0^\infty \frac{\alpha}{2\pi\sigma^2}e^{-(\alpha^2+2\alpha A\cos v)/2\sigma^2}d\alpha \quad \text{(A.9.4)}$$

$$= e^{-\rho}\left[\frac{\sqrt{\rho}\cos v}{2\sqrt{\pi}}\exp\left[-\rho(1-\cos^2 v)\right]\mathrm{Erf}c(-\sqrt{\rho}\cos v)\right]$$

where $\rho = A^2/2\sigma^2$ and $\mathrm{Erf}c(x) = 1 - \mathrm{Erf}(x)$. To evaluate (A.9.1) we use the expansion

$$Q(a\cos v) = \frac{1}{2} - \frac{1}{\pi}\sum_{n=0}^{\infty}(-1)^n\frac{\Gamma(n+\frac{1}{2})}{(2n+1)!}a^{2n+1}{}_1F_1\left(n+\frac{1}{2}, 2n+2, -a^2\right) \quad \text{(A.9.5)}$$
$$\times \cos(2n+1)v$$

where $\Gamma(x)$ is the Gamma function [1, p. 253] and, ${}_1F_1$ is the hypergeometric series [1, p. 556]

$${}_1F_1(a, b, z) = \sum_{k=0}^{\infty}\frac{\Gamma(a+k)}{\Gamma(b+k)}\cdot\frac{z^k}{k!} \quad \text{(A.9.6)}$$

Substituting (A.9.5) in (A.9.1), and using the integral identity

$$\int_0^{2\pi}\cos[(2n+1)v]p(v)dv = \rho^{2n+1}\frac{\Gamma(n+\frac{3}{2})}{(2n+1)!}{}_1F_1\left(n+\frac{1}{2}, 2n+2, -\rho_1^2\right) \quad \text{(A.9.7)}$$

produces equation (4.7.11) of Chapter 4.

A.10 MASK

In MASK the data words are encoded into carriers with one of M amplitude levels $\{A_i\}$. The carriers therefore have the form

$$c(t) = A_i\cos(\omega_c t + \phi) \quad 0 \leqslant t \leqslant T_w \quad \text{(A.10.1)}$$

For any set $\{A_i\}$ the carrier $c(t)$ corresponds to a T_w sec carrier burst, and therefore always occupies a bandwidth of $2/T_w$ Hz. The average power of the signal set is

$$\overline{P}_c = \frac{1}{M}\sum_{i=1}^{M}(A_i^2/2) \quad \text{(A.10.2)}$$

If the amplitude levels A_i are all evenly spaced over positive and negative amplitude values, each separated by distance Δ volts, we have $A_i = (2i - 1)(\Delta/2)$, $1 \leqslant i \leqslant M/2$, and $A_i = A_{i-(M/2)}$, $M/2 \leqslant i \leqslant M$. The average power of this set is then

$$\overline{P}_c = \frac{\Delta^2(M^2 - 1)}{12} \tag{A.10.3}$$

Decoding in MASK is achieved by phase-coherent carrier referencing, followed by word integration, to produce the variable

$$z = A_j T_w + n \tag{A.10.4}$$

where n has variance $N_0 T_w/2$, and A_j is the transmitted amplitude during $(0, T_w)$. A word decision is based on which $A_i T_w$ product z is closest. An error occurs if n causes z to be outside the interval $(A_j + \Delta/2,\ A_j - \Delta/2)$. For Gaussian noise this occurs with probability

$$\begin{aligned} \text{PWE} &= \frac{1}{M}\left[(M-2)2Q\left(\frac{\Delta T_w}{\sqrt{2N_0T_w}}\right) + 2Q\left(\frac{\Delta T_w}{\sqrt{2N_0T_w}}\right)\right] \\ &= \frac{M-1}{M}\left[2Q\left(\frac{\Delta T_w}{\sqrt{2N_0T_w}}\right)\right] \end{aligned} \tag{A.10.5}$$

When written in terms of the average power in (A.10.3) we obtain

$$\text{PWE} = \left(\frac{M-1}{M}\right)2Q\left[\left(\frac{6\overline{E}_w}{(M^2-1)N_0}\right)^{1/2}\right] \tag{A.10.6}$$

where $\overline{E}_w = \overline{P}_c T_w$ is the average word energy over the signal set. This result is included in Table 2.4 in Chapter 2.

REFERENCES

1. A. Abramowitz, and I. Stegun, *Handbook of Mathematical Functions* (Washington, D.C.: National Bureau of Standards, 1965), chapter 26.

2. R. Fang, and O. Shimbo, "Unified Analysis of a Class of Digital Systems in Noise and Interference," *IEEE Trans. on Comm.*, vol. COM-21 (October 1973).

3. K, Yao, and E. Biglieri, "Multidimensional Moment Error Bounds for Digital Communication Systems," *IEEE Trans. on Info. Theory*, vol. IT-26 (July 1980).

4. S.A. Rhodes, "Effect of Noisy Phase Reference on Coherent Detection of QPSK," *IEEE Trans. on Comm.*, vol. COM-22 (August 1974), pp. 1046–1055.

5. A. Papoulis, "Probability, Random Variables, and Random Processes," (New York: McGraw-Hill, 1965).

6. R. Gagliardi, *Introduction to Communication Engineering* (New York: Wiley, 1978), chapter 7.

7. W. Lindsey, and M. Simon, *Telecommunication System Design* (Englewood Cliffs, N.J.: Prentice-Hall, 1973.

8. C. Marcum, "Tables of the Q-function," Rand Corp. Research Memo RN 399, January 1950.

9. L. Brennan, and I. Reed, "A Recursive Method for Computing the Q-Functions," *IEEE Trans. on Info. Theory*, vol. IT-11 (April, 1965).

B

Carrier Recovery and Bit Timing

Carrier recovery (sometimes referred to as **phase referencing**) is the operation of extracting a phase coherent reference carrier from an observed noisy received carrier. **Bit timing** is the operation of extracting a time coherent bit rate clock from an observed noisy data-modulated waveform. Both of these operations are fundamental to digital communications. In this appendix we review the basic analysis associated with both these operations.

B.1 CARRIER RECOVERY

Carrier recovery is achieved by forcing a local voltage controlled oscillator (VCO) to track the phase of a received carrier. The VCO output can then be used as a receiver reference source for decoding operations. The VCO and the received carrier are said to be phase locked, or phase coherent, if the phase error (phase difference) of the two carriers, when referred to the received carrier frequency, is small ($\leq 20°$).

Phase tracking of an unmodulated carrier is achieved via the **phase locked loop (PLL)** shown in Figure B.1a. Let the loop input be written as

$$x(t) = A \cos(\omega_c t + \psi(t)) + n(t) \tag{B.1.1}$$

where $\psi(t)$ is the phase to be tracked, and $n(t)$ is again white noise of one-sided spectral level N_0 in a wide bandwidth around the carrier frequency ω_c. The VCO, at rest frequency ω_0, is frequency-multiplied to ω_c to track the phase of the received carrier. A phase comparator determines the instantaneous phase error between the two carriers. This error voltage is then filtered and used to correct the phase of the VCO. If the phase comparator is a phase detector with gain $K_m g(\psi)$, the phase error voltage appears as*

*If the phase comparator is a phase *mixer*, then $g(\psi)$ is replaced by $\sin(\psi)$, and $e(t)$ is multiplied by the carrier amplitude A. [see Reference 4, chapter 9]. This multiplies K_m by A and scales the spectrum of $n_m(t)$. These conversions are easily accounted for in all subsequent equations.

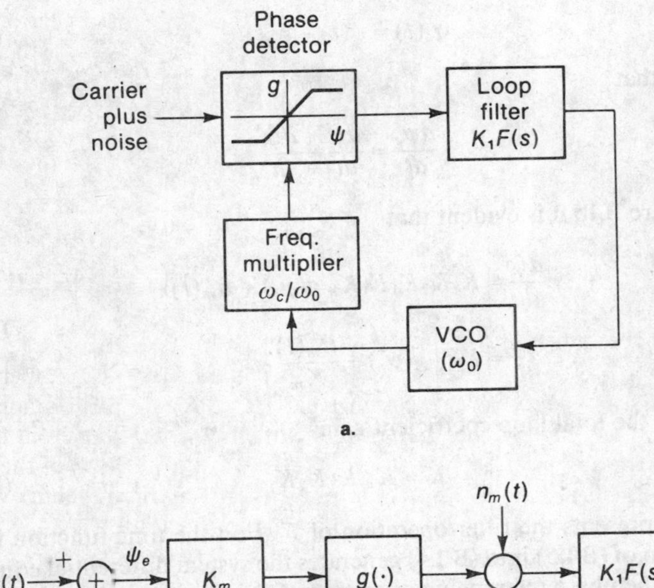

Figure B.1. Phase lock tracking loop for unmodulated carrier. (a) Block diagram. (b) Equivalent phase model.

$$e(t) = K_m g[\psi(t) - \hat{\psi}(t)] + n_m(t) \tag{B.1.2}$$

where $g(\psi)$ is the nonlinear phase conversion function, $\hat{\psi}(t)$ is the VCO phase, and $n_m(t)$ is the mixer output noise. The latter is a baseband white noise process of two-sided spectral level $K_m^2 N_0/A^2$. The voltage $e(t)$ is filtered by the loop filter function $K_1F(s)$ and used to adjust the frequency of the VCO. The PLL therefore has the equivalent phase model shown in Figure B.1b. Note that the VCO is effectively replaced by an integrator to account for the conversion from frequency control at its input to phase variations at its output. If we define the tracking phase error at frequency ω_c as

$$\psi_e(t) = \psi(t) - \hat{\psi}(t) \tag{B.1.3}$$

it follows that

$$\frac{d\psi_e}{dt} = \frac{d\psi}{dt} - \frac{d\hat{\psi}}{dt} \tag{B.1.4}$$

From Figure B.1b it is evident that

$$\begin{aligned} \frac{d\hat{\psi}}{dt} &= K_f K_2 K_1 F\{K_m g(\psi_e) + n_m(t)\} \\ &= KF\left\{ g(\psi_e) + \frac{n_m(t)}{K_m} \right\} \end{aligned} \tag{B.1.5}$$

where K is the total loop coefficient gain

$$K = K_m K_1 K_2 K_f \tag{B.1.6}$$

and $F\{\cdot\}$ represents the filter operation of $F(s)$ on the time function in $\{\cdot\}$. Substitution of (B.1.5) into (B.1.4) generates the system differential equation describing the phase referencing operation of the phase lock loop,

$$\frac{d\psi_e}{dt} + KF\{g(\psi_e)\} = \frac{d\psi}{dt} - KF\left\{ \frac{n_m(t)}{K_m} \right\} \tag{B.1.7}$$

Note that the equation is a nonlinear, stochastic differential equation forced by the phase dynamics $d\psi/dt$ of the received carrier and the filtered random noise $n_m(t)$. If the phase error is small ($\psi_e \gtrsim 20°$), the loop is said to be *in-lock*, and the system can be linearized by assuming $g(\psi_e) \approx \psi_e$. The nonlinear phase system in Figure B.1b then becomes a linear feedback system, as shown in Figure B.2. The inputs to the loop are the input phase process $\psi(t)$, the input noise $n_m(t)$, and any other phase variations superimposed on the received carrier or VCO, such as oscillator phase noise. We see that the phase error $\psi_e(t)$ of the PLL evolves as a superposition of the contributions from all phase sources. Figure B.2 includes the addition of the phase noises of the carrier and the VCO, each adding directly at the points shown. Phase error can be computed by determining the response at the error point due to each input. This error will have a deterministic part (due to tracking phase dynamics in $\psi(t)$) and a random part (due to tracking the phase noise and thermal noise inputs). Each of these error responses will depend on the loop gain function defined as

$$H(\omega) = \frac{KF(\omega)/j\omega}{1 + KF(\omega)/j\omega} \tag{B.1.8}$$

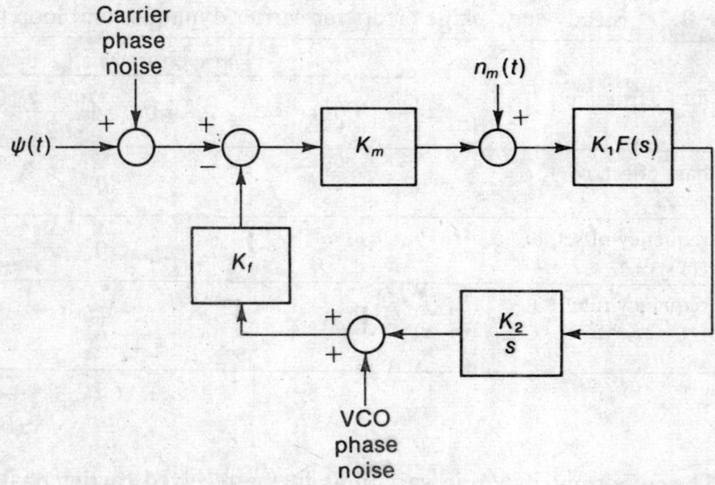

Figure B.2. Linear phase model with phase noise.

Table B.1 summarizes the resulting form for $H(\omega)$ for some common loop filter functions $F(\omega)$.

Table B.1. Tabulation of loop-filter function $(F(\omega))$, loop gain function $(H(\omega))$, and loop noise bandwidth B_L.

Loop filter, $F(\omega)$	$H(\omega)$	B_L
1	$\dfrac{K}{j\omega + K}$	$\dfrac{K}{4}$
$\dfrac{j\omega\tau_2 + 1}{j\omega\tau_1 + 1}$	$\dfrac{1 + j\left(\dfrac{2\zeta}{\omega_n} - \dfrac{1}{K}\right)\omega}{-\left(\dfrac{\omega}{\omega_n}\right)^2 + \dfrac{2\zeta}{\omega_n}j\omega + 1}$ $\omega_n^2 = K/\tau_1$ $2\zeta\omega_n = \dfrac{1 + K\tau_2}{\tau_1}$	$\dfrac{\omega_n}{8\zeta}\left[1 + \left(2\zeta - \dfrac{\omega_n^2}{K}\right)^2\right]$
$\dfrac{j\omega\tau_2 + 1}{j\omega\tau_1}$	$\dfrac{\left(1 + \dfrac{2\zeta}{\omega_n}j\omega\right)}{-\left(\dfrac{\omega}{\omega_n}\right)^2 + \left(\dfrac{2\zeta}{\omega_n}\right)j\omega + 1}$	$\dfrac{\omega_n}{8\zeta}(1 + 4\zeta^2)$

Table B.2. Steady-state phase errors for carrier dynamics and loop filters.

Phase Dynamic	Phase error	
	$F(\omega) = 1$	$F(\omega) = \frac{j\omega + b}{j\omega}$
Phase offset, ψ_0 $\psi = \psi_0$	0	0
Frequency offset, ω_d $\psi(t) = \omega_d t$	$\frac{\omega_d}{K}$	0
Frequency rate $\psi(t) = \dot{\omega}_d t^2/2$	∞	$\frac{\dot{\omega}_d}{K}$

The important dynamic variations in the received carrier phase $\psi(t)$ are phase offsets, frequency offsets (doppler), and linear frequency changes. These lead to constant phase errors depending on the type of loop. Table B.2 summarizes the resulting phase error values of several loops due to each type of offset. An infinite value implies the loop error will increase without bound, and therefore the loop cannot track that particular offset. The ability to track, however, improves as the loop order is increased, while the residual error decreases with loop gain.

A closely related parameter is the time it takes to reduce an initial phase or frequency offset to the phase-error value stated. This is often referred to as the loop **pull-in time**, or loop **acquisition time**. For a second-order loop with a carrier frequency offset of Ω rps from the expected carrier frequency, the acquisition time to reduce the initial frequency error to the zero value in Table B.2 is given by

$$T_{\text{acq}} = \frac{\Omega^2}{2\zeta\omega_n^3} \tag{B.1.9}$$

Hence frequency pull-in time increases as the square of the frequency offsets, but decreases as the cube of the loop natural frequency ω_n. This means frequency acquisition is improved by using wider bandwidth loops.

Random phase error is due to the cumulative effect of all noises entering the loop. Hence the phase error variance (about the mean errors in Table B.2) is given by

$$\sigma_e^2 = \left(\frac{N_0}{A^2}\right)\frac{1}{2\pi}\int_{-\infty}^{\infty} |H(\omega)|^2 d\omega$$

$$+\left(\frac{\omega_c}{\omega_0}\right)^2 \frac{1}{2\pi}\int_{-\infty}^{\infty} S_{0s}(\omega)\,|1 - H(\omega)|^2 d\omega \qquad \text{(B.1.10)}$$

$$+\frac{1}{2\pi}\int_{-\infty}^{\infty} S_c(\omega)\,|1 - H(\omega)|^2 d\omega$$

where $S_{0s}(\omega)$, $S_c(\omega)$, and N_0 are the power spectra of the loop oscillator phase noise, the carrier phase noise, and the thermal noise, respectively. Since $1 - H(j\omega)$ is an effectively high pass filtering function, we see that the phase noise outside the loop function bandwidth contributes to the tracking error, while the thermal noise inside this bandwidth is important. By defining

$$B_L = \frac{1}{2\pi}\int_0^{\infty} |H(\omega)|^2 d\omega \qquad \text{(B.1.11)}$$

as the loop noise bandwidth, the thermal noise contribution can be written more compactly as

$$\sigma_{en}^2 = \frac{1}{\rho} \qquad \text{(B.1.12)}$$

Here we have defined

$$\rho = \frac{A^2/2}{N_0 B_L} \qquad \text{(B.1.13)}$$

as the ratio of the input carrier power to thermal noise power in the loop noise bandwidth B_L. Formulas for B_L for each type of loop in Table B.1 are listed in the last column. If the carrier being tracked is phase modulated by $\theta(t)$, then the effect of the modulation on the tracking performance of the loop must be considered. The modulation reduces the strength of the carrier component being tracked, and effectively reduces the value of A in Figure B.2, depending on the type of modulation. This reduction of A to the lower value A_m is summarized in Table B.3 for several types of common modulation formats. Reduction of A to A_m increases tracking errors in Table B.2, and converts the loop CNR ρ in (B.1.13) to

$$\rho_m = \left(\frac{A_m}{A}\right)^2 \rho \qquad \text{(B.1.14)}$$

Hence, the bracket serves as a **modulation suppression factor**, which effectively reduces the carrier tracking power from the power of an unmodulated carrier.

Table B.3. Modulation suppression on tracking carrier amplitude.

Phase Modulation on Carrier	*Tracking Carrier Amplitude, A_m*
No modulation	A
Subcarrier PM, deviation Δ	$AJ_0(\Delta)$
K subcarriers PM, deviation Δ_i	$A\prod_{i=1}^{K} J_0(\Delta_i)$
Binary waveform, deviation Δ_c	$A \cos \Delta_c$
Binary waveform (Δ_c) plus K subcarriers (Δ_i)	$A \cos \Delta_c \prod_{i=1}^{K} J_0(\Delta_i)$
Random, characteristic function $C(\omega)$	$A \mid C(1) \mid$

B.2 BPSK CARRIER RECOVERY

When the received carrier is phase modulated as a BPSK carrier, there is no carrier component to be tracked (i.e., $\Delta_c = \pi/2$ and $A_m = 0$ in Table B.3), and carrier recovery cannot be obtained via a standard phase lock loop. Instead a modified system must be used, which first uses a nonlinearity to eliminate (wipe-off) the modulation while creating a carrier component having a phase variation proportional to that of the received carrier. Subsequent tracking of this residual carrier component then generates the desired carrier reference. The two common methods for achieving this BPSK carrier recovery are the **squaring loop** and the **Costas loop.**

Squaring Loops

The squaring loop system is shown in Figure B.3a. The received carrier waveform is filtered and squared prior to phase referencing. The squaring wipes off the modulation and generates a harmonic at twice the carrier frequency. This harmonic can then be phase tracked, and the VCO output can then be frequency divided by 2 to serve as a phase locked reference to the received carrier.

Let the received waveform be written as

$$y(t) = Am(t) \cos (\omega_c t + \psi(t)) + n(t) \tag{B.2.1}$$

where $m(t)$ is the BPSK modulation and $n(t)$ is again white bandpass noise of level N_0, one-sided. The filtering and squaring generates the waveform

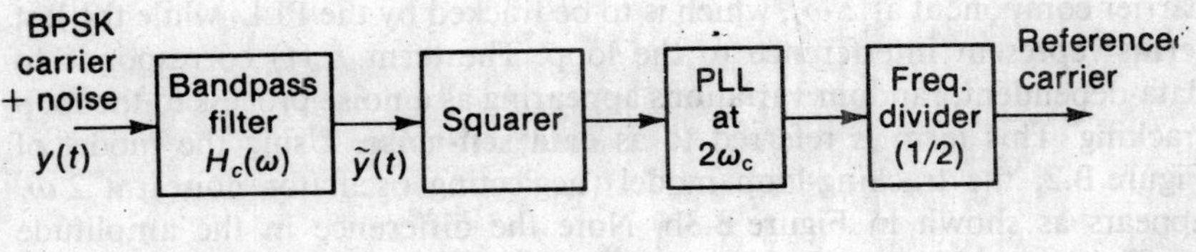

a.

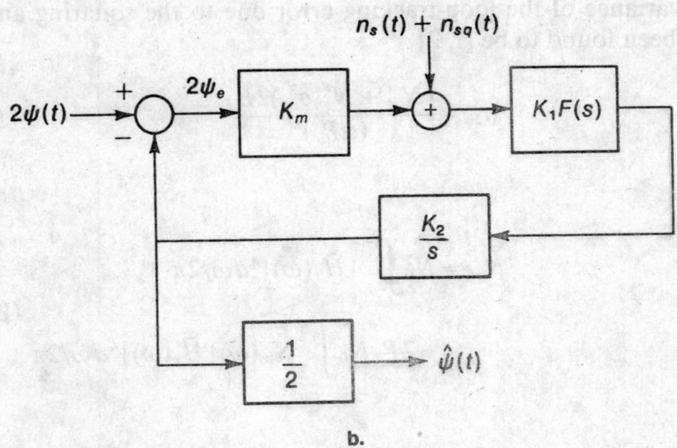

b.

Figure B.3. BPSK carrier referencing subsystem. (a) Filter-squarer system. (b) Equivalent model.

$$
\begin{aligned}
x(t) &= \tilde{y}^2(t) \\
&= A^2[\tilde{m}(t)]^2\left[\frac{1}{2}(1 + \cos(2\omega_c t + 2\psi)\right] + n_{sq}(t)
\end{aligned}
\tag{B.2.2}
$$

where the tilde denotes the effect of the filtering, and $n_{sq}(t)$ represents the signal–noise and noise–noise cross-products. Expanding out the harmonic at 2 ω_c, and neglecting low-frequency components, this becomes

$$x(t) = A^2[\overline{(\tilde{m}(t))^2}]\cos(2\omega_c t + 2\psi) + n_s(t)\cos(2\omega_c t + 2\psi) + n_{sq}(t) \tag{B.2.3}$$

where

$$\tilde{m}^2(t) = \overline{m^2(t)} + n_s(t) \tag{B.2.4}$$

with the overbar denoting time averaging. The first term in (B.2.3) is the carrier component at $2\,\omega_c$, which is to be tracked by the PLL, while the last terms represent interference to the loop. The term $n_s(t)$ corresponds to data-dependent, random variations appearing as a noise process to the loop tracking. This term is referred to as **data self-noise**. Using the model of Figure B.2, the tracking-loop model (neglecting oscillator noise) at $2\,\omega_c$ appears as shown in Figure B.3b. Note the difference in the amplitude coefficient (A^2 instead of A) and the increased noise entering the loop. The loop can now be analyzed as a standard PLL, as in Section B.1.

The variance of the loop-tracking error due to the squaring and self-noise has been found to be [1, 2]

$$\sigma_{2\psi}^2 = \frac{(N_{sq} + N_{sn}\sigma_{2\psi}^2)2B_L}{(\alpha P_c)^2} \tag{B.2.5}$$

where

$$N_{sq} = N_0^2 \int_{-\infty}^{\infty} |\tilde{H}_c(\omega)|^4 d\omega/2\pi + 2P_cN_0 \int_{-\infty}^{\infty} S_m(\omega)|\tilde{H}_c(\omega)|^4 d\omega/2\pi \tag{B.2.6a}$$

$$N_s = 4T_b \sum_{l=1}^{\infty} R_d^2(lT_b) \tag{B.2.6b}$$

$$\alpha = \frac{1}{2\pi}\int_{-\infty}^{\infty} S_m(\omega)|\tilde{H}_c(\omega)|^2 d\omega \tag{B.2.6c}$$

$$R_d(\tau) = \int_{-\infty}^{\infty} S_m(\omega)|\tilde{H}_c(\omega)|^2 e^{j\omega\tau} d\omega/2\pi \tag{B.2.6d}$$

$$P_c = A^2/2 \tag{B.2.6e}$$

$S_m(\omega)$ = Spectrum of $m(t)$

$\tilde{H}_c(\omega)$ = Low pass equivalent of $H_c(\omega)$

The spectral levels N_{sq} and N_s are due to the noise $n_{sq}(t)$ and self-noise $n_s(t)$, respectively. Equation (B.2.5) can be solved for $\sigma_{2\psi}^2$. The reference phase error at ω_c (after dividing down in frequency) is one-half the phase tracking error at $2\,\omega_c$. Hence

$$\sigma_{\psi}^2 = \sigma_{2\psi}^2/4 \tag{B.2.7}$$

Thus, solving (B.2.5),

$$\sigma_{\psi}^2 = \frac{\dfrac{N_{sq}B_L}{2(\alpha P_c)^2}}{1 - \dfrac{N_{sn}2B_L}{(\alpha P_c)^2}} \tag{B.2.8}$$

This represents the tracking error variance of a general squaring system. For most applications, the self-noise term can be neglected. For example, if $H(\omega)$ is an ideal bandpass filter centered at ω_c, with bandwidth $2/T_b$, and $m(t)$ corresponds to ideal NRZ pulses, it has been shown [3] that

$$\begin{aligned} N_{sn} &\cong P_c^2 T_b(0.031) \\ \alpha &\approx 2.8/T_b \end{aligned} \tag{B.2.9}$$

The denominator in (B.2.8) becomes

$$1 - \frac{N_{sn}2B_L}{(\alpha P_c)^2} \approx 1 - (0.031)(2.52)T_b^3 B_L \tag{B.2.10}$$

For typical $T_b B_L$ products, (B.2.10) is almost unity. Hence (B.2.8) is adequately approximated as

$$\begin{aligned} \sigma_{\psi}^2 &= \frac{N_{sq}B_L}{2(\alpha P_c)^2} \\ &= \frac{N_0 B_L}{\alpha P_c}\left[\frac{h_1}{\alpha} + \frac{N_0 h_2}{2\alpha P_c}\right] \end{aligned} \tag{B.2.11}$$

where

$$h_1 = \frac{1}{2\pi}\int_{-\infty}^{\infty} S_m(\omega)\,|\tilde{H}_c(\omega)|^4 d\omega \tag{B.2.12a}$$

$$h_2 = \frac{1}{2\pi}\int_{-\infty}^{\infty} |\tilde{H}_c(\omega)|^4 d\omega \tag{B.2.12b}$$

It is convenient to again denote

$$\begin{aligned} \rho &= \frac{P_c}{N_0 B_L} \\ \frac{E_b}{N_0} &= \frac{P_c T_b}{N_0} \end{aligned} \tag{B.2.13}$$

and write (B.2.11) as

$$\sigma_\psi^2 = \frac{1}{\rho \mathcal{S}_q} \tag{B.2.14}$$

where $\mathcal{S}_q$ is the **squaring loss**,

$$\mathcal{S}_q = \left[\frac{h_1}{\alpha} + \frac{h_2 T_b/\alpha}{2E_b/N_0}\right]^{-1} \tag{B.2.15}$$

Since $1/\rho$ is the variance in (B.1.12) for an unmodulated carrier tracking loop, $\mathcal{S}_q^{-1}$ accounts for the increased variance caused by the necessity of having to employ modulation wipe-off (i.e., filtering and squaring) with BPSK. Note that the squaring loss depends on the filter shape, the data bit waveform, and the operating E_b/N_0. If the prefilter is too wide (relative to $1/T_b$), h_1 and h_2 will increase, while if it is too narrow α decreases, and both of these increase the squaring loss. Lindsey and Simon [1] have shown that for a particular filter type and bit waveform, an optimal filter bandwidth relative to the bit rate exists for each E_b/N_0. For a typical operation ($E_b/N_0 \approx$ 8–10 dB), the required bandwidth is about $3/T_b$ Hz.

Costas Loops

A second way to achieve BPSK carrier referencing is by the use of the Costas, or quadrature, loop shown in Figure B.4. The system involves two parallel tracking loops operating simultaneously from the same VCO. One loop, called the in-phase loop, uses the VCO as in a PLL, and the second (quadrature) loop uses a 90° shifted VCO. The mixer outputs are each filtered and multiplied to form the nonlinearity for modulation wipe-off. The multiplied arm voltages are then filtered and used to control the VCO. The low pass filters in each arm must be wide enough to pass the data modulation without distortion. If the input to the Costas loop is the waveform in (B.2.1), the in-phase mixer generates

$$I(t) = Am(t)\cos\psi_e + n_{mc}(t) \tag{B.2.16a}$$

while the quadrature mixer generates

$$Q(t) = Am(t)\sin\psi_e + n_{ms}(t) \tag{B.2.16b}$$

where $n_{mc}(t)$ and $n_{ms}(t)$ are low pass demodulated noise processes. The output of the multiplier is then

$$I(t)Q(t) = \frac{A^2}{2}[m(t)]^2 \sin(2\psi_e) + n_{sq}(t) \tag{B.2.17}$$

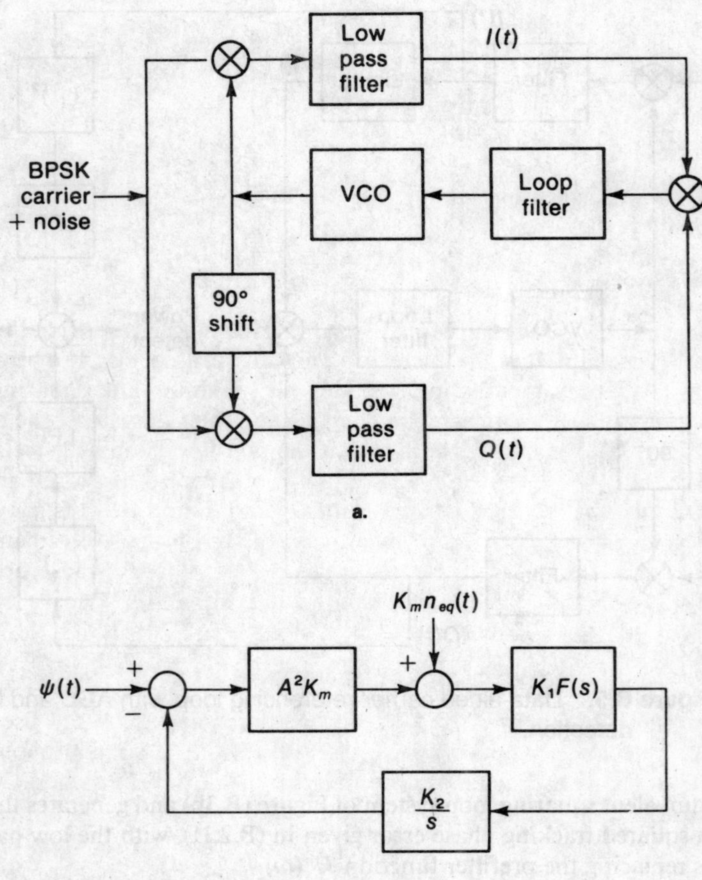

Figure B.4. BPSK Costas loop. (a) Block diagram. (b) Equivalent loop model.

where $n_{sq}(t)$ again represents all the signal and noise cross-products. When the phase error $\psi_e(t)$ is small, the Costas loop has the equivalent linear model in Figure B.4b. The mixer noises $n_{mc}(t)$ and $n_{ms}(t)$ are baseband versions of the carrier noise $n(t)$. It can be shown [4, 5] that $n_{sq}(t)$ in (B.2.17) has the identical spectrum as $n_{sq}(t)$ in (B.2.3) for the squaring loop. The frequency division by the factor of 2 can be accomplished directly in the loop gain, since the error term, $\psi - \hat{\psi}$ must be derived from the argument of the sine term in (B.2.17). Thus, the equivalent Costas loop is identical to

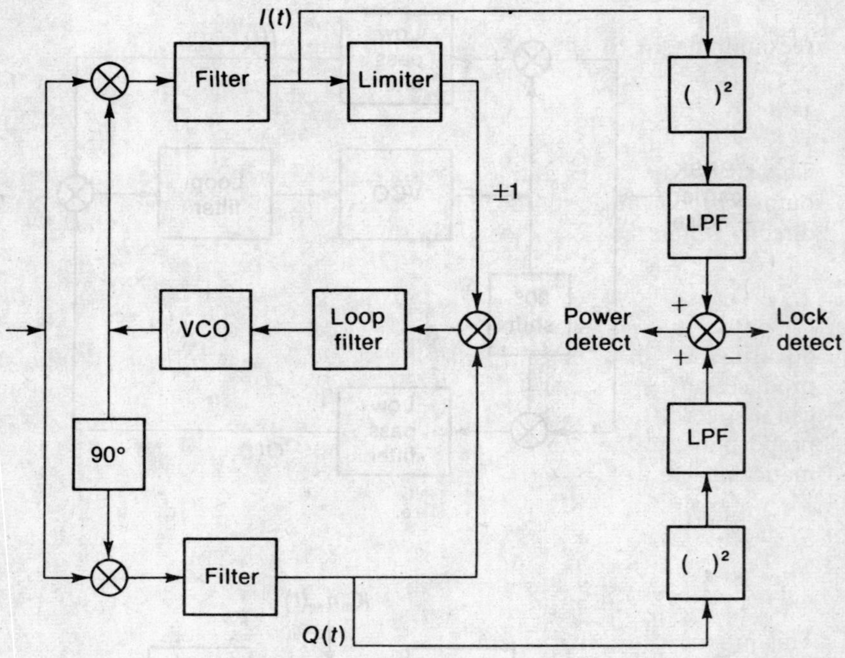

Figure B.5. Data-aided carrier referencing loop with AGC and lock detection.

the equivalent squaring loop system of Figure (B.3b) and generates the same mean squared tracking phase error given in (B.2.11), with the low pass arm filters replacing the prefilter function $\tilde{H}_c(\omega)$.

The multiplier of the Costas system can be thought of as allowing the bit polarity of the in-phase loop to correct the phase error orientation of the tracking loop, thereby removing the modulation. Often Costas loops are designed with the in-phase arm filter followed by a limiter (Figure B.5). At high SNR, the limiter output will have a sign during each bit interval that is identical to the present data bit polarity. This limiter output then multiplies the loop error and removes the loop modulation. In effect, the data bit sign is used to aid the tracking loop, and such modified systems are often called **data-aided carrier extraction** loops.

Modified Costas Loops

An interesting property of Costas loops is that the system generates signals that can be used for other auxiliary purposes as well. This can be seen by reexamining the (B.2.16) waveforms and noting the following:

1.
$$\overline{I(t)}\,|_{\psi_e=0} = Am(t) \tag{B.2.18}$$

This shows that when the loop is locked, the in-phase arm produces an output proportional to the data. Hence the data can be demodulated directly within the Costas loop after phase lock occurs.

2.
$$\overline{I^2(t)} - \overline{Q^2(t)} = A^2\overline{m^2(t)}\cos(2\psi_e) \tag{B.2.19}$$

Squaring, low pass filtering, and subtracting the arm voltages (Figure B.5) produces an output that indicates phase lock [$\cos(2\psi_e) \to 1$ as $\psi_e \to 0$] and can therefore serve as a lock detector. When $\psi_e = 0$, this generates an output proportional to the average signal power, which can also be used for automatic gain control (AGC) [6].

3.
$$\begin{aligned}\overline{I^2(t)} + \overline{Q^2(t)} &= A^2\overline{m^2(t)} + \overline{n_{ms}^2(t)} + \overline{n_{mc}^2(t)} \\ &= \text{Total power of } y(t) \text{ in (B.2.1)}\end{aligned} \tag{B.2.20}$$

This produces a measurement of the total RF input power, and therefore can be used for RF power control.

4.
$$\overline{I(t)\frac{dQ}{dt}} - \overline{Q(t)\frac{dI}{dt}} \cong [A^2\overline{m^2(t)}\cos 2\psi_e]\frac{d\psi_e}{dt} \tag{B.2.21}$$

By differentiating in each arm and cross-multiplying, a signal proportional to the frequency error, $d\psi_e/dt$, is generated. This can be used for frequency offset measurements, or for aiding in frequency acquisition [7].

B.3 QPSK PHASE REFERENCING

For a QPSK carrier, phase referencing again requires modulation wipe-off, but the required nonlinearity is slightly different. This is due to the fact that the modulated carrier, although still containing a suppressed carrier component, also contains one of four possible phases, rather than two, during each bit interval. QPSK systems therefore require a modified form of the BPSK phase referencing methods.

Fourth-Power Loops

To extract the QPSK suppressed carrier, a fourth power, instead of a squaring, system must be used, as shown in Figure B.6a. The QPSK carrier

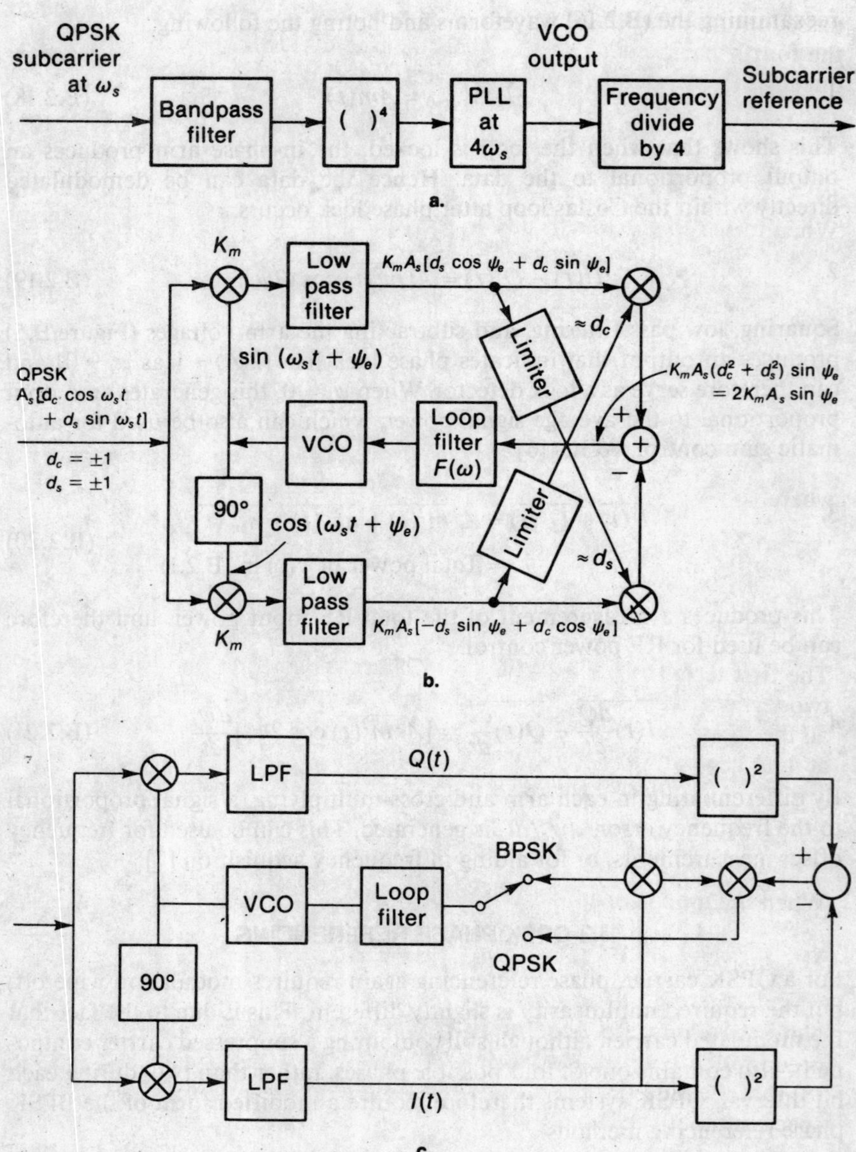

Figure B.6. QPSK carrier referencing. (a) Fourth-power loops. (b) Costas crossover loop. (c) Modified BPSK loop.

passed into the fourth-power device, and a phase lock loop can be locked to the fourth harmonic. The VCO can then be divided down by four in frequency to generate the input carrier reference. We write the input as

$$y(t) = Am_c(t)\cos(\omega_c t + \psi) + Am_s(t)\sin(\omega_c t + \psi) + n(t) \tag{B.3.1}$$

When raised to the fourth power, the fourth harmonic contains the terms

$$\begin{aligned} v_4(t) = \frac{A^4}{16} &\cos(4\omega_c t + 4\psi) \\ &+ a(t)\cos(4\omega_c t + 4\psi) \\ &+ b(t)\sin(4\omega_c t + 4\psi) \\ &+ n_4(t) \end{aligned} \tag{B.3.2}$$

where

$$a(t) = m_c^4(t) + m_s^4(t) - 2m_c^2(t)m_s^2(t) \tag{B.3.3a}$$

$$b(t) = m_c(t)m_s(t)[m_c^2(t) - m_s^2(t)] \tag{B.3.3b}$$

The first term in (B.3.2) is the fourth harmonic to be tracked. The second two terms are the self-noise at the same harmonic. The last term represents all the signal–noise cross-products in the vicinity of 4 ω_c. The tracking loop at 4 ω_c generates the tracking-error voltage

$$e(t) = \frac{A^4}{16}\sin(4\psi_e) + [a(t)\sin(4\psi_e) + b(t)\cos(4\psi_e) + n_m(t)] \tag{B.3.4}$$

When the loop is near-lock ($\psi_e \approx 0$) we have

$$e(t) \cong \frac{A^4}{16}(4\psi_e(t)) + b(t) + n_m(t) \tag{B.3.5}$$

Note that only the quadrature component of the self-noise contributes predominantly to the loop noise when the loop is in lock. It has been shown [8] that the data-dependent random process *b(t)* in (B.3.3b) typically has a spectrum that varies as

$$S_b(\omega) \approx (\omega T_b)^2 \tag{B.3.6}$$

for small ω. The contribution of the self-noise to the loop-error variance is then approximately

$$\sigma_{4\psi}^2 \cong \left(\frac{8\pi}{3}\right)^2 T_b^2 B_L^3 \tag{B.3.7}$$

where B_L is the loop bandwidth of the tracking loop. This shows that the quadrature self-noise is not white, and in fact increases as B_L^3 in the phase error variance. For most communication applications, however, $T_b B_L << 1$, and self-noise of this type is usually negligible.

The contribution of the fourth-order mixer noise $n_m(t)$ to the loop error can be computed as in the squaring loop analyses for BPSK. However, the procedure is now more complicated than it was for the squaring loop since the multiplication terms involving the QPSK carrier and noise cross-products are present in all orders up to the fourth power. It has been shown [4] that if the carrier bandpass filter in Figure B.6a has the value $B_{sc} = 2/T_b$, where T_b is the QPSK bit time, then the fourth-power loop generates the mean squared phase error at the carrier frequency of approximately

$$\sigma^2 \cong \frac{2N_0 B_L}{A^2}\left[1 + \frac{3.8}{E_b/N_0} + \frac{4.2}{(E_b/N_0)^2} + \frac{1}{(E_b/N_0)^2}\right] \tag{B.3.8}$$

The bracketed term now plays the same role for the fourth-power loop as the squaring factor in (B.2.15) for the squaring loop. We emphasize that (B.3.8) refers to the phase error between the received carrier and the divided-down reference frequency at ω_c, and the phase error in the loop at $4\,\omega_c$ has a mean squared value that is $4^2 = 16$ times larger.

Costas Crossover Loops

Carrier extraction for QPSK signals can also be derived from a modified form of the Costas loop involving loop crossover arms, as shown in Figure B.6b. The signal waveforms are shown throughout the figure. Note that each filter output contains data bits from both quadrature carriers that compose the QPSK subcarrier waveform. However, the sign of the output of the arm filters, produced by the limiters, is used to cross over and mix with the opposite arm signal. If the loop phase error is small, the output of the limiters corresponds to the cosine term of the arm filter outputs, and therefore has the sign of the data bits of the quadrature components as shown. Hence, the limiters effectively demodulate the QPSK quadrature bits, and the crossover produces a common phase error term that is canceled after subtraction, leaving a remainder error term proportional to $\sin\psi_e$. The latter signal can then be used to generate an error signal to phase control the loop VCO, thereby closing the QPSK Costas loop.

The crossover connections of the QPSK Costas loop can be redrawn in other ways. For example, the fourth-order tracking generated in (B.3.4) can be expanded as

$$\sin(4\psi_e) = 4\cos\psi_e \sin\psi_e\,[\sin^2\psi_e - \cos^2\psi_e] \tag{B.3.9}$$

In the absence of noise, and assuming ideal data pulses [$m(t) = 1$], the right side of (B.3.9) can be related to the Costas signals in (B.2.16). Hence we write

$$A^4 \sin(4\psi_e) \approx 4Q(t)I(t)[Q^2(t) - I^2(t)] \tag{B.3.10}$$

This suggests a modified Costas loop with the connection shown in Figure B.6c for QPSK carrier recovery. Note that the system is basically an extension of a PSK recovery system, and we can in fact easily convert from one to the other by simply reconnecting the VCO.

MPSK Carrier Referencing Systems

Carrier referencing systems for higher order MPSK phase modulations can be obtained by extending to higher powered nonlinearities or introducing more complicated crossover loops. A carrier with M possible carrier phases can be recovered by an Mth power device, followed by a loop tracking the Mth harmonic. The loop provides a phase coherent harmonic that can be divided by M to produce the desired reference. Since both carrier and noise are raised to the higher power, more carrier–noise cross-product terms will be generated that will again appear as noise interference to the loop tracker. Table B.4 tabulates the resulting MPSK phase reference error variance obtained in this way for 8-PSK and for the general MPSK system. Included are the previous results for BPSK and QPSK. Note the increase in error variance as the order M is increased, and the reciprocal dependence on the carrier E_b/N_0, for a given $B_L T_b$ product.

B.4 BIT TIMING

After the data modulated carrier has been demodulated to baseband via the coherent carrier reference, bit timing must be established to clock the bit or word decoding. Bit timing therefore corresponds to the operation of extracting from the demodulated baseband waveform a time-coherent clock at the bit rate or word rate of the data. Bit timing systems for performing this operation can be classified into two basic types. One involves again a nonlinearity to generate timing waveforms that can be tracked. The other uses some form of transition tracking at the bit edges and data aiding to

Table B.4. Tabulation of rms phase error σ_e^2 for MPSK carrier recovery subsystems.

Carrier Modulation Format	*Mean Squared Phase Reference Error for Carrier Recovery Subsystem*
BPSK	$B_L T_b\left[\frac{1}{E_b/N_0} + \frac{1}{E_b/N_0)^2}\right]$
QPSK	$B_L T_b\left[\frac{1}{E_b/N_0} + \frac{3.8}{(E_b/N_0)^2} + \frac{4.2}{(E_b/N_0)^3} + \frac{1}{(E_b/N_0)^4}\right]$
8-PSK	$B_L T_b\left[\frac{1}{E_b/N_0} + \frac{24.5}{(E_b/N_0)^2} + \frac{294}{(E_b/N_0)^3} + \frac{1837}{(E_b + N_0)^4} + \frac{5.8 \times 10^3}{(E_b/N_0)^5} + \frac{8.8 \times 10^3}{(E_b/N_0)^6} + \frac{5.04 \times 10^3}{(E_b/N_0)^7} + \frac{630}{(E_b/N_0)^8}\right]$
MPSK	$B_L T_b\left[\sum_{q=1}^{M} \binom{M}{q}^2 \left(\frac{q!}{M^2}\right) \frac{1}{(E_b/N_0)^q}\right]$

generate timing-error voltages. Both types of systems inherently involve modulation wipe-off and harmonic generation for clocking.

Filter-Squarer Systems

Figure B.7 shows a filter-squaring system that operates on binary modulated pulses to produce a harmonic in time synchronism with the pulse edges. Subsequent phase locking to this bit rate tone produces a coherent pulse clock. Squaring (or rectification) is needed to remove the polarity of the modulated pulses, while the filtering is used to reduce the noise and preshape the data pulses. If the binary waveform was composed of ideal, noiseless bit pulses, high pass filtering in the form of a differentiation would produce a sequence of positive and negative (according to the data bit) impulse functions at the pulse transitions. Squaring rectifies these impulses into a periodic impulse train at the bit rate, with a power level dependent on the average number of bit transitions occurring. Tracking of the bit rate harmonic by the PLL produces a VCO with zero crossings that can be used for timing markers for the bit decoding. When baseband noise is included, a pure differentiation cannot be tolerated in the prefilter because of the excessive high-frequency noise it would produce. However, if the filter is made too narrow to reduce noise, it will distort the bit pulses and decrease the harmonic power being tracked. Some consideration for the trade-off design of this prefilter has been discussed in References 8–10.

If the baseband waveform is a sequence of data-modulated pulses plus baseband noise of level N_0, the filter-squaring produces a harmonic at the bit rate frequency, plus cross-product and self-noise terms having frequency components around this frequency. The PLL tracks the harmonic, with these cross-product and self-noise waveforms appearing as interference. Holmes [9] has shown that the squared noise terms produce a timing variance in the PLL of

$$\sigma_{n \times n}^2 = \frac{B_L T_b C_n}{(E_b/N_0)^2} \text{ sec} \tag{B.4.1}$$

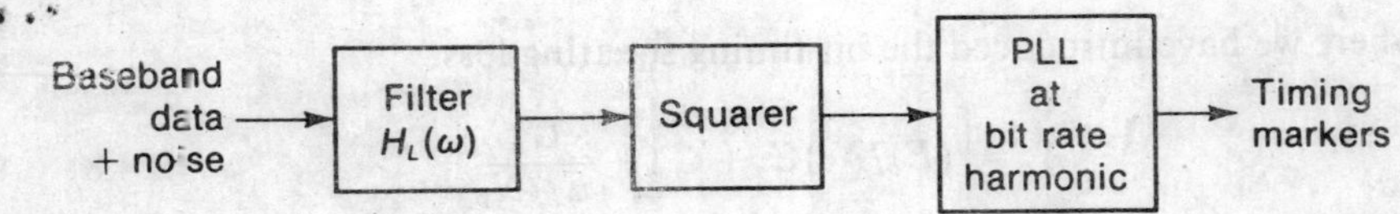

Figure B.7. Bit timing filter-squarer system.

where C_n is a coefficient dependent on the filter bandwidth, and E_b/N_0 is the baseband bit energy–to–noise level at the timing system input. For a simple RC prefilter with 3 dB frequency f_3 and NRZ pulses, C_n has the value

$$C_n = \frac{r^3\pi(1 + r^{-2})}{4(1 - e^{-2\pi r})} \tag{B.4.2}$$

where $r = f_3 T_b$. Moeneclay [10] showed the signal–noise and self-noise terms contribute a timing-error variance of

$$\sigma^2_{s\times n} = \frac{B_L T_b^3 C_{sn}}{E_b/N_0} \tag{B.4.3}$$

and

$$\sigma^2_{s\times s} = B_L T_b^3 C_s \tag{B.4.4}$$

where

$$C_{sn} = \frac{3r(4r^2 + 13r^4 - r^2 - 1)}{2\pi(1 - e^{-r})(r^2 + 1)(4r^2 + 1)(r^2 + 4)} \tag{B.4.5a}$$

$$C_s = \frac{2 + 2(1 - e^{-2\pi r})}{2\pi^2(1 - e^{-2\pi r})^2} - \frac{3(2 + e^{-2\pi r})(1 + 5r^2)}{8\pi^2 r(1 - e^{-2\pi r})(1 - r^2)(1 + 4r^2)} \tag{B.4.5b}$$

The total mean squared timing error for the filter-square bit synchronizer is then

$$\begin{aligned}\sigma^2 &= \sigma^2_{n\times n} + \sigma^2_{s\times n} + \sigma^2_{s\times s} \\ &= B_L T_b^3\left[C_s + \frac{C_{sn}}{E_b/N_0} + \frac{C_n}{(E_b/N_0)^2}\right]\end{aligned} \tag{B.4.6}$$

Normalizing σ^2 to the bit time, we can rewrite as

$$\left(\frac{\sigma}{T_b}\right)^2 = \frac{B_L T_b}{(E_b/N_0)\mathcal{S}_q} \tag{B.4.7}$$

where we have introduced the bit-timing squaring loss

$$\mathcal{S}_q = \left[(E_b/N_0)C_s + C_{sn} + \frac{C_n}{E_b/N_0}\right]^{-1} \tag{B.4.8}$$

Note that at low E_b/N_0, (B.4.7) behaves like $(E_b/N_0)^{-2}$, while, as $E_b/N_0 \to \infty$, the rms timing error decreases to an irreducible error (due to the self-noise) of

$$\left(\frac{\sigma}{T_b}\right)^2 \xrightarrow[E_b/N_0 \to \infty]{} B_L T_b C_s \tag{B.4.9}$$

It has been shown [10] that at $E_b/N_0 \approx 10$ dB, the squaring loss in (B.4.8) is minimized with a value of $r \approx 3/16$. That is, the prefilter bandwidth should be about 3/16 of the bit rate frequency $1/T_b$. For this case

$$\begin{aligned} C_s &\approx 0.017 \\ C_{sn} &\approx 0.545 \\ C_n &\approx 0.318 \end{aligned} \tag{B.4.10}$$

When these coefficients are used in (B.4.8), the normalized rms timing error in (B.4.7) plots as shown in Figure B.8 for several values of $B_L T_b$.

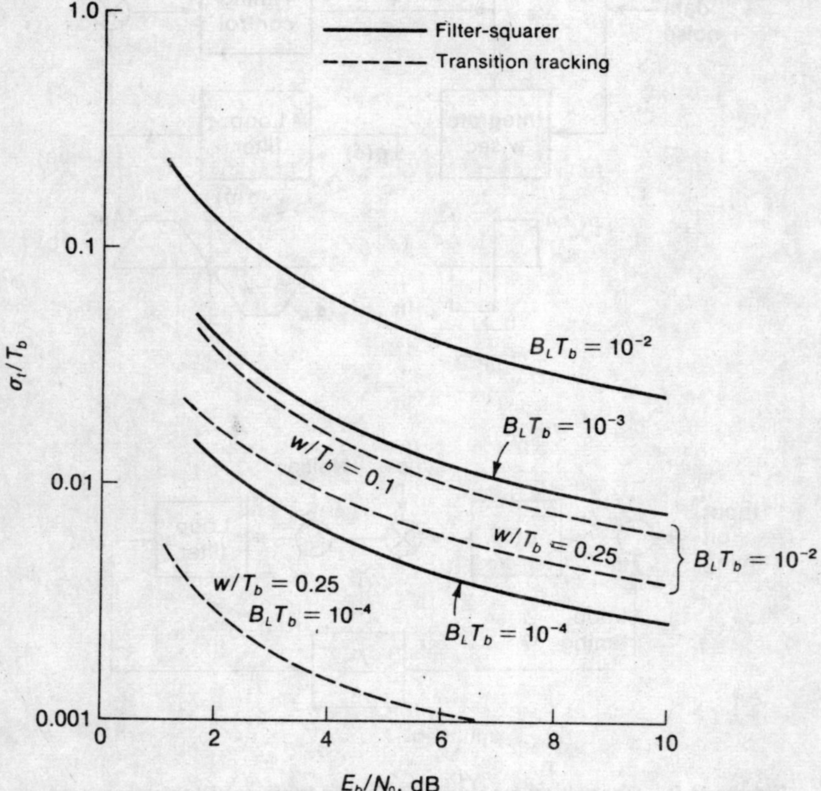

Figure B.8. Timing error vs. baseband E_b/N_0 for bit-timing systems.

Transition Tracking Systems

A second way to achieve bit timing from a modulated NRZ or Manchester bit waveform is to utilize transition tracking on the bit edges, in conjunction with bit decisioning. Transition tracking is obtained by integrating over the pulse transitions (pulse edges) to generate a timing-error voltage for feedback control. Such a system is shown in Figure B.9, where each pulse edge is integrated over a w sec integration interval. If the integration window is

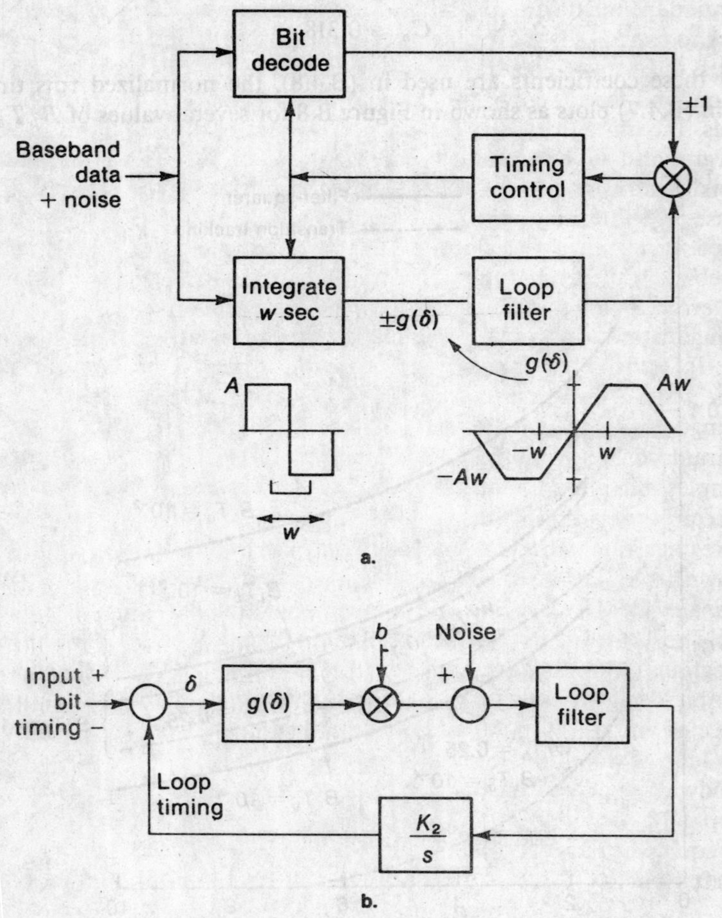

Figure B.9. Transition tracking bit-timing loop. (a) Block diagram. (b) Equivalent model.

centered exactly on the pulse edge, a zero integration value is produced because of the equal positive and negative areas. If the integration is offset by δ sec, the integration output generates the function $\pm\, g(\delta)$ shown, where the $\pm$ sign depends on the particular data bit (i.e., whether the transition changes from a positive to negative value or vice-versa). To rectify this bit sign, a bit decision is made in a separate decoding arm and used to multiply the integrator output. By inserting a one-bit delay in the loop input and by using the present bit decision, the bit polarity will always rectify the sign of the loop-error voltage, producing a timing-correction voltage of the proper sign independent of the data bit. This correction voltage is filtered and fed back to control the timing location of the integration for the next transition. Thus, the previous bit transitions are effectively used to remove the modulation, and the loop operates to hold the integrator centered on the transitions. Bit-timing markers can then be generated in synchronism with the integration for timing control. The latter system is referred to as **data-aided transition tracking**, and is the bit-timing equivalent of the suppressed carrier phase referencing system of the same type. The bit delay can also be eliminated in modified versions of the system by simply hard-limiting the baseband waveform in the upper arm and using the limiter output to invert the error. As long as the noise does not cause the bit waveform polarity to change sign during a bit, the tracking error will be properly rectified.

In transition tracking a timing-error voltage is generated each pulse time when a transition occurs. (In NRZ data, this is once per bit if the bit changes sign, but is twice per bit for Manchester data, with a transition guaranteed every mid-bit time.) The loop filter acts to smooth these error samples into a continuous loop control. In this sense the transition tracker appears as a sampling (discrete) control loop with error samples generated at regular intervals. The loop therefore has the equivalent timing model shown in Figure B.9b. The input is the timing offset of the received data bits, and the feedback variable is the relative timing position of the integrator. The function $bg(\delta)$ converts timing errors to voltages, and the loop integrates to adjust integrator timing. The multiplication by b accounts for the bit decision to rectify the error, with $b = +1$ if the bit is correctly detected and $b = -1$ if the bit is incorrectly decoded. The noise level entering the loop is the noise variance per sample ($N_0 w$) divided by the sampling bandwidth $1/T_b$, producing the effective noise level $N_0 w T_b$. Note that the loop is linear for $|\delta| \leqslant w/2$, and therefore the transition-tracking loop has an equivalent linear model with gain given by the mean slope of $bg(\delta)$ at $\delta = 0$. Hence

$$\begin{aligned}\text{Loop gain} &= \frac{Aw}{w/2}\,\mathscr{E}(b) \\ &= 2A\mathscr{E}(b)\end{aligned} \tag{B.4.11}$$

where A is the data bit amplitude. The mean of the random variable b is given by $\mathcal{E}(b) = (1)(1 - \text{PE}) + (-1)\text{PE} = 1 - 2\,\text{PE}$, where PE is the bit-decoding probability. Using the binary PSK PE in (A.2.8), (B.4.11) becomes

$$\text{Loop gain} = 2A\ \text{Erf}\left(\frac{A^2T_b}{N_0}\right)^{1/2} \tag{B.4.12}$$

With this gain inserted into the linear model, the loop can be analyzed as a standard phase lock loop with noise bandwidth B_L. The timing error variance is then

$$\sigma^2 = \frac{(N_0 w T_b)2B_L}{4A^2\text{Erf}^2(A^2T_b/N_0)^{1/2}} \tag{B.4.13}$$

The variance normalized to the bit time T_b is then

$$\left(\frac{\sigma}{T_b}\right)^2 = \frac{N_0 2B_L w/T_b}{4A^2\text{Erf}^2(A^2T_b/N_0)^{1/2}} \tag{B.4.14}$$

Again defining

$$\rho = \frac{N_0 2B_L}{A^2} = \frac{B_L T_b}{E_b/N_0} \tag{B.4.15}$$

we can write (B.4.14) as

$$\left(\frac{\sigma}{T_b}\right)^2 = \frac{1}{\rho \mathcal{S}_q} \tag{B.4.16}$$

where $\mathcal{S}_q$ is now the timing squaring loss

$$\mathcal{S}_q = \left[\frac{4\text{Erf}^2(E_b/N_0)^{1/2}}{w/T_b}\right]^{-1} \tag{B.4.17}$$

Equation (B.4.16) is also plotted in Figure B.8.

Transition-tracking performance can be improved by accumulating a sequence of m error samples prior to timing correction. (This requires replacing the filter in Figure B.9b by a digital accumulator.) Such an accumulation multiplies up the noise-voltage variance by m, but also increases the loop gain in (B.4.12) by m. The normalized timing-error variance, assuming perfect bit decisioning, is then

$$\begin{aligned}\left(\frac{\sigma}{T_b}\right)^2 &= \frac{mN_0w}{m^2 4A^2T_b^2} \\ &= \frac{(w/T_b)N_0/4}{mE_b/N_0}\end{aligned} \tag{B.4.18}$$

where w/T_b is the integration window expressed as a fraction of the bit time. Note the direct improvement as we accumulate over more samples. However, this improvement occurs only if the signal-error samples remain the same throughout the accumulation time. Hence, m is restricted to the number of bits over which the received timing variation does not change appreciably. Equation (B.4.18) is used in Equation (5.4.6) in Chapter 5.

REFERENCES

1. M. Simon, and W. Lindsey, "Optimum Performance of Suppressed Carrier Receivers with Costas Loop," *IEEE Trans. on Comm.*, (February 1977).

2. J. Holmes, *Coherent Spread Spectrum Systems* (New York: Wiley, 1982), pp. 121–129.

3. J. Layland, "An Optimum Squaring Loop Prefilter," *IEEE Trans. on Comm.*, (October 1970).

4. R. Gagliardi, *Introduction to Communication Engineering* (New York: Wiley, 1978).

5. S. Lindsey, and M. Simon, *Telecommunication Systems Engineering* (Englewood Cliffs, N.J.: Prentice-Hall, 1973).

6. R. Gagliardi, "Coupled AGC-Costas Loops with AM-PM Conversion," *IEEE Trans. on Comm.*, vol. COM-28 (January 1980).

7. L. Franks, "Carrier and Bit Synchronization in Data Communications," *IEEE Trans. on Comm.*, vol. COM-28 (August 1980).

8. F. Gardner, "Self Noise in Synchronizers," *IEEE Trans. on Comm.*, vol. COM-28 (August 1980).

9. J. Holmes, "Tracking Performance of the Filter and Square Bit Synchronizer," *IEEE Trans. on Comm.*, vol. COM-28 (August 1980).

10. M. Moeneclay, "Comments on Tracking Performance of the Filter and Square Bit Synchronizer," *IEEE Trans. on Comm.*, vol. COM-30 (February 1980).

C
Satellite Ranging Systems

Ranging systems provide a measurement of range (distance) between two points. This range measurement is achieved by processing a transmitted waveform between the two points. Although ranging is not truly a part of the satellite communication subsystem, its operation is intimately related to the carrier referencing and its waveform transmission, and processing is generally integrated directly into the communication link. In many cases, ranging performance and accuracy may ultimately limit the design of the communication subsystem.

C.1 RANGING SYSTEMS

A functional block diagram of a satellite ranging system is shown in Figure C.1. Measurement of range between two points is accomplished by transmitting a signal marker from one point to the other and back, and measuring the round-trip transit time. Since the transmitted marker travels at the speed of light,

$$\begin{aligned}[\text{Range in meters}] &= \frac{1}{2}(3 \times 10^8)(\text{round-trip time in sec}) \\ &= (150)(\text{round-trip time in } \mu\text{sec})\end{aligned} \tag{C.1.1}$$

Thus, range measurements can be made from estimates of the time between the instant of marker transmission and the instant of its return. The waveform containing the marker, called the **ranging signal**, is transmitted as an RF waveform from the earth station. At the satellite, the RF waveform is reflected, or instantaneously returned, back to ground. The returned signal is processed to recover the ranging signal and time marker, and its arrival time is compared, for the two-way range estimate, to the original transmission time. This range measurement is generally continually updated by retransmitting the ranging signal periodically, and repeating the measure-

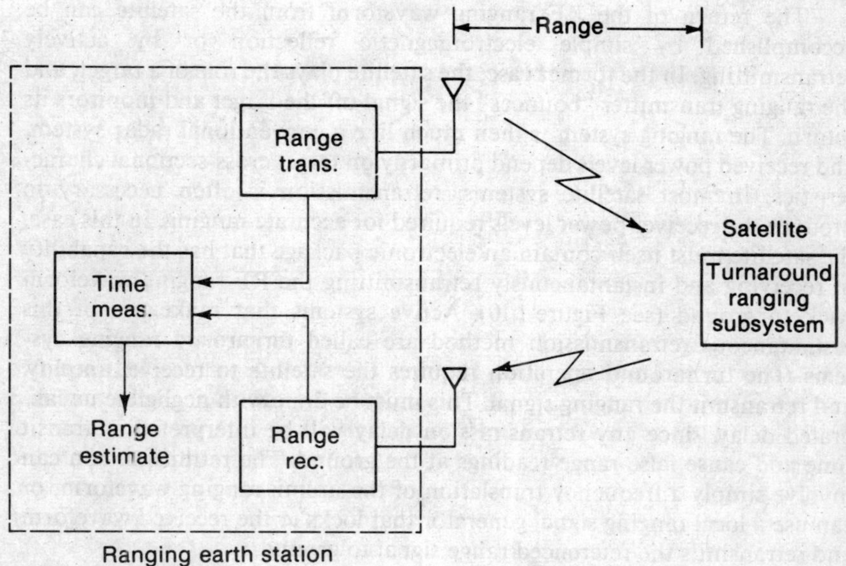

Figure C.1. Turnaround ranging system block diagram.

ment. This allows a continual measurement of the satellite range as it changes in time.

Since the returned ranging signal is invariably marred by noise, a direct time comparison between transmitted and received signals will yield range accuracies much worse than desired. For this reason, the ranging receiver attempts to align a clean version of the ranging signal with the noisy returned signal so that the time difference measurement can be made with uncontaminated waveforms. Thus, the ranging system is confronted with the task of aligning a local receiver marker sequence with a received marker sequence contained within the returned ranging signal. This alignment can be made by locking together a local version of the ranging signal with the received ranging signal. An error in the clocking of the receiver marker sequence will lead directly to an error in the measurement of the time difference, and therefore an erroneous range estimate. If the rms clocking error is $\sqrt{\epsilon^2}$ seconds, then, from (C.1.1), an rms range error of

$$\text{rms range error} = \pm(1.51)\sqrt{\epsilon^2}(10^8) \text{ meters} \tag{C.1.2}$$

will occur. Hence, clock timing accuracy determines the ultimate range accuracy.

The return of the RF ranging waveform from the satellite can be accomplished by simple electromagnetic reflection or by actively retransmitting. In the former case, the satellite plays the role of a target, and the ranging transmitter "bounces" the signal off the target and monitors its return. The ranging system is then much like a conventional radar system, and received power levels depend primarily on target cross-sectional characteristics. In most satellite systems, retransmission is often necessary to produce the receiver power levels required for accurate ranging. In this case, the satellite must itself contain an electronic package that has the capability of receiving and instantaneously retransmitting the RF ranging waveform back to ground (see Figure 1.10). Active systems that make use of this instantaneous retransmission method are called **turnaround ranging systems**. The turnaround operation requires the satellite to receive, amplify, and retransmit the ranging signal. This must be done with negligible uncalibrated delay, since any retransmission delay will be interpreted as transit time and cause false range readings at the ground. The retransmission can involve simply a frequency translation of the uplink ranging waveform, or can use a local ranging signal generator that locks to the received waveform and retransmits the referenced range signal to ground.

RF ranging waveforms are formed by modulating the desired ranging signal onto an RF carrier. Short distance (ground-to-ground) ranging systems may often use merely pulse trains as the ranging signal. Satellite systems prefer continuous ranging signals for improved power efficiency. Since a locking operation may have to be performed at both ends in a turnaround ranging system, continuous ranging signals are usually constructed as periodic digital waveforms, the latter called **range codes**. This means the ranging waveforms are formed much like the address codes used in CDMA, and the code-locking operation can be accomplished by the code-acquisition subsystems described in Chapter 7. The ranging waveforms are generated from the ranging codes by PSK modulating the code chips onto a ranging subcarrier. In this case, if the chips are w sec wide, a ranging subcarrier bandwidth of

$$B_r \cong 2/w \text{ Hz} \tag{C.1.3}$$

is required to transmit the ranging waveform.

In addition to the simplicity in code alignment procedures, digital ranging codes have the advantage that the measurement of transmitted and received time differences is computationally simplified. We need only monitor the correlation between the transmitted and local received ranging codes (Figure C.2), and count the number of code chip shifts needed to align the two. Since the chips have known time width, the number of required

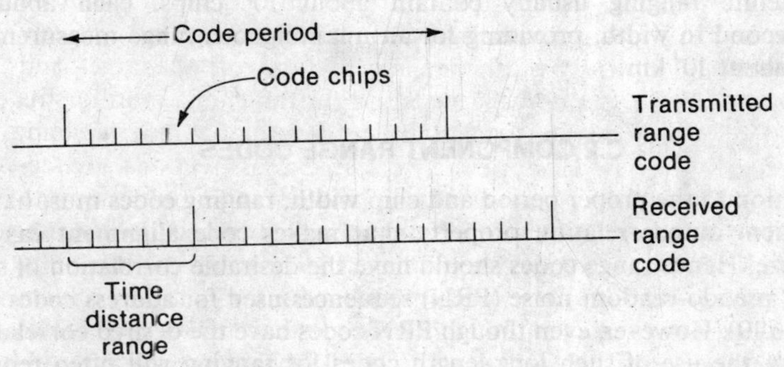

Figure C.2. Timing diagram for coded ranging signals.

chips shifts is proportional to the desired range. The narrower the ranging code pulse width, the higher the resolution in the eventual range estimate. If code alignment can be measured accurately to within a fraction η of one chip time w, then from (C.1.2) range can be measured to within

$$\text{Range accuracy} = \eta w(1.51)(10^8) \text{ meters} \tag{C.1.4}$$

Thus, the narrower the chip width the more accurate the range measurement. For example, with $\eta = 0.1$, a microsecond chip will allow range to be measured to within 16 meters. This, in turn, will require a ranging subcarrier bandwidth in (C.1.3) of about 2 MHz. Hence, ranging accuracy is achieved at the expense of ranging channel bandwidth.

Range codes differ from address codes in the manner in which the code period is selected. While address codes in CDMA usually have their code period related to bit times, the range code period is set by the range being measured. If the range is such that the round-trip travel time will exceed the range code period, the returned marker will occur after the next marker is sent. This leads to ambiguities in the subsequent range measurement. Hence range code period determines the maximum range that can be measured without ambiguities. If the range code period is T_c seconds, then the maximum range is

$$\text{Maximum range} = 1.5\,T_c(10^8) \text{ meters} \tag{C.1.5}$$

Therefore, range codes are desired with as long a period as possible to increase the maximum unambiguous ranging distance. Since the code chips should also be narrow for good measurement resolution, the long period implies long-length codes (i.e., many chips per period). Typical codes used for satellite ranging usually contain about 10^5 chips, each about 1 microsecond in width, providing for an unambiguous range measurement out to about 10^4 km.

C.2 COMPONENT RANGE CODES

In addition to the proper period and chip width, ranging codes must have a convenient autocorrelation property that makes code alignment easy to recognize. Hence range codes should have the desirable correlation of shift register pseudo-random noise (PRN) sequences used for address codes (see Figure 6.10). However, even though PRN codes have the desired correlation property, the use of such long-length codes for ranging will often require prohibitively long acquisition times, especially in systems that specifically require relatively fast range acquisition. For this reason, there is interest in using range codes that sacrifice some of the advantages of PRN correlation in order to reduce the initial range code acquisition time. One method for accomplishing this is to use ranging codes constructed from combinations of smaller length PRN codes, called **component codes**, Figure C.3a. Several methods exist [1,2] for logically combining short periodic binary codes into a long period sequence whose length is the product of the lengths of the components. This code combining is achieved by using linear or nonlinear modulo-two logic with repeated versions of the component code set, and generally requires that the component PRN codes have lengths that are relatively prime. If the combined code has been properly constructed, alignment of an individual PRN component with the entire code, and correlation over a sufficient number of chips will produce a small average correlation value. This partial correlation value is a fraction of the full code correlation. As the next component code is aligned with the code and correlated, it also produces a partial correlation that will be added to that of the first. As each component is so aligned, the correlation increases by fractional steps. until full correlation is achieved, and all components are aligned.

These partial correlation values are used by the receiver to align identical receiver components with the received code. The receiver, using the same combination logic to generate the long-length code, will therefore produce the code in exact time synchronism with the received version using the aligned components, as shown in Figure C.3b. Each partial correlation step indicates the alignment of a new component, and each component can be aligned by testing each position of its own length. Thus, a component code of length n_i will require at most n_i chip positions to be searched. Since this is true for each component, only Σn_i total positions need be searched. Hence, construction of long-length codes from shorter component

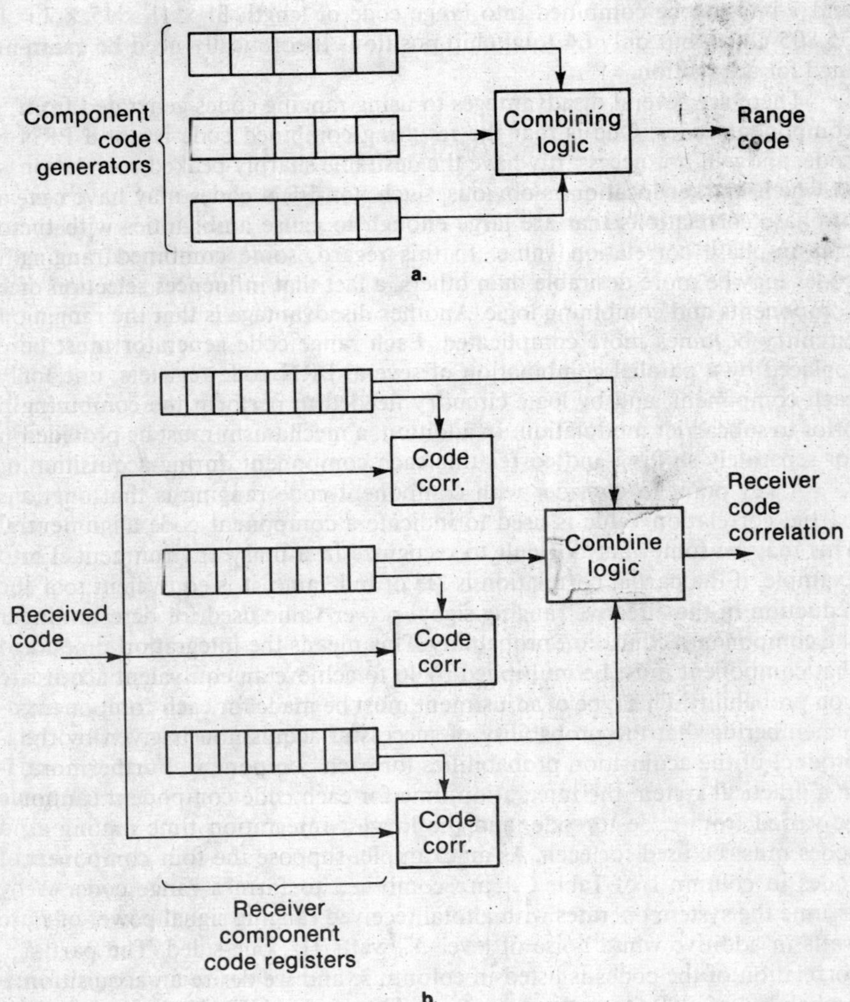

Figure C.3. Component code-ranging systems. (a) Range code generator block diagram. (b) Receiver component code correlator.

sequences have the basic advantage that while the total length is determined by the product of the code length, the acquisition time is determined by their sum. The number of chips to be searched by this method is considerably less than the length. For example, component codes of length 31, 11, 15, and 7 bits can be combined into range code of length $31 \times 11 \times 15 \times 7 = 35{,}805$ chips, but only 64 total chip positions theoretically need be examined for acquisition.

There are several disadvantages to using ranging codes generated from component codes. One is that the resulting combined code is not a PRN code, and will not necessarily have the desirable sharply peaked correlation in which marker location is obvious. Such non-PRN codes may have out-of-phase correlations that are large enough to cause ambiguities with the true in-phase correlation value. In this regard, some combined ranging codes may be more desirable than others, a fact that influences selection of components and combining logic. Another disadvantage is that the ranging circuitry becomes more complicated. Each range code generator must be replaced by a parallel combination of several PRN code registers, one for each component, and by logic circuitry needed to perform the combining prior to subcarrier modulation. In addition, a mechanism must be provided for separately shifting and correlating each component during acquisition.

A key point to consider with component code ranging is that only a partial correlation value is used to indicate a component code alignment. This may be somewhat difficult to recognize in a noisy environment. For example, if the partial correlation is .25 of full value, it is equivalent to a $\frac{1}{16}$ reduction in the effective ranging signal power value used for determining the component acquisition probability. This means the integration time for that component must be multiplied by 16 to achieve an equivalent acquisition probability. This type of adjustment must be made for each component, remembering that the probability of successful acquisition is given by the product of the acquisition probabilities for each component. Furthermore, in a practical system the integration time for each code component cannot be varied from code to code, and the longest integration time among all codes must be used for each. As an example, suppose the four component codes in column 1 of Table C.1 are combined to form a range code. We assume the system operates with a total received ranging signal power of P_r watts in additive white noise of level N_0 watts/Hz, one-sided. The partial correlation of the codes is listed in column 3, and we desire an acquisition probability of .999 for each component. The required E_c/N_0 for each code is listed in column 4, obtained from Figure 2.29 for each code length. The required code acquisition time is then determined by the maximum E_c/N_0 and the smallest partial correlation value. Hence,

$$\text{Time to acquire} = \left(\frac{N_0}{P_r}\right)\left(\frac{1}{\frac{1}{4}}\right)^2 (4.5) \qquad \text{(C.2.1)}$$

where P_r is range code power. For a given value of P_r/N_0, the required

Table C.1. Tabulation of component code parameters.

Component Code Length	*log₂ (length)*	*Partial Correlation Value*	*Required (E_c/N_0)*
7	2.8	$\frac{1}{4}$	4.5
11	3.46	$\frac{1}{4}$	3.8
15	3.91	$\frac{1}{6}$	3.5
31	4.95	$\frac{1}{6}$	3.0

acquisition time can be computed from (C.2.1). While (C.2.1) indicates an increase in the acquisition time as P_r/N_0 is reduced, it implies that acquisition will be achieved at any value of P_r/N_0 if enough time is allowed. In a practical system, however, one must be concerned with the ability to phase reference (properly demodulate the PSK-coded subcarrier) as P_r/N_0 is reduced. The discussion of the carrier referencing analysis in Appendix B is applicable here. The ability to maintain phase referencing with the partially correlated signal values and the loop noise bandwidth will determine the minimal value of P_r/N_0 for successful code acquisition.

C.3 TONE-RANGING SYSTEMS

Another ranging technique used to reduce acquisition time makes use of sinusoid or square wave harmonics. The operation is referred to as **side tone acquisition**, and the system is sometimes called **tone ranging**. Tone ranging systems take advantage of the phase relation between harmonics to quickly resolve ambiguities and avoid the multiposition search associated with coded acquisition. Consider a sequence of N harmonic signals $\{S_i(t)\}$, as in Figure C.4. (The figure shows square waves, but the discussion pertains to sine waves of the same period as well.) We show three such harmonics, each at one-half the frequency of the previous. That is, if f_i is the frequency of the harmonic $S_i(t)$

$$f_i = \frac{f_1}{2^{i-1}} \tag{C.3.1}$$

where f_1 is the clock (highest) frequency. At the ranging transmitter these harmonics are aligned so that the transmitter marker can be interpreted as the point in time where each harmonic simultaneously has a positive-going

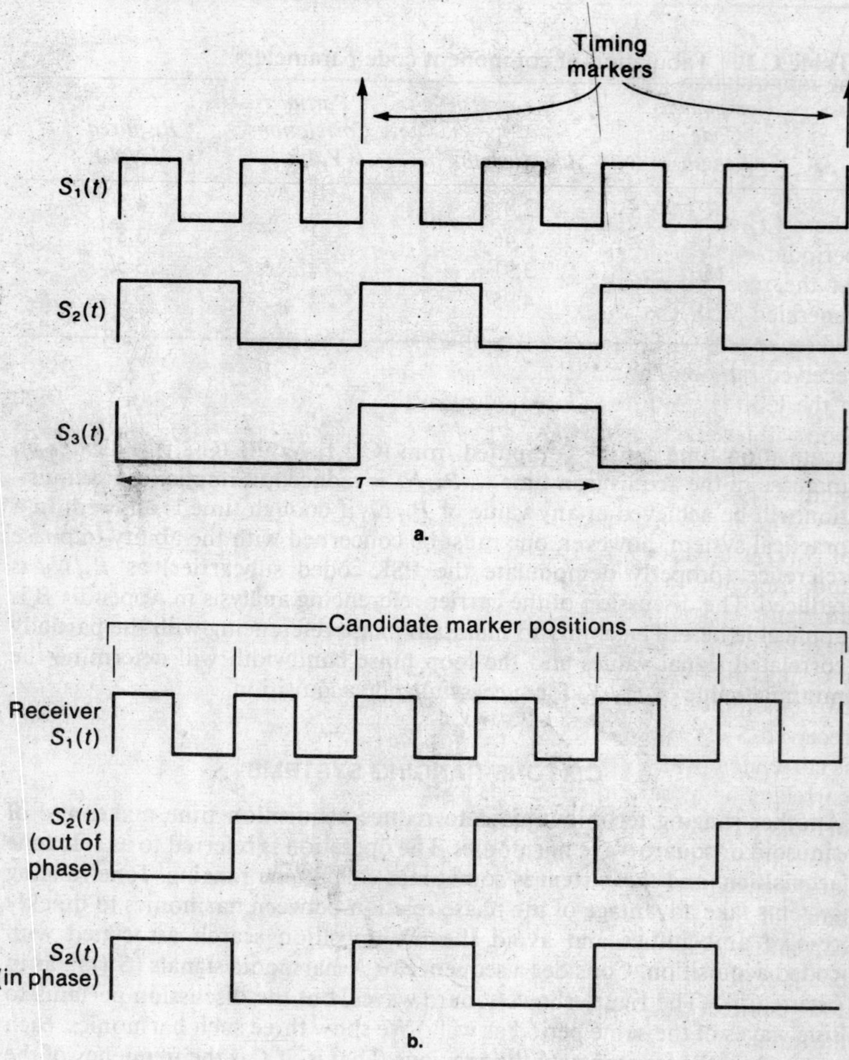

Figure C.4. Tone ranging waveform diagram (square waves). (a) All tones in phase. (b) Out-of-phase tones.

zero crossing. Only one such point occurs during each period of the lowest harmonic, $S_N(t)$. Hence, the lowest harmonic determines the periodicity of the markers. The set of phase-aligned harmonics are then summed to form the range signal

$$r(t) = \sum_{i=1}^{N} a_i S_i(t) \tag{C.3.2}$$

where $\{a_i\}$ are the square wave amplitudes. The range signal in (C.3.2) is periodic with period $\tau = l/f_N$ sec, that is, the period of the lowest harmonic. At the receiver ranging subsystem, Figure C.5, the same harmonics are generated with the same phase relationship, but with an arbitrary time reference point. The first receiver harmonic $S_1(t)$ is first phase locked to the received ranging signal, using either a sine wave or square wave clock loop. If the loop bandwidth is less than the harmonic frequency separation, the loop will track the clock harmonic only at f_1 in (C.3.2), and the receiver and received versions of $S_1(t)$ will be brought (theoretically) into phase alignment.

Within the total acquisition period of τ sec, each positive zero crossing of $S_1(t)$ is a candidate time reference point of the received ranging signal, and, therefore, $\tau f_1 = f_1/f_N = 2^{N-1}$ ambiguity points must be resolved. This ambiguity resolution is provided by the remaining harmonics. Since the next harmonic, $S_2(t)$, is time-locked to the first harmonic (its positive zero crossings are aligned with those of $S_1(t)$), we see from Figure C.4b that only two possibilities can occur: the receiver $S_2(t)$ is exactly in phase with the received $S_2(t)$, or it is exactly 180° out of phase. If the local harmonic $S_2(t)$ is correlated over a period with the received ranging signal in (C.3.2), it will correlate with only the second harmonic, since all the harmonics are orthogonal. Thus, because of the harmonic phasing, a correlation of $S_2(t)$ with $r(t)$ will produce either a large positive in-phase correlation value or a large negative out-of-phase correlation. The in-phase or out-of-phase possibility of $S_2(t)$ can therefore be determined by a single polarity test on the correlation of $S_2(t)$ and the received ranging signal. If $S_2(t)$ is decided as being in phase, it is left alone. If it is decided as out of phase, it is shifted by 180° (shifted forward by one-half its period) to be brought into second harmonic alignment.

We now have $S_1(t)$ and $S_2(t)$ properly aligned with the corresponding components of the received ranging signal. Since the negative-going zero crossings of $S_2(t)$ cannot be marker locations, only the positive zero crossings common to both $S_1(t)$ and $S_2(t)$ signify possible marker positions. This conclusion eliminates one-half of the original ambiguity points of $S_1(t)$. Thus, by a single polarity decision test on the correlation of $S_2(t)$, we now need only consider $2^{N-1}/2$ possible ambiguity points. The procedure is now repeated with $S_3(t)$. This latter is generated in phase synchronism with $S_2(t)$, and correlated with the received waveform. A polarity decision on the

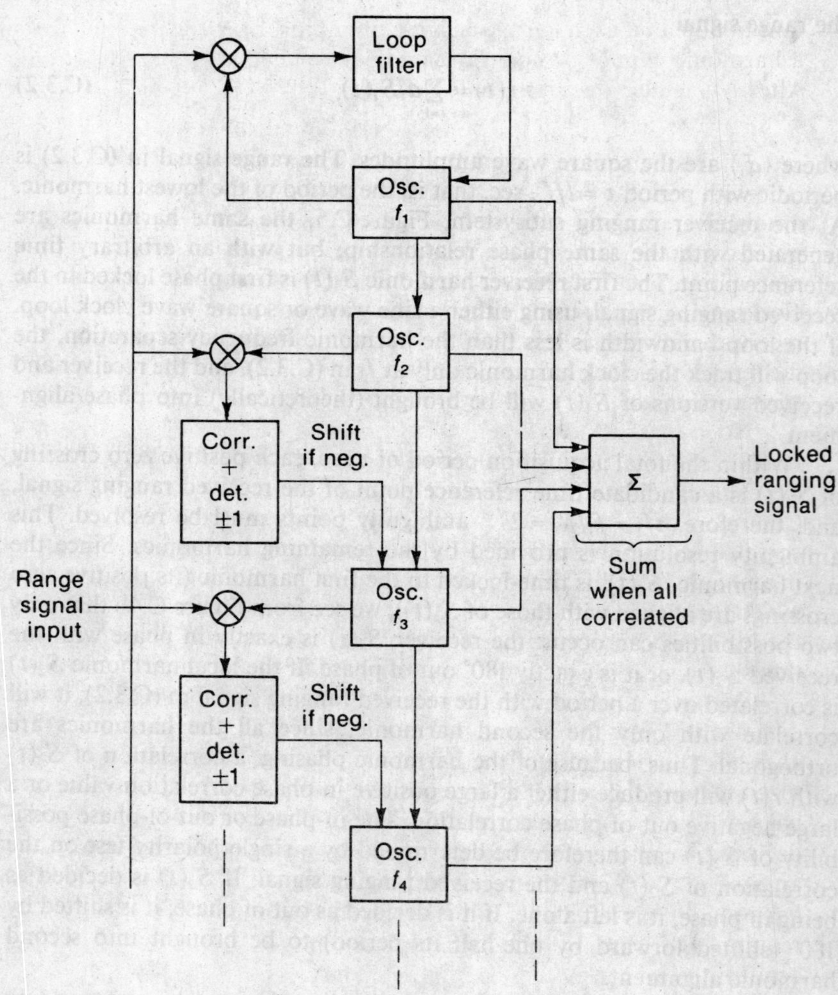

Figure C.5. Tone range receiver correlator.

correlation output will determine if $S_3(t)$ is in or out of phase. This allows us to align $S_3(t)$, which again eliminates one-half the remaining ambiguity points, leaving only $2^{N-1}/2^2$ possibilities. By continuing in this manner—each time correlating, deciding, and aligning the subsequent harmonic—we continually reduce the remaining candidate points by one-half. It is important to note that each harmonic alignment must be made in sequence, since a harmonic cannot be correlated until the previous one has been aligned. After $N - 1$ such decisions, only

$$\frac{f_1\tau}{2^{N-1}} = \frac{f_1}{f_N 2^{N-1}} = \frac{2^{N-1}}{2^{N-1}} = 1 \tag{C.3.3}$$

ambiguity point will remain. If all polarity decisions were correct, this last point correctly identifies the marker position. The correct marker position now allows continual generation of the receiver timing markers, and the clocking of the highest harmonic maintains the timing, so that receiver and received markers are synchronized. These timing markers can then be used for repeated range measurements by comparing to the time markers of the transmitted signal.

Note that in tone ranging the original 2^{N-1} ambiguity points are resolved by $N - 1$ binary polarity decisions made in sequence. Conversely, we can say $f_1\tau$ ambiguities were resolved by $\log_2 (f_1\tau)$ binary decisions. Contrast this with the PRN ML acquisition schemes, which required a correlation at each of the ambiguity points. Hence, a substantial reduction in ambiguity decisioning is achieved by tone ranging. Acquisition systems in which the number of ambiguity decisions to be made is proportional to only the log of the number of ambiguity points are referred to as **rapid acquisition systems.**

We have interpreted the operation of the tone ranging receiver by the diagram of Figure C.5. That is, the binary polarity decisions are used to align the harmonics, which are then used to reconstruct the time synchronized ranging signal in (C.3.2). However, we can also interpret the individual harmonic polarity decisions as digits of a binary word. The sequence of decisions then formulate a complete word, and the word uniquely identifies an ambiguity point. In this sense, the decisions are not used to align a harmonic, but rather to enumerate a location. Since k ambiguity points require $\log_2 k$ binary digits for unique representation, we see that rapid acquisition systems, such as tone ranging, resolve ambiguities with the minimal number of receiver decisions.

The key parameters characterizing any acquisition system are the acquisition probability, the time to acquire, and the signal power levels. Since acquisition is successful in tone ranging only if each harmonic polarity decision is correct, the probability of acquisition is then

$$PAC = \prod_{i=2}^{N} \mathrm{PC}_i \tag{C.3.4}$$

where PC_i is the probability of correctly deciding the phase of the ith harmonic. Since this is simply an antipodel binary decision,

$$\mathrm{PC}_i = Q\left[\left(\frac{2a_i^2 T_i}{N_0}\right)^{1/2}\right] \tag{C.3.5}$$

where T_i is the correlation time of the ith harmonic. The total acquisition time is then the sum of the $\{T_i\}$. However, practical limitations will require that each harmonic use the same integration time. Hence,

$$\begin{aligned} \text{Acquisition time} &= (N-1)\left[\max_i T_i\right] \\ &= \log_2(f_1\tau)\left[\max_i T_i\right] \end{aligned} \tag{C.3.6}$$

We see that the total time to acquire is directly related to the number of harmonics, which in turn is logarithmically proportional to the clock frequency and ranging period. The former defines the highest harmonic and the latter the lowest harmonic, and the number of decisions depends on the required number of harmonics that must be inserted between. The latter also determines the complexity of the acquisition receiver in Figure C.5. A basic disadvantage of tone ranging is that the total ranging power must be divided among all harmonics. Hence, the power levels a_i^2 in (C.3.2) is only a fraction of the available ranging power, and this power per harmonic varies inversely as the number of harmonics. In particular, even after successful acquisition, only a fraction of the ranging power is available for the clock, and range accuracy is degraded over that of a coded system. In some cases, the clock is given a significant fraction of the total power, at the expense of longer integration times in (C.3.5).

Transmission of tone ranging signals requires a bandwidth necessary to send all harmonics simultaneously. For sinusoidal harmonics, this requires a bandwidth extending from the lowest harmonic, f_N, to the highest f_1. The lowest tone may in fact be quite low if the maximum range is long. For example, if the range is on the order of 20,000 km, then $f_N = 1/\tau = 3 \times 10^8/2(2 \times 10^7) = 7.5$ Hz. For square waves, the upper bandedge must be at least $2f_1$ to avoid pulse rounding of the higher harmonics. The ranging signal must be modulated on the RF, and demodulated prior to ranging processing. More serious is the dynamic voltage range of the tone ranging signal, since the signals are arithmetically summed in (C.3.2). Even square waves will produce a multilevel-voltage waveform, which makes it somewhat disadvantageous compared to the convenient bipolar nature of coded signals. Hard-limiting of the tone ranging signal to produce binary signals causes harmonic power suppression that must be accounted for in (C.3.5).

The harmonics in (C.3.2) were taken as half frequencies. By using higher submultiples, the number of required harmonics, and the number of corresponding decisions, between the highest and the lowest can be reduced. If each harmonic was $1/k$ of the previous, then only $\log_k (f_1 \tau)$ harmonics are required. However, each harmonic will have one of k possible phase shifts relative to its corresponding received harmonic when correlating. Hence, a decision on one of k phase values, instead of an antipodal decision, must be made. This is identical to word detecting with polyphase block-coded signalling. The harmonic detection probabilities in (C.3.4) must now be replaced by the general polyphase results of Section A.5. Recall there that the effective detection energy was reduced by the number of phase states to be distinguished. This means integration time must be increased by the same factor to compensate. Hence, use of higher order submultiple harmonics reduces the number of harmonics, but increases the length of integration time per harmonic for decisioning.

REFERENCES

1. S.W. Golomb et al., *Digital Communications with Space Applications* (Englewood Cliffs, N.J.: Prentice-Hall, 1964), chapter 6.

2. W. Lindsey, and M. Simon, *Telecommunications System Engineering* (Englewood Cliffs, N.J.: Prentice-Hall, 1974), chapter 4.

D

Correlation Analysis of a Nonlinear Device

In Section 5.2 we considered a class of nonlinear devices whose output waveform $y(t)$ can be written in terms of its input waveform $x(t)$ as

$$y(t) = \frac{1}{2\pi}\int_{-\infty}^{\infty} G(\omega)e^{j\omega x(t)}d\omega \tag{D.1}$$

Here $G(\omega)$ is the Fourier transform of the device nonlinearity. Many of the nonlinearities encountered in communication systems fall into this classification. In this appendix, we examine the autocorrelation function of the output $y(t)$ when the input waveform is a random process. The case of most interest is when $x(t)$ is a carrier waveform with additive Gaussian noise. The autocorrelation of $y(t)$ is given formally by

$$\begin{aligned} R_y(\tau) &= \mathscr{E}[y(t)y(t+\tau)] \\ &= \frac{1}{2\pi}\int_{-\infty}^{\infty}\int_{-\infty}^{\infty} G(\omega_1)G(\omega_2)\psi_x(\omega_1, \omega_2, \tau)d\omega_1\, d\omega_2 \end{aligned} \tag{D.2}$$

where

$$\psi_x(\omega_1, \omega_2, \tau) = \mathscr{E}\{\exp[j\omega_1 x(t) + j\omega_2 x(t+\tau)]\} \tag{D.3}$$

is again the second characteristic function of the input process $x(t)$. For the case where $x(t)$ is composed of the sum of a modulated carrier, $a(t)\cos[\omega_c t + \theta(t)]$, plus independent bandpass Gaussian noise $n(t)$, (D.3) factors as

$$\psi_x(\omega_1, \omega_2, \tau) = \psi_c(\omega_1, \omega_2, \tau)\psi_n(\omega_1, \omega_2, \tau) \tag{D.4}$$

where ψ_c and ψ_n are the evaluation of (D.3) with the carrier and noise separately inserted. For the carrier term, we can use the Jacobi–Anger identity to expand the exponentials first. Subsequent averaging then yields

$$\psi_c(\omega_1, \omega_2, \tau) = \sum_{q=0}^{\infty} \epsilon_q \mathcal{E}[I_q(j\omega_1 a(t)) I_q(j\omega_2 a(t+\tau)) R_c(\tau, q) \qquad \text{(D.5a)}$$

where

$$R_c(\tau, q) = \mathcal{E}[\cos(q\omega_c t + q\theta(t))\cos(q\omega_c t + q\omega_c \tau + q\theta(t+\tau))] \qquad \text{(D.5b)}$$

The characteristic function of a Gaussian process is

$$\Psi_n(\omega_1, \omega_2, \tau) = \exp -\tfrac{1}{2}[R_n(0)\omega_1^2 + R_n(0)\omega_2^2 + 2R_n(\tau)\omega_1\omega_2] \qquad \text{(D.6)}$$

where $R_n(\tau)$ is the autocorrelation function of the noise process. Substituting (D.6) into (D.2) and expanding exp $(R_n(\tau)\omega_1\omega_2]$ yields

$$R_y(\tau) = \sum_{q=0}^{\infty} \sum_{i=0}^{\infty} \frac{\epsilon_q \epsilon_i}{i!} \mathcal{E}[h_{qi}(t) h_{qi}(t+\tau)] R_n^i(\tau) R_c(\tau, q) \qquad \text{(D.7)}$$

with

$$h_{qi}(t) = \frac{1}{2\pi} \int_{-\infty}^{\infty} G(\omega)\omega^i I_q[j\omega a(t)] e^{-R_n(0)\omega^2/2} d\omega \qquad \text{(D.8)}$$

Equation (D.8) represents the general expression for output autocorrelation of a nonlinear device having transform $G(\omega)$, operating on a carrier plus noise waveform. Note that $R_y(\tau)$ appears as a sum of terms over the integers q and i and generates the various combinations of the signal and noise cross-product terms of the output. The corresponding power spectrum of the nonlinearity output can be obtained by transforming the preceding autocorrelation term by term. A bandpass nonlinearity would produce only the frequency components in the vicinity of the carrier frequency. The signal component in this region would correspond to the ($q = 1$, $i = 0$) term in (D.7), whereas the noise and interference would involve any of the remainder terms having frequency components in this zone. By properly determining the power of the signal component and the combined power of the noise and cross-produce interference terms, the effective signal-to-noise ratio of the device output can be computed.

The result in (D.7) simplifies for specific types of modulated carriers. For AM with a uniformly distributed phase angle and a stationary amplitude modulating process,

$$R_c(\tau, q) = \frac{1}{\epsilon_a}[\cos(q\omega_c \tau)] \qquad \text{(D.9)}$$

and

$$R_y(\tau) = \sum_{q=0}^{\infty} \sum_{i=0}^{\infty} \frac{\epsilon_i}{i!} R_n^i(\tau) [\mathscr{E}[h_{qi}(t) h_{qi}(t+\tau)]] \cos(q\omega_c \tau) \tag{D.10}$$

where $h_{qi}(t)$ is given in (D.8), and the average $\mathscr{E}$ is over the statistics of the amplitude modulation. For angle modulation,

$$R_y(\tau) = \sum_{q=0}^{\infty} \sum_{i=0}^{\infty} \frac{\epsilon_q \epsilon_i}{i!} (h_{qi})^2 R_n^i(\tau) R_c(\tau, q) \tag{D.11}$$

with h_{qi} given in (D.8) with $a(t) = A$. The various values of q yield the harmonics of the carrier waveform, whereas the sum over i produces the various convolutions of the noise with itself. A bandpass nonlinearity would produce a carrier component at its output, having an autocorrelation function

$$2h_{10}^2 \mathscr{E}\{\cos[\omega_I \tau + \theta(t+\tau) - \theta(t)]\} \tag{D.12}$$

The power in this component is obtained by setting $\tau = 0$. Hence

$$\begin{aligned} \begin{bmatrix} \text{Output carrier} \\ \text{signal power} \end{bmatrix} &= 2h_{10}^2 \\ &= 2\left[\frac{1}{2\pi}\int_{-\infty}^{\infty} G(\omega) I_1(j\omega A) e^{-R_n(0)\omega^2/2} d\omega\right]^2 \end{aligned} \tag{D.13}$$

Equation (D.13) gives the carrier power output of a general bandpass nonlinear device when the input corresponds to an angle-modulated carrier plus Gaussian noise. The particular form of the nonlinearity enters through its transform function $G(\omega)$. As an example, a hard-limiting device has the transform

$$G(\omega) = \frac{2}{j\omega} \tag{D.14}$$

and (D.13) is then

$$2h_{10}^2 = \left[\frac{1}{\pi}\int_0^{\infty}\left(\frac{1}{j\omega}\right) I_1(j\omega A) e^{-R_n(0)\omega^2/2} d\omega\right]^2 \tag{D.15}$$

The preceding can be integrated directly to yield

$$2h_{10}^2 = \frac{2}{\pi}\rho e^{-\rho}\left[I_0\left(\frac{\rho}{2}\right) + I_1\left(\frac{\rho}{2}\right)\right]^2 \tag{D.16}$$

where $\rho = A^2/2R_n(0)$. A saturating (soft-limiting) gain device can be conveniently modeled by the gain function

$$y(t) = \text{Erf}\left[\frac{x(t)}{b}\right] \qquad x(t) > 0$$
$$= -\text{Erf}\left[\frac{|x(t)|}{b}\right] \qquad x(t) < 0 \tag{D.17}$$

where Erf(x) is the Gaussian error function and b is a normalizing parameter determining the saturation level. The Fourier transform of (D.17) is given by

$$G(\omega) = \frac{2}{j\omega}e^{-b^2\omega^2/2} \tag{D.18}$$

This differs from the hard-limiting transfer function only by the exponential term. When (D.18) is used in (D.13), we obtain

$$2h_{10}^2 = \left[\frac{1}{\pi}\int_0^\infty \left(\frac{1}{j\omega}\right) I_1(j\omega A)e^{-[R_n(0)+b^2]\omega^2/2}\,d\omega\right]^2 \tag{D.19}$$

When compared to (D.15), we see that the integral differs only in the addition of the b^2 to the integrand exponential. This simply converts $R_n(0)$ to $[R_n(0) + b^2]$, which is equivalent to increasing the input noise power by b^2. The integration in (D.16) is again valid, with ρ now redefined as $\rho = A^2/2[R_n(0) + b^2]$.

Consider now the extension to the case of a general nonlinearity when K modulated carriers appear at the input with Gaussian noise. In this case we would have

$$\psi_c(s_1, s_2, \tau) = \mathscr{E}\left\{\exp\left[js_1\sum_{i=1}^{K} a_i \cos[\omega_i t + \theta_i(t)] + js_2\sum_{i=1}^{K_1} a_i \cos[\omega_i t + \omega_i\tau + \theta_i(t+\tau)]\right]\right\} \tag{D.20}$$

where a_i, ω_i, and $\theta_i(t)$ are the amplitudes, frequencies, and phase modulations of the individual carriers, and the expectation is over the statistics of the modulation. Applying the Jacobi–Anger expansion and making use of the statistical independence of the carriers, we obtain

$$\Psi_c(s_1, s_2, \tau) = \sum_{m_k=0}^{\infty} \cdots \sum_{m_1=0}^{\infty} (\epsilon_{m_1} \cdots \epsilon_{m_K}) \prod_{i=1}^{K} I_{m_i}(a_i s_1) I_{m_i}(a_i s_2) \times \prod_{i=1}^{K} R_{c_i}(m_i, \omega_i, \tau) \tag{D.21}$$

where $\epsilon_0 = 1$, $\epsilon_m = 2, m > 0$, and

$$R_{c_i}(m, \omega_i, \tau) \triangleq \frac{1}{2}\mathscr{E}\{\cos[m\omega_i\tau + m(\phi_i(t) - \phi_i(t+\tau))]\} \tag{D.22}$$

Here $R_{c_i}(m, \omega, \tau)$ is simply the correlation function of a modulated carrier with frequency ω and with its entire phase argument multiplied by m. The fact that the phase modulations are stationary makes the carrier process itself stationary. Equation (D.21) is simply the kth order extension of our earlier result in (D.5). Substitution of (D.21) into (D.2) then yields

$$R_y(\tau) = \sum_{i=0}^{\infty} \frac{R_n^i(\tau)}{i!} \sum_{m_K=0}^{\infty} \cdots \sum_{m_1=0}^{\infty} \epsilon h_i^2(m_1, m_2, \ldots, m_K) \prod_{q=1}^{K} R_{c_q}(m_q, \omega_q, \tau) \tag{D.23}$$

where $\epsilon = \prod_{q=1}^{K} \epsilon_{m_i}$, and

$$h_i(m_1, \ldots, m_K) \triangleq \frac{1}{2\pi_j} \int_{-\infty}^{\infty} G(\omega)\omega^i e^{\sigma_n^2\omega^2/2} \left[\prod_{q=1}^{K} I_{m_q}(a_q\omega)\right] d\omega \tag{D.24}$$

By letting $\omega = jx$, $I_m(ja\omega) = j^m J_m(a\omega)$, this integral can be rewritten instead as

$$h_i(m_1, \ldots, m_K) = \frac{1}{2\pi} j^{(i+m_1+\ldots+m_K-1)} \int_{-\infty}^{\infty} G(x)x^i \left[\prod_{q=1}^{K} J_{m_q}(a_q x)\right] e^{-\sigma_n^2 x^2/2} dx \tag{D.25}$$

To model the saturating power amplifier of Figure 4.20 we use the soft-limiting characteristic of (D.17), whose transform is given in (D.18). For this model (D.25) becomes

$$h_i(m_1, \ldots, m_k) = \frac{V_L}{\pi} j^{(i+m_1+\ldots+m_k-1)} \int_{-\infty}^{\infty} x^{i-1} \prod_{q=1}^{K} J_{m_q}(a_q x) e^{-(\sigma_n^2 + b^2)X^2/2} dx \tag{D.26}$$

Since $J_m(x)$ is an even function when m is even and is an odd function when m is odd, (D.26) will integrate to a nonzero value only if

$$i + |m_1| + |m_2| + \cdots + |m_k| = \text{odd number} \tag{D.27}$$

For this condition,

$$j^{(i+m_1+\cdots+m_k-1)} = (\pm 1)^2 = 1 \tag{D.28}$$

and we can ignore this coefficient in evaluating (D.26). Thus the saturating amplifier of Figure 4.20 is described by the output correlation function

$$R_y(\tau) = V_L^2 \sum_{i=0}^{\infty} \sum_{m_k=0}^{\infty} \cdots \sum_{m_1=0}^{\infty} \frac{R_n^i(\tau)}{i!} h_i^2(m_1,\ldots,m_k) \left[\prod_{q=1}^{k} R_{c_q}(m_q, \omega_q, \tau) \right] \quad \text{(D.29)}$$

where

$$h_i(m_1,\ldots,m_k) = \frac{1}{\pi^2} \int_{-\infty}^{\infty} x^{i-1} \prod_{q=1}^{k} J_{m_q}(a_q x) e^{-(\sigma_n^2 + b^2)x^2/2} dx \quad \text{(D.30)}$$

Equation (D.29) is useful in our discussion of satellite amplifiers in Chapters 4 and 5.

Index